Distribution of State and Local Civilian Employees by Region, 1997

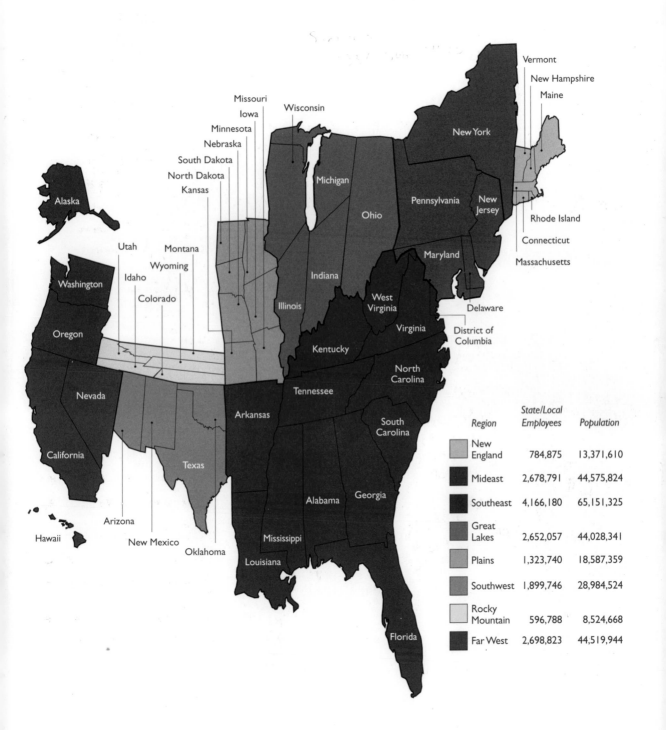

Region	State/Local Employees	Population
New England	784,875	13,371,610
Mideast	2,678,791	44,575,824
Southeast	4,166,180	65,151,325
Great Lakes	2,652,057	44,028,341
Plains	1,323,740	18,587,359
Southwest	1,899,746	28,984,524
Rocky Mountain	596,788	8,524,668
Far West	2,698,823	44,519,944

Public Administration in America

Public Administration in America

SEVENTH EDITION

Michael E. Milakovich
University of Miami, Florida

George J. Gordon
Illinois State University

BEDFORD/ST. MARTIN'S   Boston ♦ New York

For Bedford/St. Martin's

Executive Editor for History and Political Science: Katherine E. Kurzman
Developmental Editor: Amy McConathy
Senior Editor, Publishing Services: Douglas Bell
Production Supervisor: Cheryl Mamaril
Project Management: Stratford Publishing Services, Inc.
Text Design: Publisher's Studio/Stratford Publishing Services, Inc.
Cover Design: Donna Lee Dennison
Composition: Stratford Publishing Services, Inc.
Printing and Binding: RR Donnelley & Sons Company

President: Charles H. Christensen
Editorial Director: Joan E. Feinberg
Director of Marketing: Karen R. Melton
Director of Editing, Design, and Production: Marcia Cohen
Manager, Publishing Services: Emily Berleth

Library of Congress Catalog Card Number: 00-104006

Manufactured in the United States of America.

6   5   4   3   2   1
f   e   d   c   b   a

For information, write: Bedford/St. Martin's, 75 Arlington Street, Boston, MA 02116
(617-399-4000)

ISBN: 0-312-24972-1

Acknowledgments
Acknowledgments and copyrights appear at the back of the book on page 596,
which constitutes an extension of the copyright page.

Preface

This book is written for interested citizens, government officials, undergraduate and graduate students, and all others seeking to better understand the academic field and applied practice of public administration. The subject reflects multiple perspectives and has complex roots in many different academic disciplines and "real world" fields of endeavor. That by itself should alert the reader to one of the essential features of public administration: there are many sides to it, with a wide variety of issues, questions, practices, and themes, that have commanded attention (both in and out of the field) for more than a century. Public administration is both a subject for academic study and an increasingly challenging aspect of public service.

In the following pages, we discuss many themes and controversial features of contemporary public policy and administration. One recurring focus is on the distinction between the political and managerial aspects of the field, and the need to understand the importance of each. Another emphasis is on the day-to-day challenges facing leaders and managers in the public and nonprofit service sector, such as dealing with complex and sensitive personnel issues, budgetary and legal constraints, assuring ethical decision making, maintaining a professional and respected workforce, delivering quality services, and ensuring high levels of measurable productivity in government programs. We also describe continuing initiatives to "reinvent government," a movement that has gained considerable strength at all levels of government in the United States during the 1990s. Among other things, this movement emphasizes a redefinition of the relationship between citizen and government; "entrepreneurial" thinking, innovation and creativity; "empowering" public employees to enable them to do their best work; eliminating "unnecessary" regulation; achieving results with fewer resources; and serving government's "customers" efficiently and well. Reinvention efforts have resulted in substantial changes in the ways government organizations operate; and the results of change are visible at all levels of government. Another related theme is the increased concern with ethics and integrity in both the selection of appointed and elected public officials and in decisions made by governmental institutions and agencies. This concern has intensified in the public sector and includes a focus on various types of ethical considerations that enter into both political and administrative decisions as well as an examination of ways to promote more ethical behavior, responsiveness, and accountability among public administrators. A final theme is the exponential growth of information technology (IT) to enhance knowledge, improve access, and facilitate communication between citizens, elected officials, and public administrators. Today, new interactive technologies exist that were not even available a few years ago. The Internet, World Wide Web, and teleconferencing offer the potential for all citizens to participate responsibly in public decision making. New technologies are being applied worldwide to achieve greater access to decision makers, improve efficiency in government, and influence the outcome of public issues.

We will also devote considerable attention to more specific, management-related topics in the field. These include, among others, continuity and change in complex relationships between national, state, and local governments (Chapter 4); management challenges, organizational changes, and leadership responsibilities in public organizations (Chapters 5–7); both old and new personnel management concerns (Chapter 8); ongoing tensions in the budgetary process, including continuing attention to budget deficits and government spending (Chapter 9); the emerging attention to government productivity and to customer service standards in the public sector (Chapter 10); and government regulation, privatization, and deregulation (Chapter 11). In the concluding chapter (Chapter 12), we will look back at the field, and attempt to integrate the various themes and subject matters covered in this text, as well as look ahead to emerging issues and concerns.

Twenty-First Century Public Administration

There have been major changes in the academic field of public administration as well as in the practical world of government service since the sixth edition of this book was published in 1998. What characterizes public administration at the beginning of the twenty-first century is the scope and rapidity of change affecting virtually all aspects of governmental activity. The rapid integration of technology is but one element of this transformation; others include a reexamination of basic social values; reconsideration of social insurance and "entitlement" programs; reassessing government's role in changing social and economic environments; growing emphasis on serving customers, measuring performance, encouraging job training and productive employment; new approaches to budgetary dilemmas; a bipartisan concern with balancing the federal budget; a politically charged debate about how to spend the anticipated budget *surplus;* freer trade; protecting the environment, combating crime, and incremental health care reform (among many other things); state and local government officials' willingness to experiment with new approaches; and widespread frustration among many citizens about all governments' capacities to manage and successfully reform a diverse range of public programs. Thus, public administration, which is always somewhat difficult to understand under the best of circumstances, is even more challenging for today's student because of the turbulence that characterizes so many administrative operations, controversies, and challenges. In this context, it is vital for all those seeking greater information about the field to better understand the way the public perceives the profession, the forces for change (such as the Clinton administration's efforts to reinvent government), and the often larger forces resisting change or urging radical change (bureaucratic inertia and ideological opposition). In addition, all students of the field must appreciate the ethical dilemmas present in their current or future roles as public administrators.

Finally, three themes are very much at the heart of contemporary public administration and of our discussion in the book: the degree of accountability of public administrative agencies, the measures of efficiency and ethical guidelines used by public agencies and public managers to perform their duties, and the results or effectiveness of programs in the real world of public management. To some extent, these concerns have been with us since the administrative state began to emerge in the late nineteenth century. But they have taken on greater urgency as we move into the twenty-first century. This blend of old and new is an integral part of public administration: old concerns never entirely disappear and new concerns usually have some roots in continuing issues. Nevertheless, what is new now — and what may emerge in the immediate future — may result in greater change, in a short time span, than in many previous periods of rapid change and uncertainty.

What's New in the Seventh Edition?

Those who have used previous editions of *Public Administration in America* will notice that the changes for the seventh edition begin with a return to hardcover and an increased trim size. A fresh new design for this edition provides a better format for charts, graphs, and tables and a look that is much more light and appealing, creating a book students will want to keep as a future reference in the context of their work lives.

For this edition, we have undertaken a consolidation of previous material, as well as provided thoroughly updated new material. Coverage in the seventh edition has been organized in twelve chapters within three parts. Chapters 2 and 13 have been combined in order to present a more cohesive discussion of democracy and the political system. Chapters 7 and 8 have also been combined in order to present the challenges of administrative leadership and bureaucratic leadership together in one chapter. Updated material includes results and implications of the 1998 congressional election, a complete analysis of President Clinton's second term, and discussions of current policy issues such as entitlement reform, affirmative action, accountability, regulatory reform, customer service quality standards, and ethical decision making in government. Updated material is also present in the ongoing discussions of changing values, federalism, organizational development, human resources, budgeting, total quality management, regulation, and administrative law.

We have also incorporated new and streamlined apparatus to present important information more accessibly. The end-of-chapter material has been reorganized, and feature boxes, charts, graphs, tables, and running heads have all been redesigned. We have also provided new glossary terms in the margins for easier reference by students. Key terms are **boldfaced** in the text and defined in the margins of each chapter. These key terms also appear in end-of-chapter material, and are cross-referenced in the glossary so students can find a term easily and understand it in a variety of contexts. Also new are the end-of-chapter On-Line Resources. An annotated list of the most useful World Wide Web sites from a variety of government and nonprofit organizations provides more in-depth information on issues relevant to each chapter as well as a starting place for research. Chapter-opening epigraphs feature quotes from scholars and politicians such as Ronald Reagan and Bill Clinton, and present students with a high-interest theme for each chapter. Also, boxed features have been reorganized under new headings. All boxed features now come under one of these five headings: Background Briefing, Intergovernmental Relations, Ethical and Leadership Challenges for Public Managers, Labor-Management Relations, and Productivity and Service Quality Improvement.

Finally, we have added a new appendix listing selected academic, professional, and public-interest organizations, job-search links, and relevant journals for research in public administration. This is designed to help students with the postgraduation job search and to keep them abreast of the most current issues and legislation.

Acknowledgments

We are indebted to the many individuals who contributed in myriad ways to the preparation of this and the earlier editions. Valuable research and feedback was provided by Melanie Nathanson, Dawn Dress, Robert Ortiz, Jason Harr, Carrie Edmondson, Richard Newmark, Miriam Singer, Terry Pearl, Ellyn Broden, Eileen Damaso Taube, Bevin Horn, Beto Negriel, Scott Mendelsberg, Larry Milov, Mary Manzano, Suzanne Torriente, Gamel Sabet, Ann Shaw, Bill Soloman, Shayna Owen, George Gonzalez, Leslie Swanson, Dan Wall, Pam Anderson, Carlos Atienza, and Alina Tejeda Houdak. Faculty colleagues at our two universities and elsewhere who were especially helpful include Bob Brantley, Ann Cohen, Gen. Robert L. Dilworth (ret.), Thomas E. Eimermann, Juliet Gainsborough, Albert C. Hyde, Donald Klingner, Nancy S. Lind, Elizabeth Rexford, Frederick J. Roberts, Dragan Stefanovic, Stuart Streichler, James H. Svara, Nathan Teske, and Jonathan P. West.

Still others who were generous with time, energy, and information on our behalf include Jonathan Breul of the Executive Office of the President; Jay Chatzkel of the National Academy of Public Administration; David Grinberg of the U.S. Office of Management and Budget; Paul Hershey and Jackie McCormick of the U.S. Office of Personnel Management; and Alan V. Stevens of the U.S. Bureau of the Census.

The reviews commissioned by Bedford/St. Martin's were uniformly helpful in their critiques; the topic coverage in this book is stronger, more accurate, and more complete because of the insights and recommendations of the following readers: Cary R. Covington, University of Iowa; Steven M. Neuse, University of Arkansas; and John P. Stewart, Penn State University. Also deserving of recognition, and sincere thanks, are Amy McConathy, Katherine Kurzman, and Doug Bell of Bedford/St. Martin's. Cindy, Nicole, and Tiffany Milakovich, and Myra, Dan, and Rachel Gordon, were endlessly patient and supportive, and we are grateful — on this project, as on so many others before! These individuals richly deserve much of the credit for whatever strengths are present in the book; ours alone is the responsibility for its weaknesses.

This book is dedicated (by Milakovich) to Beth and Eli Milakovich for their discipline, humor, patience and values, and (by Gordon) to the memories of Roscoe C. Martin and Hibbert R. Roberts. We owe them a great debt, a debt we will never be able to fully repay. The same may be said of our wives, Cindy Milakovich and Myra Gordon.

Michael E. Milakovich
Coral Gables, Florida

George J. Gordon
Normal, Illinois

To the Student

This text will help you expand your knowledge and understanding of what public administration is all about. Several features of this book will aid you in your studies. Chapter summaries present restatements of key points covered in the chapters. References are grouped at the end of the text; an effort has been made to furnish extensive source material in the hope that you will become familiar with the literature in this field.

A new feature of this edition is **boldfaced** key terms and concepts noted in the text and defined in the margins of each chapter. This glossary of terms will help you review key concepts, techniques, laws, and institutions pertaining to public administration. A list of suggested reading at the end of each chapter notes important sources for further research and information. In addition, this edition includes many uniform resource locators (URLs), hyperlinked Internet Web sites, and on-line resources to assist students seeking additional knowledge about the field, finding jobs, obtaining additional information, and preparing research papers for courses in political science, public policy, and public administration. A new appendix is also available, listing professional organizations and journals for research and job searches.

Note to Instructors

Public Administration in America, seventh edition, is accompanied by an instructor's manual that contains, for each chapter, summaries and multiple-choice, true/false, and essay questions.

Contents

About the Authors

MICHAEL E. MILAKOVICH is professor of political science at the University of Miami, Coral Gables, Florida. A life member of the American Society for Public Administration, he serves as an expert witness in state and federal courts and advises public and nonprofit organizations on policy analysis and quality improvement strategies. He is a member of the board of directors of the National Center for Public Productivity.

His articles have appeared in the *American Review of Public Administration, National Productivity Review, Crime and Delinquency, Health Care Management Review, Public Productivity and Management Review, North Carolina Review of Business and Economics, National Civic Review*, and the *Journal of Health and Human Resource Administration*. He is the author of *Improving Service Quality: Achieving High Performance in the Public and Private Sectors* (1995), *Florida State and Local Government* (1993), and *U.S. vs. Crime in the Streets*, with Tom and Tania Cronin (1981). He has consulted with various judicial, governmental, and health care agencies both in the Unites States and abroad.

GEORGE J. GORDON is professor of political science at Illinois State University at Normal and is active in political and civic affairs. He served as a Democratic presidential elector from the state of Illinois in 1992 and was elected to the McLean County Board in 1996. He also served as section head of the Public Administration Section at the 1997 Convention of the Midwest Political Science Association. His articles on federalism and intergovernmental relations have appeared in *Publius: The Journal of Federalism; Public Administration Quarterly;* and the *Journal of the American Planning Association*.

PART I

The Context, Nature, and Structure of Public Administration in America

This opening section explores essential facts and concepts in public administration in order to set the stage for further detailed discussion of the subject. The central themes are (1) the roles and functions of public bureaucracies within the larger governmental system, (2) the impact of politics within that larger system on administrative actions and decisions, and (3) the critical, and increasing, importance of productivity improvement and effective management at all levels of government. In Chapter 1, we will first describe the most common structural arrangements of executive-branch agencies, stressing the growth of government generally and public administration in particular. We will explore similarities and differences between public and private administration, taking note of some ways in which they overlap in practice. We will then examine public administration as a field of study, especially its evolution from a relatively uncomplicated field in the early 1900s to the complex and rapidly changing discipline it is in the 2000s.

In Chapter 2, we establish the governmental system in which public administration operates, consider traditional conceptions of how public agencies ought to function and then compare them with the broad realities of American bureaucracy, and discuss why the differences are important. We then examine the underlying values in American administrative practice. Of central importance are the tensions between *political values* — such as individual freedom to choose, fair representation, and popular control — and *administrative values* — such as efficiency, economy, and the ideal of "political" (usually meaning partisan) neutrality. The discussion focuses on selected current value conflicts that pose difficult challenges for a society striving to be democratic while becoming increasingly bureaucratic in dealing with pressing social issues. Among these issues are the need for accountability, the extent of citizen participation in decision making, access to information about public issues, and how we define representativeness. In addition, we analyze the impact of the mass media, social change, and technology on our values.

Chapter 3 focuses on the nature and exercise of bureaucratic power and discusses various issues involved in the rise of what has become known as the "bureaucratic state." The discussion centers on the dispersal of power throughout government and what that means for public administrators, the foundations of bureaucratic power, the political implications of structure, bureaucrats as political actors as well as public managers, and dilemmas of political and administrative accountability. Bureaucrats are seen as active participants in a broad range of political interactions that allow for considerable variety and complexity in the manner of their involvement.

Chapter 4 deals with the dynamic nature of federalism and intergovernmental (national–state–local) relations. A description of the formal federal setting is followed by an examination of intergovernmental relations within federalism. Particular attention is given to fiscal and administrative relations among the different levels and units of government, the divisive issue of unfunded mandates (federal programs *without* funds to support them), regulatory reform and devolution of federal program authority to states and local governments. The evolution of American federalism has profoundly affected the management of government programs at all levels, and it is essential that we understand how the two are interrelated. Federalism is an important structural element of public administration which, in turn, creates a challenging organizational dynamic among local, state, and federal stakeholders.

Chapter 1

Approaching the Study of
Public Administration

> *The time has come where there has to be a change of direction in
> this country, and it's going to begin with reducing government
> spending. . . . You can cut layers and layers without hitting muscle
> fiber. Keep trying. That's what we were sent here for.*
>
> Ronald Reagan, then president-elect, early in 1981

The governor and elected comptroller of a state publicly disagree with each
other on the condition of state government finances, taking issue especially over
the question of projected revenues. A police officer is injured in a traffic accident
while pursuing a car that has been reported stolen. A metropolitan transit
authority allocates funds for an extensive study designed to assist local governments in the region with long-range transportation (and economic development) planning. The U.S. Postal Service made a *profit* of $363 million in 1999,
allowing it to postpone further rate increases until 2001. A candidate for state
government office runs successfully on her pledge to *abolish* the office after being
elected! Local government bargaining teams engage in round-the-clock negotiations with a firefighters' union in an effort to avert a threatened strike only days
away. The president and Congress fail to agree on federal budget priorities and,
as a result, national parks must close, economic reports are delayed, and social
security recipients fail to receive benefits. Sound familiar?

What do these examples — none of them hypothetical — have in common?
All of them represent various aspects of public administration, one of the most
rapidly growing dimensions of the American governmental process and one with
increasing influence both inside and outside of government.

Public administration in America today is a large enterprise made up of thousands of smaller units that encompasses the everyday activities of literally millions of government employees at all levels. Their decisions touch the daily lives

of virtually every American. The growth of government activity and public bureaucracy is one of the most significant social phenomena of recent decades and has become the subject of considerable discussion among scholars and practitioners. At the same time, politicians of every stripe have criticized the bureaucracy: in 1976, Jimmy Carter promised to "clean up the bureaucratic mess in Washington"; in 1980, Ronald Reagan promised to "get the federal government off your backs"; George Bush dared us to "Read my lips" in 1988; and, in 1996, Bill Clinton declared that "the era of Big Government is over." Many other politicians have run successfully "against" the bureaucracy. The "taxpayers' revolt" that surfaced swiftly and intensely in the late 1970s was in part a reaction against perceived bureaucratic excesses. It has even been suggested that the language of bureaucracy (its jargon) has harmed the English language as a whole. In one way or another, most of us are familiar — if not always comfortable — with government bureaucracy.

bureaucracy
(1) a formal organizational arrangement characterized by division of labor, job specialization with no functional overlap, exercise of authority through a vertical hierarchy (chain of command), and a system of internal rules, regulations, and record keeping; (2) in common usage, the administrative branch of government (national, state, or local) in the United States; also, individual administrative agencies of those governments.

Our awareness of bureaucracy varies according to the situations in which we find ourselves. This awareness is usually higher when we fill out our income tax returns (especially when we have to pay additional tax on April 15), apply for government loans to finance a college education, seek federal assistance after a natural disaster, or deal directly with that most visible of street-level bureaucrats, a police officer. We are less conscious of the role of **bureaucracy** under other circumstances. (Key terms and concepts are highlighted in **bold** print, defined in the margins, and listed at the end of each chapter.) Much bureaucratic decision making is obscure or just not directly meaningful to us. Consider, for example, decisions by the U.S. Department of Education (DOE) to change eligibility formulas for determining student loans. Proposals such as these may be important and may even lend legitimacy to the final actions taken by public agencies, but they typically generate little publicity or public attention by themselves. Some of the most important work of government agencies takes place away from public view. Yet *everyone* has a general opinion — usually negative — about bureaucracy and politics. (See Box 1–1, "The Meaning of 'Bureaucracy.'")

Regardless of our level of awareness concerning particular bureaucratic activities or decisions, the institution of bureaucracy evokes strong feelings among millions of Americans. Mention of "the bureaucracy" usually elicits a strong response; bureaucrats are unpopular with many of those they serve. Bureaucracy has been blamed for many of society's current ills, for several reasons: government agencies are clearly influential; in all but a handful of cases, bureaucrats are not elected by the public; and bureaucrats are convenient, increasingly visible targets. We hear a great deal about the growing power of bureaucracy and bureaucrats, the arbitrary nature of many decisions, the lack of government accountability, corruption, questionable ethics, poor service quality, impersonal treatment, and cases of simple incompetence.

Our attitudes toward both public and private bureaucracies (that is, toward all large organizations) have been affected by the larger complex of feelings and reactions toward government as a whole and toward other major institutions in

BOX I–I   BACKGROUND BRIEFING

The Meaning of "Bureaucracy"

A *bureaucracy* or a *bureaucratic organization* is characterized by an internal division of labor, specialization of work performed, a vertical hierarchy or chain of command, well-defined routines for carrying out operating tasks, reliance on precedents (previous actions) in resolving problems, and a clear set of rules regarding managerial control over organizational activities. It is assumed that most of those working in a bureaucracy are professionals in their specialties, and that their occupational loyalties rest with their organizations rather than with a political party or other external affiliation. Because much of public management in American governments occurs within bureaucratic structures, there is a tendency to use *bureaucracy* as just another term for public administration or public management; but it has a more specific meaning than either of those, particularly with regard to the form or structure of administrative agencies (see Chapter 5).

American society, such as business, labor, the mass media, and education. The confidence of Americans in their institutions has declined significantly since the 1960s, a decade of divisive social conflict — the war in Vietnam, student protest, racial violence — followed by Watergate and a decade of economic decline — the energy crisis, recession, and the rampant inflation of the 1970s. The 1980s brought a new Republican administration to Washington and optimism based on tax cuts, higher corporate profits, and less regulation of the economy. The inevitable "downsizing" of many jobs resulting from a slowing economy significantly influenced people's feelings about their leaders and institutions in the 1990s. To the extent that governmental activity was directed toward trying to deal with these problems but was perceived by the public to be ineffective, public confidence was adversely affected. So, too, were the electoral fortunes of incumbent presidents seeking second terms: Gerald Ford, a Republican, in 1976, Jimmy Carter, a Democrat, in 1980, and George Bush, another Republican, in 1992. Public trust in government has become a major issue, and the level of trust has declined measurably from that of forty years ago. Bureaucracy has become a focal point of discontent not only because of its obvious power but also because of its waste and mismanagement of scarce resources, its relatively obscure decision processes, and the degree to which it is insulated from direct (elective) political controls. Protests against the action of local school boards and police departments, impatience with inefficiency and red tape, and public response to regulatory actions all testify to the intensity of feeling and, more generally, to growing *frustration* and a widening sense of *distance* between the people and their governing institutions.

As economic conditions improved during the 1990s, public attitudes toward government also began to change for the better, notably in the form of rising support for government deregulation and for reductions in government spending. Shifts in public opinion also reflect faith and trust in government and are associated with confidence in government's ability to maintain economic growth and resolve basic social issues. Expressions of trust or mistrust in government largely reflect feelings about the incumbent national administration. Thus, as efforts to curb inflation bore fruit in the early 1980s, public confidence in government surged upward noticeably, but to a level still below that of the 1960s. Public trust in government reflects the national "mood" and declined from the mid-1980s until the early 1990s. Perhaps as a result of the reinvention efforts initiated by the Clinton administration, trust has moved up sharply since the mid-1990s (see Figure 1–1). For selected federal agencies, such as the U.S. Coast Guard, the Federal Emergency Management Agency (FEMA), the National Park Service, and the Social Security Administration, public trust and evaluation of service quality have improved dramatically. So, too, has the strength of the

FIGURE 1–1   Trust in Government and National Mood

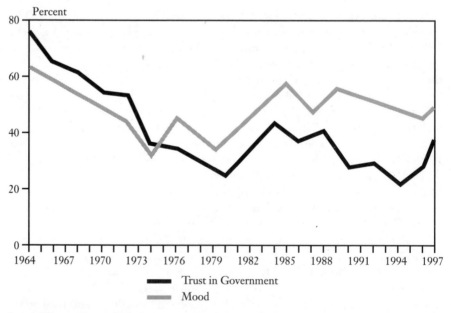

SOURCE: "Deconstructing Distrust: How Americans View Government" (*The Pew Research Center,* 1997), p. 4. Reprinted with permission.

domestic economy. In contrast, a worsening economy in the early 1990s was a major factor in Bill Clinton's victory over George Bush in the presidential election of 1992. The Clinton-Gore victory in 1996, the first time in thirty-two years that Democrats have been reelected for a second presidential term, reflected a positive national mood about the future of the economy, lower federal budget deficits, more jobs, and continued low rates of inflation. The election also reinforced a public preference for "divided government," with Republicans maintaining majorities in the U.S. House of Representatives and Senate as well as many statehouses.

Whether public attitudes toward government bureaucracy and bureaucrats have followed broader opinion patterns exactly is unclear. What is certain, however, is that the public's regard for public administrators has fallen far below what it was sixty years ago, when the civil service was considered an esteemed profession. During the Great Depression of the 1930s, then during and after World War II, public administrators and their organizations enjoyed greater public confidence than they do today. The general public, through its elected officials, looked to the administrative apparatus of government to take on increasing responsibility. Congress, state legislatures, and city councils, as well as presidents, governors, and mayors, all delegate growing amounts of discretionary **authority** to administrative officials, in effect directing them to make the day-to-day choices involved in applying laws. No national referendum was held on the question, "Should bureaucrats be given more responsibility?" But public acceptance of greater governmental involvement in a wider range of societal activities outweighed any opposition to growth of government in general and government bureaucracy in particular. Indeed, once bureaucratic involvement in policy making began to increase, heightened public demand for government services ensured continuation of greater administrative activity, at least until the early 1980s.

authority power defined according to a legal and institutional framework and vested in a formal structure (a nation, organization, profession, or the like); power exercised through recognized, legitimate channels.

The sharp decline in bureaucracy's public standing has also coincided with greater demands for a wider range of public services, increasing complexity in the nation's problems and (ironically) much higher levels of competence and professionalism among government workers. Both Jimmy Carter and Ronald Reagan, even as they tried to reduce the size and role of bureaucracies, acknowledged the honesty, integrity, and demonstrated talents of the vast majority of administrative officials. George Bush was even more openly supportive of public administrators, and Bill Clinton has placed considerable emphasis on "empowering" federal employees so that they may do their best work. Clinton has gone farther than any recent President in suggesting that it was "time to shift from topdown bureaucracy to **entrepreneurial government** that generates change from the bottom up. *We must reward the people and ideas that work, and get rid of those that don't.*"[1]

entrepreneurial government emphasizes productivity management, measurable performance, privatization, and change.

Public administration scholar Charles Goodsell has suggested that government bureaucracies and administrators do not, in fact, deserve such harsh criticism.[2] The essence of his argument is that, despite shortcomings inevitably found in such complex organizations, America's government bureaucracies perform quite well. This is the case whether bureaucratic performance is measured by objective standards, in comparison with that in most of the other nations of the world, or (as noted earlier) in terms of citizens' satisfaction with their dealings with government administrators. Goodsell summarizes his position this way:

> Any large, immensely complex, and far-flung set of institutions will be riddled with individual instances of inefficiency, maladministration, arrogance, and even abuse of power. But, in this country, *these deficiencies are particularized rather than generalized, occur within tolerable ranges of proportionate incidence, and are minor compared to many bureaucracies of the world.* In fact most nations, especially continent-sized ones like our own, would do almost anything to possess an equivalent social asset. . . . [A strong case for bureaucracy may be made] by describing . . . the *very substantial merit and record of achievement and democratic responsibility* associated with American public administration.[3]

Goodsell thus focuses attention on the sometimes unthinking criticisms of bureaucracy that have characterized much of our national dialogue in the recent past. Scapegoating bureaucracy only makes it more difficult for us to acquire a clearer understanding of *what* it really is and *how* it really operates in our governmental system and our society at large.

At the same time, when people vent their frustrations on bureaucracy in general, there is surprisingly strong evidence of favorable citizen reaction to direct dealings with individual bureaucrats.[4] It has even been suggested by a reputable observer that public administrators *"could not be engaged in more important or more honorable work . . . however they may be judged by the public they serve."*[5] Why, then, have these officials lost so much prestige? Part of the answer is that they may appear to constitute something of a government "elite" in an era when the angry and cynical voice of the people is heard more forcefully. Or, perhaps, the very complexity of the problems currently confronting government decreases the likelihood of *complete* solutions, despite the serious efforts of more competent people. The more complex the problems, the greater the discretionary authority vested in bureaucracies to attempt to deal with them. Finally, perhaps, the public has come to expect *too much* from government (sometimes encouraged by the mass media and public officials themselves) and has made bureaucrats into scapegoats for not meeting public expectations. Whether bureaucrats are deserving of blame for these sentiments is another matter.

What Is Public Administration?

Public administration may be defined as *all processes, organizations, and individuals* (the latter acting in official positions and roles) *associated with carrying out laws and other rules adopted or issued by legislatures, executives, and courts.* This definition should be understood to include considerable administrative involvement in for-

---

public administration
(1) all processes, organizations, and individuals acting in official positions associated with carrying out laws and other rules adopted or issues by legislatures, executives, and courts (many activities are also concerned with formulations of these rules); (2) a field of academic study and professional training leading to public-service careers at all levels of government.

mulation as well as implementation of legislation and executive orders; we will discuss this more fully later. Public administration is simultaneously a field of academic study and of professional training, from which substantial numbers of government employees currently are drawn.

Note that this definition does not limit the participants in public administration to administrative personnel, or even to people in government. It can and does refer to a varied assortment of **stakeholders,** that is, individuals and groups with an interest in the consequences of administrative action. Among stakeholders, the foremost perhaps are the administrators themselves. Also included are members of the legislature, legislative committees, and their staffs; higher executives in the administrative apparatus of government; judges; political party officials whose partisan interests overlap extensively with issues of public policy; lobbyists (that is, leaders and members of interest groups) seeking from the government various policies, regulations, and actions; mass media personnel (particularly in their watchdog role over the actions and decisions of public officials); and members of society at large who, even when they are not well organized, can have some impact on the directions of various public policies. Furthermore, public administration involves all those just mentioned in shifting patterns of reciprocal (mutual) relationships — in state, local, and federal governments as well as in national-state-local (that is, intergovernmental) relations. The politics of administration involves agency interactions with those *outside* the formal structure as well as interactions among those *within* administrative agencies; we are concerned with both.

> **stakeholders** bureaucrats, elected officials, groups of citizens, and organized and unorganized interests affected by the decisions of federal, state, and local governments; those having a stake in the outcome of public policies; see also **interest groups, issue networks, subsystem.**

THE MANAGERIAL ROLE

Let us consider another dimension of public administration: the *managerial,* or *management,* side. Although the emphasis in this book is on the "politics of bureaucracy," as some have called it,[6] management practice has always occupied a place of major importance in the discipline of public administration and is becoming increasingly important in making government both efficient and effective. Managerial aspects of public administration have as their primary focus the *internal* workings of government agencies, that is, all the structures, dynamics, and processes connected with operating government programs. The terms *public administration* (as used in this text) and **public management** are both concerned with implementing policies and programs enacted through authoritative institutions of government. But, even though they may appear to be interchangeable terms, the latter emphasizes methods of organizing for internal control and direction for maximum effectiveness, whereas the former addresses a broader range of civic and social concerns.

> **public management** a field of practice and study central to public administration that emphasizes internal operations of public agencies and focuses on managerial concerns related to control and direction, such as planning, organizational maintenance, information systems, budgeting personnel management, performance evaluation, and productivity improvement.

Despite these differences, there is general agreement that managerial skills are essential to operate public agencies. Networking and organizing skills that can be performed with more or less competence are the indispensable foundation on which actual operations are built and sustained. An important point for

information technology (IT)   refers to the use of computers, linked-area network (LAN) systems, the World Wide Web, and the Internet to improve the delivery of government services and enhance the capacity of individuals and organizations to communicate and to gather information.

reverse pyramid   a conception of organization structure, especially in service organizations, whereby managerial duties focus on providing necessary support to frontline employees (particularly those whose work centers around information and information technology) who deal directly with individuals seeking the organization's services.

the public manager is that *action* is expected, even if it is not necessarily advisable or convenient. Managers must often take actions to move the organization in the face of strict deadlines within a range of choices that is far less than ideal. These elements make up a large part of the public manager's existence in, and contribution to, the totality of public administration.

During the 1990s, a number of new concerns have emerged in the field of management, concerns that came increasingly to the attention of both public and private managers. For example, the need became even more apparent for improving the skills of employees dealing with information and **information technology (IT)**; with such individuals constituting a larger proportion of many organizations' personnel, this need could (or should) not go unattended.[7] Another concern is the growing emphasis on individual *character* and *leadership* (stable personalities providing vision and direction for an organization) as opposed to simply managing established, routine operations (see Chapter 7). There is also a new emphasis on improving the quality of services provided in both public and private organizations and, with it, the possibility of a new conception of the relationship among managers, their frontline service providers, and the "customers" (that is, the recipients of services). Unlike the traditional top-down bureaucratic chain of command, this conception envisions a **reverse pyramid** with line workers responsive to customers in public service organizations, and managers' at the base of the triangle, supporting the frontline employee (at the point or tip of the triangle). Another concern is the prospect of transforming organizational structures themselves — given the many changes in information and its uses — service provision, and the roles of managers and leaders.[8] Still other concerns for managers include the challenge of providing career development and job enrichment for employees, encouraging participatory management, and applying emergent total quality customer service management techniques to the tasks of running large, complex bureaucratic organizations. Public managerial responsibilities have become more complicated and, at the same time, more challenging and potentially beneficial to employees, citizens, managers, and their organizations.

Principal Structures of the National Executive Branch

CONSTITUTION OF THE UNITED STATES

The Constitution is silent on the subjects of public administration and management, except to refer to the president's responsibility to "faithfully execute the laws." The structures that exist today are products of congressional action, as are many of the procedures followed within public administration. The national executive branch is organized primarily into five major types of agencies, four formal bases, or foundations of organization and four broad categories of administrative employees. These deserve consideration because they affect both the way administrative entities function and the content of policies they help to enact.

At first glance, questions of organizational structure may not appear to carry many political overtones. But formal organizational arrangements do not simply appear, and they are not neutral in their consequences.[9] The choice of organizational structure may both reflect and promote some interests over others because a particular structure is the product of decisions reached through the political process by a particular majority coalition, whether directly (as through congressional action) or indirectly (as when the president proposes executive reorganization). Those who organize or reorganize an agency in a certain way obviously have reasons for doing so, one of which is usually promotion of their own policy interests. For example, President George Bush highlighted his concern for our nation's military veterans and expanded the access of veterans' groups to top policymakers in Washington by creating the Department of Veterans Affairs in March 1989 (see Chapter 3). Similarly, the decision to separate the Social Security Administration as an independent agency from the U.S. Department of Health and Human Services (effective in March 1995) recognized the importance of disabled, elderly, retired persons, and all others who might be eligible for supplemental social insurance income.

CABINET-LEVEL DEPARTMENTS

Sometimes referred to as just departments, they are the most visible, though not necessarily the largest, national executive organizations; this is also true in most states and localities. As of mid-1999, there were fourteen departments in the national executive branch — for example, the departments of State, Defense, Commerce, the Treasury, Justice, Labor, and the Interior (see Figure 1–2). The newest department is Veterans Affairs; it replaced the Veterans Administration, previously an independent entity. Each department is headed by a secretary and a series of top-level subordinates, all of whom are appointed by the president with the approval of the Senate (such approval is rarely withheld). Their main function is to supply policy leadership to their respective departments on behalf of the president but, in practice, they also speak to the president for their departments (see Chapter 7).

Departments are composed of many smaller administrative units with a variety of titles, such as bureau, office, administration, and service. Within the Department of Transportation, for example, one finds such diverse units as the Urban Mass Transportation Administration (UMTA), the Federal Aviation Administration (FAA), and the U.S. Coast Guard; the Bureau of Land Management (BLM) is subsumed within the Interior Department; and the Health Care Financing Administration (HCFA), the Public Health Service (PHS), and (most significant) the Food and Drug Administration (FDA) are all part of the Department of Health and Human Services (see Figure 1–3). The fact that bureaus or

FIGURE 1-2   Organization Chart of the Government of the United States

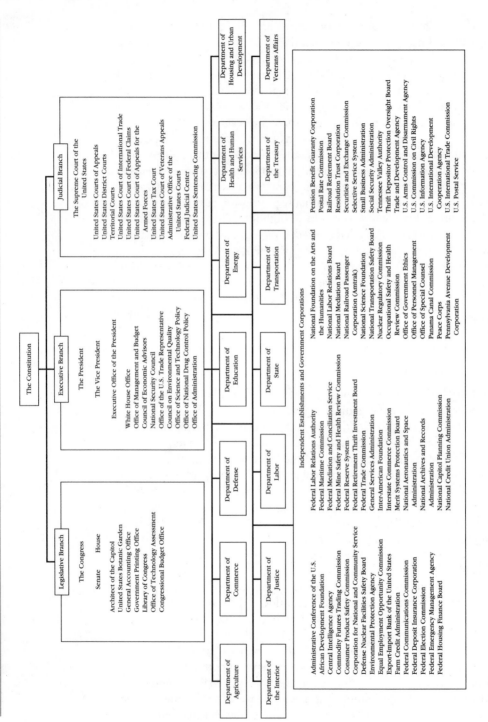

SOURCE: *U.S. Government Manual* (Washington, D.C.: U.S. Government Printing Office, 1998), p. 22.

FIGURE 1–3   **Organization Chart, U.S. Department of Health and Human Services**

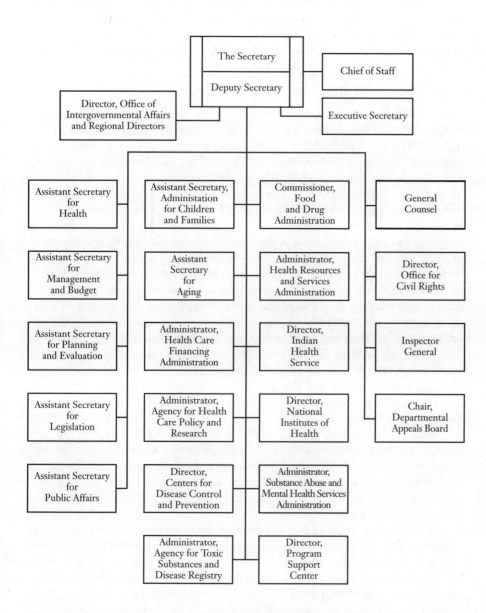

SOURCE: *U.S. Government Manual* (Washington, D.C.: U.S. Government Printing Office, 1998), p. 272.

offices are located within the same departmental structure does not necessarily mean that they work cooperatively on any one venture; in fact, conflict among agencies within the same department is not uncommon (though efforts have been made to reduce such conflict). Finally, departments and their subunits generally are responsible for carrying out specific operating programs enacted by Congress; they have, and attempt to maintain, fairly specific program jurisdictions (areas of programmatic responsibility) and often concrete program objectives.

INDEPENDENT REGULATORY BOARDS AND COMMISSIONS

Among such organizations are the Federal Trade Commission (FTC), Federal Reserve Board (FRB), National Labor Relations Board (NLRB), and U.S. International Trade Commission. They are a second major type of administrative entity and differ from cabinet-level departments in a number of important ways. First, they have a different function — namely, to oversee and regulate activities of various parts of the private economic sector. Second, their leadership is plural rather than singular; that is, they are headed by a board or commission of several individuals (usually five to nine) instead of a secretary. Third, they are designed to be somewhat independent of other institutions and political forces. Members of these entities are appointed by the president with Senate approval (as are senior department officials) but have more legal protection than do Cabinet members against dismissal by the president; in addition, they normally serve a term of office longer than that of the appointing president. In relation to Congress, these entities are supposedly somewhat freer to do their jobs than are departments and their subunits; in practice, this is questionable, but the design does have some impact. Finally, these entities are designed to regulate private-sector enterprises in a detached and objective manner and are expected to prevent abuses, corruption, and the like. Some controversy has existed, however, over just how detached and objective these organizations have been in relation to those they regulate.

Independent regulatory boards and commissions are not, however, the only government entities having regulative responsibilities. A phenomenon of considerable importance is the growth of government regulation since 1960 through a wide variety of other administrative instruments. Examples include the Federal Aviation Administration (FAA), state departments of transportation, the National Transportation Safety Board (NTSB), and the U.S. Food and Drug Administration (FDA). These agencies play important roles in their respective policy areas with regard to the setting of rules and standards for those in the private sector. The increasing incidence of government regulation has spawned rising political discontent over the scope and content of regulatory activity. As part of their reinventing government initiative, President Clinton and Vice President Gore ordered a cost-benefit analysis of what were called "important" regulations, and called for the dissolution of those that were deemed "insignificant." The purpose of this ongoing review is to "get rid of the bad rules and make the good ones eas-

ier to understand."[10] Sorting out the necessary from the unnecessary is a task —
involving significant discretionary authority — heavily influenced by private
interests, congressional intent, and procedures governing regulatory agencies,
boards, and commissions. In Chapter 11, we will explore the politics of regulatory reform more fully.

GOVERNMENT CORPORATIONS

These are national, state, or local government organizations that are identical to
private corporations in most of their structures and operations except one: they
are government-owned. Also, while some (such as Amtrak and local public utilities) seek to make a profit, others (such as the Federal Deposit Insurance Corporation and the Lower Colorado River Authority of the state of Texas) do not.
These are conceived as corporate entities for a number of reasons. First, their
legislative charters allow them somewhat greater latitude in day-to-day operations than other agencies enjoy. Government corporations also have the power
to acquire, develop, and dispose of real estate and other kinds of property while
acting in their own names (rather than in the name of the parent government).
Finally, they can bring suit in a court of law and are legally liable to be sued, also
in their own names. They are each headed by a board of directors, much as private corporations are, and are engaged in a wide variety of governmental activities. Three of the newest such entities are Amtrak, the Corporation for Public
Broadcasting, and the U.S. Postal Service; two of the oldest, both founded in the
1930s, are the Federal Deposit Insurance Corporation (FDIC) and the Tennessee Valley Authority (TVA).[11]

EXECUTIVE OFFICE OF THE PRESIDENT (EOP)

The EOP is a collection of administrative bodies that are physically and organi-
zationally housed close to the office of the president and designed precisely to
work for the president. Several of these entities are especially prominent and
important. (1) The White House Office, located at 1600 Pennsylvania Avenue,
consists of the president's key staff aides and staff directors. (2) The **Office of
Management and Budget (OMB)** assists the president in assembling budget
requests for the entire executive branch and forwards them to Capitol Hill as the
president's annual budget message, coordinates operating and regulatory programs, develops high-quality executive talent, and improves management
processes throughout the executive branch. (3) The Council of Economic Advisors (CEA) is the president's principal research arm for economic policy; it frequently influences the president's economic thinking (not surprisingly, since
presidents usually appoint to the CEA economists who reflect their own economic philosophies). (4) Entities such as the National Security Council (NSC),
designed originally as forums for generating a broad overview of policy directions, consist of the president, vice president, key cabinet secretaries, and other

**Office of Management
and Budget (OMB)**
an important entity in the
Executive Office of the
President that assists the
president in assembling
executive-branch budget
requests, coordinating
programs, developing
executive talent, and
supervising program
management processes in
national government
agencies.

officials. The formal purpose of these entities is to monitor and assess administration policies. Most of these entities become directly involved in policy making to a greater or lesser degree, according to each president's preferences. As staffs have grown larger, however, actions can be (and increasingly have been) taken without direct presidential supervision, as the Iran-Contra affair involving the NSC clearly illustrates (for elaboration see Chapter 7).[12]

Finally, there are miscellaneous independent agencies that have no bureaucratic departmental "home" but fit no other category we have discussed. Among these are the Office of Personnel Management (OPM) and the Merit Systems Protection Board (MSPB), formerly combined as the U.S. Civil Service Commission, which together oversee the national government's personnel system; the General Services Administration (GSA), the government's office of property and supply; and the Environmental Protection Agency (EPA).

The foundations of organization, mentioned earlier, are function, geographic area, clientele, and work process. The most common organizational foundation is according to *function*, indicating that an agency is concerned with a fairly distinct policy area but not limited to a particular *geographic* area. Organization according to geography indicates that an agency's work is in a specific region; examples include TVA, the Pacific Command of the Navy, and the Southern Command of the U.S. Army.

CLIENTELE-BASED AGENCIES

These are agencies that appear to address problems of a specific segment of the population, such as the (old) Veterans Administration (VA) or the Bureau of Indian Affairs (BIA) and the "new" Social Security Administration (SSA), which became an independent agency on March 31, 1995. The label *clientele-based agency* may be misleading for two reasons. First, every agency has a clientele of some kind — a group or groups in the general population on whose behalf many of the agency's programs are conducted. For example, farmers are clients of the Department of Agriculture, skilled and semiskilled laborers are associated with the Labor Department, and coal interests are linked to the Bureau of Mines. Similarly, the decision to reestablish a separate Social Security Administration, as it had been before merging with the Department of Health, Education and Welfare in 1953, recognized the increasing political influence of its clientele as well as the importance of its $426 billion annual budget.

The label also may be misleading because these clienteles may not always be *satisfied* clienteles. The VA and the BIA are, in fact, excellent illustrations of agencies whose clienteles have complained about some aspect of agency performance. In 1975, various veterans' groups and individual veterans protested vigorously about the VA's alleged shortcomings in awarding and processing veterans' benefits, to the point that a virtual sit-in took place in the VA director's office. Likewise, the BIA was, for a time, a principal target of the American

Indian Movement and others who expressed dissatisfaction with government management of Native American problems on and off the reservation. With both the VA and the BIA, a clientele was the most dissatisfied group — a not uncommon situation in bureaucratic politics. Likewise, the decision to re-create an independent SSA anticipated the growing controversy over the future of federal Social Security retirement benefits and Medicare, the federally funded health care program for the elderly.

WORK PROCESS AGENCIES

These agencies engage predominantly (if not exclusively) in data gathering and analysis for some higher-ranking official or office and rarely if ever participate formally in policy making (although their work can have policy implications). Agencies such as the Economic Research Staff of the Department of Agriculture, the Economic Studies Division of the Federal Energy Regulatory Commission, the U.S. Census Bureau, and the Soils Research Staff of the U.S. Geological Survey fall into this category.

Individual administrators occupying the multitude of positions in the various agencies can be categorized several different ways. For example, most national government administrators are *merit* employees, which means that they are presumably hired, retained, and promoted because they have the skills and training necessary to perform their jobs. Of the approximately 2.7 million full-time civilian employees in the federal government, about 92 percent work under a merit system of some kind. The remaining 8 percent include unionized employees not subject to merit hiring procedures (such as blue-collar workers in shipyards and weapons factories) as well as *political appointees,* some of whom can be removed by the president. In the latter group, numbering some 2,500 individuals, are the highest-ranking officials of the executive branch, including cabinet secretaries and undersecretaries, regulatory commissioners, and EOP personnel (see Chapter 8). Another way of viewing administrative employees is as either *specialists* or *generalists.* The term *specialist* refers to employees at lower and middle levels of the formal hierarchy whose responsibilities center on fairly specific programmatic areas. The term *generalist* is used to describe those in the higher ranks of an agency whose responsibilities cover a wider cross section of activities within the agency, involving some degree of supervision of various specialists in the ranks below.

The national executive branch, then, is organized primarily into five major types of agencies, with four formal bases of organization (function being the most common) and four broad categories of employees. State and local governments are different, though, and are worth considering briefly for the same reasons that we have examined the national executive branch: the administrative structure has some impact on the way the machinery of government functions and on the content of policies it helps to implement.

State and Local Government Structures

In general, states and larger local governments resemble the national government in composition and organization of their executive-branch agencies. Most states now have numerous cabinet-level departments; states also have a wide variety of regulatory bodies, some government corporations, and miscellaneous agencies. Similarly, most governors have fairly strong executive-office staffs responsive to the governor's leadership (see Chapter 7).

There are nearly 87,500 governments in the United States and except for the federal and state governments, *all* are local governments such as cities, counties, townships, a school or special districts. Individual state and local governments are smaller and more numerous than their federal government counterparts. There are also more elected local officials than federal ones: 96 percent of all 513,200 elected officials serve on elected boards or commissions in states or local districts (Table 1–1). These elected governments are small units averaging only about six elected representatives per government. States and communities also vary in terms of climate, economies, geography, population size, topography, type of government, and urbanization, as well as the individual characteristics of residents. For example, the state of Hawaii has only twenty-one governments (and only one municipal or city government) as compared to the state of Illinois with 6,723 governments. Citizens of Hawaii have just 1.7 governments per 10,000 residents, while citizens of North Dakota have almost 243 governments. These extreme variations among states and local governments reflect a history of independence from the federal government and a tradition of self-governance and local control.

TABLE 1–1	The Number of Governments and Elected Officials in the United States			
Level of Government		*Elected Officials*		*(Percent)*
Federal	1	National	542	(3.8)
State	50	State	18,828	
Local	87,444	Local	493,830	(96.2)
Special districts	34,683	Special districts	84,089	(17)
Municipalities	19,372	Municipalities	135,531	(27)
Townships	16,629	Townships	126,958	(26)
School districts	13,726	School districts	88,434	(18)
Counties	3,043	Counties	58,818	(12)
TOTAL	87,495		513,200	(100)

SOURCE: U.S. Census, *Governments Integrated Directory (GID)* (Washington, D.C., 1997) <http://www.census.gov/govs/www/gid.html>; U.S. Census, *1992 Census of Elected Officials* (Washington, D.C., 1995) <http://www.census.gov/govs/www/gid.html>

Some state agency structures reflect past or present influences of particular interest groups more than those in Washington do. One example was Pennsylvania's powerful Department of Mines and Mineral Industries, indicative of the role played in that state's economy by coal mine owners over the years. Another is the Illinois' Department of Aging, created in the mid-1970s in response to the emergence of a growing constituency with common problems of senior citizenship. These so-called special interests have "their" agencies in the national government, of course, but a pattern found in many states is the creation of somewhat higher-level agencies in response to constituency pressures. Another distinctive feature of several state executive structures is greater legislative control over some individual agencies' budgets and personnel, in comparison to Congress's hold over national government agencies. This varies, however, from state to state.

Larger cities like New York, Chicago, Houston, Philadelphia, Boston, and Los Angeles have bureaucratic arrangements not unlike those in state and national governments. (One example, Los Angeles' government organization, is illustrated in Figure 1–4.) There is a great deal of administrative specialization, a directly elected chief executive (mayor) with a highly developed executive-office staff, and similar bases of organization.

There are, however, some differences between local governments and state and national governments. Local party politics frequently plays a more prominent role in shaping municipal policy making (notably in Chicago, Boston, and New York), and local public employee unions have a great deal of influence in many cities (see Chapter 8). Activity of local governments is more heavily oriented to providing such essential services as water, sewage disposal and sanitation, and police and fire protection than to broader policy concerns, such as education, health care, welfare reform, and mass transit development.

In smaller communities, as well as in many counties and townships, bureaucratic structures are not very numerous or sophisticated. This can sometimes (although not always) mean that professional expertise is not as firmly established in local government as it is in most state governments and the national government. This lack of expertise is often reflected in the limited quantity and quality of programs enacted by many local governments, a pattern particularly visible in some rural county governments, many smaller towns and villages, and most special districts (although with declining frequency). As noted earlier, many local governments concentrate on providing basic urban services, with less emphasis on the sort of operating programs and regulatory activities that characterize state and national administration. The larger the unit of local government, the more likely its bureaucracy is to resemble state and national administrative agencies.

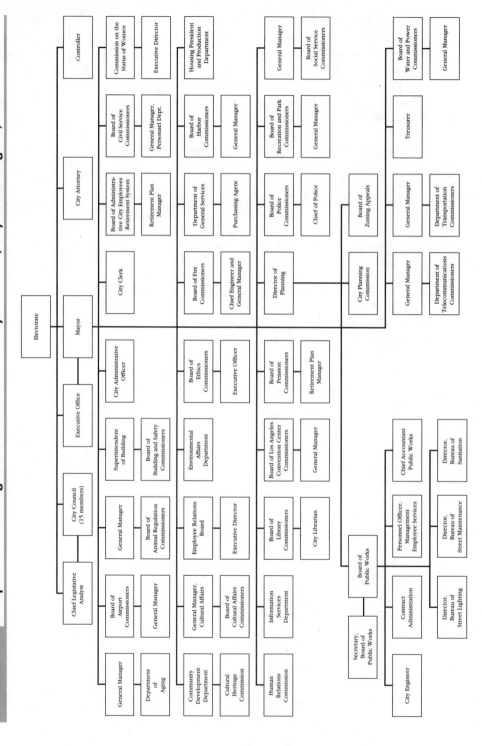

FIGURE 1–4   Adapted from an Organization Chart of the Mayor's Office, City of Los Angeles, 1996

Explaining the Growth of Government Bureaucracy

The reasons for the growth of public administrative functions are not readily apparent. A number of possibilities exist, each of which is worth examining for the influence it may have had on the expansion of public administrative agencies.

One explanation commonly cited is that, beginning in the 1800s and continuing today, *technological complexity* gradually exceeded the capacities of legislative bodies and of political generalists to cope successfully. This view assumes that professional specialization in a host of fields (including the physical and social sciences, management itself, and professions such as law and medicine), in effect, invaded the public service just as it assumed far greater importance in society at large. Thus, as both the nation's problems and methods of addressing them became more complex, specialized bureaucracies became more necessary in the process of discharging government's responsibilities — or so the argument runs. To some extent, technological complexity has had an important effect on bureaucracy (see Chapter 2), but whether it alone triggered bureaucratic growth is not certain.

According to a second view, *public pressures* helped create a diversified and responsive bureaucracy, primarily because economic and social interests (stakeholders) became increasingly diverse throughout our society and government began to recognize those interests. Political scientist James Q. Wilson has referred to the phenomenon of **clientelism,** a term that describes the relationships between individual government agencies and particular economic groupings, a pattern that first appeared about the time of the Civil War. Wilson cites another political scientist, Richard L. Schott, who noted that "whereas earlier departments had been formed around specialized governmental functions (foreign affairs, war, finance, and the like), the new departments of this period — Agriculture, Labor, and Commerce — were devoted to the interests and aspirations of particular economic groups."[13] That trend has intensified in this century to such a degree that it is now entirely appropriate to speak of bureaucratic clienteles or constituencies in the same sense as legislative constituencies. (See Chapter 3 for an elaboration of this theme.) This view, then, suggests that bureaucracies have been created or disestablished in response to popular demand for government action or inaction in specific policy fields.

A third explanation, which has its roots in the disciplines of economics and international relations, maintains that governmental responses to *crisis situations* (such as economic depressions or military conflicts) cause both revenues and expenditures of government to move sharply upward. More important, after the crisis has passed, the levels do not return to their precrisis status, and new ideas of what is acceptable emerge, resulting in new "routine" levels of government activity. As we shall see in Chapter 9 on government budgeting, national government expenditure levels underwent precisely this sort of shift after the Civil War and again after World War II, with political acceptability of the change generally high in both cases. This explanation indirectly emphasizes society's increasing

clientelism a phenomenon whereby patterns of regularized relationships develop and are maintained in the political process between individual government agencies and particular economic groupings; e.g., departments of agriculture, labor, and commerce, working with farm groups, labor groups, and business organizations, respectively.

readiness to turn to government for managing responses to major (and, perhaps, not so major) problems.

One final explanation, which also dates back to the late 1800s, overlaps all the previous ones. As the private economy became both more national in scope and more industrial in nature compared to the period before 1850, there developed a need for (and an implicit base of public acceptance of) *greater regulation* by the national government of private economic activities. Many of those regulative actions spawned new ones that, combined with the other forces at work (particularly crisis-related actions), led to the steady growth of public administrative entities. All four of these explanations appear to have some merit; together, they paint a clearer picture of how government bureaucracy has reached its present scope. Considering "how we got here" may be useful in light of contemporary efforts to deregulate, privatize, or impose curbs or restraints on administrative agencies.

Public and Private Administration: Similarities and Differences

Many similarities exist between administrative activities in the public and private sectors. In fact, many elements of public administration have their roots in the private sector. There are those who assume that whatever differences exist are relatively minor and that what works effectively in one setting will also work in the other; thus, for example, the recurring themes that we should make government more businesslike, provide public services equal to the best in business, and bring sound management methods from business into government. But the notion that there are few if any important differences between public and private administration is undergoing intense scrutiny. There is no consensus about the nature of "publicness" in organizations. Scholars are divided over the importance of an organization's public or private status.[14] This has led to increasing reliance on **nonprofit, or "third-sector," organizations** to deliver government services. Although some parallels do exist, there are also critical differences between the public and private sectors.

First the similarities. In both settings, managers and those to whom they are accountable have an interest in running programs and other activities that are properly designed, appropriately directed to meeting their intended goals, efficient in expenditure of organizational resources, and effective in their impacts. Public and private managers are both concerned with meeting their *staffing* needs, *motivating* subordinates, obtaining *financing*, and otherwise conducting their operations so as to promote the survival and maximum impact of their programs. All this involves some "politics," both internal and external to the organization. There are agreements to be reached and maintained, elements of persuasion and coercion to be weighed, and gains and losses to be realized. The president of the Ford Motor Company and the secretary of Health and Human

nonprofit, or "third-sector," organizations nongovernmental tax-exempt institutions, such as churches, hospitals, private colleges and universities, the United Way, and the Boy Scouts and Girl Scouts, which provide quasi-governmental services to many local communities using volunteers.

Services — as well as Ford's chief research engineer and the administrator at the U.S. Food and Drug Administration — have to be concerned with many of these same managerial issues, which must be carefully planned for and acted on to promote the organization's interest.

On the other hand, important elements of the managerial environment (including its "politics") differ for public and private managers.[15] One fundamental difference is that, in the private sector, products or services are furnished to individuals based on their own needs or wants in exchange for a direct (usually monetary) payment — a quid pro quo transaction. In the public sector, however, the goal of the manager historically has been to operate programs or provide services on a collective basis (rather than directly to individuals), supported in the great majority of cases by tax revenues, not direct payments (such as user charges or fees) for services rendered (although this has been changing since the 1970s). Another key difference is that private organizations define their markets and set their own broad goals, whereas public organizations and managers are obligated to pursue goals *set for them by their legislatures*. Public managers have relatively little freedom to alter basic organizational goals. Thus, while private managers can use an internal measure (the bottom line of profit or loss) to evaluate their organization's performance, public managers are subject ultimately to evaluation by outside forces (especially the legislature, the chief executive, the courts, and often the public itself), and it is those outside forces — not open markets — that have the critical last word in judging how well a public organization fulfills its responsibilities. Public managers, moreover, have been evaluated in somewhat nebulous and ill-defined terms. Until recently, for example, many managers have had more incentive to focus on satisfying interested clienteles and on holding and expanding political support than on substantive performance by itself. Meaningful, objective performance measures were largely lacking in the public sector until the mid-1970s, even where managers have sought to use them. New emphases on efficiency, productivity, and accountability for results have produced fresh concern for such measures (see Chapter 10) — another sign of increasing similarity between public and private organizations.

Other differences also exist. For one thing, many public organizations have held a virtual monopoly on providing certain essential public services and, consequently, have been able to survive without necessarily providing highest-quality performance of their functions (although that, too, has clearly begun to change). Another difference is that achieving results in the public sector must compete for administrators' attention with political and procedural concerns. Values such as participation and public accountability make it necessary for public managers to divide their attention between the *results* they seek and *how to obtain* those results. It is difficult to achieve maximum economy and efficiency while keeping a wary eye on possible political repercussions — and many public managers must do just that.

In contrast to the narrowly focused profit-oriented concern shared by most of private-sector management, there are often conflicting incentives among citizens, elected representatives, and administrative supervisors and leaders. If a consensus is lacking on *what* is to be done and *why* (not to mention *how*, as noted earlier), an organization will not function with the same smoothness it would if incentives were agreed on. Just as economic measures of performance have no counterpart in the public sector, general economic incentives have no parallel either.

Furthermore, most public organizations suffer from diffuse responsibility, often resulting in absence of accountability for decisions made. Separation of powers between branches of government is one factor in this, but fragmented executive-branch authority in most large governments (including those at the local level) is another. In contrast, centralized executive responsibility is a key feature of many profit-oriented organizations. (It should be noted, however, that exceptions to this generalization exist in both types of organization.) Also, unlike private organizations, public organizations entrust a fair amount of decision-making responsibility to citizen groups, courts, and various types of boards or commissions. Thus, an absolutely clear chain of command is not possible because of numerous opportunities for outside pressures to influence the power hierarchies (although some chief executives have tried to minimize those external pressures while enhancing their own leadership effectiveness; see Chapter 7).

There are still other important differences. Public-sector managers frequently must operate within structures designed by other groups (in some states, these can include private interest groups as well as government entities), work with people whose careers are in many respects outside management's control, and accomplish their goals in less time than is usually allowed corporate managers. Unlike many private managers, public managers must operate in a "goldfish bowl" of publicity in which they are subject to scrutiny and criticism from the press, others outside the agency, and the general public. As for the media spotlight, public managers must cope with critical comments from outside, regardless of how well others understand agency purposes, empathize with operating difficulties, or consider political constraints on the manager. Conversely, the skilled public manager may be able to turn the media, as well as critical stakeholders, to the agency's side, which can make it easier to recruit new staff, acquire more operating funds, or perhaps prevent potential critics from gaining credibility. At times, private managers may have to face the same types of public criticism or have similar opportunities to generate good press. But, for the most part, their activities are significantly less exposed to public view until the final product or service has been delivered and evaluated.

In comparing the changing roles of public, private, and nonprofit sectors, two other dimensions merit consideration. In practice, these sectors are becoming increasingly interdependent: one example of this is the multibillion-dollar government bailout of failed savings and loan institutions in the late 1980s and early 1990s. There is also a growing tendency for governments (especially on the local level) to enter into contractual arrangements with private firms for delivery of certain services, such as corrections, garbage collection, and fire protection.

For many, the distinction between public and private is becoming less important as functions overlap. There has been a considerable blurring of what many still believe to be a well-defined boundary between the two sectors. Nonetheless, a growing body of scholarly opinion holds that public organizations, and the roles of those who occupy key decision-making positions within them, are distinctive in important respects and that we need to develop a broader conceptual understanding of their design, function, and behavior.

Thus, although many administrative activities are common to both public and private sectors, major differences are also evident. As a result, there are obvious limits to how much the public sector can borrow advantageously from the private sector to improve the management of public affairs. As we shall see, however, those limits are breaking down as governments everywhere are being asked to do more with less (and, increasingly, to do *less* with less). At the same time, options are expanding as public administrators are able to choose from a much wider range of strategies to address public problems. This has led to greater interest in, and experimentation with, **privatization,** as well as direct delivery of services through third-sector nonprofit agencies. Even these emerging realities, however, do not change the fact that significant (and perhaps enduring) differences exist between public and private management.[16]

privatization a practice in which governments either join with, or yield responsibility outright to, private-sector enterprises, for provision of services previously managed and financed by public entities; a pattern especially evident in local government service provision, though with growing appeal at other levels of government. See also **contracting out.**

Public Administration as a Field of Study

The principal focus of public administration as a field of academic study has changed often since its emergence in the late 1800s. Changing and overlapping conceptions of the subject sometimes reflected and sometimes preceded evolution in administrative practice in the real world of government, and cross-fertilization of ideas between practitioners and academics has been prominent throughout the twentieth century. Because so many public administrators were trained in formal academic programs (thus increasing the impact that academic disciplines have had on government administrative practices), it is useful to review major emphases that have characterized and helped shape the academic field.[17]

In its earliest period, from roughly 1887 to 1933, public administration was viewed as distinct and separate from politics, more akin to business and business methods than to anything political. In his classic essay, *The Study of Administration*, Woodrow Wilson wrote that administration "is removed from the hurry and strife of politics. . . . Administrative questions are not political questions. Although politics sets the tasks for administration, it should not be suffered to manipulate its offices."[18] The concept of a dichotomy between politics and administration was widely accepted during this period, based not only on the writings of Wilson but also on the first textbook in the field, published by Frank Goodnow in 1900 and significantly entitled *Politics and Administration*. The bureaucracy was to administer, in an impartial and nonpolitical fashion, the programs created by the legislative branch, subject only to judicial interpretation.

The dichotomy between politics and administration was reiterated in Leonard D. White's *Introduction to the Study of Public Administration*, published in 1926. White summarized the conventional wisdom of administrative theory: Politics and administration were separate; management could be studied scientifically to discover the best methods of operation; public administration was capable of becoming a value-free science; and politically neutral administration should be focused exclusively on attainment of economy and efficiency in government.

The next phase in the development of the discipline was the movement toward discovering fundamental "principles" of administration. This offshoot of the scientific approach to administration was based on the belief that there existed certain permanent principles of administration that, if they could only be discovered and applied, could transform the performance of administrative tasks. Publication in 1927 of F. W. Willoughby's *Principles of Public Administration* marked the beginning of a decade in which identifying and correctly applying these principles was the predominant concern of many, both inside and outside of academic circles. Luther Gulick and Lyndall Urwick's *Papers on the Science of Administration*, published in 1937, defined seven principles that have become professional watchwords: planning, organizing, staffing, directing, coordinating, reporting, and budgeting (collectively known by the acronym **POSDCORB**). Gulick and Urwick reemphasized the importance of these administrative principles, declared their applicability to almost any human organization, regardless of what the organization was or why it existed, and stressed the fundamental desirability of efficiency as the underlying goal for administrative "science."[19]

POSDCORB acronym standing for the professional watchwords of administration: **P**lanning, **O**rganizing, **S**taffing, **D**irecting, **CO**ordinating, **R**eporting, **B**udgeting.

Even as Gulick and Urwick wrote these words, however, the dominant themes of public administration were changing. The orthodoxy of the first thirty years or so of the twentieth century — that is, the willingness of most of those in public administration to "embrace, without basic skepticism, the Wilsonian dichotomy"[20] between politics and administration — was no longer as widely shared as it had been. The New Deal of Franklin D. Roosevelt, accompanied by a vastly expanded governmental role and the creation of scores of new administrative agencies in Washington, significantly changed the social and political contexts of public administration and sparked a crisis in the field. There were three major developments in the period 1933–1945: (1) a "drastic expansion in the public conception of the obligations and responsibilities of government in social and economic affairs"; (2) the emergence of an "enduring emphasis upon presidential leadership"; and (3) a change in the nature of the federal system, with a shift to "the national scene [of] the responsibility for most of the important policy decisions" in the economy and society at large.[21] According to political scientist Alan Altshuler, Roosevelt had demonstrated "that patronage might be of great value in aiding a vigorous President to push through programs of social and economic reform."[22] Emphasis on nonpartisan neutrality could have obstructed presidential leadership in achieving social reforms supported by many academics. Blurring the politics–administration dichotomy caused considerable turmoil in the study of public administration as the discipline was cast loose from its original intellectual moorings without a clear alternative direction.

In the 1940s, with World War II commanding an even greater commitment in terms of government activity, the turmoil increased. Academics who worked for national government agencies during the war effort took back to their post-war campuses a considerably altered perspective on what was important to teach about administration, especially in relation to the political process and public administration's explicit role in making public policy.[23] During this same period (less than a decade after Gulick and Urwick had published their *Papers*), the principles of administration were coming under increasing fire. Critics claimed that the principles were logically inconsistent and potentially contradictory and that they gave no clues concerning how to choose the one most appropriate for particular situations. For example, one principle held that, for purposes of control, workers should be grouped according to either function, work process, clientele, or geography. There was nothing to suggest standards for using one instead of another nor whether these were mutually exclusive categories.[24] (As we have seen, however, these four categories are still used in government bureaucracy.) Critiques of this sort came from many scholars in the field but, in 1946 and 1947, few scholars had greater impact than Herbert Simon. In "The Proverbs of Administration,"[25] Simon likened the principles to contradictory proverbs or paired opposites. For example, Simon pointed out that, while "Look before you leap" is a useful proverb, so also is "He who hesitates is lost." Both are memorable, often applicable, and *mutually exclusive*, without any hint of how to choose between them. Simon argued that the principles underlying these proverbs were much the same; that is, they were interesting but of little practical value in defining administrative processes. His book *Administrative Behavior* (1947) developed this line of argument further and contributed significantly to the weakening of the principles approach.

No comparable set of values replaced the POSDCORB principles, but different concerns began to emerge. Through the 1940s and into the 1950s, public administration found its relationship to political science — its parent discipline — to be one of growing uneasiness. Political science itself was undergoing significant changes in the post–World War II period. Most of these changes were in the direction of developing more sophisticated, empirical (including statistical) methods of researching political phenomena but were always based on the assumption that objectivity in research methodology was of the highest importance.

The problem for public administration in this "behavioral" era was that many functions and processes of administration do not lend themselves to the same sorts of quantitative research as do, for example, legislative voting patterns, election data, and public opinion surveys. Altshuler points out that administrative decision making is frequently informal and that many decisions are made in partial or total secrecy. He also states that the exact values of administrators and the alternatives they consider are difficult to identify and analyze and that the traditional emphasis on efficiency (which has by no means disappeared) contrasts sharply with the core concerns of modern political science.[26] Consequently, public administration became, in Altshuler's words, a "rather peripheral subfield of political science," with many questioning its place in the larger discipline.

Another related development was the growth of research into administrative and organizational behavior; this research sought to examine all sorts of organizations, not only (or even necessarily) *public* entities. This movement worked from the assumption that the social psychology of organizations made less important the question of precisely what kind of organization was to be studied and sought to integrate research from not only social psychology but also business administration, information science, sociology, and statistics. This field, currently known as **organizational development,** represents an attempt to synthesize much of what is known about organized group behavior within the boundaries of formal organizations.

Altshuler questions whether this direction — as valuable as it has been in furthering our understanding of human behavior in an increasingly organized society — has resulted in research findings that have political relevance, that is, relevance to the research directions of contemporary political science.[27] Public administration scholar Nicholas Henry goes further than Altshuler, asserting that public administration declared its intellectual and institutional independence from political science and business administrative science, moving instead toward the establishment of autonomous departments or programs.[28]

Public administration as an academic field of study, then, is far from a settled discipline.[29] The boundaries between it and other fields are blurred, and there are many loose ends in terms of what to study and how. Public administration has a history of conflict with its parent discipline (political science), and growing controversy exists over just where public administration belongs intellectually and institutionally. It is within this volatile setting that we take up our study of public administration.

organizational development a theory of organization that concentrates on increasing the ability of an organization to solve internal problems of organizational behavior as one of its routine functions; primarily concerned with identification and analysis of such problems.

A Word About This Book

Two brief comments are in order about what to look for in this book. First, three essential and recurring themes appear in the following pages: (1) maintaining the *ethics* and *accountability* of public administrators within the context of the larger political system, (2) increasing the internal *efficiency* and *economy* of public resources, and (3) improving the *effectiveness* or *results* of public programs — especially through the application of information technology — in the real world of public management. An effort is made to treat these issues separately, but it is inevitable that they overlap, both in our treatment of them and in the working environments of public administration.

Second, the discussion of public bureaucracy and management can and does go on at three different (but interrelated) levels of analysis, that is, with a focus on three distinct dimensions of the administrative process. One is the *role and function of government bureaucracy in society at large* — what differences large, complex, and influential agencies make in a nation founded on diffuse notions of popular rule (note the implicit importance of the accountability theme). A second dimension or level of analysis is the *management of public organizations*, broadly defined as issues and challenges confronting the individual public manager. A third topic is the *role of the individual* — the contribution, in whatever form, of a person working as a public administrator and the problems and opportunities associated with that role. All these are ultimately interrelated, and explaining why that is so is a major purpose of this book.

Summary

Public administration has become a prominent and influential force in American government and society. Most of us are familiar with bureaucracy, and many of our most pressing current political issues are related to administrative agencies and actions. Public administration is the set of processes, organizations, and individuals associated with implementing laws and other rules enacted by legislatures, executives, and courts. It also includes administrative agency involvement in the formulation of many of these rules, as well as their application. Public administration is simultaneously an academic field of study and an active field of training. Public administration and its politics involve interactions both internal and external to the formal agency structure. Public administration is also characterized by a distinctly managerial component, focusing on the internal dynamics of public organizations. Public managers need certain skills, including management of information technology, personnel, and budgeting. A successful public manager must direct both short- and long-term activities and is responsible for defining and bringing about action. Most managers operate within a bureaucratic and political environment that shapes both formal structure and operational policies of their organizations.

Public administration in the national government is characterized by several different types of agencies, and ways of categorizing administrative employees; each of these may affect what agencies do and how they do it. The principal agencies are cabinet-level departments, independent regulatory boards and commissions, government corporations, divisions of the executive office of the president, and other miscellaneous agencies. These are most commonly organized according to function but can also be organized according to geographic area, clientele served, or work process. Administrative personnel can be classified according to whether they were hired through merit procedures or political appointment and whether they are specialists or generalists.

The organizational structure of state and local executive branches is generally comparable to that of the national government. In larger states and local governments, some essentials of organization are the same as those at the national and state levels. But the influence of local political parties and employee unions and the nature of government activity serve to differentiate local governments from the national government. Smaller local governments usually have less extensive bureaucratic development and less professional expertise than the national government.

Several explanations have been advanced for the rise of government bureaucracy, including: technological complexity, public pressures in an increasingly diverse society, and government responses to social and economic crises. Greater public acceptance of regulation over the years has reinforced the impact of these factors on the growth of bureaucracy.

Many similarities, and a number of more significant differences, exist between public and private management. Two of the most important differences are that public managers must pursue broad goals set by others and evaluated by outside forces; neither is true of private managers. In addition, public managers generally cannot design their own organization's structures or control the careers of many subordinates. They generally have far less time than private managers to accomplish their goals and must operate under considerable public scrutiny. Both public and private managers are expected to be similarly competent, effective, and efficient in producing results. There is growing overlap of the two sectors.

As an academic field of study, public administration has been shaped by several major and partially overlapping schools of thought: (1) the politics–administration dichotomy; (2) the pursuit of economy and efficiency as the key objectives of public administration; (3) the search for principles of administration; (4) rejection of the principles approach; (5) a turning toward different perspectives on administrative behavior (such as social and psychological factors in internal organizational processes); (6) growing ferment regarding the links between public administration and its parent discipline, political science; and (7) developing trends that seem to carry the study of administration away from political science and allied fields of administrative study and toward disciplinary autonomy. This book will focus on the interrelationships between politics and public administration, with attention to managerial aspects as well.

KEY TERMS AND CONCEPTS

bureaucracy	Office of Management and Budget
authority	(OMB)
entrepreneurial government	clientelism
public administration	nonprofit, or "third-sector,"
stakeholders	organizations
public management	privatization
information technology (IT)	POSDCORB
reverse pyramid	organizational development

SUGGESTED READING

Barzelay, Michael, with Babak Armajani. *Breaking Through Bureaucracy*. Berkeley, Calif.: University of California Press, 1992.

Goodsell, Charles T. *The Case for Bureaucracy: A Public Administration Polemic*. 3rd ed. Chatham, N.J.: Chatham House, 1994.

King, Cheryl Simrell, and Camilla Stivers, eds. *Government is Us: Public Administration in an Anti-Government Era*. Thousand Oaks, Calif.: Sage Publications, 1998.

Mosher, Frederick C., ed. *American Public Administration: Past, Present, Future*. University, Ala.: University of Alabama Press, 1975.

Nye, Joseph S., Philip D. Zelikow, and David C. King, eds. *Why People Don't Trust Government*. Cambridge, Mass.: Harvard University Press, 1997.

Ostrom, Vincent. *The Intellectual Crisis in American Public Administration*. 2nd ed. University, Ala.: University of Alabama Press, 1989.

Perry, James L., ed. *Handbook of Public Administration*. 2nd ed. San Francisco: Jossey-Bass, 1996.

Stillman, Richard J. II *The American Bureaucracy: The Core of Modern Government*. 2nd ed. Chicago: Nelson-Hall, 1996.

Tolchin, Susan J. *The Angry American: How Voter Rage Is Changing the Nation*. Boulder, Colo.: Westview Press, 1996.

Waldo, Dwight. *The Enterprise of Public Administration*. Novato, Calif.: Chandler & Sharp, 1980.

Wamsley, Gary, et al. *Refounding Democratic Public Administration*. Newbury Park, Calif.: Sage, 1996.

White, Leonard D. *Introduction to the Study of Public Administration*. New York: Macmillan, 1926.

ON-LINE RESOURCES:
Approaching the Study of Public Administration

Federal Computer Products Center
(National Technical Information Service)

http://www.ntis.gov/fcpc/

The current inventory of computer products includes more than 1,200 titles, datafiles, software on diskettes, CD-ROMs, and magnetic tape. Most of the Center's products are developed or sponsored by the federal government. However, NTIS does announce products developed by state governments and in a few cases by private sector organizations and distributed by NTIS.

Federal Government Information Sharing Project (U.S. Department of Education)

http://govinfo.kerr.orst.edu/index.html

This site provides interactive access to government-produced demographic, economic, and education data.

Federal Government Resources on the Web (University of Michigan's Documents Center)

http://www.lib.umich.edu/libhome/Documents.center/federal.html

This site contains many relevant links to United States federal government information. Useful items include the congressional directories with e-mail addresses.

Federal Research and Educational Opportunities

http://www.sciencewise.com/fedix/

FEDIX is an outreach tool for participation agencies to provide information to educational and research organizations.

Fedstats (Federal Interagency Council on Statistical Policy)

http://www.fedstats.gov/

This site is well organized and user-friendly with links to more than seventy federal agencies that produce statistics of interest to the public. It provides easy access to the full range of statistics and information produced by these agencies for public use.

FEDWORLD Information Network (U.S. Department of Commerce, National Technical Information Service)

http://www.fedworld.gov/

FEDWORD enables users to find useful federal sites for everyday needs. This is one of the premier government Web sites, serving as the jump station for all other government divisions.

Government Information Xchange

http://www.info.gov/

Using the Government Information Xchange's Federal Yellow Pages, one can access a clearinghouse of printable forms on useful topics, including copyright forms, tax forms, federal student aid forms, Social Security forms, voter registration forms, etc.

Index to Federal, State, and Local Web Sites

http://www.searchgov.com

> Comprehensive site linking Congress, executive agencies, and state and local governments.

Library of Congress Home Page

http://www.loc.gov/

> This site is an authoritative source of government information on the executive branch, Congress, judicial branch, and state and local governments (U.S.).

Public Administration Review

http://www.niu.edu/ext/par/

> Public Administration Review is a journal for practitioners, scholars, teachers, and trainers interested in the public sector and public-sector management. Articles identify and analyze current trends, provide a factual basis for decision making, stimulate discussion, and make the literature in the field available in an easily accessible format.

Statistical Abstract of the United States
(U.S. Government Printing Office)

http://www.census.gov/statab/www/

> Perhaps the single most useful collection of statistical information available in a small package, this site includes hundreds of statistical tables on areas such as population, economics, and social factors, with references to the original sources. An index to the tables provides easy access.

U.S. Census Bureau: The Official Statistics

http://www.census.gov

> This site offers Internet access to an astounding amount of demographic, social, an economic data. The search engine allows for pinpointing relevant statistical tables and reports and the site is updated almost daily with newly released reports.

U.S. Government Agencies Directory

http://www.lib.lsu.edu/gov/fedgov.html

> This directory provides a list of federal agencies on the Internet.

U.S. Government Manual Online

http://www.access.gpo.gov/nara/browse-gm.html

On-line access to the federal government's official handbook.

U.S. Office of Management and Budget Home Page

http://www.whitehouse.gov/OMB/

At this site you can read the federal budget and other publications.

U.S. Postal Service

http://www.usps.gov

The official Web site of the Postal Service.

The White House

http://www.whitehouse.gov/

Official White House site with numerous links to federal executive agencies.

For further information on the political environment of public administration see: Bedford/St. Martin's Home Page

http://www.bedfordstmartins.com

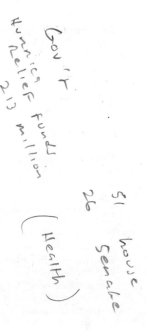

Chapter 2

Public Administration, Democracy, and the Political System: Conflicting Values and Social Change

The exercise of discretionary power, the making of value choices, is a characteristic and increasing function of administrators and bureaucrats; they are thus importantly engaged in politics.

Wallace S. Sayre, "Premises of Public Administration: Past and Emerging," 1958.

The decisions of public administrators do not take place in a vacuum. They are powerfully influenced by broader economic, social, and governmental processes — the constitutional allocations of political power, the exercise of power by those inside and outside of government, and the overall roles assigned to elected officials, judges, and appointed administrators in governing the nation. In turn, the *governmental system* (like all other human institutions) is continuously being reshaped by society's values and beliefs (both past and present) about what should be done and how it should be done. A major influence on these beliefs is the social setting of government, including society's basic values, the extent of popular agreement on them, how directly they relate to the conduct of government, and how government reflects and shapes them. The values of other institutions in society (such as business, education, and the mass media) also shape government and public administration. Conflicting values create demands and expectations that may need to be met through government action. For example, the public demands a commitment to public safety, national security, and education, as well as ethical conduct from elected and nonelected administrators; it also expects the government to conduct its affairs in a "businesslike" manner, with a high degree of economy and efficiency.

Another set of issues that surfaced in the early 1990s centered around the widespread public perception that government was functioning less and less effectively and that many small problems within government bureaucracy had

reinventing government the Clinton administration initiative based on the best-selling 1992 book *Reinventing Government: How the Entrepreneurial Spirit Is Transforming the Public Sector,* by David Osborne and Ted Gaebler. The book documents successful public-sector efforts to apply market-based, quality, and customer service principles to government. See also **National Partnership for Reinventing Government (NPRG)** (formerly the National Performance Review).

National Partnership for Reinventing Government (NPRG) formerly the National Performance Review, NPRG is the Clinton administration's effort to reform the federal government. For an overview, see the NPRG's Internet home page, <http://www.npr.gov>.

combined and multiplied into larger ones. In particular, calls for **reinventing government** were heard, suggesting that government should give its utmost attention to "serving its customers well," and should try to instill an "entrepreneurial spirit" into as many of its operations as possible. Journalist David Osborne attracted a considerable following with facile prescriptions for *Reinventing Government* (coauthored with former city manager Ted Gaebler) and *Banishing Bureaucracy* (coauthored with Peter Plastrick),[1] much of the content of which has been endorsed publicly by many people at all levels, both inside and outside of government. There is no question that these authors caught the imagination of many in this country who are anxious to see some kind of change in government operations.

The questions raised by this clarion call are numerous and will be addressed throughout this book, but a central question can be identified here: *Does this movement represent a fundamental shift in the administrative values underlying governmental practice in the United States, or is it merely a passing trend?* Over the years, many administrative practices have been established, altered, revised again, and then perhaps made routine or even discarded. Such changes are relatively easy to identify and describe. However, it is far more difficult to say with certainty when value shifts occur and, when they do occur, if they are going to be temporary or permanent. This is particularly true during periods of profound cynicism and distrust about all government actions. The ultimate measure of success for this effort, however, will be a change in public attitudes about the ability of government agencies to cope with basic social expectations.[2]

Since 1993, the Clinton administration has expended considerable resources to "reinvent government" — that is, drastically altering the ways the federal government conducts its affairs and interacts with the "customers" (citizens) it serves. Under the direction of Vice President Albert Gore, the **National Partnership for Reinventing Government (NPRG)**— formerly the National Performance Review — has succeeded in reducing the number of federal workers by 375,000, increasing the efficiency of the federal executive branch, cutting layers of supervisory management, eliminating 16,000 pages of unnecessary regulations, setting performance standards for federal executive agencies, and saving the taxpayers nearly $140 billion in lower operating expenses.

Public administration has been sharply affected by changes in values concerning the role of government, in administrative concepts (including reinventing government and infusing an entrepreneurial spirit into government activities) and, in general, social values and public demands. On the one hand, *modern bureaucracy is the result of past evolution in theory and practice.* In general, institutional change tends to be cumulative: as patterns of behavior come and go, they leave behind carryover effects, which then mingle with, and become indistinguishable from, the patterns that replace them. So it is with contemporary administrative policies and machinery, in which much of what we do today reflects lingering influences of the past. On the other hand, *social values and established institutional patterns are undergoing rapid, unpredictable, and turbulent change.* Today, many basic values are changing, such as those relating to marriage and family life, sex roles, respect for authority, job security, "entitlements," material possessions, the environment, and human rights. For traditional institutions (including bureaucracy) to respond to such social upheaval is a large order, and much recent criticism of bureaucracy focuses on its apparent failure to do so.

Out of all this has come a renewed interest in *democratic values* as they pertain to public trust and control of government institutions. With the tremendous expansion of government bureaucracies have come clearer distinctions between *political values*, such as equality, fairness, representation, participation, patriotism, and accountability; *social values*, such as concern for others, civic duty, individual achievement, and morality; and *administrative values*, such as political neutrality, secrecy, economy, efficiency, rationality, rule of law, and expertise. Some of America's traditional values — democracy, equality, freedom of speech and religious expression, and the belief that America has a special moral responsibility internationally — have remained constant throughout decades of social change. Other values, such as duty to one's country, social conformity, respectability, accepted norms of sexual morality, and the work ethic, have declined in importance for many people. Values *gaining* in importance during this same era include respect for diversity, pluralism, greater acceptance of individual differences, wider choices in personal lifestyles, concern for the environment, emphasis on quality of work life, belief in technology as a solution to many problems, putting family ahead of career and personal ambition, assuming individual responsibility for health care and retirement, and protecting the rights of women and children. As greater numbers of interests espouse different and often conflicting values, it becomes less and less likely that all groups in society as a whole will share a common set of *value preferences*. As always, when different values conflict, it is more difficult to compromise and reach consensus. In this chapter, we examine those value conflicts as they pertain to public administration and then deal more extensively with specific problems in this area.

Equally important to the context of public administration is social change in, among other things, the makeup of the population; the nature of the economy; social relationships (such as marriage, child rearing, divorce, the generation gap); and where people choose to live (such as city or suburb, Sun Belt or Snow Belt). Social change is important because emerging social arrangements and patterns of behavior are inevitably accompanied by new problems with which government policymakers must contend. It is also important because, as society changes, so do our values, expectations, and priorities.

The Political System and Government Bureaucracy

In this section, we will review several traditional conceptions relating to bureaucratic activity and will briefly discuss how our political system has affected American bureaucracies in light of these conceptions. This is an introductory treatment only, for our complex political processes cannot be described adequately in a few words; the same is true of the impacts of that political complexity on our public administrative institutions. Even this brief discussion, however, will help to set the stage for a fuller exploration of the political values that underlie our governmental processes, the administrative values that have helped to shape the conduct of public administration, and the many facets of social change.

Traditional Conceptions of Bureaucracy in Government

Bureaucracy has traditionally been conceived of in terms of implementing directives of other government institutions as a servant of political forces *external* to it but not as a political force in its own right. This notion of **bureaucratic neutrality** is central to an understanding of the way executive-branch bureaucracies have been designed to function in Western governments for over a century. A number of companion assumptions have also been evident in administrative practice.

First, bureaucratic behavior is assumed to follow the intent of the legislature in the form of legislative enactments and guidelines for implementation. With **legislative intent** assumed as a principal guiding force, the bureaucracy's responsibility to the legislature is clearly established: it relies on the legislature for substantive policy direction and for financial and political support. The legislature, in turn, looks to the bureaucracy for faithful and competent administration of the laws.

Second, there is a legitimate function of **legislative oversight,** or supervision, of bureaucratic behavior that logically complements legislative intent. In other words, the legislature is expected to supervise the work of the bureaucracy. Present in both assumptions is the expectation that the bureaucracy is distinctly subordinate to the will and initiative of other parts of the government.

Third, bureaucratic behavior is assumed to be subject to direction by the chief executive of the government. The apparent contradiction between chief-executive direction and legislative direction of the bureaucracy stems from the fact that these traditional assumptions were derived from **parliamentary forms of government.** In parliamentary forms of government, the chief executive and top-level ministers are themselves members of the legislature. Parliamentary government is practiced in most democratic nations, and the chief executive (prime minister or premier) is usually the leader of the majority party in the legislature (parliament). In this situation, bureaucratic responsiveness to the chief executive and to the legislature are one and the same thing. There is, however, a real contradiction — and often, a conflict — between chief-executive and legislative control of the bureaucracy in a system such as ours. In the United States, the chief executive and top-level executives are independent of the legislature. In fact, they are almost always *prohibited* from serving in the legislature at the same time that they hold executive office. Republican candidate Bob Dole (R-Kansas) resigned his position as majority leader of the Senate in order to run for the presidency in 1996.

bureaucratic neutrality a central feature of bureaucracy whereby it carries out directives of other institutions of government (such as the chief executive or the legislature) in a politically neutral way, without acting as a political force in its own right; a traditional notion concerning bureaucratic behavior in Western governments; also called *political neutrality*.

legislative intent the goals, purposes, and objectives of a legislative body, given concrete form in its enactments (though actual intent may change over time); bureaucracies are assumed to follow legislative intent in implementing laws.

legislative oversight the process by which a legislative body supervises or oversees the work of the bureaucracy in order to ensure its conformity with legislative intent.

parliamentary form of government a form of government practiced in most democratic nations, including France, Germany, the United Kingdom, and Japan in which the chief executive and top-level ministers are themselves members of the legislature.

Finally, it was traditionally assumed that the bureaucracy would be a neutral, professional, competent structure staffed by specialists in both general administrative processes and their respective specific policy areas. The notion of a competent bureaucracy responding in a *politically neutral* manner to the initiatives of executives and legislators external to it seems to conform to the image of administration held by many Americans and has had a powerful influence on administrative design and practice in this country. The "inaccuracy" of this image is the focus of the next section of this chapter. (See also Chapters 3, 8, and 10.)

The Dynamics of Policy Making in the United States

There is little question in many parliamentary governments about how, by whom, and through what channels authority is exercised. In the United States, however, such questions take on added importance because, in our system, there are no similarly convenient answers. Government power and authority in America are, by design, highly fragmented and scattered, for the framers of the Constitution feared nothing as much as excessive concentrations of power. Therefore, they did all they could to divide power among the different branches of the national government, and they gave each branch various means of checking the power of the other two. The division of power is called **checks and balances.** Such a division of power within national, state, and (to a lesser extent) local governments places bureaucracy in this country in a very different position from the one it occupies in parliamentary systems.

The making of public policy in the United States and the bureaucracy's participation in that process are characterized by a number of major features. For one thing, the process lacks a centralized mechanism that comprehensively directs traffic. Rather, many centers of power are scattered throughout the executive and legislative branches. This lack of centralization produces a great deal of slack in the decision-making system. That is, in the absence of tight legislative or executive control, there are many opportunities for lower-ranking executives to affect implementation of a law. This phenomenon of **administrative discretion** is widespread, arising not only from structural separation of powers but also from conflicts that characterize executive-legislative relations and from statutory language that is often broad or even vague.

It follows that there are many **power vacuums** throughout the decision-making process. This is the basis for some, but not all, of the conflict between president and Congress and between many governors and their legislatures. The existence of a power vacuum also allows those involved in the decision-making process to compete for relatively small amounts of power, thereby increasing their influence (if they can) a little at a time. Among the most active contenders for these small quantities of power are interest groups and bureaucratic agencies, both of which seek to dominate policy making in the areas of greatest concern to them.

checks and balances a governing principle, following from separation of powers, which creates overlapping and interlocking functions among the executive, legislative, and judicial branches of government. These include: the president's power to veto an act of Congress (and Congress's power to override a presidential veto by a two-thirds majority); the Senate's power to confirm or reject presidential appointments to executive and judicial positions; and the power of the courts to determine the constitutionality of the actions of other branches.

administrative discretion the ability of individual administrators in a bureaucracy to make significant choices affecting management and operation of programs for which they are responsible; particularly evident in systems with separation of powers. Related terms: *discretionary authority, discretionary power.*

power vacuum where power to govern is splintered, there will inevitably be attempts by some to exercise that power which is not clearly defined and is, therefore, "up for grabs."

It is not only formal governmental power that is fragmented and scattered in American politics. So, too, is the ability to influence policy making in specific subject areas. In other words, there is no one overarching policy process in which the same top government officials make all decisions and take responsibility for them. Rather, the policy-making process is broken into many parts, and responsibility over each component is determined by a combination of factors. In such a setting, it is not uncommon for public administrators to become significant players in the political game, to assume an advocacy stance, and to take initiatives that influence the long-term development of policies, especially in specific programs under their jurisdictions.

Thus, bureaucracy in American government differs from traditional notions of bureaucracy in important ways. First, it functions in a system in which power is far from centralized. Second, bureaucracy has had at its disposal, for many years, a great deal of discretionary power in making day-to-day decisions and in dealing with broader policy questions. Third, accountability is enforced through multiple channels as a result of the fragmentation of higher political authority.

How does all this affect the behavior of public administrators? It is impossible to answer that question entirely in a few words, but two general observations suggest the nature of the political environment. First, bureaucracies often have independent momentum with which political leaders must contend if they are to influence bureaucratic activity — hardly the conditions suggested by traditional conceptions of bureaucracy. Top executives are not always able to command the civilian bureaucracy to act. Quite the contrary, senior appointed officials are viewed as part-timers, whose influence on the "permanent" bureaucracy is limited. One advantage of this situation, however, is that public bureaucracies can more easily develop continuity in their operations because career employees are directed more by strong "institutional memory" than by the influence of any one appointed senior official. (See Chapters 7 and 8.) Second, bureaucratic activity focuses predominantly on the respective areas of agency jurisdiction; a bureaucracy will usually contest any significant change in the policy area for which it is responsible. Both of these phenomena indicate the nonneutral stance of American public bureaucracy. This is one of the most important differences between American bureaucratic practice and any ideal model of bureaucracy against which it might be measured.

Political Values

Our discussion of political and administrative values has three purposes: (1) to understand the fundamental beliefs underlying American government and public bureaucracy, (2) to recognize the impact of values on public administration, and (3) to see the ways in which these values conflict conceptually — and how that conflict affects the conduct of public administration.

As used here and in Chapter 1, the term *political values* refers to basic beliefs and assumptions not only about politics and the political system but also about appropriate government relationships to private activity, especially economic activity. Links to economic activity fall under the heading of political values and are relevant to a discussion of public administration because of increasing governmental responsibility in regulating business and industry.

In general, the United States is regarded politically as a **liberal democracy** and economically as a **capitalist system.**[2] The two concepts of **popular sovereignty** and **limited government** are central to the notion of liberal democracy. Popular sovereignty — government by the ultimate consent of the governed — implies some degree of popular participation in voting and other political actions. Although this does not necessarily mean mass or universal political involvement, America has, in fact, expanded voting rights over the years. The specific vehicle for popular rule has been representative government. Initially, Americans emphasized legislative **representation,** which is stressed by the Constitution. More recently, concern has grown for political representation and demographic **representativeness,** notably in administrative organizations and processes. This concern has principally taken the form of efforts to promote affirmative action in hiring, with the goal a public service that, in the words of Bill Clinton, "looks like America." These subtle changes in meaning have cumulatively made it more difficult to determine whether democratic or administrative values are being maintained. Conceptual uncertainty about values also makes it more difficult to deal with accusations that we are not living up to our own standards of democratic government. For example, defining representativeness in a particular way might, in effect, include one group while *excluding* another from decision making, and the excluded might well dispute the existence of representativeness. Public discontent with affirmative action and preferential hiring policies has prompted groups in many states to challenge these policies by placing them on the ballot to be decided through public initiative and referenda. In recent decades, as the public grew dissatisfied with the degree of popular control over bureaucracy, greater representativeness in bureaucracy was seized on as one remedy that had considerable appeal. Political scientist Herbert Kaufman has gone so far as to suggest that "the quest for representativeness . . . centers *primarily* on administrative agencies."[4]

The second central concept, limited government, reflects the predominant view of those who framed the Constitution that government poses a basic threat to individual liberties. In their experience with the British government, these men had endured the suppression of their personal liberties, and they wanted to prevent that from happening again. Therefore, they incorporated into the Constitution four devices that effectively limit government: (1) *separation of powers* among the executive, legislative, and judicial branches of government; (2) a system of *checks and balances* in which the exercise of even a fundamental power by one branch requires the involvement of a second branch; (3) *federalism,* a division

---

liberal democracy
a fundamental form of political arrangement founded on the concepts of popular sovereignty and limited government.

capitalist system an economic system where the means of production are owned by private citizens.

popular sovereignty government by the ultimate consent of the governed, which implies some degree of popular participation in voting and other political actions; does not necessarily mean mass or universal political involvement.

limited government refers to devices built into the Constitution that effectively limit the power of government over individual citizens.

representation a principle of legislative selection based on the number of inhabitants or amount of territory in a legislative district; *adequate, fair,* and *equal* representation has become a major objective of many who feel they were denied it in the past and now seek greater influence, particularly in administrative decision making.

representativeness groups that have been relatively powerless should be represented in government positions in proportion to their numbers in the population.

of powers between government levels in which certain powers are allotted to the national government while others are retained by the states (which are to some degree independent of control by the national government); and (4) *judicial review*, the process by which courts can invalidate, on constitutional grounds, the laws and actions of other government entities. In addition to this fragmentation of government powers, the Bill of Rights (the first ten amendments to the Constitution) established broad areas of protection for individual liberties against encroachment by official government actions.

individualism   a philosophical belief in the worth and dignity of the individual, particularly as part of a political order; holds that government and politics should regard the well-being and aspirations of individuals as more important than those of government.

Two related concepts widely reflected in American society are **individualism** and **pluralism.** Our emphasis on the individual is evident in the complex of protections for civil rights and liberties, but individualism also implies the right to participate meaningfully in the political process. The theory and practice of pluralism stresses group organization as a means of securing protection for broad group interests in society. Furthermore, it assumes that groups of citizens have the right to organize to advance their interests, that groups with differing interests will bargain with one another, and that the resulting compromises will benefit the community and the nation as a whole. The rights of all citizens to "organize to advance their interests" links the Bill of Rights, individualism, and pluralism, suggesting that individual freedom includes the right to become active in organized interest groups.

pluralism   a social and political concept stressing the appropriateness of group organization, and diversity of groups and their activities, as a means of protecting broad group interest in society; assumes that groups are good and that bargaining and competition among them will benefit the public interest.

Directly related to individualism and pluralism is the capitalist notion of political and economic *competition*, which exists primarily among groups but is also found among individuals. Limited government suggests that economic competition will be loosely regulated by government; in theory, market competition itself will establish boundaries of acceptable behavior among the competitors and will allocate the fruits of victory. Geared to private profit and general economic growth, these economic doctrines fit very comfortably with capitalist theories. They emphasize maximum freedom for private entrepreneurs (individuals) and minimal government involvement in the decisions and operations of the private economic sector. Two assumptions link capitalism to political values of limited government, individualism, and pluralism: (1) the individual is assumed to be both self-sufficient and capable of being self-governing (thus minimizing the need for government), and (2) the individual is thought to be better off both politically and economically if government intervention is restricted.

During the twentieth century, government's relationship to the economy changed dramatically, and what was once minimal involvement increased. Have limited government and capitalism, then, been lost? Some argue that they have. Others suggest that government programs for economic development and social welfare are neither radical nor brand-new ideas, and that governments have a responsibility within the broader framework of capitalism to ensure economic well-being and social justice, as well as providing for the common defense and ensuring domestic tranquillity.

It should be noted that our values generally emphasize *how* things are accomplished more than *what* is accomplished. Our political values stress the importance of means, not ends. The end does not justify the means; rather, procedures are valued for their own sake, and fair procedure lends legitimacy to what is done. Hence our commitment to due process of law — although there is an inevitable gap between ideal and reality. Our ideology does not attempt to define specifically what is good or correct public policy. We leave it to the political process to formulate policy while we concentrate on ensuring that the process is characterized by some degree of public access to decision making and decision makers, a certain amount of equity in the distribution of political and economic benefits, and a great deal of market competition among diverse interests. The amount of access, equity, or competition that exists is itself a matter requiring resolution. These values serve as standards against which political reality is measured; only rarely do realities match the rhetoric or thinking. But that does not alter the importance of these political values or their influence on what we may try to accomplish through the implementation of public policy.

A major political value in America has been **representative democracy,** and increasing emphasis has been placed on democratizing the political process. What that entails has not always been clear, however. Some elements of democracy are universally supported (or nearly so), whereas others are the subject of controversy. Most agree, for example, that *majority rule* and *minority rights* are fundamental. The former enables the political system to make and implement binding decisions through popular control; the latter permits those not in the majority the freedom to voice their political views and otherwise to be politically active. Directly related to these principles are the constitutional guarantees of a "free marketplace of political ideas" — that is, the freedom to speak, write, and publish political concepts and commentaries, including those out of favor with officials and the majority of citizens. Most of us would, at least, pay lip service to free expression of ideas. (Numerous studies of public opinion suggest, however, that many Americans are inconsistent in their willingness to allow free expression of unpopular ideas, such as Communist ideology or advocacy of elective abortion.) Most would also agree that democracy requires widespread participation in the election of public officials by means of voting and active participation in political campaigns.

One element emphasized in the last half-century as essential to democratic government is *direct participation* in making and administering important decisions by those affected most directly by them.[5] Initially, there was considerable resistance to this idea (both in the abstract and in practice) in light of the extensive reallocation of political resources and power that would be required. Nevertheless, calls for **participatory democracy** in general and participative management in particular have met with increasingly positive responses. Where it has been implemented, direct participation has had the effect of increasing the number of decision makers — such as citizens giving testimony at public hearings and participating in managing program operations, and emerging forms of voluntarism — at the same time that it altered decision-making mechanisms (and very often the content of some decisions). Whether representative

representative democracy   representatives are nominated and elected from individual districts. They compose a legislature that makes binding decisions for its society.

participatory democracy   a political and philosophical belief in direct involvement by affected citizens in the processes of governmental decision making; believed by some to be essential to the existence of democratic government. A related term is *citizen participation.*

democracy requires widespread direct participation is open to debate, but merely raising the question has had an impact on our thinking about democracy and on the ways some government decisions have come to be made.

Another idea about democratic government, closely related to direct participation, was an expanded definition of what constitutes "representativeness" in our major institutions. The claim was made, with some justification, that numerous groups in the population — women, gays, lesbians, African Americans, and Latinos in particular — had been regularly excluded from decision making in government, business, industry, the legal system, religious hierarchies, labor organizations, and political parties. It was argued that these institutions had not been sufficiently responsive to the needs, interests, and preferences of such groups. This systematic exclusion from power needed to be corrected, and increased direct representation of these groups in key decision-making positions was advocated as the most appropriate remedy. Not surprisingly, considerable tension has been generated over this policy ever since it entered the political arena. Although many governments at all levels have moved steadily to increase representativeness (or diversity) in the workforce, many citizens remain uneasy for a variety of reasons. Starting in the early 1970s, national government guidelines for **affirmative action** to remedy past discrimination were implemented. Educational institutions, local police forces, collegiate athletics, and other programs and institutions that wished to receive federal funds had to comply with those guidelines. But compliance was often grudging at best and was accompanied only intermittently by changes in the attitudes and values in question. Furthermore, with the aid of a number of Supreme Court appointments by the Reagan and Bush administrations and several subsequent lower-court decisions, some parts of the policy have been successfully reversed. (The controversy over affirmative action as a public policy is discussed in Chapter 8.)

Furthermore, issues involving economic competition and regulation, public participation, and popular representativeness have recently tended to center (though not exclusively) on the roles of administrative entities. One crucial debate in the 1980s (as noted in Chapter 1) focused on the manner, scope, specificity, and implications of government (mainly administrative) regulation of the economy. There are still other links between political values and public administration. One is the diversity of interest groups, which increases the potential for alliances with those in positions of influence in the government (see Chapter 3). Another is renewed concern for democratic values and political accountability; this interest leads to new questions about administrative discretion, ethics, and effective control of bureaucracies.

Public administration in America has been profoundly affected by the evolution of, and recent upheavals in, political values. It has been shaped in part by the devices that limit government (i.e., separation of powers, checks and balances, federalism, and judicial review) while also having a profound effect on those devices. In particular, government bureaucracies have both contributed to, and

affirmative action
in the context of public personnel administration, a policy or program designed to bring into public service greater numbers of citizens who were largely excluded from public employment in previous years; also, the use of goals and timetables for hiring and promoting women, blacks, and other minorities as part of an equal employment opportunity program.

benefited from, what some have called the tilt toward the executive branch of government (and away from Congress) during much of the twentieth century. It is clear that if public administration had been shaped solely by changing political values and the interplay of political forces, it would have been altered considerably from its earliest forms and practices in the nineteenth century. However, administrative values have also figured prominently in its evolution, and it is on these values that we now focus our discussion.

Administrative Values

American public administration is grounded in certain fundamental assumptions that have dominated administrative thinking for more than a century. Chief among them are the following.[6] First, it has been freely assumed that politics and administration are separate and distinct. Political determination of broad policy directions and administrative management of public programs have been thought of as different processes controlled by different hands. From the founding of the Republic to the early twentieth century, public administrators viewed their role as subordinate and responsive to prevailing majorities in legislatures and to chief executives' proposals and directives. Their duty was not to initiate but to act on the initiatives of others. Administration was to be not only politically neutral but also passive. This conception of bureaucracy is not unlike that of a finely tuned machine that is activated only when someone else pushes the button.

Another common assumption, since the reforms of the late nineteenth century, has been that partisan politics should not intrude on processes of management. This idea has persisted even though political control of administration was considered entirely appropriate and even consistent with bureaucratic neutrality. It was also assumed, in the early 1900s, that administrative processes and functions (based on business practices) could be studied scientifically and that such an examination would yield various principles to guide administrative conduct. The purpose of developing a "science of administration" was to increase economy and efficiency in government and to use these principles as the main measures of administrative performance. Companion values have included an emphasis on merit (instead of political loyalty tests) as the primary basis for hiring, faith in the work ethic and in statistical evaluations of work performance, and a belief that a basic social consensus (other than the profit motive) underlies public administrative processes.

These values first emerged around 1900, in the era of government reform that followed a period of some seventy-five years in which politics and administration were deeply intertwined. Government administrative jobs had been crudely bartered in exchange for favors and support, and the guiding principle in public personnel administration had been "To the victors belong the spoils of victory." The reform effort was based on the belief that all kinds of politics could have *only* adverse effects on administration and that, therefore, a separation of politics and administration was absolutely necessary.

Heavily politicized administration had indeed been wasteful and inefficient, and there had been undeniably negative effects on the quality and effectiveness of government action. It should be emphasized, however, that attempts to separate politics and administration, pursue economy and efficiency, and discover enduring principles of administration were not merely passing fancies. They dominated virtually all the major approaches to administration from the turn of the century until after World War II, and remain present in large segments of the general population even today. Some reformers and others who seek to bring better management practices into government still cling to the doctrines of economy and efficiency almost as a matter of faith. And presidents from Teddy Roosevelt to Bill Clinton (not to mention numerous other politicians) have found it politically advantageous to speak of improved government performance and efficiency as goals of their tenure in public office.

There are, however, some problems created by administrative values that stress separation of politics and administration (see Chapter 1) while at the same time emphasizing efficiency in government operations. First, these approaches are not all consistent with the political values articulated by the Constitution. The framers of our government did *not* seek to establish an extensive bureaucratic structure, nor (as far as we can tell) did they foresee the development of one:

> They placed their faith in periodic elections, legislatures, and an elected chief executive rather than in a bureaucracy, however pure and efficient. There is nothing to suggest that they believed sound administration could compensate for bad political decisions. Redressing grievances and bad political decisions [was] the function of the political process, rather than of administrative machinery.[7]

Thus, the dichotomy between politics and administration probably would have been seen by the framers as either undesirable (since government through the political process was central to the constitutional scheme) or impossible. (It is also likely, however, that they would have objected equally to the blatant politicizing of administration that occurred during the mid-1800s.) It seems probable that they would have been suspicious of any developments that insulated important decision makers, such as administrators, from effective control by, *and accountability to*, the voters or the voters' elected representatives. Yet the administrative values that we have discussed here seem to create precisely that sort of insulation.

Second, it has become clear, on the basis of a substantial body of research since World War II, that public administration is not merely machinery for implementing decisions made by other government institutions. As we noted earlier in this chapter, public agencies and administrators have both the authority and the power of initiative to make a host of decisions, both large and small, that have real impacts on public policy. Instituted a century ago in response to unmistakable partisan excesses, protections against undue manipulation have given rise to the possibility of *administrative excesses*. Because control over policy making (in all but the smallest governments) is indirect, it is therefore more difficult for elected leaders and their immediate subordinates to exercise.

Third, there is some tension (if not outright conflict) between the major emphases of the Constitution and those of administrative values. Perhaps, above all else, the framers sought to prevent unchecked exercise of power by any institution of government or by government as a whole. Although they undoubtedly would not have advocated deliberate waste or wanton corruption, they were far more concerned with preventing growth of concentrated power, regardless of who wielded the power or with what degree of effectiveness or efficiency. Thus, they fragmented the formal powers of government in order to create a certain amount of inevitable — and calculated — *inefficiency*. Furthermore, as noted previously, the framers placed great reliance on the political process and on representative institutions (especially legislatures) as devices for resolving conflicts and representing the sovereign people. At the same time, however, they sought to make the new national government effective and competent within its sphere of activity; their interest in creating limited government was tempered by the fear that it would be unable to act at all, thus permitting unchecked social discord and chaos. In sum, the framers contemplated a political system that could both tolerate and benefit from somewhat inefficient exercise of power (the benefit being the government's decreased ability to infringe on individual liberties). The framers also desired a political system that would freely resort to the political process for making decisions and solving problems and that, when necessary, would be able to act.[8]

The underlying values of administration, on the other hand, clearly point toward efficiency, not merely as a desirable feature of government operation but as a key standard for evaluating government performance.[9] The reformers who first sought to increase efficiency in government associated most forms of politics with inefficiency (in many instances, rightly so) and consequently were largely "antipolitics." Their values strongly favored political neutrality as a key feature of both the composition and operation of public administrative agencies and, thus, also as a major remedy for inefficiency. (It should be noted, however, that these reform efforts had political effects. In particular, they narrowed channels of access to government employment for those who could not meet criteria of merit, and built public organizations around a predominantly white, middle-class ethic.)

Political scientist Douglas Yates explored more fully the conflicts between these two sets of parallel, yet distinctive values (Yates treats them, with somewhat more precision, as normative models of **pluralist democracy** and **administrative efficiency**). He summarizes the main conflicts as follows:

1. In the pluralist model, power is dispersed and divided; in the efficiency model, power is concentrated. Related to this, in the pluralist model,

pluralist democracy a normative model of administrative activity characterized by dispersion of power and suspicion of any concentration of power; by exercise of power on the part of politicians, interest groups, and citizens; by political bargaining and accommodation; and by an emphasis on individuals' and political actors' own determination of interest as the basis for policy making; the principal alternative to the administrative efficiency model.

administrative efficiency a normative model of administrative activity, characterized by concentration of power (especially in the hands of chief executives); centralization of governmental policy making, exercise of power by experts and professional bureaucrats, separation of politics and administration, and emphasis on technical or scientific rationality (arrived at by detached expert analysis); the principal alternative to the pluralist democracy model.

governmental policy making is decentralized; in the efficiency model it is centralized.

2. In the pluralist model, there is suspicion of executive power (in fact, of any concentration of power); in the efficiency model, great emphasis is placed on centralizing power in the hands of the chief executive [for the sake of accountability].

3. In the pluralist model, power is given to politicians, interest groups, and citizens; in the efficiency model, much power is given to experts and professional bureaucrats.

4. In the pluralist model, political bargaining and accommodation are considered to be at the heart of the democratic process; in the efficiency model, there is a strong urge to keep politics out of administration.

5. The pluralist model emphasizes individuals' and political actors' own determination of interest . . . the efficiency model emphasizes technical or scientific rationality (which can be better discovered by detached expert analysis than by consulting the desires of voters and politicians).[10]

It is small wonder, then, that, whereas both sets of values have continued to influence American government, inconsistencies between them have been difficult to reconcile. The result, a structurally fragmented government operating on broadly democratic principles, makes some *inefficiency* more likely than overall efficiency. On the other hand, efforts to maintain efficiency of operations while holding administrators accountable have met with considerable success. Attempts to reconcile these values merit our continued attention.[11] The conflicts inherent in the application of these explanatory models contribute daily to the operational decisions of public managers (see Box 2–1, "The Public Manager: An Overview"). These models also reveal the complexity of dealing with public issues and reflect citizen expectations (and frustrations) often associated with democratic government.

Democratic Government: Needs and Constraints

Popular control of government has always been a matter of considerable importance in American politics. The founding fathers emphasized the legislative and, to a lesser extent, executive branches of government — which, in principle, could be held directly accountable to voters through periodic elections. This mechanism did not assume a large bureaucracy or broad-scale participation in anything other than the electoral process. This relatively simple, clear-cut arrangement for accountability and popular control has become responsive to other kinds of political pressure. Thus, it is not surprising that there is fresh concern about public access to government and influence over what government does.

BOX 2-1   ETHICAL AND LEADERSHIP CHALLENGES FOR PUBLIC MANAGERS

The Public Manager: An Overview

Several major points should be made about the public manager's job:

1. The public manager inhabits an intensely political environment. Political processes do not abruptly stop at the door of a bureaucracy; the manager's job and environment are *essentially* political, requiring a primary emphasis on the task of managing political and administrative conflict.
2. The public manager's job also contains a *variety of political dimensions,* including building support with the chief executive, dealing with related departments and interest groups, bargaining with the legislature, managing and coordinating a fragmented structure of bureaucratic subunits, and (in the national government) trying to oversee and coordinate policy subsystems extending to the operations of state and city governments.
3. The manager's primary role is to deal with competing organizational pressures and to manage political conflict. In some cases, the manager will employ strategies of conflict resolution. At other times, the task will be to convert the negative, adversary features of conflict into something more positive, namely, cooperation, compromise, and coalition building among both political and administrative actors. (This process of conversion is often what we have in mind when we speak of leadership.)
4. In managing this political conflict, the manager faces many of the same issues that worry an advocate of pluralist democracy and, in a general way, would-be controllers of the bureaucracy. He or she has to worry about the fragmentation of bureaucratic activity, especially where it leads to strongly segmented bureaucratic structures and insulated concentrations of power. No less than the ordinary citizen, the public manager needs to "open up" the bureaucracy in order to achieve any real penetration into its operations. Finally, the public manager, along with the pluralist democrat, must worry about the balance of power among different groups: whether desirable levels of competition and bargaining exist, whether certain interests overwhelm other groups in the policy-making process, whether citizens' complaints and demands are heard and registered. In sum, the public manager, far from being the *clerk of a narrow efficiency,* faces the problems of *both* pluralist democracy and administrative efficiency.

SOURCE: Adapted and reprinted by permission of the publishers from *Bureaucratic Democracy: The Search for Democracy and Efficiency in American Government,* by Douglas Yates, Cambridge, Mass.: Harvard University Press. Copyright © 1982 by the President and Fellows of Harvard College.

Democratic government requires at least the presence, in a political system, of popular sovereignty, substantial equality among its citizens, consultation between government and citizens over proposed major courses of action, and majority rule. Increasingly, *equality of opportunity* is also regarded as a prerequisite for a political system to be truly democratic. In a more specific, operational sense, democracy may be said to require the following: (1) freedom of expression, (2) citizen participation in decision making, (3) a free press and uncensored mass media to hold government accountable for its decisions, (4) an independent judiciary, and (5) regular, free elections to encourage participation and political accountability. The meaning and scope of these values, however, have varied over time.

In the 1700s, *political participation* referred to voting and holding public office and was limited by such qualifications as property ownership, wealth, education, social status, race, and gender. Beginning in the 1830s, eligibility for participation was broadened, so that today, virtually every citizen eighteen years of age or older can vote and otherwise become involved in politics. Lately, participation has taken on another, more controversial dimension — *mandatory inclusion* of various population groups in governmental decision making.

Debates over the meaning and scope of participation are nothing new and may indeed be inevitable in a democracy. Political scientist Emmette Redford observed, more than three decades ago, that, although participation is a key element of "democratic morality," a number of questions about it still exist.[12] One concerns *who* should participate, with near-universal participation recommended by the true believer in democracy (the pure "democrat"). Another question centers on the *scope* of participation — at what stages of policy making and in what ways participation is to occur. Another dilemma for the aspiring democrat is whether *opportunities to participate* should be afforded equally to those with high stakes in government decisions and those with little interest in specific policies. Such issues complicate the structuring of channels of participation, but a commitment to making participation possible must exist before the issues can be addressed.

accountability a political principle according to which agencies or organizations, such as those in government, are subject to some form of external control, causing them to give a general account of, and for, their actions; an essential concept in democratic public administration.

Accountability once meant holding officials generally responsible for their actions through direct elective mechanisms, as in the case of legislators, or through indirect machinery in which elected officials held others to account on behalf of the public. Now, however, the meaning of accountability is less clear. The issue of *to whom* officials are *actually* accountable is a complex one, making it difficult to determine whether they can, in fact, be made to answer to the general public for what they do. Complicating matters further have been the isolated, but highly publicized, instances of serious abuses of power (such as the Rodney King incident in Los Angeles). Widespread ownership of cameras and expanded use of amateur video photography have given a whole new meaning to the term "mass media," have provided a direct method of recording the actions of government officials, with or without permission, and have fueled the debate about official conduct and public accountability.

Holding government officials accountable for their actions and conduct is crucial to democratic government, even more so when substantial responsibility is entrusted to nonelected (administrative) personnel. This rationale underlies the need for openness in government operations, public scrutiny, and **freedom of information (FOI)** and **sunshine laws,** all of which increase the public's ability to inquire successfully into the activities of bureaucracy and other branches of government. The glare of publicity has long been known as one means of enforcing accountability, by making possible a better-informed citizenry that can then act more intelligently and purposefully. **Sunset laws** add another dimension to accountability. By requiring positive legislative action to renew agency mandates, there is a virtual guarantee that some examination of agency performance will take place. It should be emphasized, however, that merely routine reviews and near-universal renewals of agency authorizations will not serve the purposes of sunset legislation. Only careful, thorough, and demanding examinations will do.

The use of sunset laws, in particular, as an instrument of accountability is part of a widespread resurgence of legislative efforts to hold executives accountable. In the best tradition of those who first shaped the political system, the public once again seems to be looking to its legislative representatives to bring about greater popular control over executive-branch agencies. In both state and national government, increasing numbers of legislators seem inclined to respond positively to public pressures and, in some cases, to lead public opinion as well as follow it. Further, legislative entities (such as the U.S. General Accounting Office) that conduct general oversight activities and issue critical reports have been granted increasing authority to discipline administrative agencies. It should be noted also that agencies such as the Office of Management and Budget (OMB) and state bureaus of the budget ("mini-OMBs") are increasingly active in seeking to hold operating bureaucracies more accountable. These, too, have acquired more authority of late to carry out that function.

Accountability is hampered by the prevalence of technical subject matter in government decision making. In many respects, this limits the potential for accountability to those able to understand an issue and the implications of different proposed solutions. A case in point is energy policy, where one thing that stands out is a need for more and better information for decision maker and citizen alike. Few among us comprehend all the intricacies of natural-gas pricing, the politics of oil supply here and abroad, and so on. If we the people cannot monitor government decisions, who can be held accountable for them? There is no easy answer.[13]

Accountability is also made more difficult by the fact that administrators must frequently face situations in which *competing criteria for decision* are very much in evidence. For example, it has been noted that, in allocating public housing, there are contradictory goals that create conflicts in the possible approaches to decision making: *equity* (treating like cases alike on the basis of rules) and *responsiveness* (making exceptions for persons whose needs require that rules be

freedom of Information (FOI) laws   legislation passed by Congress and some state legislatures establishing procedures through which private citizens may gain access to a wide variety of records and files from government agencies; a principal instrument for breaking down bureaucratic secrecy in American public administration.

sunshine law   an act passed by Congress and by some states and localities requiring that various legislative proceedings (especially those of committees and subcommittees) and various administrative proceedings be held in public rather than behind closed doors; one device for increasing openness and accountability.

sunset law   provision in laws that government agencies and programs have a specific termination date.

stretched). How does one reconcile these desirable but conflicting objectives? By one set standard, to which all adhere? By situation ethics? By following dictates based on the *kinds* of need? Again, there is no single or easy answer. Note, also, that the "equity-responsiveness tension" can be found in numerous other settings as well (for example, personnel management, making grants and loans, and the college or university classroom).

Disagreement with specific policies notwithstanding, the larger concern is for maintaining democratic norms and practices in a complex governmental system within a diverse and rapidly changing society. Today, many fear that democratic values, however defined, are endangered by government actions that take place *without* popular control and consent. Government institutions are clearly under pressure "from the people" — left, right, and center — to stay within the public's political reach. (Witness the brief but strong support for the Buchanan and Perot populist movements during the 1992 and 1996 elections, and the efforts of the Clinton–Gore administrations to make government both more responsive and more effective.) Difficulties in maintaining democracy, however, are hardly new. Assuming that democracy implies fairly equitable access to decision makers, widespread opportunity to exert influence in the political process, and clear public preferences about public policy, the realities of American democracy have fallen short of the ideal for some time.

Access and influence are unevenly distributed throughout the population, with the wealthy having a better chance than the poor to gain a hearing in official channels. Both major political parties advocate campaign finance reform, albeit with protections for *their own* loyal contributors. In fact, most contributors give money to candidates and political parties for the express purpose of gaining access to those in office after electoral decisions are made. Similarly, *influence* in the political process (partly dependent on access) is clearly enjoyed by some more than others. Besides money, a key factor seems to be organization; well-organized groups have long been acknowledged as having the advantage in exercising political influence. Reform is difficult because of the dominance of organized over unorganized interests. Large institutions — corporations, government agencies, and colleges and universities — will always place their institutional interests over the interests of individuals. This makes it impossible to sustain a claim of comparable influence among different groups in a system in which organization and political power go hand in hand.[14]

Finally, in many cases, clear public preferences on policy questions simply do not exist. Contrary to popular belief, voters usually do not confer *policy mandates* — clear statements of policy preference — when they go to the polls. The Clinton victory over Dole in 1996 (as well as Ronald Reagan's landslide over Walter Mondale in 1984 and Nixon's over George McGovern in 1972) were substantial, but many of those voting for the winners clearly did not agree with their every policy position. Rather, in many instances, they voted *against* the candidate of the opposition party. The narrower electoral victories, such as Bill

Clinton over George Bush in 1992 and Bush's victory over Michael Dukakis in 1988, said even less about voters' policy preferences.

If policy mandates are vague, the process of defining the "public interest" is even more so. One can argue (as Ross Perot did in his unsuccessful presidential campaigns) that the public is the ultimate "owner" of government institutions and that institutions should serve the owner's interest — the public interest — but defining and gaining agreement on what that is as a practical matter is not easy. In a pluralist democratic society, various contesting forces claim to be acting in and for the public interest, and each may have a legitimate claim to some part of larger societal values. Also, it is not clear whether the public interest is some generalized view of societal good or the sum total of all private interests, which are themselves inconsistent with one another.

Democracy and Public Administration

Democracy, as we have noted, requires mechanisms for *both* participation and accountability, ensured by an independent judiciary, uncensored media, and free elections. Public administration, however, poses troublesome problems for any such system. It does not accord with the notion of elected public officials because most bureaucrats are not elected, and it has usually emphasized limited access, expertise, and knowledge over accountability, participation, and democratic control. Growing societal complexity and increasing administrative responsibilities have virtually required more specialization and larger numbers of bureaucratic professionals, as well as new and varied forms of indirect public administrative activity (contracts, grants, loans, performance partnerships, tax expenditures, and regulation). At the same time, disadvantaged groups and others have turned to government bureaucracy more frequently for various kinds of aid — ironically, often while voicing grievances *against* many of the same agencies — and to demand a greater role in making policies that affect them. The result has been a collision between the need for professionalism and technical competence, and insistent demands for citizen participation in policy making.[15] Bureaucratic accountability in such a system has to be achieved largely, if not entirely, through *indirect* popular influence via the legislature and chief executive. When technical expertise is required, it is very difficult, though not impossible, to reconcile accountability and participation in the policy-making process. In the same way, and raising some of the same issues, it is difficult to build both popular control and administrative discretion into the policy process.[16]

The concerns that have come to center on bureaucracy include, besides issues of accountability and participation, the question of representativeness. In addition, the general disposition of bureaucrats and bureaucracies to operate behind a veil of secrecy, in the best tradition of Max Weber, has triggered efforts to open their activities to public scrutiny. Two such efforts are state and national

FOI laws and so-called sunshine laws requiring that public business be conducted in open forums.

FREEDOM OF INFORMATION LAWS

The relationship between governmental accountability and popular access to government information was recognized five decades ago. Congress, in the Administrative Procedure Act of 1946, attempted to open up the bureaucracy by encouraging distribution of information to the public on a need-to-know basis. According to that principle, the burden rested with the inquiring citizen to demonstrate that information was needed from the bureaucracy; the presumption was that information could be safeguarded by the bureaucracy unless a strong case was made to the contrary. As long as popular trust of bureaucracy remained high and no major interests felt harmed or threatened, that arrangement was satisfactory. At the same time, bureaucratic secrecy went largely unchallenged, and little information filtered out of the bureaucracy when agency personnel decided to restrict it.

By the 1960s, the situation had changed. Increasing government activity bred rising citizen concern about administrative decision making, which, in turn, sparked calls for greater access to hard-to-get information. Congress responded, after some delay and without strong presidential leadership, by passing the Freedom of Information Act (FOIA) in 1966, based on the principle that the "timely provision of information to the American people, upon their own petition, is a requisite and proper duty of government."[17] The law presumed a right to know, with some limitations on information to be made available (most relating to national security). The effect of this statute was to increase the potential for citizen access to a wide variety of government records and files.

Thus, the burden appeared to be shifted from those seeking information to agency personnel who might wish to restrict its release. In practice, administrative personnel did not enthusiastically comply with provisions of the act in the first decade of its operation, moving Congress to criticize the bureaucracy for "foot-dragging." Amendments adopted in 1974 were designed to ensure faithful implementation of the act, and some improvement followed. Congress acted again *without* leadership from the president — indeed, the amendments were passed over a presidential veto! (Lack of forceful leadership from the White House, under any president, may explain some of the bureaucratic reluctance to conform to the new requirements.) And, despite the improvement noted, widespread delay in releasing information persisted. Gradually, however, a combination of congressional oversight and educational efforts in the executive branch succeeded in lessening resistance by bureaucrats and increasing compliance with the FOIA. Thus, definite gains in information acquisition by private citizens were achieved only after Congress demonstrated its commitment to the ideal of "democratic morality." In the 1980s, however, the Reagan and Bush administrations gave less attention and emphasis to freedom of information as a high priority — and, indeed, were accused by FOIA advocates of deliberately tightening government policies regarding availability of information on the grounds, especially, of national security.

The value of this statute is increasingly recognized as a means of exposing mismanagement. Under FOIA procedures it was disclosed, in the mid-1980s, that (1) the Energy Department had decided to build a heavy-water nuclear reactor using what proved to be the worst of five possible designs; (2) the Veterans Administration had spent $700,000 to renovate office space that was never used; (3) the Tennessee Valley Authority had given over $3 million to a development agency that may have been operating illegally; (4) the National Archives had tolerated certain fire and safety violations; (5) spoiled and diseased meat had been sold to the school lunch program; and (6) some defense contractors were charging lobbying and public relations expenses to government contracts.[18] None of these actions was a grave threat to the nation's welfare, but all demonstrated a need for substantive improvement in public management. Most important, agency accountability was greatly enhanced simply because information about agency behavior could be brought to light.[19] One further observation is in order: At least the *spirit*, if not the "letter," of the FOIA was very much in evidence in the disclosure of information regarding American victims of U.S. nuclear testing in the 1950s. This information, which came to light in 1993 and 1994, sparked a controversy that highlights the tensions often present between the people's interest in *obtaining* information, on the one hand, and a governmental interest (whether seen as legitimate or not, whether well regarded or not) in *protecting* information. In this case the government's interest was generally seen as entirely self-serving and clearly *not* in the public interest.

The FOIA-related record during the Clinton administration appears to be somewhat mixed.[20] Proponents of greater access to government information have seen some of these developments as very positive; other developments are viewed less favorably; and there have been frustrating instances of evasion that are cause for concern. (Obviously, some — but not all — of the following directly involved the president himself.) Bill Clinton drew praise during the 1992 campaign for pledging openness in government and, in October 1993, took a major step to fulfill that pledge by formally reversing a twelve-year policy of withholding government information from the press. The president, with Attorney General Janet Reno, issued new FOIA policy directives that, among other things, established a presumption of openness in the executive branch and directed that the Justice Department no longer defend other executive-branch agencies challenged under provisions of the FOIA. The attorney general also issued new procedures governing Justice Department responses to FOIA requests for some department documents. The Office of Management and Budget (OMB) created a new policy under which executive-branch agencies must make government information, in electronic form, accessible to scholars and librarians, among others. And in mid-1993, the U.S. Supreme Court ruled that FBI records are not automatically confidential, especially if a criminal defendant seeks access to relevant records as part of an effort to establish his or her innocence.

On the other hand, the Clinton administration, and others in the national government, have been criticized on various grounds regarding freedom of information policy. For example, the Health Care Task Force conducted some of its deliberations in secrecy, which seemed to contradict the Clinton emphasis on openness. The Clinton administration also revised FOIA policy to exempt the personal computer files of government employees. On one occasion, the administration — while publicly praising the FOIA — rejected a reporter's request to obtain salaries of White House staff members. The Supreme Court, in late 1991, ruled that complete disclosure of reports on Haitian refugees was not necessary under FOIA provisions. Also, it was reported in mid-1991 that requests for documents under FOIA guidelines were often delayed, sometimes for considerable periods of time. And a controversy surfaced over a memo allegedly circulated in 1989 within the National Aeronautics and Space Administration (NASA) that suggested ways to evade FOIA inquiries. Yet another controversy was triggered by former Middle East hostage Terry Anderson, who charged in 1993 that he was repeatedly denied access to government records containing information about his own captivity. Finally, some raised FOIA alarms when, during the Whitewater inquiry in 1993–1996, a Clinton lawyer placed some Whitewater documents in Justice Department hands under "ground rules" that prevented public access to those documents under the terms of the FOIA.

A number of other issues have emerged that will demand our attention in the immediate future. First, access to on-line electronic data is thought by most observers, including many members of Congress, to be protected under the FOIA, but many troubling questions remain to be answered (some with privacy implications).[21] Second, there is growing unease about the possibility that privatizing government services (see Chapter 10) has created greatly diminished public access to information about those services, because no FOIA provisions automatically extend to private-sector entities.[22] Nearly forty states have also passed FOIA statutes, with varying degrees of effectiveness. Free and open exchange of information is crucial both for economic development and for necessary innovations in society. Clearly, freedom of information continues to have substantial importance, in the eyes of both government officials and those who, for myriad reasons, wish to monitor what government does.

Sunshine Laws

Sunshine laws, which have been passed at all levels of government and apply mainly to legislative proceedings, have also been enacted for administrative agencies. Regulatory agencies at the national level operate "in the sunshine," although they are required to do so by judicial rather than legislative action. In all fifty states, open-meeting laws are on the books, applying to state legislative committees, state executive branches and independent agencies, and local governments. As with freedom of information laws, the greatest potential beneficiaries are organized groups of citizens who seek to monitor administrative activities. City councils, county commissions, and local school boards have been at the center of controversies over open meetings at least as often as state or national entities. Both FOIA statutes and sunshine laws have succeeded at all levels in opening government to greater public scrutiny, but — perhaps not surprisingly — they have fallen short of what was hoped for them by their strongest advocates. Government behavior can be changed only gradually, if experience with these devices is any guide.

There is growing concern, also, that government and bureaucracy are not doing enough to protect individual privacy and to ensure that government records concerning affairs of private citizens are fair and accurate. This is a particularly sensitive issue in view of electronic information capabilities. Before the 1960s, information might have been available to government, but it was costly and time-consuming to have it on hand or to organize it. Computers, however, make retrieval and cross-referencing of information not only possible but quick and convenient. A principal concern is the extent and diversity of personal information that is now stored on computers of public and private organizations — Social Security data, credit ratings and transactions, driver's license information, medical records, income figures, and so on.

Both national and state governments have taken action to better safeguard an individual's right to privacy. Legislation at the national level includes the Freedom of Information Act, the Fair Credit Reporting Act, the Family Educational Rights and Privacy Act, the Privacy Act of 1974, and the Fair Credit Billing Act. Congress has established the Privacy Protection Study Commission to look into intrusions on individual privacy by agencies outside the national executive branch. Over half a dozen states have enacted privacy laws, and an even larger number have adopted their own versions of the Fair Credit Reporting Act. In short, there has been considerable government activity in this area, but concern persists that Big Brother still may have too much access to personal records. Indeed, there are growing fears that "hackers" in *both* the public and private sectors may be in a position to invade our privacy to a far greater extent than ever before. (Note, again, the potential links to freedom of information policy regarding access to electronic data).[23]

Dimensions of Democratic Administration

In the following section, we will examine in greater depth selected areas in public administration that pose particular challenges for the maintenance of democratic norms and practices. We will consider each of the following: (1) citizen participation, (2) bureaucratic representativeness, (3) bureaucratic responsiveness, and (4) administrative effectiveness as a threat to personal freedom.

CITIZEN PARTICIPATION

The ideology of citizen participation has firm roots among our political values, especially *participatory democracy*. The push for greater citizen participation in government decision making was born in the 1960s out of related movements for civil rights, "black liberation," and decentralization of urban government structures. It originated in demands by nonwhites for a larger voice in determining policies and programs directly affecting them. The urban poor, at least during the 1960s, concentrated on organizing themselves and confronting those in power with demands for change. Their participation was formally incorporated in both the planning and implementation of federal Model Cities and community-action programs and in other programs since then.

The forms and practices of citizen participation are numerous, ranging from advising agencies to attending hearings to actual decision making. In addition to making statements at meetings held by administrative agencies, individuals may take part in budget and other legislative hearings, and in initiatives and referenda; serve on advisory committees; participate in focus groups and respond to citizen surveys; and, in some cases, sit on governing boards of operating activities funded by government entities. Also, in the delivery of human services, individuals act as *coproducers* of the services by their deep involvement in program operations (this refers to services such as unemployment compensation, welfare, garbage collection, and education).[24] Viewing the citizen as coproducer is a different but highly relevant conception of participation that should not be overlooked. The same kind of active role is an essential ingredient in the more contemporary attempts to provide improved customer service and empower local communities to act in their own interests.

Specific purposes of participation can include some or all of the following: (1) providing information to citizens; (2) receiving information from or about citizens; (3) improving public decision processes, programs, projects, and services; (4) enhancing public acceptance of governmental activities; (5) altering patterns of political power and allocations of public resources; (6) protecting individual and minority group rights and interests; and (7) delaying or avoiding difficult public policy decisions. (Redistributing power and resources and protecting minority interests were central to the demands of urban nonwhites in the 1960s.) Although some of these purposes are mutually incompatible, all are directed generally toward reducing citizen alienation from government. This is a form of grassroots involvement that can also be used to hold public officials accountable.

Ideological differences about citizen participation and debates over its place in governing are related conceptually to the continuing debate in American politics over centralization and decentralization (see Chapters 4 and 5). Particularly as practiced in the federal system during the past quarter century, citizen participation represents an application of the decentralist principle, which assumes value and purpose in delegating decision-making authority to affected persons and groups. Decentralization as a mode of operation clearly permits wider par-

ticipation; it gives greater assurance that the existing spectrum of opinion will
receive a hearing; and it lends more legitimacy to both the process and the outcomes of decision making. Because federalism itself was designed as a bulwark
against intrusive centralization, the concept of decentralization obviously has a
place in operations under a federal system. Citizen participation, fostered by
many national programs, has been a key mechanism used to promote decentralization of operating responsibility.

The concept of participation has been applied in different ways to varying
problems. **Community control** focused on neighborhood management of
schools and delivery of other essential urban services, principally in nonwhite
ghetto areas of major American cities.[25] In other places, neighborhood and citizen action organizations sprang up for the purpose of "preserving neighborhood
character" and sometimes redevelopment of physical structures in the neighborhood. For example, there have been concerted efforts to prevent construction of
interstate highway projects that would cut through, or perhaps level, parts of
established urban neighborhoods. One such case involves a continuing conflict
in Los Angeles, California, over construction of the Century Freeway (Interstate
105) through neighborhoods in the south-central parts of Los Angeles County
and nine other cities. The proposed stretch of road would almost certainly have
an adverse impact on neighborhood residents, so the seventeen-mile project was
delayed by court action for ten years. It was finally completed in 1993 and is six
lanes wide, heavily landscaped, noise-attenuated, and was built under strict affirmative action guidelines. Another case centered on a proposal to construct a
bridge between the communities of Rye and Oyster Bay, New York, across Long
Island Sound. In this case, a coalition of citizen action groups succeeded in
defeating the proposal, which had the backing of powerful interests and individuals, such as the late Governor Nelson Rockefeller, former New York Port
Authority head William Ronan, and the late Robert Moses, longtime power
behind the scenes in New York City. Many other examples can also be cited:
community groups protesting bank *redlining* (the practice attributed to some
financial institutions that excludes some areas of a community from eligibility for
loans); cattle ranchers in western states joining forces with Native Americans and
antinuclear groups against uranium mining by energy conglomerates; citizen
groups protesting toxic waste disposal; and residential associations trying to
attract (or repel) commercial enterprises.[26] Organized tax protest movements,
the Ruby Ridge, Idaho, and Waco, Texas, incidents, and the bombing of the Federal Building in Oklahoma City illustrate the extremes to which some groups
have gone to protest actions of government agencies.

Citizen participation has also been incorporated into formal mechanisms for
decision making. At the national level, for example, public participation in regulatory proceedings has been increasing, although with considerable variation in
regulators' responses and opportunities provided to citizen groups, such as consumer organizations. Agencies and commissions undoubtedly have legal discretionary authority to decide just how much public participation (if any) to permit

community control
legal requirements that
groups affected by political
decisions must be repre-
sented on decision-making
boards and commissions.

public-interest groups (PIGs) organized lobbying groups which represent collective interests, i.e., nonbusiness or labor, in influencing public policy. Examples are Common Cause and Greenpeace.

and, particularly, whether and how to finance participation by those with limited resources. Nonetheless, there has been considerable frustration on the part of so-called **public-interest groups (PIGs),** which have been slow to gain access to regulatory proceedings. Agencies and commissions with consumer protection as a high priority are more likely to offer assistance, whereas those in highly technical fields are more likely to resist. And, at the local level, participation is now more regularized, especially in zoning enforcement, environmental protection, and planning and design of urban communities.

Some other dimensions of citizen participation are worth noting. First, the matter of who is to participate and to what extent is not only a problem of democratic ideals, as discussed earlier; it has potentially important implications in a strictly operating sense. In antipoverty programs of the mid- and late 1960s, "maximum feasible participation of the poor" was called for, but there was bitter debate over who constituted "the poor," and how they were to be selected and incorporated into program operations. Furthermore, in almost all studies of citizen participation, it has been found that

> groups of individuals active in such programs (1) represent organized interests likely to have been previously active in agency affairs, (2) include a large component of spokesmen for other government agencies, (3) represent a rather limited range of potential publics affected by programs, and (4) tend toward the well-educated, affluent middle- to upper-class individuals.
>
> Viewed in terms of the ideological program goals, programs seldom appear to . . . produce a great socioeconomic diversity among participating interests.[27]

Second, there is a distinct possibility that officials and agencies will co-opt citizen action groups. On more than one occasion, what began as a good-faith effort to build greater participation into a decision-making process ended up as more show than substance, symbolic politics at its worst, with the newer groups occupying a place of greater visibility but little increased power. Officially sponsored citizen participation tends to be **co-optation** and tokenism rather than representation. In sum, nothing is automatic about the manner in which participation and representation are practiced.

co-optation a process in organizational relations whereby one group or organization acquires the ability to influence activities of another, usually for a considerable period of time.

Third, decentralizing and localizing control over governmental programs has not been a guarantee of either increased participation at the local level or more democratic operations. (The links between decentralization and increased participation are noted in Chapter 5; the point here is that those links should not be assumed to exist automatically.) Indeed, government at the grass roots may be *less* democratic than in a larger and more diverse political system.[28] The dangers of domination by a small minority of elite local citizens are very real, regardless of official mandates or unofficial expectations. It also has been observed that citizen participation can become a "bureaucratic ideology," to be used "against the elected officers of representative government."[29] Similarly, citizen participation may be used to transfer decision-making authority from elected officials with broader interests in the community at large to nonelected local groups that lack broader civic obligations and responsibilities. All such observations clearly imply a hazard inherent in citizen participation: the potential for citizen interests to become primarily self-serving rather than representative of broader interests in the community or society.

A fourth concern is that agency personnel, in their enthusiasm for satisfying immediate citizen action demands, may initiate responses that prove to be short-sighted when judged by more rigorous criteria over time. Although public administrators may wish to respond, or appear to respond, to new and powerful interests such as citizen action groups, there is danger that they may act hastily before the consequences of actions can be fully assessed by those most likely to be affected by the action. Compounding this potential difficulty is a tendency for citizen groups to scorn cost-benefit analysis as an instrument of evaluation of their own proposals. Cost-benefit analysis is not always an appropriate evaluative tool, but it can often strengthen one's case, particularly under current conditions of fiscal stress, or at least increase a group's credibility in a political dialogue.

Fifth, if citizen participation is designed to help keep bureaucracy responsible to the general public, it has had only a mixed record of success. Citizen groups seem to have the greatest impact when they have the political power to make bureaucrats listen and when group values most nearly match those of the bureaucracy. But because of limitations on citizens' expertise, time, and access, citizen inputs are likely to have a disappointing effect in attaining bureaucratic responsibility.[30]

Sixth, citizen participation and its impact will be affected by the degree to which contacts with those in government are characterized by confrontation as opposed to negotiation, by a sense of "us against them" as opposed to a perceived community of interests. Tension in a political system is not uncommon, but a democratic system virtually requires that tension not be constant. Barring fundamental shifts in the locus of power in a particular decision-making system, continuous confrontation will soon reach a point of diminishing returns for those seeking access and influence.

Finally, a widely accepted concept affecting participation is citizen *input*, about which a cautionary note is in order. Many of us seem to assume that we should seek "greater input" into the mechanisms of decision making. (The term is borrowed from computer science, where input makes a major difference in results.) However, the concept of input involves an implicit acknowledgment that *somebody else* is running the machine. In other words, those who seek input are admitting to a *subordinate* position in decision making. How to get action with too many voices "in action" is a real dilemma for decision makers. There are other possibilities — coproduction, **empowerment**, partnership, and full control, for example — for which input is an inappropriate concept. To think only in terms of input, in short, serves to limit the variety of ways that participation can occur and to confirm the power of those already holding it.

Citizen participation, in sum, has dramatically modified decision making in a host of policy areas and has taken its place as a major feature of democratic

empowerment an approach to citizen participation or management that stresses extended customer satisfaction, examines relationships among existing management processes, seeks to improve internal agency communications, and responds to valid customer demands; in exchange for the authority to make decisions at the point of customer contact, all "empowered" employees must be thoroughly trained, and the results must be carefully monitored.

administration. Although those in positions of power have often yielded only grudgingly to citizen groups, it is unlikely that the gains that have been made will be rolled back. If anything, the near future seems to hold promise of still greater citizen empowerment.[31]

BUREAUCRATIC REPRESENTATIVENESS

There are, first of all, several approaches to representation.[32] Should constituents' opinions and preferences be conveyed to government officials and reflected faithfully in legislative voting, or should a representative exercise independent judgment and individual conscience in making decisions? The former, which has been labeled the "delegate role," maximizes the public's impact on decision making but does not take advantage of the representative's potentially superior knowledge of details and of subtleties in making choices. The latter, labeled the "trustee role," emphasizes the representative's capabilities and the public's trust that their interests will be faithfully served (thus the label *trustee*). In both instances, we are depending on our representatives to somehow serve the public interest. Unfortunately, it is rarely clear how elected officials make their decisions and to *whose* voices they listen when they do act as delegates. Thus, in its most basic dimension, there is ambiguity concerning representation.

That ambiguity is complicated considerably when the focus shifts to the administrative context. Because bureaucracies in American politics are acknowledged to have a representative function, it follows that answers to the same sorts of questions must be found. But, historically, bureaucratic agencies have served narrow clienteles with specialized interests. An agency's representation of those interests — and its accountability to them — can be quite complete without its serving the larger political system. How, then, can these administrative patterns be reconciled with democratic values that emphasize broad popular representation? These are not "new" issues. Political scientist Emmette Redford attempted to supply some answers to this dilemma in the late 1960s. Central to the argument is the following proposition: *"The attainment of the democratic ideal in the world of administration depends much less on majority votes than on the inclusiveness of the representation of interests in the interaction process among decision makers."*[33] Redford develops that proposition this way:

> The process can be called democratic only if the interaction process is broadly inclusive at *two levels of decision making:* first, at the level of political superstructure, where basic decisions on rules for society and roles for actors in the administrative state are made, and second, at the level of program specialization to which much of the decision making of the administrative state has been committed. The interaction process must include the participation of several types of leaders who through the diversities reflected in their participation and the influence of non-leaders upon them give representation to the manifold common and varied interests within the society.[34]

Thus, the degree to which representation is *inclusive of existing interests in the society* is, in this view, a key test for how democratic administrative processes will be. Underlying this is another concern: the extent of effective *access* afforded to those *not* already a part of the interaction process, consistent with the norm of inclusiveness. Both access and regularized interactions are crucial to democratization of administration, especially regarding the opportunity for newer or weaker groups to gain a hearing for their interests and grievances.

Another essential difficulty in representation concerns the delegation of authority. In a fundamental sense, we delegate our authority to Congress and to state and local legislatures to make our laws, knowing as we do that representation of our every view is imperfect. Legislatures, in turn, have delegated vast amounts of authority to bureaucracies (and to chief executives), further removing decision-making power from the source of authority — that is, the people. When authority is delegated, it must be either very precisely defined and limited, which tends to be impractical and defeats the purpose of delegating, or else *discretionary*, with those who exercise it largely deciding how it should be used.

Once discretion enters the picture, which it clearly does in administrative decision making, the representational quality of decisions may be diminished. This is especially true where expertise, technical competence, and rationality are highly prized values, as they are in much of our bureaucratic structure. We come back, then, to a dilemma that troubles much of democratic administration: *the conflict between professionalism and participation/representation.* Increasingly in recent years, "the people" have grown to resent "somebody else" making a judgment about what is best for them. Most of the time, that "somebody" is a professional operating within a bureaucracy. Thus, discretionary authority exercised by bureaucratic "trustees" increases the chance that the general public's feelings will not be as well represented as they might be under conditions of reduced (professional) discretion.

Another aspect of discretion should be noted. If, as one observer has pointed out, "good administration consists of making [bureaucracy] *predictably and reliably responsive*" to the wishes of the public,[35] then large areas of discretionary authority clearly get in the way of predictability. The only way to make bureaucracy more predictable, given our past history of delegating authority, is to reduce dramatically the discretion technical experts in the bureaucracy are permitted to exercise. This would require a fundamental reassessment of the kind of bureaucracy — and expertise — we want. Such a reassessment may have already begun with the current emphasis on reinventing government in Washington, but it has yet to spread to states and local governments, where most of the discretionary authority resides.

Finally, bureaucratic representation is inhibited by longtime practices insulating administrative personnel from direct political pressures. Conceptually, politics and representation of the public's feelings are virtually synonymous, and to hamper political interchange is to place limits on popular representation.[36]

Whether the U.S. civil service is, in fact, representative of the population at large is a debatable — and debated — issue.

Several studies suggest that national government civil servants are imperfectly representative of the public at large in demographic (and perhaps political) terms, as senior civil servants certainly are. Yet, given the professional nature of their work, we might expect that to be the case — at least concerning income, education, and certain issue positions. On the other hand, considering the changes already in motion regarding recruitment, promotion, and the like, it is not surprising that we are seeing greater demographic representativeness.

By the late 1980s, a separate study showed stronger Republican partisanship than was the case in the early or mid-1970s or the early 1980s (which is not surprising after Reagan's landslide victory in 1984). The study found that top administrators were much more likely than before to view the national government's role in economic affairs as a limited one, that differences of views among officials of different agencies had virtually disappeared (in a comparison of these results to those of a 1970 study conducted by the same two scholars), and that the views of top civil servants still clashed, to some extent, with those of the Reagan appointees. These findings can be accounted for by the substantially more systematic approach of the Reagan administration in trying to staff executive positions with individuals fully committed to the Reagan agenda. They also suggest, however, that, although career civil servants are likely to be affected by the presence of a presidential administration which has "a substantial degree of coherence in its overall program goals and its personnel system, and [that] appears for the moment to have strong political momentum," the views of career employees still *do not* "exactly mirror those of the presidential administration."[37]

The issue of representativeness obviously has many sides to it. Women and ethnic minorities, in particular, have taken the virtually unanimous position that greater representativeness is needed to enhance general understanding within the civil service of problems confronting women and minority groups. Furthermore, theirs is a call for *advocacy* of their cause as a central activity of female and minority administrators. In general, the effort to increase representativeness based on sex and race is founded on the belief — perhaps quite valid — that government would otherwise ignore their concerns in program design and management.[38]

BUREAUCRATIC RESPONSIVENESS

The responsiveness of public officials to popular sentiments depends on the presence of several factors in the governmental process. For one thing, it depends fundamentally on the people's assumptions about what *is* and what *should be* in the conduct of government and public policy making. It is not only a matter of what we establish very loosely as our governmental and societal objectives (and those objectives will conflict!), it is also what we take for granted in our expectations about governmental activity.

Second, responsiveness requires meaningful access to the *right* decision makers and a legitimate opportunity to be heard. *Access* is a key step in the policy process and, without it, responsiveness cannot be ensured. A key issue regarding access, is — and will continue to be — whether it should be granted or denied by virtue of an individual's (or group's) payment of a "retainer" in the form of a preelection campaign contribution.

Third, government and its agencies have to be *able* to respond to policy and program demands, even assuming that they are willing to do so. Politically, financially, and administratively, agencies must be equipped to deliver services or otherwise satisfy public demands placed on them.

There are two major constraints on responsiveness. The first concerns public expectations. Ideally, public expectations should be realistic, reasonable, and manageable. Admittedly, anyone in government can hide behind excuses of unrealistic, unreasonable, or unmanageable public desires to avoid tackling hard problems that may, by objective standards, need attention. But the point here is that there may actually be conditions that, for legitimate reasons, are difficult to deal with, for example, crime, environmental pollution, poverty, or nuclear waste disposal. If people assume that a problem can be solved and it is not solved, the government may be accused (not entirely fairly) of being unresponsive to public wants. Despite our skepticism, inability to act can be an operating reality for a government agency — perhaps as a result of lack of jurisdiction, limited funds, political opposition, or merely difficulties in "making the ordinary happen" (see Chapter 10).

The second constraint on responsiveness is that government agencies cannot — or, at least, do not — respond equally to different societal interests. Inevitably, some groups view government as unresponsive because it does not respond to *them*. And they are often correct in that assessment. The main point, however, is that government is not simply responsive; it is *responsive to* specific sets of interests and preferences that exist in society at large. Especially in the context of limited resources (fiscal and otherwise), government cannot be responsive to each and every interest or need, and it is rarely able to satisfy fully those interests to which it does respond.

Administrative Effectiveness and Personal Liberty

One other topic deserves brief treatment: the possibility that, as government machinery is strengthened, it may acquire additional potential for diluting individual liberties. This does not necessarily occur as the product of deliberate decision in the highest councils of government. It can result simply from overzealous implementation of perceived mandates by an individual agency or bureaucrat. It is an even greater possibility when strong public sentiment supports an agency in doing a job that inherently threatens individual liberties.

A leading example is law enforcement agencies. In their zeal for "fighting crime," there is danger that the FBI, state law enforcement agencies, or local police may infringe on Bill of Rights protections. This is a serious concern of many people, involving such issues as search and seizure procedures, wiretapping, profiling, and priorities of national security versus individual privacy. The essential point is that, as the machinery of government grows stronger — whether or not it is supported by popular majorities — the *potential* for infringement of all sorts on individual rights grows apace. This causes operating problems for those in public administration but, because of the basic values at issue, all of society is ultimately involved.

Social Change and Public Administration

social-demographic changes shifts in the population and economies of various regions that impact the delivery of public services.

The social setting of public administration, like the context of values, has both direct and indirect impacts, and changes in that setting, like changes in values, carry with them potentially far-reaching implications. Several **social-demographic changes** during the past fifty years have been of particular importance in shaping contemporary public administration.

The most obvious changes are population growth and shifts in the demographic makeup of the population. We have become a nation of nearly 280 million inhabitants, from less than half that many a century ago and less than two-thirds of that number (151 million) in 1950.[39] This striking growth in numbers has been paralleled by increases in demands for public services. More often than not, these demands have been directed at administrative agencies (especially at the state and local level), such as police officers, firefighters, teachers and other educators, sanitation workers, and health services personnel. Related to, complicating, and intensifying this increased demand for service is a second development: the continuing concentration of people in urban areas. The greatest population growth occurred in suburban rings around larger cities, mainly in the Southeast, Northwest, and Southwest.

Perhaps more important have been major shifts in both population and economic activity from the Northeast/Midwest (Snow Belt) to the South/West (Sun Belt). During the 1970s, population growth increased faster outside the Snow Belt as states in this region lost nearly 1 million manufacturing jobs. In the 1980s, more than 90 percent of the nation's population growth occurred outside the Snow Belt. Such changes continued during the 1990s and entail serious social, economic, policy, and administrative implications for regions on both ends of the migration streams. Even within the Sun Belt, growth has been concentrated in particular areas. In Florida, for example, the coastal population doubled between 1964 and 1984, and today, 10 million people live in that state's Atlantic and Gulf Coast counties. Similarly, the population of the seventeen coastal counties of Texas increased by 64 percent in the period 1960–1984 and now numbers 4 million people. These general population trends in the Sun Belt continued well into the 1990s.

Several other important demographic shifts should also be mentioned. First, during the 1970s, the proportion of African Americans living in central cities declined (from 59 percent to 55 percent of all African Americans). This was the first time that any decline of that significance had occurred since the great influx of African Americans to northern cities during World War II. Second, more than 10 percent of the U.S. population age five or older speak a foreign language at home, and half of those individuals speak Spanish as their first language. Third, after a period of declining birthrates, a small echo of the post–World War II baby boom has now appeared; consequently, the school-age population, which shrank during most of the 1970s, has begun to grow again. These changes pose new and complex problems for those who administer government programs in education, economic development, housing, and other social service areas.

Technological change has become increasingly important to public administration. We have experienced a revolution in electronic communications in terms of instantaneously linking widely separated parts of the world via the Internet, World Wide Web, and satellites. Mass communications capabilities now allow literally millions of people to witness an event simultaneously. Technology, in the form of automation and other advances, has also permitted mass production and the distribution of durable goods on a larger scale than ever before. The **knowledge explosion** is another dimension of technological change and is giving rise to both the education industry and the expansion of private- and government-sponsored scientific research. Government regulation of, and participation in, increasingly complex technologies (such as the space program, control of environmental pollution and toxic wastes, and energy research) require more and more sophisticated and specialized bureaucracies. This drastic alteration in responsibilities has had a permanent effect on the nature and course of American public administration.[40]

The need for increased specialization is evident throughout much of both public and private administration. As tasks and skills become more complex, mastering any one of them demands more of an individual's time and attention, thus possibly hampering acquisition of broad skills. Of course, specialization is a core value in traditional conceptions of public bureaucracy; thus, movement toward greater specialization represents the extension of an existing feature rather than a new one. It has been a very important consequence for public administration that specialists both inside and outside of government have been able to be — indeed, have *had* to be — in closer working contact with one another as part of the policy-making process. Technology has allowed for the creation of electronic networks that make it very easy for computer network users to make contact with others on the network and to exchange data. This reinforces the dual patterns of *more informed* decision making that results from the use of various knowledge resources that can be brought to bear, and of *less centrally directed* decision making (due to the limited ability of top executives to comprehend fully all the specialties of the people in their organizations). Patterns of decentralization have been identified as a significant offshoot of the knowledge explosion that has become so much a part of American life.[41]

technological change rapidly emerging patterns of change (related in part to the knowledge explosion) in communication, medical, and transportation technologies, among others, with significant implications both for the societal challenges confronting government and for the means and resources increasingly available to government for conducting public affairs.

knowledge explosion a social phenomenon of the past forty years, particularly in Western industrial nations, creating new technologies and vast new areas of research and education; examples include biogenetic engineering, space exploration, mass communications, nuclear technology, mass production, and energy research (see also Chapter 12).

The desire for specialization is a major reason for fragmenting and compartmentalizing decision-making responsibility within a bureaucracy. Specialization gives a staff or organization considerable discretionary authority within its jurisdiction. To the extent that personnel systems are based on job-related competence that includes increasingly specialized knowledge, these tendencies toward specialization are likely to be reinforced.

Political decisions to address new problems, or to identify as problems certain conditions already present in society, have almost always enlarged the responsibilities of administrative bodies. This suggests that many of today's challenges, such as environmental pollution, energy use and conservation, population growth and stability, welfare reform and mass transit (to name only a few major ones), have actually been with us for some time. In all of these cases, changes in societal values preceded identification of the problems. Even though certain situations may not as yet have been widely regarded as areas requiring public action, there is still debate over the scope and nature of particular governmental actions to address them. Administrative entities empowered to deal with these problems are thus drawn into controversies surrounding the nature of the problems themselves as well as the methods used to resolve them.

In sum, the combined effects on bureaucracy of population growth and geographic redistribution, vast changes in our knowledge and technological capabilities, specialization, and the rise of new, complex social problems have been profound and probably irreversible. Many of these changes are global in nature and impact governments in many different countries. Clearly, change in American society has led to new, unforeseen, and complex pressures on our machinery of government at all levels.

Summary

Calls for "reinventing government" have found a broad and receptive audience inside and outside of government and it is likely that reform efforts will continue for some years to come. Contemporary public administration is being shaped by the larger political system of which it is a part, by past and present political and administrative values, and by technology and social change. Traditional conceptions of bureaucracy and its role in government include: (1) political neutrality in carrying out decisions, (2) legislative intent as a principal guiding force, (3) legislative oversight, (4) direction by the chief executive of administrative activities (which, in a system of separation of powers, creates the possibility of conflict over control of bureaucracy), and (5) professional competence. Although they form the core of our beliefs about public administration, these conceptions are not altogether accurate.

The fragmented nature of policy making forces administrators to function in a political environment where: (1) there is no central policy coordinator with total control, (2) administrators possess considerable discretion, and (3) not all decision-making power or authority is clearly allocated. In such a setting, public administrators are often politically active and take policy initiatives that are not neutral, thus departing from traditional views about bureaucratic roles and functions. Furthermore, bureaucratic activity is organized around jurisdiction over particular policy areas; bureaucracies seek to prevent changes in jurisdiction that might harm their interests or those of their supporters.

Politically, our system of government is a liberal democracy; economically, it is based on free enterprise and capitalism. Throughout our history, key political values have included popular sovereignty, limited government, individualism, and pluralism. We have also emphasized individual liberty and democratic principles such as majority rule, minority rights, and the free exchange of political ideas. Two related concepts — representation and representativeness — have taken on new meanings, leading to definitional uncertainty. More controversial issues are direct voter participation and a broadened definition of representativeness in public decision making. For the most part, our political values have fit comfortably with the economic doctrines of capitalism. Although increasingly regulative, government economic policies have sought to sustain competition and protect the rewards of competitive success.

Major objectives of a politically neutral "science of administration" have included separation of politics and administration, scientific management and administrative principles, and, most important, attainment of economy and efficiency in government. These values were the basis of administrative reform in the late nineteenth and early twentieth centuries, and were a reaction against practices of the early to mid-nineteenth century. These values have had continuing popular appeal and have been used quite effectively as part of campaign oratory by candidates for public office.

However, our political and administrative values are not entirely consistent with each other. The framers of the Constitution assumed that there would be effective political control over all important decision makers by the voters or their elected representatives, whereas the reformers intended to insulate administration from direct political control. Such insulation has become cause for concern as administrators have assumed or been delegated ever greater policy-making responsibility and authority. In addition, one set of values is based on the assumption that individual liberty and the public interest are best served by keeping government restrained — and therefore unable to infringe upon our freedoms. The other set of values, however, is geared toward improving the ability of government agencies to operate efficiently — and also in the public interest. Changes in particular values have intensified existing pressures on administrative institutions, especially in recent years.

Public administration is particularly troublesome for a democratic system. Most bureaucrats are not elected. Expertise and knowledge are emphasized over participation. Specialization and professionalism are valued. Participation and professionalism often conflict, and it is difficult to incorporate both accountability and participation into administrative policy making. Accountability and access requires government openness to public scrutiny. In this connection, freedom of information and sunshine laws have been enacted. Sunset laws help legislative bodies hold executive-branch agencies accountable. Accountability is made more difficult by the technical subject matter in so much government activity.

Major dimensions of democratic administration include (1) citizen participation, (2) bureaucratic representativeness, (3) responsiveness, and (4) administrative effectiveness as a threat to personal freedoms. Citizen participation originated with efforts on the part of the urban poor (and some others) to obtain a greater voice in government decisions affecting their lives. It has now been adapted to the purposes of many other groups, white as well as nonwhite, more affluent and less affluent. Citizen participation has taken many forms; it has also been incorporated into formal mechanisms for decision making. Citizen participation has had substantive impact on government decisions, but it also has its constraints, including the possibility of co-optation of citizens, limits on citizen time and access, and tokenism.

Representation and representativeness in government generally, and public administration specifically, have recently been given more attention. Bureaucratic representation is ambiguous, although it has been suggested that democratic morality is best served by promoting broadly inclusive representation of interests in interactions among decision makers. Closely related is the need for access to decision makers, especially for weaker interests. The representativeness of government bureaucracy, a continuing concern, has been said to enhance bureaucratic effectiveness and responsiveness. Representativeness of minorities, emphasized since the late 1960s, has increased in the civil service, although with what effects is not entirely clear.

Bureaucratic responsiveness depends on popular assumptions about what is and should be in the conduct of government, meaningful access to decision makers, and agencies' ability to respond to public demands. Public expectations can affect how responsive government is thought to be. Also, government cannot or will not respond equally to every interest in society.

Effectiveness of administrative machinery may pose a threat to individual liberties under some circumstances. Concerns about public administration and democratic government include the possible misuse of administrative secrecy, a traditional feature of bureaucracy, to violate the constitutional rights of individual citizens. Another recent emphasis is on the need to protect individual privacy against government invasion and against misuse of personal information. The Internet and its capabilities have made this an increasingly vital issue.

In addition to adapting to changing trends in political and economic thought, public administration has also had to adapt to rapid social change. Especially during the beginning of the twenty-first century, public administration must deal with rapid population growth and urbanization, increased specialization, the emergence of new social problems, and complex technological advances.

KEY TERMS AND CONCEPTS

reinventing government	pluralism
National Partnership for Reinventing Government (NPRG)	representative democracy
	participatory democracy
bureaucratic neutrality	affirmative action
legislative intent	pluralist democracy
legislative oversight	administrative efficiency
parliamentary forms of government	accountability
checks and balances	freedom of information (FOI) laws
administrative discretion	sunshine laws
power vacuum	sunset laws
liberal democracy	community control
capitalist system	public-interest groups (PIGs)
popular sovereignty	co-optation
limited government	empowerment
representation	social-demographic changes
representativeness	technological change
individualism	knowledge explosion

SUGGESTED READING

Dodd, Lawrence C., and Richard L. Schott. *Congress and the Administrative State.* New York: Wiley, 1979.

Ingraham, Particia W., James R. Thompson, and Ronald Sanders, eds. *Transforming Government: Lessons From the Reinvention Laboratories.* San Francisco, Jossey-Bass, 1998.

Kearns, Kevin P. *Managing for Accountability.* San Francisco: Jossey-Bass, 1996.

Kettl, Donald F. *Government by Proxy: (Mis?)Managing Federal Programs.* Washington, D.C.: CQ Press, 1988.

Kettl, Donald F., and John J. DiIulio, eds. *Inside the Reinvention Machine.* Washington, D.C.: The Brookings Institution, 1995.

Kweit, Mary Grisez, and Robert W. Kweit. *Implementing Citizen Participation in a Bureaucratic Society: A Contingency Approach.* New York: Praeger, 1982.

Light, Paul. *Monitoring Government.* Washington, D.C.: The Brookings Institution, 1996.

Martin, Roscoe C. *Grass Roots.* University, Ala.: University of Alabama Press, 1957.

———, ed. *Public Administration and Democracy.* Syracuse, N.Y.: Syracuse University Press, 1965.

Osborne, David, and Ted Gaebler. *Reinventing Government*. Reading, Mass.: Addison-Wesley, 1992.

Osborne, David, and Peter Plastrik. *Banishing Bureaucracy: Five Strategies for Reinventing Government*. Reading, Mass.: Addison-Wesley, 1997.

Perry, James L., ed. *Handbook of Public Administration*. San Francisco: Jossey-Bass, 1996.

Redford, Emmette S. *Democracy in the Administrative State*. New York: Oxford University Press, 1969.

Rohr, John A. *To Run a Constitution: The Legitimacy of the Administrative State*. Lawrence, Kansas: University Press of Kansas, 1986.

Rosen, Bernard. *Holding Government Bureaucracies Accountable*. 3rd ed. Westport, Conn.: Greenwood Press, 1998.

Sears, David O., and Jack Citrin. *Tax Revolt: Something for Nothing in California*. Enlarged ed. Cambridge, Mass.: Harvard University Press, 1985.

Seidman, Harold, and Robert Gilmour. *Politics, Position, and Power: From the Positive to the Regulatory State*. 4th ed. New York: Oxford University Press, 1986.

Sheldon, D. R. *Achieving Accountability in Business and Government*. Westport, Conn.: Quorum Books, 1996.

Stillman, Richard J., II, ed. *The American Constitution and the Administrative State: Constitutionalism in the Late 20th Century*. Washington, D.C.: University Press of America, 1989.

Waldo, Dwight. *The Administrative State: A Study of the Political Theory of American Public Administration*. 2nd ed. New York: Holmes and Meier, 1984.

Wamsley, Gary L., et al. *Refounding Public Administration*. Newbury Park, Calif.: Sage, 1990.

Yates, Douglas. *Bureaucratic Democracy: The Search for Efficiency and Democracy in American Government*. Cambridge, Mass.: Harvard University Press, 1982; paperback edition, 1987.

ON-LINE RESOURCES:
Public Administration, Democracy, and the Political System

Alliance for Redesigning Government

http://www.alliance.napawash.org/alliance/index.html

The Alliance is a nonprofit center of a national network and clearinghouse for state, local, and federal innovations, and scholars who advocate performance-based, results-driven governance.

Center for Civic Networking
http://www.civic.net/ccn.html

A nonprofit organization dedicated to applying information infrastructure to the broad public good, particularly by putting information infrastructure to work within local communities to improve delivery of local government services, improve access to information that people need in order to function as informed citizens, broaden citizen participation in governance, and stimulate economic and community development.

Center for the Study of Values in Public Life
http://divweb.harvard.edu/csvpl/

Teaching and research center founded to examine the values that shape public debates, policies, and institutional practices.

Congressional Accountability Project
http://www.essential.org/orgs/CAP/CAP.html

Congressional watchdog group.

In Our Path
http://www.outtacontext.com/iop/

This is a fascinating photo documentary (now Web site) about the controversy surrounding the construction of the Century Freeway in Los Angeles.

Institute for the Study of Civic Values
http://www.libertynet.org/edcivic/iscvhome.html

Evolving collection of on-line resources dedicated to supporting civic life and citizen participation in collaboration with a growing number of individuals and organizations.

Government Accountability Project
http://www.whistleblower.org

The mission of the Government Accountability Project is to protect the public interest and promote government and corporate accountability by advancing occupational free speech, defending whistle-blowers, and empowering citizen activists.

Governments on the WWW
http://www.gksoft.com/govt/en/us.html

Comprehensive and frequently updated database of government institutions on the World Wide Web: parliaments, ministries, embassies, courts, city councils, central banks, and multigovernment institutions. Frequently updated.

National Academy of Public Administration (NAPA)

http://www.napawash.org/

NAPA is a nonpartisan, nonprofit organization chartered by Congress to improve government performance. Information regarding NAPA, including a list of publications, congressional testimony, news releases, and other pertinent information, can be found on this site.

National Association of Schools of Public Affairs and Administration (NASPAA)

http://www.naspaa.org

Accrediting association for schools of public affairs and administration.

National Partnership for Reinventing Government (NPRG)

http://www.npr.gov/

Excellent source for information on federal executive agency reinvention efforts, including numerous case studies and links to other related sites.

U.S. Department of Commerce

http://www.doc.gov/

The executive branch agency charged with promoting job creation, economic growth, sustainable development, and improved living standards for all Americans.

U.S. General Accounting Office

http://www.gao.gov

The official Web site of Congress's investigative arm.

For further information on public administration, democracy, and the political system see: Bedford/St. Martin's Home Page

http://www.bedfordstmartins.com

Chapter 3

Bureaucratic Politics
and Bureaucratic Power

> *Economy and efficiency are demonstrably not the prime purposes*
> *of public administration. . . . Supreme Court Justice Louis D.*
> *Brandeis emphasized that 'the doctrine of separation of powers was*
> *adopted, not to promote efficiency but to preclude the exercise of*
> *arbitrary power.' The basic issues of . . . organization and admin-*
> *istration relate to power: who shall control it and to what ends?*

> Harold Seidman and Robert Gilmour, *Politics, Position, and Power:*
> *From the Positive to the Regulatory State*, 1986

In this chapter, we resume our discussion of the politics of American public administration. Here, we shall deal with five principal themes. First, we will consider the *political environment* in which bureaucracy functions. Second, we will examine *foundations* of bureaucratic power, especially the use of expertise in a particular field to build, retain, and mobilize support for administrative agencies and programs. Third, we will look at *subsystem politics*, a term that refers to the ways in which bureaucrats enter directly into alliances with others inside and outside of government in order to pursue shared (or at least complementary) programmatic and political objectives. Fourth, we will discuss the emergence of *issues networks* and how they influence policy development. Fifth, we will consider the challenge of establishing the *accountability* of nonelected government officials (i.e., most bureaucrats), identify several limitations on bureaucratic accountability, and suggest how those limitations can be overcome.

The Political Environment of Bureaucratic Power

Like most other government institutions, administrative agencies function within a complex framework of widely scattered legal and political power. Both the formal structure of governmental power and the actual competition for power reflect a *lack of centralization* in the political system. The formal framework includes constitutional traditions such as separation of powers, checks and balances, federalism, and judicial review. Competition for power includes conflicts among and within the branches of government (especially within Congress), factional conflict within the two major political parties, and continual jockeying for position and influence among interest groups. This dispersal of power is sustained and supported by the noncentralized nature of American society, with its strong cultural emphases on individualism and pluralism. This prevailing political culture is accompanied by acceptance of individualism and group competition as appropriate mechanisms for achieving success in politics and other pursuits.

Wide dispersal of political power both constrains and creates opportunities for *stakeholders* — diverse interested individuals, groups, and institutions — to seek and acquire leverage in a policy arena. The major problem facing any group or agency is that competition for influence in a particular subject area is usually fierce because, at the same time, many other groups and agencies are also seeking to have their preferences adopted as public policy.

Take, for example, a proposed change in government health care policy. This area is of considerable interest to the medical profession, pharmaceuticals manufacturers, hospitals, medical equipment dealers, insurance companies, patients, the uninsured, and consumer groups. Others with a stake in health care policy include labor unions whose members are covered by company-paid health plans, stockholders of drug companies, nonphysicians employed by health care providers, and government agencies — such as the national Department of Health and Human Services (DHHS) and state and national health regulatory commissions — that have responsibilities affecting, and affected by, decisions on health care policy issues.

The key to understanding why bureaucratic agencies are forced to play political roles is the lack of cohesive political majorities within the two houses of Congress and the resultant "fuzziness" in programmatic mandates often enacted by Congress.[1] Political scientist Norton Long, writing over fifty years ago, observed that "it is a commonplace that the American party system provides neither a mandate for a platform nor a mandate for leadership. . . . The mandate that the parties do not supply must be attained through public relations and the mobilization of group support."[2] Long went on to suggest that the parties fail to provide "either a clear-cut decision as to what [administrative agencies] should do or an adequately mobilized political support for a course of action."[3] He continued:

> The weakness in party structure both permits and makes necessary the present dimensions of the political activities of the administrative branch — permits because it fails to protect administration from pressures and fails to provide adequate direction and support, makes necessary because it fails to develop a consensus on a leadership and a program that makes possible administration on the basis of accepted decisional premises.[4]

Thus Congress, lacking majorities that can speak with clear and consistent voices for sustained periods of time, is characterized instead by shifting political coalitions, the composition of which varies from one issue (and even one vote) to the next.

Another factor contributing to the lack of clarity in legislative mandates to government agencies is the inability of legislatures as institutions — and of individual legislators — to define precisely the exact steps required to put into effect a desired policy or program:

> Legislators, not being technical experts, frequently write laws embodying goals that are exemplary but [that] lack details. Skeletal legislation, as it is frequently called, is phrased in occasionally grand and, therefore, fuzzy terms. The implementing agency is told by the legislature [in national, state, or local government] to provide a *safe* environment for workers, to see that school children are served meals with *adequate* nutritional content, . . . to *assist the visually impaired*, to maintain *adequate* income levels, and so on.[5]

Most of the time — but especially when basic statutory language is ambiguous — legislators delegate to administrators the authority necessary to breathe life and specific meaning into such provisions of the law and then to implement them. (Ambiguous language can also be the result of political compromises. For example, it is always easier to agree on support for "quality education" than to define exactly what that is.) For whatever reason, then, the usual pattern is legislative enactment of statutes that are phrased in general terms, accompanied by legislative delegation of authority (to define and implement those statutes) to administrative agencies.

Thus, agencies are placed in the position of making judgments about legislative intent and program management. These decisions carry with them significant political implications. Congress, however, does not simply leave bureaucrats to their own devices. As noted in Chapter 2, *legislative oversight* is a legitimate function of Congress, one that can sometimes result in fairly strict control by a legislative committee or subcommittee of actions taken by administrators under its jurisdiction. (Other potential controls will be examined in the discussion of bureaucratic accountability later in this chapter.)

Presidents, who might be expected to provide leadership for bureaucracy from a solid base of political support, ordinarily lack the sort of backing that would permit them to take unequivocal policy positions. Presidents have the largest constituencies and therefore must be, if not all things to all groups, at least many things to many of them. Administrative decisions are inevitably impacted by the need to serve so many varied interests. This can also pose a considerable challenge to administrators seeking to carry out directives from the chief executive as well as the legislature.

For a variety of reasons, chief executives of public agencies (presidents, governors, mayors) may seek to avoid a leading role in giving detailed direction to administrative implementation of public policy. For administrators, there are both advantages and disadvantages to this course of action: on the one hand, administrators are not bound to follow every executive dictate exactly; on the other hand, they are not able to rely routinely on presidential, gubernatorial, or mayoral power or prestige for political support.

Before discussing the principal political resources of administrative agencies, some other generalizations concerning the political environment of bureaucratic power should be noted. First, formal definitions of agency power or responsibility are not likely to reveal the complete scope of actual power or influence. Second, although bureaucratic agencies generally occupy a power position somewhere between total independence from president and Congress and total domination by either or both, the amount of independence they have in any specific situation is also heavily influenced by the power relationships they have with other political actors and institutions. Agencies with relatively low political standing may be dependent on the support of Congress or the president in order to function adequately, thus running the risk of allowing others to dominate their decisions. Those with higher standing or stronger backing from other supporters are better able to stand on their own in relation to Capitol Hill and the White House. These generalizations also hold true in state and local politics.

Third, the acquisition and exercise of bureaucratic power are frequently characterized by conflicts among agencies over program **jurisdiction,** the area of responsibility assigned to an agency by Congress or the president. The study of **bureaucratic imperialism,** that is, the tendency of agencies to expand their program responsibilities, suggests that such expansionism arises because administrative politicians need to maintain a sufficient power base for their agencies. *"Power is organized around constituency and constituency around jurisdiction."*[6] In their quest for "sufficient power," bureaucratic agencies seek support from permanent and semipermanent coalitions of constituency groups (that is, **interest groups**), which in turn are organized to pursue policy objectives of their own. To secure backing from such groups, administrative agencies must manage government programs of interest to these potentially supportive constituencies. Thus, agencies always seek to obtain control over programs that have strong support from influential constituencies.

Bureaucratic imperialism, however, is neither universal nor automatic; for example, an agency may deny, in its own interests, that it has legal authority to exercise powers within some specified "unpopular" area of jurisdiction. The point is not that agencies are inherently imperialistic or nonimperialistic but rather that an agency's decisions regarding program jurisdiction usually take into account potential repercussions. Thus, conflicts over agency jurisdiction are serious contests for political power.

Finally, governmental institutions, including administrative agencies, have at least two roles to play in the exercise of power and decision-making authority. These roles overlap but are conceptually distinct and can sometimes conflict. On the one hand, the institutions may act as *unified entities* seeking to maximize their

jurisdiction   in bureaucratic politics, the area of programmatic responsibility assigned to an agency by the legislature or chief executive; also, a term used to describe the territory within the boundaries of a government entity, such as "a local jurisdiction."

bureaucratic imperialism   the tendency of agencies to try to expand their program responsibilities.

interest groups   private organizations representing a portion (usually small) of the general adult population; they exist in order to pursue particular public policy objectives and seek to influence government activity so as to achieve their objectives.

influence and their share of available political rewards and benefits. On the other hand, government institutions also serve as *arenas of political competition*, within which various forces contend for dominant influence in decision-making processes. This is especially evident in Congress, where rival political coalitions are frequently in noisy dispute over well-publicized issues. Media reports that "Congress voted today to . . ." really mean that a majority coalition was successfully formed on a given vote. Also at issue every time Congress makes a decision is control of the way the question is presented, possible amendments, use of numerous tactics to speed up or delay consideration, and other tactical questions. There is far less visible conflict in the bureaucracy than in Congress, but this pattern of conflict resolution is much the same, complete with conflict over shaping the issue, moving it along or foot-dragging, and so forth. Like Congress, the bureaucracy operates within a complex web of political forces and must respond to the external (and frequently internal) pressures brought to bear on the administration of government programs.

Ordinarily, administrative agencies try to strike a manageable balance between, on the one hand, what they *can* and *want to* do to further their own programmatic interests and, on the other, what they *must do* to ensure their survival and prosperity, however that is defined. Achieving such a balance requires a willingness to compromise, a sure instinct for deciding when to seek a larger or smaller share of the pie, and an ability to read both long- and short-term political forecasts accurately. In addition to those internal skills, however, an agency must first have and maintain the two crucial foundations or sources of bureaucratic power mentioned earlier: expertise in the subject matter of its program responsibilities, and political support. Let us consider each of these in turn.

Foundations of Power: Bureaucratic Expertise

A major foundation of bureaucratic power is the collective expertise an agency can bring to bear on programs for which it is responsible. As various facets of society have become more complex and interdependent and as technological advances have followed one another with astounding speed, the people with know-how — the experts — have acquired increasing influence because of their specialized knowledge. Government is obviously subject to the same forces as the rest of society; this is particularly true of technological change. As a result, government experts now play larger roles in numerous public policy decisions.

Political scientist Francis Rourke has suggested that the influence of experts rests on five major components[7]: (1) full-time attention by experts to a problem or subject-matter area; (2) specialization in the subject; (3) a monopoly on information in the subject area that, if successfully maintained by only one staff of experts, makes these specialists indispensable in any decision making involving their subject; (4) a pattern of increasing reliance on bureaucratic experts for technical advice; and (5) increasing control by experts of bureaucratic discretion.

The last three of these components deserve discussion. Although a monopoly on information is desirable from a particular agency's point of view, it is rarely achieved in practice. This is partly because no agency controls all governmental sources of information on any given subject, partly because government does not control all information sources in society, and partly because information — itself a source of power and influence — is the subject of intense interagency competition. Thus, when expert staff members have a monopoly on information relevant to making a given decision, their influence increases. Conversely, influence can be more effectively contested when there is greater diversity of information sources.[8]

Reliance on expert advice, although on the increase, is not without limits; the influence of experts, therefore, is similarly constrained. Not every agency decision revolves around technical criteria or data. Even when an issue does involve technical data, top-level administrators, for political or other reasons, may prefer a decision that is not the best according to technical criteria (see Chapter 6). Thus, in many agencies, expert advisers play a role that, although important and influential, also has its limitations.

Two aspects of the experts' increasing control of bureaucratic discretion are worth noting. First, by exercising discretion, an expert maximizes the ability to decide just how vigorously or casually to implement the public policies over which the agency has jurisdiction. Second, bureaucratic discretion enables agency experts to influence policy decisions by defining the decisional alternatives from which higher-level officials choose the course to be followed. To the extent that responsible policymakers permit bureaucratic experts to define available alternatives, they strengthen the experts' influence through the power to decide what is and is not included among the alternatives presented.

Experts possess another useful resource: their ability to employ the language of their respective trades, speaking in terms and concepts unfamiliar to most of us. This use of **specialized language** (some might call it *jargon*) has become a common phenomenon among experts inside and outside of government, and poses problems for the layman who seeks to understand complex developments and issues. By using jargon, bureaucratic experts make it very difficult for others to challenge them on their own territory, so to speak; if we cannot fathom what they have proposed, how can we argue against it? This resource, moreover, has been greatly enhanced by the fact that, in countless cases, proposals put forward by experts have yielded very positive and beneficial results. As Rourke has noted, this combination of obscurity of means and clarity of results has helped consolidate the position, prestige, and influence of experts in government agencies.[9]

In recent years, however, the obscurity of means that previously was a source of strength for experts has contributed to growing public disenchantment with "big government," bureaucracy, and experts in general. With the increasing desire for broader public involvement in decision making (see Chapter 2) has come a greater unwillingness to take the experts' word and a more insistent demand

specialized language
technical vocabulary used by bureaucratic agencies, one effect of which is to restrict access and outside influence.

that experts make clear to the general public exactly what they are doing, proposing, and advocating. The Clinton administration's vision of *Common Sense Government*,[10] as part of the larger effort to reinvent government, sought to "put customers first" by eliminating unnecessary obstacles to delivering public services. In the long run, public reactions and attitudes may have more effect on the influence and power of government experts than any characteristics or actions of the experts themselves.

Foundations of Power: Political Support

Political support for an administrative agency has a number of key dimensions. First, and perhaps foremost, the legislature is a major potential source of support that must be carefully and continuously cultivated. In most instances, an agency derives its principal backing from one subdivision (usually a committee or subcommittee with authority to oversee the agency's operations) rather than from the legislature as a whole. Most agencies are faced with the task of continually generating and maintaining the support of committees, subcommittees, and even individual members. They attempt to do this in a number of ways. Some of these methods are: (1) responding promptly to requests for information, (2) effectively promoting and managing programs in which legislators are known to have an interest, (3) cooperating administratively with legislators' electoral needs, and (4) anticipating legislative preferences regarding the operations of particular programs.

A second source of support is the executive branch, which is composed of the president, governor, or mayor and other administrators and agencies formally lodged in the executive hierarchy. Executive influence can be decisive in determining success or failure, and an agency will make every effort to win favor in both the short and long run. An important corollary of presidential or vice presidential backing at the national level is favorable reviews of agency budget requests by the Office of Management and Budget (OMB), which molds the executive-branch budget proposals submitted to Congress each year. Although the OMB does not itself allocate funds to the agencies, its support can enable an agency to concentrate on persuading Congress (which does hold the purse strings) to back its programs financially. The best position for an agency to be in is one in which its programmatic responsibilities have a high priority on presidential policy agendas year in and year out but, as suggested earlier, few agencies enjoy this kind of support. Far more common is a pattern in which agencies and their programs compete for support and settle for a "win some, lose some" record. Support for an agency can be earned, among other ways, by giving stronger agency support to programs that are administered by the agency and are consistent with the current administration's policy priorities; by sharing, at least on the surface, chief-executive concerns about how programs are managed (as many agencies did in response to Vice President Albert Gore's reinvention initiatives for the federal government); and by avoiding public conflict with the chief executive over policy and program priorities.

A second means of acquiring executive-branch support is by allying with another agency or agencies in quest of common objectives. Such interagency alliances tend to be limited in scope and duration. Because most agencies are very protective of their program jurisdictions and because there is an element of risk that a cooperating agency might also be a potential rival, most agencies enter into alliances with others rather carefully, even though they may share limited objectives. An example of such a bureaucratic alliance is the periodic coalition formed by the Army, Navy, and Air Force in opposition to cuts in defense appropriations, even as each is contending with the others for a greater share of the fiscal pie. But these are occasional alliances brought about by specific and passing needs; they do not usually outweigh more enduring differences among agencies. In sum, although cooperation with other agencies may indeed be a means of acquiring support, it has its limitations. The agencies with which cooperation would be most logical in terms of programmatic interest are the very ones with the greatest potential for conflict over jurisdictional responsibilities.

A third major source of support, which is carefully cultivated, is constituent or clientele groups that look to the agency for satisfaction of their policy demands. These *interest groups* represent an organized expression of political opinion by a portion — usually a small one — of the adult population.[11] They tend to be groups directly affected by the agency's operations, which therefore have a tangible stake in its policy decisions, rule making, or programmatic output. The political relationship that usually develops between an agency and such a group is one of *reciprocity*, in which each has some political commodity from which the other can benefit. The agency's greatest strength is its expertise and the control it exercises over particular government programs that are of interest to the group. In turn, the group has political resources that it makes available to the agency in return for agency attention to its needs and desires. The group may provide channels of communication to other influential individuals and groups, help the agency sell its program to Congress and the president, or aid the agency in anticipating changes in the political environment that would present problems or provide opportunities. Such agency-clientele group relationships exist, among many others, between the Pentagon and defense contractors, the Social Security Administration and senior citizen groups, the Department of Agriculture and the tobacco industry, the Maritime Administration and the shipping industry, state commerce commissions and private business associations, and both state and national departments of labor and the labor movement.

Administrative agencies often have more than one constituent group, creating both advantages and disadvantages. A principal advantage is that, with multiple sources of support, an agency can operate more effectively in the political process without having to rely too heavily on any one source of assistance. A corresponding disadvantage stems from the fact that various clientele groups often have differing interests, which lead them to demand different things from an agency or to demand the same things but not in the same order of priority. Not infrequently, an agency faces a situation in which satisfying one group's preferences will seriously interfere with its ability to satisfy those of another.

An agency must also deal with Congress or a specific committee as though it were a clientele group with demands and expectations that must be satisfied. An agency is well advised to consider congressional clientele groups as among its most important, especially when it is confronted with conflicting sets of demands. In other words, it is unwise to regularly disregard the demands of Congress, even if this means making other (private) clientele groups unhappy. (As we shall see later in this chapter, however, agencies have some means at their disposal to avoid being caught [most of the time] in a squeeze between their congressional and private clientele groups.)

In state politics, agencies are frequently tied even more closely to private interest groups. When the governor has somewhat limited formal powers or informal influence, or when the state legislature is relatively passive or weak, support from interest groups is often the greatest (and sometimes the only) source of strength for an administrative agency. Even in states with strong governors and legislatures — such as New York, California, Illinois, and Michigan — the support of key interest groups can benefit an agency significantly. For example, the Illinois Agricultural Association, the state component of the American Farm Bureau Federation, is a vital source of political strength for the state Department of Agriculture; in California, farm organizations help sustain both the Department of Agriculture and the Department of Water Resources. In return, of course, these agencies are expected to advocate and defend the interests of their supporters, such as irrigation for California's farmers. These relationships often become at least semipermanent.

One other aspect of agency-clientele relationships is quite important. As noted earlier, administrative organizations cherish, and thus strive to maintain, their control over particular programs. Sometimes, however, an agency may have to give up some of this control to outside influences, such as legislators or private clientele groups, in return for continuing political support. If this surrender is temporary, an agency loses little and may gain a great deal in the long run. If the agency fails to regain control, however, it is said to have undergone co-optation, whereby a set of outside interests acquires the ability to influence the agency's long-term policies. If this happens, all the agency's substantive policies may be subject to influence, not just those of most direct concern to the outside group or groups.

Numerous examples of co-optation may be cited. In developing relationships between some urban community-action groups and municipal administrations (i.e., "city hall"), city government leaders have occasionally succeeded in co-opting a group's leadership by acceding to some of their demands and giving them greater political visibility in exchange for moderating other demands. This has occurred especially in communities like Chicago that have well-entrenched local political organizations, where community-action groups choose to settle for "half a loaf" rather than risk forfeiting all chance to have some impact on the way decisions are made and resources allocated in the city government system. Powerful government structures are capable of co-opting nongovernmental groups. In addition, co-optation can work both ways, in that a government agency can be co-opted by stronger nongovernmental groups. Either way, co-optation involves a surrender by a weaker entity to a stronger one of some power to shape the course of the weaker entity's long-term activities.

A fourth source of political support or opposition for an administrative agency is the general public. The potential influence of the unorganized public is great; if mobilized and concentrated on a particular issue, public opinion can decisively tilt the political balance of power in one direction. The problem for any stakeholder is to mobilize the public successfully, which is no easy task. Ordinarily, most Americans pay scant attention to public issues unless and until the issues affect them personally.

Yet the public's attention can be directed to a pending major policy decision, and the public's feelings about it can be aroused. In some instances, expression of public opinion has forced a decision to be made — for example, withdrawing troops from an unpopular engagement, making an effort to combat environmental pollution, and taking steps to reduce government budget deficits. Without broad public demand and backing, these policy directions, which represented significant changes from earlier policies, could not have been proposed or sustained through the political process. In short, public support can be a valuable political resource to strengthen the positions of those in government. Numerous public-opinion studies have suggested that, when the general public has strong feelings on a matter of importance to large numbers of people, the governmental response is usually consistent with those feelings. An agency supported by broad public opinion can, by using public sentiment, generate support for itself and its programs.

In political terms, an agency's overall task can best be understood as controlling its programmatic responsibilities while simultaneously maintaining adequate support for its operations. This must be accomplished without making any of the agency's clientele groups seriously dissatisfied with the way it is performing its functions. This is far from easy to do, and it is the exception rather than the rule when an agency succeeds on all fronts. More frequent is the pattern of agency adaptation to, and accommodation of, particularly strong interests. Political backing can usually be obtained from these powerful groups in sufficient strength to outweigh any losses incurred by diminished program support among weaker clientele groups.

The Politics of Organizational Structure

Another dimension of the political setting in which agencies operate is the particular form of administrative organization. As noted in Chapter 1, structural arrangements can have political implications for administrative agencies. Here we will take a closer look at the political significance of structural arrangements, using as illustrations the U.S. Department of Education (DOE), established in 1977 by the Carter administration, and the Department of Veterans Affairs (DVA), created in 1988 by the Veterans Affairs Act and supported by the Bush administration.

Organizational form can signify a number of things. First, a particular **organizational structure** demonstrates commitment to one set of policy objectives instead of another. It can also foreshadow adoption of a distinct policy direction, either in an individual policy area or in broader policy terms. President Carter's decision to reorganize existing education agencies — bringing most of them into the DOE from the agency then called the Department of Health, Education, and Welfare (HEW) — signaled an increased emphasis on dealing with broad educational problems and issues. Previous organizational arrangements seemed to suggest that education, while important, was *no more important* than policy matters involving health, Social Security, or welfare. Also, as a practical matter, education concerns frequently had to compete with interest groups promoting these related issues for the attention of the Secretary of HEW and of other top leaders. Following the establishment of the DOE, the HEW was reorganized and renamed the Department of Health and Human Services (DHHS).

Another example of organizational structure reflecting policy direction was President Bush's active support of legislation to promote the Veterans Administration (VA) to cabinet status as the Department of Veterans Affairs (DVA). That action was taken in opposition to career administrators and even some influential leaders of the president's own party. It contradicted the general strategy of other Republican policies (such as the "New Federalism" of the 1980s) that were designed to reduce bureaucracy, save expenses, and weaken federal management of government programs. Despite these concerns and intraparty inconsistencies, however, the DVA was organized, largely in response to pressures from veterans' groups.

Second, a particular structure helps to order priorities by promoting some programs over others. Jimmy Carter's merger of existing education agencies into the DOE changed both symbolism and reality in the administrative politics of education. As mentioned earlier, the relatively higher priority of education was highlighted by the creation of a cabinet department to deal with it; such status carries with it increased prestige, not to mention visibility, both of which can be very useful to an agency. Furthermore, that sort of commitment from the chief executive, combined with more prominent organizational status, often leads to increased access to committees and influence in the legislature.

Finally, while a particular structure may provide greater access to influence for some interests, it could mean less for others. This is perhaps the most vivid lesson of the formation of the DOE. The campaign for its creation was led by the National Education Association (NEA), an influential interest group that represents hundreds of thousands of teachers across the country. Presidential

organizational structure the types of organizational unit designed to achieve a particular policy goal (see Chapter 1).

candidate Jimmy Carter, who was known to be sympathetic to many of the NEA's policy positions, pledged early in his presidential campaign to create a new education department. In turn, the NEA was one of Carter's staunchest supporters for the presidency. Obviously, the creation of the department for which so many teachers had campaigned substantially increased the degree of access to educational policymakers enjoyed by the NEA in particular and by teachers in general. The importance of access cannot be overestimated, as evidenced by the NEA's strong negative reaction to Ronald Reagan's proposed elimination of the DOE in 1981. During the Reagan and Bush administrations (1981–1993), groups supporting education policy were able to fend off repeated attempts to abolish or diminish the power of the DOE. Even popular presidents can encounter resistance to their policy initiatives when powerful interests converge around strong issues.

With this in mind, we should recall comments made earlier about agency jurisdiction and how it relates to *access* and agency structure. Structure and jurisdiction are at least indirectly related and, while changes in jurisdiction may not necessarily be accompanied by a change in structure, any change in structure will inevitably result in some reallocation of program jurisdiction.

Access and jurisdiction are also related. Clientele groups have meaningful access, at best, only to those administrators responsible for the programs with which these groups are concerned. Changes in jurisdiction, however, will often force affected clienteles to reestablish lines of access. Such changes could cause difficulties for these groups, especially in persuading new working partners to their points of view. Furthermore, clienteles normally prefer to have all related programs clustered under one administrative umbrella because that allows them to influence the full range of programs. It is also likely that such an arrangement will be managed by administrators sympathetic to programs for which they are responsible. Scattering the same programs among different agencies and administrators may result in more hostile treatment of both programs and clienteles.

These generalizations apply with equal force to the executive branches of state and local governments and to some specific circumstances and issues in the politics of organization. When state and local governments reorganize, downsize, or reinvent programs and policies, they are also subject to shifting coalitions and political struggles over power and administrative jurisdiction. This is clearly illustrated by the periodic effort in cities and towns across the country to redefine the form of local government structure to be adopted. This controversy has its roots in the late nineteenth and early twentieth centuries, when growing concentrations of European immigrants appeared in America's larger cities, as well as some smaller ones. Their arrival was accompanied by more — and more powerful — political party organizations and their "bosses."

The effort to reform American municipal government, according to the rhetoric of the time, was designed to bring about "economy and efficiency" in government, "to take the politics out of local government," and to promote "good government in the interests of the whole community." Municipal reform, then as now, usually involved one or more of the following structural arrangements: (1) the method of selecting the chief executive, that is, whether to have a popularly elected mayor or a professional city manager chosen by, and responsible to, the city council; (2) the extent of the chief executive's powers — this usually meant whether the office of the mayor was formally strong or weak; (3) whether municipal elections were to have candidates selected by political parties or on a nonpartisan basis; and (4) whether members of the city council were to be elected from specific geographic areas of the city, that is, by districts or wards, or selected at large.

Political rhetoric aside, decisions about these fundamental arrangements carry with them major implications for the distribution of local political power. For example, citywide minorities have little chance of winning representation in at-large council elections but a better chance in district or ward elections (provided ward boundaries were drawn up to reflect, rather than fragment, their population concentrations). Similarly, there are numerous instances in which a chief executive elected under the strong-mayor form was almost certain to be more politically sympathetic to ethnic or minority concerns than one chosen under a weak-mayor or city-manager form. It seems clear that group preferences for or against structural reform were not arrived at by chance but arose out of perceived group self-interest. This perception occurs because ethnic voters constitute the political majority in many cities that employ the strong-mayor form.

In sum, there are clear winners and losers in this facet of politics as in all others. Organizational structures, jurisdiction, and access in different settings reflect the relative power of competing forces, race and ethnic conflicts, and values. The politics surrounding structural arrangements are anything but neutral.

Bureaucrats as Politicians:
Subsystem Politics in America

We now turn to an examination of how bureaucrats manage their political alliances. Such regular collaboration often leads to the establishment of semipermanent ties. These political roles are relevant to agency efforts to secure needed support from interested clientele groups and various committees, subcommittees, and individual members of Congress, state legislatures, school boards, or city commissions.

One place to begin this analysis is to consider certain important parallels between the national government bureaucracy and the U.S. Congress. These institutions have three features in common that are important in this context. First, within both, there is a well-established pattern of *division of labor*; that is, the work to be done is divided among numerous smaller, specialized units. In Congress, these units are the committees and subcommittees of each chamber; in the bureaucracy, they are the multitude of bureaus, staffs, branches, and divisions that make up larger executive agencies. Second, the divisions within both Congress and the bureaucracy are organized primarily according to function and deal with general areas of policy concern, such as education, housing, labor, or defense. Third, the *specialized* nature of these smaller units is the principal source of their influence in the policy-making process.

It is a pervasive unwritten rule of Washington political life that, all other things being equal, larger institutions defer to the judgments of their more specialized units. This pattern of regularized respect for experts means that, in the great majority of cases, these units tend to be focal points of important decision making. In Congress, although bills passed by the full House and Senate must be identical, committee proposals usually form the core of bills that eventually reach passage. Amendment of committee proposals is possible, but the initial form of legislation carries some weight, and key committee and subcommittee members often influence the entire process of deliberation in the full chamber. In the bureaucracy, specialized personnel (the experts described earlier) wield considerable influence in the formulation of proposals that make their way up the formal hierarchical ladder (and to Congress as well) and into the daily processes of program implementation.

In short, it is misleading to assume that influence is concentrated only "at the top" in either Congress or the bureaucracy. The fine details of lawmaking, and of legislative oversight of executive departments, are the responsibility of subject-matter committees and subcommittees of Congress, each assigned jurisdiction over particular administrative agencies and their programs. Only rarely do such matters engage the attention of the full House or Senate. Similarly, the "nuts and bolts" of administration are normally concentrated in the lower levels of government organizations, not at the top or even very near it. Thus, in the broad picture of policy making in Washington, there is a high degree of fragmentation, with many small centers of influence operating in their respective areas of expertise.

Plainly, bureaucratic expertise is a source of bureaucratic power. Members of Congress also seek to become specialized, for two reasons. First, they are encouraged to do so by constituent interests on the grounds that this is the best route to influence in Congress. Second, they quickly recognize that, by becoming influential, they can do more for their voters back home. For sound political reasons, most seek to join congressional committees that have jurisdiction over areas of public policy affecting their electoral constituencies. A representative from rural Kansas, for example, is likely to apply for membership on the House Agriculture Committee, hoping also to be on its subcommittee dealing with subsidies for wheat farmers, wheat export policies, and so on. A representative from a constituency with sizable concentrations of low-income and minority groups in a large city would be likely to seek assignment to the Banking, Finance, and Urban Affairs Committee or perhaps to the Education and Labor Committee; both deal directly with the problems of urban constituents. Likewise, a senator from a state with a major port or a rail transportation center would cherish a position on the Commerce, Science, and Transportation Committee. And so it goes, all through Congress.

Obviously, members of Congress do not always get their first choices of assignment. But in pursuit of their own electoral fortunes and policy objectives, legislators are attracted to those committees in which they can have the most impact in policy areas that interest them personally and in which they can maximize their influence in support of **constituency** interests that could be decisive in their reelection bids. (Note that this implies selective attention to constituency interests, often focusing on objectives and preferences of influential friends and allies before — or at the expense of — objectives and preferences of others less powerful who live in the same constituency.) This naturally leads to increased contact between legislators and others interested in the same policy areas; administrators in agencies with jurisdiction over relevant programs; interest groups that, even more than legislators or bureaucrats, have specialized interests at the core of their existence and activities; and other members of Congress with one or more similar public policy interests.

> **constituency** any group or organization interested in the work and actions of a given official, agency, or organization, and a potential source of support for it; also, the interests (and sometimes geographic area) served by an elected or appointed public official.

This coalition of shared specialized interests produces the potential for pooling political resources by individuals and small groups in different parts of the policy-making arena in order to achieve common purposes. Hundreds of quiet, informal alliances have grown up in this manner, with the term *policy subsystem* — or simply *subsystem* — used to describe them.

What is a **subsystem?** It is defined here as *any political alliance uniting some members of an administrative agency, a congressional committee or subcommittee, and an interest group with shared values and preferences in the same substantive area of public policy making* (see Figure 3–1). Subsystems are informal alliances or coalitions that link individuals in different parts of the formal policy structure.[12] Their members usually have some influence in the policy-making process, in part because of their formal or official positions — bureau chief, committee or subcommittee chair, or committee member. The essential strength of a subsystem, however, lies in its ability to combine the benefits of bureaucratic expertise, congressional leverage, and interest group capabilities in organizing and communicating the opinions of those most concerned with a particular public issue. All subsystems have that potential; some, of course, are far more powerful than others.

> **subsystem** in the context of American politics (especially at the national level), any political alliance uniting some members of an administrative agency, a legislative committee or subcommittee, and an interest group according to shared values and preferences in the same substantive area of policy making; sometimes called an **iron triangle** (see p. 91).

One example of a very influential subsystem is the so-called *medical-industrial complex,* composed of doctors, hospitals, insurance companies, pharmaceutical and medical equipment manufacturers, the U.S. Department of Health and Human Services staff, influential members of House and Senate health and social affairs committees, and each chamber's appropriations subcommittee on Medicare and Social Security expenditures. Parallel executive departments, private insurers, health care professionals, and legislators at the state and local government level are also active stakeholders in this subsystem. The presence in this subsystem of large industries supplying hospital and medical equipment, prescription drugs, and public health care assistance to the poor (through Medicaid)

FIGURE 3–1   Relative Importance of Relationships
in Subsystem Politics

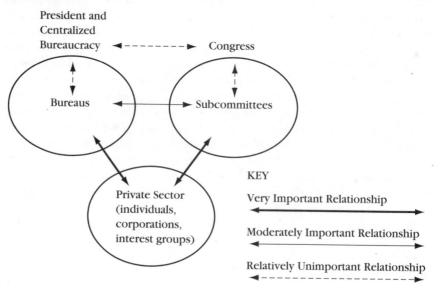

SOURCE: Randall B. Ripley and Grace A. Franklin, *Congress, the Bureaucracy, and Public Policy,* 5th ed. (Pacific Grove, Calif.: Brooks/Cole, 1991), p. 102.

and the elderly (through Medicare) significantly expands the number of affiliated legislators. Numerous public and private interest groups, such as the American Medical Association (AMA), the American Association of Retired Persons (AARP), and the American Hospital Association (AHA), direct their lobbying efforts toward key members of congressional committees. Thus, members of these committees are not the only legislators who might belong to a subsystem; other legislators may belong to a subsystem in order to advocate the interests of their constituencies.

Another example of a subsystem is the "highway lobby." Members of the House Public Works and Transportation Committee, officials of the Bureau of Public Roads, and such powerful interest groups as auto manufacturers, auto workers' unions, long-distance truckers, tire companies and their unions, road contractors and their unions, and oil companies and their unions, as well as members of Congress from these groups' states, have a common interest in maintaining and expanding highway usage. States represented include Michigan, Missouri, California, Texas, and Oklahoma, and some key legislators come from those states. It is not surprising, then, that Congress has only reluctantly allocated funds collected from gasoline and road taxes to be used for the expansion of mass transit systems. This political subsystem ardently opposes gasoline tax increases as a source of federal, state, or local government revenue. Not surprisingly, these same groups opposed a temporary *reduction* in the gasoline tax in order to relieve consumer complaints about the high costs of fuel during the run up of prices in the winter of 1999–2000.

Subsystem activity tends to remain behind the scenes. Policy decisions are reached in a spirit of friendly, quiet cooperation among various interested and influential persons; many of their decisions turn out to be key. Bureaucrats derive considerable benefit from this arrangement because they can usually count on adequate support both from inside government (Congress) and from outside (interest groups). Sometimes referred to as the **iron triangle,** the three-sided relationship (Figure 3–1) allows any one component of the subsystem to activate an effort toward common objectives with the full cooperation of the others. Unless challenged from outside — by other subsystems, the media, or perhaps the president — a subsystem is often able to dominate a policy-making arena.

iron triangle   see **subsystem,** p. 89.

Admittedly, however, even a strong subsystem cannot ignore the possibility that rivals may emerge. For example, the powerful tobacco lobby has lost considerable influence in the continuing controversies over required health warnings on cigarette packages, payments for the health care of individuals afflicted with smoking-related illnesses, and sales of its products to teenagers; similarly, automobile-exhaust-emission controls, fleet mileage requirements, and air bags were imposed over the objections of auto manufacturers. Under routine circumstances, however, subsystems, including their administrative supporters, exercise decisive influence in the policy-making process.

Several changes in the environment of subsystem politics have become increasingly noticeable, especially in the past dozen years. One is the process by which House and Senate leaders refer a bill to more than one congressional committee; this is known as **multiple referral.**[13] While the Senate requires unanimous consent for such a step (a rare occurrence in that chamber), the practice has become more common in the House. The chamber leadership may refer bills *jointly* (that is, concurrently) to two or more committees; a referral may be *sequential*, going first to one committee, then to another; or a *split* referral may occur, with different parts of the same bill being considered by different committees. One effect of multiple referrals is to strengthen the influence of the chamber's leaders (the Speaker of the House and the Senate majority leader), at the expense of committee — and therefore subsystem — control over the decision-making process regarding a particular bill. Therefore, to the extent that multiple referrals become even more common — which is, of course, uncertain — subsystem influence might be reduced still further.

multiple referral   a legislative tactic that has strengthened the power of Congress over policy subsystems.

There are other developments that, like multiple referrals, point to a continued weakening of subsystems as pressures rise for more sharply focused, and therefore more *centrally directed*, congressional responses to a wide variety of policy challenges. One such challenge most evident in debates over budgetary issues is the increasing influence of votes in the full chamber rather than in

gridlock   derived from term referring to traffic that is so congested that cars cannot move; government is so divided that no consistent policy direction can be established.

partisanship   political party pressures on elected members of Congress, state legislature, or local boards and commissions.

subcommittees and committees. Another, which was especially noticeable in the weeks of **gridlock** between President Clinton and the Republican-controlled Congress, leading to shutdowns of government operations, resulted in the increased use of what one observer calls "special crisis-focused leadership summits."[14] These are also employed at the expense of committee influence in shaping both decision agendas and decisions themselves. Finally, the role of **partisanship** in congressional decision making has become somewhat more prominent in recent years. This indicates that members of Congress may be subject to stronger pressures to respond to *party* rather than to *committee* leaders, thus weakening members' committee and subsystem decision-making roles.

For several reasons, the influence of similar alliances is often less extensive in state and local policy-making than in national politics, even taking into account the changes just discussed. First, in many state legislatures, individual committees do not have the same kind of independent standing or jurisdictional control over policy areas that U.S. congressional committees have. Policy-making is more centralized in the hands of legislative leaders, making any interest group relationship with an individual committee less productive. Second, in many states and localities, the policy-making process is dominated by less diverse groups than is the case nationally and, consequently, the process lacks the intense competitiveness for access, influence, and power that characterizes Washington politics. Therefore, the necessity to develop close working relations with an individual committee or agency is not as great. Third, especially in local government, the policy process is not only less visible but much more informal than at the national level. For many established interest groups (particularly the stronger ones), there are fairly regular opportunities for consultation on policy preferences, so that the influence of these groups is often felt throughout local government, not in just one part of it. Thus, though some elements of subsystem politics can be found in state and local governments, the general patterns identifiable in the national policy process do not operate to the same extent on other governmental levels.

issue networks   in the context of American politics (especially at the national level), open and fluid groupings of various political actors (in and out of government) attempting to influence policy; "shared-knowledge" groups having to do with some aspect or problem of public policy; lacking in the degree of permanence, commonality of interests, and internal cohesion characteristic of subsystems.

"Issue Networks" and Subsystems: Similarities and Differences

Subsystem politics has been the subject of informed discussion since the late 1950s. More recently, however, several observers have noted still another pattern of interaction developing in the policy process: the phenomenon of so-called **issue networks,** which, like subsystems, involve a variety of political actors attempting jointly to influence the course of public policy. Unlike subsystems, however, issue networks are more open and fluid groupings of individuals both inside and outside of government. In political scientist Hugh Heclo's words, an issue network is "a *shared-knowledge* group having to do with some aspect [or problem] of public policy"[15] — but without the degree of permanence characteristic of subsystem alliances. Such a "floating" network may exist only when a policy question emerges that activates a wide range of interests; members of the network may not deal with one another regularly outside their network contacts; and, significantly, they may not agree on the nature of the policy problem or on possible solutions to it. In all these respects, issue networks differ from subsystems.

Examples of issue networks include the various groups and public officials involved in specific policies, such as those dealing with AIDS research: university medical research departments, state medical associations, hospitals and hospital organizations, U.S. Public Health Service personnel, and nutrition specialists, among others; and homosexuals in the military: Department of Defense program managers, gay-rights groups, and civil rights groups interested in preventing discrimination and ensuring benefits to dependents of military personnel. In these examples, many of the participants could not reach even general agreement on policy directions merely by activating the network. Rather, once a policy question was perceived as affecting a broad range of interests, groups and individuals advocating those interests jumped into the fray over policy development, thus creating the network as a means of addressing the policy issues at hand. This was especially true of the AIDS research policy under President Reagan and the policy on gays in the military under President Clinton. It is not surprising that neither policy was clearly defined under such circumstances.

The foundation of shared knowledge that unites network participants often does not lead to the creation of a "shared-action" coalition or a "shared-belief" (conventional interest) group. Like subsystems, such networks function with relative autonomy but, unlike subsystems, "rarely in any controlled, well-organized way,"[16] or even with agreement on policy content among the principals involved. Thus, issue networks contribute further and in somewhat new ways to the fragmentation present in national policy making. Expanded use of the Internet and World Wide Web has led to an increase in the number of issue networks and shared knowledge groups.

Bureaucratic Power and Political Accountability: More Questions Than Answers

Having discussed the political context of bureaucratic power, key sources of that power, and the informal alliances through which much of that power is exercised, let us now consider to what extent bureaucracy is, or can be made, accountable for what it does or fails to do. In Chapter 2, it was suggested that political accountability of the bureaucracy is enforced through multiple channels, both legislative and executive. As we have seen, political interests in the legislature and in the executive branch are frequently in conflict with one another, making it, at best, difficult to enforce accountability consistently or effectively. The situation is made more complex by the fact that most bureaucracies operate under authority delegated by *both* the chief executive and the legislative branch and have considerable discretion to make independent choices. The difficulty is further compounded by the hybrid systems of personnel management found in different parts of the executive hierarchy in the national government and in many states and localities. Frequently, top-echelon executives owe their positions to appointment through political channels, but the bulk of their subordinates are hired and usually retained through job competence–related merit procedures. In state and local government, the mix of *political* and *merit* employees in a bureaucracy varies widely, and the presence of public employee unions and collective bargaining raises other issues of bureaucratic accountability.

Another factor limiting accountability is the inability of top executives to command whole-hearted responses from administrative subordinates. A substantial portion of the work of top executives is inspecting, monitoring, and overseeing the activities of their staffs in an effort to bring about as much congruence as possible between presidential directives and the performance of executive agencies. In particular, the executive operates under severe handicaps in this effort. Because of time constraints, the necessity of concentrating on a limited number of general policy priorities, and the complexity of administrative operations, a considerable proportion of bureaucratic activity escapes close examination by the White House. Furthermore, as noted by journalist David Broder, subsystems represent "powerful centrifugal forces" in the nation's capital. Broder writes: "The interest groups that benefit from specific programs, the agency bureaucracies that run those programs and the congressional subcommittee members and staffs who create, finance, and oversee those programs are *tenaciously resistant to directives from the president.*"[17] Thus, the task of holding bureaucracy accountable for its actions assumes formidable proportions.

bureaucratic accountability principles of political accountability applied in an effort to control bureaucratic power.

Bureaucratic accountability implies several things. First, in a legal and constitutional sense, it implies that a political entity — in this case, the bureaucracy — is not beyond the control of other entities in a checks-and-balances system or, ultimately, beyond reach of the consent of the governed. Also, accountability implies that, to the extent that such an entity exercises delegated authority and discretion in decision making (as bureaucracy certainly does), it also has some responsibility to adhere to the broad will of the governed, however that will has been expressed. This also assumes that "the public will" and the achievement of accountability can be defined (see Chapter 2).

Although it may be possible in theory to define these concepts and circumstances, in practice it is difficult to do so with certainty or finality. One approach is to interpret election results as reflecting the will of the majority and to define bureaucratic accountability as responsiveness to the chief executive (president, governor, mayor), who is dominant in setting policy directions and standards. Opponents of a given chief executive or of executive power in general would resist such definition, however, looking instead to legislatures and sometimes to the judiciary to lay out broad guidelines for measuring bureaucratic accountability. Political conflict over criteria of accountability ensures less than complete adherence to whatever standards prevail at a particular time.

Therefore, it is not simply a matter of bureaucracy being or not being "accountable." Rather, bureaucracy and all other institutions of government can be accountable only to officials or to institutions *outside* themselves. Furthermore, the question, Accountable *for what?* must also be answered in meaningful ways (see Chapter 10 for a discussion of program evaluation methods and techniques). Also, the bureaucracy cannot be viewed as a whole; its many subparts have institutional bases, lives, and priorities of their own. All these factors act as constraints on the political accountability of bureaucratic power.

Is it impossible, then, to speak in practical terms of accountability? No, it is not. Allowing for limitations such as those just outlined, it is possible not only to prescribe in theory but to describe in fact some forms and aspects of accountability that characterize political relationships between bureaucracy and other parts of the American polity — although these, too, have their limitations.

First, both the president and Congress have many instruments of control at their disposal. The president's arsenal includes (1) powers of appointment and dismissal that, restricted to the very top positions, give him the ability to staff key leadership posts in the executive branch; (2) considerable initiative in lawmaking, which helps shape the legislative environment surrounding bureaucratic implementation of congressional enactments (this includes congressional delegation of authority to the president to formulate rules and regulations under which the bureaucracy functions); (3) the Executive Office of the President (EOP), through which the president can make known his preferences and intentions to the bureaucracy, directly and indirectly; (4) specific entities of the EOP, notably the White House Office and the Office of Management and Budget (OMB), which carry the full prestige of the presidency when they interact with the bureaucracy and, in the case of OMB, can exert financial leverage that can be persuasive; (5) access to the mass media, through which the president can generate favorable or unfavorable publicity; (6) power to initiate bureaucratic restructuring, an unwelcome course of action for most agencies though, in the past, it has been used sparingly (see the comments earlier in this chapter regarding structure, jurisdiction, and clientele politics); and (7) the **line-item veto**, a favorite way for conservatives to trim budgets. Shrewd presidents have used these instruments to win support for their initiatives, though the process often requires significant expenditure of political capital. In general, governors, local executives, and state and local legislatures have less extensive powers over their bureaucracies.

Congress also has many tools at its disposal with which to conduct legislative oversight of administration.[18] These include (1) appropriations power, the classic power of the purse, and the implied (sometimes real) threat that it can represent to an agency's fiscal well-being; (2) power to conduct legislative postaudits of agency spending and program effectiveness through the General Accounting Office (GAO), headed by the comptroller-general and operating under the

line-item veto a constitutional power available to more than forty of America's governors — and, on a limited basis to the president — with which they may disapprove a specific expenditure item within an appropriations bill instead of having to accept or reject the entire bill.

direction of Congress; (3) hearings before congressional committees in which bureaucrats may have to answer very specifically for their actions (most notably during budget hearings before appropriations committees and subcommittees); and (4) occasional devices such as senatorial confirmation of presidential appointees and special committee investigations. These are not perfect instruments, but they do afford Congress many opportunities to look into details of bureaucratic activities and to maintain a degree of control over the administrative apparatus.

Partly because of bureau-clientele ties, a number of studies have questioned whether legislative oversight — as currently conducted — is even minimally effective as a means of holding bureaucracies accountable to the political system at large. The core concern of those raising this possibility is that *changes within Congress itself* have produced a markedly reduced capacity for congressional supervision of administrative activities. These changes include an emphasis on wider participation by members of Congress in policy-making processes, a resultant dispersion of power within Congress from its standing committees to much more numerous, and more autonomous, subcommittees, and a tendency to devote more of their time to constituent services or **casework** in pursuit of their own reelection. Casework provides a form of "feedback" between citizen and legislator, and may assist in the early identification of problems with government programs. There has also emerged a generalized pattern of behavior in which legislators regularly call on administrative agencies (and their clientele groups) to facilitate the rendering of services to the public. Administrative agencies benefit during the appropriations process from effectively responding to members' requests for service to their constituents.

Formal responsibility for legislative oversight has also passed from full committees to subcommittees but, although more hearings have been held and more pages filled with testimony, the net effect has been one of *less effective oversight*. This is attributable to members of Congress simultaneously becoming (1) more dependent on agencies and interest groups as they call on these groups for increased constituent service and (2) less inclined to "challenge the existing relationships between agencies and interest groups" and, thus, "less likely to investigate agencies' implementation of policy unless that implementation flies in the face of these major interest groups."[19]

If congressional supervision of the bureaucracy via subcommittees is indeed less reliable now than in the past, bureaucratic autonomy may be greater than is ideal. We might describe this pattern and others like it as cases in which the *microinstitutions* (committees and subcommittees) within Congress are unable or unwilling to hold agencies accountable for their actions. But it appears that, as a *macroinstitution*, Congress is also rather limited in its oversight capabilities. This limitation exists principally because legislators often lack incentive to use available oversight instruments (and frequently have incentive *not* to use them) and because some instruments of congressional control have proved to be fairly "weak reeds." This is especially true with regard to appropriations: individual

casework   refers to services performed by legislators and their staff on behalf of constituents.

members jealously guard their own capacities for largesse but fail to oversee expenditures as a whole.

Congress lost one oversight instrument that it had employed, on occasion, for over fifty years — the legislative veto — when the Supreme Court declared it unconstitutional by a 7–2 ruling in *Immigration and Naturalization Service v. Chadha*, 103 S. Ct. 2764 (1983). Included in more than two hundred statutes enacted between 1932 and 1983, this veto required the executive branch to inform Congress of the actions that the executive branch planned to take in implementing a new law and to receive approval from Congress of the actions before actually carrying them out. Within a fixed time period, usually sixty to ninety days, one or both chambers of Congress had the option to vote down, by simple majority, a proposed administrative action. But the veto was increasingly criticized, mainly on the grounds that it unconstitutionally intruded on the president's authority to direct executive-branch agencies. Critics of the veto assumed that only the president should have authority to direct activities of the executive branch. This assumption, however, contradicts both established legal tradition within the framework of separation of powers and a variety of congressional practices, such as GAO audits and studies and committee hearings and investigations, designed to promote Congress's influence over administration of the laws. The 1983 ruling articulated a legal doctrine of near-total separation of powers, which had not existed before *Chadha* and has not operated since *Chadha*. In the first year after the Court's ruling, Congress enacted thirty provisions *allowing* legislative vetoes of agency decisions (most in the form of committee review of proposed agency actions).[20] This is perhaps testimony to the strength of our commitment to the concept of checks and balances and to separation of powers, and also to our long-standing belief that Congress is obligated to use a variety of instruments to ensure that laws are faithfully executed by administrative agencies.

In sum, although there may be telling weaknesses in legislative oversight of government bureaucracies, they are not beyond remedy, and there may be alternative means of supervising administrative agencies. This discussion highlights one aspect of the situation that merits explicit emphasis: If we are not content with administrative agencies' behavior, we might do well to pressure Congress to make the desired changes. Indeed, one authoritative observer argues that Congress has already strengthened its own oversight capacity, leading to congressional oversight that is more consistent and effective than many seem to believe.[21] In any event, as political scientist Morris Fiorina notes, "United States congressmen gave us the Washington establishment. Ultimately, only they can take it away."[22]

Some other mechanisms of accountability also exist. Bureaucracies are legally accountable to the courts for their observance of individual rights and liberties, whether in their investigative capacities (especially where regulatory agencies are concerned) or in the course of routine legislative activities. In this respect, they hardly differ from the president and Congress, in that the courts have the ultimate say in defining acceptable legal boundaries of governmental behavior. It is symptomatic of the growth of the bureaucracy and of its impact on our national life that the most rapidly expanding area of court litigation has been in administrative law, in which cases arise out of administrative rules and regulations and their application to individuals, groups, and public and private enterprises (see Chapter 11).

The courts have taken on a more activist role in recent years, not only maintaining traditional constitutional guarantees but also, in some instances, taking over direct supervision of state prisons, mental hospitals, highway patrols, and other institutions in order to remedy violations of the constitutional rights of prisoners, mental patients, and other citizens that had occurred as part of routine administrative processes.[23] In the words of one observer: **"Judicial review** has passed from matters of procedure to matters of both procedure and substance. . . . Courts have not merely sat in judgment on administrative action but on inaction as well; they have required agencies to do things the agencies themselves had declined to do."[24] Other examples of judicial activism include appointing expert witnesses, dismissing jurors for poor conduct, suggesting areas of inquiry during civil cases, ordering payment of fees for research, and transferring prisoners held in overcrowded city jails to state prisons. Whether such activism on the part of the courts is desirable from all standpoints has been questioned.

Bureaucratic agencies are also held to account, as part of our constitutional scheme, by the mass media. The news media's interest in bureaucratic activity is founded on a basic premise of free government and on a powerful ethic of American journalism: that a free press, acting in an adversarial relationship to public officials, serves as a watchdog over government actions. In particular, the investigatory potential of the news media makes bureaucracies wary. Part of an agency's strength is good public relations, and adverse publicity resulting from a media investigation — even if unwarranted and even if successfully counteracted — can damage an agency's political standing. Thus, the mere possibility of such an inquiry is enough to prompt most agencies to exercise considerable caution. Increasing numbers of governments, notably state and local institutions, have employed "media consultants" or public relations specialists to handle the volume of such inquiries.

As in the case of bureaucracy–legislature interactions, relationships between administrators and the media are often two-sided. This creates the possibility that the press, far from maintaining a critical and objective perspective, may become involved in continuing relationships, the principal product of which is an ability to publicize agency programs. Under such circumstances, it is still possible for a reporter, editor, or publisher to investigate or critique agency performance. But if an agency official continually provides good copy for a reporter and also provides inside tips or leads on stories that the reporter can take credit for "breaking," it is less likely that an agency will be subjected to the feared spotlight of publicity. This is politics on an intensely interpersonal level, but it can matter a great deal in determining how much and what kind of information will come to public attention about a given agency.[25]

judicial review   the constitutional power of the courts to review the actions of executive agencies, legislatures, or decisions of lower courts to determine whether judges, legislators, or administrators acted appropriately.

Finally, there is some measure of bureaucratic accountability directly to the public. Although the general populace rarely has direct access to, or control over, a given bureaucratic entity, a widespread public outcry over bureaucrats' actions can have an effect. Ordinarily, this requires public pressure on other divisions of government to get them to restrict the actions of an agency. Such pressure must be sustained over a sufficient period of time and with sufficient intensity to overcome resistance from the agency and its supporters, but it can be done.

ADMINISTRATIVE DISCRETION AND POLITICAL ACCOUNTABILITY: AN ALTERNATIVE PERSPECTIVE

In discussions of how concerned citizens might hold bureaucrats and their agencies accountable, there is often an implicit assumption that more accountability and control are needed in order to keep these officials in line and that their natural tendency is to go astray unless they are closely watched. There is no question, of course, that, in our system of checks and balances, every government entity must *ultimately* be held to account. In recent decades, however, that principle (as applied to administrative agencies) seems to have acquired an additional dimension that is not necessarily accurate. Many people seem to assume — wrongly — that administrative discretion can *only* be abused, at the expense of the public interest, and can serve no useful or constructive purpose. Many also bemoan the fact that neither Congress nor the president is able or willing to control administrative actions fully or effectively. This point of view seems to suggest that elected officials can act only beneficially whereas administrators can be expected to act only in a narrowly focused, inefficient, destructive, and otherwise irresponsible fashion. (Recall Charles Goodsell's remarks about perceived bureaucratic shortcomings compared to the realities, quoted in Chapter 1.) There is, indeed, reason to wonder how much truth there is in this view of discretion.

For one thing, administrative discretion was an important, though often overlooked, element in the thinking and writing of administrative reformers of a century ago. Woodrow Wilson, one of the foremost reformers, argued, in his classic essay "The Study of Administration" (1887), that administrators should be granted "large powers and unhampered discretion" — both "administrative energy and administrative discretion"[26] — as essential elements of their functioning in accordance with the notion of "political" neutrality. His expectation was that, given the opportunity, administrators would exercise competent professional judgment as they carried out their assigned duties. This would serve the public interest (because sound public policy would result) and, in turn, the interests of elected officials of either political party (who could then take the credit for effective governance). In sum, he saw discretion as necessary for administrative *effectiveness* as well as ensuring political neutrality.

If exercised positively, administrative discretion has one very positive aspect: Program managers are often better able than legislators or judges to make decisions on the basis of the broader public interest — and, according to Wilson's nineteenth-century view, most administrators are capable of doing so most of the time. Interference with administrative discretion by congressional restraints and controls actually brings about the kind of narrow responsiveness to private interests that such controls seem designed to prevent. There are two reasons for this. First, interest groups often usurp public power through the manipulation of iron triangle relationships (see Figure 3–1), exercising considerable influence through both committees and issue networks. Second, as noted previously, legislators are strongly inclined to look after their own policy priorities and constituency interests; in the process, they pressure administrators to conform to their wishes. Thus, it is possible that if oversight of administration is left to legislators acting primarily in their committee roles, the actions taken by administrators may be more narrowly conceived and implemented than would be the case if those same administrators were given more freedom.

This is not, by any means, a call for the complete autonomy of administrators. There is ample reason to be as concerned about "discretionary" abuses of power or fraud or corruption among public administrators as among any other government officials. However, we might do well to place greater implicit faith in administrators than we now do if we want them to be able to act responsibly. Under these circumstances, it would still be possible to hold them ultimately accountable, consistent with our scheme of government and with public expectations for accountability, at least as effectively as we do at the present time.[27]

Summary

Bureaucratic power is exercised in the context of widely dispersed political power. Neither the legislature nor the chief executive has a power base that is sufficiently unified to permit decisive control over the bureaucracy. Administrative agencies are keenly interested in building power bases of their own, and they seek to acquire programs that bring with them constituency support for their activities. Agencies are frequently centers of conflict and must seek to maintain themselves through adaptation to the pressures that are placed on them. How well they succeed is an important determinant of their long-term survival.

The major foundations of bureaucratic power are (1) expertise in the programs they administer and (2) adequate political support. The impact of bureaucratic expertise stems from full-time attention to a specialized subject-matter area, a monopoly or near-monopoly on relevant information, a pattern of reliance on experts for technical advice, and experts' growing control of administrative discretion. The experts' prestige has also helped consolidate the influence they wield in the government. Sources of political support include key legislative committees and subcommittees, chief executives and their staffs, other executive agencies (especially those directly under the chief executive), clientele groups that follow agency affairs because of their own interest in the same program areas, and the general public, which can occasionally be mobilized on behalf of particular agency objectives.

Organizational structure is politically significant in a number of respects: (1) It demonstrates commitment, symbolic or substantive, to particular policy objectives; (2) it can signal adoption of specific policy directions; (3) it serves to order political priorities by emphasizing some programs over others; and (4) it can provide different degrees of access to decision makers. The politics of organization is also significant in settings other than executive-branch arrangements.

Subsystem politics in America is built around coalitions that bring together interest group representatives and government officials who share common interests and policy preferences. A subsystem ordinarily includes congressional committee or subcommittee members, representatives of interest groups, and bureaucrats from the responsible administrative agency. Because both Congress and the bureaucracy generally divide work among subunits whose expertise they respect, quiet, informal alliances (subsystems) of specialists often dominate their respective policy arenas. Bureaucrats contribute expertise to their subsystems and receive in return an opportunity to share control of a policy area. Similar patterns of collaboration exist in state and local politics but usually not in precisely this form or to the same extent. Issue networks and shared-knowledge groups are also different from subsystems but add to the fragmentation in national policy making.

Promoting accountability of bureaucratic power is not an easy task. Because bureaucracies operate under delegated executive and legislative authority, tight controls from either are difficult to impose, and tight controls from both would be likely to conflict. Accountability suggests that bureaucracy is, or should be, answerable for its actions to other institutions and to the public. This is difficult to put into practice because of the noncentralized nature of both government and bureaucracy. The president and Congress (and their state and local counterparts) each have methods for influencing bureaucratic behavior that, although somewhat effective, require continuing effort and vigilance.

In recent years, some have questioned whether Congress is still able to exercise meaningful oversight in terms of maintaining accountability to the political system at large. The mass media also have the ability to uncover and publicize information adverse to agency political interests. In addition, bureaucratic agencies are accountable to the courts in that the agencies' actions are limited (and sometimes mandated) by legal guidelines laid down in judicial decisions. Finally, the general public can be mobilized either in support of, or in opposition to, actions taken in the administrative process.

All these instruments of accountability have some impact on bureaucratic behavior, but none is perfect. It is also possible that more, not less, administrative discretion would serve the political system well, providing for pursuit of both the broader public interest and administrative accountability.

KEY TERMS AND CONCEPTS

jurisdiction	multiple referral
bureaucratic imperialism	gridlock
interest groups	partisanship
specialized language	issue networks
organizational structure	bureaucratic accountability
constituency	line-item veto
subsystem	casework
iron triangle	judicial review

SUGGESTED READING

Aberbach, Joel D. *Keeping a Watchful Eye: The Politics of Congressional Oversight.* Washington, D.C.: The Brookings Institution, 1990.

Berry, Jeffrey M. *The Interest Group Society.* 3rd ed. New York: Longman, 1997.

Browne, William P. *Groups, Interests, and Public Policy.* Washington, D.C.: Georgetown University Press, 1998.

Chandler, Ralph Clark, ed. *A Centennial History of the Administrative State.* New York: The Free Press, 1987.

Fiorina, Morris P. *Congress: Keystone of the Washington Establishment.* 2nd Ed. New Haven: Yale University Press, 1989.

Fisher, Louis. "The Administrative World of *Chadha* and *Bowsher.*" *Public Administration Review,* 47 (May/June 1987), 213–19.

———. *The Politics of Shared Power.* 2nd ed. Washington, D.C.: CQ Press, 1987, Chapter 4.

Fritschler, A. Lee, and James M. Hoefler. *Smoking and Politics: Policy Making and the Federal Bureaucracy.* 5th ed. Upper Saddle River, N.J.: Prentice-Hall, 1995.

Garvey, Gerald. *Facing the Bureaucracy: Living and Dying in a Public Agency.* San Francisco: Jossey-Bass, 1993.

Kaufman, Herbert, with the collaboration of Michael Couzens. *Administrative Feedback: Monitoring Subordinates' Behavior.* Washington, D.C.: The Brookings Institution, 1973.

Kearns, Kevin P. *Managing for Accountability: Preserving the Public Trust in Public and Non-Profit Organizations.* San Francisco: Jossey-Bass, 1996.

Neu, C. Richard, Robert H. Anderson, and Tora K. Bikson. *Sending Your Government a Message: E-mail Communication Between Citizens and Government.* Santa Monica, Calif.: Rand Corporation, 1999.

Pfeffer, Jeffrey. *Managing with Power: Politics and Influence in Organizations.* Boston: Harvard Business School Press, 1992.

Rosen, Bernard. *Holding Government Bureaucracies Accountable.* 3rd ed. Westport, Conn.: Greenwood, 1998.

Seidman, Harold, and Robert Gilmour. *Politics, Position, and Power: From the Positive to the Regulatory State.* 4th ed. New York: Oxford University Press, 1986.

Truman, David B. *The Governmental Process.* 1951. Reprint, New York: Alfred A. Knopf, 1981.

Wood, Dan B., and Richard W. Waterman. *Bureaucratic Dynamics.* Boulder, Colo.: Westview Press, 1994.

ON-LINE RESOURCES:
Bureaucratic Politics and Bureaucratic Power

American Association of Retired Persons (AARP)

http://www.aarp.org/

Nonprofit, nonpartisan association dedicated to shaping and enriching the experience of aging for members and for all Americans. Founded in 1958, AARP is the nation's largest organization of midlife and older persons, with more than 30 million members.

American Hospital Association (AHA)

http://www.aha.org/

Interest group representing hospitals and health care organizations.

American Medical Association (AMA)

http://www.ama-assn.org/

Interest group representing doctors.

American Political Science Association (APSA)

http://www.apsanet.org/

APSA is the world's largest organization devoted to the study of politics, with 13,000 members in seventy countries.

Citizens for an Alternative Tax System

http://www.american.net/com/7star/cats/afr.html.

Citizens for an Alternative Tax System (CATS) is a national grassroots nonprofit organization committed to bringing about the end of the income tax and the IRS by replacing both with a national retail sales tax (NRST).

Citizens for a Sound Economy

http://www.cse.org/cse

> Interest group dedicated to free markets and limited government.

Concord Coalition

http://www.concordcoalition.org

> Formed by former U.S. Senators, this group seeks to eliminate federal budget deficits while preserving social programs.

League of Women Voters of the United States

http://www.lwv.org/

> The League of Women Voters, a nonpartisan political organization, encourages the informed and active participation of citizens in government, works to increase understanding of major public policy issues, and influences public policy through education and advocacy.

Legislative Information on the Internet

http://thomas.loc.gov/

> Summarizes the bills being discussed on the floor every week. Each listing explains the bill's subject matter, the committee assigned to it, and its current status. The site has bills organized under topics ranging from abortion to welfare, and thoroughly describes how bills are considered by the House and Senate.

National Conference of State Legislatures

http://lcweb.loc.gov/global/state/stategov.html

> NCSL is a bipartisan organization dedicated to serving the lawmakers and staffs of the nation's states, commonwealths, and territories. It is a source for research, publications, consulting services, meetings, and seminars as well as the national conduit for lawmakers to comminicate with one another and share ideas.

National Education Association (NEA)

http://www.nationaleducationassociation.com/

> Interest group representing teachers and local education associations.

Supreme Court of the United States

http://www.supremecourtus.gov/

The official Web site of the Supreme Court has information on its calendar/schedules, how to obtain opinions, justice biographies, and links to related sites.

U.S. Department of Health and Human Services

http://www.dhhs.gov/

The federal government's principal agency for protecting the health of Americans and providing human services. Operates/oversees more than three hundred programs including the National Institutes for Health, the Centers for Disease Control and Prevention, Medicare, Head Start, the Administration on Aging, and many others.

U.S. Department of Veterans Affairs

http://www.va.gov

Information on this executive branch agency's programs and services including benefits for veterans, news, congressional testimony, and state/local affiliates.

For further information on bureaucratic politics and power see:
Bedford/St. Martin's Home Page

http://www.bedfordstmartins.com

Chapter 4

Federalism and Intergovernmental Relations

I think it is quite an interesting thing that we have this impressive array of people to come to a conference on federalism, a topic that probably ten or twenty years ago would have been viewed as a substitute for a sleeping pill.

An excerpt from President Clinton's speech at the Forum of Federation Conference in Mont-Tremblant, Canada, October 8, 1999

Federalism is a widely recognized feature of American government. The federal system comprises a national government and various state governments existing *independently* of each other in the same territory while commanding the loyalties of the same individuals as citizens of both state *and* nation. Under the Constitution, the powers of all governments are drawn from the same fundamental source — the sovereign people — and are exercised concurrently. States, in turn, are composed of numerous subjurisdictions, such as counties, cities, municipalities, townships, and special districts, which are *dependent* entities chartered by the state. The original rationale for establishing a federal system in the United States was to prevent the concentration of power in a strong national government; the states were viewed as counterweights and protectors of individual liberties against a central power.

The nature and operation of federalism have been the subject of much controversy since the founding of the Republic. Referring to our basic governmental structure, Vice President Albert Gore observed that "America was born angry at government. We were so sick of the [distant and insensitive] English crown . . . we quit colonialism before we had something else lined up."[1] Indeed, this nation was later torn by a civil war that resulted from conflict over the twin issues of slavery and the extent of the states' authority to oppose the national government. Since the New Deal, and with rising emphasis in the last few years, many Americans (including public officials of both major political parties) have expressed concern about the wide-ranging authority of the national government. These concerns focus, among other things, on how the expansion of that authority has affected state and local government powers. In turn, the states' relations with — and influence over — their respective local governments have increased in importance. There have also been growing concerns about citizens' power to retain a significant measure of control over governmental structures at all levels in the federal system.

Public administration is at the heart of many of the questions and controversies that have characterized contemporary federalism. The two have had a reciprocal effect on one another. The administration of national government programs requires recognition of, and accommodation to, the existence, prerogatives, and preferences of states and localities that have their own decision-making apparatus and political majorities. At the same time, the growth of bureaucracy at all levels of government has helped to reshape the federal system.

In this chapter, our concerns will include (1) the definition of **federalism** and a brief historical review of its evolution; (2) the rise of **intergovernmental relations (IGR),** the multitude of formal and informal contacts among governmental entities throughout the federal system, and the ways in which these have modified federalism as a formal concept; (3) the expansion, after 1960, of financial assistance from the national government to states and localities, with accompanying shifts in leverage exerted by the former over the latter, and, since 1980, changes in national government aid, together with *reduced* leverage in the hands of national officials for pursuing national goals through state and local action; (4) administrative and political consequences of increased intergovernmental aid, especially administrative complexity and bureaucratic controls accompanying national government grants, and the resulting political conflicts, including a rising public backlash against both government **unfunded mandates** and the professional public administrators responsible for managing intergovernmental programs; (5) growing concern about managing IGR and the grants system; and (6) questions about the future course of IGR, including the impacts of diminished national government fiscal support for many of its own activities as well as those at state and local levels.

Before we begin, a comment is in order about one key term in this discussion, namely, *federal.* Technically, *federal* describes the formal relationships among different levels of government and various qualities or characteristics of those relationships. In a more colloquial sense, however, many people refer to the national government as "the federal government." Such usage, which has roots in debates over ratification of the Constitution in the 1780s, can lead to confused thinking about contemporary federalism and IGR. In this chapter and elsewhere, when reference is made to the *national government,* that is generally the phrase employed; *federal* is used in its more technical sense, for the sake of clarity.

federalism a constitutional division of governmental power between a central or national government and regional governmental units (such as states), with each having some independent authority over its citizens.

intergovernmental relations (IGR) all the activities and interactions occurring between or among governmental units of all types and levels within the American federal system.

unfunded mandates federal (or state) laws or regulations that impose requirements on other governments, often involving expenditures by affected governments, without providing funds for implementation.

The Nature of Federalism: The Formal Setting

The most elementary definition of *federalism* suggests that it is a *constitutional* division of governmental power between a central or national government and a set of regional units (such as the American states, Canadian provinces, and Swiss cantons); that, under a federal arrangement, both the national and regional governments have some independent as well as some shared powers over their citizens; that neither government owes its legal existence to the other (as local governments in the United States do to the states); and that, as a matter of law, neither may dictate to the other(s) in matters of structural organization, fiscal policies, or definition of essential functions. This definition clearly implies that the regional governments have substantial independence from the national government but that both may exercise powers of government directly over their citizens. It leaves unanswered, however, some pertinent questions about how authority is to be exercised *simultaneously* by different units of government sharing jurisdiction over the same territory and citizenry.

Federalism is also an explicitly *political* arrangement. This relates in important ways to how power in a governmental system is distributed, structured, and exercised. A federal arrangement is designed to restrain and counteract centralized power through multiple centers where decisions are made in widely scattered geographic regions. Such a system, with separate, legitimate, and authoritative government units operating individually within the same overall territory, makes it less likely that a central government could achieve an excessive concentration of power, which might endanger individual freedoms. Finally, federalism has an increasingly important *fiscal/administrative* dimension. This pertains both to the operations of government programs that have impact on at least one other level or unit of government and to the growing complexity and interdependency of programs created, funded, and managed by different governments. Later in this chapter, we will treat the phenomenon of intergovernmental fiscal relations in considerably more detail.

In the early 1800s, the U.S. Supreme Court defined some essential boundaries in national–state relations, with long-term implications. The fundamental issue was the scope of national authority, particularly when it overlapped and conflicted with state powers. Specific questions included whether states could tax national government agencies (they cannot, under *McCulloch v. Maryland*, 4 Wheaton 316 [1819]); whether the national power to regulate interstate commerce superseded state regulatory actions, setting up conflicting rules (it does, with some exceptions); and whether the states could interfere in any way with national enforcement of national laws (they cannot). Some other issues were resolved in Congress and by presidential action. The question of slavery, however, proved insoluble through the political system. This failure, coupled with irreconcilable differences (related to slavery) over national versus state sovereignty, resulted in the secession of the South and the creation of a confederation of eleven states. The Civil War followed, culminating in a Union victory that was both military and political: slavery was ended, the Union was preserved, and a federal — not confederate (state-centered) — system was reaffirmed.

The next half-century was a time of transition in American federalism. Many basic decisions affecting the legal structuring of federalism were resolved and, as government generally became more active in dealing with problems of society, some forms of joint or overlapping governmental activities became more common. A number of new national programs combined participation by (especially) state governments with use of the first cash grants-in-aid from the national government to the states; early examples included agricultural extension programs in 1914, federal aid for state highways in 1916, and the Vocational Education Act of 1917. Fundamental structural-legal questions were receding in importance, but modern intergovernmental relations was still being defined within the broader context of federalism.

Intergovernmental Relations: The Action Side of Federalism

Intergovernmental relations is a relatively new term, having come into common usage only in the past sixty years. It designates "an important body of activities or interactions occurring between governmental units of all types and levels within the [United States] federal system."[2] In political scientist Deil Wright's words, intergovernmental relations embrace "all the permutations and combinations of relations among the units of government in our system."[3] These include national–state and interstate relations (the areas traditionally emphasized in the study of federalism), as well as national–local, state–local, interlocal, and national–state–local relations. In addition, other key features of IGR are worth noting.

One is the fact that the consequences of intergovernmental relations are often unpredictable and decision making is hidden from public view. There is no direct electorate and decisions shift from year-to-year with no particular direction. There is no policy-making body, no executive, no legislative, and no judiciary to oversee the results of billions of dollars transferred to states and local governments from the federal government. Predictably, this lack of consistency leads to considerable inequities in the distribution of federal money to states and cities.

A second feature of IGR is that, although we speak of intergovernmental relations in the abstract, the individual actions and attitudes of elected and appointed officials determine what kind of relations exist between units of government. Understanding intergovernmental relations has to be formulated largely in the context of human relations and human behavior. Who the officials are, the roles they play in the governmental process, their policy views, and the interests they seek to promote all have a bearing on the conduct of IGR.

Third, IGR does not refer only to occasional interactions, single contacts, or formal agreements. Rather, it is a continuous series of informal contacts and exchanges of information and views among government officials aimed at solving shared multigovernmental problems. Virtually all policy areas have an intergovernmental dimension, and some are almost totally the product of shared policy formulation, implementation, or financing. Examples of such policy areas include air and water pollution, criminal justice, public housing, agriculture, education, and transportation. That policy is fashioned through intergovernmental processes, however, does not always mean that government officials agree with one another on all or even most major aspects of a program. IGR can be cooperative, competitive, conflicting, or a combination of all three and still be IGR.

Another key feature of IGR is the involvement of public and private, government and nongovernment officials, at all levels. Clearly involved are chief executives and legislators in Washington, state capitals, county seats, and city halls, since they formally promote and enact the programs that constitute IGR. As appointed administrators at all levels of government have assumed greater responsibility and as IGR has become more pervasive, intergovernmental *administrative* relations have taken on ever greater significance. (An issue of some importance in IGR, discussed later in this chapter, concerns the degree to which influence has become concentrated in the administrative arm of government at all levels without effective means of control by elected officials.) Although we speak of *intergovernmental* relations, many public purposes are accomplished through nongovernmental institutions and organizations. Thus, IGR, properly understood, also includes the public functions of organizations not formally part of any government (voluntary action groups, civic organizations, The United Way, and so on).

Action in the federal system is often taken on selected parts of a general problem rather than on the total problem area; that is, decisions are *fragmented* rather than *comprehensive*. Governments are prone to act in response to relatively specific pressures for narrow objectives and find it difficult and politically "unprofitable" to do otherwise. Thus, although government policies exist in areas such as water quality and air pollution, no *one* policy governs the nation's approach to environmental quality. Similarly, there are policies concerning urban mass transit and public housing, but there is no *one* overall urban policy. A major reason for this is the ability of literally hundreds of governmental agencies at all levels to act independently of one another. When a policy emerges, it is usually in incomplete form and, in the majority of cases, lacks a centrally coordinated direction.[4] Contributing to this, of course, is the fact (discussed in Chapter 2) that the national government itself is far from a monolithic entity. According to Russell L. Hanson,

> The structure of intergovernmental relations is . . . a federal one in which the powers and responsibilities of government in general are shared among specific governments. However, *the sharing of power and responsibility is not equal, nor is it unalterable.* As a result, the structure of authority [in IGR] tends to be rather

loose, and it invites frequent clashes between governments over the right to make certain kinds of decisions. *Conflict often arises in the course of day-to-day interactions between governments* as they seek to define and redefine their relationships with one another in order to satisfy the demands of their respective citizenries.[5]

As a result, a wide spectrum of political opinions and issue preferences are reflected in the multitude of national government activities. It is thus inaccurate to speak of what *the* national government desires, intends to do, or is actually doing. The same may be said, though perhaps to a lesser extent, of many state and local governments as well. Thus, when different governments *do* try to integrate their efforts through cooperative activity, their joint undertakings may well be based on a foundation of programs that are not consistent in intent, design, or execution. Intergovernmental relations are characterized both by this lack of central direction and by some efforts in recent years to overcome it.

Thus, IGR involves virtually all governments and public officials, is highly informal and very dependent on human interactions, and involves the nonprofit and private sectors. The role of the courts (especially the U.S. Supreme Court) in shaping federalism has become more prominent as a number of key decisions have been handed down in the past two decades.

The Courts and Intergovernmental Relations

Does the rise to prominence of intergovernmental relations mean that the legal side of federalism is no longer of any consequence? No, quite the contrary. Both national and state judiciaries have been called on increasingly to resolve federalism-related disputes. Indeed, the U.S. Supreme Court has handed down a number of significant rulings in areas such as state and local personnel management practices, local regulation of handguns, and the impacts of congressional action on state and local government policies. These rulings have directly addressed the powers that may be exercised by different governments in the federal system and the constitutional protections that the Supreme Court has said do or do not exist for those powers.

For example, in 1983, the Court ruled in *Equal Employment Opportunity Commission (EEOC) v. Wyoming* (460 U.S. 226) that, under provisions of the national Age Discrimination in Employment Act, the state of Wyoming could not require its game wardens to retire at age 55. The Court thus sustained Congress's use of the commerce clause in the U.S. Constitution as a basis for limiting the powers of the states in personnel matters. Also in 1983, the Court left standing an appellate court decision in *Quilici v. Village of Morton Grove* (104 S. Ct. 194), upholding the right of a municipal government (in this case, Morton Grove, Illinois) to ban the possession of handguns within city limits.

More significantly, in 1985, the Court ruled, in a 5–4 decision, that, when setting terms and conditions of employment for their employees, state and local governments are subject to the minimum-wage and overtime requirements of the *national* government's Fair Labor Standards Act. The Court's opinion in *Garcia v. San Antonio Metropolitan Transit Authority* (469 U.S. 528) held that nothing in the wage and overtime requirements is "destructive of state sovereignty or violative of any constitutional provision," a forthright assertion of national government authority in an area that some regard as central to state and local government management.[6] Equally important, the Court ruled, in the same case, that state sovereignty (seemingly protected by the Tenth Amendment to the Constitution) did not prevent Congress from exercising far-reaching powers under the commerce clause[7] — a legal view suggested by the decision in the Wyoming case and reaffirmed in *South Carolina v. Baker,* 485 U.S. 505 (1988), dealing with Congress's authority to tax interest earned on state and local government bonds.

The federal government has attempted to influence the policies of states and local governments in several ways. For many controversial areas such as civil rights, federal judges have acted to enforce federal mandates. For example, the Supreme Court ruled, in *Schneidewind v. ANR Pipeline Co.,* 485 U.S. 293 (1988), that state authority to regulate how natural gas companies issue securities to finance their operations was preempted by federal law (also under the commerce clause).[8] **Preemptions** are legal actions by federal courts or agencies to preclude enforcement of a state or local law or regulation. These direct assumptions of power have increased significantly during the past two decades.

preemptions the assumption of state or local program authority by the federal government.

In 1984, the U.S. Supreme Court handed down another significant federalism-related decision. The Court, by a 5–4 margin, sharply limited the power of other national government courts by ruling that the lower courts have no authority to order state officials to obey state laws. The decision in *Pennhurst State School and Hospital v. Halderman,* 104 S. Ct. 900 (1984), greatly expanded the scope of the Eleventh Amendment, the relatively obscure provision giving state governments immunity from being sued in U.S. courts without the states' consent. Prior to this decision, the Court had repeatedly maintained that the amendment did not apply to suits charging individual state officials with violating the law. Unlike some of the cases mentioned earlier and contrary to many American legal trends of the previous generation, this decision strengthened the ability of state officials to operate independently within the federal framework. (This ruling's implications for the administration of state-based criminal justice agencies, welfare to "workfare" initiatives, and civil rights statutes alone are considerable.)

It is not only the Supreme Court or national government courts that have had an impact on IGR. For example, a U.S. district court ruled that the state of Indiana was responsible for paying the transportation (busing) costs of the Indianapolis school system, which had been sued successfully by local minority groups for racial discrimination. The court ruled that the discrimination in question was a result of the state's role in creating UNIGOV, the metropolitan government of greater Indianapolis. Consequently, the state was liable for the costs of busing to overcome the effects of the resulting segregation.[9] Also, the California Court of Appeal ruled that a San Francisco handgun ordinance similar to the one passed in *Morton Grove* conflicted with state laws allowing firearms to be kept in businesses and private homes without a license. These and subsequent cases raised further questions about the relationship between the federal government and state and local governments.

The courts, then, have been highly influential in shaping the organization and operation of the federal system. The continuing expansion of IGR has served only to increase the reach of judicial decision making since more governments and their actions are potentially affected by any given ruling. This expansion is testimony to the increased complexity within American federalism, and it is that subject to which we now turn our attention.

Contemporary Intergovernmental Relations: The Rise of Complexity

It was under Franklin Roosevelt, a Democrat, in the 1930s and 1940s that national government activity underwent a quantum leap in terms of scope and diversity, and intergovernmental relations became more closely interwoven with general (and more centralized) governmental undertakings. With little fanfare, but steadily, intergovernmental aid and joint efforts became more important components of public policy making. Thus, for example, national government grants for rural highway construction and maintenance (begun in 1916) became more numerous; grants for urban renewal became more widespread; and direct aid to urban governments for airport construction and other transportation purposes also appeared on the scene.[10] After the Depression, federally funded state and local social welfare, along with farm support and public assistance bureaucracies, gradually replaced voluntary sources for aiding those in need. In the 1950s, under Republican Dwight Eisenhower, the pace of national government expansion slackened but did not stop completely. Significantly, it was just after Eisenhower took office in 1953 that the Department of Health, Education and Welfare (HEW) was created, paving the way for later expansion of grants and other provisions relating to social services. Throughout the period 1930–1960, increased national government activity and the rising importance of IGR paralleled one another and often coincided. With the advent of the 1960s, however, IGR experienced its own quantum leap into new forms and new impacts.

In the last four decades, the structure of intergovernmental relations has been transformed by the rapid proliferation of financial transactions among different levels of government; by the development of new and often permanent linkages among program administrators at all levels; by the establishment of new forms of government at what is called the "substate regional level" — such as local-level "special districts" (providing many services, including water, education, and transportation), economic development districts, and health planning agencies; and by issuance of literally thousands of rules, guidelines, and regulations — collectively known as mandates and often accompanying fiscal aid packages — to hundreds of governmental units (see Chapters 10 and 11). This expansion of national government power has sparked political controversy of various kinds, resulting from the complexity associated with increasing numbers of federal grants and their accompanying regulations. Despite the best efforts of state and local elected officials to keep pace with the rapidly changing rules of the game, there is growing concern that the national government may have acquired excessive influence over state and local decisions. Also, many citizens apparently believe that these same complexities have weakened the people's control over many of the activities and decisions of government that affect their daily lives either directly or indirectly; part of the effort to "reinvent government" stems from this perception. In recent years, IGR has been affected (though more indirectly) by another change: the growing service-delivery roles of nonprofit community organizations and various for-profit organizations in the private sector. These developments have also posed immense new challenges to those responsible for effectively administering government programs in a constantly changing environment. That these developments have been largely interrelated has made coping with them all the more difficult.

In the following discussion, several principal themes stand out. One is the importance, in this context and in broader terms, of government purposes organized by *function*. Functional alliances have tended to dominate contemporary IGR and, as a result, have become centers of ongoing controversy. A second theme, closely linked to the first, is the growing political and managerial struggle between elected public officials and administrative/functional specialists (and their respective political allies) for control of major IGR program directions. A third, broader theme focuses on the tensions between forces promoting greater *centralization* in the general governmental system and those favoring *decentralization* (including a lessening of national government regulation of state and local government activity). Nowhere is that issue more crucial than in the federalism/IGR realm since a prime purpose of federalism is to prevent excessive centralization of governmental authority. Deliberate efforts both to centralize and to decentralize government programs have been numerous. Calls for downsizing, decentralization, and deregulation have been gaining ground, especially since the early 1980s, and reinventing government implicitly (if not explicitly) puts considerable emphasis on decentralizing government functions in order to put them within easier reach of popular control. All these themes have fiscal, administrative, and political dimensions.

fiscal federalism   the complex of financial transactions, transfers of funds, and accompanying rules and regulations that increasingly characterizes national–state, national–local, and state–local relations.

Intergovernmental Fiscal Relations

Intergovernmental fiscal relations, also referred to as **fiscal federalism,** are central to contemporary IGR. While there have been some forms of financial aid from one governmental level to another throughout American history, the scope of such transactions has expanded rapidly and dramatically in the past forty years. This applies to national government aid to states and localities and, to a lesser extent, to state aid to local governments.

Intergovernmental aid has taken on greater importance for a relatively simple reason. Traditionally, many state and local governments have had weaker economic bases and less productive systems of taxation than the national government has. Yet, the former provide the great bulk of public services in health, education, welfare, housing, highway construction, police protection, parks and recreation, conservation, and agricultural services. The national government, with far stronger fiscal resources and revenue-generating capacity, delivers directly only a few public services.[11] These include Social Security benefits, postal services, federal law enforcement, veterans' payments, and farm subsidies. In essence, the national government, with the greatest tax resources, delivers the fewest direct services; local governments, with the narrowest and weakest tax bases, are frequently the most heavily laden with costly service obligations (police, fire, streets and roads, sewage and sanitation, water, and utilities); the states fall between them. (It should be noted that the national government — through *mandated* grants, contracts, loans, regulations, and the like — now has many avenues of *indirect* service provision.[12])

There are two basic reasons for the revenue-raising disparity among different governmental levels. First, local and state governments have limited geographic areas — often dependent on one or two products or services — from which to extract revenues (for instance, tourism in Florida and coal in West Virginia). A more diversified economy is a more stable and productive source of government income, and only the national government has access to the nation's full range of economic resources.

Second, different types of taxes yield different amounts of revenue from the same income base. The most responsive, or *elastic*, tax (a tax that shows the greatest increase in revenue for a given rise in taxable income) is the *graduated income tax* (so called because the tax rate rises as income increases). Somewhat less elastic is the *sales tax*, which levies a flat percentage rate on the price of purchased goods; some sales taxes are general and allow few exemptions, while others are selective and apply only to certain items. Least elastic is the *personal property tax*, which is levied on real estate and other personal belongings. The national government is the principal user of the graduated income tax. States rely heavily on sales and other excise taxes (though increasingly, state revenues are also derived from nongraduated or "flat-rate" income taxes). Local governments, including special districts, depend most heavily on personal property taxes (though sales and wage taxes have come into increasing use by many local governments).[13]

Thus, the government with the broadest tax base, the national government, also uses the most efficient generator of revenue, whereas the governments with the narrowest and least diversified tax base, local governments, employ the least elastic tax, with the states again falling between the two. The result is a **fiscal mismatch** between the service needs and fiscal capacities of different levels of

fiscal mismatch differences in the capacities of various governments to raise revenues, in relation to those governments' respective abilities to pay for public services which they are responsible for delivering.

government and among different governments at the same level in terms of their varying abilities to pay for needed public services (for example, wealthy school districts versus less affluent ones). Rising service demands on government at all levels have placed a particular strain on those governments least able to expand their tax revenues rapidly, that is, local units. The consequence of all this has been increasing demand for aid from higher levels of government to help pay for proliferating government services.

GRANTS-IN-AID

The growing needs of state and local government during the first half of the twentieth century coincided with rising congressional and executive-branch interest in expanding and upgrading available public services at all levels of government. By the 1960s, the stage was set for the national government (and some state governments) to utilize financial assistance on a much larger scale than before as a means to expand public services. The principal device adopted to bring all this about was the grant-in-aid, which had been an established mechanism for thirty years and was now to be given a substantially enlarged role.

grants-in-aid money payments furnished by a higher to a lower level of government to be used for specified purposes and subject to conditions spelled out in law or administrative regulation.

Grants-in-aid are money payments furnished by a higher to a lower level of government to be used for specified purposes and subject to conditions spelled out in law or administrative regulation. Cash transfers are used most widely by the national government, although states also make some use of them. When John F. Kennedy was inaugurated in 1961, only forty-five separate grant authorizations (statutes) existed. (Under each authorization, multiple allocations of funds can be made.) But in the period 1965–1966, when Lyndon B. Johnson commanded decisive Democratic majorities in both chambers of Congress, he took advantage of the opportunity to legislate a host of new federally directed grant programs as he pursued his vision of the "Great Society." By the time Richard Nixon entered the White House (only eight years after the start of Kennedy's term), the number of grants had mushroomed to about four hundred. Using the criterion of separate authorizations, the U.S. Advisory Commission on Intergovernmental Relations (ACIR) estimated that almost 540 grant programs existed in fiscal year (FY) 1981. During the Reagan administration, the number of grants dropped to about 400 by FY 1985, with significant adverse implications for state and local delivery of many public services and for the fiscal well-being of many state and local jurisdictions. The number increased again, however, to 478 grant programs in FY 1989 and to nearly 600 in FY 1996. Grants have financed state and local programs in virtually every major domestic policy area — urban renewal, highway construction and maintenance, mass transit, education, criminal justice, recreation, public health, and so on.

Equally dramatic is the increase in dollar amounts appropriated under national grant programs. In FY 1960, the figure was about $7 billion; by 1970, it had risen to $24 billion; five years later, it was almost $50 billion; by FY 1981, it was just under $95 billion; and, in FY 1997, it was approximately $234 billion.

Despite the Reagan administration's success in slowing the rate of growth in spending for grants, under both presidents Bush and Clinton, the number of grant programs increased, along with the funds appropriated for them (see Table 4–1).

National grants-in-aid were originally enacted to achieve certain broad purposes.[14] These included (1) establishing minimum nationwide standards for programs operating in all parts of the country, (2) equalizing resources among the states by redistributing proportionately more money to poorer states, (3) improving state and local program delivery, (4) concentrating research resources on problems that cross government boundary lines (such as air and water pollution) or that attract interest from numerous governments, and (5) increasing public services without enlarging the scope of the national government or its apparent role in domestic politics. Other purposes have included improving the

TABLE 4–1 Federal Grants-in-Aid to Individuals and as a Percentage of State and Local Outlays and Total Federal Outlays: 1970–1998

[For fiscal year ending in year shown; Minus sign (–) indicates decrease]

| | | | Current Dollars | | | | | Constant (1992) Dollars[1] | |
| | | | Grants to Individuals | | Grants as Percent of — | | | | |
Year	Total Grants (mil. dol.)	Annual Percent Change[2]	Total (mil. dol.)	Percent of Total Grants	State-Local Govt. Outlays[3]	Federal Outlays	Gross Domestic Product	Total Grants (mil. dol.)	Annual Percent Change[2]
1970	24,065	19.3	8,727	36.3	19.0	12.3	2.4	86.9	11.8
1975	49,791	14.8	18,762	33.7	23.5	15.0	3.2	126.6	3.3
1980	91,385	9.6	32,652	35.7	26.3	15.5	3.4	155.7	−1.1
1985	105,852	8.5	49,352	46.6	21.3	11.2	2.6	135.6	4.7
1990	135,325	11.0	77,132	57.0	18.7	10.8	2.4	144.7	6.2
1991	154,519	14.2	92,497	59.9	19.5	11.7	2.6	158.6	9.6
1992	178,065	15.2	112,185	63.0	20.8	12.9	2.9	178.1	12.3
1993	193,612	8.7	124,289	64.2	21.2	13.7	3.0	168.7	6.0
1994	210,596	8.8	135,232	64.2	21.8	14.4	3.1	200.5	6.3
1995	224,991	6.8	145,793	64.8	22.2	14.8	3.1	208.2	3.8
1996	227,811	1.3	147,598	64.8	21.4	14.6	3.0	205.5	−1.3
1997	234,160	2.8	148,847	63.6	21.2	14.6	2.9	205.8	0.1
1998 (est.)	250,992	7.2	161,063	64.2	20.5	15.0	3.0	215.9	4.9

[1]Constant dollars are dollar amounts of public and private income, expenditures, costs, etc., expressed in terms of dollar values in a given (base) year, and assumed to be unchanged (constant) since that year; thus, constant-dollar figures do not reflect changes in the price of goods and services (and in the value of the dollar) between the base year and any subsequent time period; the alternative to constant-dollar figures is current dollars — that is, dollar amounts that reflect changes in prices of goods and services, and changes in the value of the dollar.

[2]Average annual percent change from prior year shown. For explanation, see Guide to Tabular Presentation, 1970, change from 1969.

[3]Outlays as defined in the national income and product accounts.

SOURCE: Office of Management and Budget, based on *Historical Tables, Budget of the United States Government, FY 99.*

structure and operation of state and local agencies (such as merit personnel practices or better planning), demonstration and experimentation in national policy, encouragement of general social objectives (such as nondiscrimination in hiring), and provision of services to otherwise underserviced portions of the population.

The importance of grants-in-aid in the total picture of domestic programs is suggested by the fact that throughout the 1970s and 1980s these grants provided about *one-fourth* of state-local revenues each fiscal year. That proportion began to decline in the early 1980s, following Ronald Reagan's election to the presidency (see Table 4–1). And, today, there are clear indications that the problem of revenue generation in state and local governments — while taking on greater importance than before — is likely to be addressed by a different combination of approaches. Congress and the president have agreed on spending reductions to balance the federal budget, and the national government has shown little inclination to resume higher levels of aid. By the late 1990s, grants provided only *one-fifth* of state-local revenues. Plainly, state and local officials will not be able to rely on federal grants as much as they have in the past. Growth has been further constrained by pressures to reduce taxes, robust state government economies, and widespread public opposition to increased federal government spending.

Despite the prospects for limited growth, the advantages attributed to grant-in-aid programs are numerous. First, the national government affords a single focal point for bringing about a greater degree of concerted action on a policy problem. Second, political minorities in states and localities have an opportunity to seek some measure of national support for their policy demands, as African Americans and other social-political minorities did in the 1960s. Third, grants-in-aid are an appropriate way to deal with *nationwide* problems; many policy questions are interrelated in terms of their impact, such as those linking highways, urban transportation, and air pollution or education, unemployment, poverty, and welfare. Although a fully coordinated attack on such sets of problems has yet to be mounted (and is not likely to be), a greater degree of consistency is possible at the national level than among fifty separate states and 87,000 local governments.

Finally, and perhaps most important, it has been suggested that national funds assist states and localities with programs and projects that benefit citizens outside the borders of the recipient government. These so-called *ripple effects* — more formally known as **externalities** — justify national monetary support for state or local efforts because of the wider benefits realized from them. Three examples illustrate the point: (1) a state job-training center, whose graduates may find employment in other states; (2) a state park system (such as Kentucky's, which is one of the best) that attracts tourists and vacationers from a much wider geographic area; and (3) local education systems that, in a mobile society such as ours, are undoubtedly investing in the future productivity and contributions of persons who will reap the benefits of their education elsewhere. Because the nation as a whole gains from such investments of state and local funds, there is good reason to add grant funding from the national treasury.

externalities the economic consequences or impacts of federal grants-in-aid at the regional and local level.

Grants-in-aid have taken several forms; we "can usefully categorize grant programs along two dimensions":[15] (1) the degree of discretion national government administrative officials possess in distributing funds, and (2) the "degree of restriction imposed on the use of [national government] funds."[16] Administrative discretion in distributing funds is least under **formula grants,** created by legislation that clearly specifies the criteria (standards) for determining eligibility to receive the funds. Depending on the purpose of a grant, these criteria might include population, unemployment rates, or the percentage of the population living in poverty. Administrative discretion is much greater in the case of **project grants;** with these, agency officials have wide latitude in deciding which states or local governments will receive funding and how much each will get. Formula and project grants are subtypes of **categorical grants** — the most commonly used kind of national government assistance programs to state and local governments. Of the nearly six hundred categoricals in existence, three-fourths are project grants, available by application; the remaining one-fourth are formula grants, for purposes such as aid to the blind and disabled (an ongoing concern common to many government jurisdictions). On the other hand, although individual project grants outnumber formula grants, the dollar amounts available under formula grants exceed those of project grants.

Grants can also be distinguished with regard to how freely recipient governments can use national government funds. Under categorical grants, states and local governments can spend the money only for certain clearly designated "categories" of expenditure, leaving very little room for adjustments on the part of a recipient government. The extreme specificity of categorical grants has been described as "hardening of the categories," which

> created such proliferation of minutely targeted grants that . . . a local government wishing to improve its recreational amenities ha[s] to make separate applications to several different agencies if its total program include[s] buying land for park purposes; building a swimming pool on it; operating an activity center for senior citizens; putting in trees and shrubbery; and purchasing sports equipment. In the area of urban transportation, there are [or have been] separate categorical grant programs covering car pool demonstration projects; urban transportation planning; urban area traffic operations improvement; urban mass transportation basic grants (based on a formula for fund distribution); and mass transit grants (on a project application basis).[17]

With about six hundred such grants operative at the present time, the categorical grant business has become immensely complicated, and is difficult for even experienced professionals to comprehend at times (see Table 4–2 for a comparison of the scope of categorical grant assistance before 1960 and in FY 1993).

With grants-in-aid of all types, the proportion of total expenditure paid by the national government varies considerably. Congress defines some grants as representing important national initiatives and sets the national government share at 100 percent. Other grants require dollar-for-dollar matching funds by

formula grant a type of national government grant-in-aid available to states and local governments for purposes that are ongoing and common to many government jurisdictions; distributed according to a set formula that treats all applicants uniformly, at least in principle; has the effect of reducing grantors' administrative discretion. Examples are aid to the blind and aid to the elderly.

project grant a form of grant-in-aid available by application to states and localities for an individual project; more numerous than formula grants but with less overall funding by the federal government.

categorical grant a form of grant-in-aid with purposes narrowly defined by the grantor, leaving the recipient relatively little choice as to how the grant funding is to used, substantively or procedurally.

TABLE 4–2	The Scope of National Aid Has Increased Dramatically

		1993 — Categorical Grants for Everything	
Prior to 1960 — Few and Far Between		Budget Subfunction	Number of Programs
1787	Education land grants	National defense	6
1862	Agricultural education (land grant colleges)	General science, space, and technology	1
1914	Agricultural extension	Energy	13
	■ 50–50 matching	Water resources	2
	■ state plan approved	Conservation and land	
	■ first modern conditional money grant	management	13
		Recreational resources	10
1916	Federal aid highways	Pollution control and	
1917	Vocational education	abatement	29
1921	Public health assistance	Other natural resources	19
1935	Social Security	Farm income stabilization	2
1935	Public assistance	Agricultural research and	
1937	Housing	services	11
1946	Airport aid	Mortgage credit and deposit	
1946	Hospital and medical facilities	insurance	1
		Other advancement of	
1948	Water pollution control	commerce	7
1949	Urban renewal	Ground transportation	26
1950	Federal impact school aid	Air transportation	1
1954	State and local planning assistance	Water transportation	2
		Other transportation	4
1954	Small watershed protection	Community development	7
1955	Air pollution control	Area and regional development	22
1956	Library aid	Disaster relief and insurance	8
1958	College student aid	Elementary, secondary, and	
		vocational education	84
		Higher education	10
		Research and general education aids	16
		Training and employment	8
		Other labor services	2
		Social services	80
		Health	100
		Income security	34
		Veterans benefits and services	5
		General management, multiple functions, and other	55
		Total	578

SOURCES: ACIR, *In Brief: The Federal Role in the Federal System: The Dynamics of Growth* (Washington, D.C.: ACIR, December 1980), pp. 2–3; U.S. Advisory Commission on Intergovernmental Relations, *Characteristics of Federal Grant-in-Aid Programs to State and Local Governments: Grants Funded, FY 1993,* Table 4 (Washington, D.C.: U.S. Government Printing Office, 1993).

the recipient government, which doubles the total amount of money available to the recipient. Some other grant allocations require recipients to share the burden to some extent but not fifty-fifty (sometimes as little as 1 percent of the total). The national share, then, is at least one-half and can cover the total.

Several other observations should be made with reference to Tables 4–1 and 4–2. First, in FY 1993, only twenty-one categorical grant programs accounted for 80 percent of total spending for categoricals, and another two dozen programs accounted for another 10 percent of spending. These included the **Medicaid** program, child nutrition grants, wastewater treatment plant construction, Aid to Families with Dependent Children (AFDC), training and employment programs, low-rent public housing, and community development programs. (Under the Welfare Reform Act of 1996, AFDC programs are now administered as formula grants by the states, with federal standards.) Still, nearly 90 percent of the funds allocated for categoricals was taken by the largest forty-five programs (fewer than 10 percent of the total number of programs.) Second, spending for intergovernmental aid has risen at the rate of about 5 percent annually since 1982. A sharp aid reduction occurred between FY 1981 and 1982 before spending levels began edging upward again. Also, national government assistance as a proportion both of state/local revenues and expenditures began to decline after FY 1980, but that proportionate decline has continued even though grant spending has generally increased.[18]

Medicaid federal health care program operated by the states to assist the poor.

Expansion of grants-in-aid was accompanied by qualitative and administrative changes: (1) there were increasing numbers of project grants; (2) there was an increased variety of matching-grant formulas; (3) it became possible to apply for multiple-function instead of single-function grants, although the number of these was small; (4) Congress broadened the eligibility of grant recipients and increased joint-recipient possibilities; (5) aid was concentrated in large urban areas and directed to the urban poor in numerous new ventures; (6) there was increased national aid not only to governments but also to private institutions, including corporations, universities, and nonprofit organizations; and (7) the national government made funding available specifically to assist state and local jurisdictions in improving both their planning capabilities and their actual planning activities.[19] All these changes grew out of an expanding emphasis on achieving national goals under the direction of the national government.[20]

Prior to the 1960s, aid had been used primarily to supplement the policy actions of states and localities. Under Kennedy and then Johnson, however, presidential and congressional initiatives were couched more in terms of *national* purposes. Given this emphasis, it was deemed entirely appropriate to write into grant legislation substantive and procedural requirements (mandates) that would promote those purposes.[21] Administration of these programs remained predominantly in the hands of state and local governments, but the national role in defining the uses of grant funds was clearly becoming decisive in determining general policy directions and many specific state and local program activities.

During the Clinton administration (1993–2001) funding for grants-in-aid increased slightly to around 15 percent of total federal spending.

While major changes were unfolding in national categorical programs, another development was also evident, namely, the continued expansion of state aid to local governments. Not only were states contributing increasing amounts to local government functions (especially to school districts and to the growing suburbs), but states were also making much of the funding available in the form of *revenue sharing*, that is, funds drawn from the respective state treasuries and allocated to local governments with few if any "strings" attached. Many states also established the practice (still in use across the country) of returning to each local government a portion of state sales-tax revenues, in proportion to the amount of sales-tax revenue collected within each locality. Thus, from the local perspective, state and national governments, in their differing methods of organizing fiscal assistance to local governments, have moved in somewhat opposite directions during the past thirty-five years. This is not to say, however, that states have given their local governments free rein to allocate funds — far from it. Nevertheless, key features of state aid, especially categorical grants, differ in significant respects from those of national aid.

CATEGORICAL GRANTS AND ADMINISTRATIVE COMPLEXITY

In the preceding discussion of grants-in-aid, we noted a number of administrative dimensions, including the objectives of providing more and better public services, with growing emphasis recently on efficiency and effectiveness — both squarely in our administrative traditions; establishing minimum uniform programmatic standards nationwide; enhancing both the procedure and the substance of state and local programs; and strengthening the planning function. How all this should be accomplished, however, was and still is a serious question. The use of categorical grants rather than some other instrument of assistance contributed directly to increased interdependence, reliance on political bargaining, and the rise of administrative complexity. This is so because of historical patterns in grants management that are worth reviewing.

Today, states receive more than two-thirds of all formula grants and act as conduits for the majority of project grants to local governments. As Congress deliberated over expansion of successive aid programs, a principal concern was ensuring that the national purposes of programs were not lost by dividing up administrative responsibility among fragmented state agencies. One way to prevent such jurisdictional jostling would have been through the assertion of strong **gubernatorial** prerogatives, whereby the appropriate state agencies were designated to receive given grant funds and to administer program activities under congressional authorization. Most governors, however, were ill equipped to serve that function, especially in the early years of grant activity, when the operations of state executive branches often lacked unified direction and were hampered by partisan politics and administrative chaos.

gubernatorial a term which refers to anything concerning the office of state governor — for example, gubernatorial authority or gubernatorial influence.

One response from the national level was the **single state agency requirement.** Only one agency is designated to administer national grants and to establish direct relationships with its counterpart in the national government bureaucracy. This provision first appeared in the 1916 Highway Act and was duplicated the following year in the Vocational Education Act. Currently applicable laws either name a specific state agency or call for one to be designated in policy areas such as child welfare, library services, urban planning, water-pollution control, civil defense, and law enforcement assistance. Thus, for most of the twentieth century, the administration of grant funds was largely in the hands of professional administrative personnel in individual agencies.

As the grant-in-aid system grew more specialized, national agency personnel came to work even more closely with their state and local counterparts. Partly as a result of national grant policies, the latter were now much more professionalized than they had been in the past, operating under state merit systems that had created a contingent of administrators whose backgrounds, interests, and professional competencies were similar to those of national government administrators. Parallel relationships were formed between officials of the Bureau of Public Roads and state and local highway department personnel; national educational administrators and their counterparts in state departments of education and officials in local school districts; and Agriculture Department staffs with state and, especially, county agricultural officials. This process of strengthening intergovernmental administrative linkages led to a situation largely invisible to the general public but fraught with consequences for the governmental process. Political scientists Harold Seidman and Robert Gilmour, among others, have suggested that what we have in a number of important functional areas are "largely self-governing professional guilds"[22] composed of bureaucrats at all levels with common programmatic concerns. The ACIR, describing the same phenomenon, coined the term **vertical functional autocracies,**[23] the *autocracy* label signifying not only the agencies' operating autonomy from chief executives and legislators but also the extent of agency control over essential program decisions.

The development of intergovernmental administrative ties gave rise to a new label for the federal system. Previously, dual federalism was likened to a *layer cake,* with different levels of government clearly distinguished from one another; and growing cooperation was likened to a *marble cake,* with functions of different levels of government intermingled. The new vertical administrative patterns gave rise to the term **picket-fence federalism,** illustrated in Figure 4–1. Former North Carolina Governor (and later U.S. Senator) Terry Sanford provided this definition:

> The lines of authority, the concerns and interests, the flow of money, and the direction of programs run straight down like a number of pickets stuck into the ground. There is, as in a picket fence, a connecting cross slat, but that does little to support anything. In this metaphor it stands for the governments. It holds the pickets in line; it does not bring them together. The picket-like programs are not connected at the bottom.[24]

single state agency requirement a requirement contained in federal grants designating only one agency to administer national grants, and to establish direct relationships with its counterpart in the national government bureaucracy.

vertical functional autocracies associations of federal, state, and local professional administrators who manage intergovernmental programs; also referred to as **picket-fence federalism.**

picket-fence federalism a term describing a key dimension of American federalism — intergovernmental administrative relationships among bureaucratic specialists and their clientele groups in the same substantive areas; suggests that allied bureaucrats at different levels of government exercise considerable power over intergovernmental programs. See also **vertical functional autocracies.**

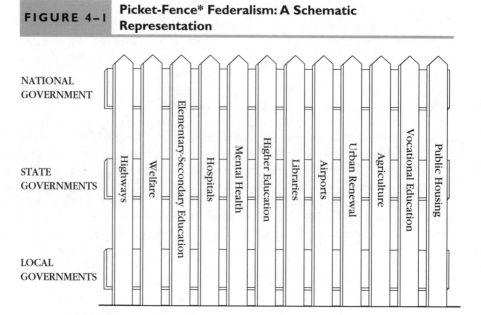

FIGURE 4–1   **Picket-Fence* Federalism: A Schematic Representation**

*Each picket represents the political and administrative ties among specialists in each policy area at all three levels of government.

SOURCE: Adapted from *Understanding Intergovernmental Relations*, 3rd. ed., by Deil S. Wright. Copyright © 1988, 1982, 1978, by Wadsworth, Inc. Reprinted by permission of Brooks/Cole Publishing Company, Pacific Grove, CA 93950.

Bureaucratic officials within each of these pickets, together with their clientele groups at all levels, do not always agree, of course, on the substance and procedures of programs they administer. But the responsibility for formulating many basic policies and for resolving many of the conflicts that arise rests largely — and often exclusively — within the discretion of these functional groupings. How that situation can be reconciled with democratic values of public accountability and control is an important question and one not easily answered. One hopeful sign, however, has been noted: The pickets may have already been somewhat altered. Only ten years after Sanford used the picket-fence label for the first time, David Walker of the ACIR suggested a variation, namely, *bamboo-fence federalism.* Walker asserted that this new label more accurately "captures the vertical functionalism, continuing professionalism, [and] greater flexibility and realism" of contemporary public administrators, even though most still give primary emphasis to their functional concerns, including the protection of programmatic interests as a high priority.[25]

CATEGORICAL GRANTS: GROWING DISSATISFACTION

The tremendous proliferation of grants, the rise of vertical functional autocracies, picket- or bamboo-fence federalism and, particularly, the duplicative and overlapping nature of so many available grants soon led to a growing chorus of concern about management of grants and about the impacts they were having on recipient governments. (See Box 4–1, "Categorical Grants: The Most Common Criticisms.")

BOX 4–1   INTERGOVERNMENTAL RELATIONS

Categorical Grants: The Most Common Criticisms*

1. The proliferation of project grants has conflicted with equalizing governmental resources; applying successfully for such grants has required professional skills (the "art of *grantsmanship*") most likely to be found in already affluent states and communities.
2. Restricting categorical aid uses has distorted state and local policy priorities. (Some have argued, however, that even if true, categorical grants were *designed* to induce states and localities to become active in policy areas where they had not moved on their own.)
3. State and local leaders might gradually yield policy *initiative* to aid grantors in Congress and the bureaucracy, increasingly waiting for "Washington" to establish new policies.
4. The national government did (and does) not aid all public services; thus, greater *inequality* of available services often has resulted.
5. States and localities required to put up matching funds to receive aid have had a harder time meeting their other (unaided) service obligations. This has been especially important for financially pressed cities, which spend considerable sums on public services that Congress has not supported through grant funding to any great degree (e.g., fire protection and sidewalk maintenance). In contrast, suburbs often have devoted much of their budgets to strongly aided functions (e.g., education, parks, and public health programs).
6. Many state and local officials have objected to the paperwork, uncertainty, and delays associated with applying for categorical aid. Application forms are often complex and difficult to fill out. Worse, sometimes aid has been approved after expenditures dependent on that aid already have been made. Worse still, a grant occasionally has been *disapproved* after state or local funds were spent.
7. Coordination of hundreds of grants spread across scores of agencies has been a persistent problem (see text).

*That these criticisms are often expressed does not necessarily mean that they are accurate.

These criticisms suggest several dimensions of the politics of grants.[26] One is provision of essential public services, and equality or inequality among (and sometimes within) jurisdictions in the levels of those services. Another concerns tensions among different levels and units of government over setting program priorities, and program management. A third dimension is the procedural pitfalls that can hamper applicant governments in their efforts to obtain grant assistance. Many state and local officials tell horror stories about rejection of applications on seemingly narrow technical grounds, about having to resubmit applications because a relatively minor section was improperly filled out, and so forth. Underlying all such concerns, however, is a common theme: considerable conflict between elected state and local officials ("generalists") and the specialists of their own bureaucracies as well as those in the national government's administrative agencies (see Figure 4–1). Much of the criticism came from state and local chief executives and legislators and was directed explicitly toward the greater control that bureaucrats at all levels were coming to have over government aid programs. As the criticisms grew in intensity and became a partisan issue dividing Democrats and Republicans, the critics increasingly gained the attention of the Congress and, significantly, the president.

Increasing attention was also given to the problem of grant coordination that resulted from the sheer number of grants and the variety of grant sources within the national bureaucracy. The availability of urban transportation grants from different national agencies for similar, often overlapping purposes made it difficult to select the most appropriate grant program. Also, many general development projects in states and communities had component parts funded independently by separate national agencies. As a result, a grant applicant was faced with applying separately for each part of the overall project, thereby running the risk of applications being approved for some portions of the project but not for others.

Furthermore, most national aid-granting agencies did not have much (if any) knowledge of what other programs were being funded by other agencies; at the other end of the aid pipeline, most recipient governments knew or cared little about what funds other governments were receiving, or even applying for. Grant applications were being reviewed and approved or rejected by national agencies with no means of keeping track of which states and localities were asking for aid, for what purposes it was requested, and how much aid was distributed. Nor were there any provisions for systematically monitoring which agencies were responsible for programs with similar purposes or for determining the actual results, if any, of grant funds. Meanwhile, state and local officials were chafing under what many considered unreasonable guidelines for spending grant money, as well as the problems they encountered in obtaining funding in the first place.

The problems of coordination have been compounded at the recipient end of the aid pipelines by growing intergovernmental administrative linkages in *horizontal* as well as vertical dimensions. Various types of contracting arrangements, consortia, cooperative agreements, regional interagency councils, commissions, multijurisdiction functional agencies, ad hoc planning groups, temporary clearing houses, and a multitude of other intergovernmental structures have been created to administer federal programs. Interstate compacts, such as the New York Port Authority, have come into greater prominence; other regional bodies crossing state lines, created by either state or national governments, have also been established. Likewise, there has been an increase in the phenomenon of *substate regionalism*. Special districts of all kinds (excepting school districts) have proliferated in recent years — many in response to national government encouragement — for a variety of purposes, such as planning, review of grant applications, economic development, public health, and provision of care for the aging. Here, again, the picket-fence analogy is evident because national, state, and local administrative officials all have active roles in substate regional functions. The formation of these nearly independent federal-local government systems poses considerable administrative difficulties because it frees districts to compete (often successfully) for grant monies available to all other types of local government. Thus, these systems are also woven into the pattern of functionally organized administrative relationships but, at the same time, they are among the most invisible and least accountable of all forms of government.

Grant Reform: Multiple Efforts, More Complexity

By the late 1970s, pressures were mounting for changes in the grant-in-aid system, particularly in grants management. Although various concepts and options had been explored from time to time, few actions had been taken. The changes that followed, and that have continued up to the present, have emphasized efforts to reduce the programmatic influence of the national government, through both fiscal and administrative reform. We will consider these, and their major components, in turn.

FISCAL REFORM: GENERAL REVENUE SHARING

During the late 1960s, political reaction mounted to the strings (conditions and specifications) attached to grant-in-aid funding. Increasingly, state and local elected officials sought financial assistance that would permit them greater discretion in spending decisions. The Nixon proposal for general revenue-sharing (GRS) appeared to meet such demands. General revenue sharing deemphasized concern for national policies, goals, and standards; defined state and local rather than national majorities as the key decision makers about program spending; and built into the intergovernmental fiscal system greater discretion for state and local elected officials. But, despite attracting quite a following among state and local officials, GRS never lived up to its advance billing.

The principle behind revenue sharing was a simple one: A portion of tax revenues would be returned to states and to general-purpose local governments according to a prescribed formula defined by Congress and automatically followed each year. Revenue-sharing funds would be allocated with no strings attached, and recipient governments could use the money for almost any purpose. There would also be no need for a state or locality to apply for the funds; once the formula was determined, the funds would be available with no uncertainty and no delay. Such an arrangement seemed to respond directly to the sharpest criticisms of the grant-in-aid system. In particular, revenue sharing seemed to represent a way for local political majorities, through their elected officials, to reassert their priorities in local and state spending and not to be bound to grant programs with which they increasingly disagreed on both policy and procedural grounds.

One of the reasons, of course, for its appeal was precisely that GRS would allow officials of recipient governments to exercise wide latitude in deciding how to spend the funds; however, some of those officials proved wiser than others. For example, some communities applied GRS monies to special projects, usually construction projects of limited scope or duration, while others, often out of necessity, incorporated GRS funds into their operating budgets. Those who confined their funding to capital improvement turned out to be better off when the flow of funds stopped in 1986.[27]

Even when GRS was most strongly supported at the White House, it represented only a small proportion of total spending for intergovernmental aid (less than 5 percent). Ronald Reagan, however, opposed extending revenue sharing, and Congress did not renew the program. Reagan's willingness to allow general revenue sharing to lapse was apparently due to two policy preferences: (1) an overriding interest in reducing national government spending and growing annual budget deficits; and (2) a commitment to another alternative to categoricals, namely, block grants.

FISCAL REFORM: BLOCK GRANTS

If general revenue sharing represented a departure from existing categorical aid and its attendant problems, block grants were a more modest attempt (at least initially) to "decategorize" federal grants and "devolve" authority to states and localities.[28] **Block grants,** while also given out for use in a specific policy area (such as community development, public assistance, or health care), leave much more discretion and flexibility in the use of such funds in the hands of recipient governments. They represent a middle way between the alleged restrictiveness of categorical grants and the elimination of all national-level influence and responsibility in intergovernmental aid. In general, block grants have the following features: (1) recipient jurisdictions have fairly wide discretion within the designated program area; (2) administration, reporting, planning, and other program features are designed to minimize grantor supervision and control; (3) most allocation provisions are based on a formula, which is also intended to limit grantor discretion as well as to decrease fiscal uncertainty for the grantees;

block grants a form of grant-in-aid under which the purposes to be served by the funding are defined very broadly by the grantor, leaving considerable discretion and flexibility in the hands of the recipient.

(4) eligibility provisions are fairly precise, tending to favor general local governments as opposed to special districts, and generalist officials over program specialists; and (5) matching-fund requirements are usually relatively low.[29] The original block-grant concept retained the notion that national goals were to be pursued in a program area through expenditure of allocated funds; the ACIR has noted that block grants "do not imply a hands-off [national] role, nor one confined to purely procedural matters."[30] These observations were clearly descriptive of the block grants of the 1960s and 1970s.

The Reagan administration's block grants, however, differed from the earlier ones in several important respects.[31] One obvious difference was the increase from five such grants in FY 1981 to twelve in FY 1984. More important was the explicit link between establishment of block grants and elimination of categoricals. Creation of block grants was accompanied by a reduction in the number of categorical programs from 534 in FY 1981 to 404 in FY 1984 — a decrease of about 24 percent.[32] In 1981–1982 alone, seventy-seven categoricals were consolidated into nine new or revised block grants, and another sixty categorical programs were terminated outright.

A third difference is that these block grants were accompanied by a decline not only in the number of categoricals but also in total spending for intergovernmental assistance. In its efforts to slow the growth of national government spending, the Reagan administration made many of its early spending cuts in intergovernmental aid — although aid levels increased slowly after the first wave of reductions (see Table 4–1). Moreover, there is evidence that the block-grant strategy was used implicitly to cut spending and not simply to alter the degree of program control exercised by government administrators through categorical grants. Neither George Bush nor Bill Clinton, however, adopted that course of action, at least to the same extent. Block grants (especially under Clinton) have been allowed to operate as more of a "freestanding" form of fiscal assistance, without strong links to any apparent federalism-related strategy.

A fourth difference is the contractual nature of the new block grants, involving contracts between national and state governments. The use of state–national contracts reflects a prevailing emphasis on increasing the states' role within a broader vision of a "revitalized" (and considerably revamped) federal system. This emphasis suggests yet another difference between "old" and "new" block grants: the implicit subordination of national purposes to those of the states, if not outright abandonment (at least in the Reagan years) of national control over program spending under block grants.

Under the Bush administration, the shifts (both ideological and administrative) toward a stronger state role were reaffirmed and consolidated. Significantly, however, George Bush did little to expand the changes that Ronald Reagan set in motion. In FY 1991, for example, Bush proposed increasing block-grant funding by the modest sum of $15 million, with the explicit proviso that state governors be given exclusive responsibility for deciding how the funds would be used. This proposal typified the overall approach of the Bush administration toward intergovernmental change: the allocation of generally small amounts of money to these programs in a manner consistent with the philosophical directions defined in the previous administration. The total amounts appropriated for both categoricals and block grants increased somewhat but with more attention to budgetary constraints than to explicitly intergovernmental concerns.

Likewise, the Clinton administration has had to grapple with budgetary concerns and has seemingly tried to do so with only minimal attention to IGR. Early in his first term of office, Clinton advocated terminating or consolidating some one hundred and fifty existing grant programs (a somewhat unusual step for a Democratic president). In the FY 1995 budget, however, President Clinton proposed a combination of programs in selected programmatic areas that represented some expansion of funding to state and local governments. These included assistance for education, job training, and public works. Current budgetary constraints, however, make it highly unlikely that any president of either major party will soon be able to propose major increases in funding for a wide range of intergovernmental programs.

FISCAL REFORM: IMPACTS OF CHANGE

Both general revenue sharing and block grants were introduced on the national political scene amid considerable fanfare; both were advanced as important solutions to major problems associated with the existing grants system, such as confusion, overlapping, red tape, inequities, and rigidity. With three decades of experience behind us (including a number of evaluations of both approaches), it is useful to assess the pros and cons in more substantive terms in order to measure just how close the rhetoric came to the realities. It is also useful to consider some consequences that few observers forecast.

Various studies of GRS and block grants suggested the following patterns of use: (1) more funding was allocated to existing operating programs than to new ones; (2) the largest category of use in smaller communities was capital expenditures — for new municipal buildings, waterworks, even public golf courses; (3) keeping tax rates stable in inflationary times was a major concern of many local decision makers in considering how to use these funds; (4) local political majorities became, if anything, stronger and more entrenched; and (5) alleviating poverty in larger cities (a major aim of many categoricals in the 1960s) was not a primary purpose of either GRS or block grants. A major consequence of the shift to this form of aid was a decline in public policy concern for needy minorities, many of whose members were concentrated in the poorest central cities. The distinction between local political majorities and minorities as primary beneficiaries of GRS/block grants and categorical grants, respectively, was a significant one; the effects of the grants on each of these recipients form a crucial corollary to debates over types of national government assistance. The politics of fiscal federalism overlaps such policy fields as urban policy and civil rights. To "increase the flexibility of state and local governments" (meaning their elected officials) is to deemphasize the policy concerns (much more prevalent in the 1960s than now) with problems of urban minority groups and, more generally, with problems of poverty.[33]

In addition to these general impacts, neither "generation" of block grants has operated precisely in the manner predicted by their strongest advocates. Soon after being enacted, the early block grants showed signs of what some called "creeping categorization" — a pattern of various abuses discovered in the course of grant implementation, followed by the gradual reassertion of national agency control in order to prevent further abuse. In recent years, both old and new block-grant programs have taken unexpected turns.[34] One observer summarized some of the impressions (and frustrations) of block-grant operations as viewed from the local level:

> Seemingly secure entitlement block grants can quickly crumble, as CETA (Comprehensive Education and Training Act) and LEAA [Law Enforcement Assistance Administration] . . . have. Seemingly simple programs can become more [complex and] categorical, as CETA, LEAA, and, to a lesser extent, CDBG (Community Development Block Grant) have. Promises of "local" autonomy can vanish into thin air as state grant and contracting procedures — and [national] statutes, regulations, and administrative discretion — intervene. In reality, the most significant issue of the Reagan block grants from a local perspective is not grant consolidation, state control, or loosened mandates. Rather, it is funding level.[35]

To the extent that the last contention is true, the current debates over federalism and IGR — at least with respect to intergovernmental aid — are essentially debates about government budgeting and spending reductions. That focus may rob us of an opportunity that arises only infrequently, namely, to make decisions consciously (and, one would hope, thoughtfully) on the merits of possible changes of direction in American federalism. Given the focus on deficit reduction, budget considerations will have a prominent place in any future discussion about possible change in the role of the national government in relation to states and localities; so, also, will the concerns for reinventing government, which could produce new directions for transferring power and raising revenue at the state and local government levels.

Both general revenue sharing and block grants have achieved, at least in part, what their proponents intended for them: to loosen the conditions attached to aid from Washington. However, powerful forces will continue to support increases in categorical aid. This fact is reflected in the perpetuation of nearly six hundred such programs; together, they make up about 75 percent of all intergovernmental funding by the national government. This reflects congressional interest in defining and targeting national aid in ways favored by members of Congress, even though their decisions may or may not match the preferences of state and local elected officials, or even those of the public at large. Thus, the debate is likely to continue for some time over the direction of intergovernmental aid.

ADMINISTRATIVE REFORM: PARTICIPATION AND COORDINATION

Other efforts begun in the 1960s to reduce national government influence have taken two directions. The first of these, chronologically, was the movement for *citizen participation* in administrative decision making, especially where decisions on expenditures of grant funds were concerned. By incorporating such requirements into a large number of grant authorizations, Congress was responding to substantial pressures from previously underrepresented constituencies, notably poorer urban minority groups (see Chapter 2). The underlying assumption was that government officials had been insensitive to the needs of aid recipients in the past and that, as aid categories multiplied, it would be necessary to expand clientele representation. Thus, in many grants as well as GRS, provision was made for public hearings, and sometimes for more formalized participation, at crucial points in the decision-making process. The promise of citizen participation may well have been greater than the realization of it, not least because some administrators may have succeeded in co-opting potential adversaries from citizen groups.

Another approach to bringing the grants system (and functional specialists) under better control centered on achieving better *coordination* among proliferating aid programs. The earliest efforts focused on coordination among aid applicants and stressed regionwide coordinative mechanisms. A number of efforts were made to promote better communication among aid applicants (especially at the local level). Despite some protests, these efforts were deemed necessary by many in Congress and federal agencies because of widespread local and state unwillingness to consider the effects of their own programs and planning on those of neighboring jurisdictions. Improving coordination through better communication was a consistent theme in the IGR arena (see Chapter 5 for a general discussion of coordination).

Emphasis has also been placed on more information and training. Information resources currently available to grant seekers include the "bible" of grantsmanship, the Catalog of Federal Domestic Assistance (CFDA), published by the national government; a computerized information system based largely on the CFDA, known as the Federal Awards Assistance Data System (FAADS); and publications of the Grants Management Advisory Service in Washington and the Grantsmanship Center in Los Angeles. Training is receiving more attention from government bodies at all levels, as well as from nongovernmental organizations such as the National Assistance Management Association (NAMA).

ADMINISTRATIVE REFORM: CHANGE AND CONTINUITY

More than any other recent president, Ronald Reagan actively sought to change the way national government agencies conducted their intergovernmental activities. By making frequent use of presidential executive orders, he attempted to alter many features of national–state and national–local relations that existed when he first took office. During his second term (1985–1989), President Reagan took more explicit steps to promote his conception of "New Federalism" — a view of the federal system that, if fully adopted, would limit executive-agency activities in contemporary IGR and instead return to a position that favored heightened state government activity and influence. National government departments and agencies were told to consider the effects of their regulatory and legislative policies on state and local governments in an effort to improve the management of state-administered federal programs. During George Bush's presidency, executive-branch agencies were advised

> to pursue further . . . relief to State and local governments by providing administrative flexibility, promoting efficiency through Governmentwide common rulemaking, cutting . . . red tape, decentralizing the decisionmaking process, and seeking State and local government views in the development of [national government agency] rules.[36]

In all these formulations, there is the clear assumption that national programs and procedures have had generally adverse effects on state and local governments, and that both states and localities should be in the forefront of planning and managing future intergovernmental programs.[37]

The Clinton administration came to office in 1993 without the same ideological commitment to state and local government predominance that the two previous administrations had, but Clinton (like Reagan, a former governor) was eager to apply to the national government many lessons learned during his experience with state government.[38] In addition, President Clinton (in part from budget/deficit concerns) has exhibited some of the same inclinations as Reagan and Bush did toward downsizing, and devolving functions from, the national government. Nevertheless, President Clinton strengthened some national government initiatives for funding intergovernmental activities, especially in policy areas such as education, environmental protection, transportation, and infrastructure improvements. Significantly, however, the Clinton administration spoke consistently of moving decision authority "closer to the people" by allowing state and local governments greater flexibility in managing their programs. We may be approaching a middle ground between the Reagan–Bush state-centered approaches and those of previous "generations" of Democratic presidents — which espoused stronger national government control and direction of intergovernmental funds.

Prospects and Issues in IGR: A Look Ahead

Admittedly, any attempt to forecast even the near future in IGR is a highly speculative venture. But there are already certain indications. One issue that has been addressed by both academics and politicians is the extent to which *intergovernmental regulation* has become part of IGR.[39] These regulations, which have become far more numerous since the 1960s, have been enacted as part of national government bureaucracies' efforts to direct implementation of categorical grant assistance programs. In most instances, the regulations are designed to implement other national government legislation aimed at achieving wide-ranging social and economic objectives (see Table 4–3).

Political scientist Donald Kettl explains the rise of **regulatory federalism**:

regulatory federalism
an approach to intergovernmental relations under which federal agencies use regulations as opposed to grants to influence state and local governments.

> The [national] government cannot constitutionally order state and local governments to examine the environmental impact of projects they propose or to keep their financial records in specified ways. The . . . government can, however, set those standards as conditions for [both categorical and block] grants.[40]

TABLE 4–3   Selected National Government Statutes with Regulatory Impact on State and Local Governments

Title	Objective
Age Discrimination in Employment Act (1974)	Prevent discrimination on the basis of age in state and local government employment
Americans with Disabilities Act (1990)	Comprehensive civil rights law to provide access to public accommodations and facilities for physically disabled persons
Civil Rights Act of 1964 (Title VI)	Prevent discrimination on the basis of race, color, or national origin in nationally assisted programs
Clean Air Act Amendments of 1970	Establish nationwide air quality and emissions standards
Davis–Bacon Act (1931)	Ensure that locally prevailing wages are paid to construction workers employed under national government contracts and financial assistance programs
Equal Employment Opportunity Act of 1972	Prevent discrimination on the basis of race, color, religion, sex, or national origin in state and local government employment
Family and Medical Leave Act (1993)	Offer 12 weeks of unpaid leave within a 12-month period, with job protection and continued health care coverage in certain situations
Federal Water Pollution Control Act Amendments of 1972	Establish national government effluent limitations to control the discharge of pollutants
National Environmental Policy Act of 1969	Ensure consideration of the environmental impact of major national government actions
Resource Conservation and Recovery Act of 1976	Establish standards for the control of hazardous wastes

SOURCE: Adapted from U.S. Advisory Commission on Intergovernmental Relations, *Regulatory Federalism: Policy, Process, Impact and Reform,* Report A-95 (Washington, D.C.: U.S. Government Printing Office, February 1984), pp. 19–21.

Literally hundreds of such regulations now exist. An examination of a small sampling of them may help to convey the scope of this regulation.[41] Under statutory authority from Congress, for example, the Environmental Protection Agency (EPA) may prescribe the treatment local governments must give to their drinking water, as well as the inspections some states must conduct on automobile emission controls. Health care regulations govern the operation of Medicaid programs run by state governments with funding by the national government. National mine-safety regulations set standards for the operation of state and local gravel pits. One reason for the creation of new special-purpose local "quasi governments" (such as regional health planning organizations) was a regulatory requirement imposed by agency officials who distrusted — and therefore wanted to bypass — traditional local political institutions. Professor Kettl summarizes the consequences:

> In all of these areas, the [national] government has spun out elaborate requirements about who can make decisions, who must be consulted, and even how records of performance must be filed. Rules stipulate who must benefit from [nationally] aided programs, and how state and local governments must administer those benefits. These regulations have created a wide channel of [national] influence over the most intimate details of state and local operations. They have also made state and local governments front-line administrators for numerous national programs.[42]

(The point has been made, however, that such regulations often have positive substantive aspects as well; the experience of numerous states has "indicated how important — and useful — [national] requirements [turn] out to be.")[43] The central challenge for reforming IGR is to reduce the number of so-called "unproductive" regulations without abolishing those serving important national purposes.

Two varieties of regulations have developed: (1) so-called *crosscutting rules*, which apply across the board to many national aid programs, and (2) *program-based rules* that apply to individual programs. Some rules, such as the 1931 Davis–Bacon Act, govern administrative and fiscal policy; other rules, such as those accompanying the 1990 Americans with Disabilities Act and the 1993 Family and Medical Leave Act, govern social and economic policy[44] (see Table 4–3).

Two particular aspects of regulatory federalism deserve mention. One is the concern that many mandated activities are costly — for example, paying prevailing wages (determined by the U.S. Labor Department) on construction projects receiving national government funds, or providing "reasonable accommodation" for access by the physically handicapped — and that governments imposing such mandates have not been supplying necessary funding. This has placed numerous local governments and private organizations in increasingly difficult financial positions since the intergovernmental aid is not sufficient to pay for mandated activities. The federal government has little systematic data concerning the cumulative costs it imposes on state and local governments. A study by the U.S.

Conference of Mayors, published in October l993, claimed that an average of *12 percent* of all municipal budgets is devoted to meeting the financial obligations associated with mandates. As mentioned earlier, these unfunded mandates (legal requirements that states and local governments must undertake a specific activity or provide a service meeting minimum national standards) cover a very wide range of public policy areas, including community development, environmental pollution, transportation, public health and safety, and public housing.

The reaction to mandates among state and local officials began to heat up in the early 1990s, to such a point that President Clinton issued an executive order in late 1993 calling for a slowdown in the issuance of new mandates. The administration also intensified "mandate relief efforts" in early 1994 by announcing a series of steps designed to further ease pressures. Many state and local officials, however, wanted even more action.[45] Congress responded with the passage of the *Unfunded Mandates Reform Act of 1995* (P.L. 104–4) making it more difficult for Congress to impose new laws, rules, or regulations that would add significantly to state or local government costs.

The other aspect of the mandating question, however, is the widely shared impression that national government mandates have been the hardest to bear. Though there is obvious variety among the fifty states, a study commissioned by one state legislature and intended to highlight the extent of federal mandates on local governments found instead that four-fifths of the burden (in this case, in the education field) was imposed by state rather than national government law. This does not downgrade the significance of the mandating issue in general; it does, however, suggest that grouping national and state mandates together may foster false impressions about some aspects of the extent of the problem.[46]

In the l990s, increased attention was paid to such problems of intergovernmental regulation, and steps have been taken to ease the burden — especially that on local governments. A major effort begun under the Bush administration that was maintained and expanded under Bill Clinton is the elimination of many of the more detailed (and, many say, more burdensome) regulations. President Clinton and Vice President Gore told government regulatory agencies to cut obsolete regulations and to act like partners with affected businesses, states, and local governments. Clinton and Gore claimed that agencies are eliminating and simplifying thousands of pages of federal regulations. While not all of these regulations affect local government directly, the fact that the effort is being made sends a clear signal to state and local officials that attempts at reform are under way. That this is happening under a Democratic president is also significant; it makes it much less likely that a president in the near future, of either party, will find it acceptable to reimpose major new regulations on local governments and their officials.

Intergovernmental Relations and Public Administration

The diffuse nature of federalism (which is perhaps not as diffuse now as it was in the past) has combined with growing intergovernmental ties in all directions to create an unquestionably complex situation. Public administration has been altered, perhaps permanently, by rapid change in intergovernmental relations.

For example, it is clear that the patterns of political influence termed *subsystem politics* in the national government (see Chapter 3) have been extended into intergovernmental politics. Despite recent efforts to gain greater control of their bureaucracies, most chief executives have failed to stem the growth of vertical functional bureaucratic linkages — the "autocracies" referred to by ACIR. One reason for the inability of a president or governor to overcome the institutional strength of bureaucracies is precisely that the latter can call on political support from at least one other level or unit of government much more easily than a chief executive can. Intergovernmental administrative relations, in other words, have served to strengthen existing bureaucratic autonomy at every level of government. (Whether that general pattern will continue unabated is an important and intriguing question.)

A second area of serious concern for public administration is fiscal relations, especially the financial difficulties of some American governments. Problems like those experienced at various times in New York City, Miami, Detroit, Cleveland, and Orange County, California, as well as other major cities and counties (and some smaller ones), may come to hound political leaders, administrators, and citizens in other communities as they struggle to avoid fiscal chaos caused by antitax sentiments among voters, declining property-tax bases, and escalating service costs. Although intergovernmental aid can do much to bail out a city here and a suburb there, a real question exists as to whether costs imposed by inflation, tax limitation movements, and rising service needs can, in fact, be met over the long term by infusions of aid. At the core of the problem is the fact that recipient governments can easily develop a continuing dependency on such aid (whether from national or state sources), which may not always be available. Programs funded in whole or in part through intergovernmental aid face more sharp cuts or even curtailment as funding declines or ceases. Program cuts, efficiency, priority setting, strategic planning, and "entrepreneurial thinking" are relatively new concerns in public administration — in degree, at least — arising out of the very real fiscal crunch enveloping all levels of government.

A third area of concern is control over grants-in-aid and other funding. A stark reality of intergovernmental relations is the existence of bureaucratic — and "interbureaucratic" — controls on much of the money flowing from one level to another. These controls raise questions about public accountability and about the ability of chief executives to coordinate spending effectively. Public administrators have considerable discretionary authority over public spending; this authority has affected the age-old issue of fiscal responsibility and accountability. A related concern is that, until the last decade, some government institutions (such as state legislatures) have lacked any real access to key decision makers or any impact on decisions regarding intergovernmental funding. For the most part, bureaucrats are in the driver's seat when it comes to categorical grant funding, still by far the largest part of intergovernmental aid. Whether the situation will stay that way is unclear, given new pressures on both intergovernmental aid and the administrators in charge of intergovernmental programs.

Other emerging patterns in contemporary IGR include some decline in the relative prominence of fiscal and grant-related issues and a corresponding rise in the importance of (among others) intergovernmental regulatory issues and the role of the courts in settling federalism-related questions. There is also growing recognition of a disturbing possibility that increased coordination among local governments — a worthwhile objective — may prove to be elusive in the long run.[47]

Finally, scholars in the field of federalism will, in all likelihood, continue their efforts to bring some intellectual order out of the seeming chaos that has occurred in IGR just since 1960. For example, there have been spirited debates about the *degree of centralization* appropriate as a remedy for bureaucratic control of categorical grants; also at issue is the question of just how functional or dysfunctional contemporary IGR has become.[48] It is no exaggeration to suggest that few areas of governance in this country are as complex or as challenging as this one has proved to be.

Summary

Federalism, in its original meaning, defined an arrangement of governments in which a central government and regional units each had some independent standing in the governmental system. Federalism has important constitutional, political, fiscal, and administrative dimensions. Our federal system has evolved through a variety of choices and changes and, today, intergovernmental relations are predominant on the federal scene.

In the past forty years, contemporary IGR has become highly complex. Contributing to the complexity are the present grants system, functional alliances among program administrators, and continuing tensions between political executives and functional specialists (and their respective clienteles). Bureaucratic activity at all levels is central to IGR and to fiscal federalism. This role of bureaucracy is also one reason why those seeking to reinvent government focus some attention on the various aspects of complexity within IGR.

Categorical grants are the most widely used form of fiscal assistance. Besides being used to achieve a wide range of programmatic purposes, these grants also have served to encourage a number of changes in the behavior of recipient governments (such as upgrading personnel systems, fostering planning, and promoting nondiscrimination). From the early 1960s to the late 1980s, categorical grants of both project and formula types were increasingly used to promote explicitly national purposes.

That led to considerable administrative complexity. Political and administrative choices made early in the history of cash grants set a precedent for "single state agency" relationships with national agencies in charge of a given grant program. A sequence of events was thus set in motion that led to the creation of self-governing guilds (also called vertical functional autocracies) and picket- or bamboo-fence federalism. These allied interests gradually consolidated control over grant programs, causing a political reaction that sparked a continuing search for ways to control those guilds. Coordination is increasingly difficult to achieve, however, given the proliferation of politically potent government units and of both horizontal and vertical linkages among them.

Grant reform has occurred in several ways. Fiscal reforms included the use of general revenue sharing and block grants (though neither has ever approached categorical grants in scope or funding). Since the presidency of Ronald Reagan, block grants have assumed new importance. Administrative reforms have taken the form of either decentralization (in particular, through increased citizen participation) or efforts to improve coordination and management of the grants system. Improved information and communication have also been stressed.

Issues to be dealt with in the immediate future include intergovernmental deregulation, unfunded mandates, and changes in the extent of bureaucratic autonomy at all levels of government. Also important will be questions of continuing fiscal constraints facing government across the board, IGR-related policy directions of the current administration, and the challenge of maintaining governmental accountability in the federal system. Continued complexity in intergovernmental relations is a certainty.

KEY TERMS AND CONCEPTS

federalism	project grants
intergovernmental relations (IGR)	categorical grants
unfunded mandates	Medicaid
preemptions	gubernatorial
fiscal federalism	single state agency requirement
fiscal mismatch	vertical functional autocracies
grants-in-aid	picket-fence federalism
externalities	block grants
formula grants	regulatory federalism

SUGGESTED READING

Anton, Thomas J. *American Federalism and Public Policy: How the System Works.* Philadelphia: Temple University Press, 1989.

Conlan, Timothy J. *New Federalism: Intergovernmental Reform from Nixon to Reagan.* Washington, D.C.: The Brookings Institution, 1988.

————. *From New Federalism to Devolution: Twenty-Five Years of Intergovernmental Reform.* Washington D.C.: The Brookings Institution, 1998.

Cook, Brian J. *Bureaucracy and Self-Government.* Baltimore: Johns Hopkins University Press, 1996.

Elazar, Daniel J. *American Federalism: A View from the States.* 3rd ed. New York: Harper & Row, 1984.

Howitt, Arnold M. *Managing Federalism: Studies in Intergovernmental Relations.* Washington, D.C.: Congressional Quarterly Press, 1984.

Kettl, Donald F. *The Regulation of American Federalism* (paperback text edition). Baltimore: Johns Hopkins University Press, 1987.

Ostrom, Vincent. *The Meaning of American Federalism: Constituting a Self-Governing Society.* San Francisco: ICS Press, 1991.

O'Toole, Laurence J., ed. *American Intergovernmental Relations: Foundations, Perspectives, and Issues.* 3rd ed. Washington, D.C.: Congressional Quarterly Press, 2000.

Peterson, Paul E. *The Price of Federalism.* Washington, D.C.: The Brookings Institution, 1995.

Peterson, Paul E., Barry G. Rabe, and Kenneth K. Wong. *When Federalism Works.* Washington, D.C.: The Brookings Institution, 1986.

Posner, Paul L. *The Politics of Unfunded Mandates: Whither Federalism?* Washington, D.C.: Georgetown University Press, 1998.

Riker, William H. *The Development of American Federalism.* Boston: Kluwer Academic Publishers, 1987.

Walker, David B. *The Rebirth of Federalism.* Chatham, N.J.: Chatham House, 1995.

Wright, Deil S. *Understanding Intergovernmental Relations.* 3rd ed. Monterey, Calif.: Brooks/Cole, 1988.

Wright, Deil S., and Harvey L. White, eds. *Federalism and Intergovernmental Relations.* Washington, D.C.: American Society for Public Administration, 1984.

ON-LINE RESOURCES:
Federalism and Intergovernmental Relations

Assessing the New Federalism Project

http://newfederalism.urban.org/

The Urban Institute's state-by-state multiyear research project provides public access to over 5,000 indicators of policies to analyze the devolution of responsibility for social programs from the federal government to the states, focusing primarily on health care, income security, job training, and social services.

Catalogue of Federal Domestic Assistance Programs

http://www.cfda.gov/public/cat-highlights.asp

Catalog contains descriptions of 1,424 assistance programs administered by fifty-seven federal agencies.

Center for the Study of Federalism (Temple University)

http://www.temple.edu/federalism

An interdisciplinary research and educational institute committed to the study of federal principles, institutions, and processes as practical ways to organize political power.

City and County Data Book

http://fisher.lib.virginia.edu/ccdb/

This resource provides Internet access to the electronic versions of the 1988 and 1994 County and City Data Books. The site allows visitors to create custom printouts and/or customized data subsets.

Council of State Governments (CSG)

http://www.statesnews.org/

State News is presented like a newspaper with extensive links to state and local government Web sites. There are also links to databases, regional offices of the CSG, and information about policy areas.

Federalism Research Group

http://rockinst.org/fedres.htm

The Rockefeller Institute of Government of the State University of New York at Albany investigates the management resources, capabilities, and problems of state government as they attempt to implement social programs.

Government on Line

http://www.gol.org/

Information service linking state and local government and the information technology industry. Provides government executives with summary information about successful programs and the ability to learn more in specific areas of interest.

International City/County Management Association (ICMA)

http://www.icma.org/othersites/othersites.cfm/

Professional and educational organization representing appointed managers and administrators of local governments throughout the world.

Library of Congress State and Local Government Home Page

http://lcweb.loc.gov/global/state/stategov.html

Authoritative site with links to all states, research institutes, and comprehensive multistate and local association Web sites.

National Association of Counties (NACo)

http://www.naco.org/counties/index.cfm/

Created in 1935, NACo represents the nation's 3,066 counties in Washington. NACo's membership totals over 1,800 counties, representing over 75 percent of the nation's population. Databases and linked Web sites provide insights on how government programs are actually working at the local level.

National Conference of State Legislatures (NCSL)

http://lcweb.loc.gov/global/state/stategov.html

NCSL is a bipartisan organization dedicated to serving the lawmakers and staffs of the nation's states, commonwealths, and territories. It is a source for research, publications, consulting services, meetings, and seminars, as well as the national conduit for lawmakers to communicate with one another and share ideas.

National Governors Association (NGA)

http://www.nga.org

The NGA Web site has useful information about the passage and implementation of federal-state policies such as welfare reform, including links to federal agencies, best practices, research findings, state information, and home pages of the fifty states.

National League of Cities (NLC)

http://www.nlc.org

The mission of the NLC is to strengthen and promote cities as centers of opportunity, leadership, and governance. NLC was established in 1924 by and for reform-minded state municipal leagues. NLC now represents 49 leagues, more than 1,500 member cities, and, through the membership of the state municipal leagues, more than 18,000 cities and towns of all sizes.

State and Local Gateway

http://www.statelocal.gov/

An interagency project in cooperation with the National Partnership for Reinventing Government; links to information on reinvention initiatives in the states by policy areas such as education, health, transportation, and workfare development.

U.S. Conference of Mayors (USCM)

http://www.usmayors.org/uscm/home.html

The officials nonpartisan organization of cities with populations of 30,000 or over. There are about 1,050 such cities and each is represented by a chief elected official, the mayor. The USCM Web site contains This Week with Mayors, best practices, newspaper, meet the mayors section, and Washington updates.

For further information on federalism and intergovernmental relations see: Bedford/St. Martin's Home Page

http://www.bedfordstmartins.com

PART II

Managing and Leading Public Organizations

As public organizations are being asked to do more with fewer resources, greater attention has been focused on better understanding of internal dynamics, leadership, and behavior within organizations. This section deals with efforts to improve management, addressing the related subjects of organization theory and behavior, decision making, ethics, and administrative leadership. Chapter 5 reviews the evolution of organization theory, beginning with late nineteenth-century writings and following developments in theory and practice up to the present. Organization theory has moved from a formalistic, relatively mechanistic view of organizations to more diverse and comprehensive concepts, reflecting increasingly complex awareness of human behavior and the need for everyone in an organization to learn as they respond to their environments. In addition, important internal dynamics of organization are discussed, including communication, coordination, centralization and decentralization, line and staff functions, "tall" and "flat" hierarchies, and alternative forms of organization structure.

Chapter 6 examines administrative decision making — the formal and informal considerations that enter into decision processes and how decision makers deal with them. Ethics, the meaning of *rationality*, alternatives to the rational approach, the impact of personal and organizational goals, and other influences in the decisional environment are reviewed.

Chapter 7 focuses on chief executives and their leadership of bureaucracies at national, state, and local levels, and analyzes administrative leadership tasks within organizations. Similarities and differences are given careful attention, particularly with regard to policy development, implementation, changing leadership styles, and coping with declining resources. In addition, we summarize the characteristics and behaviors that facilitate effective leadership in public agencies. How chief executives interact with those in administrative agencies, what defines a good leader, and how their actions affect bureaucratic operations are also discussed.

Chapter 5

Organizational Theory

As a citizen interested in government and as a former legislator, I had long believed that too many governmental programs are botched because they are started in haste without adequate planning or establishment of goals. Too often they never really attack the targeted problems.

Jimmy Carter, then governor of Georgia, to the
National Governors Conference, June 1974

Organization theory deals with the formal structure, internal workings, and external environment of complex human behavior within organizations. As a field spanning several disciplines, it prescribes how work and workers ought to be organized and attempts to explain the actual consequences of organizational behavior (including individual behavior) on work done and on the organization itself.

The formal study of organizations — which spans the fields of business administration, sociology, political science, economics, and psychology, as well as public administration — has evolved over nearly a century. Assumptions about work and workers in an organizational setting have changed; numerous (and often contradictory) hypotheses and research findings have emerged about what motivates workers and how different incentives affect various tasks, employees, and situations; and a variety of views has existed regarding the reciprocal impacts of organizations and the environments in which they operate. Some of the following discussion will be familiar to anyone who has worked in an organization — which, in our society, means most of us.

Categorizing major organization theories is not easy. On one level, they can be distinguished according to whether they concentrate on the needs, objectives, methods, problems and values of management; on the personal and social needs and values of workers within organizations; or on the attempts by organizations to adapt to their social, political, or economic environments. On another level, it is possible to identify numerous specific theories, each with its own principal assumptions and emphases. Some of these theories overlap to an extent, sharing certain values and viewpoints while differing significantly in other respects. We will examine four major areas of organization theory: (1) formal theories, (2) the human relations school, (3) organizational humanism, and (4) modern organization theory.

Formal Theories of Organization

hierarchy a characteristic of formal bureaucratic organizations; a clear vertical "chain of command" in which each unit is subordinate to the one above it and superior to the one below it; one of the most common features of governmental and other bureaucratic organizations.

Although formal organization theory, as we understand it, originated in the late nineteenth century, some formative thinking on the subject dates back many centuries. In fact, such concepts of organization were largely derived from the highly structured arrangements of military forces and from rigidly structured ecclesiastical organizations. Most notably, the idea of a **hierarchy** (chain of command) — found in the great majority of contemporary organizations — springs from ancient military and religious roots. Some other features of formal theory (such as the need for control and for defining certain set procedures or "rituals") also originated in very early organizations. The most prominent model of bureaucracy as an explicit form of social organization, however, was formulated by German sociologist Max Weber (1864–1920) late in the nineteenth century. Although widely known in Europe during the early twentieth century, Weber's work was not translated into English until the 1940s.

Max Weber and the Bureaucratic Model

Weber's model was intended to identify the components of a well-structured government bureaucracy. He prescribed the following key elements:

1. *Division of labor and functional specialization* — work is divided according to type and purpose, with clear areas of jurisdiction marked out for each working unit and an emphasis on elimination of overlapping and duplication of functions;
2. *Hierarchy* — a clear vertical chain of command in which each unit is subordinate to the one above it and superior to the one below it;
3. *Formal framework of rules and procedures* — designed to ensure stability, predictability, and impersonality in bureaucratic operations (and thus equal treatment for all who deal with the organization), as well as reliability of performance;
4. *Maintenance of files and other records* — to ensure that actions taken are both appropriate to the situation and consistent with past actions in similar circumstances; and
5. *Professionalization* — employees are (a) appointed (not elected) on the basis of their qualifications and job-related skills, (b) full-time and

career-oriented civil service, and (c) paid a regular salary and provided with benefits such as health insurance and a retirement pension.[1]

In addition to these explicit components, Weber obviously intended a government bureaucracy of the type just described to be endowed with sufficient *legal* and *political* authority to function adequately. His model of bureaucracy is, in fact, based on both legal and *rational* authority[2] derived from a fixed central point in the political process and is assumed to function under that authority. It is important to understand that Weber's presentation should be viewed in the context of the late nineteenth century and the rampant **patronage** systems that existed at the time. His model proposed a solution to the existing situation and a blueprint for professional and effectively managed organization.

This model of bureaucracy represented an effort by Weber both to describe and prescribe what he saw as the *ideal* form of organization then emerging in early twentieth-century Europe. It is clearly a formalistic model and lacks dimensions later recognized as important, such as informal lines of authority, internal communication, customer feedback, concern for individual behavior, and motivation in the bureaucracy. Also, Weber himself indicated that the model was not meant to apply to all conceivable organizational situations. It represented only a broad framework rather than an all-encompassing model, complete in every detail. Despite these limitations, however, the Weberian model was the first effort to define systematically the dimensions of this new form of social organization and to prescribe or explain its operations in abstract and theoretical terms.

One of the central goals of Weber's model was to make possible an optimum degree of *control* in an organization. The quest for control lay at the heart of virtually every element of the model. In particular, the *formalism* suggested by rules, procedures, and files, along with the exercise of authority through a hierarchy, point to Weber's overriding concern for organizations that would be both smoothly functioning and effectively managed. In this **formal theory of organization** and in others proposed at the time, to the extent that management concerns are emphasized, the ultimate goal is control from the top down over *all* organizational activities and needs. Consequently, in order to facilitate control, there is a preoccupation with encouraging *uniformity* rather than permitting diversity — in values as well as behavior — within the organization. In today's complex, diverse, and regulated society, this generalization has important political, as well as managerial, applications and implications, especially for well-educated "knowledge workers" in large bureaucracies.

Nonetheless, a comparison of the Weberian model to contemporary American public administration illustrates the model's attractiveness as a yardstick against which to measure actual administrative arrangements and the limitations on its applicability to very different times and circumstances. American public bureaucracies have operated within a formal framework of vertical hierarchy; extensive division of labor and specialization; specific rules, procedures, and

patronage selection of public officials on the basis of political loyalty rather than merit, objective examination, or professional competence.

formal theory of organization stresses formal, structural arrangements within organizations, and "correct" or "scientific" methods to be followed in order to achieve the highest degree of organizational efficiency; examples include Weber's theory of bureaucracy and Taylor's "scientific management" approach.

routines; and a high degree of professionalization, complete with extensive merit systems, career emphases, and salary and fringe benefits. Yet, in spite of these similarities, there are equally prominent differences.

First, although the formal bureaucratic structure is hierarchical, those within that hierarchy respond to commands, incentives, and decisions that arise from outside it. Thus, the hierarchy is often only one of the chains of command active in the bureaucracy (a reflection of our political diversity).

Second, Weber's division of labor and specialization were designed to reduce **functional overlap** among bureaucratic units, so that any functions performed by a given entity were the responsibility of *only* that entity; in Weber's view, this was in the best interests of efficient operation. In contrast, American bureaucracy is shot through with functional overlap in spite of its specialization. This reflects (among other things) overlapping political jurisdictions and societal interests. For example, an occupational retraining program could logically be placed under the authority of either the Department of Labor (since the program is vocationally focused) or of Education (since it emphasizes training, a DOE responsibility in programs not related to labor). Furthermore, functional overlap is practically guaranteed in a federal system in which separate governments organize their bureaucracies independently. (As described in Chapter 4, managing intergovernmental programs is especially challenging.)

Third, the kind of professionalization foreseen by Weber has been only partially achieved in American bureaucracy; this has been due in part to matters of definition. Weber's European "professionals" were so defined because they were making the bureaucracy their lifelong careers, were competent to perform the tasks for which they were hired, and were paid in the manner in which other professionals were paid. American bureaucracy differs from this European ideal in two respects. First, there is a wide variety of personnel systems, ranging from the fully developed **merit system** in which job-related competence is the most important qualification for employment, to the most open, deliberate patronage system in which political loyalty and connections are the major criteria in personnel decisions. The U.S. Civil Service, several states (such as Minnesota, California, and Wisconsin), and many cities headed by city managers make personnel decisions largely on a merit basis. Patronage is found in many other states, as well as in numerous urban and rural governments throughout the country — sometimes even when a merit system appears to be in operation.

The second departure from the Weberian ideal of professionalism is that more and more specialized professions in the private sector — law, medicine, engineering, social and physical sciences, and business management — are represented among government employees. Whereas Weber seemed to envision a *professional bureaucrat,* the American experience has produced *bureaucratic professionals* — specialists trained in various private-sector professions who find careers in the public service. Weber's conception appears to be narrower than the American reality with regard to the scope and diversity of skills of bureaucrats, as well as the variety of their professional loyalties.

---

functional overlap a phenomenon of contemporary American bureaucracy whereby functions performed by one bureaucratic entity may also be performed by another; conflicts with Weber's notions of division of labor and specialization.

---

merit system a system of selection (and, ideally, evaluation) of administrative officials on the basis of job-related competence, as measured by examinations and professional competence.

A further implication of professionalization is that employees of a Weberian bureaucracy would be judged by their *continuing* competence in their jobs. In this regard, American *merit systems* also diverge from Weber's model. In the majority of cases, those who secure a merit position need only to serve a probationary period (usually six to eighteen months) before earning job security. How rapidly one rises through the ranks or how easily one can transfer to a new position may well be affected by periodic evaluations of competence, but it is still the exception rather than the rule to find a public employee dismissed solely for incompetence on the job.

Finally, Weber placed considerable emphasis on career employment. It is only since 1955, however, that the national government and some states and localities have attempted to structure their personnel systems so as to foster a career emphasis as an integral part of public-sector employment (see Chapter 8).

In summary, even though American public administration has emulated many elements of Weber's model, the applicability of that model in the United States is limited in important respects. The fundamental strength of Weber's model is that it defined and described bureaucracy as a structure of social organization and as a means of promoting hierarchical control, and that it paved the way for further theory, explanation, and prescription regarding large and complex organizations.

FREDERICK WINSLOW TAYLOR AND "SCIENTIFIC MANAGEMENT"

In contrast to Weber's ideal model, the United States bureaucracy was not designed for efficiency, but for accountability and equity, with divided lines of authority and limited discretionary power. Such deliberate inefficiency was largely dictated by the constitution and the existing political culture. The development of Frederick W. Taylor's (1856–1915) theory of **scientific management**[3] marked the beginning of the managerial tradition in organization theory. Taylor's theory was designed to assist private-sector management in adapting production practices to the needs of an emerging industrial economy in the early 1900s. Prior to Taylor's research, there was little systematic organization of work in private industry; his writings became the principal source of ideas on the subject. Unlike Weber, Taylor focused on private industry and prescribed a "science" of management that incorporated specific steps and procedures for implementation. (Weber's more abstract model of bureaucracy did not specify actual operations.) Both men, however, emphasized formal structure and rules, dealt hardly at all with customers or with employees' working environment, and directly or indirectly equated the control needs of those at the top of the hierarchy with the needs of the organization as a whole.

The theory of scientific management rested on four underlying values. The first was *efficiency* in production, which involved obtaining the maximum benefit or gain possible from a given investment of resources. The second was *rationality*

scientific management a formal theory of organization developed by Frederick Winslow Taylor in the early 1900s; concerned with achieving efficiency in production, rational work procedures, maximum productivity, and profit; focused on management's responsibilities and on "scientifically" developed work procedures, based on "time and motion" studies.

in work procedures, which addressed the arrangement of work in the most direct relationship to objectives. The third was *productivity*, which meant maintaining the highest production levels possible. The fourth was *profit*, which Taylor conceived of as the ultimate objective of everyone within the organization. These values formed the framework within which the remainder of his theory was applied.

Taylor made several other critical assumptions. He viewed organizational authority as *highly centralized* at top management levels. He assumed a hierarchy of midlevel managers and supervisors through which top management conveyed orders to those below. And he thought that, at each level of the organization, responsibility and authority were fixed at a central point. Taylor also believed that there was only "one best way" to perform a particular task, and that, through scientific research, that method could be discovered and applied. Taylor maintained that the ideal method for performing a certain task could be taught to workers responsible for that task and that selection of workers for their capabilities would be the most rational way to achieve the organization's overall objectives.

According to Taylor, management needed to do three things to increase productivity (and thus profits). First, the most efficient tools and procedures had to be developed. Here, Taylor relied on so-called *time-and-motion studies*, which concentrated on identifying the most economical set of physical movements associated with each step of a work process. Taylor was a pioneer in such studies, although he was only one of a number of researchers in this area.[4] Second, in teaching the new techniques to workers, emphasis was to be placed on *standardizing procedures* in order to enable workers to discharge their responsibilities routinely yet efficiently. Third, criteria that emphasized *task-related capabilities* needed to be developed for, and applied to, the worker selection process. Note, again, that top management was to be entirely responsible for implementing this "science" of administration.

As with any model or theory, there were shortcomings in the application of scientific management to industry and, later, to government. A theoretical shortcoming that received considerable attention from later scholars was that, under scientific management, workers were seen as mere cogs in the industrial machine, with motives and incentives that were purely financial and with no other needs on or off the job that were worthy of incorporation into the theory. An important alternative perspective on Taylor and his work has been advanced by Hindy Lauer Schachter, who argues that Taylorism included important elements of what later emerged as both human relations and organizational humanism.[5] (Although Taylor also viewed management in rather one-dimensional terms, critiques of his theory — and of Weber's — have concentrated on the consequences of viewing workers too narrowly.)

Taylor's theory encountered significant difficulties when American industry tried to implement it. Taylor had assumed that management and labor would share the same objectives and that there would be no conflict or disagreement over organizing to achieve them. He believed that management would naturally seek efficiency, rationality, and productivity in order to maximize profits. Taylor thought that labor would support those same goals because, at the time, laborers were paid by the piece (that is, they received a certain sum for each item produced) and would earn more money as production increased. Thus, Taylor projected a united labor–management interest in his science of management. The problem was that this unity of interest was assumed without accounting for how it might be affected by the law of supply and demand. Taylor projected that demand for a product would always keep pace with supply and, thus, that maximum productivity would always be a goal of both management and workers. In practice, however, production levels sometimes exceeded market demand for a product. When this occurred, management laid off some workers, retaining only the number needed on the job for each to maintain maximum productivity without causing total output to exceed demand. This touched off vigorous opposition by workers who were "downsized" and by their labor unions (then in their infancy). Most industrial managers had enough power to withstand labor's reaction, but Taylor's theory came under increasing criticism.

Nevertheless, Taylor and his disciples had inaugurated a new direction in organization theory and management practice. Scientific management took hold not only in the private sector but also in public administration. For a time, the values of efficiency, rationality, and productivity were virtually official doctrine in the national bureaucracy; eventually, an important body of theory in public administration evolved largely from Taylor's work. Scientific management has had a lasting influence on organization theory. It has directly shaped the values and structures in numerous private and public enterprises, and has indirectly influenced organization theory as other theories either followed from it or developed in reaction to it. In particular, scientific management is generally regarded as having had tangible impact on the *principles approach* to public administration.

THE "PRINCIPLES" AND OTHER EARLY WRITINGS

Leonard D. White, in his *Introduction to the Study of Public Administration* (1926), was clearly influenced by Taylor in asserting that management procedures could be studied scientifically to discover the best method of operation. This was not only White's view — it was commonly held by most scholars of public administration of that period. Together with the politics–administration dichotomy, the quest for economy and efficiency, and the notion of public administration as a value-free science, the scientific study of management practices was at the core of public administration theory.

Other elements of Taylorism appeared in the *principles of administration* approach, which became prominent in the 1930s. The very effort to discover principles was itself derived from the scientific approach to management, and individual principles reflected Taylor's continuing influence on the study of organizations, both public and private. The writings of Henri Fayol, F.W.

Willoughby, and the team of Luther Gulick and Lyndall Urwick[6] set forth the essential themes of the principles approach. The major themes were as follows:

1. *Unity of command* — direction by a single individual at each level of an organization and at the top of the structure;
2. *Hierarchy* — the vertical ordering of superior-subordinate relations in an organization, with a clearly defined chain of command;
3. *Functional specialization* — division of labor and subject-matter specialization as a main contributor to work efficiency;
4. *Narrow span of control* — each supervisor having responsibility for the activities of a limited number of subordinates;
5. *Authority parallel with responsibility* — each responsible official endowed with the authority necessary to direct operations in the particular organizational unit; and
6. *Rational organizational arrangement* — plan the organization according to function or purpose, geographic area, process performed, or people served (clientele).[7]

As we saw in Chapter 1, the principles were increasingly criticized as being inconsistent and inapplicable and eventually became outdated by developments in both theory and practice. These developments were not limited to public administration. In particular, new approaches in psychology and sociology focused attention on those who made up the workforce of an organization. The **human relations** approach constituted the next major phase in the evolution of organization theory and signaled the advent of the informal tradition. Those who embraced this approach did so because they were increasingly dissatisfied with one or more dimensions of scientific management. This triggered an intense controversy over the nature of organizations and over what aspects of organization were most appropriate as building blocks for successful management. In a sense, that controversy, begun in the late 1920s and early 1930s, continues to the present day.

human relations
theories of organization that stress workers' non-economic needs and motivations on the job, seek to identify these needs and how to satisfy them, and focus on working conditions and social interactions among workers.

The Human Relations School

The informal and formal traditions differ from each other in both major assumptions and principal research directions. Whereas formal theories assumed that workers were rational in their actions and motivations and sought to maximize their gains in economic terms, informal theories looked beyond economic motivations and viewed workers as having noneconomic needs on the job and as being motivated (at least potentially) through satisfaction of those needs. Thus, researchers in the informal school sought to determine which noneconomic factors in the work situation, broadly defined, might have impact — and what kinds of impact — on workers and their performance.

THE HAWTHORNE STUDIES

The first major studies of the human relations approach were conducted at the Western Electric plant in Hawthorne, Illinois, between 1927 and 1932.[8] Elton Mayo and his associates at the Harvard Business School began the study in order to measure the effects of worker fatigue on production. But it was expanded over a period of five years and resulted in a set of findings about productivity and other job-related factors not based solely on economic reward. Specifically, the study centered on how workers reacted to actions of management, how variations in physical working conditions affected output, and how social interactions among workers affected their job performance. It is significant that, initially, Mayo did not intend to examine all these relationships; an investigation of them became necessary after early results of the study did not turn out as expected.

In one experiment, male workers making parts of telephone switches were paid by the piece and, hence, according to Taylor's theory, were expected to try to maximize their production output. To the surprise of both Mayo and the management of Western Electric, production stabilized well below the expected level, primarily because of the workers' reluctance to increase it beyond a certain point. This appeared to be a result of their fear of layoffs, and nothing management did or said could change their attitude — or their level of productivity. This turn of events was totally unexpected and was not explained by anything in the theory of scientific management.

Another experiment involved varying the physical surroundings of a group of female telephone-relay assemblers and observing changes in output. It was predicted that improvements in working conditions would lead to greater output and that changes for the worse would cause a drop in productivity. This same experiment was also conducted with the men making switches. The results, however, did not conform to expectations on two counts. First, the women's production levels rose after each change in working conditions, regardless of whether conditions had been improved (better lighting, bigger working area, more frequent rest breaks) or worsened. Apparently, the women were responding to the attention they received as the subjects of an experiment. (Such a reaction has become known as the **Hawthorne or "halo" effect**.) More to the point, as long as management consistently paid attention to the women and their work, they seemed ready to produce at steadily higher levels. The second unexpected result was that the members of the male work group reacted entirely differently from the way that the women did. No matter what changes were made in working conditions, the men seemed to lag behind their previous level of productivity. These findings, which ran counter to the concepts of scientific management, suggested that a new theory was needed.

Mayo and his associates concluded that, within the formal organizational framework, there was an informal social substructure of groups and teams that tangibly influenced the behavior and motivations of the workers. Among the men, for example, there was pressure not to produce too much or too little and

Hawthorne or "halo" effect   tendency of those being observed to change their behavior to meet the expectations of researchers; named after a factory in Hawthorne, Illinois, where studies took place in the late 1920s and early 1930s.

not to get too closely tied to management.[9] There was also, quite clearly, pressure to conform to the group's production target level in preference to any levels set by management. Among both men and women, there was pressure to regard oneself as a team member and to react to management in those terms rather than strictly as an individual. This was very important in light of contrary assumptions made about workers by Taylor and other formal theorists. The work of the Mayo researchers also revealed the importance of noneconomic incentives and motivations on the job, in contrast to the "rational economic" assumptions of formal theorists.[10]

In sum, the Hawthorne studies opened the way to investigation of factors other than formal organizational structure and operations, and established the importance of social structure and worker interaction. These studies became the basis for the human relations school of organization theory, which stressed the social and psychological dimensions of organizations, particularly the satisfactions workers derived from the work situation and effective motivating forces on the job.

LEADERSHIP IN ORGANIZATIONS

A major emphasis in the human relations school during the 1930s was the study of organizational leadership, and how — if at all — leadership affected workers' behavior and the organization's general performance. Two of the most influential scholars in the field were Chester Barnard and Kurt Lewin. Barnard examined the nature of authority within organizations, concentrating on leader–follower interaction; Lewin studied different leadership styles and their effects on subordinates.

Chester Barnard spent his professional life in executive positions in the private sector (e.g., as president of the New Jersey Bell Telephone Company). Writing on the basis of that experience, he theorized that leadership could not be exercised by those at the top of a hierarchy solely at their discretion. Rather, leadership's effectiveness depended largely on the willingness of others (i.e., followers) to accept and respond to it. Barnard maintained that workers had a social-psychological **zone of acceptance** (or "zone of indifference").[11] His main point was that followers can greatly influence the nature and effectiveness of leadership over them. (This perspective is linked to the rise of teams, quality circles, group rewards, and other types of empowered work groups, treated later in this chapter.) Whatever the amount of legal, political, or organizational authority leaders possess, their *operating* authority is granted, in effect, by followers.

zone of acceptance refers to the extent to which a follower is willing to be led and to obey the leader's commands or directives; concept originally proposed by Chester Barnard, who wrote about leadership in the 1930s.

Barnard's view of leadership also included the idea that leaders and followers each had something sought by the other and could, in effect, bargain to their mutual advantage. Organization leaders could offer appropriate incentives to workers, and workers could contribute to the welfare of the organization through improved job performance. This early version of what has come to be known as exchange theory[12] reflected Barnard's opinion that coercive leadership relying on negative incentives, such as punishments or wage reductions, was less effective than supportive leadership offering positive inducements. In other words, Barnard thought that, as a motivator, the carrot was more effective than the stick.

Kurt Lewin, founder of the Group Dynamics School at the University of Iowa in the 1930s, conducted a series of experiments designed to test the effects of different types of leaders on the work output and group atmosphere of ten-year-old boys.[13] Lewin and his associates trained adult leaders in three leadership styles and then rotated the different leaders among groups of boys who were making masks. The leadership styles were (1) *authoritarian* — a threatening, intimidating, coercive leader who permitted no "nonsense" in the work group (thus suppressing the natural high-spiritedness of young boys), who specialized in finding fault with individual workers, and who resorted to scapegoating when things went wrong; (2) *laissez-faire* (hands-off) — a distant, nonthreatening leader who gave no direction, said nothing concerning cooperation among the workers or the need to keep on working, and gave no encouragement to the boys; and (3) *democratic* — a leader who stressed the job "we" had to do, maintained a relaxed and informal atmosphere, was very positive and supportive, encouraged the boys to do their best, lavished praise for work well done, and encouraged those who were more proficient at mask making to assist those who were still having some difficulty.

To the extent that it is possible to draw firm conclusions from a study in which ten-year-old boys were the subjects, the principal findings in the Iowa experiments were revealing. First, productivity was greatest under the authoritarian leader, with the democratic leader second, and the laissez-faire leader third. The only exception to this pattern was during "leader-out" periods, during which the leader left the group on its own. In those periods, groups under democratic leadership maintained the highest levels of production, and the production of authoritarian-led groups fell off sharply (as expected) without the coercive motivation of the authoritarian leader. Second, interaction among group members and levels of group satisfaction with the work experience varied dramatically according to the style of leadership. Democratic leadership was clearly the most conducive to interpersonal cooperation, group integration, and worker satisfaction. Authoritarian leadership led to considerable hostility among some group members, apathy on the part of others, and very high tensions. Laissez-faire leadership had the smallest impact on worker behavior and attitudes.

As in all such research, there are limitations on the findings of these experiments, chief among them the extent to which these findings can be applied to other, more complex situations. Many tasks in business, industry, and government are more complicated than making masks, and the personal and psychological needs of adults differ from those of ten-year-old boys. Hierarchical organizations with multiple layers of leaders and followers present different problems of group motivation, and a workforce of adults that is socially, economically, ethnically, and professionally diverse is far more difficult to deal with than a homogeneous group of boys.

Yet the findings of this experiment and the conceptions suggested by Barnard both pointed to the possible importance of leadership as another variable in getting the most and the best out of workers. Like the concern for working conditions and social interaction, this represented a fertile new field of inquiry, with some reason to think that "better leadership" might well help to make a better organization (see Chapter 7). That the Iowa results may not be universally applicable does not, by any means, reduce their significance in the study of organizations.

CRITIQUES OF THE HUMAN RELATIONS SCHOOL

More recent scholars have devoted some attention to shortcomings in the human relations school of organization theory. The principal criticisms have revolved around three points. The first and most commonly noted charge is that this theory fails to take into account the potential for conflict between workers and managers.[14] Critics have pointed out that, although "good human relations" are advanced as the remedy for just about any difficulty between employers and employees, it is not enough simply to make the worker feel important in situations that involve basic conflicts about conditions of employment, such as the extent of control, long-range goals, work methods, and specific task assignments. In this respect, human relations proponents and formal theorists were guilty of the same oversight — that is, neither approach seemed to acknowledge that work-related conflict was a real possibility that had to be dealt with.

Second, the human relations school seemed to discount almost entirely the effects of formal structure on the members of the organization. Also, the rational-economic incentives so much in favor with formal theorists were given little if any emphasis in these later formulations. This is not surprising since it was formal theory with which the human relations school was in sharpest conceptual disagreement. The human relations approach, after all, produced the first body of theory to take issue with the Weber–Taylor–Fayol–Gulick approach. Even so, there is some accuracy in such criticisms. Other studies confirmed that organizational structures, monetary incentives, and wage or salary differentials affected the amount of conflict and tension between labor and management.

Third, it has been argued that the kind and complexity of technologies employed in an organization are considerably more important in shaping informal social structure and human interaction than the factors that Mayo, Lewin, and others regarded as pivotal. Robert Blauner, in particular, made this point persuasively, stressing impersonal factors (i.e., technology) as crucial.[15] It is possible, however, that this does not really contradict the findings of human relations studies. Writing in the 1960s, Blauner was observing an organizational environment in which technology played a much bigger part than it had during the 1930s, when emphasis on human relations first emerged. Still, this view does suggest that, as factors in the work situation change, theories that previously were useful for analyzing organizations may have decreased applicability. In the 1990s, and at present, new technologies — such as database management, advanced fiber optics, videoconferencing, and data compression — are having an even greater impact in the workplace and are affecting on-the-job individual and group relationships.

These are not, however, the first critiques of the human relations approach. Another body of research, begun in the 1940s and 1950s, contributed a different perspective on the worker's place in the organization and on what satisfactions and motivations existed in the work situation. Known as organizational, or industrial, humanism, this approach was concerned with the organizational factors that contributed to the psychological and psychosocial health of the worker. In particular, it defined the worker's relationship to the work itself as an important variable in maintaining motivation and job satisfaction: this approach differed significantly from those that had emphasized worker–supervisor or worker–worker interactions. **Organizational humanism** marked a turning point, serving as something of a bridge between the human relations approach and what we refer to as modern organization theory.

Organizational Humanism

Organizational humanism was based on several assumptions that differed from those of both formal organization theory and the human relations school. The first was that work held some *intrinsic* interest that would itself serve to motivate the worker to perform it well. According to the second, individuals worked to satisfy both off-the-job and on-the-job needs and desires. This suggested that workers sought satisfactions in their work, and that achieving those satisfactions was a separate and distinct objective related to the most fundamental reasons for working. The third assumption was that work was a central life interest to the worker, not merely something to be tolerated or endured for *extrinsic* rewards.

A fourth assumption, following directly from the notion of the centrality of work and of on-the-job satisfactions, proved to be a harbinger of things to come in contemporary organization theory. It was assumed that management was better advised to promote positive motivation (through delegating responsibility, permitting discretion and creativity on the job, and involving the worker in important policy decisions affecting the work environment) than to conclude that workers were inherently uninterested in their work and would avoid doing it if possible. The latter view of workers was an implicit part of formal theories of organization, and even human relations scholars seemed to share it to some extent. Organizational humanists, however, assumed the opposite. They did so in light of their research findings, which showed that authoritarian management practices designed to control lazy, irresponsible employees resulted in unhappy and frustrated workers and poor work performance.

organizational humanism   a set of organization theories stressing that work holds intrinsic interest for the worker, that workers seek satisfaction in their work, that they want to work rather than avoid it, and that they can be motivated through systems of positive incentives (such as participation in decision making and public recognition for work well done).

Theory Y   model of
organizational behavior
that stresses self-motivation, participation, and
intrinsic (internal) job
rewards.

Theory X   model of
behavior within organiza-
tions that assumes that
workers need to be
motivated by extrinsic
(external) rewards or
sanctions (punishments).

Douglas McGregor, who was among the pioneers of organizational human-ism, argued that workers could be self-motivating from their own interest in the work and their own inclination to perform it.[16] McGregor's **Theory Y** was in sharp contrast to what he called **Theory X,** which maintained that workers were lazy, wanted to avoid work, and needed to be forced to do it; see Table 5–1 for summaries of Theories X and Y. Another major figure among organizational humanists was social psychologist Chris Argyris, whose view of work as a central life interest was fundamental to this approach.[17] Argyris also pointed out that the need of workers to identify with their work is another source of motivation to perform it well.

The writings of Rensis Likert emphasized employee participation in as many phases of management as possible, directed by a leader or leaders in the demo-cratic mold (which was consistent with Kurt Lewin's findings). And Frederick Herzberg, in a study of over two hundred accountants and engineers and some nonprofessional employees in a Pittsburgh firm, found that motivators such as salary, fringe benefits, good lighting, and adequate facilities served only to meet workers' minimum expectations, without producing real satisfaction on the job. What *did* yield personal satisfaction were such things as recognition for good job performance, opportunity to take initiative and exhibit creativity, and responsi-bility entrusted to individual workers and groups of workers. Because they were the most satisfying aspects of the jobs, these intangibles (according to Herzberg's

---

TABLE 5–1   Theory X and Theory Y: A Summary

Underlying Belief System: Theory X

1. Most work is distasteful for most people.
2. Most people prefer close and continuous direction.
3. Most people can exercise little or no creativity in solving organizational problems.
4. Motivation occurs mostly or only as a response to "bread-and-butter" issues — threat of punishment — and is strictly an individual matter.

Underlying Belief System: Theory Y

1. Most people can find work as natural as play, if conditions permit.
2. Most people prefer and can provide self-control in achieving organizational objectives.
3. Most people can exercise significant creativity in solving organizational problems.
4. Motivation often occurs in response to ego and social rewards, particularly under conditions of full employment, and motivation is often dependent upon groups.

SOURCE: Reproduced by permission of the publisher, F.E. Peacock Publishers, Inc., Itasca, Illinois. From Robert T. Golembiewski and Michael Cohen, eds., *People in Public Service: A Reader in Public Personnel Administration,* 1970 copyright, p. 380.

study) proved to be far better motivators than such tangible features as salary or fringe benefits.[18]

Some of the most important research in organizational humanism was done by Abraham Maslow. He wrote of "self-actualizing" workers who achieved the highest degree of self-fulfillment on the job through maximum use of their creative capacities and individual independence.[19] According to Maslow, the worker had a **hierarchy of needs,** in which each level had to be satisfied before the individual could go on to the next one (see Figure 5–1). The first level of the hierarchy included *physiological needs* such as food, shelter, and the basic means of survival. Next was minimum *job security*, in the form of a reasonable assurance (but not necessarily a guarantee) of continued employment. After these essentials came *social* needs, which included group acceptance both on and off the job, as well as positive and supportive interpersonal relationships. *Ego satisfaction* and *independence needs* represented the fourth level of Maslow's hierarchy; these were derived from accomplishments in one's work and public recognition of them. (A management practice of some importance in this regard is "public praise, private criticism" for an employee.) Finally, Maslow's highest level was *self-actualization* — feelings of personal fulfillment that resulted from independent, creative, and responsible job performance.

As the worker satisfied the needs of one level, he or she was seen as being further motivated to work toward satisfying the needs of the next higher level. Thus, Maslow placed his emphasis on interactions among the essential needs of the employee on and off the job, the work being done, the attitude of both management and employee toward work performance, and the relationships among employees in the work situation. In a sense, Maslow incorporated into a larger and more complex scheme those aspects of the human relations approach that centered on interpersonal interactions among workers. Like other formulations in organizational humanism, the hierarchy of needs assumed that worker

hierarchy of needs
a psychological concept formulated by Abraham Maslow holding that workers have different kinds of needs that must be satisfied in sequence — basic survival needs, job security, social needs, ego needs, and personal fulfillment in the job.

FIGURE 5–1   Maslow's Hierarchy of Needs

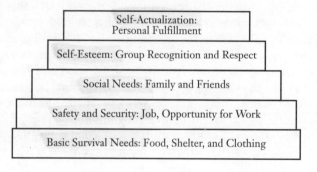

Self-Actualization:
Personal Fulfillment

Self-Esteem: Group Recognition and Respect

Social Needs: Family and Friends

Safety and Security: Job, Opportunity for Work

Basic Survival Needs: Food, Shelter, and Clothing

satisfaction could be affected by many factors in the organization, both close to the work situation itself and more distant from it. It should be noted, however, that Maslow did not assume that all employees would be motivated by the same essential needs and interactions.

Organizational humanism did not escape criticism, however. Robert Dubin found, for example, that fewer than 10 percent of the workers he studied in an industrial work group preferred the informality, job-centeredness, and independence on the job so highly valued in organizational humanism.[20] He suggested that different workers have widely varying needs and that no one approach could successfully meet all of them. Some workers needed strong direction from a leader, not independence; lack of direction caused them to be anxious and frustrated in their work. Some really did work for the money. Others simply did not get along with their coworkers; in these situations, an emphasis on group interaction would cause additional problems instead of solving existing ones. Still others did not especially want to participate in organizational decision making. Finally, there were those who sought to achieve certain needs without continuing to strive for higher-level satisfactions, thus posing motivation problems for managers relying on Maslow's formulations. (Maslow had acknowledged the possibility that such a situation could arise.) In sum, Dubin suggested that placing too much faith in "one-size-fits-all" organizational humanism should be avoided. The varied needs of employees had to be taken into account.

Another critique of organizational humanism came from two sociologists who questioned some assumptions about the need for workers to "self-actualize" in their jobs and to participate in organizational decision making. H. Roy Kaplan and Curt Tausky maintained that some of the assumptions of organizational humanism seem to have been grounded more in *ideological* beliefs than in empirical data and that, according to mounting evidence, they do not stand up to empirical research and testing.[21] According to Kaplan and Tausky, many organizational humanists mistakenly viewed employee motivations and satisfaction one-dimensionally and failed to recognize that, for some, work was not intrinsically interesting and fulfilling, creativity and independence were not valued, and monetary and other tangible benefits were of the first order of importance. Kaplan and Tausky's is a wide-ranging challenge that echoes, to some degree, Dubin's earlier critique.

A third, related criticism of organizational humanism was that the *kind* of work being done — routine or nonroutine, individualized or small-group or assembly-line — greatly affects the possibilities for motivating and satisfying workers. It often appears that the more routine the task, the greater the possibility for worker dissatisfaction (or, at least, for frustration and boredom). That phenomenon alone limits the applicability of organizational humanism.

On the other hand, there may be ways to combat this problem. One approach is to make more systematic the recognition for employees doing routinized tasks; the "employee of the month" award, complete with a prime parking space or the individual's photograph hung in the front office, is a familiar example of this. Another device is to alter the routine work situation, such as on an auto assembly line, and give workers the opportunity to form their own work groups, which then proceed to assemble a single automobile (or other product) "from the ground up." This may reduce on-the-job boredom and frustration while increasing the sense of participation in, and identity with, the service provided or the product being turned out — in the best tradition of organizational humanism. Such programs in auto factories are in wider use in parts of western Europe than in the United States; whether they could successfully be put into practice on this side of the Atlantic is not clear. Nevertheless, when examined separately from the kind of supervision or the backgrounds of the workers, the nature of particular tasks appears to be relevant in explaining the success or failure of organizational humanism in different work situations.

Modern Organization Theory

Modern organization theory differs from all previous approaches in four key respects. First, there is a deliberate effort to separate facts from values (assuming that is possible) and to study organization behavior empirically. Proponents of earlier approaches made quite a few assumptions that were grounded in the predominant economic or social values of the time, the perceived needs of management or labor, anecdotal evidence, or simple common sense. In contrast, modern organization theorists make every effort to minimize the impact of their own values on the phenomena under study.

Second, modern organization theorists make extensive use of empirical research methods unavailable even thirty years ago. These include the use of statistics, information retrieval systems, computer simulations, and quantitative techniques. Such methods permit more sophisticated insights into the operation of organizations and the needs of all "customers," not just those occupying official positions within government agencies.

Third, modern organization theory is constructed on an interdisciplinary basis; it draws on the varied approaches of sociology, organizational psychology, public administration, business, and information science. This greatly broadens the perspectives that can be developed concerning organizational behavior and the management of large, complex enterprises.

Fourth, modern organization theory attempts to generalize about organizations in terms sufficiently broad to be applicable to many different kinds of enterprises, including businesses, hospitals, universities, interest groups of all kinds, labor unions, voluntary agencies, and community-based organizations. In order to make such generalizations, it is necessary to use abstract formulations that can account for characteristics common to dissimilar organizations. Thus, features such as information generation and transmission, informal group processes, power relationships, environmental stability or turbulence, and decision making become the currency, so to speak, of generalized organization

modern organization theory a body of theory emphasizing empirical examination of organizational behavior, interdisciplinary research employing varied approaches, and attempts to arrive at generalizations applicable to many different kinds of organizations.

theory. We will examine briefly some of the major approaches that have been developed.

A pioneering study that ushered in the modern period of organization theory was conducted by John Pfiffner and Frank Sherwood.[22] They described organizations as being characterized by a series of interrelated networks superimposed on a formal structure. They also discussed, among other features, formal and informal communications systems, group dynamics, relative power of different parts of the organization, and decision processes. Theirs was the first comprehensive effort to integrate a variety of approaches, and it set the stage for a tremendous expansion in information about organizations and in specific approaches to studying them.

systems theory a theory of social organizations, holding that organizations — like biological organisms — may behave according to inputs from their environment, outputs resulting from organizational activity, and feedback leading to further inputs; also, that change in any one part of a group or organizational system affects all other parts.

A general approach shared by virtually all modern theories is the systems approach, or **systems theory.** In the context of modern social science, a system refers to "any organized collection of parts united by prescribed interactions and designed [at least ideally] for the accomplishment of a specific goal or general purpose."[23] This definition is equally applicable to an automobile engine, a hospital, the Department of the Interior, or a major industrial firm. (The last three, of course, are *social* systems that are subject to sociological, political, and psychological analyses of their functions and effectiveness.) For any biological, mechanical, or social entity, the systems approach generally assumes the existence of *inputs, some means of responding* to those inputs, *outputs, feedback* from the environment in response to system outputs, and *further inputs* into the system stemming from feedback (see Figure 5–2 for an application of this approach to politics). For an organization, inputs might consist of demands for some action, resources

FIGURE 5-2   A Simplified Model of a Political System

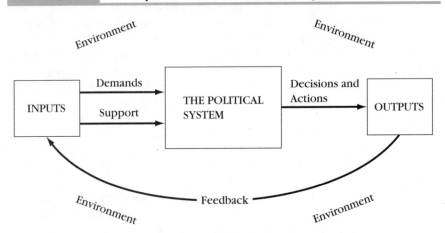

Source: From David Easton, *A Framework for Political Analysis.* Copyright © 1965, 1979 David Easton, reprinted with permission of the University of Chicago Press.

to pursue organizational objectives, underlying values of those outside the organization (and within it), and support for, or at least passive acceptance of, the organization's essential structure and goals. The means of responding to inputs would include all formal and informal decision mechanisms, judgments about how — or even whether — to respond to particular inputs, the history of the organization in similar circumstances, the organization's inclination (or lack of it) to follow precedent, and the availability of necessary resources. Outputs could refer to the rendering of services by the organization, symbolic steps taken to maintain favorable images of the organization, rules and regulations for which it has proper authority, and adjustments to demands for change or to reallocations of resources (by a legislature, for example).[24]

A crucial distinction that has been drawn regarding the application of systems theory to complex organizations is between *closed* and *open* systems.[25] **Closed systems** are essentially simple systems that have very few internal variables and relationships among them and little or no vulnerability to forces in the external environment. The primary objectives of those managing closed systems are the elimination of uncertainty, optimum use of resources that contribute to the overall result, and predictability of outcomes. Many formal (closed-system) theories focused on the concepts of *planning* or *controlling* behavior within organizations. Control, stability, and predictability were the cornerstones of these theories of organization, which may once have worked effectively in a relatively simple and predictable world, with few external factors impacting internal processes.

Open-systems theory proceeds from very different logical premises, which many scholars argue are more appropriate to the study of contemporary organizations (including public administrative agencies) than the premises that underlie closed-systems theory. Open systems are seen as highly complex, interdependent, and characterized by an *expectation of change* and uncertainty, internally and externally. This view is based on the fact that, in organizational theorist James Thompson's words, "a system contains more variables than we can comprehend at one time, [and] some of the variables are subject to influences we cannot control or predict."[26] As a result, the elimination of uncertainty is not considered a viable organizational objective, and the very nature of an organization is vastly different. Again, quoting Thompson:

> Approached as a natural [open] system, the complex organization is a set of interdependent parts which together make up a whole because each contributes something and receives something from the whole, which in turn is interdependent with some larger environment. Central to the natural-system approach is the concept of **homeostasis,** or self-stabilization, which spontaneously, or naturally, governs the necessary relationships among parts and activities and thereby keeps the system viable in the face of disturbances stemming from the environment.[27]

An obvious difference between closed and open systems is the way each allows external environments to impact the organization. Open-systems theory,

closed systems organizations that, in systems theory, have very few internal variables and relationships among those variables, and little or no vulnerability to forces in the external environment.

open-systems theory a theory of organization that views organizations not as simple, "closed" bureaucratic structures separate from their surroundings, but as highly complex entities, facing considerable uncertainty in their operations, and constantly interacting with their environment; assumes that organizational components will seek an "equilibrium" among the forces pressing on them and their own responses to those forces (see also **homeostasis**).

homeostasis a concept within open-systems theory referring to a process of spontaneous self-stabilization in the relationships among various parts and activities of a complex organization, thereby keeping it functioning in the face of disturbances in the organization's environment.

information theory
a modern theory of organization that views organizations as requiring constant input of information in order to continue functioning systematically and productively; assumes that a lack of information will lead to chaos or randomness in organizational operations.

game theory   a modern theory viewing organizational behavior in terms of competition among members for resources; based on distinctly mathematical assumptions and employing statistical data collection methods.

cybernetics   emphasizes organizational feedback that triggers appropriate adaptive responses throughout an organization; a thermostat operates on the same principle.

organizational change
a theory of organization that focuses on those characteristics of an organization that promote or hinder change; assumes that demands for change originate in the external environment, and that the organization should be in the best position to respond to them.

like some other modern theories, assumes considerable interdependence between organizations and their environments, with changes in the latter triggering adaptive responses within the organizations. Thus, a private firm will alter its marketing priorities in response to changing consumer preferences; a government agency can turn public criticism in its favor by providing for enlarged areas of citizen or employee participation in decision making. In such instances, the formal "boundaries" of the organization do not exclude others who are not formally members of it; in fact, those inside the organization are willing to tailor their activities to meet externally imposed needs or wants. Also, because open systems continuously interact with their environments, there is a constant need to seek *homeostasis* (or equilibrium) by balancing pressures and responses, demands and resources, and worker incentives and contributions (to use Barnard's formulation). All this is in the long-term interest of organizational stability, which permits continued functioning in the manner expected by leaders, workers, customers, and other external clienteles. In sum, open-systems theory — in sharp contrast to Weber's self-contained, closed bureaucracy — defines organizations as a great deal more than just formal structures, interpersonal relations, or worker involvement in the job. It treats organizations as whole beings, complex in their makeup and constant in their interactions with the surrounding environment.[28]

Other approaches that are based on the systems framework deal with organizations in a similarly broad-gauged fashion. For example, **information theory** is based on the view that organizations require information to prevent them from evolving to a state of chaos or randomness in their operations. **Game theory** addresses itself to competition among members of an organization for gains and losses, in terms of resources and access to resources; game theory is distinctly mathematical in orientation and methods. The concept of the self-regulating organization is advanced in **cybernetics**[29] (see Table 5–2).

Mention should also be made of some other approaches as well. **Organizational change** concentrates on the characteristics within an organization that promote or retard change in response to, or in anticipation of, changes in demands from the external environment, particularly with regard to needs and desires for the services produced by the organization.[30] In contrast, "organizational development" focuses on analysis of organizational problems and formulation of possible solutions.[31] It aims to increase the capacity of an organization to identify, analyze, and solve internal problems as a regular function within its ongoing routines, using a social-psychological approach somewhat reminiscent of human relations approaches. *Management according to task* conceives of organizations that do not follow a single structure or format from top to bottom.[32] Rather, depending on the set of tasks in a particular unit of the organization, that unit will be shaped structurally, socially, and technologically in the most appropriate manner. Thus, in a large and complex organization, there is likely to be considerable diversity in the arrangements of different units.

TABLE 5-2   Common Characteristics of Open Systems

Characteristic	Examples
1. Open systems import some form of energy from the external environment.	1. Cells receive oxygen from the bloodstream; the body takes in oxygen from the external world; organizations must draw renewed supplies of energy from other institutions or people or the material environment.
2. Open systems transform the energy available to them.	2. The body converts starch and sugar into heat and action; organizations create a new product or process materials or train people or provide a service.
3. Open systems "export" some product into the environment.	3. Biological organisms "export" carbon monoxide; the engineering firm constructs a bridge.
4. The pattern of activities of the energy exchange has a cyclical character: the product export furnishes the source of energy for the repetition of the cycle of activities.	4. Industry utilizes raw materials and human labor to turn out a product that is marketed, and the profit is used to obtain more raw materials and labor to perpetuate the cycle of activities; the voluntary organization provides satisfactions to its members, who are further motivated to continue their activities.
5. To survive, open systems must arrest the process of inevitable degeneration (*entropy*) by acquiring more energy from the external environment than they expend.	5. Prisoners on a starvation diet husband their energy to stretch their limited intake of food; organizations attempt to acquire a comfortable margin, or reserve, in their needed resources.
6. Open systems receive information and negative feedback from their environments and must simplify all such data by coding it into a limited number of recognizable categories.	6. Individuals receive instructions, warning signals, pleasurable feelings, and the like; a thermostat regulates room temperature by a feedback mechanism; an automated power plant supplies and distributes electricity also through feedback.
7. Open systems maintain some constancy in energy exchange, and in relations among their respective parts, so that the essential character of the system is preserved (even if it expands).	7. Body temperature remains the same, despite varying external conditions; human physiological functions are maintained evenly by endocrine glands.
8. Open systems tend toward differentiation and elaboration.	8. The human body evolves from very simple cells; organizations move toward greater specialization of functions (e.g., medicine).
9. As differentiation proceeds, it is offset by two processes that bring the system together for unified functioning: *integration* and *coordination*.	9. In small groups, integration is achieved through shared norms and values; in large organizations, coordination occurs through fixed controls, e.g., setting priorities, establishing routines, scheduling activities.
10. Open systems can reach a final state from differing initial conditions and by a variety of paths.	10. Some biological organisms can develop from a variety of initial forms.

Theory Z Japanese management system that stresses deliberative, "bottom-up" collective accountability and decision making, long-term planning, and closer relationships among managers and workers.

More recently, three other emphases have emerged in modern organization theory. One bears the label **Theory Z** and refers to patterns of organization and operation characteristic of many contemporary Japanese corporations (and some Japanese municipal governments).[33] Proponents of Theory Z assume that productivity is a problem of social or managerial organization; rather than by technological change, productivity can be improved by greater communication, feedback, and involvement of workers. Once the organization is committed to real involvement of employees in self-managed work teams, the key ingredients become trust, subtlety, and mutual support. The key values and characteristics of Theory Z are summarized in Table 5–3.

Theory Z is suggestive of some beliefs present in our earlier thinking and is decidedly different from others. For example, the involvement of workers is reminiscent of organizational humanism, and the positive consequences of workers having confidence in their managers echo the human relations approach. On the other hand, American theories put little or no emphasis on managers knowing the private lives of employees (the so-called holistic or all-encompassing approach), generalist career paths, or collective accountability. Nevertheless, the perceived successes of Japanese manufacturing firms have drawn international attention to extended and modified versions of Theory Z and to its extension, **total quality management (TQM).** The potential of these two theories for application in American public-sector organizations is being increasingly examined, and its application to public policy will be covered in more detail in Chapter 11.[34]

total quality management (TQM) a management approach that encourages organization-wide commitment, teamwork, and better quality of results by providing incentives to increase the success of the whole enterprise. Elements of TQM include commitment to meeting customer-driven quality standards; employee participation or empowerment to make decisions at the point closest to the customer; actions based on data, facts, outcome measures, results, and statistical analysis; commitment to process and continuous quality improvements; and organizational changes and teamwork to encourage implementation of the above elements.

TABLE 5-3   Values and Characteristics of Theory Z

Values	Characteristics
1. Emphasis on trust, subtlety, and intimacy	1. Permanent rather than short-term employment
2. Increased involvement of workers leads to increased productivity	2. Slow rather than rapid promotions
3. If workers have confidence in their managers and believe their organizations are just and equiable, they will function well in uncertain environments, take risks for their organizations, and make personal sacrifices	3. General rather than specialized career paths
	4. Collective decision making
	5. Collective accountability
	6. Decision making is "bottom up"
	7. Decisions are made slowly at each level, but final plans are rapidly implemented
4. Good managers know the private lives of their employees	

SOURCE: Adapted from Clyde McKee, "An Analysis of 'Theory Z': How It Is Used in Japan's Public Sector," paper delivered at the 1983 annual meeting of the American Political Science Association, Chicago, September 1983. Reprinted by permission of Clyde McKee, Trinity College, Hartford, Connecticut.

Another Japanese practice occasionally found in American public agencies is *quality circles.*[35] Not surprisingly, this practice reflects some of the same assumptions evident in Theory Z and TQM in public agencies. Quality circles are small groups of workers who meet on a regular basis to identify, analyze, and solve problems they experience in their jobs. Most range in size from three to fifteen and come from the same work area; thus, members are familiar with the problems identified by the group. "Through quality circles, workers serve as 'in-house' consultants on how to improve conditions and results. The objectives for the circles are to: (1) enhance the quality of goods and services produced by [their] members; (2) solve workplace problems; (3) develop a closer identification with the goals of the organization; and (4) improve communication between supervisors and workers."[36] In quality circles, as in Theory Z, there are echoes of earlier American organization theories (such as improving relationships between supervisors and workers). This is not surprising since the underlying principles of **systems analysis** and **statistical process control (SPC)** were taught by Americans recruited to assist the Japanese in rebuilding their war-torn economy following World War II.

Together with total quality management and process reengineering, "organizational learning" and "continuous learning theory" reflect significant change in the evolving discipline of organizational behavior. These theories suggest that all organizations, like individuals, have the capacity to learn and grow from interactions with their environments. Those committed to fostering continuous learning can create opportunities, policies, and resources to support individual growth and development. Organizational behavior can be transformed in the same way in which individuals learn from contacts with systems, processes, expanded training, and educational opportunities. **Learning organizations** are built on many of the same assumptions as those of earlier theories, including shared vision, consistent values, dedication to customer service, and competence. Vital elements that must be taught include systems thinking, personal mastery, shared visioning, team-based learning, and problem solving. Creating a *continuous learning environment* will become especially important as more service organizations, including governments, evolve into nonbureaucratic, boundaryless, decentralized, knowledge-based organizations in the twenty-first century.[37] (See Box 5–1, "Hampton, Virginia, Case Study.")

As useful as organizational theories are in explaining many aspects of human behavior within organizations, they cannot possibly encompass all the dynamics of actual operations in large and complex enterprises. They do, however, suggest a theoretical framework for understanding a wide range of internal variables related to organization design, communication, coordination, and effective leadership styles.

systems analysis an analytical technique designed to permit comprehensive investigation of the impacts within a given system of changing one or more elements of that system; in the context of analyzing policies, emphasizes overall objectives, surrounding environments, available resources, and system components.

statistical process control (SPC) the use of statistics to control critical processes within organizations; frequently used with TQM and Theory Z Japanese management techniques.

learning organizations a concept of organizations emphasizing the importance of encouraging new patterns of thinking and interaction within organizations to foster continuous learning and personal development; see On-Line Resources at end of chapter for sources.

BOX 5–1   ETHICAL AND LEADERSHIP CHALLENGES
FOR PUBLIC MANAGERS

Hampton, Virginia, Case Study

The city government of Hampton, Virginia, provides a good example of how a *learning organization* has been institutionalized in the public sector. In terms of overall performance, Hampton can show less cost for services than most communities. The city government was one of five U.S. municipalities chosen to participate in Vice President Albert Gore's National Performance Review and regularly finishes first or second among other Virginia cities in this region. Customer satisfaction levels with municipal services (which are checked continuously) are extremely high; 85 percent of Hampton's citizens rate city employees' service as above average.

What is particularly interesting about Hampton's city government is that teams can spring up on their own cross-functionally (across departmental boundaries) and then dissolve naturally when their tasks are completed. There are many permanent work teams operating, as well as over one hundred temporary configurations related to employee problem-solving groups, task forces, and committees. This represents a significant amount of team activity, given a city workforce of about 2,000 employees. Cross-functionality is emphasized, and community service is frequently the focus of team undertakings. More than 1,400 employees participated in community projects during 1993. City employees even assumed the task of building a community golf course, rather than contracting it out, saving the city millions of dollars.

Hampton orients itself on a different mental model [from the one] most organizations practice in America. "Turf" issues have largely disappeared, with most decision-making and planning bodies operating cross-functionally. It was not easy to get there. To arrive at a point where self-managed teams became commonplace and knowledge was widely shared required the "unlearning" of traditional (Weberian) formal management principles, such as those dealing with hierarchy and span of control. The city manager, Robert O'Neill, does not know on any given day how many teams are operating. He is also blessed with political leadership that leaves day-to-day operations to him and to city employees. Such broad use of teams without political interference unlocks myriad opportunities for learning to occur through shared responsibility and action.

In 1995, Hampton received special recognition for its efforts in human resources. It was one of just ten Optima Award winners from across the United States; these prestigious awards were created by the *Personnel Journal* in 1991 and cannot be applied for. Established business reputation and results are what count. Hampton was the only public-sector award winner and captured the top award for General Excellence. To earn this award, the city had to outrank the other award winners, including Intel Corporation, PepsiCo, Inc., Colgate-Palmolive, and 3M Company. What clearly thrust Hampton to the forefront was its successful institutionalization of a learning culture, one centered on shared power, value added, flexibility, and a tolerance for risk and failure. Hampton has, in effect, become a learning community, involving people who naturally interact and relish learning together. In this cooperative environment, employees have even taken it upon themselves to tutor fellow employees in basic literary skills. It is a caring community in which self-development activity is nurtured and encouraged, and teams members learn from each other.

SOURCE: Adapted from Robert L. Dilworth, "Institutionalizing Learning Organizations in the Public Sector," *Public Productivity and Management Review,* Vol. 19, No. 4, June, 1996, pp. 412–413.

Organizational Dynamics and Behavior

In the course of daily activities, many possibilities exist for assigning work, deciding how managerial objectives are transmitted to others, delegating responsibility, and making many similar choices. For example, the way subordinates are regarded by managers affects the modes of communication that are used to convey directives (that is, whether managers issue "marching orders" or set out program objectives with flexibility in how best to achieve goals). In another example, the application of Theory X, Y, or Z would dictate the operating responsibility that management chooses to delegate to others. In most public organizations, proponents of these theories interact simultaneously and often conflict, reflecting individual managerial experience and styles.

These concerns are part of the dynamics of organization and affect both individual and group behavior. Two topics can be classified as *process* issues: (1) **communication,** a vital function in organizational life; and (2) **coordination** of activities internally or across organizational lines. Both are central not only to traditional thinking and effective operations in practice but also to processes of change within organizations. Four other topics to be discussed are appropriately labeled *design issues* because they are relevant to the formal structuring of organizations. They are: (1) *line* (substantive or policy-focused) and *staff* (support or advisory) activities, and how they are related — and differentiated — in practical terms; (2) *centralization* versus *decentralization* in assigning responsibility and in overseeing operations; (3) the implications of *tall* versus *flat* hierarchies for managing a workforce (that is, the practical differences between organizations having

communication vital formal and informal processes of interacting within and between individuals and units within an organization, and between organizations.

coordination the process of bringing together divided labor; efforts to achieve coordination often involve emphasis on common or compatible objectives, harmonious working relationships, and the like; linked to issues involving communication, centralization-decentralization, federalism, and leadership.

few structural layers and those having many); and (4) the possibilities of *alternative forms of organization.*

COMMUNICATION: FORMAL AND INFORMAL

In recent decades, few topics have received more attention in both academic and practitioner literature than communication. (In this discussion, "communication" refers to the *field* and *process* of communication, where the plural, "communications," refers to individual *messages* sent or received.) In the contexts of large and small groups, interpersonal relations, communication theory, the general political realm, and even relations between nations, communication has been the focus of intensive research as well as practical application.[38] This attention is not unprecedented, however, particularly in the context of public organizations. Every major theory of organization has included (explicitly or implicitly) assumptions about the nature, roles, and processes of communication in a given organizational setting. Observers of organizations traditionally approached the subject by attempting to define the various kinds and flows of communication. More recently, as the scope and substance of the field have been altered, more attention has been given to social and psychological dimensions aiding or retarding effective communication.

There are many types of organizational communications. One of the most important distinctions is between *formal* and *informal*. **Formal communications** (1) originate in the authority of an organization official who attempts to influence some element of collective activity, (2) are directed to a particular audience within the organization, (3) follow proper organizational channels to the audience, and (4) constitute a building block in the continuing effort to officially state organizational policies, purposes, missions, strategies, and tactics. Formal communications are usually written, so that they become part of a permanent record of activity. They range from broad policy statements to specific operating memoranda.

Informal communications, on the other hand, take varied forms: (1) They may come from many sources (not necessarily individuals acting in an official capacity); (2) although they are directed toward a selected audience, others may also become aware of the message; (3) they may follow official channels of communication, but often those who send them deliberately avoid those channels; and (4) they are concerned with organizational life and activity (like formal communications) but reflect a wider range of thinking and actions on the part of members of the organization. Informal communications supplement official messages and can even become a more reliable guide to what organizations actually do. Formal memorandums are the skeletal framework of organizational intent and activity. Less structured contacts, such as those among friends and coworkers or through friends discussing agency projects or the last staff meeting over lunch, facilitate the multitude of actual operations built around the policy directions set in formal communications.

formal communication official written documentation within an organization including electronic mail, memoranda, minutes of meetings, and records; forms the framework for organizational intent and activity.

informal communication all forms of communication, other than official written documentation, among members of an organization; supplements official communications within an organization.

In a bureaucracy with a vertical chain of command, established communication routes traditionally follow hierarchical lines of authority. That is, formal communications are more closely associated with the arrangements and structures on the organization chart than informal communications are. However, it should be noted that formal communications are not confined to vertical organizational channels. A common and increasing phenomenon is **lateral or cross-functional communication,** which cuts across the vertical hierarchy yet is still conducted relatively formally. Thus, even as the chiefs of different (and potentially competing) divisions within an agency pursue their respective programmatic objectives, discovering that they have a common objective can prompt them to stay in touch, both formally and informally, in an effort to promote their mutual interests.

lateral or cross-functional communication patterns of oral and written communication within organizational networks that are interdisciplinary and typically cut across vertical layers of hierarchy.

Messages do not merely travel top to bottom in an organization, given the presence of both formal and informal lateral communication possibilities. Still more important, however, is *upward* communication, which goes against the traditional direction of formal channels but is becoming ever more crucial to the effective functioning of organizations large and small. This has a number of important dimensions.

First, every organization has *feedback* mechanisms — some means of transmitting information from those who received messages to those who sent them. Virtually every communication system provides for feedback, at least in theory; these feedback mechanisms can be highly formalized and sophisticated or they can be informal. The problem for the top-level manager and others is to ensure that they will be able to learn via feedback what effects their own communications have had. Feedback mechanisms can range from suggestion boxes, individual conversations, or an open-door policy by supervisors to regularized consultations between management and subordinates, surveys of employee opinion, or surveys of citizens about the quality of the services provided by a public organization. These "voice of the customer" surveys are becoming increasingly useful to senior managers as feedback mechanisms from internal employees who provide services, as well as from external recipients of services.

A second factor, complicating the feedback process, is the strong tendency for good news to travel freely up the line but for bad news to be suppressed, rerouted, or rewritten. The desire of lower-level units and personnel to present a favorable image to those higher up accounts for this phenomenon. But, in the interest of their own effectiveness, higher-level managers ordinarily need to know both good and bad news. Managers must have a clear understanding of all that is going on in their organizations in order to be able to correct existing problems, anticipate future difficulties, and iron out internal conflicts that may hamper organizational activity. Too often, those who have knowledge that might be deemed negative do not report it to their supervisors for fear of the consequences.

To overcome the natural reluctance to report bad news to superiors, managers can initiate something akin to a "no-fault" or forgiving information policy (within limits). Such a policy encourages employees to bring problems that are unmanageable at lower levels to the attention of higher management but without fear of retribution or faultfinding as a penalty. To be successful, such feedback would have to develop in the context of positive, supportive, trust-based interactions between superiors and subordinates; the democratic leadership style is more conducive to this sort of communication than other styles (see also Chapter 7). Negative feedback is often lacking precisely because the types of general organizational relationships that would facilitate it have not been developed and maintained. Top management must take deliberate steps to make such feedback possible, regardless of the possible consequences. (In this regard, see discussion of "whistle-blowers" in Chapters 6 and 7.)

In this era of more democratic and participatory management in public and private sectors, all employees are being asked to address a wider range of organizational problems. Whether formal or informal, upward flows of communication have increased in importance and can contribute measurably to the effective functioning of an organization. Without accurate feedback from employees, the probability increases that management decisions will be based on false or misleading information.

DIMENSIONS OF COMMUNICATION

Although achieving better communication is a goal to which many subscribe almost on faith, it may be useful to consider various aspects of the process; such an examination may yield a fuller understanding of the potential and the pitfalls. We will briefly examine (in order) the prerequisites, purposes, obstacles (and their remedies), and consequences associated with better communication.

There are, first of all, several kinds of *prerequisites*, including the transmitter of a message, the message itself, the medium through which it is sent, and a receiver mechanism of some sort. Considerable research has been done on how the medium and especially the receiver influence the understanding of messages sent; the late Marshall McLuhan's work is a leading example of this kind of research on mechanistic communication models.[39] Other kinds of prerequisites, however, are equally important, including the individual desire to communicate clearly, a *shared* interest in achieving common understanding among those communicating with one another, and organizational arrangements that facilitate message transmittal. In short, simply wanting to improve communication is not enough. This is especially true in a diverse work environment where those involved lack common definitions of the terms employed or shared understanding of the concepts and assumptions underlying the information transmitted. (That problem significantly affects all types of organizations having difficulty communicating with those receiving services. In the college classroom, for example, professors and students sometimes have communication problems.)

The *purposes* of communication may seem obvious, yet they can be as varied as the people communicating. Many of us may use communications for purposes less constructive than achieving human understanding and organizational effectiveness or promoting the public interest. For example, the use of **gobbledygook** is often a major impediment to clear communication in organizations.[40] Although some gobbledygook just seems to happen, sometimes its use may be carefully calculated by those employing it; the more they confuse potential opposition, the more they may be able to *de*fuse it. The same is true of the use of professional jargon, or what has been labeled "bureaucratese." Gobbledygook may be one way to fend off criticism; if listeners cannot understand what is said, they cannot take issue with it. For whatever reasons, a considerable amount of gobbledygook still exists in government communications.

On the other hand, the crisp memo is a weapon of considerable potency in bureaucratic politics. It is widely acknowledged in all large organizations that one can be influential through carefully conceived, well-written, and brief memorandums to key decision makers. In many respects, memo writing and its potential represent everything gobbledygook does not: clarity of expression, sharpening understanding of available options, and the deliberate shaping of opinions. How clear the meaning of a communication is, then, depends heavily on how clear the sender intended it to be — and why!

Obstacles to effective communication can be found among both senders and receivers of messages. One obstacle, already noted, is *lack of clarity* on the part of the sender as a result of poor word choices, failure to explain the purposes of the communication, inadequate explanation of actions to be taken, and the like. Another problem is *lack of accurate or complete relay of a message* (as in the games "telephone" and "rumor clinic"); the more layers there are in the structure of an organization, the more likely it is that messages will be distorted. A third obstacle is *failure of the receiver to listen or to read*, a human failing related to our tendency to screen out negative or unwanted information; related to this is *reluctance to accept the contents of the message* if it goes against the receiver's opinions on the subject of the message. Still another problem is *failure of the receiver to act appropriately* on the message if he or she fails to comprehend its importance fully. Compounding all these is the possibility (very real in large, complex organizations) that great distance will separate sender from receiver(s), making it difficult to determine the effectiveness of messages sent.

Numerous *remedies* are available to the communication-conscious manager, but they must be chosen carefully; none can be counted on to completely overcome all obstacles to communication. One remedy is formal training in communication skills for all employees. Another is more specifically targeted training for higher-level managers, designed to make them sensitive to the need for continual monitoring of messages passing through their divisions; this might be coupled with a program of incentives for improving communication flows. A third device, which can be used by top management personnel, is spot-checking activities at lower levels of the organization to be sure that directives have been received and are being acted on. (All electronic or "e-mail" systems now allow the sender to check the exact time a message was received.) If such monitoring

gobbledygook
misleading jargon or meaningless technical terms often used to purposely obscure communications within organizations.

from the top occurs through normal channels, it may suffer from the same problem posed for regular communications, namely, imperfect relaying. Modern information technologies aid in shortening the distances among decentralized, often isolated agencies and public service functions, allowing managers to go outside the usual channels in following up on their directives. But perhaps the most important factor in improving communication is a clear perception on the part of employees that top management is committed to maintaining effective flows of communication and that the process is explicitly valued for the contributions everyone can make to organizational operations.

The *consequences* of communication, like its purposes, cannot simply be assumed. Although many people think that better communication will solve problems and conflicts, that is not necessarily true. At the root of most communication problems are perception and credibility issues. Certain attitudes and behaviors are essential to break down mistrust and establish clear lines of communication. It is possible, of course, that improving communication will produce beneficial results in an organization, in the ways that have already been discussed. On the other hand, communicating more clearly can complicate matters as well. The circumstances of communication strongly influence which kinds of results actually occur.

For example, if interpersonal hostilities exist between two employees and the hostile feelings are temporary, it may be wiser not to express those feelings. After some time has passed and both people have had a chance to cool off, talking things out may then help resolve the problem without things being said that both parties might later regret. For two employees who have a running feud, refraining from communicating may be one short-term measure that makes it possible for them to continue functioning somewhat normally. Similarly, part of organizational politics is knowing when not to speak openly about some problem if doing so would only exacerbate the situation. It is perhaps better — even in the long run — not to try solving the problem if the attempt is unlikely to succeed and if making the effort brings to the forefront some interpersonal or substantive disagreements that are better left in the background.

Of most relevance to the public administrator, the communication processes in public bureaucracies generally occur within the context of what some have labeled the **bargaining or political model** of communication. To the extent that public administration is viewed as a distinctively political process, this model of communication seems to apply. Administrators do seek monopolies on key information; they do conduct their communication activities with an eye to maximum political gain; and so on. According to this conception, the communication process becomes another weapon in the administrator's political arsenal; clear communication of ideas, actions, or intentions could easily conflict with attaining political objectives.

On the other hand, an alternative model of communication that is equally relevant to public administration merits attention. Although the political model is widely applicable, a **consensual or consensus-building model** may be useful

---

bargaining or political model of communication assumes the presence in an organization of considerable sustained conflict, strong tendencies toward secrecy, and motives of expediency on the part of most individuals.

consensual or consensus-building model of communication assumes that by cooperation instead of power struggles and political trade-offs, administrators may seek to reach agreement with potential adversaries as a means of furthering mutual aims.

at some points in the administrative process. Under such circumstances, it is useful to communicate openly about both differences and areas of agreement. In this setting, communication should be open and clearly inclined toward sharing rather than guarding information, even if doing so leads to recognition of disagreement. The key to successful use of this model is the common will to understand and overcome differences. There may be political risks in employing this approach, but a judgment must be made about whether those risks are worth taking.

A manager choosing between these communication models must take several things into consideration. Among them are the relative probabilities of achieving organization goals with one or the other approach, the chances of reaching consensus with another agency (or agencies), and the sensitivity of information that would be shared if the consensus-building model is used. Other concerns could include the longer-range needs of the organization for political support from others, the agency's credibility in the administrative-political process, and the reliability of potential allies as working partners.

What, then, is the importance of communication? Clearly, the basic processes serve to facilitate management of large enterprises in a number of ways. These include:

1. Defining and fulfilling objectives;
2. Determining the division and assignment of responsibilities across the full range of functions in the organization;
3. Identifying problems and opportunities in ongoing programs;
4. Anticipating long-term and short-term options (ideally with their attendant costs and benefits — see Chapter 6);
5. Motivating employees and pinpointing morale problems;
6. Soliciting ideas from individuals throughout the organization; and
7. Resolving conflicts as (or before) they occur.

As with many other human activities, the particular styles and mechanisms of communication may influence the content and purpose of the message, the degree of effectiveness, and the consequences for the organization as a whole.[41]

COORDINATION

Like communication, the concept of *coordination* has almost universal appeal in the abstract. Obviously, a large and complex organization must achieve a minimally adequate degree of coordination in its multiple activities if there is to be any chance of consistency in the impacts of those activities. Put another way: If the right hand is ever to know what the left hand is doing, activities need to be coordinated at various points in the process. The need for coordination varies according to the type of service provided and the geographic location of the public agency. Coordination problems become more serious as organizations undergo growth, increase in complexity, and experience internal differentiation of functions. Organizational communication can be important here, it should be noted. And coordination can occur in different ways.

What exactly is *coordination?* Various definitions have been advanced, most of them emphasizing notions such as common goals and interests, compatible objectives, and harmonious collaboration among different groups or organizations.[42] Essentially, however, coordination is the *process of bringing together divided labor.* It is the opposite of division of labor and the organizational cure for it where it is necessary to integrate the activities of different entities — whether separate agencies of the same government, agencies of different governments (or governments themselves), or elements of the public and private sectors. Having compatible objectives or working jointly may help to facilitate the coordinative process, but the basic task can still be carried out even under less than favorable conditions (such as conflict, hostility, and apathy).

If we consider coordination in light of prerequisites, purposes, obstacles, remedies, and consequences, as we did with communication, some similarities — but also some differences — are evident between the two phenomena. At the risk of oversimplification, it may be said that the prerequisites are virtually the same — channels and mechanisms for coordination must be purposefully established and maintained, just as for communication. The difficulty of accomplishing this varies with the degree of organizational autonomy possessed by the entities being coordinated. As far as purposes are concerned, there is probably less variety in the objectives of those who desire coordination than in the objectives of those who seek to improve communication. Whereas communication can serve to mislead or confuse as well as to clarify, coordination is almost always designed to clear away difficulties in organizational activity.

It should be noted, however, that many individuals and groups may resist would-be coordinators' efforts to clear away perceived difficulties. For their own reasons and priorities, some people both inside and outside of organizations may prefer to engage in their assigned activities without bending their purposes to some larger, better-coordinated undertaking. Such behaviors demonstrate the validity of the observation that "coordination is rarely neutral. To the extent that it results in mutual agreement or a decision on some policy, course of action, or inaction, inevitably it advances some interests at the expense of others or more than others."[43] Thus, those who seek better coordination must deal with those who would plant obstacles in their path. Those obstacles to coordination merit our attention, as do their remedies.

One obstacle is differing perceptions of program goals. This, in turn, leads to varied degrees of commitment to a coordination process that assumes substantial goal consensus among major participants. Other obstacles are divergent preferences on major or minor aspects of implementation; conflicting priorities, even when substantive agreement on the total program exists; unequal fiscal capabilities; conflicting political pressures on program agencies; poor organization; breakdowns in communication; and inept leadership.[44] In addition, *legal auton-*

omy can lead to a situation in which some or all of the obstacles mentioned may be present but little can be done to cause the relevant officials to coordinate their efforts; this is especially evident when many separate local government jurisdictions exist in a single metropolitan area. In other words, coordinating across organizational (including governmental) boundaries is more difficult than intra-organizational coordination.

Overcoming these obstacles is not easy, but a number of remedies do exist. One is improved communication; that can be an implicit reason for focusing on communication problems. In the abstract, there is every reason to hope that better communication — on objectives, tactics, perceived problems, or opportunities — can indeed lead to a better "meshing of the gears" among agencies and their activities. But whether better communication actually facilitates coordination depends to a large extent on the amount of conflict (both real and potential) present in the entities' relationships. Limited areas of conflict would permit the use of the consensus-building model of communication, which would tend to improve coordination. Significant conflict, however, would probably lead to use of the political model of communication and, in that event, the impulse to hoard information would work against the effort to coordinate more fully. Even in the absence of conflict, however, the will to improve coordination must be present among key personnel in the affected organizations or units.

Another remedy for coordination problems is the exercise of leadership in at least two important ways. First, responsible managers can devote leadership resources and exert their influence in support of coordination, clearly demonstrating their concern for improving it. Relevant managerial functions include goal setting and building consensus supportive of common goals; conflict management aimed at containing and resolving internal disputes before they reach a level of intensity harmful to organizational effectiveness; and information management. Second, on an interpersonal level, managers of different organizations or agencies can initiate efforts to coordinate activities of their respective entities, thus establishing the context for a more formalized coordinative process. Their success ultimately depends on their personal commitment and their ability to go back to their organizations and build support there for coordination in the manner described above (see also Chapter 7).

Organizational arrangements for strengthening coordination fall into two principal categories. One is *central coordination*, in which decisions are rendered by a coordinative entity or individual. The other is *mutual adjustment* (sometimes termed *lateral coordination*), in which there exist "consultation, sharing of information, and negotiation among equals."[45] (Note the presumption of the consensus-building model of communication.) A third possibility also exists, "a combination of these — a process in which lateral coordination is expedited, facilitated, and even coerced by leadership and pressure from an independent or higher-level coordinator."[46]

Overall, then, coordination, like communication, is often highly prized but just as often is achieved only with conceptual and operational difficulties. The more complex the organization, the greater the challenge to those who would achieve coordination of activity among its various parts.[47]

LINE AND STAFF FUNCTIONS

line functions substantive activities of an organization, related to programs or policies for which the organization is formally responsible, and usually having direct impact on outside clienteles; the work of an organization directed toward fulfilling its formal mission(s).

staff functions originally defined to include all of an organization's support and advisory activities that facilitated the carrying out of "line" responsibilities and functions; more recently, redefined by some to focus on planning, research, and advisory activities (thus excluding budgeting, personnel, purchasing, and other functions once grouped under the "staff" heading).

The notions of **line functions** and staff functions in an organization can be traced back to very traditional treatments of formal organization. They deal with programs or policies having *direct impact* on outside clienteles and are ultimately accountable to a superior in the performance of substantive responsibilities. This definition has been widely accepted in public administration ever since the *principles* approach emerged during the 1930s. In the same period, **staff functions** were originally defined as consisting of support and advisory activities undergirding the ability of line personnel to carry out their duties. These could be, for example, financial and budgetary, personnel administration, planning, purchasing, and legal counsel. More recently, however, the notion of staff activities has undergone some revision (it should be noted, however, that these revisions have not been accepted by all experts in the field and outside observers). With the work of Leonard D. White in the 1940s, *staff* came to mean the planning, research, and advisory activities essential to the long-term well-being of an organization.[48] A new term — *auxiliary* — was coined to describe the remaining activities that would need to be performed in all units (such as budgeting, personnel, and purchasing). The interrelationships among *line, staff, and auxiliary* activities (especially between the first two) have continued to be an important concern in public administration.

Several areas of interaction between functions are important in public administration organizations. First, the activities of such diverse units in any organization require some degree of coordination. The likelihood of conflict is greatest between line and staff personnel; the most obvious point of potential clash is in their very different time perspectives and their order of priorities. Line personnel are usually concerned with the immediate, the concrete, the here and now, and the substantive aspects of activity, whereas those engaged in longer-range planning typically concern themselves with where the agency may be going five or ten years hence. Thus, top management must at least integrate their activities, if not directly attempt to link them operationally.

Second, some kinds of conflicts between the different types of personnel are virtually unavoidable. For example, an agency budget officer, who is responsible for reducing costs and keeping budget requests in line with projected estimates, may have to cut funds, which may result in a variety of complaints. The bureau chief may believe that top management (i.e., the budget officer) is not sufficiently aware of, or sensitive to, the importance of the bureau's work. At the same time, the budget officer may come to regard the bureau as a reckless spender of scarce departmental dollars. In another example, a reform-minded city manager's attempts to centralize the purchasing function may infuriate department directors who have their own arrangements with suppliers and resent giving up their authority and discretion.

Finally, these traditional distinctions are increasingly seen as less important in an era of rapid change inside and outside of organizations. In particular, as long-term strategic planning has taken on greater legitimacy — and has become a more significant part of the thinking of top-level line managers — the planning function has become more closely integrated with daily operations. Reciprocal understanding is growing, blurring old distinctions between line and staff. In their demands for more and better program analysis before policy commitments are made, many political leaders have further enhanced the position of staff personnel vis-à-vis their line counterparts. Thus, as societal demands and management techniques have changed, the distinctions between line and staff functions have become increasingly less significant.

Centralization and Decentralization

The degree of **centralization** in an organization affects all other aspects of organizational life. Traditional management approaches have stressed how top managers exercise their powers in the interest of economy, efficiency, or effectiveness. The easy assumption of this thinking has been that it is entirely appropriate to centralize authority in an organization. Especially in recent years, however, much has been said, written, and accomplished in support of the value of **decentralization** in administration. It is useful to understand what each concept means before going on to discuss why decentralization has become so much more popular.

centralization an organizational pattern focused on concentrating power at the top on an organization.

decentralization an organizational pattern focused on distributing power broadly within an organization.

In its extreme form, centralized management means that all essential decision making and implementation are the concentrated responsibility of those at the top. Communication and coordination become one-way streets, from the top down (except for structured feedback). Nothing of any consequence goes on that is not under the direct control of top management. Some entities still function in this way, but many others at all levels of government and in the private sector do not. As the scope and complexity of many organizations have increased, it has become necessary to delegate considerable amounts of operating authority to line managers (and occasionally to others), whose position in the organization is some distance from top management.

In general, most employees seek a larger voice in organizational affairs. The decentralization of decision-making authority effectively responds to this desire without forcing top management to relinquish either oversight capacity or ultimate authority. Even if employees of a public agency have not pressed for internal decentralization, the national government has encouraged it by responding to the demands of external clienteles, especially in cases involving the poor, and by increasing citizen participation in decision making. Concepts of citizen participation, neighborhood empowerment, and community activism trace their origins in part to congressional decisions intended to broaden opportunities for citizens to become more self-sufficient and less dependent on government. Thus, decentralization strategies often result in increased internal complexity. Generally, although ultimate policy and administrative responsibility remain with top managers, many day-to-day operating decisions are delegated to others at lower ranks within the organization. Depending on the degree of decentralization, some or all of the programmatic activities are supervised by middle-level managers operating under discretionary authority from senior management. Communication becomes a multichannel affair, with all manner of messages, directives, and informal contacts. While still partly a central responsibility (and perhaps more so, in light of the dispersal of authority), coordination is also likely to involve lateral (or cross-functional) coordination to a significant degree. It is also probable that top management will show greater willingness to include a wider range of employees in mapping out long-term strategies. If centralization is analogous to *centripetal* force — that is gravitational force that pulls all objects to the center — decentralization has as its analog the *centrifugal* aspects of physics, in which the major thrust of the system is away from the center. In practice, a decentralized system of organization is one with *both* centripetal and centrifugal forces at work. It might be noted that these issues were — and still are — central to the continuing debate over American federalism, as well as to specific forms of administrative organization. In recent years, initiatives aimed at reinventing government have stressed employee empowerment, devolution, and decentralization, together with teamwork, participatory management, labor–management cooperation, customer service, and employee enrichment programs. Much of what is said in the following section about the significance of centralization and decentralization also applies to the foundation and operation of the federal system.

SIGNIFICANCE OF CENTRALIZATION VERSUS DECENTRALIZATION

There can be little doubt that the degree of centralization in an organization (or, for that matter, a political system) can make a difference in how things are done. But what *is* that difference? What purposes and values are served by greater or lesser centralization?

Clearly, effective control and internal program consistency are enhanced by centralization; so, too, is *accountability* for actions of individuals within organizations. If authority is highly centralized, there can be little question as to whose values and assumptions shape organizational goals. Centralization also decreases the likelihood that management prerogatives will be challenged directly from below. Orderly operations within the organization are similarly facilitated whenever management responsibility is centralized.

On the other hand, centralization — even as it may facilitate control — often carries with it a certain lack of flexibility and adaptability, especially in large enterprises. According to many observers, one of the advantages of decentralization is that it enables middle-level managers in the field to act as organizational *sensors* — able to detect new problems or opportunities, in a position to respond on the spot to particular policy needs, and so on. Especially in an age of diversity and change, organizational adaptiveness may depend in large measure on the speed with which changes in the environment are detected and brought to the attention of top management and subsequent adjustments provided for. In many settings — large government bureaucracies, private corporations dependent on changing markets, local government service-delivery mechanisms faced with changing citizen demands — the need for this sort of adaptive capability is so great that it demands some sacrifice of central control. In short, the most important need is an organization's survival amid uncertainty and change.

Another function served by decentralization pertains to a political–philosophical question: *To what degree are the members of an organization or other system meaningful participants in affairs of governance?* Political systems, both ancient and modern, have confronted this question and have responded in many different ways. In democratic systems, suspicion of centralist control runs very deep, prompting many to equate decentralization in government with popular rule in one form or another. In our society, that doctrine has recently been joined to theories about organizational life; the result has been considerable emphasis on greater participation (through decentralization) by many who were previously excluded from organizational decision making. In general, it is thought that democratic participation enhances the quality of decisions reached and increases the probability that affected clienteles or "customers" will accept those decisions. Whether those expectations are realistic or well founded is another question.

Here again, however, there is another side to the coin. For just as top management might have to choose between control and flexibility, those who preach the virtues of decentralization must be alert to the possibility that, *in a decentralized organization, it will be more difficult to hold accountable those who actually make decisions.* The astute leader may find it possible to put through desired policy while avoiding accountability by pointing to the decentralized nature of the decision-making process in which many others also took part. There is the further prospect that *co-optation* will occur, thus reducing criticism or opposition by giving critics or opponents a stake in the decision process. Their co-optation would have important political consequences (in any setting) for the maintenance of meaningful opposition and the existence of informed, critical debate over proposed policy directions.

Thus, decentralization (like anything else) is far from an unmixed blessing and should not be viewed as a panacea that will solve all an organization's ills. Note, in this connection, the conceptual links between our discussion of centralization and decentralization and our treatment in Chapter 2 of the *administrative efficiency* and *pluralist democracy models*. Advocates of centralization seek to apply the administrative efficiency model, whether consciously or not; arguments in favor of one are virtually identical to arguments in favor of the other. Similarly, those committed to decentralization implicitly favor the democracy model and its underlying assumptions and rationales.[49] Equally important is the fact that the centralization–decentralization debate cuts across a wide spectrum. It is as appropriate to questions of large-scale political arrangements (such as democratic governance or federal systems) as it is to smaller-scale organizational concerns, including the extent to which practices like *democratic* or *participative management* are encouraged within an organization.

In any discussion of decentralization, the caveat of the late Paul Appleby (former assistant to the Secretary of Agriculture and a leading scholar in public administration) is well worth noting. He wrote that nothing can be decentralized until it has first been centralized.[50] This suggests — or *should* suggest — that a central authority capable of *decentralizing* is also theoretically capable of *recentralizing!* Thus, decentralization can occur only in the context of previous centralization — not the most comforting thought for those who place their faith in decentralization as the appropriate remedy for abuse of centralized power. In many instances, the "center" can assume responsibilities that had been delegated elsewhere if decentralized operations are interfering with other values or objectives that are deemed important by those at the center. It is one of the pitfalls affecting the whole concept of decentralization in organizations.

The feeling is still widespread, however, that decentralization has sufficient advantages to warrant taking the attendant risks. It is significant that many top-level managers share that opinion.

Tall versus Flat Hierarchies

Most people associate bureaucracy with a distinct chain of command through which a number of essential tasks can be effectively coordinated. These include exerting managerial control, providing for division of labor, and sending and receiving communications. Much of the literature on the subject assumes that a bureaucratic structure implicitly embraces many layers of organization in a "tall" hierarchy. Only in more recent decades has much attention been given to "flat," or "delayered," hierarchical arrangements, and to some of the differences between flat and tall organizations.

span of control   the number of people an individual supervises within a subunit of the organization. Each supervisor should have only a limited number of subordinates to oversee. This expands the chain of command to produce the needed ratio of supervisors to subordinates at each level, in the interest of overall coordination.

Tall hierarchies evolved out of a combination of circumstances and organizational factors present in many early bureaucracies. Among the most important was, first, the *diversity* of tasks being performed within the same organization, therefore requiring significant horizontal and vertical differentiation of each division or unit from all others. Second, the principle known as narrow **span of control** combined with task diversity and interdependence of activities to encourage the growth of tall hierarchies. Third, that higher-level employees in many early organizations were regarded as more professional than those at lower echelons gave impetus to the tendency to differentiate clearly between top and bottom in the organization structure. Finally, spurred by growing complexity both of internal tasks and technologies and of external environments, more modern organizations tended to exhibit intensified patterns of centralized hierarchy.

Flat hierarchies were not unknown even in the early 1900s, however, and recently have become more common. A flat hierarchy is one in which either top management is conducted in a collegial, "board of directors" fashion, or all subordinate units below the highest level of the organization are regarded as hierarchical equals, or both. An early example of a flat hierarchy was the commission system in some local governments, in which each commissioner was the organizational equal of all the others and responsibility for municipal leadership and management was shared coequally. A more contemporary organizational example is that of the scientific research team; although there is probably a division of labor among team members and a coordinator of team efforts, no one leader is officially designated or informally acknowledged as such by team members. Also, decision making is a function shared on the basis of mutual respect for each other's expertise (to some extent, this is similar to organizational humanism and quality circles). Another example is the small professional staff in a nonprofit social service agency (such as a local Girl Scout office), which depends on the active participation of dedicated volunteers in the community. Other examples are found in state and national advisory commissions, blue-ribbon citizens' panels, and the like (see Figure 5–3).

FIGURE 5–3 Tall and Flat Hierarchies

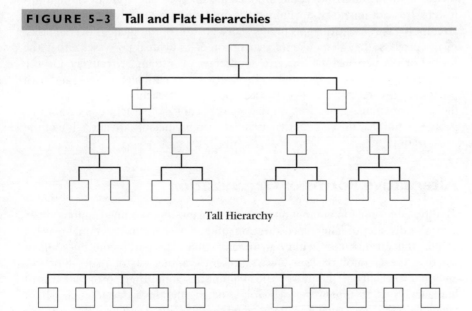

Tall Hierarchy

Flat Hierarchy

SIGNIFICANCE OF TALL VERSUS FLAT HIERARCHIES

Among the most important differences between these two types of structures, communication problems in a tall hierarchy stand out. In general, the more layers an organization has, the less likely it is for messages to reach all levels undistorted. For lower-level employees and customers, the problem of access to those at higher ranks is closely related to this difficulty in communication. Obviously, these problems are greater in taller hierarchies and create the very real possibility that many employees will be alienated from organization leadership (depending, of course, on how top managers conduct employee relations). Furthermore, as already suggested, problems of coordination are usually greater in the presence of organizational complexity; a tall hierarchy can contribute to the development of both those situations. Finally, issues of centralization and decentralization are more pressing in tall than in flat hierarchies.

Flat hierarchies are not, however, without their drawbacks. If organizational tasks become more diverse, there may not be enough flexibility in the structure to permit the reflection of that diversity, resulting in operating problems among individuals and staffs that are too closely crowded together. A second possible disadvantage lies in the existence of interpersonal hostilities on the same operating level of a flat hierarchy; again, there may not be enough distance to shield the organization effectively against the adverse consequences of such feelings, thus allowing the functioning of the organization as a whole to be disrupted. Finally, flat hierarchies (particularly in smaller organizational settings that have some sort of chain of command) could produce too many leaders and not enough followers. It is not unknown for individuals operating on roughly equal footing to attempt to take charge (inappropriately) of a portion of the agency's overall tasks; in the process, they demonstrate that no other individual possesses either the formal or the personal authority to counteract the attempt effectively. On the other hand, such a development can be dealt with in a tall hierarchy — and with potentially greater impact — partly because there are channels designed to handle such situations. Thus, we find that neither choice of structure is without its problems and that the choices that are made can predictably affect the life of the organization.

Alternative Forms of Organization

Traditional formulations about bureaucratic organization assumed (among other things) a division of labor, specialization, and an absence of functional overlap among the various units within an organization. Apart from the question of whether these conditions are always present, another set of issues has now emerged to challenge the most basic assumptions about the appropriateness of bureaucracy as an organizing principle. Specifically, three developments have taken place that have encouraged informed thinking about various alternatives to bureaucracy as a form of organization.

First, the *rise of new technologies* such as the Internet and World Wide Web have significantly altered and expanded the substantive tasks of both public and private organizations. Scientific and other professional research and expertise, in a host of fields, have affected so much of public policy making that it is difficult to imagine transportation, conservation, agriculture, urban planning, housing, or national defense (to name but a few) without them. The technologies involved in operating an organization (such as wireless communications, psychological profiles and testing, computer applications, and other quantitative aids) have themselves spawned a number of new specialties in the field of management alone. The result has been a proliferation of new and different organizational units devoted to functions that were unknown in most organizations just a few years ago. It has also spawned the development of software to address these problems. Examples of how technological change has affected organizations include the following: an insurance company contains a medical rehabilitation unit that concentrates on support services for vocationally disabled individuals insured by the company; almost any large state government department has within it an office of planning and analysis whose job it is (as a "staff" entity) to look past immediate challenges and anticipate the future; and a corporate legal office includes a paralegal unit that assists in research and administrative services essential to providing high-quality legal work. Much of this technology allows public administrators to "work smarter, not harder" while concentrating their efforts in other areas of importance.

Second, the *growth of complex knowledge* has been characterized by *increasing interdependence of fields of knowledge;* the same is true of the staffs of specialists in those various fields. Thus, in the university setting, interdisciplinary plans of study and research are increasingly common. So also are interdependent teams of experts acting as consultants to industry or government organizations. Under such circumstances, hierarchical channels of authority would be highly dysfunctional and would tend to interfere with the accomplishment of stated objectives. Other organizational forms have had to be developed.

Third, the *rise of professionalism* in many occupations has triggered an emphasis on professionalism itself in public organizational activities. Consequently, this has strengthened organizational tendencies toward diversity and created the need for different styles of management among diverse professionals. By itself, professionalism might have made bureaucratic hierarchy somewhat inappropriate as a principle of organization but, in combination with the factors mentioned above, many claim that such a hierarchy has been made all the more unworkable.

What, then, are some of the alternative forms of organization? Several directions (if not specific structures) have been suggested. One is the call for "an end to hierarchy and competition";[51] this is a clarion call for sweeping change in the ways we approach both structure and incentive systems within modern organizations. A second approach has been suggested by public administration scholar Warren Bennis, who has argued that Weber-style bureaucratic structure may have been entirely adequate and appropriate for dealing with routine and predictable tasks in a stable environment (such as the early 1900s) but that, given the unpredictable nature of contemporary organizational life, coupled with a far more turbulent social environment, organizations need new forms of management and leadership.[52]

Bennis sees an *end to hierarchical leadership* because no one leader is capable of mastering the complex and diverse technologies present in so many organizations. And, because of technological needs, managers will increasingly become *coordinators* or *facilitators* among teams of experts operating within an almost horizontal (rather than a traditional, vertical) chain of command. According to Bennis, this clearly suggests a participative style of management;[53] if the chain of command runs horizontally, it virtually requires a view of organization members as equals, not as superiors and subordinates. The concept of a "series of interconnected teams" already operates in many computer software companies, aerospace industries, blue-ribbon commissions, and numerous professional consulting firms that have considerable influence on the policy-making process.

One other possibility, referred to in Chapter 1, is that public organizations might come to reflect the *reverse pyramid* associated with so-called knowledge workers (those whose work centers around information and information technology) in service-providing organizations.[54] Rather than a hierarchy characteristic of traditional bureaucracies, this reverse structure defines managers as sources of support, principally for their frontline employees who deal directly with anyone seeking services provided by the organization. Such a structure assumes a greater degree of decentralization, accountability, and participatory management than is found in traditional hierarchies; it also implicitly assumes an open rather than a closed system, one that is in nearly constant interaction with its surrounding social environment. Because of the changing nature of organizations and the growing service demands on many government organizations, the reverse pyramid may indeed be found in increasing numbers of government structures.

Organization Theory and Behavior in Perspective

The theories and realities of organization are all in a state of continuous change. In this chapter, we have seen many proposals for organizational arrangements; none of them, however, solves all the problems that existed before or is free of its own shortcomings. Yet we seem never to cease trying — to devise the communication channel that is one step better, to bring about coordination of programs and projects that will be truly effective, to establish the nonbureaucratic structure that will not suffer from *lack* of formal direction and leadership. In the midst of such variety and richness in the possibilities available, it may be that our single biggest problem is learning how to select the proper devices, forms, and tools to fit particular organizational and functional needs. That would require broadening management skills and training in directions that are not now clearly perceived; it also has implications for our choices on larger questions of power, authority, and self-governance. As we discussed in Chapter 2, choices made that pertain directly to administration will be made in the larger "force field" of values that surrounds all our institutions. It is evident that both general and specific values are in an evolutionary process.

In spite of its intellectual diversity, the subject of organizational theory has been characterized by a unifying theme: the attempt to identify the elements in an organization's existence that are most important to the successful attainment of its goals. What those elements are, what the goals are, and even what constitutes the organization itself have not been agreed on. The overlapping series of schools or approaches has given us a wide range of ideas from which to choose. Furthermore, the evolution of organizational theory has reflected changing emphases in a host of academic disciplines, in business and industry, and in society at large concerning what is important and how to go about achieving it.

Several general comments are in order. First, the various approaches to organization theory have clearly overlapped chronologically and, more to the point, intellectually. The human relations school, while departing significantly from Weber and Taylor, assumed the existence of the same formal, hierarchical structure. Organizational humanism borrowed from the human relations approach. Quality circles, Theory Z, learning organizations, and total quality management have incorporated some elements of organizational humanism. Learning theory encompasses aspects of systems thinking and total quality management. Thus, various strands of theoretical development have often been woven together as parts of different fabrics, so to speak. Each theory is neither self-contained nor totally self-explanatory.

Second, although various approaches may fall out of favor among organization theorists of a particular period, those approaches do not necessarily cease to have any influence. On the contrary, the influence of organization theories is generally cumulative; at any given time, one may find in existing organizations some offshoots of earlier belief and practice. For example, although Weber's and Taylor's ideas of formal theory no longer predominate among contemporary scholars, they have had a powerful influence in shaping many public and private institutions and, significantly, are still influential (however indirectly) in the thinking of many people. The same is true of the principles of administration and the human relations approach, both of which still carry some weight in theory and practice.

Furthermore, the emerging "newer" tradition avoids the closed versus open-system dilemma and views the organization, in James Thompson's words as a "problem-facing and problem-solving phenomenon . . . focusing on organizational processes related to choice of courses of action in an environment which does not fully disclose the alternatives available or the consequences of those alternatives."[55] Thus, most organizations are neither fully closed nor fully open systems. In an increasingly interdependent world, the former is impractical, if not impossible; the latter, although still possible, would produce a situation in which any organization would be overwhelmed by the inflows of energy and information, rendering it ineffectual at best. In this mixed view of organizations, then, external environments are regarded as very important; at the same time, organizations are seen as attempting to cope internally with enormous (and growing) uncertainty as they try to learn from the environment and successfully cope with change.

Finally, the evolution of organization theory has included a marked shift in assumptions about organizational leaders and followers — from a formal hierarchical relationship in which orders were transmitted and obeyed to much more diverse and diffuse arrangements in which more participation and team direction is accepted as a matter of course. The control emphasis has had to yield (at least partially) to other values, further complicating our understanding of how organizations can be effectively operated and posing new challenges to managers themselves.[56]

Organization theory and practice have grown more complex over the years as they paralleled actual developments in organizations throughout modern society. As more knowledge has been brought to bear, it is not surprising that, today we are confronted by both greater diversity of approaches and less certainty about the nature of large-scale organizations and the behavior of people within them. That trend is likely to continue.

Summary

Organization theory focuses on formal and informal structures, internal dynamics, and surrounding social environments of complex human organizations. Spanning several academic disciplines, it has emphasized, at different times, the needs of management, the needs and motivations of workers, and the relationships between organizations and their environments. Four major areas of organization theory are (1) formal theory, (2) human relations, (3) organizational humanism, and (4) modern organization theory.

Weber's formal model of bureaucracy incorporated the concepts of hierarchy, division of labor and functional specialization, detailed rules and procedures, maintenance of files, professionalization, and adequate legal and political authority. Control was a central purpose of this model. American public administration differs from the formal model as a result of commands from outside the formal hierarchy, the extent of functional overlap among agencies, less than complete operation of merit personnel systems, diversity of substantive professional expertise, loose requirements for continuing competence, and late development of career emphasis. Early in this century, scientific management theories were proposed to meet the growing needs of private industry. Authority was concentrated in management's hands, and there was "one best way" to perform each task; efficiency, rationality, productivity, and profit were foremost. In both theory and practice, scientific management encountered some difficulties though it gained wide acceptance in both private and public organizations. Early efforts to discover principles of administration were based on these same theories.

The human relations school, the first of the "informal" theories, was launched with the Hawthorne studies in the late 1920s and early 1930s. A major emphasis of the human relations school was the effect of leadership on worker performance and social interaction. The leadership function was viewed as offering positive incentives to workers in exchange for their contributions to the organization and its work.

Organizational humanism was founded on four central assumptions: (1) work was (or could be made) intrinsically interesting to the worker; (2) workers sought satisfactions in their jobs; (3) work was a central life interest to the worker and not merely a means to financial gain; and (4) greater worker involvement in management — through the delegation of responsibility, opportunities for creativity and independence, and inclusion in important policy decisions — could serve as positive motivation to improve worker performance and satisfaction.

Modern organization theory is characterized by an effort to separate facts from values, apply empirical research methods (including the use of statistical data and computers), incorporate information from diverse sources, and respond to complexity in the formulation and application of theory. Contributions to modern theory have come from such concepts as process integration, open-systems theory, information theory, cybernetics, organization development, Theory Z, TQM, and learning theory.

The dynamics of organization help shape how daily activities are carried on within organizations and include: (1) communication, (2) coordination, (3) line and staff functions, (4) centralization and decentralization, (5) tall and flat hierarchies, and (6) alternative forms of organization.

Communication is a crucial process in any organization and has been studied closely in recent years. Organizations are characterized by both formal and informal communications; the former carry with them more of the formal authority of top-level managers, whereas the latter may include almost anything other than communications "through channels." Lateral communications are often encouraged to facilitate the spread of information about activities throughout the organization. Prerequisites of communication include appropriate channels, a shared interest in clear communication, and common usage of terms by both sender and receiver. Purposes can include everything from promoting harmony, understanding, and cooperation to serving defensiveness and self-interest.

Coordination is another important function, one that brings together divided labor in an organization. Like communication and cooperation, coordination has its prerequisites, purposes, obstacles, remedies, and consequences; to date, most attention has focused on obstacles and remedies. Communication and leadership are often utilized in efforts to achieve better coordination. Organizational arrangements include central coordination, mutual adjustment through lateral coordination, and combinations of these two.

Line and staff functions are among the most traditional conceptions in the study of organizations. Line activities have been defined almost universally as pertaining to the policy responsibilities of the organization. Staff activities originally referred to support and advisory operations (such as budgeting, personnel, planning, and purchasing), but a further distinction has been drawn more recently between planning or research activities (which are classified as *staff*) and all other support functions (which are grouped under the rubric of *auxiliary*).

Centralization and decentralization are sources of tension in most organizations. In the past, many organizations exhibited a high degree of centralization; more recently, the trend has been toward decentralizing agency activities. Centralization has the advantage of enhancing effective control and consistency of activities; it has the disadvantage of lacking flexibility and adaptiveness to employee and "customer" needs. Decentralization exhibits the converse characteristics (intermittent control, some lack of consistency, but also greater flexibility); it also affords greater opportunities for meaningful participation by more people in the organization.

Tall hierarchies have been characteristic, for the most part, of government bureaucracies. Flat hierarchies, which emphasize collegial decision making and organization and which were not unknown in the past, are gaining in both recognition and actual use.

In recent years, alternatives to the bureaucratic form of organization have been suggested more frequently on the grounds that bureaucracy is no longer an appropriate way to structure organizations. Reasons cited range from the rise of new technologies and organizational functions to the development of professionalization within public administration. Suggested alternatives to traditional bureaucratic forms include a task force or project-team arrangement, a somewhat more permanent matrix organization, and the reverse-pyramid model.

Organization theory seeks to identify the elements crucial to organizational success. There has been both chronological and intellectual overlap from one body of theory to the next, and most theories have left their imprint on society even after passing from prominence among theorists. The complexity of modern organization theory parallels the complexity of real-world organizations in an era of accelerating change.

KEY TERMS AND CONCEPTS

hierarchy	scientific management
patronage	human relations
formal theory of organization	Hawthorne or "halo" effect
functional overlap	zone of acceptance
merit system	organizational humanism

Theory Y

Theory X

hierarchy of needs

modern organization theory

systems theory

closed systems

open-systems theory

homeostasis

information theory

game theory

cybernetics

organizational change

Theory Z

total quality management (TQM)

systems analysis

statistical process control (SPC)

learning organizations

communication

coordination

formal communication

informal communication

lateral or cross-functional
communication

gobbledygook

bargaining or political model

consensual or consensus-building
model

line functions

staff functions

centralization

decentralization

span of control

SUGGESTED READING

Argyris, Chris. *Integrating the Individual and the Organization.* New Brunswick, N.J.: Transaction Publishers, 1990.

———, *Knowledge for Action: A Guide to Overcoming Barriers to Organizational Change.* San Francisco: Jossey-Bass, 1993.

Ban, Carolyn. *How Do Public Managers Manage?* San Francisco: Jossey-Bass, 1995.

Barnard, Chester. *The Functions of the Executive.* Cambridge, Mass.: Harvard University Press, 1938.

Bozeman, Barry. *All Organizations Are Public: Bridging Public and Private Organizational Theories.* San Francisco: Jossey-Bass, 1987.

Brudney, Jeffrey L., Laurence J. O'Toole, and Hal G. Rainey, eds. *Advancing Public Management: New Developments in Theory, Methods, and Practice.* Baltimore, Md.: Georgetown University Press, 2000.

Davis, Charles R. *Organizational Theories and Public Administration.* Westport, Conn.: Praeger, 1996.

Downs, Anthony. *Inside Bureaucracy.* Boston: Little, Brown, 1967; reprint edition published by Waveland Press, Prospect Heights, Ill., 1994.

Garnett, James L. *Communicating for Results in Government: A Strategic Approach for Public Managers.* San Francisco: Jossey-Bass, 1992.

Goldhaber, Gerald M. *Organizational Communication.* 5th ed. Dubuque, Iowa: Wm. C. Brown, 1990.

Graham, Cole Blease, Jr., and Steven W. Hayes. *Managing the Public Sector.* 2nd ed. Washington, D.C.: Congressional Quarterly Press, 1992.

Hummel, Ralph. *The Bureaucratic Experience: A Critique of Life in the Modern Organization.* 4th ed. New York: St. Martin's Press, 1994.

Lane, Frederick S., ed. *Current Issues in Public Administration.* 6th ed. Boston: Bedford/St. Martin's, 1999.

Likert, Rensis. *New Patterns of Management.* New York: McGraw-Hill, 1961.

March, James G., and Herbert A. Simon. *Organizations.* New York: Wiley, 1958.

Maslow, Abraham H. *Motivation and Personality.* 2nd ed. New York: Harper & Row, 1970.

Meyer, C. Kenneth, and Charles H. Brown. *Practicing Public Management: A Casebook.* 2nd ed. New York: St. Martin's Press, 1989.

Peters, Guy. *The Future of Governing.* Lawrence: University Press of Kansas, 1996.

Rainey, Hal G. *Understanding and Managing Public Organizations.* 2nd ed. San Francisco: Jossey-Bass, 1996.

Senge, Peter M. *The Fifth Discipline: The Art and Practice of the Learning Organization.* New York: Doubleday, 1990.

Senge, Peter M., Charlotte Roberts, Richard Ross, Bryan Smith, and Art Kleiner. *The Fifth Discipline Fieldbook.* New York: Currency Doubleday, 1994.

Simon, Herbert A. *Administrative Behavior: A Study of Decision-Making Processes in Administrative Organizations.* 4th ed. New York: The Free Press, 1997.

Stivers, Camilla. *Gender Images in Public Administration: Legitimacy and the Administrative State.* Newbury Park, Calif.: Sage, 1993.

Thompson, James D. *Organizations in Action.* New York: McGraw-Hill, 1967.

ON-LINE RESOURCES:
Organizational Theory

Academy of Management On-Line

http://www.aom.pace.edu/

The official site for this professional society, which is primarily composed of professors who teach and research management.

Association for Quality and Participation (AQP)

http://www.aqp.org.

An international nonprofit membership association dedicated to improving workplaces through quality and participation practices.

@Brint.com

http://www.brint.com/orgLrng.htm

Commercial business technology and knowledge management site for information about knowledge management and learning organizations.

Encyclopedia of Organizational Theory

http://www.stanford.edu/~krollag/org_site/encyclop/encyclo.html

Extensive alphabetical listing of topics related to organizational theory.

Frederick W. Taylor

http://www.lib.stevens-tech.edu/collections/taylor

A site dedicated to the writings of Frederick Winslow Taylor.

Herbert A. Simon

http://http://kungfu.psy.cmu.edu/psy/faculty/hsimon/hsimon.html

This site is dedicated to the research of academic Herbert A. Simon, including his research on economics and management.

Learning Organizations (MIT)

http://www.learning-org.com

Learn more about learning organizations in this Web site.

Max Weber

http://msumusik.mursurky.edu/~felwell/http/weber/whome.htm

A reference site dedicated to Max Weber and sociological theory, organized by a sociology professor at Murray State University.

Organizational Development Network

http://www.odnet.org/

The OD Network Web site is sponsored by the OD Network and is provided as a service to the community of organization development practitioners.

Organizational Learning

http://www.albany.edu/faculty/pm157/teaching/topics/orglearn.html

This site contains organizations, articles, consultants, and more on the topic of organizational learning.

Quality Digest

http://www.qualitydigest.com

This site is part of the Quality Management WebRing and is dedicated to the discussion of quality management.

Quality Resources On-Line

http://www.quality.org/

> An Associated Quality Consultants, Inc., Web site where you can browse Internet services on the issue of quality.

The Society for Organizational Learning

http://learning.mit.edu/olc/sol_faq.html

> The Society for Organizational Learning is a global learning community dedicated to building knowledge about fundamental institutional change through integrating research, capacity building, and practice. This site's purpose is to discover, integrate, and implement theories and practices for the interdependent development of people and their institutions.

Stanford Learning and Organization Web

http://www.stanford.edu/group/SLOW/

> The Stanford Learning Organization Web (SLOW) is an informal network of researchers, staff, and students along with colleagues and friends from the corporate world interested in the nature and development of learning organizations.

W. Edwards Deming Institute

http://www.deming.org

> A nonprofit institute founded by the late quality management consultant and bearing his name. Its aim is to foster understanding of the Deming system and to advance commerce, prosperity, and international peace.

For further information on organizational theory see: Bedford/St. Martin's Home Page

http://www.bedfordstmartins.com

Chapter 6

Decision Making in Administration

If you can't stand the heat you better get out of the kitchen.

Harry S. Truman to the Aero Club of Washington,
quoting a colleague from Truman's days as a county judge,
December 27, 1952

The making of decisions is at the heart of public administration. How decisions are made in a bureaucracy, by whom, by what standards, at what cost, and for whose benefit are questions of continuing interest as well as occasional controversy. The scramble for influence over decisions, the accessibility of decision makers, the actions of those making and affected by government decisions, the ethical standards maintained and the values applied by public administrators, as well as the accountability of decision makers, all attest to the importance attached to the decision-making process.

The substance of decisions, as well as the procedures by which they are made and applied, leaves a lasting imprint on administrative politics. In this chapter, we will discuss the general nature of bureaucratic decisions, principal approaches to decision making, the impacts of different kinds of goals, ethical considerations of decision making, major features of the surrounding environment that ordinarily enter into the process, and how different sorts of political pressures affect the way many administrative decisions are made.

The Nature of Decisions

Organizational **decision making** involves making a choice to alter some existing condition, choosing one course of action in preference to others, expending

decision making
a process in which choices are made to change (or leave unchanged) an existing condition, and to select a course of action most appropriate to achieving a desired objective (however formalized or informal the objective may be), while minimizing risk and uncertainty to the extent deemed possible; the process may be characterized by widely varying degrees of self-conscious "rationality," or by willingness of the decision maker to decide incrementally, without insisting on assessment of all possible alternatives, or by some combinations of approaches.

some amount of organizational or individual resources to implement the decision, and acting with the expectation of gaining something desirable. Some decisions are made to leave things as they are rather than to change them, but theoretically the mere fact that a decision was called for not to change something alters the overall situation. The definition of decision making suggests that a decision is not a single, self-contained event; rather, it is "the product of a complex social process generally extending over a considerable period of time . . . Decision making includes attention-directing or intelligence processes that determine the occasions of decision, processes for discovering and designing possible courses of action and processes for evaluating alternatives and choosing them."[1] Thus, a decision entails a series of other choices that may rightly be regarded as part of it.

It is assumed that a decision maker selects the course of action most appropriate to achieving a desired result or objective; deciding what is most appropriate, however, is often difficult. There is always some uncertainty as to the eventual outcome of a decision; as a result, a degree of risk (however small) is involved in implementing that decision. Concerns that are central to the decision-making process, therefore, include (1) increasing potential gains, (2) monitoring the ongoing decisional process, and (3) reducing the resource expenditure, uncertainty, and risk involved in achieving whatever gains are made.[2]

In this chapter, we will discuss decisions about relatively important, even fundamental, matters in organizational life. But it should be noted that the great majority of all decisions are more or less routine and based on previously adopted policy. Routine decisions have the advantage of requiring little time or mental energy to make; they can be made according to regular schedules (Should we hire our usual extra summer help?) or where clear need exists (Should we send out the snowplows?), without having to "start fresh" each time. The central risk involved in routine decision making is that decision makers may fail to perceive a need to reconsider existing policy or program assumptions on which routine decisions are based.

For example, in an agency dependent on extra personnel to meet seasonal demand (such as the U.S. National Park Service), the number of extra people needed should not *automatically* be based on prior experience. If, say, the price of park admission rises five dollars per person, the Park Service personnel director may reasonably assume that fewer staff aides will have to be hired because the flow of visitors is very likely to diminish. Similarly, sending out the snowplows as a routine response to a midwestern snowstorm might have to be reexamined if a city is confronted with a fiscal crunch (as many now are). Work crew layoffs, reduced gasoline allocations, fewer streets plowed, fewer plows in operation — under nonroutine circumstances, all these options might have to be explored. Thus, maintaining routines that are inappropriate to changing conditions may only complicate the problems to which they were first addressed and may lead to new problems.

Approaches to Decision Making:
Concepts and Controversies

Few issues have occupied such a central place in the literature of public administration or have generated so much debate as the question of *how* to make decisions. Arguments have raged over such issues as the importance and relevance of goal setting, the capacities of decision makers to absorb information and use it objectively, the scope and types of data that decision makers ought to use in order to make good decisions, and the consequences of employing different approaches to decision making. Models that are applicable to administrative organizations have been derived from a variety of disciplines, notably economics and political science. Some have stressed statistical techniques, utilizing quantitative data and (allegedly) value-free measures of decision alternatives. Others, said by their advocates to be both more realistic and more effective, suggest that decisions can and should be made without first having to define every goal that might be served by a given action; these models also recommend the use of more informal measures of decision choices. Still other models have been advanced that attempt to integrate the strong points of existing models into new perspectives on, and approaches to, decision making.

The debate surrounding how decisions should be made is marked by intense disagreement. Issues of decision making are far from settled, and new contributions to the literature continue to appear. New controversies and directions have recently emerged, especially in government, that are reshaping many long-standing assumptions about how decisions should (and *can*) be made. These include efforts supporting empowerment of citizens, better service to government's customers, and devolving decision-making power to nongovernmental entities. Other issues (such as the impacts of past decisions on a current choice) also affect decision making and further complicate matters. The complexity and importance of the subject make it imperative that the student of public administration understand the nature of the controversies surrounding decision making, as well as key aspects of the process itself. The following section explores the principal approaches to decision making, criticisms of each, considers other dimensions of the process, and concludes by examining a consciously political approach to decision making.

RATIONALITY IN DECISION MAKING:
THE CLASSICAL/ECONOMIC MODEL

The **rational** approach is derived from economic models of decision making. According to this classical outlook, decision makers are consciously rational; that is, they order their behavior so that it is "reasonably directed toward the achievement of conscious goals."[3] Another crucial dimension of economic rationality is the concept of *efficiency* — "maximizing output for a given input [of scarce

rational decision making is derived from economic theories of how to make the "best" decisions; involves efforts to move toward consciously held goals in a way that requires the smallest input of scarce resources; assumes the ability to separate ends from means, rank all alternatives, gather all possible data, and objectively weigh alternatives; stresses rationality in the process of reaching decisions.

resources], or minimizing input for a given output."[4] In the words of political economist Anthony Downs:

> Economic analysis thus consists of two major steps: discovery of the *ends a decision maker is pursuing* and analysis of which means of attaining them are most reasonable, i.e., require the least input of scarce resources. . . . Thus, whenever economists refer to a "rational man" they are not designating a man whose thought processes consist exclusively of logical propositions, or a man without prejudices, or a man whose emotions are inoperative. In normal usage all of these could be considered rational men. But the economic definition refers solely to a man who moves toward his goals in a way which, to the best of his knowledge, *uses the least possible input of scarce resources per unit of valued output.*[5]

In terms of actual behavior, a rational man or woman (1) can always make a decision when presented with a range of alternatives; (2) knows the probable consequences of choosing each alternative; (3) ranks all alternatives in an order of preference, so that each is preferred, equal, or inferior to other options included in the ranking; (4) always chooses the highest-ranked alternative; and (5) always makes the same decision each time the same alternatives are available. Such an individual would normally try to separate ends (goals) clearly from means (methods) while concentrating on one or a few primary goals; pursuing too many goals simultaneously would frustrate efforts to attain them and to measure the efficiency and rationality of the process. Also, the rational decision maker would seek to gather all possible data pertaining to the range of alternatives and objectively weigh alternative solutions before selecting the best possible one (maximizing). The analysis and methodology must be comprehensive, with precise evaluation procedures, quantification of measures and relative values, and statistics.

cost-benefit analysis technique designed to measure relative gains and losses resulting from alternative policy or program options; emphasizes identification of the most desirable cost-benefit ratio, in quantitative or other terms.

Maximizing utility value and pursuing self-interest objectives are fundamental aspects of the rational-comprehensive model of decision making. Also, important are the relationships that are assumed to exist between means and ends (and that enable the decision maker to choose the most rational means for achieving the specified end) and the relationships between *costs and benefits* involved, in the interest of efficiency. **Cost-benefit analysis** and specification of **cost-benefit ratios** for each alternative presume the ability to assign a quantitative value to each alternative in a ranking and to distinguish clearly among the values assigned. In theory, this makes it possible to determine the optimum (best) ratio of benefits to costs, thus enabling the decision maker to make the final best choice.

cost-benefit ratios the proportional relationship between expenditure of a given quantity of resources and the benefits derived therefrom; a guideline for choosing among alternatives, of greatest relevance to the rational model of decision making.

This model essentially stresses the rationality of the decision-making *process* as *value-neutral* without reference to whether goals are also rational. The test of a good decision is that "it can be shown to be the most appropriate means to [achieving] desired ends,"[6] judging in long-term perspectives. It is *procedural* criteria that must be satisfied in order to assess decision making as being rational; the decision outcome is distinctly secondary. (The analytical steps in the method are similar to the seven-step policy analysis approach outlined in Box 10–1, p. 396.)

For several decades, the rational model has had a powerful influence on decision theory and on the art and craft of practical decision making. It was not until the late 1950s that questions and criticisms began to be raised about the model and alternative approaches to decision making were suggested. Two principal themes were sounded: (1) that the rational model lacks practical applicability outside the realm of economic theory, and (2) that it is less desirable than other possible models as a mode of operation, especially in public administrative organizations.

CRITIQUES OF THE RATIONAL MODEL

The practicality of the rational model has been questioned on numerous grounds.[7] Most critiques are based on the proposition that it is not possible — and never has been — to construct a purely rational, that is, value-neutral, decision-making process for any but the simplest, lowest-level decisions. Among the impediments to rationality suggested by the model's critics are the impossibility of distinguishing facts from values and of analytically separating ends from means, the improbability of obtaining agreement among decision makers on predetermined goals, the changing and ambiguous nature of many political and administrative goals (we will examine this more fully, later in this chapter), the pressures of time to make a decision when it is needed, and the ability of decision makers to handle only a limited amount of information at any one time. Other problems include the difficulty of giving one's undivided attention to a single problem or decision; the costs of information acquisition; failure to secure all possible data because of time constraints, excessive cost, or oversight; defects in communication processes; and the inability to predict all the consequences of a given choice, which contributes to inevitable uncertainties during and after the decision process.

Still other handicaps include competition among decision makers and their organizations for resources, preventing any one entity from achieving maximum utility; the need to deal with different aspects of the same problem — for example, the funding and location of a new public sports arena or capital and operating budgets for a mass transit system; lack of precision in measuring various costs, benefits, and side effects; and uncertainties in the sociopolitical environment that affect substantive problems and the availability of both alternatives and resources.

The other major criticism of the rational model was that it required activities and calculations that *were not possible* in decision-making processes. The first and principal spokesman for this view was political scientist Charles Lindblom, who first articulated his position in 1959.[8] Lindblom argued that decision makers do not have to seek prior goal consensus in order to make sound decisions for the short run; furthermore, because goals can rarely be agreed on in advance, even trying to achieve consensus makes the pursuit of reasonable decisions just that much more difficult. Lindblom referred to this facetiously as the science of "muddling through" a decision, also noting that the means–ends analysis called for in the rational model is impossible if means and ends are confused (as, he suggested, they inevitably are). Also, public administrators cannot look to the general public to set and articulate meaningful policy goals (see Chapter 10) because public opinion is highly ambiguous and diverse; even if identifiable goals do exist, they do not serve as clear guides to administrative decision making. Finally, many broad (and even worthy) public goals may conflict with one another.

INCREMENTALISM AND MIXED SCANNING: RESPONSE AND COUNTERRESPONSE

As we have seen, major criticisms of the rational model centered on several of its basic assumptions: the quest for maximizing utility, emphasis on long-term consequences at the expense of short-term changes, the need to formulate explicit goals, and a heavy bias in favor of economic, that is, market-driven, conceptualizations of costs, benefits, and their relationships. A number of scholars have expanded on these criticisms and have argued that individual decisions, and change in general, are produced by an "incremental" process. **Incrementalism,** in contrast to rationality, stresses decision making through a series of limited, successive comparisons with a relatively narrow range of alternatives rather than a comprehensive range; it uses the status quo, not abstract goals, as the key point of reference for decisions. Incrementalism focuses primarily on short-term rather than long-term effects, on the most crucial consequences of an action rather than on all conceivable results, and on less formalized methods of measuring costs and benefits.

> **incrementalism**
> a model of decision making that stresses making decisions through limited successive comparisons, in contrast to the rational model; also focuses on simplifying choices rather than aspiring to complete problem analyses, on the status quo rather than abstract goals as a key point of reference, on "satisficing" rather than "maximizing" and on remedying ills rather than seeking positive goals.

Differences between rationalists and incrementalists are very sharp. First, the rationalist attempts to maximize benefits in all phases of decision making, whereas the incrementalist tries to "satisfice" (to use economist Herbert Simon's term). To "satisfice" is to reach a decision that is satisfactory, yielding benefits that suffice to meet the situational needs of the decision maker. In other words, a decision maker who satisfices is one who is willing to "settle for good-enough answers in despair at finding best answers."[9] The incremental decision maker accepts that it may not be possible to get everything out of a given decision and that settling for "half a loaf" is not unreasonable. Furthermore, the incrementalist maintains that it is *irrational* to expect success every time a decision is made, because doing so increases the risks — and consequences — of failure and expends resources too rapidly and because rationality itself would not be cost-effective (assuming, again, that rationality is possible).

Second, although incrementalism does not dismiss the importance of long-term consequences, it emphasizes short-term needs and problems. Incrementalists are comfortable filling the role of troubleshooters, responding to immediate pressures and seeking to alleviate the worst of them. Charles Lindblom, perhaps the leading spokesman for this school of thought, speaks of serial analyses — that is, repeated and ongoing analyses — rather than one comprehensive analysis as called for in the rationalist view. He maintains that making *continual incremental adjustments* in both the definition of a problem and the formulation of solutions is a reasonable and effective method of solving problems and making decisions.

Third, Lindblom and others suggest that the emphasis in the rational model on comprehensive evaluation of how a given decision would affect all other decisions is unrealistic. They contend that it is impossible to account in advance for all the ways in which a particular course of action will affect other decision-making processes and their outcomes.

Incrementalism may also have a practical advantage for public administrators as they try to deal with executive orders or legislative requirements, which often are ambiguous. Making decisions incrementally may enable administrators to satisfy the minimal expectations while gaining time to determine more specifically what effects the directives will have in practice. Under conditions of uncertainty of all kinds, it is difficult at best to pursue a classical/economic rational course.

Most important, those who have advocated the incremental approach reject the notion that only "efficiency" models of decision making are legitimate. They argue that noneconomic models and modes of decision making have intrinsic value and that, in some circumstances, using economic models might well be inappropriate and irrational. Furthermore, they claim that the incremental model allows for measures of costs, benefits, and side effects of decisions that are not economic or even necessarily quantitative. Incrementalists acknowledge that this approach permits *subjective values* to influence decisions, but they justify that on the grounds that subjectivity can never be eliminated entirely. They maintain that it is better to openly incorporate sound subjective judgment than to attempt self-consciously to exclude all traces of subjectivity. At the same time, incrementalists strongly endorse the need for adequate and good-quality data, for choosing sound courses of action, and so on. The difference is that they are prepared to make decisions even when the ideal conditions called for by the rationalists do not exist, which, they maintain, happens in an overwhelming majority of decision-making situations.

The incremental approach itself has come under fire. Two critics, in particular, stand out — one for identifying a serious shortcoming, the other for elaborating on the criticism of the first and outlining a third approach to decision making. Yehezkel Dror, in a pointed response to Lindblom, emphasized that marginal changes acceptable to incrementalists may *not* suffice to meet real and growing policy demands and that, as policy needs change, decision makers may have to develop innovations bolder than those apparently contemplated by supporters of the incremental approach.[10] Dror's message is that, if incrementalists focus solely or even primarily on small-scale changes designed to meet disjointed and short-run needs, they are likely to overlook larger needs and demands, with subsequent decisions even more likely to "miss the mark" in one or more policy/problem areas.

Dror also criticized incrementalism for making more acceptable the forces in human organizations that tend toward inertia and maintenance of the status quo. His comments suggest that, in incrementalism, one can find justification for the behavior of Downs's "conserver" — the bureaucrat who is chiefly interested in maintaining power, prestige, and income and who takes a cautious, low-risk approach to decision making. Dror clearly leaned toward a view of bureaucratic behavior that encourages both responsiveness to larger-scale needs and innovativeness in seeking solutions; he found incrementalism wanting in both respects.

mixed scanning
a model of decision making that combines the rational-comprehensive model's emphasis on fundamental choices and long-term consequences with the incrementalists' emphasis on changing only what needs to be changed in the immediate situation; emphasizes short-term decisions.

Amitai Etzioni expanded on Dror's criticisms of the incremental model and offered an alternative approach, which he labeled **mixed scanning**.[11] Etzioni's chief criticism of the incremental approach was its apparent failure to distinguish between fundamental and nonfundamental decisions. He suggested that, for nonfundamental decision making, the incremental approach was entirely valid and appropriate but that, in making fundamental decisions, a wider perceptual horizon was needed. More important, he believed that incrementalists tended to decide only nonfundamental matters — stemming from their emphasis on the troubleshooter approach to solving problems — and, as a result, promoted a general aimlessness in overall policy. Etzioni suggested a twofold or mixed approach to decision making that incorporates some elements of both the rational-comprehensive and incremental approaches.

Etzioni's mixed-scanning model can best be understood through his analogy involving a high-altitude weather satellite in orbit around the earth. Onboard the satellite are two cameras — one equipped with a wide-angle lens that can scan a large area and record major weather patterns, the other equipped with a narrow-angle lens capable of zeroing in on turbulence and examining it in much finer detail. Examination by the narrow-lens camera is contingent on the wide-lens camera's having first discovered large systems of turbulent weather. Conversely, the wide-lens camera is incapable of detailed analysis of storm centers and other phenomena. In sum, either camera without the other would supply some useful information, but much more can be obtained when they are used in combination. Further, the analysis provided by the narrow-lens camera is more intelligible when meteorologists have some idea of the total weather system's size, location, and boundary — that is, when they have a meaningful context for the detailed data. So it is with decision making:

> Fundamental decisions are made by exploring the main alternatives the actor sees in view of his conception of his goals, but — unlike what rationalism would indicate — details and specifications are omitted so that an overview is feasible. *Incremental decisions are made but within the context set by fundamental decisions (and fundamental reviews).* Thus, each of the two elements in mixed-scanning helps to reduce the effects of the particular shortcomings of the other; incrementalism reduces the unrealistic aspects of rationalism by limiting the details required in

fundamental decisions, and . . . rationalism helps to overcome the conservative slant of incrementalism by exploring longer-run alternatives.[12]

This prescription for decision making has, in turn, been criticized in several ways. First, it is difficult to identify "a big or little decision" because the consequences are often unknown at the time a decision is being made. From that, one might infer that, while fundamental decisions may be relatively easy to recognize, problems can develop when a seemingly minor choice turns out to have led to unexpectedly significant outcomes. In this context, perhaps too much emphasis has been placed on differences between fundamental and incremental decisions, implicitly undercutting the mixed-scanning model.

Contrary to the interpretation given it by many observers, incrementalism is not, by definition, concerned with change only in small steps, nor is it biased against large-scale alterations in the status quo. Change by increments, according to this view, is a matter of degree as well as substance. Lindblom acknowledged criticisms that "doing better usually means turning away from incrementalism" by arguing that incrementalists "believe that for complex problem solving, it usually means *practicing incrementalism more skillfully* and turning away from it only rarely."[13] Contrary to the assumptions of the rational model, no one can hope to analyze a complex problem completely, and calculated analytic strategies designed to simplify complex problems hold more promise of success than do attempts at comprehensive "scientific" analysis. Incremental analysis can and should focus on immediate problem solving rather than long-term goals. It is that line of reasoning that challenges the mixed-scanning model. Incrementalists believe that relying on rationality produces worse analysis and decisions than does strategic analysis. In sum, Lindblom would fault mixed scanning for its failure to reject the rational model completely, while defending incrementalism as a viable approach to decisions of either large or small consequence.[14]

We will refer to these models later in this chapter. Now we turn to another dimension of decision making that also merits discussion.

The Problem of Goals

One does not have to subscribe to the rational model of decision making to acknowledge that, in one form or another, all programs are managed, agencies receive and spend public funds, individuals engage in myriad activities, and administrative routines are carried on in order to fulfill some kind of purpose or purposes. In this sense, the goals of various organizations range from the most concrete to the most ambiguous formulations; they may be substantive or symbolic, individual or organizational or suborganizational, and they may be held by those inside the organization or imposed from outside. Agency personnel may consciously select particular objectives, or others outside the agency may come to regard it as pursuing certain goals because of its programmatic choices (incre-mentalists argue that the latter occurs quite frequently). Formally, of course, the goals pursued by a public agency are defined in the first instance by legislatures (as noted previously). Similarly, measures of success or failure in achieving for-mal agency goals are devised and applied by at least some outsiders.

The types of goals that can be pursued by agency personnel acting collec-tively or by individuals seeking their own ends through administrative action (or inaction) vary greatly. We will seek to give some order to this subject by examin-ing organizational goals, broadly defined, and then considering impacts of per-sonal goals of employees in public agencies.

ORGANIZATIONAL GOALS

Many casual observers of government organizations seem to believe that they exist to achieve only certain kinds of goals, such as substantive programmatic objectives (for example, adequate health care or safe, reasonably priced air travel) and that they act out of a desire to satisfy a broad public interest. Other observers assume, in contrast, that government bureaucracies act as interest groups, are concerned only with their own survival, and take a limited view of the public interest. Neither view is totally wrong, but both fail to account for the complex-ity of goals within government agencies.

Survival and maintenance are indeed principal goals of virtually all organiza-tions, governmental or otherwise. (To draw an analogy to human behavior, sur-vival is a fundamental instinct but not the sole purpose of our existence.) Administrative agencies, like other organizations, have as one of their goals maintenance of their own position. Such inward-oriented goals, which have been termed **reflexive**,[15] are supported by those aspects of an organization's behavior and programs that have primary impact *internally* rather than exter-nally. Agencies pursue such goals by trying to persuade a significant constituency that their functions are essential either to society at large or to an important seg-ment of society.

Administrative agencies are, of course, concerned with **substantive** goals. All government organizations seek to achieve program objectives, whether popular or unpopular, visible or obscure, major or minor. Program objectives appear to be the raison d'être (the reason for existence) of administrative agencies and, in many cases, they constitute a powerful argument for an agency's existence. Goals can also lend **legitimacy** to organization activities both within and outside the formal organizational structure. Thus, goals become the rationale for legitimiz-ing those serving the organization and for those seeking to understand the courses of action that the organization follows. This type of goal has been labeled **transitive** in that there is an intended programmatic impact on the envi-ronment beyond the organization itself.[16] In advancing its cause through the political process, an agency will emphasize substantive goals — their importance

reflexive an orga-nizational or individual goal related primarily to survival and maintenance; "inward oriented" as opposed to a goal focusing on external impacts.

substantive an organiza-tional goal focusing on the accomplishment of tangible programmatic objectives.

legitimacy the accep-tance of an institution or individual such as a gov-ernment, family member, or state governor as having the legal and publicly recognized right to make and enforce binding decisions.

transitive an organizational goal that, if achieved, would have an impact on an organiza-tion's external environ-ment; a goal concerned more with external than with internal consequences of organizational actions.

to particular clienteles and to the whole society — and the agency's performance in pursuit of them.

Political scientist Lawrence Mohr has suggested an alternative conception of organizational goals that narrows and sharpens what is meant by the terms. In Mohr's view, we may accurately label as "organizational goals" only those on which there is widespread consensus of intent (agreement as to purpose) among a large majority of organization members, and that relate to "mainstreams" of organizational behavior.[17] Mohr maintains that these goals must be identified on the basis of empirical investigation rather than superficial reading of official pronouncements, informal discussion with leaders or members, or intuitive judgements. He raises the possibility of being able to identify such organizational goals empirically and precisely, and he stresses the necessity of doing so. Without identifying goals in this manner, Mohr says, the result of any inquiry into the goals of an organization are likely to be misleading, or at best incomplete. The implication of this conception of goals is this: if organizational goals are formulated by achieving a consensus of intent, then by definition there is substantial overlap between personal and organizational goals. Were this the commonly accepted and applied definition of organizational goals, the leader's task in this regard would be virtually nonexistent.

Research in the human relations school of organization theory, as well as later studies, suggest that where there are differences between an organization's official and actual goals, it is group norms among members that account for those differences and designate *actual* goals. Where leaders rely heavily on member preferences as part of goal definition, chances are greater that personal and organizational goals can be reconciled at least to some degree. This is because the followership can be expected to respond favorably to a leadership willing "include them in" on so basic a question as the goals of *their* organization. Leaders are therefore well advised to focus on the task of goal definition. If the results here are positive, other leadership tasks will be more readily accomplished.

Pursuit of program goals is not without its subtleties, however. In practice, an agency may emphasize substantive goals and others that are largely "symbolic." **Symbolic goals** (and some substantive goals) are valuable because of the political support they can attract; in effect, the agency adopts the goals of persons outside it. (See Chapter 10, Public Policy and Management.) Frequently, an agency goal can be both substantive and symbolic, with merit in objective terms as well as beneficial political consequences. Finally, it is common to find agencies saying that they are trying to accomplish a worthy but unreachable goal — for example, total eradication of illiteracy in the United States — yet continued pursuit of that objective yields benefits to both the agency and society. Many citizens and public officials support efforts to wipe out illiteracy and are willing to appropriate public funds to agencies with jurisdiction to carry on the struggle, which benefits at least some of those who cannot read or write.

symbolic goals
organizational objectives reflecting broad, popular political purposes; frequently unattainable.

Another dimension of substantive goals is the tricky question of goal attainment. How do we know when a goal has been met, and what happens to the agency in charge of a program when its goal has been reached? Achievement of organizational goals can be detrimental to an agency's continued operation. If an agency accomplishes its purposes, some might question the further need for it. On the other hand, if, in order to avoid that embarrassing dilemma, an agency does not act vigorously to "solve the problem," it risks the wrath of supporters in the legislative and executive branches, as well as clientele groups. Fortunately for most agencies, the dilemma is not insoluble because of the breadth of many goals and the different dimensions of goal attainment situations.

For many public agencies, goals are not objectively attainable. It is possible to view organizational goals conceptually as *aims*, or sets of values to be pursued, rather than as tangible objectives to be achieved. In this sense, *goals* are sets of broad policy directions in which organization members seek to move without necessarily expecting to accomplish them, whereas objectives are more limited, achievable purposes that are related to the larger goals. Adequate health care, for example, is an abstract goal; attracting more doctors and building another hospital are concrete objectives that move the organization (or community or state or nation) closer to that goal. Using this example, is it possible to reach the goal of adequate health care so that efforts to achieve it may cease? Not really, for two reasons. One is that definitions of adequacy have to be agreed on through the political process. There may be continuing disagreement about what is "adequate" and, consequently, about whether the goal has in fact been achieved. The other reason is that, even if it can be agreed that health care is now adequate, ongoing programs will be required to keep it that way. (Note that the latter observation implicitly undercuts the rational model.)

There may be political advantage in deliberately stating agency goals in general terms. The goal of "improving the quality of our schools" is far less likely to cause problems for a Department of Education than is a goal of ensuring that high school graduates are equipped with specific reading and writing skills and are qualified for entry-level jobs or eligible for colleges and universities according to a prescribed entrance-test score. Also, *the more generalized a goal statement, the more widely supported it is likely to be, with less chance of concerted political opposition.*

Legislative language establishing agency goals can be imprecise as a result of uncertainty about specific meanings and the frequent need for compromise. For example, a health program in the Department of Health and Human Services could have minimizing heart disease and related ailments among adult Americans as its overall goal. This is a laudable goal; no one would quarrel with it. But who is to say that the minimum has been reached and by what measures? Such language is quite common in legislation and administrative regulations (see Chapter 3). Under these circumstances, all an agency with such responsibilities needs to show is that it has had some success in putting across its message (get more exercise, stop smoking, have regular checkups, etc.), with some resultant reduction in heart disease and related ailments, and it is likely to be able to sustain itself and its programs. Most agencies start with a combination of goals, and many branch out into new but related areas. Thus, agency goals may undergo substantial and permanent modification at the instigation of decision makers outside the agency.

One other major point should be made about organizational goals. When public bureaucracies are repeatedly criticized for failure to reach their goals, they may develop a tendency to articulate publicly goals that they know they can reach. Bureaucracies also know that they may suffer politically from excessive attachment to goals that turn out to be unpopular. In short, politics may influence the choice of official or unofficial organizational goals. An agency may adopt as official goals only objectives that, in the judgment of its leaders, will produce the requisite political support for its operations. This does not happen universally, but the fact that it *can* happen should serve as a warning not to view goals as abstract, permanent, or sacred statements that are above politics or somehow separate from the interests of the agencies.

PERSONAL GOALS

In addition to organizational goals, the personal motivations of employees must be considered. Most individuals have personal goals. Besides the basic drives for earning a decent living and job security, individual motivation may relate to opportunities for professional advancement or personal self-improvement. Or, as Anthony Downs and Arnold Meltsner each note, job performance can be related to an overzealous attachment to a particular policy direction.[18] In other words, personal goals can affect an organization's goals in two ways: (1) individuals might devote more time and energy to pursuing their own goals than those of the organization, and (2) they might come into conflict with others in the organization over such matters as advancement through the ranks or policy-related organization activities. Interpersonal conflicts or office politics diverts attention and resources from the effort to attain organizational objectives.

Anthony Downs has suggested five types of bureaucratic employees, each characterized by a particular combination of goals.[19] Two types, *climbers* and *conservers*, act purely out of self-interest. Climbers are interested in increasing their power, income, and prestige; conservers seek to maximize their job security and maintain the power, income, and prestige that they already have. The three other types are, in Downs's phrase, "mixed-motive officials, [who] combine self-interest and altruistic loyalty to larger values. The main difference among the three types of mixed-motive officials is the breadth of the larger values to which they are loyal."[20] Downs calls them *zealots*, *advocates*, and *statesmen*, who focus, respectively, on relatively narrow policies or concepts, on a set of wider functions or on a wider organization, and on the general welfare or public interest, broadly defined.

Although Downs's formulation is admittedly hypothetical and idealized, Meltsner's analysis of federal bureaucrats found noticeable similarities to Downs's typology.[21] The essential point here is that the greater the variety of bureaucratic types and motives, the more difficult it is to attain official organizational objectives because so many other unofficial objectives are present. Also, potential for internal conflict is increased with the variety of bureaucratic types, and a higher level of conflict will inhibit attainment of both official and unofficial goals.

From the standpoint of an organization's ability to fulfill its official objectives and manage its programs effectively, the ideal situation is one in which there is a high degree of **goal congruence** among all organization members. If leaders are agreed on objectives and priorities and can count on unified support from employees in attaining shared objectives, an organization's chances of success are obviously enhanced. Such congruence, however, is the exception rather than the rule, even within the leadership. Also, within the framework of the organization at large, there are likely to be numerous small groups, each with its own particularistic goals, which may be given greater weight than those of the wider organization. The importance of small-group goals has been emphasized in the findings of Elton Mayo and his associates in the Hawthorne experiments and by John Pfiffner and Frank Sherwood in their studies a quarter of a century later (see Chapter 5).[22] All this makes it even less likely that substantial goal congruence will exist. (Moreover, goal congruence can become too much of a good thing by discouraging fresh thinking about organization directions and actions and stifling the sort of open dialogue that often gives rise to creative and useful new ideas.[23] See the discussion of groupthink later in this chapter.)

goal congruence
agreement on fundamental goals; in the context of an organization, refers to the extent of agreement among leaders and followers in the organization on central objectives; in practice, its absence in many instances creates internal tensions and difficulties in goal definition.

Ethical Dimensions of Decision Making

In pursuit of personal (and even organizational) goals, it is not uncommon to find examples of administrative behavior that raise serious questions about the ethical propriety of tactics used or courses of action followed. Such instances, fortunately, do not make up the bulk of administrative decision making, but they occur frequently enough to warrant discussion here. Evaluating decisions according to standards of ethical behavior has a long history in American government. In recent decades, it has become a matter of greater urgency and concern for many, in and out of government — even as we have become aware of numerous examples of government behavior widely characterized as unethical.

But just what is *ethical* behavior? Unfortunately, as noted in Chapter 2, there is no single answer to that question. Yet several efforts have been made to define, in sufficiently broad terms, the ethical behavior that a majority of Americans would perceive as acceptable in the public service. Another effort was made in the mid-1980s by the **American Society for Public Administration (ASPA)**, which formally adopted a **Code of Ethics** applicable to official conduct in virtually any administrative agency or setting (see Box 6–1, "American Society for Public Administration: Code of Ethics"). For further information on ASPA, see On-Line Resources at the end of this chapter.

American Society for Public Administration (ASPA) Code of Ethics
effort by the nation's leading professional association of public administrators to draw up and enforce a set of standards for official conduct.

BOX 6-1   ETHICAL AND LEADERSHIP CHALLENGES FOR PUBLIC MANAGERS

American Society for Public Administration: Code of Ethics

The American Society for Public Administration (ASPA) exists to advance the science, processes, and art of public administration. The Society affirms its responsibility to develop the spirit of professionalism within its membership, and to increase the public awareness of ethical principles in public service by its example. To this end, we, the members of the Society, commit ourselves to the following principles:

I Serve the Public Interest

Serve the public, beyond serving oneself.
ASPA members are committed to:

1. Exercise discretionary authority to promote the public interest.
2. Oppose all forms of discrimination and harassment, and promote affirmative action.
3. Recognize and support the public's right to know the public's business.
4. Involve citizens in policy decision-making.
5. Exercise compassion, benevolence, fairness and optimism.
6. Respond to the public in ways that are complete, clear, and easy to understand.
7. Assist citizens in their dealings with government.
8. Be prepared to make decisions that may not be popular.

II Respect the Constitution and the Law

Respect, support, and study government constitutions   and laws that define responsibilities of public agencies, employees, and all citizens.
ASPA members are committed to:

1. Understand and apply legislation and regulations rele-vant to their professional role.
2. Work to improve and change laws and policies that are counter-productive or obsolete.
3. Eliminate unlawful discrimination.
4. Prevent all forms of mismanagement of public funds by establishing and maintaining strong fiscal and manage-ment controls, and by supporting audits and investiga-tive activities.
5. Respect and protect privileged information.
6. Encourage and facilitate legitimate dissent activities in government and protect the whistleblowing rights of public employees.
7. Promote constitutional principles of equality, fairness, representativeness, responsiveness and due process in protecting citizens' rights.

III Demonstrate Personal Integrity

Demonstrate the highest standards in all activities to inspire public confidence and trust in public service.
ASPA members are committed to:

1. Maintain truthfulness and honesty and to not compro-mise them for advancement, honor, or personal gain.
2. Ensure that others receive credit for their work and contributions.
3. Zealously guard against conflict of interest or its ap-pearance: e.g., nepotism, improper outside employ-ment, misuse of public resources or the acceptance of gifts.
4. Respect superiors, subordinates, colleagues and the public.
5. Take responsibility for their own errors.
6. Conduct official acts without partisanship.

IV Promote Ethical Organizations

Strengthen organizational capabilities to apply ethics, effi-ciency and effectiveness in serving the public.
ASPA members are committed to:

1. Enhance organizational capacity for open communica-tion, creativity, and dedication.
2. Subordinate institutional loyalties to the public good.
3. Establish procedures that promote ethical behavior and hold individuals and organizations accountable for their conduct.
4. Provide organization members with an administrative means for dissent, assurance of due process and safe-guards against reprisal.
5. Promote merit principles that protect against arbitrary and capricious actions.
6. Promote organizational accountability through appro-priate controls and procedures.
7. Encourage organizations to adopt, distribute, and peri-odically review a code of ethics as a living document.

V Strive for Professional Excellence

Strengthen individual capabilities and encourage the professional development of others.
ASPA members are committed to:

1. Provide support and encouragement to upgrade competence.
2. Accept as a personal duty the responsibility to keep up to date on emerging issues and potential problems.
3. Encourage others, throughout their careers, to participate in professional activities and associations.
4. Allocate time to meet with students and provide a bridge between classroom studies and the realities of public service.

Enforcement of the Code of Ethics shall be conducted in accordance with Article I, Section 4 of ASPA's Bylaws.
In 1981 the American Society for Public Administration's National Council adopted a set of moral principles. Three years later in 1984, the Council approved a Code of Ethics for ASPA members. In 1994 the Code was revised.

SOURCE: American Society for Public Administration, 1120 G. Street, NW. Suite 700. Washington D.C. 20005-3885. Used with permission.

Foremost among the provisions of the ASPA Code of Ethics are imperatives for public administrators to "serve the public, beyond serving oneself"; to conduct themselves in a manner that inspires "public confidence and trust"; to strengthen organizational "capabilities to apply ethics, efficiency and effectiveness" in serving the public; and to exercise discretionary authority "to promote the public interest." Such provisions clearly emphasize the *public* and *ethical* obligations of government administrators — a theme that is the underlying foundation for this, and perhaps any, workable code of ethics.

Some years ago, political scientist Stephen K. Bailey suggested that people need certain attitudes and moral qualities in order to behave ethically in the public service. The first attitude is an awareness of moral ambiguity in decision making. The second is appreciation of the contextual forces at play in decision situations. The third attitude is a conception of the "paradox of procedures," that is, an understanding of the need for orderly and rational procedures balanced against an understanding that procedures (red tape) can sometimes be an impediment to responsiveness and public accountability. The moral qualities are (1) *optimism*, including a willingness to take risks; (2) *courage*, including the courage to avoid special favors, to make decisions that are unpopular, and the ability to decide under pressure; and (3) *charity*, that is, being fair and placing principle above personal needs for recognition, status, and power.[24]

Obviously, such considerations are not much in evidence when public officials (at any level) engage in various forms of questionable behavior. Former Reagan White House aide Michael Deaver, for example, was convicted in late 1987 of lying under oath to Congress and to a grand jury about his lobbying activities. Deaver was suspected of having illegally used his official and personal ties with President Reagan on behalf of his lobbying activities (though no formal charges to that effect were filed). Another case involving ethical issues centered on Lt. Col. Oliver North, who (with others) was "charged with conspiring to defraud the United States and trying to thwart congressional inquiries into the funding of Nicaragua's contra rebels."[25] North was accused, among other things, of shredding classified documents and other sensitive materials and of lying under oath to Congress. Similarly, a Pentagon contracting scandal broke in 1988, revolving around the possibility that "private consultants, hired by defense contracting firms, paid bribes to government employees for inside information that gave them an advantage in securing multimillion-dollar contracts."[26] Another example of unethical behavior involved a major scandal at the U.S. Department of Housing and Urban Development (HUD) in 1989. Information uncovered in records and testimony gathered by congressional investigators and by HUD included the following items: Marilyn Harrell, a consultant under contract with HUD to handle HUD property sales in Washington's Maryland suburbs, told Congress that she had stolen $5.5 million from such sales and claimed to have given the money to charitable organizations[27] (hence her nickname: "Robin HUD" — misleading perhaps because, among other things, Ms. Harrell paid for a swimming pool with some of the money); and one HUD regional administrator "became a real estate firm's chief executive after making housing recommendations that earned the company millions."[28] Finally, in the summer of 1994, former U.S. Secretary of Agriculture Mike Espy came under investigation and later resigned for allegedly accepting various gifts (travel, tickets to sports events, and the like) from companies regulated by the Department of Agriculture. President Clinton had "ethics" problems with the Congress in 1998 over the issue of whether or not he lied about his White House affair with Monica Lewinsky. In 1999, the president was impeached by the House of Representatives; he was subsequently tried and acquitted by the Senate in 1999 because there were not enough votes to remove him from office.

All such behaviors are unethical, for several reasons. They involve violating basic values, such as telling the truth and making decisions based on the objective merits of a case. They clearly suggest a callous disregard for the concept of the public interest, which public servants are obligated to promote and pursue. Finally, they harm essential public-service concepts such as operating within the laws of the land and remaining accountable to higher levels of authority (and to the legislature) for one's official actions. (We should keep in mind, however, that, as serious as these cases were, the great majority of decisions made by public officials — at all levels — do *not* involve breaching the public trust.)

Another aspect of ethics is the question of **internal (personal) checks** versus **external (legal-institutional) checks** on the behavior of individual administrators. Over the years, a debate has gone on about whether one or the other type of control is more effective for ensuring ethical behavior, accountability, and responsibility. The classic exchange on this subject took place more than fifty years ago between political scientists Carl Friedrich and Herman Finer.[29] Friedrich argued, essentially, that administrators are responsible if they are responsive to two dominant factors: technical knowledge and popular (majority) sentiment. He urged reliance on these criteria for assessing responsibility, laying little if any stress on mechanisms for ensuring adherence to those standards. Finer, writing a year later, criticized the absence in Friedrich's formulations of any institutional safeguards for administrative responsibility. He suggested that, while Friedrich defined responsibility as a "sense of responsibility, largely unsanctioned, except by deference or loyalty to professional standards," he (Finer) regarded it as "an arrangement of correction and punishment even up to dismissal both of politicians and officials."[30] Finer went on to warn that "sooner or later there is an abuse of power when external punitive controls are lacking."[31]

Thus, the central question, as framed in this exchange, is whether responsibility can be achieved by reliance on internal checks primarily or whether it *requires* political checks and sanctions in addition to the individual administrator's own ethical sense. Recent commentaries take the position that *both* types are needed. One central point made by a number of observers can be summed up as follows: "The public has to be able to rely on the self-discipline of the great majority of public servants. Otherwise *the official restraints and sanctions must be so numerous and so cumbersome* that effective public administration is impaired

internal (personal) checks   personal values of, and actions taken by, individuals who are concerned with behaving in an ethical and moral manner.

external (legal-institutional) checks   codes of conduct, laws, rules, and statutes that serve as safeguards to ensure that individual actions are ethical.

greatly."[32] The essential point is that, while there may be some things we can —
and perhaps must — do to try to ensure ethical actions in the public service, the
ultimate safeguard is in the character and inclinations of bureaucrats themselves.

A crucial distinction in this regard is between private and public morality.
John Courtney Murray, the great American Jesuit philosopher, wrote that "one
of the most dangerous misconceptions of the modern world is the idea that the
same standards that govern individual morality should also govern national
morality."[33] Behavior offensive to private morality, for example, could conceiv-
ably be moral according to standards of public morality. But what is "public
morality?" For an answer, we must look to a basic distinction between those
clothed with the authority of official position and all others; a crucial difference
is that *government has a monopoly on the legitimate use of force*. This means that government may use force when necessary to apprehend suspected criminals, that it
may utilize the death penalty as long as it is constitutional to do so, and that it
may order its soldiers to kill those of another country in wartime. We judge these
acts by standards very different from those applied to private citizens because the
contexts of governmental versus individual actions are different. With power, of
course, should go responsibility — some sense that there are different sorts of
limits on behavior because of one's *public* obligations.

Joseph Califano, a former White House counselor and Secretary of Health
and Human Services, provides a Watergate-related example:

> Patrick Gray can equivocate in statements to the press, campaign while Acting
> FBI Director for the Republican Presidential candidate, and destroy "politically
> dynamite" documents, but his Catholic upbringing and schooling did not permit
> him to lie under oath because that involves personal morality and perhaps serious
> sin. The Haldeman and Ehrlichman letters of resignation pay lip service to public
> morality, but protest their private morality as though *that were the ultimate stan-
> dard by which their exercise of the public trust* should be judged.[34]

And that is the point: the public trust and its exercise add an entirely different
dimension to what individuals do in official capacities or in matters related to
government decisions. The public trust imposes obligations on public officials
over and above those arising from private moral codes.[35] This may explain why
President Clinton, despite the eventual admission that he lied to his wife and to
Congress about the Lewinsky affair, never suffered a major loss of public trust in
opinion polls measuring his job performance as president.

One other example further illustrates confusion of public and private morality. The case involved the late Mayor Richard J. Daley of Chicago and two of his
sons, who were employed by an insurance firm in suburban Evanston. It came to
light that the firm had been awarded millions of dollars' worth of Chicago city
government insurance contracts without competitive bidding. When questioned
by reporters about this, Daley explained that any father would do what he could
to help his sons! True enough and, by Daley's strict personal moral code, entirely
appropriate. But because of his public position and power, there were at least

some who regarded this as a breach of public trust because other insurance firms were also (corporate) citizens of Chicago and public morality requires a government to deal equitably with all its citizens. And that, Daley clearly had not done.

What, then, can we say of **political corruption?** Corruption is offensive to many traditions of private morality, yet rooting it out is very difficult. There is one overriding truth about corruption: According to the standards many of us apply, *corruption is universal* in the sense that virtually every political system has had its share of political favoritism, private arrangements between public figures, and out-and-out thievery and bribery. We find this offensive — it runs counter to our Western standards; but without trying to justify it, we should note that not everyone reacts the way we do. In many parts of the world, what we call corruption is part of the routine of politics — and business and other enterprises, for that matter. Yet it is appropriate to combat it if, in fact, corruption violates *our* expectations of what our officials should and should not do.

Corruption is commonplace in government, and many states and localities are impacted. Deals are made quietly, contracts awarded, jobs created, votes bartered for (and occasionally stolen), offices bandied about, power exerted, contributors rewarded, and so on, all on the basis of various forms of favoritism. The battle over municipal reform (see Chapter 3) has centered on making it possible to stamp out corruption in government. Our image of corruption seems to emphasize big-city politics, but the fact is that, in rural America, there is the same kind of favoritism toward friends and rewards for political loyalty as in the city. *Patronage* is rampant in some states, barely visible in others. The remarkable thing is that so much has been done to make the conduct of government more honest and open.[36]

One other observation is in order. Corruption, as a practical matter, is a *form of privilege* indulged in by those in positions of power, wealth, and influence for mutual gain. As such, it is inherently antidemocratic and unethical because it concentrates power and its benefits in relatively few hands. If democracy is founded in large part on a premise of political equality, corruption is offensive to *that* value as well as to ethical values. Ultimately, this is another good reason for being concerned with corruption in a democratic government, one at least as relevant as ethical considerations.

political corruption all forms of bribery, favoritism, kickbacks, and legal as well as illegal rewards; commonly associated with reward systems where partisan patronage is in use; more generally, patterns of behavior in government associated with providing access, tangible benefits, etc., to some more than others, on an "insider" basis.

The Ethical Setting: New Emphasis on an Old Challenge

One of the most pressing problems confronting public managers in the late twentieth century is the challenge of defining, establishing, and maintaining a high level of ethical behavior among government employees. This is an especially sensitive problem for government, perhaps even more than for business or other private-sector institutions. Almost by definition, government is designed —

and widely expected — to serve the needs and interests of the full range of society, not just those who may seek a particular product or service as they might from the private sector. Ethical behavior on the part of public servants can enhance workforce effectiveness, improve employee morale, and promote better public relations. It may also serve to set a standard for the behavior of others outside government (though that may not be viewed as a major purpose). Indeed, in recent decades, ethical behavior has taken on new importance, in part because of the widespread public cynicism about government, a pervasive distrust that almost invites government employees to be anything but ethical in their daily activities and operations.

There have been impressive efforts on the part of government employees and (significantly) many employee associations to raise the ethical standards of conduct in the public workplace. For example, both the American Society for Public Administration (ASPA) and the International City/County Management Association (ICMA) have established and widely circulated organizational codes of ethics. Administrators have made, and continue to make, systematic efforts to familiarize public employees with these codes, to train employees in what is expected of the ethical public servant, and to monitor employees' behavior for compliance. First and foremost, of course, it has been necessary to identify what is meant by "behavioral ethics" or "ethical standards." Although there is room for debate, substantial consensus currently exists on some essentials. Furthermore, there appears to be considerable agreement about how to make codes of ethics operational in the workplace. We will address each of these efforts in turn.[37]

Many observers of administrative ethics suggest that professional conduct, personal honesty, and concern for serving the public and respecting both law and democratic principles are at the center of those beliefs. Among other things, professional conduct describes an employee's actions regarding professional excellence, merit-based employment decisions, commitment to government service, professional development, conforming to professional codes (such as the legal or medical profession's canons of ethics), and interpersonal skills. Other professional duties might also be cited, such as protecting the health, safety, and welfare of the public; promoting safety in the workplace; and acting with empathy and understanding toward others (both coworkers and those who seek to use the services offered by a particular agency). Other responsibilities might include ensuring employee privacy, applying fairness in making job assignments, monitoring and preventing sexual harassment, maintaining honesty and accuracy in financial reporting, protecting so-called **whistle-blowers** (those who publicly report cases of fraud, abuse, or mismanagement in their organizations), and providing employees with leave for education or child care.

Ethical behavior emphasizing *personal honesty* and *integrity* calls for avoiding any personal gain that results from the fulfillment of one's duties (these conflicts of interest, though, can sometimes be difficult to define and monitor), dedicating oneself to honesty and integrity, maintaining open and truthful relationships,

whistle-blowers those who make any disclosure of legal violations, mismanagement, gross waste of funds, abuse of authority, or dangers to public health or safety, whether the disclosure is made within or outside the formal chain of command.

and respecting the confidentiality of information. (Note that it is possible, as in the case of confidentiality, for some ethical standards and behaviors to be regarded as both professional and personal.) In general, it can be said that standards of personal honesty in the government workplace involve many of the same elements as they do in private life. Public standards, however, are usually of greater importance than private standards because of the nature of government work, which takes place in an open setting, where personal dishonesty may have impacts far beyond one individual's behavior or punishment.

Finally, respect for the law and democratic principles (what has been termed the "political" aspect of ethics) may be said to underlie both professional and personal dimensions. This refers to what might generally be expected of public employees *in their official capacities* as public servants — by their superiors, their subordinates, and the people they serve. These aspects involve a commitment to maintaining open (and usually participatory) modes of decision making, conducting official business in a consensus-building fashion whenever possible, complying with all relevant laws and regulations (and encouraging others to do likewise), and impartially distributing the benefits and burdens associated with the agency's services. That this list of ethical considerations is long indicates the scope of concern presently found in the public service, as well as the difficulty confronting an individual administrator in living up to all these ethical standards.

IMPLEMENTING ETHICS

How, then, do public managers concerned with ethics go about promoting appropriate attitudes and behaviors within their workforce? Not surprisingly, there is no single, easy answer; a number of approaches have been employed. One is formal adoption of a code of ethics or policy statement in order at least to signal an organization's seriousness of intent regarding the promotion of ethical conduct. A related phenomenon is development of codes of ethics by professional associations (as noted earlier); these codes can affect the actions of association members (such as attorneys) who are employed in the public sector. Another approach that has come into greater use is the requirement of financial disclosure in order to minimize the possibility of monetary conflicts of interest. A fourth approach prohibits employees from accepting outside honoraria (payments for individual services, such as giving lectures); a fifth requires administrative approval of professional activities outside of the organization; and a sixth approach establishes in-house ethics training for all employees (on a mandatory or voluntary basis). Perhaps the most important element in strengthening ethical conduct in government agencies, however, is what some have called the "moral leadership" of both top-ranking organization leaders and those in middle management. In other words, leading by example appears to hold the greatest potential for leaders to influence public administrators in the desired ethical directions. These ethical considerations may be said to constitute the ethical environment of public administrators' everyday activities.

Decisions in the Balance:
The Environment of Choice

In addition to questions concerning goals, models, and ethics, a number of other considerations are involved in reaching decisions. First is the matter of the resources necessary to implement a decision. The decision maker must consider both what kinds and what quantity of resources will be expended in pursuing a particular course of action. A decision to take some organizational action may require expenditures of time, personnel, money, and what we might call *political capital* (influence, prestige, and so on). The responsible official must have a reasonably clear idea — the clearer the better — of just how much it will cost in terms of *all* these resources.

Decision makers also must establish whether potential benefits are worth probable costs. This requires answering some difficult questions: Do we have sufficient time to devote to this enterprise, given our other responsibilities? Will our political supporters go along with us, or will we encounter pressure to do it differently or perhaps not at all? Are we sufficiently certain about the probable benefits we can derive? At times, decision makers may have to choose between two mutually exclusive benefits (either this gain or that one, but not both), to decide whether to seek something now or later (entailing the risk that it might be difficult now, but impossible later), and (especially in government) to weigh the impact of values that are not central to the specific decisional equation (setting a bad political precedent, losing faith and trust in elected officials, damaging democratic traditions, and so on).

A corollary concern is how to measure both costs and benefits or to ascertain whether meaningful measures are even available. One of the most tangible measures is in dollar terms, particularly regarding costs. However, there has always been considerable debate, both in the academic community and in government, over different ways to measure costs and benefits, separately and in relation to each other, and over the political implications of using different sets of measures.

Finally, decision makers may base their decisions on different grounds, singly or in combination. Three such grounds are most prominent. One is *substantive* grounds, with decisions made on the merits of the question. For example, a decision concerning the design of a highway linking two major cities, using efficiency criteria, would focus on the "shortest distance between two points" in terms of mileage, travel time, and construction costs and time. A second basis is *political* grounds — that is, net gain or loss measured by changes in political support or resources. In the example of the highway, the decision as to a specific route might be affected by the discovery that following a straight line between the cities would take it across some valuable farmland owned by an influential politician or a contributor to the election campaigns of incumbent officeholders. In this case, the "shortest distance" might well include a generous curve around the perimeter of the farm property, even if this meant that total dollar costs, mileage, and construction time would increase. Also relevant to political grounds for decision making are values such as popular representation and accountability. A third basis for decision is *organizational*. For example, if the government's highway engineers felt strongly that a detour around the farm property would detract from economy, efficiency, sensible roadway design, and scenic value, the responsible decision maker would have to weigh the possible effect on the engineers' morale of deciding to build the curve anyway.

Note that different considerations produce the need for a prior decision — namely, which factor(s) should be given predominant weight in the final decision. The question in the highway example is: Can the organization better afford to have on its hands an angry politician, demoralized professional employees, or displeased consumers (users of the highway)? There is no easy or automatic solution to such a dilemma. Other factors would have to be taken into account, such as who else would be pleased or displeased with a particular decision. In hundreds of administrative decisions — some routine, some not — the same sorts of considerations apply. The less routine a decision is, the more carefully such questions must be weighed.

A comment is in order about the types of decision makers who are likely to be concerned with the different grounds for decisions. Normally, organizational *experts* (such as highway engineers) have as their highest priority the substance of a decision or issue rather than concerns of politics or of the organization as a whole. This is in keeping with the main task of substantive specialists — to concentrate on the subject matter of their area of expertise. Those more highly placed in an organization, however, whether higher-ranking specialists or so-called political generalists, ordinarily have a different order of priorities, giving greater weight to political and organizational aspects of decision making. This is not to say that top-level officials are ignorant of, or oblivious to, the merits of a question, as we have used that term, or that specialists care little for politics. It is to say, however, that generalists are often inclined toward a more balancing process, weighing and choosing from among a greater number of decisional criteria.

Many generalists are appointed directly through political channels or are otherwise politically connected to a greater extent than most experts are; consequently, they are under more constraint to act with sensitivity toward their political mentors and allies (and adversaries). At the same time, their concern for the organization as a whole prompts them to be watchful of the morale of specialists who are likely to be dissatisfied with political decision making that runs counter to their expert opinion and preference. Some tensions within a bureaucracy are due to these variations in approaches to decision making in different parts of the organization.

In addition to the considerations already discussed, there is normally a *time factor* in decision making. Time is a key resource in both making and implementing a decision; it is therefore necessary to allow for sufficient time at every stage of deliberation and action. There are two significant time considerations. First, the amount of time in which to reach a decision is not unlimited. Time constraints — especially during an emergency or crisis — can profoundly affect the ability of decision makers to gather and analyze information and to project and compare consequences of different alternatives, ultimately affecting the course of action selected. Second, decisions can have long-term and short-term consequences that may have to be dealt with. For instance, anticipated benefits frequently are long-term, whereas costs are short-term; thus, in the immediate future, the latter will probably outweigh the former. A case in point is job training for the unemployed; it takes time for them, as with any new worker, to become fully productive employees, and per-capita costs of training can run very high. How quickly and with how much certainty benefits will be derived would have to be considered. Politically, a decision that yields some gain right away and carries with it the promise of better things yet to come is the most defensible. The essential point is that time is a relevant consideration in assessing the costs and benefits of a given course of action.

Central to all these decision-making elements is the quantity and quality of information available. All decision makers need enough information to serve as a basis for making reasoned choices, and most try to gather as much information as possible before making a final decision. The ideal situation (the rational-model setting) would be one in which an official had total access to, and could verify the accuracy of, all data directly related to the decisional alternatives under consideration, including comprehensive projections of all possible consequences resulting from each proposed course of action. In practice, decision makers must "muddle through," consciously settling for less than complete information, usually because a decision is needed promptly. Or they may try to postpone a decision, pending the acquisition of more information that will reduce the risk of making mistakes. Even officials or agencies enjoying strong political support seek to accumulate hard data to back their decisions; a recurring pattern of faulty or inadequate data could endanger that support. Information, in sum, is needed to make decisions that are supportable both objectively and politically.

decision analysis the use of formal mathematical and statistical tools and techniques, especially computers and sophisticated computer models and simulations, to improve decision making.

The uses to which information is put are also important. The role of **decision analysis** has assumed great prominence in the last forty years, relying on a wide variety of new techniques. Herbert Simon noted advances through which "many classes of administrative decisions have been formalized, mathematics has been applied to determine the characteristics of the 'best' or 'good' decisions, and myriad arithmetic calculations are carried out routinely to reach the actual decisions from day to day."[38] Simon and others have noted two significant developments that have facilitated use of such techniques: the improvement and wider use of sample survey techniques (to gather empirically defensible information on the public policy problems) and the rapid increase in the data-processing capacity of electronic computers (which seem to go through new "generations" every three or four years).[39] In addition, much greater use has been made of the experimental method in investigations of decision making.[40] In short, the *need for information*, while growing rapidly, has been joined to burgeoning *technologies* of decision making (see Chapter 2). This has resulted in vastly expanded information capability.

Technology may also have created an illusion of greater capabilities than we actually have. For example, malfunctions can and do occur in the myriad technological systems that underpin decision making. When these happen, data necessary to an informed decision can be inaccurate, with the predictable consequence that, at a minimum, the decision reached will be inappropriate to the problem because the problem will have been incorrectly defined and presented. Such a malfunction could have grave consequences.

Computer capabilities may also blind us to the simple reality that human judgment is still valuable in making decisions and that computers are no substitute for it. Electronic computers, although very useful, should not be relied on totally as a basis for decisions. They should also serve to remind us that computers are no better than the people who manufacture them, program them, and input the use of data. Experience can contribute to one's judgmental capacity; so, too, can breadth of training, perceptiveness, sensitivity, and capacity for continued learning. It is the interactions between individual competencies and computer technology that lead to the most effective decisions.

There are several other significant limitations on the acquisition and use of information. Perhaps most important is the fact that we live in a world of imperfect information. It is futile to mount a search for literally *all* the information that might be obtained on a subject, and most decision makers have somewhat more modest ambitions. Compounding the problem, communication of information is often less than clear and is subject to human error at the point of origin and at the receiving end, even when both parties desire full mutual understanding[41] (see Chapter 5).

Another crucial limitation on information resources has been the cost of obtaining information. Information costs include the personnel and time that must be devoted to its acquisition, organization, and presentation. Acquisition costs, in particular, can become prohibitive. The greatest value of the computer as an information storage and retrieval system — and of on-line data services — is the enormous saving in time and money it makes possible in obtaining a quantity of data compared to the investment necessary to gather the same amount of data by older methods. (This, incidentally, is a clear example of long-term benefit making worthwhile a high short-term cost — in this case, the cost of installing computerized information systems.)

The last major limitation stems from the conscious and (especially) unconscious biases of those who send, relay, and receive information. We tend to attach high importance to objective information, yet there is great difficulty in interpreting information with complete objectivity. Even the most fair-minded individuals have subjective values that color their perceptions of data, images, or phenomena. Existing preferences can shape responses, or even receptiveness, to particular information. Thus, pure objectivity in data interpretation is an impossibility and, as a result, absolutely objective information is beyond our grasp.

Finally, there is the problem of deliberate distortion of information. Information is a source of power, and it is often in the best interests of an agency or official to provide only information that will have a positive political effect. We may debate the utility and wisdom of political interference with objectivity in information, but it is undeniably a significant constraint. With enough effort, deliberate distortions can be discovered and corrected, but that effort can require large investments of resources and, consequently, is made only irregularly. In sum, motives of self-interest can seriously impair objective use of data.

Decision makers also face other kinds of problems. For one thing, decision making is strongly influenced by previous decisions and by policies already in effect. In other words, some alternatives are not available because of past decision making. Instead of starting with a clean slate, decision makers must work within the confines allowed by past choices. An example would be a decision to implement an affirmative action plan in local government hiring, which might effectively foreclose any contrary options five or ten years later. The same would be true of a local decision to sell bonds for a capital construction project, or for the army to change its basic emphasis on the weaponry it needs for ground warfare.

Another problem is unanticipated consequences in spite of efforts to foresee all the outcomes of each decision. Sometimes the projected outcome does not occur; sometimes there are unintended side effects that develop along with the projected outcome; sometimes only the side effects occur. If these unanticipated results turn out to be serious, they can cause intense problems and political repercussions. This happened in California during the early 1990s as a result of speculative investments in high-risk bonds used to finance capital improvements in 180 local governments. The resultant $2 billion loss in Orange County, California, lowered bond ratings, hampered growth, and affected millions of taxpayers.

Yet another potential pitfall in decision-making processes is the phenomenon of **groupthink,** defined by social psychologist Irving Janis as "a mode of thinking that people engage in when they are deeply involved in a cohesive in-group, when members' strivings for unanimity override their motivation to realistically appraise alternative courses of action."[42] This phenomenon is most likely to be evident in small groups of decision makers. The two basic elements in most potential groupthink situations are group cohesiveness and a tendency toward unanimity, or at least toward making any dissident member feel conspicuous and uncomfortable. Two other factors are the degree to which a cohesive group of decision makers becomes insulated from other influences in the decision-making process and the extent to which a cohesive group's leader promotes one preferred solution (even when that leader genuinely does not want group members to be "yes-men" and the members try to resist unanimity). In essence, any cohesive "in-group" of individuals who generally think along similar lines can be a breeding ground for groupthink; some politicians need to surround themselves with advisers fitting this description. Familiarity with one's high-level advisers can facilitate the advisory process but can also repress critical analysis — the thoughtful dissenting voice that can cause those in the majority to reexamine

groupthink   a mode of thinking that people engage in when they are deeply involved in a cohesive in-group, when members striving for unanimity override their motivation to realistically appraise alternative courses of action; facilitated by insulation of the decision group from others in the organization, and by the group's leader promoting one preferred solution or course of action.

BOX 6–2   ETHICAL AND LEADERSHIP CHALLENGES FOR PUBLIC MANAGERS

One Way to Combat "Groupthink": Lessons from the State Department

An institutionalized practice for the encouragement and preservation of dissent has been in effect since 1972 at the State Department. Known as the "Dissent Channel," it provides that employees here or abroad who dissent from policy recommendations of their superiors can invoke a special channel for memoranda or messages. This channel ensures: (a) that top-level officers in the Secretary's office will know about the dissent; (b) that the dissenter gets an acknowledgment within a week; and (c) that the dissenter gets a substantive response after senior decision makers (often including the Secretary, who gets a copy of each message) have reviewed the dissenter's views and reasons. The strongest admonitions are made to Departmental superiors never to penalize dissenters for taking advantage of this channel. Ten to fourteen messages per year are sent through this channel, and it clearly has enriched the State Department's policy process.

SOURCE: Adapted from testimony of Charles Bingham, Member, Special Panel on the Senior Executive Service, American Society for Public Administration, February 28, 1984; *The Senior Executive Service,* Hearings before the Subcommittee on Civil Service, Committee on Post Office and Civil Service, U.S. House of Representatives, 98th Congress, 2nd Session (Washington, D.C.: U.S. Government Printing Office, 1984), pp. 284–85.

their assumptions and commitments — with consequent errors in decisional outcomes.[43] (See Box 6–2, "One Way to Combat 'Groupthink': Lessons from the State Department.")

Finally, decision making involves **sunk costs** — certain irrecoverable costs resulting from commitment of past resources. The realities of sunk costs raise the stakes in decision making. The term sunk costs has two meanings. First, a given resource or commodity, once spent, cannot be spent again. For example, a piece of land committed to use as an approach ramp to a superhighway obviously cannot also be used as a hospital site. Second, sunk costs suggest that once a decision has been made to proceed in a particular policy direction, certain costs would be incurred if that direction were to be reversed later. An analogy would be a motorist at a fork in the road, pondering which one leads to his or her destination. If the motorist makes the wrong choice, it will take extra time, gasoline, and wear-and-tear on the car to return to the junction and resume the trip, this time in the right direction. In administration, too, investment of extra resources and some political risk are required to reverse a policy direction. It is often easier to maintain a given policy course than to change it; to a degree, this explains why administrative agencies resist having to modify what they are doing.[44] If,

sunk costs in the context of organizational resources committed to a given decision, any cost involved in the decision that is irrecoverable; resources of the organization are lessened by that amount if it later reverses its decision.

however, the costs of *not* changing direction approach or exceed the costs of changing, an agency would be far more likely to adapt its policy. In any event, sunk costs represent an additional factor to be taken into account in the course of making and implementing decisions.

IMPLICATIONS OF THE DECISION ENVIRONMENT

Given the variable nature of goals — and of such elements in the decision environment as resource availability, competing grounds for decision, information constraints, and sunk costs — it would appear that the requisite conditions for the rational decision model are found rarely, if at all. However, though rationality as process is unlikely to be found in administrative decision making, reasonable, sensible, and productive decisions are not only possible, they occur frequently. Decision makers face difficult problems, particularly in a social and political environment filled with uncertainty and change. They can and must try to reduce the effects of that uncertainty so that decisions are useful and appropriate in solving the problems at hand and in anticipating longer-term needs. Multiple methodologies might help them in their efforts. But the rational model, as a whole process, is likely to be applicable only in very limited instances.

DECISION MAKING: LINKS TO ORGANIZATION THEORY

As all organizations try to cope with the uncertainty thrust on them by the external environment, they must develop processes for *searching and learning*, as well as for deciding. They must set limits to its definitions of situations — and make

bounded rationality
the notion that there are prescribed boundaries, controls, or upper and lower limits on the decision-making abilities of individuals within organizations.

decisions within the framework of **bounded rationality.** This notion of bounded (limited) rationality, so crucial to the recent reshaping of organization theory, overlaps the incrementalist and mixed-scanning approaches to decision making, with acceptance of satisficing rather than maximizing very much at the heart of it.[45] Thus, developments in the art of making decisions have been paralleled — indeed, caused in part — by evolving conceptions of complex organizations.

With the rise of so many new pressures on government decision making — and especially for enhanced accountability of public administrators — it seems clear that the continuous-learning model may be applicable to a greater extent than ever before. Reinventing government calls for potentially major changes in the decision routines of literally thousands of government entities at all levels. "Empowerment" of administrators and citizens (whether or not directly a part of agency clienteles) means that policy and program preferences of many individuals and groups outside public agencies will become intermingled with those of agency personnel. And any efforts to streamline or scale back government activity (meaning government organizations and the personnel employed there) have a disruptive effect — for better or worse — on the manner in which decisions are considered and made. To the extent that these various pressures have an impact on administrative decision making, it is more and more unlikely that anything close to goal consensus can be achieved, either internally or externally. Without goal consensus, of course, pure-form decisional rationality is impossible — according to the criteria used by the rationalists themselves.

Political Rationality: A Contradiction in Terms?

We have been speaking for the most part of decision makers in the abstract and of models of decision making applied to theoretical situations. We now take up a question central to our overall concern in this book: whether it is possible to achieve *any* sort or degree of rationality in a public administrative system permeated by political influences and pressures. Can administrators who act at least partially in response to political stimuli be said to be acting rationally, in any sense, when they make decisions? Can *politics* and *rational decision making* be made to coexist or, at least, not totally contradict each other?

Much of the literature on rational decision making in economics and political science suggests that the answer to such questions is no. Politics is frequently represented as *interfering* with rational processes, outweighing more objective considerations, and overriding "neutral" or "nonpolitical" measurements, requirements, and data. When political considerations predominate in decision making, as they frequently do, the stigma of irrationality is attached to the process and the outcomes. To dispute this characterization of *politicized* decision making requires a significant modification of the meaning of rationality. In particular, what must be changed is the "currency" of rationality, the criteria by which rationality is defined and measured.

Plainly stated, rationality has traditionally been an economic measure, and the currency has been implicitly or explicitly quantitative. For many years, most economists — and many others — have assumed that economic-quantitative rationality is sufficient as an overall definition of the concept. Recently, however, the possibility has been raised that there may be other, equally valid, forms of rationality, specifically **political rationality**.[46] This is to say that political and economic choices are often conceived in different terms and directed toward fulfilling different kinds of objectives and should therefore be evaluated according to different criteria. More to the point, it is not rational — by any standard — to pursue the politically impossible.

In a political setting, a decision maker's need for support assumes central importance and the political costs and benefits of decisions are crucial. Political benefits that might accrue to a decision maker are self-evident: obtaining short-term policy rewards, enhanced power over future decisions; added access to, and earlier inclusion in, the decision-making process (given that both access and involvement are meaningful); and so on. Political costs, however, are less obvious and need explicit categorization, which political scientist Aaron Wildavsky provided:

political rationality
a concept advanced by Aaron Wildavsky suggesting that behavior of decision makers may be entirely rational when judged by criteria of political costs, benefits, and consequences, even if irrational according to economic criteria; emphasizes that political criteria for "rationality" have validity.

Exchange costs are incurred by a political leader when he [or she] needs the support of other people to get a policy adopted. He has to pay for this assistance by using up resources in the form of favors (patronage, logrolling) or coercive moves (threats or acts to veto or remove from office). By supporting a policy and influencing others to do the same, a politician antagonizes some people and may suffer their retaliation. If these *hostility costs* mount they may turn into reelection costs — actions that decrease his chances (or those of his friends) of being elected or reelected to office. *Election costs*, in turn, may become *policy costs* through inability to command the necessary formal powers to accomplish the desired policy objectives. [We] may also talk about *reputation costs*, i.e., not only loss of popularity with segments of the electorate but also loss of esteem and effectiveness with other participants in the political system and loss of ability to secure policies other than the one immediately under consideration.[47]

It is apparent that, as stated here, political benefits are rarely measurable in quantifiable terms. The one set of political costs that might be measurable numerically is reelection costs, but it is difficult to determine from voting data how particular actions by politicians affect the ballot choices of thousands of voters. This lack of easy measurability, however, does not diminish the impact political costs have on the behavior of governmental decision makers, including those in bureaucracy.

There is a widespread tendency, even among some political scientists, to scornfully dismiss or downgrade as "irrational" any behavior or decision not clearly directed toward achieving the *best* results. But if criteria of political rationality were to be used — that is, establishing cost-benefit ratios in political terms — such behavior and decisional outcomes might be perfectly "rational." Perhaps most important, decisions made and measured by even the most objective economic-quantitative criteria have political implications; for example, an economically rational tax reform law will benefit some more than others. The mistake all too frequently made in and out of government is ignoring or denigrating those implications because they somehow "pollute" the "truly objective" decisions based on only the most "neutral" of considerations.[48] In every instance, *the choice of criteria* by which to measure decisional outcomes has political significance because of the ever-present possibility that adherence to a particular set of criteria (including quantitative data) will ultimately favor the interests of one group over those of other groups.

Another observer who has made a similar point from a different perspective is Martin Landau.[49] He questions the traditional inclination to minimize organizational duplication and overlap in the name of efficiency, and he points out that such practices, rather than being rational, may prove to be quite irrational. He suggests, first, that duplication of organizational features may make overall performance more reliable in the event that any one part breaks down. As an example, he cites an automobile with dual braking systems; the secondary system may seem to be just so much extra baggage, so uneconomical, so wasteful — until the primary braking system fails![50] Within human organizations, training more than one individual or staff member in essentially the same tasks fits the same description of "rational duplication"; the alternative is increased risk of organizational breakdown, should any one part fail. Second, Landau asserts that overlapping parts may improve performance by allowing for greater adaptability within the organization as a whole. His examples of rational overlapping include biological organisms that can adapt and survive in the face of a failing part and, significantly, the U.S. Constitution.

Why the Constitution as an example of rational overlap? Because our framework of government was calculated from the outset to be overlapping (and, for that matter, duplicative) in the interest of preventing political tyranny, that most efficient of governmental methods. Separation of powers and checks and balances were both designed to prevent any one branch of government from becoming predominant. And what are checks and balances except *deliberately designed overlap* in the execution of essential government functions? Similarly, our structure of federalism is clearly duplicative, yet the purpose is the same: to prevent undue concentration of power. From Landau we can infer that in working toward the accomplishment of clearly delineated political goals (in this example, preventing concentration of power), some structural and behavioral arrangements may be politically rational and defensible even though they might appear quite irrational in economic or other "value-neutral" terms. Above all, both Landau and Wildavsky challenge the application of economic criteria to the measurement of political phenomena, as well as the assumption that economic rationality is, by definition, superior to political rationality.

In sum, then, *political rationality* is not at all a contradiction in terms. We can accept the propositions that politics is legitimately concerned with enabling the decision processes of government to function adequately, that basing decisions on political grounds is as valid as basing them on other grounds, and that rationality according to the currency of politics is as defensible as rationality in economic terms. Political rationality, when appropriately conceived and applied, can be a useful tool for evaluating both the processes and the outcomes of organizational decision making.

Organized Anarchies: The "Garbage Can" Model

One other perspective on decision making explains many of the gaps left by the preceding perspectives. Michael Cohen, James March, and Johan Olsen studied decision processes of organizations confronted with ambiguity in the organizational setting — that is, in circumstances in which organizations have "goals that are unclear, technologies that are imperfectly understood, histories that are difficult to interpret, and participants who wander in and out."[51] Terming such entities **organized anarchies,** Cohen, March, and Olsen developed the **garbage can theory of organizational choice** (their term).

organized anarchies
organizations in which goals are unclear, technologies are imperfectly understood, histories are difficult to interpret, and participants wander in and out; decision making in such organizations is characterized by pervasive ambiguity, with so much uncertainty in the decision-making process that traditional theories about coping with uncertainty do not apply.

garbage can theory of organizational choice
a theory of organizational decision making applicable to organizations in which goals are unclear, technologies are imperfectly understood, histories are difficult to interpret, and participants wander in and out; such "organized anarchies" operate under conditions of pervasive ambiguity, with so much uncertainty in the decision-making process that traditional theories about coping with uncertainty do not apply.

pervasive ambiguity
a situation of long-term uncertainty that pervades the decision-making environment of an organization.

The garbage can theory appears to have two principal emphases. First, under conditions of **pervasive ambiguity,** organizations behave in ways that contradict conventional assumptions about organizational choice. Second, so many organizations now operate under conditions of ambiguity and behave so unpredictably (in light of traditional theories) that the garbage can explanation might account for collective behaviors that deviate from expected patterns. The garbage can model, in short, assumes that pervasive ambiguity introduces *so much uncertainty* into decision processes that the assumptions of traditional theories about coping with uncertainty do not apply. As a result, decisions made in the "garbage can" must be more flexibly implemented than decisions made under conditions of greater certainty, for there will be more uncertainty in the implementation as well.

In short, the organized anarchy/garbage can model refers to almost random streams of "people, problems, and solutions." Because these three streams are treated in the model as independent of each other, the choice of an appropriate solution to any given problem, or an appropriate decision maker to resolve the problem, is as much a product of *chance* as it is of rationality in some settings — and perhaps more so. In light of recent events in and surrounding many public organizations, this model may be the most appropriate perspective (even more than Thompson's "bounded rationality") from which to understand the complexity of government decision making in the twenty-first century.

Summary

Decision making involves attempts to bring about a change to achieve some gain by means of a particular course of action that requires expenditure of a certain amount of resources. There is some unavoidable uncertainty and, therefore, some risk involved, and most decision makers seek to minimize both. Most decisions are of a relatively routine nature, though care should be taken not to allow routines to dominate. A significant debate, still ongoing, surrounds how actually to make decisions. The rational model, derived from classical economics, assumes that decision makers consciously pursue known goals and seek to achieve them in the most efficient manner possible. Rational behavior includes quantifying and ranking alternatives, separating ends from means, comprehensively analyzing data, and seeking to maximize utility. Rationality, in this model, refers to the process of making decisions, not to goals or outcomes.

Criticisms of the rational model have centered on its lack of practical applicability as a method of administrative decision making. Impediments to rationality are said to include distinguishing facts from values, the ambiguous nature of goals, time pressures, costs of information acquisition, and pervasive uncertainty. One critique holds that rationality is not possible because goals cannot be, and should not have to be, agreed on in advance of decisions.

Two major alternatives to the rational model have been suggested. Incrementalism emphasizes decision making through limited successive comparisons, aiming to satisfice rather than to maximize, to meet short-term needs, and to maintain flexibility in responding to problems. Mixed scanning, on the other hand, counters that incrementalism is not sufficiently innovative, that it is too supportive of the status quo, and that it is inadequate as an approach to fundamental decisions. Defenders of incrementalism respond that their approach is viable in dealing with both changes and problems, large and small.

Organizational goals, though often ambiguous, can influence administrative behavior and can, in turn, be affected by political considerations. Key goals may include agency survival and maintenance (reflexive goals), accomplishment of substantive program objectives that influence the external environment (transitive goals), and symbolic goals. Agencies seek to articulate their goals in relatively general fashion and may be deliberately unclear about some of them to preserve political support. Efforts to achieve certain kinds of goals may have to be ongoing because of the nature of the problem. Also, some goals may be determined by the extent to which political support can be generated for them. The personal goals of agency employees usually vary considerably, thus making goal congruence between individuals and organizations difficult to achieve.

Ethical considerations in decision making have assumed greater importance in recent decades despite some uncertainty in defining what constitutes ethical behavior. An effort by the ASPA to define a code of ethics for administrators emphasizes the public obligations of public administrators (for example, acting in the public interest and avoiding undue personal gain and conflicts of interest). Ethical behavior is more likely to be achieved if bureaucrats are aware of the moral ambiguities in decision making, if they appreciate contextual forces in decision situations, and if they understand that orderly and rational procedures, although important, should not become ends in themselves. The personal character of bureaucrats is a crucial factor, but legal-institutional checks are also needed to promote morality and responsibility in the public service. In addition, there are differences between private and public morality. The latter is based on the idea that special responsibilities accompany exercise of the public trust and legitimate use of force. Among government employees, ethical behavior has come to be regarded as an increasingly important aspect of administrative activity. Professional conduct, personal honesty, and respecting law and democratic principles are at the heart of concerns about ethical behavior. Many governments and professional associations have adopted codes of ethics and formal policy statements, require financial disclosure, or have implemented ethics training. Most important is the expectation of "moral leadership" from organization leaders and middle managers.

The major considerations in the decision process are (1) goals and ethics; (2) the resources necessary to achieve goals; (3) projected benefits; (4) the cost-benefit ratio; (5) substantive, political, and organizational grounds for decisions; (6) the time element; (7) the quality and quantity of information available; (8) the role of decision analysis and its supporting technologies; (9) past decisions and policies; (10) the prospect of unanticipated consequences and efforts to avoid them; (11) the need to avoid groupthink; and (12) sunk costs — resources expended in having made and implemented a decisional commitment and resources that would be necessary to alter it. On balance, these considerations seem to point toward a decision process in which the rational model cannot prevail. The debate over appropriate models of decision making is part of the larger evolution of contemporary organization theory — as well as an indicator of the many changes currently taking place inside and outside of most government organizations.

Another critique of rationality is founded on the premise that economic-quantitative measures may not always be appropriate in determining what is rational. By using a set of explicitly political measures, political rationality is possible. What is politically rational may not be economically rational, and vice versa, and applying economic concepts of rationality to political phenomena may be misleading. The garbage can theory of organizational choice suggests an alternative perspective on the effects of decisional ambiguity on an organization's activities — ambiguity that, if anything, is on the increase.

KEY TERMS AND CONCEPTS

decision making
rational
cost-benefit analysis
cost-benefit ratios
incrementalism
mixed scanning
reflexive
substantive
legitimacy
transitive
symbolic goals
goal congruence
American Society for Public
    Administration (ASPA)
    Code of Ethics

internal (personal) checks
external (legal-institutional) checks
political corruption
whistle-blowers
decision analysis
groupthink
sunk costs
bounded rationality
political rationality
organized anarchies
garbage can theory of organizational
    choice
pervasive ambiguity

SUGGESTED READING

Adams, Guy B., and Danny Balfour, *Unmasking Administrative Evil.* Thousand Oaks, Calif.: Sage Publications, 1998.

Bowman, James S. *Ethical Frontiers in Public Management: Seeking New Strategies for Resolving Ethical Dilemmas.* San Francisco: Jossey-Bass, 1991.

Choi, Young B. *Paradigms and Conventions: Uncertainty, Decision Making, and Entrepreneurship.* Ann Arbor: University of Michigan Press, 1993.

Cohen, Michael D., James G. March, and Johan P. Olsen. "People, Problems, Solutions, and the Ambiguity of Relevance." In James G. March and Johan P. Olsen, eds., *Ambiguity and Choice in Organizations.* Bergen, Norway: Universitetsforlaget, 1976, pp. 24–37.

Downs, Anthony. *Inside Bureaucracy.* Boston: Little, Brown, 1967; reprint edition published by Waveland Press, Prospect Heights, Ill., 1994, Chapter 8.

Etzioni, Amitai. "Mixed Scanning: A 'Third' Approach to Decision Making." *Public Administration Review,* 27 (December 1967), 385–92.

Garofalo, Charles, and Dean Geuras. *Ethics in the Public Sector: The Moral Mind at Work.* Baltimore, Md.: Georgetown University Press, 1999.

Heineman, Robert A., William T. Bluhm, Steven A. Peterson, and Edward N. Kearny. *The World of the Policy Analyst: Rationality, Values, and Politics.* 2nd ed. Chatham, New Jersey: Chatham House, 1997.

Janis, Irving L. *Groupthink.* 2nd ed. Boston: Houghton Mifflin, 1982.

Koteen, Jack. *Strategic Management in Public and Non-Profit Organizations.* 2nd ed. Westport, Conn.: Praeger, 1997.

Lindblom, Charles E. "The Science of 'Muddling Through.'" *Public Administration Review,* 19 (Spring 1959), 79–88.

———. "Still Muddling, Not Yet Through." *Public Administration Review,* 39 (November/December 1979), 517–26.

Moore, Mark. *Creating Public Value: Strategic Management in Government.* Cambridge, Mass.: Harvard University Press, 1995.

Moore, Mark, and Malcolm Sparrow. *Ethics in Government: The Moral Challenge of Public Leadership.* Englewood Cliffs, N.J.: Prentice-Hall, 1990.

Rohr, John A. *Ethics for Bureaucrats: An Essay on Law and Values.* 2nd ed., revised and expanded. New York: Marcel Dekker, 1989.

Simon, Herbert A., Robin L. Marris, and Massimo Egidi. *Economics, Bounded Rationality, and the Cognitive Revolution.* Brookfield, Vt.: E. Elgar Publishing, 1992.

Swan, Wallace. "Decision Making." In Thomas D. Lynch, ed., *Organization Theory and Management.* New York: Marcel Dekker, 1983, pp. 47–79.

Van Wart, Montgomery. *Changing Public Sector Values.* New York: Marcel Dekker, 1998.

ON-LINE RESOURCES:
Decision Making in Administration

American Society for Public Administration (ASPA)

http://www.aspanet.org/

Diverse professional association linking over 10,000 academics, students, and public administrators. Excellent source for current research, jobs, learning, and information exchange.

Center for the Advancement of Applied Ethics (Carnegie Mellon University)

http://caae.phil.cmu.edu/caae/Home/CAAE.html

This is the official site for the Center for the Advancement of Applied Ethics, a research and development center that focuses on teaching people practical methods for analyzing and responding to real ethical problems.

Center for Public Integrity

http://www.publicintegrity.org/

The Center for Public Integrity is a nonpartisan, nonprofit organization based in Washington, D.C., whose mission is to examine public service and ethics-related issues.

Center for the Study of Ethics in Professions

http://www.iit.edu/departments/csep/

Information on the Center for the Study of Ethics in the Professions at the Illinois Institute of Technology.

Decision Analysis Society Home Page (Duke University)

http://faculty.fuqua.duke.edu/daweb

The Society for Decision Analysis promotes the development and use of logical methods for the improvement of decision making in public and private enterprise. Members include practitioners, educators, and researchers with backgrounds in engineering, business, economics, statistics, psychology, and other social and applied sciences.

Decision Sciences Institute

http://dsi.gsu.edu/

The Decision Sciences Institute is an interdisciplinary, international organization dedicated to the advancement of the science and practice of education and research about business decisions.

Ethics (University of Chicago)

http://www.journals.uchicago.edu/Ethics/

The on-line version of *Ethics*, an international journal of social, political, and legal philosophy from the University of Chicago Press.

Journal of Ethics — On Line (DePaul University)

http://www.depaul.edu/ethics/ethg1.html

An on-line journal featuring cutting edge research in the field of business and professional ethics.

Office of Government Ethics

http://www.usoge.gov/index.html

The official site for the United States Office of Government Ethics.

Society for Judgment and Decision Making

http://www.sjdm.org/sjdm/

The Society for Judgment and Decision Making is an interdisciplinary academic organization dedicated to the study of normative, descriptive, and prescriptive theories of decisions. Its members include psychologists, economists, organizational researchers, decision analysts, and other decision researchers.

For further information on decision making and ethics within organizations see: Bedford/St. Martin's Home Page

http://www.bedfordstmartins.com

Chapter 7

Chief Executives
and the Challenges of
Administrative Leadership

*The task of the president is to set before the American people
the unfinished public business of our country.*

John F. Kennedy, on the eve of his election in 1960

The quality and style of leadership practiced by elected and appointed public administrators are key factors in how public agencies perform their duties and achieve their goals. Some aspects of leadership have already been examined including the distinction between management and leadership and on the effects that leaders have on the work of their subordinates in a variety of organizational settings. These studies focus on leadership in formal settings, where those in charge of a work group or unit had close contact with those they supervised. Another dimension of leadership with important consequences for public administrative activity is how elected or appointed chief executives (and their immediate subordinates) influence administrative behavior from a more distant position (in organizational terms) and how those executives interact with bureaucracies they attempt to lead.

The roles played by chief executives (presidents, governors, mayors, city managers, and county executives) as leaders of their governments' bureaucracies have not been studied as fully as some of their other functions. Yet, as the presence of public bureaucracies and their effects throughout society have grown, accountability, character, efficiency, and results have become salient concerns.[1] More to the point, chief executives (together with judges and legislators) have increasingly been regarded as logical choices for the task of maintaining some measure of operational control and accountability within their administrative establishments. To a great extent, electoral outcomes — that is, whether elected executives remain in office — are determined by public perceptions of these leadership criteria.

We will consider various challenges of leadership as they affect what elected officials and public administrators do. We should keep in mind as we proceed that, in bureaucracies where the "value-neutral professional model" predominates, various leadership dimensions are distinctly different in how these agencies operate and in how public administrators respond to both appointed and elected officials' efforts to lead them. In addition, we will address the ways in which chief executives seek to lead their respective bureaucracies, and will discuss changing definitions of leadership and the roles of leadership in the ranks of administrators.

The Context of Administrative Leadership

American chief executives stand apart from the executive-branch agencies they are expected to lead. Unlike most modern bureaucrats, these leaders and their immediate subordinates obtain their positions through elections (either partisan or nonpartisan) or are answerable directly to elected officials (cabinet secretaries and undersecretaries, other high-level political appointees, county administrators, and city managers). These officials are responsible, in the eyes of most of the public, for the operations of the bureaucracies that make up their respective executive branches. Historically, they have also taken much of the "heat" for programmatic failure. At the same time, however, they are not really a permanent part of their bureaucratic structures, which are highly fragmented by function, operate autonomously (see Chapter 3), and depend on chief executives for only some of their political support.

Chief executives are clearly expected to set general policy directions and to provide the leadership necessary to manage government agencies and programs. If they are to fulfill those expectations, they need some measure of effective influence, if not control, over bureaucratic agencies that are not primarily interested in the executive's political success or failure. Chief executives require deliberate strategies, and various forms of leverage, in dealing with administrative agencies if they are to succeed in directing administrative behavior toward fulfillment of their policy objectives.

Certainly, in the formulation of broad policy directions, executive leadership has been evident, especially in the past two decades; presidential, gubernatorial, and local executive initiatives have been commonplace and have come to be regarded as marking the opening round of policy deliberations on many issues. The ability of chief executives to influence their bureaucracies significantly cannot, however, be taken for granted. Where the chief executive controls most of the key mechanisms of governmental and political party power — such as party nominations for office, patronage in government hiring, and awarding of government contracts — we can expect to find relatively responsive bureaucracies.

Examples of such chief executives are Governor Huey Long of Louisiana during the 1930s and the late Mayor Richard J. Daley of Chicago.[2] The degree of chief executive control over the bureaucracy may vary with the extent of such powers — comparisons among state governors are revealing in this respect[3] — but there are other factors involved as well.

Chief executives' control over the bureaucracy is frequently challenged by the legislative branch and others (such as opposition party spokespersons) who seek a voice in agency decisions. More important, in most instances, their authority to lead is challenged from within by the legislature, interest groups, or bureaucrats themselves. Presidents (and most governors and many mayors) have diverse and frequently disunited coalitions of political support that do not enable them to operate with a free hand or to speak with a consistent voice. Bureaucracies, on the other hand, have a limited range of policy interests because they are more specialized. By concentrating its efforts in one policy area, an agency can develop clientele support and expertise and can convert these diverse interests into political resources. These resources, in turn, gain the support of those in the legislature and the public who seek favorable agency treatment of their interests. Thus, agency responses to executive directives are usually calculated in terms of their effect on agency interests rather than on the interests of the chief executive. (Note that the "iron triangle" depicted in Chapter 3 does *not* include the chief executive as a major player.) Because, in most cases, an agency is not beholden to the chief executive for its political survival and because the chief executive is unlikely to risk either political resources or political defeat every time an agency fails to follow orders from above, executive leadership is much more the product of **political persuasion or "jawboning"** than of any clearly defined command authority.[4]   — to adapt his policies

To persuade public bureaucracies to follow their lead, chief executives must convince agency personnel that there will be reciprocal political and fiscal support for their specialized program interests as long as those programs are integrated acceptably within the executives' broad policy directions. A variation of the same approach involves the chief executive singling out one favored program within an agency for support, keeping alive agency hopes that other programs will be similarly favored by the executive later. In other cases, where agency programs clearly occupy a low priority on a chief executive's policy agenda, the agency may adapt *procedurally* to executive's priorities — such as trying to economize under an executive (at any level) who is emphasizing spending reductions. Even if policy differences continue to exist, both agency and chief executive advance their interests by such a tactic; this is indicative of the agency's fear of retribution from an unfriendly or hostile chief executive. Direct conflict, of course, is another possibility, although usually a last resort for both sides.

Two elements of chief-executive–bureaucracy relationships shape how the former operates to influence the latter's activities. One is the general nature of linkages between the two; the other is the specific instruments a chief executive can employ in the quest for control over bureaucratic behavior. Control from

---

political persuasion or "jawboning"

the power of the chief executive to convince legislators, administrators, and the general public that his or her policies should be adopted; jawboning is quite literally the primary tactic, i.e., talking, used by presidents, governors, or mayors to achieve this goal.

one or the other side is rarely complete, but the conflict over control and power is ongoing.

Chief Executive–Bureaucratic Linkages

Interactions between chief executives and their administrative bureaucracies take various forms, but all have some impact both on the executive's political and policy fortunes and on bureaucratic behavior. It is possible to speak of policy development and policy implementation as distinct phases of chief-executive involvement with their bureaucracies. We shall use that approach in discussing these linkages.

Policy development in broad outline is probably what chief executives do best in their capacity as leaders of bureaucracy. Yet even executives with extensive formal and political power, such as presidents and some governors, must still depend on professionals in the bureaucracy for program advice and, indeed, for proposing new programs. The chief executive's dependence on experts varies among different policy areas. "The more technically complex the work of a bureau and the more structurally autonomous it is, the less impact he has on its policy development."[5] Policy areas such as energy conservation, environmental protection, public health, or transportation require more specialized technical expertise than most chief executives possess. Another factor affecting executive dependence on bureaucracy for policy development is the diversity of information sources within the chief executives' staffs, and among those that can be called on outside government as well (for example, from issue networks). Political considerations can often reduce dependence on experts; for example, physicians' recommendations on health care policy may be offset by motives of self-interest. There may also be some choice as to *which* bureaucracy a chief executive relies on. But, in virtually every case, *some* bureau or agency helps direct policy at both the formulation and implementation stages.

Policy implementation makes chief executives even more dependent on bureaucracies. Influence over implementation is generally limited to fairly broad-gauged actions (such as budget cuts, proposed reorganizations and personnel measures) and is related also to existing institutional resources. At the national level, for example, the U.S. Office of Management and Budget (OMB) has placed greater emphasis in recent years on management improvement, including introducing specific productivity-enhancement techniques such as productivity improvement and total quality management (TQM). This creates at least the potential for more effective control over program implementation by elected chief executives. Similar developments have taken place at the state level, with the creation of departments of administration, new budget systems, and centralized planning increasingly available to governors as management tools. In recent years, large local governments (both municipal and county) have moved in this same direction.[6]

policy development
a general political and governmental process of formulating relatively concrete goals and directions for government activity and proposing an overall framework of programs related to them; usually but not always regarded as a chief executive's task.

very influence over the executive Branch

policy implementation
a general political and governmental process of carrying out programs in order to fulfill specified policy objectives; a responsibility chiefly of administrative agencies, under chief executive and/or legislative guidance; also, the activities directed toward putting a policy into effect.

Thus, most chief executives, including presidents, governors, and mayors, must contend with a dual difficulty. They must rely on *bureaucratic expertise* for much of the content of policy, especially in highly technical areas, and, at the same time, they must seek agency compliance in implementing and evaluating policy as they desire. Strengthening the tools available to chief executives for program management, coordination, and analysis of policy implementation has brought about some change, but most chief executives, as outsiders, still must induce cooperation from bureaucracy rather than being able to count on it as a matter of course.

Making the overall task of bureaucratic leadership more complex — but also possibly strengthening the chief executive as bureaucratic leader — is the fact that chief executives generally exercise leadership in three distinguishable but overlapping arenas. The broadest of the three is the public arena, in which the chief executive commonly seeks to "set the agenda" for public discussion of policy issues and concerns. A second arena is the legislative one, in which a chief executive plays a major role in proposing legislation and influencing the course of legislative deliberations. Much of Congress's business is shaped significantly by "the President's program," sent to Capitol Hill from the White House; an analogous situation often exists in many state legislatures and, to a lesser extent, in city councils. Finally, as already noted, chief executives must confront the administrative or bureaucratic arena, attempting to move administrators to effectively manage programs and policies as the chief executive wants them implemented. On leaving office, elected executives have often expressed frustration with their inability to assert their leadership over administrative agencies.

Because of the political dynamics linking these three arenas, the actions of executives in one arena may have impact in at least one other. For example, a series of major legislative successes may create a political "halo," whereby the chief executive encounters somewhat less bureaucratic resistance to his initiatives; this happened a number of times in 1981, Ronald Reagan's first year in the White House. Though our focus is on bureaucratic leadership, we also will take note of significant features of each of the other two arenas as we proceed.[7]

Chief Executives and Bureaucracies: The Instruments of Leadership

instruments, or tools, of leadership various mechanisms such as legislative support, policy initiatives, and emergency decision-making powers available to chief executives to help direct bureaucratic behavior.

The ability of chief executives to lead their bureaucracies effectively depends on a number of **instruments, or tools, of leadership,** but — as noted earlier — there is considerable variety in the extent to which any one such leader can wield these instruments, singly or in combination. Governors and mayors especially have widely varying degrees of legal powers available to them (the legal authority of mayors often varies even within the same state). Also, not all chief executives (including presidents) are inclined to use the leadership tools available to them in the same way or to the same degree.[8] Nevertheless, particular leadership instruments can prove useful to a chief executive intent on steering agency behavior in particular policy directions.

Three factors (apart from specific instruments or tools) can help to shape the leadership environment. First is the chief executive's support in the legislature (Congress, state legislature, city council, or county board). *Legislative support* or opposition can affect leadership over a bureaucracy because administrators are more inclined to follow the executive's lead if they know that members of the legislature also support that lead; the legislature, after all, is a key source of political and fiscal support for bureaucratic agencies. The second factor is the degree of (or the potential for) *policy and program initiative* exercised by the executive leader. In the twentieth century, this has become a much more visible part of the chief executive's function than in the past, in part because the public at large has clearly come to expect it of elected executive leaders. This power to initiate provides an important advantage because the way in which a question or proposal is first put forward can significantly affect the outcome of the decision process.

Another source of strength is the capability of chief executives to *respond to crisis situations*, and that capacity is reinforced by public expectations that the chief executive will coordinate and direct governmental actions in the wake of floods, hurricanes, blizzards, droughts, large fires, outbreaks of violence, and other crises. The 1997 flooding in Minnesota and North Dakota, as well as the 1994 floods in Georgia and Alabama, triggered a massive government response involving thousands of public officials, but their efforts were coordinated principally by state and local chief executives, aided by federal disaster relief and emergency management agencies. And when hurricane Andrew struck South Florida in the summer of 1992, it was the Federal Emergency Management Agency (FEMA), together with thousands of federal, state, and local executives, as well as volunteers, who directed cleanup efforts while ensuring that food, shelter, and moral support were made available as necessary to affected residents.[9]

Presidential power has been called on regularly in times of economic and military crisis — for example, Franklin Roosevelt's economic leadership during the Great Depression of the 1930s, Richard Nixon's invoking of wage and price controls in an effort to control inflation in 1970, the 444-day crisis involving Iran's seizure of American hostages during 1979–1981, and George Bush's Operation Desert Storm campaign against Iraq during the 1990–1991 Persian Gulf war. As a rule, powers created or invoked to meet specific crises do not disappear entirely after the crisis has passed. Hence, each time the president is called on to deal with a crisis, presidential powers are further enhanced. A vivid demonstration of that generalization came in 1978, when a law took effect (passed in 1976 at Gerald Ford's initiative) that ended a continuous state of national emergency dating from 1933! Presidential powers during that time had included power to seize property, to organize and control the means of production, to declare martial law, and to restrict travel. It is significant that such emergency powers can last so long after a crisis has ended. (During Operation Desert Storm, emergency war powers were restored and numerous civilian airlines crew members and air-craft were drafted into service temporarily to transport supplies and personnel to Kuwait and Saudi Arabia.)

None of these sources of strength is an unmixed blessing, however. The degree of legislative support for a chief executive may vary during his or her term; policy initiatives may be greeted with resistance by the public and the leg-islature, or a crisis may not be handled well, thus damaging the chief executive's image and prestige. (President Bush, for example, was criticized for mishandling hurricane Andrew relief efforts.) Apart from the ebb and flow of political influ-ence in the public and legislative arenas, a chief executive's influence over admin-istrative agencies is likely to depend more directly on other factors — factors that have much more influence in the everyday operations of agencies. We now turn our attention to these leadership instruments.

THE BUDGETARY ROLE

Of greater significance to virtually any chief executive is a central role in formu-lation of the executive budget — the proposals submitted by the president to Congress, and by most governors to their respective legislatures, for dollar amounts to be allocated to executive-branch agencies. (Local chief executives often, but not always, play a similar role; we will focus on the president's bud-getary role for purposes of illustration.) The president's programmatic and bud-getary priorities form the guidelines by which the OMB — working directly with and for the president, evaluates each agency's request for funds, so that it is possible for the president to influence substantially how much money is included in his budget recommendations to Congress for every agency in the executive branch. Congress, of course, is not bound by presidential recommendations for agency budgetary allocations, but it ordinarily appropriates to each agency a dol-lar amount not appreciably different from, although usually lower than, that requested by the president and the OMB.[10] In the early 1970s, another pattern emerged in which a Congress controlled by the Democrats frequently clashed with two Republican presidents over spending priorities and amounts, with the Senate especially inclined to vote larger sums than the president had asked for. Under Richard Nixon (1969–1974), this precipitated bitter conflicts over presi-dential vetoes and over Nixon's impounding (withholding authority to spend) funds appropriated by Congress (see Chapter 10).

President Jimmy Carter (1977–1981), a Democrat with a Democratic Con-gress, generated less friction on budget matters than Nixon had, although some of his proposals were treated unfavorably. Ronald Reagan, a Republican with a Republican Senate and apparent public backing (especially during his first term, 1981–1985), nevertheless encountered congressional resistance to his spending-control initiatives. President Bush took on a more conciliatory role as efforts to reduce annual budget deficits intensified in the early 1990s. President Clinton worked with Democratic congressional leaders — and often with reluctant

Republican members — before Congress accepted his budget proposals in 1993 by the slimmest of margins. This legislation included a budget-deficit reduction agreement that was to reduce national government annual deficits by nearly $500 billion by 1996. The budget conflicts between President Clinton and Congress were so intense and the divisions so deep that the proposal barely passed the House of Representatives (218–216) and Vice President Gore had to cast the deciding vote in the Senate to break a 50-50 tie. In 1995, the federal government was twice shut down because the President and Congress failed to agree on budget priorities. The deep involvement of the president testified to the role any president can assume in the budgetary process — and to the sharing of responsibility that characterizes that process. In sum, the president has considerable influence over the amounts of money received by executive agencies, but his influence — and even his legal authority — cannot be said to be absolute. There is continual competition for control of agency funding, with the president in a major leadership role.

A second function related to budgetary coordination emerged for the OMB in the 1970s, chiefly at the instigation of President Nixon. When the old Bureau of the Budget (BOB), which had existed in the Executive Office of the President since 1939, was transformed into the OMB in 1970, the change in title was not merely cosmetic. It signaled Nixon's intent to gain greater mastery over the operations and management practices of the sprawling federal bureaucracy. Even though Nixon's effort suffered from lack of an explicit strategy, he did succeed to some degree in modifying management practices and establishing presidential authority to monitor them. This set a precedent for later efforts by the Reagan, Bush, and Clinton administrations to deregulate agency authority, reduce budget deficits, and consolidate grant programs.

Another function of the OMB relating to bureaucratic agencies should be noted. When administrators seek to propose legislation for consideration by Congress, **central clearance** with the OMB is a required formality. This gives the president an opportunity to review proposals for their consistency with his legislative program. Agencies and their administrators may deal informally with Congress but, as a matter of routine, most agencies seek clearance and do not openly defy the president and OMB if clearance is denied.

Toward the end of the Carter administration, the OMB began to involve itself in numerous efforts to manage agency activities more fully. One device was limiting the paperwork requirements agencies impose on other governments and the private sector. With passage of the Paperwork Reduction Act in late 1980, a new Office of Information and Regulatory Affairs within the OMB was established, charged with reviewing all requests for information from the public made by government agencies.[11] Other steps primarily affected regulatory agencies — a focus of central concern under Ronald Reagan. Early in his term of office, Reagan put heavy emphasis on *central clearance* of proposed regulations and issued several directives that enhanced the position of presidential leadership (and control) in this regard. Other proposals put forward — some of which were

central clearance
a key role played by the Office of Management and Budget (OMB) regarding review of agency proposals for legislation to be submitted to Congress, with OMB approval required for the proposals to move forward. A similar role or pattern exists in many state governments and some local governments, in the relationships among chief executives, administrative agencies, and legislatures. Central clearance also is practiced with regard to submission of budget proposals from executive-branch agencies to legislatures, during the budget-making process.

adopted in whole or in part — included requiring cost-benefit analysis of proposed regulations, as well as so-called inflation-impact statements. The role of
the OMB as presidential staff coordinator of regulatory clearance became more
clearly defined as both Reagan and Bush pursued a policy of scaling down the
national government's role in economic regulation (see Chapter 11).

One other point should be made. During the first months of his administration, Ronald Reagan demonstrated just how great an impact a president can have
on bureaucratic agencies through his successful efforts — supported by a conservative Congress — to make deep cuts in the national government's domestic
spending. The president's fierce determination to significantly alter the nature
and scope of national government activity was reflected in the billions of dollars
cut from executive budget submissions and projections. The impacts of these
cuts, combined with fundamental changes in philosophy and program emphasis
issuing from the White House, put the entire bureaucracy on notice that it could
no longer expect to conduct business as usual. Clearly, influence over the budget
gave this president tremendous leverage over the fortunes of individual agencies.
Indeed, the uses Reagan made of presidential authority in this regard exceeded
what many observers had thought was possible (even if only as a short-term
strategy for a new president intent on achieving significant change in the manner
in which the nation was to be governed).

The budgetary influence of governors and local chief executives is predictably varied but, in general, few state or local executives can match the president's sustained impact on budget-making processes. This is true at the state
level even though, as of the mid-1980s, **executive budgets** existed — with
direct involvement of the governor — in forty-four of the fifty states.[12] In addition, most governors have acquired significant new budgetary powers under
recent revisions in state constitutions. Although their powers have increased,
most governors are not nearly as strong in budget making at the state level as the
president is at the national level.[13]

Many governors find their positions defined — and often restricted — by
formal legal and political factors. The most important of these are of state constitutional origin, reflecting an earlier age in which many constitutions were
drafted and in which powerful political and social forces favored sharp restrictions on gubernatorial powers. Among the restrictions still facing most governors are term limitations, lack of appointment power (as most cabinet officials
are elected separately), and limited budgetary control over legislatures. One former governor and U.S. senator from North Carolina has commented that "the
American governorship was conceived in mistrust and born in a strait jacket."[14]
In many instances, state government power was tightly constrained across the
board, with all branches and entities given only authority that could be rigidly
defined.

Since the mid-1960s, there has been considerable change in state constitutions, most of it favorable to the exercise of stronger gubernatorial leadership —
including leadership of state bureaucracies. Between 1964 and 1976, ten states

executive budgets
budgets prepared by chief
executives and their
central budget offices for
submission to the legislature for analysis, consideration, review, change, and
enactment.

comprehensively revised their constitutions; between 1966 and 1976, a total of twenty-seven states streamlined their amendment processes, making it easier to adjust the constitutional framework as the needs of state government required." As amending the constitution was made easier, efforts increased to update provisions bearing on the exercise of governors' powers, including some that are budget related. Though many constitutional constraints still curb the power of governors and other officials, the executive branches of most states are in a much stronger position today than they were a quarter of a century ago.

Another constitutional feature that is still in force in many states is the specific mandating of programs or allocation of funds (or both) — requirements that reduce the ability of the governor (and everyone else) to make policy choices based on the best estimates of current societal and programmatic needs. Specified in the constitutions of some states, for example, are very detailed budgetary allocations that can be changed only by a constitutional amendment. Although constitutional provisions elsewhere may not be as restrictive, they nevertheless limit gubernatorial freedom of action beyond the usual constitutional and political checks and balances.

One leadership instrument, available both to the president and (most) governors, that may be particularly useful as a source of budgetary influence is the **veto power.** The president may veto any legislation of which he disapproves, after Congress has passed it but presidential veto power is limited by the requirement that the president must approve or disapprove an entire bill. That is, even if most of a bill was acceptable to the president, with only one or a few unacceptable provisions, the president still had to sign or veto the whole bill. For this reason among others, presidents vetoed relatively infrequently, making the veto power less significant than it might have been. That is why recent presidents and the Republican *Contract with America* called for the presidential **item veto (or line-item veto).** In 1996, Congress passed, and President Clinton signed, legislation authorizing a restricted version of the presidential line-item power, limited to only the discretionary spending measures, about one-third of the total federal budget. The impact of the new law may remain "in legal limbo" for years, however, as several provisions have been challenged as unconstitutional.

All but one of the governors have a similar veto power (the governor of North Carolina has no veto authority). More important, however, forty-three governors also have an unrestricted line-item veto, enabling them to disapprove specific provisions of a bill while signing the rest of it into law. (Illinois, in addition, provides for an amendatory veto, permitting the governor not only to disapprove a provision but also to propose alternative language to the legislature; this could mean rewriting the content and even the intent of legislation if the legislature goes along with it. Two other states permit their governors to use this power for what are labeled *technical corrections*, without always distinguishing between content-related and technical changes.)

The item-veto power enables most governors to exert control with something resembling surgical precision. It permits intervention in budgetary and

veto power the constitutional power of the elected chief executive to overrule an appropriation, law or decision by the legislature. At the national government level, requires a two-thirds majority of both houses of Congress to override.

item veto (or line-item veto) a constitutional power available to more than forty of America's governors, under which they may disapprove some provisions of a bill while approving the others.

other matters of interest to functional specialists in a particular program area without forcing the disapproval of entire spending provisions, program authorizations, and the like that touch on other interests (and that the governor may wish to see become law). Essentially, it allows a chief executive greater control over spending decisions in individual program areas.[15] That is why it has more potential as a leadership tool that truly matters to program administrators in the bureaucracy and to their allies in the legislature and among interest groups.

In sum, the budget role of many governors resembles, in important respects, that of the president — but with some important differences as well. Most but not all of the differences favor presidential influence compared with that of most governors; but governors have emerged in recent decades as far more important budgetary actors in their respective states, and they are virtually certain to continue in that role.

At the local level, few mayors enjoy such influence in government budget making; in many American cities and towns, the office of mayor is more a ceremonial one than that of a working chief administrator. City managers, on the other hand, play key roles in formulating budget proposals and often succeed in winning city council approval for these proposals.[16] One contributing factor is the manager's expertise and the legitimacy this provides; another is the fact that managers are full-time professionals and, in many instances, the mayor and city council members are part-time. (The growing professionalization of county government has led, in many cases, to similar patterns of expertise — and budgetary influence — among county administrators and county managers.) Still, the budget role of local executives is somewhat more modest, relative to their respective bureaucracies, than that of either governors or presidents.

PERSONNEL CONTROLS AND CHIEF EXECUTIVE LEADERSHIP

A second important set of tools that chief executives may use to influence their bureaucracies is personnel management — overseeing the rules, organizations, and activities involved in filling administrative positions throughout the executive branch and in managing the people hired for those positions and the many tasks they perform. As in the case of budgetary practices, there is considerable variety in types of personnel systems (see Chapter 8), for example, patronage and merit systems. *Patronage* emphasizes political party or policy loyalty as a basis for making personnel decisions — hiring, on-the-job evaluation, promotions, transfers, and so on. The concept of *merit*, on the other hand, is the basis for a system under which the employee — as a career civil servant — is hired and later evaluated (and promoted, and so on) on the basis of job-related competence. The merit employee is thus presumed to place much more emphasis on career development and much less emphasis on loyalty to an individual leader. Patronage makes it easier for a chief executives to exert their will over larger segments of a bureaucracy because, in a patronage system, loyalty and responsiveness to the policy preferences and directions of a chief executive are more routinely expected of employees by top leaders and by employees. Many states prohibit by statute any elected official from ordering an appointed career civil servant to perform certain specific acts. For example, the mayor is not allowed to contact police officers directly for services other than those authorized by city ordinances or by the police chief.

Until 1883, presidents enjoyed extensive discretionary powers over appointment and dismissal of administrative employees, a power that has been largely unavailable to twentieth-century presidents because of merit reform. The president has the power to appoint some 2,500 executive-branch employees out of a total of some 2.7 million civilian employees. (Establishment of the Senior Executive Service, under the Civil Service Reform Act of 1978, increased both presidential appointment authority and the potential for presidential influence over high-ranking career bureaucrats; see Chapter 8.) Still, the president's power to appoint is more significant in the long-range execution of public policy than is his power to dismiss, because not all appointees are removable and those who are seldom find themselves actually fired. Often, but not always, the president has been able to guide the activities of these appointees, but his ability to control their respective bureaucracies through them has usually been more limited.

Limitations on presidential influence over political appointees, and on the influence of presidents and appointees alike over the bureaucracy, are complex and deserve examination. An essential element, already implied, of presidential–bureaucratic interactions is that they are not direct: there are layers of both political and career personnel between the White House, statehouses, city halls, and their respective bureaucracies. Another important factor is that cabinet officers are not merely "extensions of the presidency [with] no competing loyalties."[17] The president cannot automatically assume perfect obedience (or anywhere near that) even from a high-ranking political appointee who also has to work with the bureaucracy in order to be reasonably effective in departmental leadership. Cabinet secretaries are often pulled in opposite directions by competing political forces — the president and their own departments — because of the more focused policy interests of the latter. Secretaries of cabinet-level departments cannot be expected to act strictly as "the president's men"; as a result, a unified cabinet is unlikely. But, at the same time, a president "should [safeguard] the powers and prestige of his department heads as . . . those of his own office." To the extent that the status and authority of any department head are downgraded, he or she "is *less able* to resist the pressures brought upon him [or her] by constituencies, congressional committees, and the bureaucracy."[18]

Political appointees, in turn, have had their own difficulties in directing the activities of their respective bureaucracies. One explanation for this is that these appointees make up a "government of strangers" — certainly to their departments, often to each other and to White House staff members, and sometimes even to the president who appointed them.[19] It is more than simply a case of bureaucrats being in government longer than most political appointees, though that is part of it. Rather, newly appointed executives have to spend part of their limited time in office — two years or less for many secretaries, undersecretaries, and assistant secretaries[20] — learning both the formal and informal rules of the game in their departments. Thus, implementation of presidential policy initiatives is delayed for significant periods of time within cabinet departments — and, in politics, delay can signify ultimate defeat for a policy or program. The proposed merger of the Federal Bureau of Investigation (FBI) and the Bureau of Alcohol, Tobacco and Firearms (ATF) in 1993 was effectively stopped by delay from both agencies, even though the reorganization was recommended and endorsed as part of President Clinton's own National Performance Review.

Once having become acclimated to Washington politics, political appointees (and new presidents) are often rudely confronted with other operating realities of bureaucratic politics. One major reality is that there are important differences between modes of operation of political leaders and career officials. The former seek to accomplish many things in a short time, with what they hope is overt political appeal; they are thus interested in quick, dramatic actions, especially on first taking office. Bureaucrats, on the other hand, are predisposed toward behaviors that have been described as *gradualism, indirection,* and *political caution,* and share a concern for *maintaining relationships.* Gradualism — moving slowly — has the advantage of decreasing the possible fear associated with change. Indirection, or avoiding direct confrontations, is aimed at minimizing the potential number of sources of opposition to a program, personnel action, or implementation strategy. Political caution is designed to prevent unintentional or unwarranted identification of a career official with particular political appointees; this could easily compromise an official's career status and reputation. Finally, maintaining relationships is especially crucial for career employees, whose professional existence and effectiveness depend centrally on developing cross-agency networks.

Inevitable tensions are generated as a result of interactions among officials with these divergent approaches to discharging their public responsibilities. In particular, criticisms of the bureaucracy or of bureaucrats — across the board — are voiced by political leaders anxious to see movement in key policy areas and frustrated by a bureaucratic environment many do not understand. Among the kinder terms used to describe bureaucrats and their agencies are: *slow-moving, unresponsive,* and *disloyal* (to the chief executive). But there is a lesson here — namely, that what are regarded as inherent deficiencies of bureaucracy "are often its strengths. Effective functioning [of government] requires a high degree of stability, uniformity, and awareness of the impact of new policies, regulations, and procedures on the affected public."[21] Bureaucrats are usually in a better position to assess such impacts than are Washington's executive "strangers." Furthermore, as one observer has put it, "civil servants can provide some of their most valuable service by resisting what political appointees [and, by implication, presidents] want." **Bureaucratic resistance** based on expertise and on concern for program effectiveness — as opposed to simple obstructionism — may be the only viable alternative to letting things go wrong, and then being responsible

bureaucratic resistance self-serving feature of administrative agencies which emphasizes gradualism, slowness, and political caution when dealing with newly selected political leadership in the executive branch.

later for correcting the problem. Hugh Heclo, a long-time observer of administrative politics, sums up these tendencies this way:

> It is not simply a question of civil servants resisting any confrontations or change but of preferences for fights that do not lead to too much unnecessary antagonism and uproar — changes that do not extend uncertainty in too many directions at once. [These sorts of behavior] go beyond conventional images of bureaucratic inertia. Such tendencies can find a *good deal of justification* in an environment of complex and uncertain political leadership on the one hand and long agency tenures and individualistic job protections on the other.[22]

Some recent presidents have been surprised by the inability of their highest-level departmental political appointees to overcome these patterns of bureaucratic behavior. Because departmental appointees work more closely than presidents or White House staff with their bureaucracies, they have a tendency to take on the perspectives of their departments, often at the expense of what might be called "presidentialist perspectives."[23] This can lead to a very frustrating situation for the president, who may have expected the sort of control over his appointees that others do and who finds instead that his cabinet members serve more as "ambassadors" *from* the departments than emissaries *to* them. One consequence can be conflict among not only departments but the secretaries themselves over program jurisdiction. Another more serious result is a drain on the president's time and resources if he chooses to mediate a succession of internal conflicts. More than likely, he will delegate responsibility for mediation to others on the White House staff, or he will resign himself to having to work around such conflicts. None of these choices is especially attractive to him.

Under the Reagan administration, there were developments in Washington executive politics that may represent the start of a long-term shift in some of the patterns just discussed. Ronald Reagan, more than any other recent president, came into office not only with a firm determination to change the operations of the national government bureaucracy but also with an explicit management strategy for doing so.[24] Political scientist Richard Nathan, writing in 1983, described the principal elements of this strategy:

> The key ingredient has been the appointment of loyal and committed policy officials. But this is only one dimension. The internal organization and operation of the White House staff is another. Loyal "Reaganites" have been placed in key White House policy-making positions, with experienced Washington hands assigned to parallel posts to promote the administration's policies in the legislative process and in the media. Tensions between the White House staff and cabinet officers have been minimized through the use of cabinet councils in which cabinet members have an important policy-making role. *Appointed policy officials in agency posts have penetrated administrative operations by grabbing hold of spending, regulatory, and personnel decisions.* From the beginning, these and other administrative tactics have been used aggressively by the Reagan administration.[25]

There are several important points to be made here. First, actions taken by Reagan staff regarding career personnel demonstrated that chief executives need not rely on the ultimate instrument of dismissal to make significant changes in the behavior of career officials. Many positions were eliminated and those filling them reassigned (though there were some layoffs). These **reductions-in-force (RIFs)** sent a signal throughout the bureaucracy that, unlike some presidents, Reagan was absolutely serious about making cuts in the scope of government. It also indicated that the relative security of the career civil service could and would be breached if such breaches contributed to advancing the policy goals — especially in domestic policy — of the Reagan administration. Second, a number of Reagan's subcabinet officials remained in their positions for well over two years, reducing the impact of their being "strangers" in the executive branch. Third, the combination of budgetary and management strategies (see Chapters 9 and 10) had the effect of disrupting some of the behavior patterns associated with senior careerists. (It is much more difficult to practice gradualism or indirection, for example, when executive-branch political leadership is clearly intent on *accelerating* change and *creating* confrontation in administrative operations.)

These Reagan strategies, taken together, raised an issue of some importance — namely, whether these steps constituted excessive (and long-term) politicizing of the bureaucracy. Some critics charged that the president, in the interests of his own policy agenda, wanted presidential control to reach down to levels of the bureaucracy that previously had been largely the domain of career civil servants. There is a major difference between a president trying to influence the bureaucracy through personnel appointments on the one hand and, on the other, seeking to cement into the ranks of the bureaucracy supporters committed to one and only one policy agenda. Whether President Reagan deliberately intended to achieve the latter is not clear, but the pattern of his personnel appointments was disturbing to many observers, some of whom strongly supported the Reagan domestic policy agenda.

One other negative aspect of this management strategy has been noted by critics of the Reagan presidency: the possibility that it may have contributed to the **Iran-Contra affair**.[26] This episode, which involved the sale of weapons to Iran through third-party intermediaries and the subsequent diversion of some of the proceeds to the U.S.-backed Contra rebels in Nicaragua, involved four unpleasant possibilities. The first was that federal laws had been broken — laws banning further aid to the Contras. The second was that National Security Council officials had lied to congressional committees investigating these transactions. The third was that these officials had acted in every respect with the confidence that their president would have approved of what they were doing even if they had not been ordered to take these actions and had not even informed the president of their activities. The fourth possibility, of course, is that Ronald Reagan — as well as then vice president and successor George Bush — did, in fact, know of these activities but denied (then and later) that a link of any kind existed between the sale of arms to Iran and aid to the Contras. One of the

reductions-in-force (RIFs) systematic reductions or "downsizing" in the number of personnel positions allocated to a government agency or agencies; usually the result of higher-level personnel management policy decisions related to other policy objectives (including budget cuts and executive reorganizations).

Iran-Contra affair scandal in the Reagan–Bush administrations (1986–1987) over alleged involvement of high-level officials in the sale of weapons to Iran and the diversion of proceeds to arm the U.S.-backed "Contra" rebels in Nicaragua.

less serious implications of these possibilities is that such actions stand in stark contrast to the longer-standing traditions of the career civil service described earlier — gradualism, indirection, and political caution.

As president, George Bush was less aggressive than Ronald Reagan in attempting to direct administrative activities partly because he perceived less need to move as decisively as President Reagan had moved. Another possibility is that Bush chose to take a less threatening path in dealing with the career civil service because he had previously held a variety of top positions in the bureaucracy, including ambassador to China and director of the Central Intelligence Agency (CIA). As an insider, he had considerable personal experience working with career administrators — and perhaps a better understanding of their modes of operation. For whatever reason, his authority vis-à-vis the Washington establishment was weakened.

At the state and local levels, there are, once again, some concerns similar to those at the national level — and some substantial differences. For many governors, there are limitations on powers of appointment and dismissal for subordinate executive-branch positions. As we have seen, not even the president has unlimited authority in this respect, but the authority of individual state governors seems considerably less extensive by comparison. In many states, for example, there are boards and commissions created by the legislature to which the governor cannot name members. In other instances, appointees cannot be removed by the governor except under the most extraordinary circumstances. And most governors face the political necessity of at least tolerating appointees sponsored by political party or interest-group supporters. In fact, in some predominately rural states, a bureau or department head may be selected by a committee made up entirely or in part of persons the agency serves. A common example of this is found in the selection of many state agriculture department directors. Such committees are constituted independently of the governor, and the private interests represented exercise at least a veto — and sometimes considerably more power than that — over appointments that appear to be under gubernatorial control. Governors' control over executive-branch personnel is reduced still further by the simple fact that many states elect at least one other top-level executive official (state attorney general, treasurer, secretary of state, comptroller, or even — in a few cases — lieutenant governor) separately from the governor. The net effect is to reduce the leverage that a governor has over subordinates, thus very probably frustrating efforts to develop and implement consistent policies.

The local level presents a mixed picture, especially as local governments have become increasingly professionalized. The stereotypical image of a local boss controlling all personnel matters is now the rare exception; more common is the local government in which a merit system represents the formal mechanism for personnel management. Yet political party influences are often still felt in the local personnel process, especially in large cities. To the extent that vestiges of patronage persist, local executives may still be able to name some administrative personnel. On the whole, however, local chief executives are less influential in this respect today than in the past.

EXECUTIVE-BRANCH REORGANIZATION

reorganization
authority delegated by Congress to the executive branch to add or subtract staff positions, or to restructure organizational arrangements, to achieve policy goals as well as increased economy, efficiency, and effectiveness of bureaucratic agencies.

A third instrument of chief-executive control is periodic **reorganization** of administrative agencies. Like budgetary coordination, reorganization authority is a legacy of the reform movements of the early 1900s. Traditionally, reorganization was aimed at increasing economy and efficiency, clarifying chains of command, and the like. And, with few exceptions, presidents (and governors) who possess generous reorganization authority have approached their efforts with those objectives in mind.

Proponents of reorganization often seem to regard it as a cure-all for correcting bureaucratic ills. Reorganizations have, at various times, been touted as a means of eliminating waste and saving billions of dollars, restoring to economic health a chronically ailing maritime industry, reducing airport noise, and controlling crime in the streets.[27] Yet there is reason to suggest that such rationales may have been oversold, that reorganizations, although useful, have higher political costs and fewer benefits for a chief executive than many imagine.

One important reason for the failure of reorganizations to deliver on their promises is that the "standard reorganization strategies for rationalizing and simplifying the executive branch often clash with one another."[28] Political scientist Herbert Kaufman lists seven basic prescriptions for reorganization: (1) limiting the number of program subordinates under a given executive, (2) grouping related functions under a common command (as happened in the creation of both the Defense Department and the Department of Education), (3) increasing the number of executive staff positions, (4) granting extensive reorganization powers to elected or appointed executives, (5) insulating career public servants against political pressures, (6) decentralizing administration, and (7) expanding opportunities for public participation in the administrative process.[29] In the name of economy, efficiency, and responsiveness, these have been tried repeatedly in one form or another.

One must be selective as to which prescription to use, depending on circumstances and on the objectives. The first four prescriptions tend toward centralization of authority; the last three tend to promote dispersal of authority. More important, these prescriptions in combination involve trade-offs of advantages and disadvantages. It is impossible to reap only benefits from reorganizing without also having to cope with attendant disadvantages, and hard choices must be made about which disadvantages will be accepted in order to gain other benefits. For example, grouping related functions under a common command is at odds with protecting an agency from political pressures; similarly, increasing decentralization and public participation clashes with limiting the number of subordinates effectively involved in program administration. Adding staff positions goes against decentralization; insulating administrators against political pressures interferes with executive reorganization authority; decentralization, coupled with protection from political pressures, can severely reduce the command authority of the chief executive. Reorganizations matter most in terms of the distribution of influence, the flows of communication, and the course of policy — not in terms of economy and efficiency! Therein lies the appeal of this device for the sophisticated executive, and "the genius of the reorganizer is to know which trade-off to make at a given time."[30] It is no easy job.

In addition, there is a difference between being able to propose a package plan, subject only to legislative veto by one or both houses, and having to submit reorganization plans as part of the usual legislative process. Having to allow the legislature to amend, revise, and otherwise tinker with the proposals, even to the point of completely rewriting them, is a form — and a sign — of chief-executive weakness compared to the package approach. The president and many governors now have the option of proposing reorganization packages.

INFORMATION RESOURCES

Control over information represents a fourth broad approach to maintaining chief-executive influence over bureaucratic agencies, as well as general influence in the policy-making process. It is said that knowledge and now *information* is power and, in an era of intensive specialization, and faster access to information, that holds true as never before. The more complex the bureaucratic structure of any given executive branch, the greater the challenge to the chief executive in terms of information gathering and use. We will focus mainly on the presidency for purposes of this discussion, but it should be noted that state and local chief executives interacting with relatively complex bureaucracies will find their situations not unlike the one that confronts the president.

The president, of course, must deal increasingly with a highly specialized and expert bureaucracy (inside as well as outside the presidential establishment).[31] How then is the president to gather the facts and figures necessary to informed decision making without being dominated by, or becoming excessively dependent on, his sources of information?

To a large extent, the president is dependent on specialized bureaucratic agencies and also on information supplied by the network of presidential advisors, both those within the Executive Office of the President (EOP) and those having independent status. The president's ability to keep his information network functioning adequately while avoiding dependence on any one source of information is crucial to his retention of political leadership and policy initiative. Franklin Roosevelt was perhaps the master of this art. He ensured a constant stream of facts, ideas, suggestions, and countersuggestions by (1) centralizing decision-making responsibility in the Oval Office, (2) delegating responsibility for proposing policy alternatives rather widely so as to involve large numbers of administrators in the process of "brainstorming" for ideas, (3) actively encouraging open debate and discussion among members of his administration, and

(4) leaving just about everyone somewhat uncertain as to whose ideas might be acted on in any given situation. He also took care to follow suggestions from a variety of sources, thus demonstrating his intention to take useful ideas and follow them up irrespective of the source.[32]

Roosevelt's technique had the effect of generating more ideas than he could use, but it was to his advantage as a political leader to have that volume of information, combined with the carefully cultivated ability to make the final choices himself. Presidents since FDR have had a far more difficult task in this regard, as a result of the growth of virtually every major institution in the executive branch and the increasing power of special-interest "lobbies." There is more information than any one person can absorb and utilize; there are more competitors, both institutional and personal, for access to, and control of, information; and the greatly increased quantities of information generated by others for their own use and political advantage pose an obstacle to presidential policy direction that is difficult to surmount. As one example, President Clinton, and Hillary Rodham Clinton — as lead advocate and spokesperson for health care reform — experienced a media campaign mounted by large insurance companies opposed to the Clintons' proposals.

task forces temporary cross-functional teams responsible for achieving a particular goal, often drawn from several departments within a larger agency; typically disbanded after the goal is accomplished.

Recent presidents have tried to deal with their growing information needs by (1) increasing the information capabilities of the EOP; (2) creating specialized staffs, or **task forces,** with corresponding increases in the political and programmatic responsibilities entrusted to them; and (3) delegating greater operating authority to EOP personnel. These changes have improved the president's information base for assessing alternatives and making choices, thereby creating something of a counterforce to the information generated in other parts of the bureaucracy and elsewhere. Furthermore, the proliferation of presidential staffs has permitted more specialization within the EOP, thus strengthening the president's policy-making effectiveness vis-à-vis the expertise of the bureaucracy. Finally, by broadening the authority of assistants, the First Lady, the vice president, and staffs to speak and act on behalf of the president, Bill Clinton has enhanced his ability to transmit and acquire information through his immediate subordinates. This is important because presidents (and other chief executives) frequently encounter difficulty in transmitting and receiving accurate information through the bureaucratic hierarchy.

The strength of the governor's staff and executive office resources, including information capabilities, must also be assessed. In recent decades, many states have made considerable progress in these areas, with a consequent increase in gubernatorial effectiveness. Most of the states have a department of administration to assist the governor in directing the bureaucracy's operations and, in a number of other states the governor's personal staff has been expanded to include qualified subject-matter specialists, who strengthen the reservoir of expertise available in the executive office itself.

A major obstacle in transmitting information from one level in a hierarchy to the next is the tendency for a portion of the information to be screened out by those who receive it and, in turn, send it on. This may be done in a deliberate attempt to frustrate the will of the official sending the information, or it may be done without any particular motive — perhaps even unconsciously. Depending on how many levels there are in the structure, a great deal of information can be distorted and even lost in this manner.[33] A chief executive, or any other top-level official, cannot casually assume that his or her communications — including instructions, statements of policy, or major program directives — travel down the hierarchy simply on the strength of their having been issued. There must be follow-up (sometimes repeated checks) to ensure that communications have been received and accurately understood by those for whom they were intended (see Chapter 5).

Obtaining reliable information that gives a clear, complete picture of what is going on in the bureaucracy is the other side of the coin. A truism of administrative practice is that, unless there is some disruption in the normal routines of administration, the chief executive does not have to be informed about the details of administrative activities. Such an assumption is justified on the grounds that the chief executive's responsibilities are broader than the activities of a single bureaucratic agency and that his or her attention should be directed to individual entities only if there is some special reason for doing so. In traditional administrative thinking, this assumption is called the **exception principle**, suggesting that only exceptions to routine operations merit involvement of the chief executive. But the exception principle does not always work well in practice. For one thing, there is a strong, if natural, reluctance to communicate bad news — such as the existence of a problem that the agency knows it cannot handle on its own — through the hierarchy and, least of all, from an immediate subordinate to a superior official of that agency. Also, for its own reasons, an agency may prefer not to call attention to activities that are likely to be unpopular with its nominal superior. Therefore, for the president (or other chief executive) to have accurate, comprehensive information requires a successful effort to overcome built-in fear and resistance to a free upward flow of communication.

The president can facilitate the transmission of information to the EOP from the rest of the bureaucracy by maintaining regular follow-up checks for compliance and by requiring regular feedback from the agencies, though it is easier to establish routines of feedback than to elicit useful substantive content.[34] Administrative agencies resist supplying feedback in the same way — and for many of the same reasons — that they resist other types of upward communication. Consequently, presidential (and other) monitoring of bureaucratic activity requires deliberate, concentrated action in order to have any chance of keeping some semblance of control from the top.

Among the ways of coping with problems in acquiring information are (1) making use of external sources of information (newspapers and other media, interest groups, and so on); (2) creating overlapping substantive areas of responsibility within or among bureaus, resulting in multiple channels of information sources and presumably more reliable information; (3) using informal channels

exception principle
an assumption in traditional administrative thinking that chief executives do not have to be involved in administrative activities unless some problem or disruption of routine activity occurs — that is, where there is an exception to routine operations.

to supplement formal ones; and (4) deliberately bypassing formal structures and intermediate layers of bureaucracy to contact directly the person or persons who have the information being sought.[35] Franklin Roosevelt and John Kennedy, in particular, frequently telephoned lower-echelon bureaucrats to get from them information that was moving too slowly, or not at all, through formal hierarchical channels. Such an informal practice has two effects, both desirable from the president's point of view: it gets the particular information into his hands more quickly, and it signals the rest of the bureaucracy that the president is prepared to bypass the usual channels when he deems it necessary. The latter is likely to reduce the time required to transmit communications through channels; the threat of being bypassed can motivate those responsible for forwarding information to the president to do so with a minimum of delay, outweighing any contrary motivations to obstruct or distort.

Let us consider one other issue concerning presidents and the control of information. By simply withholding all or some information, a president can decisively influence the shape of internal deliberations, media reports, public debate, and even global confrontations. Four examples illustrate this point: (1) the previously mentioned Iran-Contra affair during the Reagan and Bush presidencies; (2) the Cuban missile crisis of 1962, when tight secrecy was essential for successfully negotiating the removal of Soviet missiles from Cuba; (3) the American buildup in Vietnam in the mid-1960s, when any information unfavorable to Lyndon Johnson's Vietnam policies was systematically withheld from the mass media and the public; and (4) the Nixon administration's secret (and illegal) domestic surveillance of anti–Vietnam War activists, civil rights organizers, and attempted burglaries to obtain confidential records of opposition candidates.

This device, however, has its limits, and failure to control information can also have major policy implications. A classic illustration involved President Kennedy's explanations of just what was promised to anti-Castro Cubans who wanted to invade Cuba at the Bay of Pigs in 1961. The invasion became a fiasco for the United States because, first, air cover promised for the landing on the beaches never materialized and, second, Kennedy's spokesmen — particularly a Pentagon press officer with years of experience on the job — denied any American involvement in either the planning or the execution of the abortive invasion. These spokesmen followed up their denials, once they were known to be false, with claims that the national interest had both required and justified their giving out false information. Another example is the attempted break-in at the Democratic election headquarters in the Watergate apartments in Washington, D.C., during the presidential election campaign in 1972. The documented falsehoods of the Nixon White House in regard to the Watergate affair also demonstrated the power of the president to influence the course of public discussion, as well as the dramatic consequences of not maintaining complete information control. The essential points are these: (1) Presidents, through their control of information, can substantially affect debate and decision in and out of government, not to mention how others perceive public issues or the president's order of priorities; and (2) conflicts over access to, and use of, information involve crucial questions of political influence, with high stakes for the president and others in politics.

A president, on the other hand, can find himself forced to react to a situation in which *he* lacks information vital to an impending decision. One such case was the **Cuban missile crisis** in 1962. President Kennedy needed to establish beyond doubt that Soviet missiles had been installed in Cuba before deciding what actions to take, actions that might have led to global nuclear war. But, despite the terrible urgency, he had difficulty obtaining the necessary photographic evidence because of the time consumed by bureaucratic processing of the information and at least one interagency squabble — over whose pilots (Air Force or CIA) would fly whose planes over the western end of Cuba, where the missiles were ultimately spotted.[36] If presidents are unable to acquire information readily in the most extraordinary circumstances, even in a potential nuclear crisis, they clearly cannot depend on routine flows of information.

Just how effective, then, is information control in the total picture of presidential leadership? The answer is mixed. In terms of public and congressional leadership by the president, control of information can be a crucial instrument. But with respect to the bureaucracy, the president's leadership is subject to greater constraints, if for no other reason than that his control of information is less secure. Individual administrators in key positions within bureaucracies could have more to do with shaping the available alternatives for presidential decisions through provision of information than any other institution or person.

Cuban missile crisis dangerous confrontation between the Soviet Union (Russia) and the United States during the Kennedy administration (1962) over the shipment and deployment of Russian nuclear missiles in Cuba.

Commonalities and Differences in Leadership Resources

The institutional, legal, and personal factors that facilitate strong executive leadership seem to operate at all levels of government, though somewhat less clearly and predictably for local executives. Strong chief executives draw much of their strength from the following general features.

First, a chief executive's political strength in the legislature, and as leader of a political party or faction, adds substantially to leadership capability in office. Research in congressional voting behavior, and to a lesser extent in state legislatures, suggests that many legislators are responsive to the initiative of the chief executive, particularly when party loyalty is invoked. Other considerations (such as policy preferences, constituency interests, and individual conscience) also play an important part in legislative decision making, but many votes are cast strictly along party lines. If a governor is strongly supported by legislators of the same party — for example, Nelson Rockefeller in New York in the 1960s[37] and Ronald Reagan in California from 1967 to 1975 — it adds measurably to gubernatorial effectiveness. If, on the other hand, a governor must constantly struggle to gain the support of his or her own partisans in the legislature, leadership capability is a good deal more constrained. The same principle holds true with equal import for local executives and presidents. It is important to note that strength in the legislature is usually tied to the amount of popular support for the chief executive.

Second, the power to initiate policy proposals and see that they are carried out politically is a key element of executive leadership. Legislatures at all levels ordinarily lack central policy formulation capabilities so that a chief executive who wishes to see his or her "public agenda" passed into law can do so in most cases. This assumes, of course, an executive leader who seeks to lead actively — an assumption that is usually, but not always, valid.

Third, the capacity to respond to crisis situations (which, by their nature, require immediate, coordinated direction) has strengthened chief executives' positions. For one thing, the public has come to expect chief executives to exercise this prerogative. Also, especially in the case of the presidency, some residual emergency powers have remained in force after particular crises have passed.

More important are specific leadership tools. First, a central role in executive budget making strengthens the overall influence of the chief executive. If budgetary "central clearance" exists, executive agencies must pay heed to the preferences of the elected executive, at least during key stages of the budget cycle.

Second, a crucial resource is control over executive-branch personnel decisions. The more extensive the authority to decide appointments and dismissals, the greater the political hold over actions of those whose tenure in office depends on pleasing their "patron" (hence the term *patronage*). Few chief executives, at any level, currently enjoy that kind of personnel domination.

Third, the ability to propose agency reorganizations enhances the chief executive's power, particularly if the legislature must accept or reject the proposals as a package. This power, however, is effective more as an implied or occasional threat because reorganization is a major step. A chief executive who attempted more than one reorganization within a short time span would encounter either the likely defeat of the proposals or reduced credibility with the legislature (or both). Reorganization authority is thus a political leadership resource of rather limited potential. Still, it is better to have it in reserve than to lack it entirely or to have to subject any reorganization proposal to the normal legislative mill.

Fourth, chief-executive information resources constitute a source of potential strength. This depends on institutional arrangements in which provision is made for adequate staff; on the skills of individuals who make up the staff; and on considerations of information availability, transmission, and control. Chief executives are generally more dependent on, rather than independent of, information sources in the bureaucracy — and, increasingly, within their own executive establishments as well. Even so, information can be a key source of executive influence.

Some chief executives have particular advantages and disadvantages that should be noted. The president, for all his difficulties with semiautonomous bureaucracies, is better off than many governors and mayors in that fewer constitutional restrictions are placed on his leadership. Many governors have a more flexible veto power than the president, whereas many mayors lack veto power altogether. The president appoints his cabinet; a governor often must work with high-level elected officials from the opposition party. Both the president and the majority of governors are their party's acknowledged leaders, a situation many mayors may envy. Most governors and local executives are limited, in a broad sense, by the fact that their governments' fiscal and administrative capabilities generally lag behind those of the national government. Moreover, many of them depend to some extent on national government assistance for a portion (sometimes a *substantial* portion) of their revenues. Although fiscal dependence is an indirect impediment to the autonomy of executive leaders, it can, in some ways, have even more adverse long-term effects on state or local policy initiatives.

The Organizational Setting of Leadership

Leadership has attracted great interest in both ancient and modern times from scholars, generals, politicians, and more casual observers. Virtually every culture, from the most primitive to the most complex, has operated within some sort of framework in which leadership functions are differentiated, identified, and exercised by some and not others. Styles of leadership have been studied and restudied; prescriptions for leadership have been written and revised; exercise of leadership has been carefully analyzed and often sharply criticized. Despite all this attention, *the question of what it takes to be an effective leader is still far from settled.* More research has been done in this century, paralleling the expansion of knowledge in such related fields as social psychology, sociology, organization theory, and political science. The subject has taken on particular urgency in the past two decades, however, as popular discontent has grown regarding the failure of leadership in existing political and social institutions.

Administrative leadership is exercised within specific organizational settings as well as in the context of the larger environment; both can significantly influence the behavior of leaders. We will first consider the impact of organizational settings, move next to traditional approaches to the study of leadership and some of the findings, and finally examine a number of roles and challenges that are, or can be, a part of the leadership function.

To focus our consideration on the exercise of leadership, we make several assumptions. First, it is assumed that the leader attains his or her position through legitimate means and remains the leader through the acquiescence of the "followership." In most cultures, groups tend to accept more readily leaders whose characteristics and abilities facilitate accomplishment of the specific tasks — for example, the captain of a swimming team is likely to be both a good swimmer and a good motivator.[38] It is also assumed, however, that the leader's legitimacy is not automatically continued, that the leader's actions contribute to, or detract from, the legitimacy the group accords him or her.

Second, our principal interest is in leaders within administrative hierarchies, where advancement through the ranks or appointments from outside the organization by top-level often elected superiors constitute the main methods of filling leadership slots.

Third, we assume that organization members have at least a minimal interest in carrying out both the organization's overall responsibilities and their own particular responsibilities as well. Furthermore, we assume that the members' job performance can be affected by the ways in which top leaders and immediate supervisors conduct themselves in the course of discharging their responsibilities. There is ample evidence supporting the view that the relationship between leaders and followers, as well as followers' personal feelings about leaders and the way they lead, can have major consequences for work performance and the general work atmosphere.[39]

Finally, the leadership roles and challenges we will discuss center on leaders who are in a position — official or unofficial — to influence significantly what happens in an organization. This is mentioned explicitly because it is frequently *not* the case; that is, some leaders are in a relatively weak position as a result of group structure and the nature of the work to be done.[40] One example of this would be a research team of equally competent and well-known scientists in which one member informally assumes overall direction of team tasks. As "first among equals," this leader would have to guide others through persuasion and participative decision making. Our concern, however, is with leaders who are significantly involved with the totality of the group or organization's existence, activities, and sense of identity, and whose leadership is accepted and acknowledged by group members.

In administrative hierarchies, leadership is a multidimensional function because of multiple levels of organization, wide variation in specific tasks and general functions, and numerous situations requiring leadership of some kind. The job of a leader within the administrative framework, therefore, is not constant. The particular combinations of needs (organizational, personal, task-oriented, political) within groups being led are rarely the same from one set of circumstances to the next.

A useful conceptual approach to the organizational setting is sociologist Talcott Parsons' suggestion that "organizations exhibit three distinct levels of responsibility and control — technical, managerial, and institutional"[41] (from the narrowest to the broadest scope). These are analogous to the distinctions drawn previously between types of decisions made by different kinds of bureaucrats (specialists or generalists) and among the varying grounds for reaching decisions (substantive, organizational, or political). Leadership in complex organizations is greatly affected by the variations in responsibility and control identified by Parsons; to understand why that is, we will elaborate on what each level signifies.

The **technical** level, or suborganization, deals with problems "focused around effective performance of the technical function" — for example, teachers

technical leadership that focuses on achieving a particular task within a subunit of an organization.

conducting their classes, a transit authority employee operating a bus on the prescribed route and running on time, or a government tax office processing income tax returns. Major concerns at this level are the nature of the technical task (such as processing materials) and "the kinds of cooperation of different people required to get the job done effectively."[42] The second, or **managerial,** level performs two functions for the technical suborganization: (1) mediating between the lower level and those who use its services, and (2) acquiring the resources necessary for carrying out technical functions, such as purchasing, hiring, and general operations. In these senses, the managers control, or administer, the technical suborganization — although such control is not strictly a one-way street. Line workers are increasingly encouraged and expected to participate. The **institutional** level of the organization develops long-term policy and provides top-level support to achieve group goals. The relationship between this level and the others bears on our earlier discussion of the relationships between chief executives and bureaucracies: In terms of "formal" controls, an organization may be relatively independent; but, in terms of the meaning of the functions performed by the organization and hence of its "rights" to command resources and to subject its customers to discipline, it is never completely "independent."

The significance of this observation is that, in *operating* terms, suborganizations at the technical and managerial levels may possess considerable autonomy and responsibility, but with ultimate responsibility and accountability vested at higher levels. (Note the further parallel between this observation and those made in Chapter 2 about the existence of considerable discretion in the making of public policy in our system.)

How is administrative leadership affected by all this? One part of the answer is that, at each of the points dividing the levels of organization (institutional from managerial and managerial from technical), "there is a qualitative break in the simple continuity of 'line' authority *because the functions at each level are qualitatively different. Those . . . at the second level are not simply lower-order spellings-out of the top-level functions.*"[43] In other words, one of the principal challenges of leadership is overseeing processes of defining, organizing, supporting, and monitoring multiple functions at multiple levels of organization, which, by their nature, tend to defy uniform methods of supervision. Responsibilities at each level must be clear enough — and flexible enough — to ensure that basic functions appropriate to that level or unit are, in fact, carried out. (Issues of centralization and decentralization, discussed in Chapter 5, are relevant here.) Particularly for elected or appointed chief executives, but for virtually any top official, these challenges must be of paramount concern.

These conceptions of organization help clarify another problem relevant to leadership, one discussed by Mary Parker Follett (1863–1933), an early student of leadership, seventy-five years ago.[44] The problem is one of *distance* within organizations, of difficulties encountered when directives must traverse a *tall* hierarchy (see Chapter 5).

managerial leadership that emphasizes midlevel supervisory skills and coordination between *technical* and senior-level *institutional* leaders.

institutional top-level leadership which is concerned primarily with achieving the long-term goals of the organization.

According to Follett, "One might say that the strength of favorable response to [an] order is in inverse ratio to the distance the order travels."[45] Follett was speaking not only of physical or geographical distance but also of the need for collaborative effort, or teamwork, between superiors and subordinates. She maintained that this could best be accomplished through face-to-face interaction, lessening both the physical distance and the tensions involved in giving orders. Such an observation, made during the 1920s (the heyday of scientific management), takes on greater significance in light of the more varied organizational functions that now exist and of Parsons' analysis of organization levels. Today, it is equally desirable, if not more so, to bridge the distances within complex organizations.

Thus, if leadership is to be effective, a deliberate effort must be made to overcome inevitable barriers inside organizations. Bear in mind, also, that the individual who may be a follower relative to higher-level officials may be a leader to others occupying subordinate positions. Multiple sets of leaders and followers operating at different levels in complex organizations complicate the tasks that each set and each leader must carry out. Thus, leadership development is equally important for followers who may "share" or coproduce some good or service within an organization.

Traditional Approaches to the Study of Leadership

traits approach a traditional method (now used less widely by scholars) of analyzing leadership in a group or organization; assumes that certain personality characteristics such as intelligence, ambition, tact, and diplomacy distinguish leaders from others in the group.

The earliest efforts to analyze leadership employed two principal approaches, centering on the *individual* leader and on the leadership situation. The **traits approach** sought to explain leadership in terms of personality characteristics, such as intelligence, ambition, ego drives, and interpersonal skills. Considerable emphasis was placed on leadership traits during the early years of the twentieth century but, in numerous studies since then, the traits approach has been found to explain little. Furthermore, contrary to the most basic assumption of this approach, leaders were not found to possess common characteristics. The traits approach was discarded by most scholarly observers (though not necessarily in the conventional wisdom about leaders) by the 1950s. Attention shifted to a seemingly more promising avenue of exploration, namely, analysis of leadership situations and how situational factors were related to what was required in a leader in a particular set of circumstances. (Interestingly, Follett had stressed the importance of situational factors in the 1920s.)

situational approach a method of analyzing leadership in a group or organization that emphasizes factors in the particular leadership situation, such as leader-follower interactions, group values, and the work being done.

The **situational approach** has become the general framework of analysis in most subsequent leadership studies. This approach does not try to explain leadership success or failure, particular styles of leadership, or why one person becomes a leader while another does not in terms of variations in personal skills and character. Rather, the situational approach emphasizes leader–follower interactions, the needs of the group or organization in the time period under study, the kind of work being done, general group values and ethics, and the like.

From this, it follows that leaders in one situation may not be cut out to be leaders in other situations. Some years ago, a successful businessman who headed the European division of a large multinational corporation was asked to serve as dean of a business school at a large private research university on the basis of his experience. The university struggled for some years to find an acceptable candidate before he took the position. But, shortly thereafter, the faculty rebelled and the university governing board realized it had made a mistake — the successful businessman was an abject failure as a dean. Not only were the specific duties different but so, too, were the types of people and their values and expectations, as well as the dean's interactions with university personnel as opposed to company employees. The point is that variations in the times, in circumstances, and in group characteristics help determine the most appropriate kinds of leadership and, to an important degree, who will lead. Personality, skills, ambition, and the rest make some difference but only in the context of the social environment, the leadership setting, and demands arising from the group.

Another general dimension of leadership is how specific styles of management affect the distribution of power, influence, and freedom of action of leaders and followers in an organization. Figure 7–1 illustrates a continuum of leadership behavior, suggesting the range of possibilities open to leaders in choosing management techniques. Such choices, like leadership effectiveness, are conditioned to a considerable extent by the nature of the organization, the tasks to be completed, and nature of the group relationships between leaders and followers. Group situations vary according to (1) *position power* of the leader, defined as the authority vested in the leader's official position; (2) *task structure* of the group — the degree to which assignments can be programmed and specified in a step-by-step fashion; and (3) leader–member *personal relationships*, based on affection, admiration, and trust of group members for the leader. Leaders who are liked by the group and have a clear-cut task and high position power are in a more favorable position than leaders who have poor relationships with group members, an unstructured task, and weak position power.[46]

But how to choose the particular leadership style most appropriate to a given situation? Recent research suggests that leadership comes from the interaction between people in a work situation and requires a combination of interpersonal and group-situational skills. For example, if tasks are clear-cut, if relations between leader and members are positive, and if official position power is considerable, a leader is best advised to be strongly directive rather than democratic and nondirective. An All-American quarterback does not call the plays by taking votes in the huddle! By the same token, the chairperson of a voluntary community service committee cannot order group members to vote in a certain way or to act according to his or her directions. This theory of leadership is important for what it suggests about what *can* be changed to improve leadership effectiveness (rank, task structure, concern for followers) and what *cannot* be changed (leader personality, work situation, organizational characteristics). Leader traits (within limits), situational dynamics, and relationships dictate the most effective

FIGURE 7–1   The Continuum of Leadership Behavior: Relations between Managers and Nonmanagers

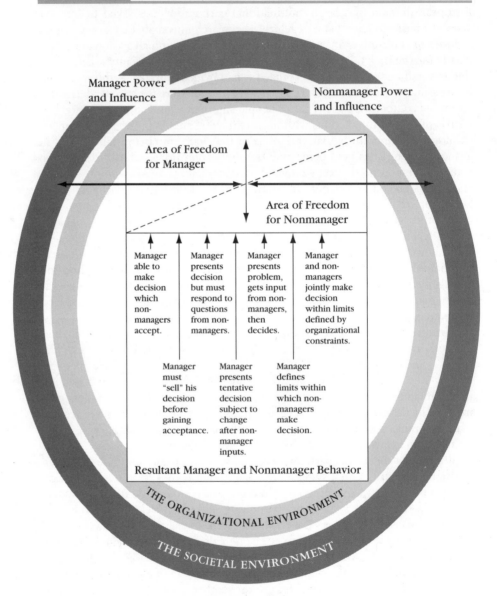

Source: Reprinted by permission of *Harvard Business Review*: An exhibit from "How to Choose a Leadership Pattern" by Robert Tannenbaum and Warren H. Schmidt, 51 (May/June 1973). Copyright 1973 by the President and Fellows of Harvard College; all rights reserved.

leadership style. The relationship between personal traits, personality, and the situation describes the most common approach to studying leadership. The most successful style must be determined almost on a case-by-case basis; it is anything but preordained.

Recent research suggests that leadership in a nonhierarchical organization is defined as a property of the social system in which individuals, groups, leaders, and followers interact. Leadership is "an outcome of *collective* meaning-making, not the result of influence of vision from an individual . . . [it] is created by people making sense and meaning of their work together, and this process, in turn, can bring leaders into being."[47] This new model of **relational leadership** encourages responsiveness to customers, grants increased nonroutine decision-making power to people with direct customer contact, and makes everyone accountable for the outcome of their work as well as for fulfilling the mission of the organization. These ideas more closely fit the model of *learning organizations* introduced in Chapter 5, requiring a flexible concept of leadership in an open rather than closed system which emphasizes continuous developmental and adaptive change.

relational leadership
leaders must not only be competent at traditional skills such as goal setting, conflict management, and motivation, but must also be able to acquire information from group members and adapt their leadership styles to fit the needs of followers.

In the early 1980s, research findings appeared that, ironically, gave renewed emphasis to the importance of personality characteristics in potential and actual leaders. This is suggestive of the traits approach, which has been out of favor among most students of leadership for some time, but there are important differences. One is the far greater sophistication and understanding we now possess of individual and group psychology. Another is the explicit link assumed in the recent research between personality and leader behavior, making assessment of personalities more meaningful. And there has been a systematic effort to identify different dimensions of leader personality in much greater detail.[48]

We turn now to challenges of leadership in an effort to describe the many facets of the leader's role. The intention here is not to make a definitive appraisal of the leader's job but rather to suggest the scope of leadership functions as they might apply to many different organizational settings. We will consider six such challenges and attempt to suggest very broadly what makes a successful leader in terms of these tasks. The purpose of examining the challenges of leadership is to illuminate the many facets of a leader's role.

Challenges of Administrative Leadership

LEADER AS DIRECTOR: RECONCILING PERSONAL AND ORGANIZATIONAL GOALS

An essential function of the **leader as director** is to bring some coherence to the multitude of activities within an organization. This is facilitated by persuading those in charge of various activities to emphasize the aspects of their work that are directed toward common organizational objectives. This can also mean that

leader as director
refers to the challenge of bringing some unity of purpose to the organization's members.

the leader defines the nature of a problem to be dealt with. Leadership to achieve common goals requires motivating others to do what is best for the organization for their own reasons. Leaders in public organizations seeking to raise customer service quality standards are thinking less in traditional bureaucratic terms, but rather like coaches, teachers, or facilitators of change. And this, in turn, requires reconciling personal and organizational goals, which (as discussed in Chapter 6) can diverge and even conflict.

The key to a leader's efforts to reconcile personal and organizational goals is to create as much psychological overlap as possible between the two. If a leader is able to induce individual members to internalize (accept as their own) general objectives of the organization, most of this task will have been accomplished. This might be done by direct and indirect persuasion, by example, or by developing members' understanding of rationales for pursuing particular objectives or adopting specific tactics. To the extent that there is conflict over goals, of course, this challenge will remain an ongoing one, with considerable potential for difficulty. The optimum situation is one in which members see pursuit of organizational goals as consistent with, and supportive of, achievement of their personal goals.

goal articulation
a process of defining and clearly expressing goals generally held by those in an organization or group; usually regarded as a function of organization or group leaders; a key step in developing support for official goals.

Goal articulation is a critical function of leadership. How goals are defined and communicated may trigger strong reactions from individual members. If reactions are negative — because of substantive disagreement, lack of consideration for members' views, or inadequate preparation — gaining members' support will be that much more difficult. Leaders often have to devote a significant amount of time, energy, and resources to winning member support for group goals, and they do not always succeed. Realistically, not all members are capable of personal commitment to the goals of the organization; as noted earlier, some members of any group may have different goals and priorities. Very often leaders must settle for grudging or reluctant cooperation, which is a far cry from genuine support.

Besides these problems, there is the possibility that leaders' personal goals may interfere with organizational performance and attainment of group objectives, though leaders, by virtue of their positions, tend to be somewhat more committed to group goals than their followers are. Enlightened leadership requires a clear vision of, and dedication to, organizational goals that outweigh any personal objectives — and this selfless commitment must be perceived as such by followers. Leaders should not underestimate the difficulty of convincing others that their direction is the proper one. Successful leadership requires sound theory, consistency, hard work, discipline, and it may entail confronting some unpleasant realities about the basic structure of the organization. Above all, a personal commitment to achieving the mission of the organization is required.

Another difficulty lies in the possibility that members' personal goals may be more important to them than the mission of the organization. The types of bureaucrats Anthony Downs labeled climbers and conservers[49] — those interested in, respectively, achieving and preserving power, prestige, and income —

attest to the possibility that highly personalized goals may predominate among some organization members (see Chapter 6). The larger the proportion of total membership that falls into these molds, the more difficult the task of directing the organization's activities toward larger goals. A related problem is determining the true state of affairs in this regard, that is, knowing what members' goals really are. Organizational goals can be separate from personal goals and from the feelings, values, and preferences of an organization's members. From this perspective, goals seem to exist independently of organization members — as something determined by persons outside the organization, as self-defining in the course of organization activities, or as the product of articulation by the leadership.

LEADER AS MOTIVATOR: THE CARROT OR THE STICK?

We discussed motivation within organizations at some length in Chapter 5. Our purpose here is to review the major themes outlined earlier and put them into perspective as part of the tasks of **leaders as motivators** who seek to inspire their followers in the most positive fashion.

leader as motivator
a key task centering on devices such as tangible benefits, positive social interaction, work interest, encouragement by job supervisors, and leadership that is self-confident, persuasive, fair, and supportive.

First, if we use the analogy of the carrot or the stick to describe one kind of choice to be made in motivating members of an organization, the stick is definitely our second choice, especially in organizations that encourage participation. A substantial body of research clearly suggests that coercive measures aimed at motivating employees by fear of punishment may have short-term impacts but are not effective in the long run.[50] Far more likely to succeed is a combination of incentives and conditions appropriate to the interests of those doing the work. On the basis of research conducted over several decades, there is reason to believe that emphasis should be given to incentives such as offering attractive salaries, fringe benefits, and working conditions; creating positive social interaction among groups of workers; and making the work as interesting and challenging as possible. The problem is that different incentives work for different people, and leaders face the continuing challenge of tailoring these motivators to the needs, preferences, and attitudes of organization members or member groups. This is important not only for accomplishing immediate goals but also for building cohesiveness in the organization through member satisfaction. It may not be possible, however, to satisfy each and every individual fully.

Some years ago, a study by the Society for the Advancement of Management sought to discover what workers in private companies felt was the single most positive feature in the behavior of their immediate supervisors. The most common response was that the supervisor had encouraged the employee in work performance. Because there is other evidence suggesting that the interaction between employees and their first-line supervisors is vital to group performance, morale, and individual job satisfaction, a positive, supportive attitude toward employees on the part of the supervisor takes on added importance. More and more organizations are realizing the importance of selecting and evaluating supervisors. Thus, leaders should be concerned about the quality of face-to-face supervision, as well as tangible benefits and incentives and the intrinsic interest the work offers.

Motivation continues to be a complex task of leadership. People respond to leadership that is clearly defined and, at the same time, persuasive, fair, and supportive. But no rule is universally applicable; exceptions are frequent, and leaders have to remain alert if they expect to cope with the full range of motivational problems that could arise in their organizations.

LEADER AS COORDINATOR/INTEGRATOR: MESHING THE GEARS

A function of growing importance for leaders in complex organizations has been coordinating and integrating the varied functions and tasks of increasingly specialized staff members. Though usually not as knowledgeable as individual technical specialists about the specialties in their organizations, **leaders as coordinators** must rely on the competence of these subordinates even as they attempt to organize the efforts of staff members into a coherent whole. If the tasks of directing and motivating members have been carried out effectively, coordinating and integrating their efforts should follow naturally — but, conceptually, there are a number of factors to be considered.

Most important is the tendency for individuals concentrating on their own particular work environment to develop **tunnel vision,** through which they see the worth of their own tasks but fail to appreciate the importance of other aspects of the organization's activity. For example, a leader attempting to change the operations of a division, staff, or branch, for the purpose of strengthening the organization's overall capacities or performance, may encounter resistance from members in that subsection who believe that their procedures and output are adequate for their purposes. Their frame of reference is their work, defined as the work of the subsection, whereas the leadership's responsibilities encompass the work of the entire organization.

As anyone with management responsibilities already knows, any attempt to change group behavior can be frustrating. It is difficult enough to change individual behavior; it can be extremely difficult to change the behavior of an organizational subgroup made up of diverse individuals. For a leader to overcome member resistance requires the ability to convey a sense of the larger issues, mission, and needs that gave rise to the leader's desire for change. In essence, this means broadening the horizons of these members to include a fuller picture of the organization in operation. The result, ideally, would be that, when actions are proposed that affect specific work units, members of those units — by understanding larger organizational purposes, would be more inclined to accept, and even to take an active part in, what their leadership is trying to do. Willingness to actively participate in work redesign requires a high level of trust between members and supervisors, often lacking in many organizations.

leader as coordinator (and integrator) involves bringing some order to the multitude of functions within a complex organization.

tunnel vision results from a fear of mistakes, missed deadlines, and focus on a narrow work environment, which limits the ability to see the organization's activities as a whole.

Mechanisms for generating ideas for work redesign include surveys, news-letters, suggestion boxes, question-and-answer sessions, and advance communication of proposed actions to members. This amounts to regularized **brainstorming** for ideas, a process that, by involving members, is likely to make final decisions more palatable to more people in the organization. Circulating information about actions already taken can also be beneficial. Not circulating information widely can result in built-up resentments, which can linger and affect subsequent organizational activities.

brainstorming free-form and creative technique for collecting and discussing ideas from all participants without criticism or judgment.

Even in the best of circumstances, leaders will have to manage diverse operations on a smoothly coordinated time schedule. Personnel, materials, financial resources, services to consumers of the organization's output (however defined), and so on, all have to be integrated into the organization's ongoing activities. In this respect, advance planning is a key leadership function, to ensure that the necessary components are on hand as needed. Every organization in existence faces that common need, and every leader is expected to meet it.

Another dimension of coordination and integration of organizational activities is the need to mesh the leadership's own tasks with those of the remainder of the organization. The need here is to avoid working at cross-purposes, making certain that leaders and followers generally share the same vision, or understanding, of the organization's mission and its intended goals. This ties in with the leader-as-director challenge in the effort to create constancy of purpose and psychological overlap among several different sets of goals. It is also linked to the role of leader as motivator in the creation of inducements designed to move members in particular directions.

In sum, organizations comprising diverse specialties and functions require efforts at the top, as well as throughout the ranks, to bring about satisfactory coordination and integration of goals. Organization members need some sense that their different functions somehow fit into a larger **shared vision** of the mission of the organization. And leaders must take responsibility for instilling that view.

shared vision a foundation of core values within which leaders, managers, and employees interact and upon which everything else in the organization is based.

LEADER AS CATALYST/INNOVATOR: POINTING THE WAY

The conception of the **leader as catalyst and innovator** — a "spark plug" or the "one who makes it happen" — which is widespread in the conventional wisdom about groups and organizations (especially sports teams), appears to have some validity. But the particular conditions prevailing in the group situation may strongly affect a leader's opportunities to stimulate group action. The best opportunities occur when the leader has influence in the group, informal support, and a relatively well-structured task at hand — when "the group is ready to be directed, and the members expect to be told what to do."[51] An example is the situation of the captain of an aircraft in its final approach before landing, when leadership decisions, instructions, and actions are crucial and no one would realistically want him (or her) to discuss or evaluate proposed options with the flight

leader as catalyst and innovator a formalized conception of the "spark plug" role in a group setting. As part of the catalyst role, a leader is also expected to introduce innovations into an organization.

crew. Other examples of well-structured tasks for which a leader is the catalyst for group action include rescue operations after a disaster, infantry combat, and a football team's last-minute drive for the winning touchdown. In these circumstances, the tasks to be performed are short-term and clearly defined; those responsible will succeed or fail within a limited time period.

Many tasks, however, are less structured, more routine, and more time-consuming. Here, too, a leader may be a successful catalyst, provided that members understand and support organizational objectives and that the leader has made clear how individual activities help promote those objectives. For example, an academic department chairman concerned about financial support for the department from the university administration may encourage faculty members to pursue research interests as well as excellence in teaching. Published articles, books, and research papers enhance a department's prestige outside the university, providing a strong argument for continued internal support. Even though such activities are conducted largely on an individual basis, a chairman can relate them to departmental well-being and thus attempt to motivate faculty members in those terms.

innovation   the introduction of something new
into an organization.

The process of **innovation** is tied to the role of a leader as catalyst because, in many instances, an organization's routine operations do not require very substantial direct participation. Indeed, delegation of authority (not responsibility for results) is a critical leadership decision. When normal procedures are all that is required, the leader is ordinarily in the background — and is best advised to remain there so as to permit members to function with some measure of independence. However, changes in routines must usually be initiated outside the group or subgroup because the routines may serve a stabilizing function inside the group and have the support of its members (see the earlier discussion of tunnel vision in the preceding section and also Chapter 6 regarding "groupthink" and routine decision making). Furthermore, routines frequently evolve in a way that reflects values and preferences of the group regarding not only the mechanics but also the very purposes of group activities. Thus, group members may interpret a proposed change in routine as a comment on their purposes as well as their procedures (which may be true). The challenge to the leader, then, is to justify adequately to group members any proposed change he or she deems necessary in the context of the larger organization.[52] Clearly, the catalyst role is important if innovation is to be brought about.

LEADER AS EXTERNAL SPOKESPERSON — AND GLADIATOR

One of the most crucial tasks for a leader is to act as representative of the organization's views and interests in the external environment. This involves articulating formal organizational positions to those outside. Ordinarily, it also includes an *advocacy role* when the organization seeks to secure additional resources or to maintain the resources it has. This spokesperson task has become more important as organizations have become more complex and is particularly so for leaders of the suborganizational units within larger hierarchical structures. The branch chief within a government bureaucracy, the manager of a plant within a large manufacturing conglomerate, and the academic department chairman within a college structure headed by a dean share a periodic need to go to bat for their organizations.

The most common setting for this role is budgetary decision making, where favorable portrayal of the organization can be decisive in influencing those who make budgetary decisions for the next fiscal year. This, however, is only the most visible kind of leadership opportunity. In fact, the **leader as gladiator** task is ongoing — standing up for the organization and its members when there is a complaint about its operation, anticipating and preparing for changes in the external environment that might adversely affect the organization, or simply keeping abreast of developments in the larger organization as they relate to the values, work, and well-being of the unit.

Few things are better for group morale than a leader who willingly and effectively defends the group's collective and individual welfare. Aside from the practical benefits such advocacy can produce, a leader's active support and defense of the organization represents, in concrete form, faith in staff members and their work. The leader, in acting as gladiator, is demonstrating that he or she is a part of the organization rather than standing aloof from it. In addition, the leader as gladiator is in effect, carrying out one of the cardinal principles of good management: Bestow praise publicly! Defense or advocacy on behalf of the organization constitutes collective rather than individual praise, but it indicates positive feedback in a strategically important form, and that is usually not lost on members of an organization.

leader as gladiator
a leadership role in which the leader seeks to promote the work of an organization, often in an effort to secure additional resources, as well as defending the organization in the external environment.

LEADER AS MANAGER OF CRISIS IN THE ORGANIZATION

Chief executives gain political strength when called on to direct governmental responses to crises of various kinds — military, economic, or natural disasters. Leaders in organizations at all levels are usually responsible for dealing with the occasional serious problem or difficulty that arises in their units or that affects one of their clienteles. Examples of the **leader as crisis manager** might include the managers of a transit district in a midwestern community faced with repeated breakdowns of district buses during a harsh winter, and a city manager confronted with deadlock in efforts to end a municipal employee strike. Such problems, although not minor, are generally limited to particular suborganizations or governments and, at least, have a definable end point.

A recently emergent dimension of leadership, however, goes beyond this sort of problem. This has to do with growing fiscal pressures on many public entities, particularly in state and local governments. Linked to all the other five roles, the leader as crisis manager must cope with an unpleasant new reality — that economic and other resources are not without limits. Also, it is clear that many citizens are unwilling to pay higher taxes in order to meet rising costs of

leader as crisis manager
involves coping with both immediate and longer-term difficulties, more serious than routine managerial challenges.

**cutback management
or "downsizing"**
current fiscal pressures on
public organizations have
spawned the need for
"downsizing" in many
places, forcing leaders
to use a variety of new
tactics. At the same time,
they must strive to main-
tain organization morale
and performance levels,
while holding to a mini-
mum the negative effects
of organizational decline.
See also **reductions-in-
force (RIF),** page 248.

government. Because it appears that resource scarcity will be with us for some
time, these leadership challenges lack the kind of end point characteristic of
more immediate difficulties. In recent years, various responses to scarcity have
been developed for administrative leaders to implement. One is the growing
practice of **cutback management or "downsizing"** which poses special difficulties for the leader responsible for carrying it out. Without growth in the economy, and perhaps with significant contractions in the public sector, leaders must
deal with unfamiliar situations that require new strategies and methods for rendering them acceptable to organization subordinates. We will treat the problem
of general resource scarcity as it relates to governmental resources in Chapter 9,
but the problems for administrative leaders stemming from tight resources,
however, are relevant here.

Various tactics exist for cutback management, addressed to the political and
economic/technical needs of the organization, both internally and externally.
Tactics designed to *resist* organizational decline include mobilizing dependent
clienteles, diversifying programs, targeting high-visibility programs for elimination (to make it politically costly for those making the decision), adopting user
charges and other means of direct funding for services where possible, retaining
internal esprit de corps and morale by developing a siege mentality, and improving productivity. Tactics designed to make downsizing smoother include cutting
programs having low prestige or those providing services to politically weak
clienteles or those run by weak subunits. It is also possible to vary leadership
styles at each stage in the downsizing process, to ask employees to sacrifice by
deferring raises or by taking early retirement, and to shift programs to other
agencies, thus reducing overall expenditures. How effective any or all of these
are, of course, is another question.

The other leader roles are profoundly affected by changes brought about by
decline and the need for cutbacks. For one thing, members of any organization
may experience a shift in personal goals, tending toward the conserver mentality
that is bent on "holding on if we can." To some extent, that can be useful, but a
leader must try to channel that motivation into useful and productive directions.
The motivator role is obviously affected, for, in the face of deteriorating
employee morale, the leader must be able to "rally the troops" in order to continue essential activities at an acceptable level of performance. The coordinator
role must be fulfilled even more effectively — with the resource base of the organization shrinking, ever more careful coordination of human and material
resources is necessary. The role of catalyst/innovator likewise is more sensitive
than ever because it falls to the leader to stimulate and direct the changes that
must be made. Ideally, this should include the leader's having previously anticipated problems of decline, so that resource reserves have been acquired as "organizational insurance." In this respect, foresight and keen judgment are valuable
leadership assets. Concern for innovation must also be manifested in another
way. Because of the possible tendency toward conserver behavior referred to earlier, organization leaders must resist pressures to conduct only "business as

usual" at the very time when complex and interdependent problems in the organization's environment cry out for innovative efforts at solving them. Leaders and their organizations are truly on the horns of a dilemma in this regard: declining resources evoke pressures for retrenchment and holding ground, but social and economic complexities underlying resource decline demand vigorous and innovative responses. No easy solutions exist to this basic dilemma, but efforts to develop answers are essential in the immediate future. Finally, and perhaps most important, the gladiator role calls for a leader's best efforts in order to reduce as much as possible adverse consequences of organizational decline for the administrative unit.

What Makes an Effective Leader?

We come back, then, to the persistent question that is at the core of most inquiries into the subject of leadership. Without claiming to have found the answers, let us suggest a number of general considerations relevant to achieving effective leadership (see Figure 7–2).

First, it appears that a leader is wise to convey to members that they are regarded as valuable to the organization and competent in their work. Many are, of course, quite competent; but the point here is that competent workers will appreciate that management has taken note of their worth, and less competent workers may work harder to live up to the leadership's expectations. The expectation of competence may, in fact, be a key factor in developing motivation to be competent.

Second, there is strong evidence that, if staff members of an organization perceive the leadership as being receptive to ideas, feedback, comments, and even complaints from below, they will be far more willing to respond to leaders' directives.[53] For one thing, communication from members gives leaders the clearest picture of what is important to employees and of their general attitudes

FIGURE 7–2   **Effective Leadership**

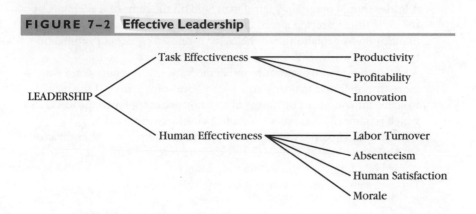

and aspirations. This cannot help but make it easier for the leaders to communicate meaningfully. More important, the leaders' willingness to listen to, and act on, useful ideas from the ranks builds a sense of cohesiveness among the members that is likely to increase each member's commitment to the organization's well-being. Without such feedback, it is virtually impossible for leaders to make the changes necessary to improve work performance.

Third, several studies suggest that the democratic leader is more effective in the broad view than any other type, with member satisfaction clearly higher in democratically led groups, and interaction among group members distinctly more relaxed and mutually supportive.[54] At the same time, the democratic leaders in these studies did not abdicate leadership functions but managed them in an open, participative, and supportive way. There is some reason to believe that such a style may work more effectively with some types of followers than with others (for example, professionals and some staff members in flat hierarchies with less formal structures) and perhaps with some types of personalities than with others. The general pattern seems to be one of fairly successful leadership direction under democratic conditions.

Fourth, a study of a work group in private industry suggests indirectly some of the leadership features to which employees may respond favorably. The study indicated that the more highly employees rated supervisors on a number of key attributes, the less employees expressed a desire for unionization. The attributes mentioned were fairness, use of authority, the ability to handle people, giving credit, readiness to discuss problems, and keeping employees informed. This combination suggests the scope of abilities demanded in many leadership situations.

At the risk of oversimplification, it is worth pointing out several other important qualities of leadership.

1. Ideally, a leader should be clear, reasonable, and consistent concerning expectations of, and standards of judgment for, member performance.
2. A leader is advised to deal openly, fairly, and equitably with all members, making distinctions among members only on work-related, not personal or life-style, criteria.
3. A leader should maintain a fairly firm hold on the reins of leadership, at the same time fostering a genuinely constructive two-way flow of communication by explaining rationales for proposed courses of action and by acting on worthwhile suggestions from members.
4. A leader should move carefully and democratically to secure consensus — more than merely a majority vote — on significant actions. One tactic is to strive for consensus by means of an extensive consultative process, which requires formal votes only when absolutely necessary.
5. The wise leader will try to prevent "empire building" and other divisive tendencies within the ranks. The goal is to prevent disunity as one step toward building cohesion within the group.
6. Cronyism and favoritism should be absolutely avoided.

7. Perhaps hardest of all, a leader can greatly influence the whole course of events in the organization by setting the tone of interactions with the members. He or she must behave in a manner consistent with the goals set for the entire organization or work group.

Although *tone* is admittedly a vague term, the leader sets some behavioral standards that often are imitated, consciously or unconsciously, by other members of the group. Clearly, this will not happen in all instances. However, where a leader has, in general, acted constructively, the chances are greatly improved that members will respond in kind, both in their attitudes and behaviors toward the leader and in their general demeanor toward one another. These generalizations have their exceptions but, as standards for positive and enlightened leadership, they appear to have much to recommend them.[55]

Of course, there are some obstacles to effective leadership. First, the situational potential for leadership may vary according to the organizational level and experience of a particular group leader. It may also vary according to the flexibility that higher-level leaders permit within the rest of the organization. The tighter the rein held on subordinates by superiors, the less chance subordinates will have to exercise leadership within their own organizational subunits. In addition, if an organization is highly structured — some would say bureaucratized — the possibilities of leadership in the manner we have described are more limited. This is so because more of the decisions concerning management of organizational affairs are already settled questions and thus are not ordinarily subject to being reopened. In this sense, bureaucracy is not conducive to leadership.

Second, individual goals may simply remain beyond the reach of the leaders' influence, though cooperation could more easily be induced from less secure members than from those with seniority, tenure, and the like. The leadership will probably have to accept some disparities between what it seeks and what individual members are willing to contribute.

Third, fighting tunnel vision and articulating a shared vision (among both members and leaders) may turn out to be a frustrating job. In organizations undergoing staff reductions, it is especially difficult to focus attention on anything other than job security.

Fourth, it is difficult to innovate in highly structured organizations, and a body of professional opinion holds that traditional management values — of the scientific management school and its conceptual descendants — hamper development of conditions conducive to innovation.[56] Additionally, values and preferences of organization members may prove to be so entrenched that leaders may have to coerce staff members to use new procedures and may fail entirely to instill new attitudes. In the face of stiff resistance, a leader must weigh the costs of coercion against the projected benefits of innovations.

Fifth, a gladiator will not always succeed in protecting his/her organization from the external environment; depending on the mix of failure and success, this could work to the leader's disadvantage both inside and outside the organization. Part of a leader's skill should lie in knowing when to fight and when not to.

Finally, effective leadership is conditioned by the particular combination of people, tasks, and organizational dynamics present in each situation. Virtually all of these leadership tasks face obstacles to their full accomplishment — in the organization's dynamics, the mix of members, and the nature of the external environment. Despite what we know about leadership, it is still not possible to construct and all-inclusive set of leadership guidelines that will cover every leadership situation. Although leadership operates within many contemporary constraints, it still occupies a place of considerable importance in organizations.

Leadership in contemporary organizations clearly operates under greater restraints from several standpoints — diminished legitimacy, declining resources, pressures for greater diversity in the workplace, public distrust, and rising turbulence internally and externally, to name only a few. Yet many still aspire to positions of leadership, and there is no question that effective leadership is essential in our attempts to cope with rapid change. Despite many things that are very different from the past, there is continuing and justifiable interest in leadership roles.

Summary

Leadership of bureaucracies makes a vital contribution to the success or failure of administrative organizations, especially from the standpoint of promoting accountability, ethics, efficiency, and results. Executive leadership differs from leadership within the ranks of administrators themselves in several different ways. American chief executives are highly visible to the public and are perceived as being able to provide political leadership and policy initiative; they are also usually considered responsible for the operations of executive-branch bureaucracies. Most chief executives lack specialized knowledge and must rely on persuasion rather than on command authority.

Linkages between chief executives and bureaucracies come into play in policy development and policy implementation. In policy development, chief executives depend on the expertise of professionals in the bureaucracy for both general program advice and specific proposals. Executive dependency increases with program complexity and bureaucratic autonomy. Bureaucracies play an even greater role in policy implementation. General factors that can contribute to chief executives' influence over bureaucracy include support in their legislatures, the degree of policy and program initiative that chief executives exercise, and their capacity to direct governmental responses to crisis situations. None of these factors is an unmixed blessing.

Other, more tangible factors that affect daily administrative operations are crucial to executive leadership. A chief executive is strengthened by having a central role in formulating the executive budget; related functions include forging a stronger role for the budget office in management coordination, requiring central clearance for legislative proposals, and exerting greater control over the regulatory process. The president's influence is greater at the federal level than that exercised by most governors, although many governors have had their budgetary powers strengthened in recent decades. Many local executives do not have comparable influence in local government budget making; city managers stand out among those who do play key budgetary roles.

Personnel controls represent a second major instrument of chief executive leadership. Executives usually have greater impact when administrators are working under a patronage system than when merit systems are in effect. Interactions among presidents, their top-level political appointees, and senior career officials are complex, involving different sets of assumptions and modes of operation on the part of each. Governors often have less control over budget and personnel than does the president, due to greater limitations on appointments and dismissals, and the fact that many states elect at least some other executive-branch officials separately from the chief executive.

Reorganization of administrative agencies may have higher costs and fewer benefits for a chief executive than is generally thought. Reorganization strategies may clash, requiring care and sophistication in their use. Chief executives are in a stronger position if they can make package proposals for agency reorganization to their legislatures; presidents and many governors currently can do so.

A major factor in chief executive influence is control over, and the uses of, information. The president and other chief executives may be dependent on bureaucratic sources of information (even within their own executive establishments), but there are ways of overcoming this dependency. Governors are in a stronger position now than in the past with regard to their information capabilities; departments of administration and governors' staff resources, in particular, have been expanded. Chief executives must closely monitor information transmittal and must also make deliberate efforts to promote feedback from those in the administrative hierarchy. Acquiring information from various sources is a continuing challenge; so, too, is control and interpretation of information. In addition, legislative backing, budget and personnel influence, reorganization authority, policy and program initiative, as well as leadership during crises are important factors underlying successful chief executives.

In complex organizations, administrative leadership is multidimensional; it is sensitive to the changing nature of the work environment, and recognizes distinctions at the technical, managerial, and institutional levels. Leaders in such settings must direct multiple functions at each level. They must also make an effort to overcome various kinds of distance within the organization.

Traditionally, leadership has been studied through two approaches. The traits approach emphasized the personality and aptitudes of individuals who were leaders, in an effort to isolate leader characteristics. This conception was followed by the situational approach, which views all organizational circumstances — structural, interpersonal, task-related, and value-based — as crucial to the kind of leadership that comes to exist. Currently, a combination of the two approaches, with emphasis on the relationships between leaders and followers, is most common in studies of leadership.

Variations in group situations may significantly affect leader effectiveness. Factors in the group situation important in this regard are position power of the leader, task structure of the group, and leader–member personal relationships. Leadership appears to be most effective where a well-liked, well-respected leader occupies a high position in a group with clearly structured tasks. Under such circumstances, leaders are best advised to be directive, giving clear instructions, rather than being democratic and nondirective. Where position power is weak, tasks not clearly defined, and personal relationships not as positive, leaders should be less directive and more democratic. To be effective, leadership must vary with circumstances in the group and the work situation.

What makes an effective leader? Among other things, an effort to convey the leader's respect for members; a willingness to hear and respond to feelings and opinions of members; a democratic style and relationship to members; attributes such as fairness, giving credit, readiness to discuss problems, and keeping members informed; consistency and equity in defining standards and judging work performance; and avoidance of pitfalls such as empire building (by either leaders or followers) and cronyism.

KEY TERMS AND CONCEPTS

political persuasion or "jawboning"	institutional
policy development	traits approach
policy implementation	situational approach
instruments, or tools, of leadership	relational leadership
central clearance	leader as director
executive budgets	goal articulation
veto power	leader as motivator
item veto (or line-item veto)	leader as coordinator
bureaucratic resistance	tunnel vision
reductions-in-force (RIFs)	brainstorming
Iran-Contra affair	shared vision
reorganization	leader as catalyst and innovator
task forces	innovation
exception principle	leader as gladiator
Cuban missile crisis	leader as crisis manager
technical	cutback management or
managerial	"downsizing"

SUGGESTED READING

Barge, J. Kevin. *Leadership: Communication Skills for Organizations and Groups.* New York: St. Martin's Press, 1994.

Bennis, Warren, and Bert Nanus. *Leaders.* New York: Perseus, 1994.

Berman, Larry, ed. *Looking Back on the Reagan Presidency.* Baltimore, Md.: The Johns Hopkins University Press, 1990.

Beyle, Thad L. *Governors and Hard Times.* Washington, D.C.: CQ Press, 1992.

Bryman, Alan. *Charisma and Leadership in Organizations.* Newbury Park, Calif.: Sage, 1992.

Bryson, John M., and Barbara C. Crosby. *Leadership for the Common Good: Tackling Public Problems in a Shared-Power World.* San Francisco.: Jossey-Bass, 1992.

Campbell, Colin, and Bert Rockman, eds. *The Clinton Legacy.* New York: Seven Bridges Press, 1999.

Cronin, Thomas E. *The State of the Presidency.* 2nd ed. Boston: Little, Brown, 1980.

Edwards, George C., III, and Stephen J. Wayne. *Presidential Leadership: Politics and Policy Making.* 4th ed. New York: St. Martin's, 1997.

Ellis, Richard, and Aaron Wildavsky. *Dilemmas of Presidential Leadership: From Washington through Lincoln.* New Brunswick, N.J.: Transaction Publishers, 1991.

Fisher, Louis. *The Politics of Shared Power: Congress and the Executive.* 4th ed. College Station, Tex.: Texas A & M University Press, 1998.

Guest, Robert H., Paul Hersey, and Kenneth H. Blanchard. *Organizational Change through Effective Leadership.* 2nd ed. Englewood Cliffs, N.J.: Prentice-Hall, 1986.

Hunt, James G. *Leadership: A New Synthesis.* Newbury Park, Calif.: Sage, 1991.

Jones, Charles O. *The Trusteeship Presidency: Jimmy Carter and the United States Congress.* Baton Rouge: Louisiana State University Press, 1988.

Kernell, Samuel. *Going Public: New Strategies of Presidential Leadership.* 3rd ed. Washington, D.C.: CQ Press, 1997.

Kouzes, James M., Barry Z. Posner, and Tom Peters. *The Leadership Challenge: How to Get Extraordinary Things Done in Organizations.* San Francisco: Jossey-Bass, 1996.

Lynch, Richard. *Lead! How Public and Nonprofit Managers Can Bring Out the Best in Themselves and Their Organizations.* San Francisco: Jossey-Bass, 1992.

Martin, David L. *Running City Hall: Municipal Administration in America.* 2nd ed. Tuscaloosa, Ala.: The University of Alabama Press, 1990.

Nathan, Richard P. *The Administrative Presidency.* New York: Wiley, 1983.

Neustadt, Richard. *Presidential Power and the Modern Presidents.* New York: The Free Press, 1991.

Pfiffner, James P., ed. *The Managerial Presidency*. Pacific Grove, Calif.: Brooks/Cole, 1991.

Rockman, Bert A. *The Leadership Question: The Presidency and the American System*. New York: Praeger, 1984.

Rosenthal, Alan. *Governors and Legislatures: Contending Powers*. Washington, D.C.: CQ Press, 1990.

Sabato, Larry. *Goodbye to Good-Time Charlie: The American Governorship Transformed*. 2nd ed. Washington, D.C.: CQ Press, 1983.

Seidman, Harold, and Robert Gilmour. *Politics, Position, and Power: From the Positive to the Regulatory State*. 4th ed. New York: Oxford University Press, 1986.

Selznick, Philip. *Leadership in Administration: A Sociological Interpretation*. Berkeley, Calif.: University of California Press, 1984.

Smith, Peter B., and Mark F. Peterson. *Leadership, Organizations, and Culture*. Newbury Park, Calif.: Sage, 1988.

Terry, Robert W. *Authentic Leadership: Courage in Action*. San Francisco: Jossey-Bass, 1993.

Waterman, Richard W. *Presidential Influence and the Administrative State*. Knoxville, Tenn.: The University of Tennessee Press, 1989.

Wildavsky, Aaron. *The Beleaguered Presidency*. New Brunswick, N.J.: Transaction Publishers, 1991.

ON-LINE RESOURCES:
Chief Executives and the Challenges of Administrative Leadership

Center for Creative Leadership
http://www.ccl.org/

The official Web site for the Center for Creative Leadership, one of the largest institutions in the world focusing solely on leadership. Its primary purpose is to generate and disseminate knowledge about leadership and leadership development.

Center for Management Development (Wichita State University)
http://www.twsu.edu/~cmd/

The Web site for the Center for Management Development at Wichita State University. This is the largest permanent training organization in Kansas and offers over 100 public seminars on topics ranging from leadership, quality improvement, teambuilding, and communications to human resources and financial management.

Council for Excellence in Government
http://www.excelgov.org/

The official Web site for the Council for Excellence in Government located in Washington, D.C.

Institute for Leadership and Institutional Effectiveness

http://www2.ncsu.edu/ncsu/cep/accee/nilie/

> The mission of this site for the National Institute for Leadership and Institutional Effectiveness is to conduct research and disseminate information on strategies to link leadership to institutional effectiveness and to improve student success through quality initiatives.

James MacGregor Burns Academy of Leadership

http://academy.umd.edu/

> The James MacGregor Burns Academy of Leadership is a multidisciplinary academic organization that fosters responsible and ethical leadership through scholarship, education, training, and development in the public interest.

Leadership Development

http://www.iel.org/leader/frl.html

> This site provides information on leadership development programs as well as information about the Institute for Educational Leadership, which strives to regularly bring together educators, civic leaders, business executives, parents, and public officials to make a difference for our children and youth.

Mary Parker Follett

http://www.plgrm.com/history/women/F/Mary_Parker_Follett.HTM

> This site has organized the most popular search engines and directories for researching the writer and lecturer Mary Parker Follett.

National Employer Leadership Council

http://www.nelc.org/nelc_home.cfm

> The National Employer Leadership Council seeks to promote efforts that combine academic courses with real-life learning to improve student achievement.

For further information on administrative leadership in organizations see: Bedford/St. Martin's Home Page

http://www.bedfordstmartins.com

PART III

The Core Functions of Public Management

This section covers four functions central to the conduct of public administration: (1) public personnel administration and human resource development (including public-sector collective bargaining), (2) the budgetary process, (3) public policy and program management, and (4) the regulatory process. Each of these represents a fundamentally important set of vital activities in administrative practice. Together, they form the core processes of public-sector operations.

The personnel and human resource development function, treated in Chapter 8, concerns, among other things, criteria and methods for hiring individuals into the public service in national, state, and local government; for training and skill development; for promoting and transferring them within the ranks; and, on occasion, for dismissing them from their jobs. Politically charged issues such as veterans' preference, patronage, and affirmative action pose difficult questions that must be answered within the domain of public personnel administration. Also, there have been significant changes in the national government's basic approaches to personnel management, stemming from the successful efforts of the National Partnership for Reinventing Government (NPRG). Furthermore, collective bargaining and union membership have emerged as a prominent and sometimes contentious aspects of public-sector labor–management relations. At all levels of government (but especially in many state and local agencies), public employee unionization and bargaining occupy a place of importance in politics and government.

The budgetary process, discussed in Chapter 9, is obviously important because of rising costs of providing government services and political conflict over allocation of increasingly limited public funds. It is important also because control over major aspects of budgeting processes represents crucial political power. In the past half-century, the political stakes in the budgetary game have risen steadily. In recent years, government officials at all levels have paid considerable attention to assessing the results of expenditures, reducing budget deficits, and gaining greater control over public spending.

Chapter 10 explores the vital subject of managing public policies and programs. This function has always been important but, in recent decades, public managers have placed new emphasis on particular managerial activities and concerns. These include planning, program analysis, implementation, program evaluation, productivity, and performance improvement in an era of political mistrust and chronic fiscal stress. At the same time, we have seen the emergence of new concerns and innovations — among them reinventing government, a renewed commitment to training and customer service, empowerment of employees, total quality management, and greater concern for results — that reflect both increased complexities and new challenges for government at all levels. This entire area reflects more sophisticated and systematic approaches to management, as well as policy problems that have become far more complex.

The regulatory process (Chapter 11) has become one of the most pervasive, complex, and controversial aspects of governmental activity in recent years. Government regulation is now carried on by a host of federal, state, and local agencies, with impacts on virtually every aspect of American economic and social life. The scope of regulation has also sparked intense pressures for deregulation, in and out of government. In other areas, such as airline safety, protection of children, and nursing home inspections, there have been some tendencies in the direction of increased regulatory activity. A related field — administrative law — has also become an important area of public administration.

Public Personnel Administration and Human Resource Development

> *. . . the government of the United States has become too big, too complex, and too pervasive in its influence on all our lives for one individual to pretend to direct the details of its important and critical programming. Competent assistants are mandatory. . . . Principal subordinates must have confidence that they and their positions are widely respected, and the chief must do his part in assuring that this is so.*
>
> President Dwight D. Eisenhower, August 1960

From the time the first executive-branch agency opened its doors, even before ratification of the Constitution, the personnel function has been a vital part of American public administration. It has evolved from a relatively obscure, often routine function of government to a prominent, frequently controversial area of administrative practice. Since the early 1800s, there has, of course, been considerable variation in the rules and regulations governing personnel policies and practices in response to the changing values and assumptions of society pertaining to proper methods of filling government positions.

Three values predominant in our approach to government have had strong, but shifting, impact on personnel practices: (1) the quest for strong executive leadership, (2) the desire for a *politically neutral*, competent public service, and (3) the belief that the composition of the public service should mirror the *demographic composition* of American society.[1] Strong executive leadership and greater representativeness have often occurred together. For example, when a strong mayor practices patronage in hiring, drawing political supporters into local bureaucracies from an ethnically diverse majority coalition, it has the effect of increasing political loyalty to the mayor in the ranks while enhancing representativeness. In such a case, both *representativeness* of social groupings and *representation* of the political majority are served through administrative appointments.

diversity   reflects the goal of many affirmative action programs to diversify the workforce to reflect the population demographics (makeup) in the affected jurisdiction.

politically neutral competence   the idea that appointments to civil service positions should be made on the basis of demonstrated job competence, and not based on age, ethnicity, gender, politics, or race.

Greater **diversity** in the workforce — which is representativeness in another form — has been a value of increasing importance in the public service. We will discuss aspects of diversity later in this chapter.

On the other hand, the quest for **politically neutral competence** — involving formal disregard of race, gender, or political party ties in filling administrative posts — has usually been carried on in opposition to advocates of strong leadership and representativeness. For example, supporters of civil service (merit) reform in the late 1800s and early 1900s harshly attacked both political "bosses" and the patronage systems that enabled them to dominate many states and cities. Significantly, most merit reformers also feared the potential influence of ethnic immigrants in many boss-run cities; part of their fervor was based on a strong desire to exclude recent immigrants from a share of political power. In short, the reformers opposed representativeness for emerging potential rivals on the political (and social) horizon. At the same time, those opposed to affirmative action, diversity, and quotas to achieve racial balance argue that race and gender are similar to political criteria, and should not be used as factors for hiring and promotion.

The case for politically neutral competence rests on the assumption that public managers should be hired and promoted on the basis of job-related skills and knowledge. Advocates of this approach contend that public programs are better administered and elected executives better served (and public funds better spent) if those in charge possess demonstrated competence in the particular program area, along with management expertise and *institutional memory* — that is, the ability to apply the lessons of past experience profitably to current tasks. Those holding this view believe that considerations such as political party loyalty — especially in hiring decisions — interfere with the quest for true managerial competence.

In response, patronage advocates stress the importance of a chief executive's ability to rely on the loyalty of his or her subordinates throughout the executive branch in order to assure efficient program implementation. Without dismissing the importance of competence, those favoring political loyalty as a key factor in making personnel decisions argue that reliance on neutral competence creates public bureaucracies largely immune to control by elected political leaders. The accountability demanded by an increasingly frustrated public suffers. This issue has been a part of public administration virtually since its founding though it has been debated more intensely at some times than at others. Since the mid-1970s, the debate has intensified once again.

public personnel administration (PPA)   the policies, processes, and procedures designed to recruit, train, and promote the men and women who manage government agencies.

human resources development (HRD)   the training and staff development of public employees; designed to improve job performance.

Public personnel administration (PPA) can be defined as "the organizations, policies, and processes used to match the needs of governmental agencies and the people who staff those agencies."[2] **Human resources development (HRD)** is also used to describe personnel functions such as training, staff development, and continuous learning that are necessary to improve service quality and productivity in complex public organizations (see Chapter 5). In the public sector, these functions differ from those in business and industry in important respects, most prominently in the need to conduct the personnel function within constraints set by other formal political institutions, by agency clienteles, by professional associations of employees and other interest groups, and by political parties and the mass media.[3] Today, PPA and HRD are no longer regarded, as they once were, as separate from the general processes of public policy-making; there are two reasons for this. First, decisions made in the personnel process have a direct bearing on who makes and implements government policies. Second, decisions have themselves become policy matters, reflecting demands for improved productivity, employee rights, affirmative action in minority hiring, and traditional merit reforms, among others. To a great extent, personnel policies and training practices have become an extension of partisan political value conflicts, and the political dimension of PPA and HRD has taken on increasing importance in recent years (see Chapter 2).

Another widely recognized problem is that rules and regulations sufficient to cover government employees in the past are no longer flexible enough. For example, separate salary schedules have had to be established in selected personnel grades for professionals in printing management, engineering and architecture, medicine and nursing, metallurgy, and veterinary medicine, among others. Another salary issue concerns the fact that, although the total size of the bureaucracy has slightly declined in recent years, the cost (mainly in salaries) of running it has risen dramatically, which is attributable both to inflation and to a larger proportion of higher-level administrators (with higher salaries) in the civil service. The National Performance Review (NPR) found that there were 850 pages of detailed rules covering personnel law, supplemented by another 1,300 pages of regulations on how to apply that law. Additionally, 10,000 pages of guidelines and 54,000 civil servants work in personnel administration positions in the federal government. The numbers and diversity of skills and training among government employees make it difficult to implement reforms in personnel procedures, such as simplification of job classification and performance evaluation.

Finally, the sheer size and scope of contemporary government make personnel and human resources concerns more important than ever before. Although the issue of "big government" is not directly tied to personnel policies, political pressures for reducing or controlling bureaucratic size affect personnel administrators and some of their decisions. This is especially important because Americans seem to mistrust large institutions (such as business, labor, and government), in part, simply because they are big. Furthermore, "whenever surveys [measuring citizen confidence in institutions] have dealt with different size levels of the same institution, they have found greater hostility to the 'big' or 'large' versions than to smaller ones."[4] This may be an explanation for the consistently higher approval ratings given by citizens to local governments over both states and the federal government.

The image of a "bloated" national bureaucracy, however, is not completely accurate. First, since 1950, civilian employment in the national government remained stable, whereas state and local government employment increased

full-time equivalent (FTE) employees the actual number of full-time government personnel plus the number of full-time people who would have been needed to work the hours put in by part-time employees.

dramatically (see Figure 8–1). Total state and local employment more than tripled, increasing from about 4 million in 1951 to over 14 million in 1998, both full-time and part-time. The figure for **full-time equivalent (FTE) employees** was 14.5 million in 1998 (see Table 8–1). During the same period, the number of national government civilian employees fluctuated, ranging from a low of 2.37 million in 1954 to just over 3.1 million in the early 1990s (full-time equivalent: about 2.6 million).

Second, the number of national civilian employees per 1,000 population also fluctuated considerably in that same period. From a high of 16.5 in 1952, it dipped to 13.2 in the mid-1960s, then rose sharply in the late 1960s before beginning another decline that brought the ratio down to 10.2 in 1998. The Clinton administration reduced national government employment even more by eliminating several layers of supervisory positions in nearly all federal executive departments. Total federal employment has decreased in all but a few functional

FIGURE 8–1   **Government Civilian Employment and Population, 1951–1995**

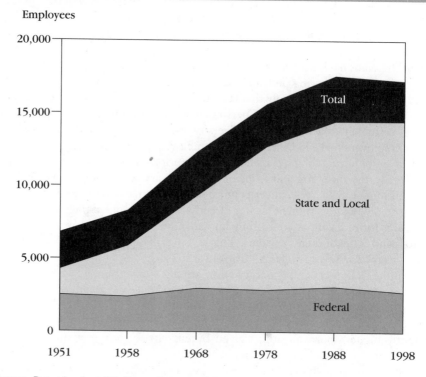

SOURCE: Data taken from U.S. Census Bureau annual sources.

TABLE 8–1   State and Local Government Employment*

Function	Full-Time Equivalent Employment	
	Amount	Percentage
Total	14,490,645	100.0
Education	7,605,851	52.4
Elementary and secondary	5,729,442	39.5
Higher education	1,668,729	11.5
Other education and libraries	207,680	1.5
Hospitals	941,280	6.4
Police protection	817,941	5.6
Streets and highways	530,097	3.6
Correction	662,654	4.5
Public welfare	477,515	3.2
Health	386,585	2.6
Financial administration	363,049	2.5
Judicial and legal	356,671	2.4
Fire protection	281,922	1.9
Parks and recreation	236,903	1.8
Central administration	254,745	1.8
Transit	191,887	1.3
Natural resources	182,191	1.3
Water supply	156,284	1.2
Sewerage	124,415	0.9
Solid waste management	108,842	0.7
Housing and community development	113,252	0.7
Social insurance administration	90,081	0.6
Electric power and gas supply	87,242	0.6
Air and water transport	50,508	0.3
All other activities	470,729	3.2

*As of October 1998.

SOURCE: U.S. Bureau of the Census. Public Employment in 1995. (Washington, D.C., U.S. Government Printing Office, 1998).

areas related to criminal justice (see Table 8–3, p. 322). Thus, increases in national government civilian employment have not kept pace with population growth, and ratios of government to civilian employment are lower now than at any time since the 1930s.

These figures, however, do not truly reflect all that has happened in the past half-century, either in terms of the numbers of public employees working under direct funding or contracts with the national government, or in terms of the scope of their activity. Twenty years ago, Joseph Califano, then Secretary of Health, Education, and Welfare (HEW), observed that, whereas his department employed some 144,000 people, it *indirectly* paid the salaries of nearly *1 million* more in state and local governments, through myriad grant-in-aid programs. Furthermore, it was estimated at the time that, if one were to add together all personnel dependent on national government funds — state and local personnel, those in the private sector employed and paid through national government contracts, consultants, and the like — the total payroll would include about *8 million people*[5] (and the number of federal "dependents" has almost certainly increased since then). If we consider the scope and impact of national government actions in this light, combined with unfunded mandates, grant-in-aid requirements, and expanded state and national regulatory responsibilities, we see that public concern about the size of government bureaucracy is not entirely groundless. It may be somewhat misplaced, in that government roles have changed substantially, but concern about size persists, and that can clearly affect personnel management.

In state and local governments, the personnel picture is a bit more complicated because of substantial numbers of employees in public education: over half of all state and local government full-time equivalent employees work in primary, secondary, or higher education.[6] State employees not in education accounted for about 20 percent, and the remainder were noneducation employees in city, county, and other local governments. Expansion of public employment at the state-local level was due in large part to a sharp rise in educational employment during the 1960s, but other state-local functional areas — such as health and hospitals, police, corrections, and fire protection — have now begun to catch up. Many states have themselves "mandated" costly expansions in various public programs, creating the need for more police, corrections officers, teachers, and learning resources.

Another feature of public personnel administration that is not reflected in head counts of government employees is the changing nature of the workforce. Since the 1960s, particularly in the national government, increasing numbers of bureaucrats have become more specialized, better educated, and more highly paid than many of their predecessors. Despite the backlash aimed at large institutions, those trends are likely to continue. The national executive branch, as well as many state and local agencies, are now managed by better-credentialed, more competent professionals and technocrats.

The national government's role — and its relationship to states, localities, and private consultants and contractors — has been affected as well. It has been suggested that it is increasingly state and local governments, along with private contractors, that actually translate national government directives into public realities (recall a similar implication in Chapter 4 regarding increased decentralization in intergovernmental relations). Expertise is not confined to the national government but, wherever it is found, its significance has become unmistakable — and is related much more closely to the expanding role of government than simply to numbers of people directly or indirectly supported by a government payroll. We will deal further with the rise of public-service partnerships, professionalism, and specialization later in this chapter.

Evolution of Public Personnel Administration

The evolution of public personnel administration, from 1789 to the present, did not occur in a social or political vacuum. Rather, development of the personnel function and of specific practices was related to other changes in public administration and society. Six major phases in the evolution of federal personnel administration have been identified and are summarized below.

1. Government by "gentlemen" reflected the powerful influence of the American quasi-aristocracy on all of politics.
2. Government by the "common man" resulted from a movement toward a more egalitarian political system.
3. Government by the "good" focused on elimination of corruption in hiring practices and equality of access to competitive entrance examinations.
4. Government by the "efficient" was characterized by maintenance of the merit system and of political neutrality and by the pursuit of management efficiency.
5. Government by "administrators" saw the development of an activist political role for public administrators.
6. Government by "professionals" has been a period of greater concern for recruiting, testing generalized skills of job applicants, and meeting the challenges of, as well as the opportunities for, increased professionalism in the public service.[7]

GOVERNMENT BY "GENTLEMEN" (1789–1829)

- Political participation was limited and **nepotism** (favoritism based on family ties) was widespread.
- Positions were filled according to a blend of patronage and merit appointment.
- Political loyalty to the chief executive was a major consideration.
- Entry was limited largely to the "gentry" of American society, to educated, white, male landowners.

nepotism a form of favoritism based on hiring family members or relatives.

GOVERNMENT BY THE "COMMON MAN" (1829–1883)

- President Andrew Jackson (1829–1837), commonly associated with this populist era, brought a full-scale spoils system to Washington.
- Government jobs were offered to those with the "right" political loyalties, without emphasis on job-related competence.
- "Establishment" credentials were not only unnecessary but were viewed as an affront to "ordinary citizens," who distrusted the "aristocracy" in government as hostile to their political interests.

- Strong executive leadership and some form of political representativeness were advocated.
- This early version of today's populist politics supported the "little people" against those with wealth, title, education, and political power. (The short-lived presidential campaigns of Patrick Buchanan and the H. Ross Perot movement in the 1990s exemplify recent populist movements, indicating how durable this phenomenon has been in our history.)
- The assassination in 1881 of President James Garfield by a frustrated (and mentally ill) office seeker was a catalyst for passage in 1883 of the **Civil Service (Pendleton) Act,** which created a bipartisan commission to administer open competitive examinations for civil service positions.
- Reformers hoped that the Pendleton Act would reduce extensive personnel turnover at each change of presidential administrations.
- Politically neutral competence was a major criterion for government service.
- The Pendleton Act de-emphasized both strong executive leadership and representativeness.

Civil Service (Pendleton) Act a law formally known as the Civil Service Act of 1883 (sponsored by Ohio Senator George Pendleton), establishing job-related competence as the primary basis for filling national government jobs; created the U.S. Civil Service Commission to oversee the new "merit" system.

egalitarianism a philosophical concept stressing individual equality in political, social, economic, and other relations; in the context of public personnel administration, the conceptual basis for "government by the common person."

GOVERNMENT BY THE "GOOD" (1883–1906)

- The period was marked by self-conscious **egalitarianism** and intensive "idealistic" changes in public personnel administration.
- Corruption in hiring practices was halted with the creation of the Civil Service Commission to enforce new rules and regulations.
- The successful drive for a merit system had to be translated into workable day-to-day arrangements.
- Government efficiency came to be viewed as the opposite of government corruption.
- The new civil service was open to anyone who could pass the competitive entrance examinations.
- The Civil Service Commission insulated the new personnel system against political pressures from Congress and the White House.
- At state and local levels, controversy surrounded reform efforts to do away with urban political machines, but many state and municipal governments were successfully reformed.
- In county governments and most rural areas, civil service reform came much later, if at all.

GOVERNMENT BY THE "EFFICIENT" AND THE NEW DEAL (1906–1937)

- The major focus was maintenance of the merit system, with political neutrality, as well as pursuit of efficiency in managing government programs.

- Separation of politics and administration was in full force, strengthened by the influence of *scientific management* on both business and public administration.
- Efficiency was the major conceptual emphasis within a package of social values that included goodness, merit, morality, neutrality, and science.
- Merit system coverage was extended from about 45 percent of the government workforce in 1900 to some 80 percent by 1930.
- Seemingly nonpoliticized administrative machinery was expanded.
- In 1933, President Franklin Roosevelt, who inherited a government bureaucracy that focused on good, effective management, began to involve agencies in planning and managing new programs, leading to basic changes in the role of government in American society.

GOVERNMENT BY "ADMINISTRATORS" (1937–1955)

- In 1939, the *American Society for Public Administration (ASPA)* was founded, and efforts were made to upgrade the level of education in the bureaucracy, to ensure that educational preparation counted for something in obtaining national government employment.
- Public administration spearheaded efforts to overcome the effects of the Great Depression and to mobilize for World War II.
- Activist administrative apparatus was able to respond to Roosevelt's vigorous New Deal policy leadership.
- Under a strong and popular president who had widespread support, the politics–administration dichotomy underwent changes in favor of representativeness.
- Allowance was made, in principle, for overlap between politics and administration without abandoning completely the idea that administration should be separated from the political process.
- The **Brownlow Report,** issued in 1937, called on the president to assume greater responsibility and authority for directing executive-branch activities and for the centralization and consolidation of responsibility throughout the executive branch.
- The report of the **Second Hoover Commission** to President Eisenhower in 1955, recommended that a "Senior Civil Service" be established, comprising about 3,000 upper-level career executives serving in administrative positions. (Not until the **Senior Executive Service (SES)** was founded in 1978 were these elements incorporated into general personnel practices in the national government).
- Public personnel administration was elevated to a place alongside other managerial tasks of traditional public administration.
- Since the early 1950s, there has been a growing interest in developing the individual skills of bureaucratic employees.

Brownlow Report recommendations for reform of the federal bureaucracy from a 1937 committee appointed by President Franklin Roosevelt, chaired by Louis Brownlow, and including respected scholars and practitioners in the emerging discipline of public administration.

Second Hoover Commission 1955 blue-ribbon commission appointed by President Eisenhower and chaired by former president Hoover to study higher-level positions in the civil service.

Senior Executive Service (SES) established in the national Civil Service Reform Act of 1978; designed to foster professional growth, mobility, and versatility among senior career officials (and some "political" appointees); incorporated into national government personnel management broad emphasis on performance appraisal and merit-pay concepts, as part of both the SES itself and broader merit-system reform (see **Civil Service Reform Act of 1978**).

GOVERNMENT BY "PROFESSIONALS" (1955 TO THE PRESENT)

- The Federal Service Entrance Examination (FSEE) was established in 1955; it was designed to provide a single point of entry into the U.S. civil service, make it possible for public servants to transfer more easily from one agency to another, and allow the Civil Service Commission to engage in more systematic recruiting, especially on college and university campuses.
- Professionalism has become widespread in the public service, so that the career needs of individuals within their professions conflict, to some extent, with the traditional emphasis on the adminstrative job itself.
- Contemporary personnel administration must take account of the needs of both public agencies and their professional employees.
- The increasing power of various professions becomes a force to be reckoned with in the administrative process.

The growth of *professionalism* in public service has contributed not only to higher government salaries but to overly narrow specialization in job classifications as well. This, in some cases, has resulted in professions having a direct voice in public policy-making, with adverse consequences for popular control and accountability. One important study in the late 1970s identified five major avenues to political power:[8] (1) election or appointment to high office, which is generally dominated by lawyers; (2) effective control (if not a near monopoly) by an individual profession of important managerial functions in an agency — for example, educators in the Office of Education, engineers in public works agencies, or foreign service officers in the State Department; (3) a professional presence in an agency but without professional domination (all agencies have legal counsel, budgeters, planners, and personnel specialists); (4) an ability to generate pressure on decision makers from fellow or allied professionals outside the governmental structure; and (5) an ability to operate through the system of intergovernmental relations by collaborating with fellow professionals in other units of government (through the "guilds," or vertical functional autocracies, described in Chapter 4). Licensing of professions, such as physicians, lawyers, insurance agents, and realtors at the state level and regulatory processes at the national level, are two areas in which professional influence is strong — too strong, according to some.

Professions such as law, medicine, and civil engineering have been described by different observers as enjoying excessive influence in formulating and implementing public policy. The lack of public accountability of such professional associations is central to criticisms of their role. There is also the possibility that loyalty to professional associations (such as the AMA for medicine or the ABA for law) may supersede loyalty to an agency as the standard by which professional employees judge their own work.[9] Individual loyalties to widely varying professional standards can create tensions within an agency that are very difficult to resolve from a broader public policy perspective.

MERIT AND PATRONAGE IN PERSPECTIVE

Politics has always played a role in personnel administration. Andrew Jackson is remembered as the father of the patronage system, though Thomas Jefferson was the first president to view partisan loyalty as an important criterion in the selection of public servants. Moreover, Jackson insisted on some competence in government employees and was not nearly as abusive in his patronage tactics as some later presidents were (notably James Buchanan and Abraham Lincoln). Franklin Roosevelt established the tradition of a strong executive who emphasized political loyalty as well as professional competence. His use of a "brain trust" of politically loyal policy advisers enhanced the respect of policy analysis and policy analysts in government.

The merit versus patronage debate arouses deep passions in many of us. The devotion of so many people to what they see as interconnected values of integrity, efficiency, economy, political neutrality, and ethical standards fosters a strong preference for merit system practices, often accompanied by contempt for patronage. Both have a rich history in American public personnel administration, yet, in the past century, merit has clearly held favor among middle- and upper-class citizens, who are the chief beneficiaries of such a system. Whether that preference will be continued or transformed in the twenty-first century is still an open question.

The distinctions between merit and patronage systems can be boiled down to a difference in defining job qualifications. Those who favor merit are fond of saying that you don't have to be qualified to get a patronage job, but that is not really true — the qualifications are usually partisan-based rather than job-related, but they are job requirements just the same. Put simply, *merit judges what you know, whereas patronage is more interested in whom you know and how you can help politically.* Each system has some clear advantages.

The most obvious advantage of a merit system is its ability to bring into the public service individuals who are considered competent (by management's standards) to perform the tasks required in a given position. Doing one's job well is valued in both the private and public sectors, and it is the root of the merit system. There is also some value in having continuity and stability in the public service (that is, "institutional memory") instead of the dramatic — and traumatic — turnovers in personnel experienced at the beginning of virtually every new administration between 1829 and 1881.

On the other hand, a patronage system also affords some advantages. The most important one, as noted earlier, is that the chief executive can command the loyalties of bureaucratic subordinates much more effectively. Every local, state, and national "boss" has had that ability, and the effect in each case has been to buttress chief-executive leadership (see Chapter 7). It is undoubtedly true that this approach yields a vastly different kind of bureaucracy, and very probably a different set of social, economic, and political priorities in public policies. But, to the extent that we value strong leadership, we may favor patronage.

The tensions between merit and patronage are rooted in a deeper philosophical and political conflict affecting how jobs are filled. The merit concept is built around the use of **achievement-oriented criteria** — that is, making personnel judgments based on the applicant's demonstrated, job-related competence. By contrast, in patronage systems (and in some other approaches to personnel decision making), judgments are based on **ascriptive criteria** — that is, attributes or characteristics of the individual other than his or her skills and knowledge. Approaches using ascriptive criteria include patronage (in which personnel decisions are based at least in part on the applicant's party or other organizational loyalties), affirmative action (in which one's race or gender is given strong consideration), veterans' preference (based on military service), and nepotism (choice influenced by kinship). Though all such approaches seem to conflict with merit principles, each is said to have certain advantages — not only for the individuals affected but also for the personnel selection system and perhaps society at large. Eventually, all managers must find ways to deal with the pressures generated by such conflicting values.[10] (We will discuss affirmative action and veterans' preference later in this chapter.)

Are merit and patronage, then, permanent and inevitable opposites? Surprisingly perhaps, the answer is no. In practice, neither merit selection nor patronage exists in a pure form. Partisan influence is not entirely unknown in merit systems although it is usually subtle. In some states and cities, the appearance of a merit system may mask an effectively functioning patronage arrangement. Knowing someone is still useful to the candidate for a merit position. By the same token, traditional patronage practices have been severely constrained by governments' need to hire individuals with specific technical skills, by reduced reliance on campaign workers in an era of media campaigns, by decreased availability of government jobs, and by a number of Supreme Court decisions limiting patronage hiring.[11] The era of the "party hack," if not gone forever, has been significantly transformed by the changing needs and restrictions of a complex technological society.

Formal Arrangements of Personnel Systems

All civil service systems are not created equal, but the national government arrangements will serve as an illustrative model for discussion of the structure of most merit personnel systems. Many state arrangements, among the nearly forty states that have merit systems, closely resemble the national government format, with some variations.

About 93 percent of all national executive-branch employees are currently covered by some merit system, most under the system administered by the **Office of Personnel Management (OPM),** which replaced the Civil Service Commission in 1979. The proportion of national executive employees working within competitive merit systems has risen steadily, if gradually from about 10

achievement-oriented criteria standards for making personnel judgments based on an individual's demonstrated, job-related competence.

ascriptive criteria standards for making personnel judgments that are based on attributes or characteristics other than skills or knowledge.

Office of Personnel Management (OPM) a key administrative unit in the national government operating under presidential direction, responsible for managing the national government personnel system, consistent with presidential personnel policy.

percent in 1884 (one year after passage of the Pendleton Act) to 85 percent in 1950, exceeding 90 percent for the first time during the 1970s.

Partly in response to prodding from the national government, state governments have gradually extended — or established — merit systems in their executive branches. For example, Congress has required states to organize **merit pay** systems in single state agencies designated as grant-in-aid recipients; the tremendous proliferation of grants has thus had the spin-off effect of strengthening merit principles in state government. The Intergovernmental Personnel Act (IPA) of 1970 greatly reinforced that requirement; most states now have many merit features built into their personnel arrangements. Local governments have been similarly affected but to a lesser extent.

The system of classifying positions is central to any personnel structuring. In the national government, jobs are classified according to 10 grades, or levels, which make up the **General Schedule (GS)** (see Table 8–2). Within each grade there are ten "steps," which are based on year of service. Grades GS-1 through GS-4 ($13,870–$24,833, as of January 2000) are lower-level positions, of the secretarial-clerical type. Grades GS-5 through GS-11 ($21,370–$50,932) cover lower-middle management posts but are divided into two subschedules: GS-6, -8, and -10 are, for the most part, technical, skilled crafts, and senior clerical positions, and GS-5, -7, -9, and -11 are professional career grades. GS-5 and -7 are the most common entry-level grades for college graduates. Grades GS-12 through -15 ($46,955–$100,897) are upper-level positions, reflecting career advancement and acceptable job competence. Senior executive positions are the so-called *supergrades*, filled by senior civil servants who earn between $110,700 and $151,800 and serve as bureau chiefs, staff directors, and so on. At the top of the personnel structure is the **Executive Schedule,** occupied by the highest-ranking career officials, those who interact on a regular basis with politically appointed administrators (see Chapter 7). Senior Executive Service executives are eligible for performance bonuses within their pay grades and, in 1998, top pay was limited by Congress to $151,800.

Promotion from one grade to the next is not automatic and, at the outset of one's career, retention in the service itself is not guaranteed. A probation period of six to eighteen months must be served before full merit protection is attained, and not all employees are put under merit. In many cases, promotion comes after one year in the service (for example, from GS-9 to -11) and, in some agencies, failure to achieve promotion in that time is a virtual invitation to leave the civil service.

In keeping with the recent emphasis on general preparation and skills, it is not difficult for an employee in the public service to transfer from one agency to another — or even from one merit system to another. Employees with more seniority (years of service) have "bumping rights" over others with less service. The Office of Personnel Management has reciprocal agreements with the Tennessee Valley Authority and Panama Canal Zone, for example, which permit employees to transfer to the other systems, and vice versa, with no loss of pension

merit pay   an approach to compensation in personnel management founded on the concept of equal pay for equal contribution; related to, and dependent on, properly designed and implemented performance appraisal systems; applied to managers and supervisors in grades GS-13 through GS-15 in the national executive branch, under provisions of the Civil Service Reform Act of 1978.

General Schedule (GS) pay scale for federal employees, based on grades and steps.

Executive Schedule compensation schedule for Federal Senior Executive Service.

TABLE 8–2   **Salary Table 2000 General Schedule (effective January 2000)**

Grade	1	2	3	4	5	6	7	8	9	10	Within-Grade Increase Amounts
				Annual Rates by Grade and Step							
1	13,870	14,332	14,794	15,252	15,715	15,986	16,440	16,900	16,918	17,351	Varies
2	15,594	15,964	16,481	16,918	17,107	17,610	18,113	18,616	19,119	19,622	Varies
3	17,015	17,582	18,149	18,716	19,283	19,850	20,417	20,984	21,551	22,118	$546
4	19,100	19,737	20,374	21,011	21,648	22,285	22,922	23,559	24,196	24,833	$613
5	21,370	22,082	22,794	23,506	24,218	24,930	25,642	26,354	27,066	27,778	$686
6	23,820	24,614	25,408	26,202	26,996	26,790	28,584	29,378	30,172	30,966	$765
7	26,470	27,352	28,234	29,116	29,998	30,880	31,762	32,644	33,526	34,408	$850
8	29,315	30,292	31,269	32,246	33,223	34,200	35,177	36,154	37,131	38,108	$941
9	32,380	33,459	34,538	35,617	36,696	37,775	38,854	39,933	41,012	42,091	$1,040
10	35,658	36,847	38,036	39,225	40,414	41,603	42,792	43,981	45,170	46,359	$1,145
11	39,178	40,484	41,790	43,096	44,402	45,708	47,014	38,320	49,626	50,932	$1,258
12	46,955	48,520	50,085	51,650	53,216	54,780	56,345	56,910	59,475	61,040	$1,508
13	55,837	57,698	59,559	61,420	63,281	65,142	56,003	68,864	70,725	72,586	$1,793
14	65,983	68,182	70,381	72,580	74,779	76,978	79,177	81,376	83,575	85,774	$2,119
15	77,614	80,201	82,788	85,375	87,962	90,549	93,136	95,723	98,310	100,897	$2,492

SOURCE: GovExec.com, <http://www.govexec.com/careers/00pay/gsbase.html>, April 14, 2000.

benefits or grade level. This interagency mobility has advantages not only for employees but also for agencies looking for varied combinations of skill and experience.

In some state merit systems, it is possible to move up the ladder very rapidly. In Illinois, for example, competitive examinations for higher-level jobs — open only to those already holding state positions — are given with some frequency. A capable individual who has landed a first job can take the examinations every time they are administered and, if successful, can achieve significant career advancement in a relatively short time. It is not unknown for an employee to move from an entry-level post to a staff director's job within four years. That is unusual, but advancement through the ranks — on the basis of on-the-job performance, competitive examinations, time in grade, and so on — is far from an impossible dream for many state government employees.

Formal Tasks of Personnel Administration

The formal tasks of personnel administration have traditionally included position classification, recruitment, examination, selection, and compensation. More recently, as management of complex organizations has become more challenging, administrators (including personnel administrators) have had to become better grounded in human resources planning, employee training, counseling, motivating employees, labor relations, interpersonal skills, social and behavioral psychology, disciplining employees, and dealing with legal constraints. All these tasks were examined by the National Performance Review under President Clinton. The NPR succeeded in vastly reducing the number of personnel rules under which agencies must work (for example, by phasing out the Federal Personnel Manual) and in decentralizing responsibility for personnel management (especially for position classification, recruitment, examination, and compensation) into the hands of individual agencies.

POSITION CLASSIFICATION

The major purpose of **position classification** is to facilitate performance of other personnel functions across a wide range of agencies within the same general personnel system. Many positions in different agencies have similar duties, so that it makes sense to group into one classification jobs with essentially the same responsibilities. Otherwise, recruitment and examination would be far more complex. Both these tasks (to be discussed in more detail shortly) have greater flexibility and value if potential employees can be evaluated in terms of their suitability for the general duties and responsibilities. Pay scales, as another example, can be set only if positions are grouped so that it is possible to award equal pay for equal work, which has been an underlying, if not completely implemented, rationale of position classification since passage of the Pendleton Act.

A written description of the responsibilities involved in a position is the basis for its classification and distinction from other jobs. But there are many obstacles to effective classification. Description of duties is relatively easy, but the exact responsibilities of a position (supervisory tasks, evaluating the work of subordinates, and expectations for initiative, innovation, or suggestions) can be elusive. How challenging the duties and responsibilities are is another ambiguous aspect of position descriptions. In an effort to counteract these problems, some weighting of the various job features — frequency of supervision, difficulty and complexity of each task, and so on — has been tried, so that classifications reflect as accurately as possible the true nature of each position. But the obstacles are not easily overcome, and many classification systems consequently (perhaps inevitably) contain some "soft spots" that require continuing attention.

There are a number of problems with position classification, even under the newer, smaller, and more responsive government structures of the 2000s. First, although an agency is responsible for classifying, according to existing schedules, the positions in that agency, there is a legitimate interest in maintaining some consistency from one agency to the next. Consequently, most states and localities, as well as the national government, provide for *reviews and audits* by a central personnel office with authority to change, if necessary, agency classifications that are out of line. (Note that this central authority has changed, at least to some

position classification a formal task of American public personnel administration, intended to classify jobs in different agencies that have essentially the same types of functions and responsibilities, based on written descriptions of duties and responsibilities.

extent, as Clinton administration recommendations for decentralization were adopted by Congress.) Second, there is concern that *narrow specialization* in many job descriptions has hampered efforts to attract into the public service qualified individuals who lack *exactly* the right combination of skills for a given position. In this respect, position classification may be said to interfere with the merit principle itself, in that job-related competence is defined too narrowly. Third, there is always the possibility that, without adequate monitoring, an existing classification system will become outdated as a result of *rapidly changing job requirements* (a position implicitly taken by the NPR). Fourth, it has been argued that, as task-oriented groups (for example, quality-improvement teams) become more common, position classification geared to hierarchical organization will itself become obsolete. These are problems that bear watching but, because most government organizations are still arranged hierarchically, position classification is likely to remain both appropriate and useful — although with some changes almost certainly in store.

An important development in the early 1990s was the set of recommendations regarding position classification emerging from a number of different sources, which examined (separately) personnel management at national and state-local levels. A common theme present in the work of both the National Performance Review (NPR) and the National Commission on the State and Local Public Service (the Winter Commission) was the need to reduce the existing complexity in classification, especially the sheer number of separate classifications (the Winter Commission noted that the problem was particularly acute in state governments[12]). Both commission reports placed emphasis on **broadbanding** job classification; that is, the recommendations urged personnel managers to consolidate existing classifications into a far smaller number, thus reducing complexity and also increasing flexibility and mobility for employees.

> **broadbanding** the consolidation of existing job classifications into fewer and broader categories, reducing complexity and specialization in job classifications.

RECRUITMENT, EXAMINATION, AND SELECTION

Attracting, testing, and choosing those who join the public service have been systematic activities of personnel administration for a relatively limited period of time. Concerns and issues involved in these areas overlap one another to some extent but deserve separate discussion.

Recruitment was something of a problem for far longer than it was recognized as such. During the early decades of this century, a combination of low pay and low prestige — not unrelated — made working for the government distinctly unattractive. The prestige problem was a matter of public values and attitudes toward government generally; even among those who favored strong administrative capabilities, "politics" was seen as unsavory, to be tolerated rather than actively joined. Although remnants of that attitude persist, the prestige of government service has increased significantly over the past few decades. Greater compensation has been both cause and effect of the change in prestige. It has thus become less difficult to arouse the interest of skilled and competent individuals in government service, but a considerable effort nonetheless had to be made.

The most important developments were the establishment of systematic ties to recruiting services on college campuses — in search of the professionally trained student as well as the liberal arts graduate — and to professional associations. At the same time, a host of requirements (filing fees, residency, and the like) that had acted to constrict access to the public service were dropped, and open competitive examinations were adopted. In a word, the recruitment process was democratized.

In recent years, the recruitment picture has changed somewhat in a number of respects. In general, the necessity to go out and beat the bushes for prospective employees has been greatly reduced; applicants for civilian jobs in the national government often outnumber vacant positions. On the other hand, the demand for qualified employees still exceeds supply in selected occupational areas (engineers, scientists, and, occasionally, secretaries and clerks) and in different parts of the country. Merely because the government job market (like that of the private sector) has tightened does not mean that there is no need to recruit for specific positions.

The *examination* process is a complex one. An examination must be broad enough to test adequately for skills that may be used in widely varying agencies yet still precise enough to be meaningful in testing specific skills and competencies. Many national agencies, as noted earlier, supplement general examinations with more specialized tests, interviews, written work submitted by the applicant, and so on. In state and local government, similar examinations are often used, with many of the same problems as well as advantages.

Most government entrance examinations are written, although it is becoming more common to incorporate both written and oral portions. Also, most tests, not unlike standardized college and graduate school entrance exams, attempt to measure both aptitude and achievement. As alternative methods of measuring competence, it is common practice to give some weight to education and experience, and, in some instances, enough of one or both can substitute for taking the initial examination. In the great majority of cases, a combination of written and oral examinations, personal interviews, education, experience, and written statements is used as the basis for evaluating prospective employees.

A central concern is the *validity* of examinations, that is, how well they actually test what they are designed to test. Another consideration is whether tests should measure specific work skills or factors such as imagination, creativity, managerial talent, and the capacity to learn and grow on the job. Clearly, for some positions, work skills deserve major emphasis whereas, for others, the second set of abilities should also be considered. (See Box 8–1, "Sample Test Questions Dealing with Administration from New York City Police Examinations.")

Of growing concern in the past two decades has been the matter of bias in testing — specifically, whether examinations have exhibited an unintentional

BOX 8-1   ETHICAL AND LEADERSHIP CHALLENGES FOR PUBLIC MANAGERS

Sample Test Questions Dealing with Administration from New York City Police Examinations*

1. "Records of attendance, case load, and individual performance are ordinarily compiled for a police department by a records unit." A plan is suggested whereby all patrol sergeants would regularly review summaries of these detailed records, insofar as they concern the men under them. The adoption of such a plan would be
   (A) inadvisable; the attention of the patrol sergeant would be unduly diverted away from the important function of patrol supervision.
   (B) advisable; the information provided by summaries of detailed records would conclusively indicate to the patrol sergeant the subordinates who should be given specific patrol assignments.
   (C) inadvisable; the original records should be reviewed in detail by the patrol sergeant if he is to derive any value from a record review procedure.
   (D) advisable; the patrol sergeant would then have information that would supplement his personal knowledge of his subordinates.

2. In planning the distribution of the patrol force of a police department, the one of the following factors that should be considered first is the
   (A) availability of supervisory personnel for each of the predetermined tours of police duty.
   (B) hourly need for police services throughout the 24 hours of the day.
   (C) determination of the types of patrol to be utilized for the most effective police effort.
   (D) division of the total area into posts determined by their relative need for police service.

3. There are some who maintain that the efficiency of a police department is determined solely by its numerical strength. This viewpoint oversimplifies a highly complex problem mainly because
   (A) enlargement of the patrol force involves a disproportionate increase in specialized units and increased need for supervision.
   (B) supervisory standards tend to decline in an enlarged department.
   (C) the selection and training of the force, and the quality of supervision, must also be considered.
   (D) the efficiency of the department is not related to its numerical strength.

*Correct answers: 1-D, 2-B, 3-C.

SOURCE: Modern Promotion Courses publications, New York City.

cultural bias that has unfairly discriminated against members of minority groups. In 1979, the Professional and Administrative Career Examination (PACE), which replaced the FSEE in 1974, became the focus of a lawsuit against OPM brought by a group of African Americans and Hispanics who alleged that it was culturally biased and that it tested for general knowledge not required for the 118 job categories for which it was used. Carter administration officials negotiated with the plaintiffs over plans to phase out the exam, and to replace it with up to 118 separate tests designed to measure specific skills for each position. Shortly before President Carter left office, the Justice Department filed its plan in U.S. district court in Washington as a consent decree to settle the suit. Acting under the consent decree, the Reagan administration abolished PACE in August of 1982.

Subsequently, OPM established a new system (known as Schedule B hiring authority) to serve as an interim replacement for PACE, pending development of alternative competitive examining procedures. However, that interim lasted well into Ronald Reagan's second term. Some viewed this (noncompetitive) hiring method as a threat to the competitive merit system. Others argued that agency use of Schedule B meant that there was no central point in the national government to which individuals could apply for jobs. Gradually, however, the picture began to change. By March 1988, OPM had developed job-related alternative examinations (in compliance with the consent decree), which accounted for just over one-half of the positions formerly filled through PACE.[13] And, under George Bush, OPM established (in May 1990) a new examination — **Administrative Careers with America (ACWA)** — which expanded still further the coverage of positions filled through this new, centrally administered exam. Although ACWA represents a step forward, those who were critical of Schedule B still consider the situation less desirable than it was during the time that PACE was in place.[14]

Selection processes vary widely from one government to another, and here, as elsewhere, the national government was the first to develop systematic procedures. There clearly is no overall pattern; merit systems are not identical, and patronage still operates in many state and local governments. But national government practice suggests what is possible — and also gives some idea of the limitations.

The normal procedure was as follows. After qualifying through examination, education, or experience, an applicant received a merit rating (GS-7 or GS-9, for example). Applicants' names were placed on a register, meaning that they were officially under consideration for appropriate positions as these became available throughout the bureaucracy. At that point, it was up to each agency to notify OPM as positions opened up. OPM then forwarded to the agency the names of those it found qualified for the particular position, and the agency took it from there.

In this procedure, two guidelines helped to shape the final decision. The first was called the **rule of three,** referring to OPM's practice of sending three names

Administrative Careers with America (ACWA) revised testing procedure for entrance examinations into the federal civil service, established in 1990 by President Bush.

rule of three a procedure usually followed by the U.S. Office of Personnel Management in narrowing the list of people most qualified for a particular job opening in a national government agency; three names are sent to the agency, which then makes the final selection based on test scores and other considerations.

at a time to agencies with one position to fill; those individuals were, literally, finalists in the competition. The other guideline — veterans' preference — helped determine whose names were included in that vital set of three because it affected total points assigned to each applicant. (In many states and localities, both the rule of three and veterans' preference are still required by law.) All veterans with the minimum passing score of 70 on the 100-point test got a 5-point bonus (with the exception, after 1979, of nondisabled military retirees at or above the rank of major or lieutenant commander); all disabled veterans received a 10-point bonus, as did Vietnam veterans; and those disabled in Vietnam received a 15-point bonus. In some cases, survivors of veterans killed in action received these bonuses as well. In many states and localities, disabled veterans still receive an absolute preference. Veterans' preference reflects the political strength of veterans' groups, as well as the generally high regard in which America's veterans have been held (although Vietnam veterans did not enjoy the same respect as did those of earlier conflicts or those of *Operation Desert Storm*, the Persian Gulf War in early 1991).

It should be noted that veterans' preference — an ascriptive personnel criterion — has had *significant* impact on the composition of the national government's workforce. Defenders of the merit system are hard-pressed to support this kind of noncompetitive generosity, even toward veterans. Many states, and hundreds of local governments as well, employ veterans' preference as a criterion for promotion as well as entry, and nearly *two-thirds* of those in senior grades of the national bureaucracy are veterans. Alan K. Campbell, OPM director under President Carter and a key architect of civil service reform, argued that veterans' preference "has damaged the quality of the senior civil service, to say nothing of discriminating against women in the [national] government."[15] (There is considerable irony here in that two different ascriptive criteria — veterans' preference and affirmative action — *clash with each other* as well as with the concept of merit.) Despite President Carter's efforts to limit this practice, veterans' preference remains largely unchanged, even with the demise of PACE.

COMPENSATION

Deciding how much to pay employees is one of the more difficult and occasionally controversial tasks confronting any government personnel system. In one sense, the task is made easier by the fact that legislatures almost always must provide pay scales and other rules of compensation, but hard decisions about what to propose remain a central responsibility of personnel administration.

There are several key considerations in determining a reasonable level of compensation. One is the necessity of paying employees enough to fulfill their minimum economic needs. Closely related is the question of compensation in proportion to the work done in terms of its importance, quality, and quantity. These can be highly subjective measures, permitting considerable disagreement about what is appropriate. A third consideration is comparability of pay scales.

This has two dimensions: (1) ensuring that wages and salaries for a given classification bear a reasonable relationship to others in the same civil service system with comparable complexity, responsibility, and skill; and (2) maintaining rates of compensation for government employees that are not dramatically different from wages and salaries paid for similar kinds of work in the private sector.

Another dimension of the pay comparability question concerns variations throughout the nation, and even within many states, in wage and salary levels paid in business and industry, which makes it difficult to align government salaries with them on a truly comparable basis. In the mid-1970s, another factor entered into this equation: cost-of-living variations and how these affected compensation. There appears to be an emerging trend — sometimes formalized, sometimes not — to tie government wage and salary levels to changes in the cost of living. As a practical matter, that avoids some tough questions, but the harm it does to the expectation that more skilled individuals will be better paid is obvious. (Later in this section, we will discuss the national government's system of "locality pay," instituted early in 1994.)

Beginning in the late 1970s and throughout the 1980s, national government salaries and wages fell farther and farther behind levels of compensation paid for comparable positions in the private sector. This resulted from both general budget cutting in the national government and, specifically, pay freezes imposed by the Reagan administration. Among those most affected were some 7,000 senior-level career executives, whose situation was aggravated by a cap on salaries. The highest salary for senior career executives, until the cap was lifted in early 1991, was just under $80,000; private-sector executives holding positions of similar responsibility (for example, directing organizations with 100,000 employees) regularly earned two and three times that figure.

During the 1980s, the pay gap for national government civil servants across the country ranged from 14 percent to nearly 30 percent, depending mainly on grade and geographic location. In a 1989 survey, the U.S. Bureau of Labor Statistics found an average pay gap of 22 percent.[16] All in all, according to the National Commission on the Public Service, "the gap between what government and the private sector pay has grown far beyond the point where government can hope to recruit and retain qualified staff, even as the federal benefits package has [also] become less attractive."[17] (See Box 8–2, "The Pay Gap in the National Government Civil Service: Dimensions of the Problem.")

Late in 1989, President Bush and Congress acted to improve the situation somewhat. Legislation passed by Congress, together with an executive order issued by the president, provided for salary boosts for top executive-branch officials ranging from about 8 percent to as much as 35 percent (most civil service raises, which took full effect in 1991, averaged just over 4 percent).[18] However, if true pay comparability is to be achieved (or even approached) for national government civil servants, much more remains to be done.

In 1993, the Clinton administration asked OPM to make recommendations regarding **locality pay** — that is, pay systems that would provide adjustments for

locality pay adjustments to federal pay scales that make allowances for higher- or lower-cost areas where employees live.

The Pay Gap in the National Government Civil Service: Dimensions of the Problem

The impact of lost purchasing power and the widening pay gap is clear. Consider the evidence:

> Over the last decade, [the National Institutes of Health] have not been able to recruit a single senior research scientist from the private or academic sectors to engage in the independent conduct of a clinical or basic biomedical research program [according to Anthony Fauci, Director, National Institutes of Health, 1988].
>
> Half the federal government's personnel officers say that inadequate compensation has become a significant hindrance in attracting the people they need.
>
> Almost 40 percent of the senior executives who left [national] government service in 1985 said their frustrations with proposed and actual changes in compensation were of "great" or "very great" importance in their decisions.
>
> Only 17 percent of the honor society graduates surveyed by the [National Commission on the Public Service] believed the national government could compete in salary with the private sector.

SOURCE: *Report and Recommendations of the National Commission on the Public Service* to the Committee on Post Office and Civil Service, U.S. House of Representatives (Washington, D.C.: U.S. Government Printing Office, 1989), p. 34.

> From 1969 to 1985 the purchasing power of corporate executives rose nearly 69 percent, while pay of senior [national government] executives registered a real decline of more than 30 percent [relative to inflation during that period].

SOURCE: *The Government's Managers: Report of the Twentieth Century Fund Task Force on the Senior Executive Service* (New York: Twentieth Century Fund, 1987), p. 11.

federal employees living in higher-cost areas. The Office of Personnel Management sent its report to the president in November 1993, and a new overall pay system went into effect in January 1994. Under the new arrangement, a total of twenty-eight area pay scales now exist in the federal civil service, for designated high-cost metropolitan (and other) areas. As the new system took effect, about 60 percent of federal employees were covered by one or another of these area scales; the remaining 40 percent are paid according to the "rest of the country" scale. According to OPM, the only federal civilian employees not covered under one of these new pay arrangements are those working overseas.

What of state and local government compensation? Generally, national government employees are paid substantially better than their state and local counterparts. Within that overall comparison, there are other variations. One is the proportion of state and local government employees working in education (see Table 8–2); another is the greater impact of public employee unions and collective bargaining on wages and salaries (which is discussed later in this chapter). In making interstate or interlocal comparisons, other factors that help explain variations in level of compensation include the degree of urbanization and industrialization in the government jurisdiction and the extent to which a bureaucracy has become professionalized. It should be noted, however, that, in some cases, state and local pay exceeds pay at the national level for similar duties. As one example, in 1989, the National Advisory Commission on Law Enforcement found that a state or local entry-level uniformed officer was paid, on the average, $24,357 per year, whereas an officer with similar duties working for the national government started at an average salary of only $15,738.[19]

Regarding pay, as with classification, both the NPR and the Winter Commission have recommended significant changes. In particular, both reports stressed the need for reducing restrictiveness in pay scales and increasing pay ranges within which individuals can receive pay increases without excessive procedural requirements, paperwork, or delays (or promotions). The rationale for such changes is simply that both managers and employees will often benefit from more flexible, and flexibly applied, pay systems.

Collective Bargaining in the Public Sector

Since the late 1950s, **collective bargaining** procedures — modeled largely after those in the private sector — have replaced traditional management-oriented — and *management-controlled* — personnel practices in many jurisdictions and at all levels of government. As a result, there have been frequent and significant shifts in effective decision-making authority on personnel matters, changes in the distribution of political and policy influence, and, on occasion, very visible implications for the delivery of even the most essential public services. In this section, we will examine (1) the general nature and dynamics of public-sector collective bargaining; (2) the sequence of steps involved in the actual process of collective bargaining between employers and employees; and (3) the impacts of collective bargaining in the public sector.

Government Labor–Management Relations: An Overview

The term **labor–management relations** — the framework for collective bargaining — suggests something quite specific about the kinds of interactions that

collective bargaining a formalized process of negotiation between "management" and "labor"; involves specified steps, in a specified sequence, aimed at reaching an agreement (usually stipulated in contractual form) on terms and conditions of employment, covering an agreed-upon period of time; a cycle that is repeated upon expiration of each labor–management contract or other agreement.

labor–management relations the formal setting in which negotiations over pay, working conditions, and benefits take place.

take place between managers and their employees. At the very least, it implies that employees have consciously chosen to organize themselves for the purpose of dealing with their superiors concerning terms and conditions of employment. Beyond that, in both public and private sectors, what is suggested is greater sharing of control over what once were strictly management's prerogatives in managing the workplace — that is, a *basic reordering* of the power to determine distribution of responsibility on the job, levels of compensation for work performed, procedures for airing and resolving grievances, conditions in the workplace, and the like. Viewed another way, labor–management relations represent a form of organizational participation permitting individuals and groups other than formal leaders to have a voice in directing the organization. Many government employees (for example, police and fire personnel) have had influence in dealing with their employers in the past. But this newer form of participation is normally governed rather strictly by contractual provisions arrived at through a joint process and ratified by both management and labor. Thus, an essential element of labor–management relations is the phenomenon of *structured relationships between formally organized participants in a shared-management process.*

This description could apply equally to industrial and governmental labor–management relations. It would, however, be a mistake, here as elsewhere in public administration, to overlook significant differences that exist between the two settings.[20] For example, top public managers are chosen through elections and political appointments, both of which are influenced by labor groups and the general public; such is not the case in private management. Another difference is the near impossibility of separating public-sector bargaining from the political process. Thus, the term **multilateral** (many-sided) **bargaining** is increasingly used in the public sector — rather than **bilateral** (two-sided) **bargaining** — reflecting the involvement of many others besides management and labor bargaining teams. A third difference is the obvious contrast in types of services provided by public and private sectors; there are different markets for each, their purposes differ, and (most important to some observers) most public organizations have had a virtual monopoly on the rendering of certain essential public services — such as police, fire, and sanitation — making the nonmonetary costs to public health and safety very high in the event of a strike or work slowdown.

A caution may be in order about important distinctions among some of the catchwords commonly used in dealing with this subject. First, not all employee organizations are formally labor unions. Other historically prominent types of organizations include various employee and professional associations (for example, of nurses and social workers). Early objectives of such groups included bettering the status of their members and improving the well-being of the respective professions. These organizations have been increasingly drawn into the arena of collective bargaining as a result of pressures from rival organizations often formed explicitly for the purpose of bargaining. For example, the National Education Association (NEA), representing about 2 million teachers, has become significantly more militant in response to the growing success of the

multilateral bargaining public-sector collective bargaining negotiations that include the broadest number of affected public employee groups.

bilateral bargaining collective bargaining negotiations in which only management and labor are represented.

American Federation of Teachers (AFT), a self-conscious labor union committed to collective bargaining.[21]

A second caveat is simply that collective bargaining, as a process, is of recent
vintage as a significant element in public employer–employee relations. In fact,
only since the 1960s has collective bargaining played an important role in public
personnel administration. A third caution is that neither collective bargaining
nor labor unionization is necessarily synonymous with public employee strikes.
Although strikes are by far the most widely reported, visible, and controversial of
all the varied aspects of public-sector labor–management relations, that should
not be permitted to obscure the fact that most labor–management interactions — including most collective bargaining processes and outcomes — do
not result in strikes by public employees. The strike issue is one component of
the total topic; although feelings often run high on that issue, one should take
care to consider other aspects of labor relations as they deserve to be considered — that is, separate from the strike question.

Finally, it should be noted that neither management nor labor is all-powerful
in decision making about management of the public workplace. Especially in
recent years, the interest of ordinary citizens has grown considerably in the contents and procedures of labor–management relations (see Figure 8–2). If nothing
else, the taxpayer still has to foot the bill (however indirectly) for costs incurred

FIGURE 8–2 Dimensions of Bargaining

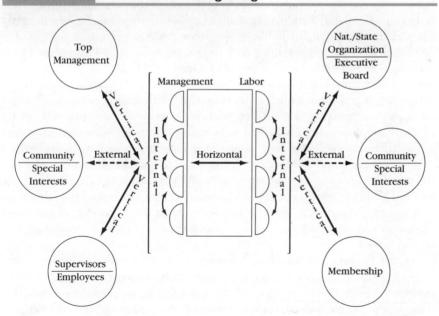

Source: Courtesy of Irving O. Dawson, and developed for the Division of Public Employee Relations,
U.S. Department of Labor.

in reaching agreements. Consequently, it is no longer the case (if it ever really was) that formal bargaining and other forms of decision making in this area can take place without some accounting being made to the ultimate board of directors, that is, the people. This is a central dimension of multilateralism in public-sector bargaining, and it has taken many forms. Two examples from the education area are instructive. In California, the state sunshine bargaining law requires that proposals be publicly disclosed before school boards may begin negotiations with teachers. And Rochester, New York, adopted a "parent involvement policy," which, among other things, invites parent participation in collective bargaining by (1) having parents work with the school board as it prepares its bargaining position before the opening of negotiations, and (2) appointing one carefully selected parent to serve on the board's bargaining team.[22] Thus, the larger reality of accountability to the general public is inescapable. And, in ways decidedly different from those of private-sector bargaining, both parties to labor–management agreements must be mindful of the impacts on the citizenry and of possible public backlash against particular provisions or the whole system of bargaining. In this era of shifting public confidence and of tighter government budgets, such concerns merit a great deal of attention from both union officials and public managers — and they are increasingly receiving that attention.

HISTORICAL DEVELOPMENT OF PUBLIC EMPLOYEE ORGANIZATIONS

Public-employee labor organizations were present in the national government as early as the 1830s, but nothing like modern *union* activity existed before the early 1900s. A turning point for public-sector labor unions — one that signaled the rapid rise of collective bargaining on a large scale — came in 1962, when President John F. Kennedy issued **Executive Order (EO) 10988.** It extended to national government employees the right to organize and to engage in collective bargaining; it provided, among other things, for withholding of union dues and for advisory arbitration of employee grievances, and prohibited union shops (in which all employees are compelled to be union members). Although this order legally altered the policy of only the national government on bargaining with its own employees, states and local governments were also challenged to reexamine and possibly change labor–management negotiation policies. Thus, although the national government was not the first to establish comprehensive new labor relations policies, Kennedy's action (which redeemed a 1960 presidential campaign pledge) served as a catalyst for change, with nationwide repercussions at all government levels.

In the national government, following Kennedy's executive order, there began a period of intensive growth in membership in most unions, spurred by deliberate efforts on the part of various union organizers to increase membership. There was a steady increase in numbers and percentages of national government employees who belonged to labor organizations representing exclusive bargaining units (those represented in negotiations by only one labor group,

Executive Order (EO) 10988 issued by President Kennedy in 1962, this order extended the right to organize and bargain collectively to all national government employees.

chosen by majority vote) or who were covered by formal labor–management agreements, during the period 1963–1992. The total number of employees in exclusive units increased nearly sixfold between 1963 and 1971 (from 180,000 to just over 1 million), with the rate of increase slowing after that date. Also, both the number and the percentage of all employees covered by formal agreements increased significantly, from some 110,000 in 1964 to over 1.2 million in 1998 — a tenfold jump. As of 1998, 1.2 million national government civilian employees (almost 60 percent of all such employees) were represented by 125 labor unions. The number of union members is not the same as the number of employees having union representation. The latter is almost always considerably higher than the former because those who do not pay union dues can also be represented in collective bargaining and are governed by any contractual agreements reached.

Growth in union membership and representation was not the only important development in the national government.[23] In the late 1960s and the 1970s, three new agencies were created by executive order to centralize decision making that had previously been in the hands of individual executive-branch agencies. These were the **Federal Labor Relations Council,** the **Federal Service Impasses Panel** (to aid in resolving negotiating impasses), and a new assistant secretary of labor for labor–management relations, who exercised responsibility for making decisions concerning, among other things, bargaining units, representation, and unfair labor practices. The **Federal Mediation and Conciliation Service** (already in existence) was given a role in mediating negotiation disputes.[24] Also, a requirement for reporting and disclosure procedures similar to those demanded of unions in private employment was imposed for the first time.

A further significant step was taken with the passage of Jimmy Carter's **Civil Service Reform Act of 1978.** One of the most important consequences of the act was to place in statutory form (in Title VII) many terms of the various executive orders, so that "presidents no longer have the authority to regulate the process on their own."[25] Title VII represents a comprehensive rather than incremental statement of labor–management regulations. Some specifics pertaining to collective bargaining included creating an independent **Federal Labor Relations Authority (FLRA),** with powers greater than those of the old Federal Labor Relations Council (including a general counsel authorized to bring unfair labor charges); bringing negotiated grievance procedures into the scope of bargaining; extending labor unions free automatic dues checkoff if authorized by the employee; requiring any agencies that issue governmentwide regulations to consult with unions before taking any action that would make a substantial change in employment conditions; and permitting judicial review of some Federal Labor Relations Authority final orders.[26] The net effect of these changes has been to put in place a complex and varied set of regulations governing a wide range of labor–management relations in the national government service. The days of unilateral personnel management, without participation of — and accommodation to — government employees represented by their unions, are long gone.

Federal Labor Relations Council created by Executive Order 11491 in 1969 to slightly expand federal workers' rights to join unions and bargain collectively.

Federal Service Impasses Panel resolves impasses when either party in collective bargaining negotiations feels that no further progress can be made toward settlement of disputed issues.

Federal Mediation and Conciliation Service mediates negotiation disputes between federal employees and managers.

Civil Service Reform Act of 1978 law designed to reinforce merit principles, protect whistle-blowers, delegate personnel authority to agencies, reward employees for measurable performance, and make it easier to discharge incompetent workers; created the **Federal Labor Relations Authority (FLRA), Office of Personnel Management (OPM), Senior Executive Service (SES),** and the Merit Systems Protection Board (MSPB).

Federal Labor Relations Authority (FLRA) replaced the Federal Labor Relations Council and increased the strength of this bipartisan, three-member panel to supervise the creation of bargaining units, union elections, and deal with labor–management relations in federal agencies.

The National Performance Review signaled an intention to take matters to an even higher level of cooperation. It recommended, in 1993, that forming a labor–management partnership be made an explicit objective of labor–management negotiations, noting in the process that such informal partnerships already existed in a number of national government agencies and that management processes were enhanced by that development.[27] Further steps in that direction have now been taken, with more of them likely to follow.

RECENT STATE AND LOCAL GOVERNMENT EXPERIENCE

At state and local levels, the labor relations picture is different in several key respects from that in the national government and the private sector. For one thing, the total number of public employees belonging to labor unions or covered by bargaining agreements far exceeds that number at the national level; in percentage terms, however, state-local unionization covers just under half of all full-time employees, compared to some 60 percent in the national government. Since the early 1960s, a tremendous increase has occurred in state-local labor organization membership in the public sector. From 1962 to 1987, union membership in the public sector grew from 1.6 million to 4.9 million. Of that total, some 1.2 million were state employees and the remaining 3.7 million worked for local governments. Just under one-half of all full time city, county, school district, township, and special district employees were unionized. By 1998, that number had fallen slightly to 44 percent of the local government workforce. The unionization rate for public employees has remained fairly constant since 1987, while membership rates have declined sharply for all major private sector industries. Thirty-seven and one-half percent of all government employees are represented by unions while the unionization rates in the private sector have dropped below 10 percent. Among occupations, public-sector union rates were highest among police officers, firefighters, and teachers. A higher proportion of blacks were members of unions (18 percent) than whites (13 percent), and on average unionized worker salaries were about one-third (32 percent) higher than nonunion employees. School districts alone accounted for 49 percent of all organized — that is, unionized — local government employees and 37 percent of all organized employees in state and local governments combined. Also, school districts and municipalities together accounted for over three-fourths of organized local employees, and almost 60 percent of those organized in both state and local governments.

The functions in state government most heavily unionized were highways, public welfare, hospitals, and police protection, each with about one-half of all employees organized; at the local level, police, fire protection, and teaching in the schools stood out above the rest. The largest state-local employee organization (with about two million members) is the National Education Association (NEA); it is perhaps significant that the NEA is traditionally the least militant of the teachers' organizations.[28] Other organizations with sizable, powerful, and stable or growing memberships include the American Federation of State, County, and Municipal Employees (AFSCME), with 1.1 million members; the American Federation of Teachers (AFT), which brings together 780,000; and the International Association of Fire Fighters (IAFF), which registers 142,000 members.

A second important difference between the state-local and national settings is the far greater complexity of state and local laws and regulations governing collective bargaining. As political scientist N. Joseph Cayer has noted, "There is no common legal framework under which state and local government labor relations are governed. Labor relations take place under policies made through common law doctrines, judicial decisions, executive orders, and statutes and ordinances."[29] Political scientist Richard Kearney has described the overall situation this way:

> These policies exhibit considerable divergence. State legislation, for instance, ranges from a single comprehensive statute providing coverage for all public employees in Iowa, to coverage of only firefighters in Wyoming, to the total prohibition of collective bargaining in North Carolina. In other states, public employees bargain under the authority of an attorney general's opinion (North Dakota), or civil service regulations (Michigan state employees).[30]

According to the AFL-CIO, twenty-three states and the District of Columbia extend full collective bargaining rights to all public employees; thirteen states protect bargaining rights for some public employees; and fourteen states do not provide for collective bargaining for any state or local government employees.[31] In sum, "the labor relations situation for public employees is different in every city, county, and state, and *the general status of public sector labor relations is still undefined.*"[32]

Thus, labor–management relations loom larger in state-local personnel management than in the national government in quantitative terms, in complexity, and with regard to use of the strike. States and localities have increasingly looked to full-time labor relations specialists for guidance and expertise. In some government jurisdictions, such specialists are given major responsibility for conducting collective bargaining with employee representatives. With or without the assistance of these experts, however, public managers have had to become more sensitive to, and skillful in dealing with, the needs and preferences — and formal demands — of their respective labor forces. In particular, they have had to learn the art of collective bargaining as a central element of personnel management.

THE COLLECTIVE BARGAINING PROCESS

The process of collective bargaining comprises a number of distinct steps and decision points, which are usually specified in some detail in government jurisdictions operating under comprehensive bargaining legislation. In such jurisdictions, the law specifies relevant organizational and administrative arrangements for implementing and enforcing the collective bargaining statute. In cases in which there is no comprehensive statutory authority, many of the same procedural steps are also found, but they lack both the detail and the implementation mechanisms characteristic of more far-reaching legislation.[33]

Whatever the steps in the actual bargaining process, it is standard for bargaining to be supervised by an agency, such as FLRA, with specific oversight responsibility. Here, too, there is considerable variety in the specific form such supervision takes. In state and local governments, a number of different arrangements are possible for supervising the bargaining process. In some states (such as Maine, New York, and Hawaii), an agency is created for the sole purpose of supervising collective bargaining as well as all other aspects of public-employee labor relations; in some other states, responsibility is assigned to personnel departments, departments of labor, or personnel boards (as in Alaska, Massachusetts, Montana, and Wisconsin). Another variation involves supervision of the overall process by a state board, but with delegation to individual departments of specific responsibility for bargaining in their respective areas; examples might include a state department of education or a local board of education.

The usual bargaining sequence consists of the following:

1. Labor organizing efforts, followed by the union seeking recognition as the bargaining agent;
2. Selection of the bargaining team by both employees and management;
3. Defining the scope of bargaining, that is, just what issues will be subject to negotiation and what will not be, within the limits set by statute or executive order;
4. Putting forward proposals and counterproposals;
5. Reaching agreement at the negotiating table (this assumes that agreement can be reached);
6. Submitting any agreement reached to a ratification vote by both employees and management;
7. In the event agreement cannot be reached, attempting to resolve impasses through **impasse procedures** (mediation, fact finding, arbitration, or referendum);
8. Dealing with the possibility — or reality — of a strike;
9. Once a contract is signed, collaborating in the implementation of its provisions (contract administration).

impasse procedures in the context of labor–management relations and collective bargaining, procedures that can be called into play when collective negotiations do not lead to agreement at the bargaining table; these include mediation, fact finding, arbitration, and referendum (in some combination, or following one another should one procedure fail to resolve the impasse).

This is, in reality, a *cycle* rather than a *sequence.* Except for the very first contractual arrangement between management and labor, these steps are repeated periodically, with considerable incentive for both sides to prepare carefully — during the last step of the cycle, namely, contract implementation — for the next round of bargaining by keeping a complete record of "all problems, disputes, grievances, and interpretations" encountered in administering the previous agreement.[34] After the process has become well established, the first two steps are normally omitted unless there arises strong sentiment among employees for a change in the organization representing them or unless it is deemed desirable by one or both sides to change the composition of their respective bargaining teams.

RELATED DIMENSIONS OF COLLECTIVE BARGAINING

An important aspect of the collective bargaining environment is the existence in most jurisdictions of a code of unfair practices. Although not a formal part of actual bargaining, or even of the scope of negotiations, such codes do play a part by restricting certain kinds of behavior by both sides that would have the effect of poisoning the atmosphere of negotiations if they did occur. Included among prohibited behaviors are such things as dismissing employees for union organizing, physical intimidation or attempted bribery to influence the outcome of union representation elections, discriminating arbitrarily against employees for nonmembership in a union, and, of course, refusing to enter into collective bargaining where it is provided for. Under terms of most labor–management agreements, any activity that may violate codes of unfair practices can become grounds for initiating grievance proceedings.

Another dimension of bargaining that has emerged only in recent years is so-called **productivity bargaining.** Following the example of the private sector, public managers have attempted, with some success, to negotiate contract provisions whereby employee wage increases are linked to various cost-cutting efforts — including increasing productivity on the job — as an alternative to layoffs. In large cities, such as New York and Washington, D.C., contracts with very specific clauses were signed during the 1970s under which labor unions agreed to help cut labor costs and increase output; in the case of the former, this was part of the mid-1970s fiscal crisis and efforts by all levels of government to prevent New York City from going into bankruptcy. In a period of growing fiscal stress for many American municipalities, productivity bargaining is a device that is likely to see increasing future use.

> **productivity bargaining**
> labor–management negotiations that link productivity improvements to employee wage increases, as an alternative to reductions-in-force.

Two other aspects of bargaining deserve mention. First, the public sector has contributed an innovation to the bargaining scene through use of computers to assist in costing out the demands of employee organizations. As a tool to aid management in assessing comprehensively what various packages would cost, computer-assisted negotiations can also help give a better overall picture of the position classification structure and the larger personnel management function. Second, in the public sector (unlike the private), there is a particular pressure of timing surrounding collective bargaining. It is necessary to conduct — and conclude — bargaining talks so that necessary funding to cover the costs of the agreement can be requested from the legislature in the normal course of the appropriations process. All the chief executive can promise, in effect, is to ask the legislature for funding; yet, in reality, although the legislature is not bound to honor such requests, its members know that much more serious labor–management problems would result if money to pay for contractual provisions were withheld for any but the most pressing of fiscal reasons. The point is, however, that, even where legislators willingly provide funds, the timetable of negotiations must be coordinated with budget timetables as well.

PUBLIC-EMPLOYEE STRIKES

Professional Air Traffic Controllers Organization (PATCO) now defunct union that once represented the nation's air traffic controllers in labor negotiations.

The phenomenon of the strike is most evident in state and local government; in fact, only postal workers and members of the **Professional Air Traffic Controllers Organization (PATCO)** have actively defied the prohibition on strikes by employees of the national government. Strike activity increased dramatically during the 1960s, but several things should be mentioned in connection with that increase. First, in earlier years strikes were far from unknown, particularly against local government; figures from the U.S. Bureau of Labor Statistics indicate that, in fiscal years (FY) 1942–1958, there were 490 work stoppages in state and local government (all but six against localities). Second, much of the increase was concentrated in a three-year period (1966–1969). Third, it appears that the labor relations situation has stabilized somewhat in states and localities. There have been fewer strikes, relative to the number of employees covered by bargaining agreements and relative to the number of agreements that are regularly negotiated at the state and local levels.

job action any action taken by employees (usually unionized) as a protest against an aspect of their work or working conditions; includes, but is not limited to, strikes or work slowdowns.

One problem in accurately conveying the extent of strike activity in the public sector is that it is sometimes difficult to say whether a strike has actually occurred. Because strikes are prohibited almost everywhere, a **job action** of some kind — of which strikes are only one variety — may take another form. One hears of the "blue flu" afflicting substantial numbers of police officers — all on the same day, with some attendant publicity beforehand — or of teachers' *sick-ins* or sanitation workers' slowdowns. What constitutes an actual strike against government employers, in short, may not be as easy to determine as one might think. Thus, a count of the number of strikes — as distinct from other kinds of job actions — must be received a bit skeptically. The count would be far higher if all types of job actions were surveyed, though that too would pose some difficulties. (See Box 8–3, "A Strike by Any Other Name . . .")

IMPLICATIONS OF COLLECTIVE BARGAINING

It is clear from this discussion of public-sector collective bargaining, and of unionism generally, that the past thirty-five years have seen unparalleled — and undoubtedly permanent — changes in many aspects of personnel management. Equally obvious are what Joseph Cayer describes as the "clear implications for financial management, budgeting, personnel, and planning, and for the roles of employees and managers in the system."[35] There are also other concerns in the 1990s related to the emphases on reinventing government and the quest for improved customer service quality. Let us look briefly at each of these.

BOX 8–3 LABOR–MANAGEMENT RELATIONS

A Strike by Any Other Name . . .

Firefighters have called in sick with the "red rash," police with the virulent "blue flu," and teachers with "chalk-dust fever."

Thousands of Pennsylvania state workers called in with severe cases of "budgetitis" in protest over receiving no paychecks for four weeks because of the state legislature's failure to enact a new budget.

In Knoxville (Tenn.), police officers threatened to engage in a "pray-in" by attending evangelist Billy Graham's Crusade each night until the city council took action on a pay proposal put forward by the Fraternal Order of Police (FOP). The local FOP president observed: "I cannot advocate work stoppages, strikes, or sick call-ins, but I am a firm believer in prayer."

SOURCE: Adapted from Richard C. Kearney, *Labor Relations in the Public Sector,* 2nd ed. (New York: Marcel Dekker, 1992), p. 270.

First, with regard to fiscal implications, two elements stand out: (1) higher personnel costs are associated with collective bargaining (though *how much* higher is not always predictable), and (2) agreements negotiated between labor and management tend to reduce somewhat the flexibility of those responsible for drawing up and approving government budgets by creating wage/salary and fringe benefit figures that can be changed only with great difficulty by budget makers after a contract is ratified by the negotiating parties. Another, broader dimension of the fiscal issue is the fact that labor organizations in comparable jurisdictions (e.g., suburban communities within the same metropolitan area) often seek comparability in pay and the like, thus adding pressure to the budgetary process in any one jurisdiction. (One response to this problem is the growing phenomenon of multiemployer bargaining referred to earlier.) And, to the extent that planning and budgeting are to be coordinated functions, they are under greater constraint because of the need to permit negotiators to decide issues that may have long-term consequences.

Second, the scope of the personnel function itself — besides having become a largely shared responsibility between management and labor — is likely to become a subject of future collective bargaining. Because the scope of bargaining can change in successive negotiation cycles, aspects of personnel management that have not been bargainable (e.g., merit system principles and work rules and regulations) could well become so. Thus, depending on how much effort labor organizations make to bargain on such issues, and on management's ability to counter such attempts effectively, the personnel function could well undergo further — and even more fundamental — change. Part of this evolution lies in what many see as the basic philosophical conflict between collective bargaining and merit principles, which, however, is not a universally held position.[36]

As for management in the public sector, collective bargaining offers both disadvantages and advantages — the former more readily noted by some observers than the latter. Assuming that management's prerogative to run the operation on its own is entirely legitimate, having to share the power to do so is a disadvantage. An accompanying problem is the difficulty management is likely to encounter in developing a consistent personnel policy among diverse groups of union and management employees in the same agency.

On the other hand, a number of distinct advantages have also been suggested. One is that bargaining requires all those interested in effective public management to deal with the management function in all its dimensions, not just whether enough money is available or whether enough authority has been delegated or whether city council will support top-level managers in this or that conflict. A second advantage lies in having to be prepared for bargaining, which forces managers and their superiors to carefully identify managerial weaknesses, in general, and negotiate on training needs, in particular, and to remedy them; otherwise, the unions might well hold the upper hand in the bargaining process. (This is complicated in cases in which supervisory and managerial unions exist — a phenomenon unique to the public sector.) Where management has previously labored under the burden of its own structural or procedural shortcomings, it can be said that collective bargaining has served the interests of governmental effectiveness by forcing attention to those shortcomings.

For public-employee unions themselves, the 1990s proved to be a challenging era. Kearney has asked if, as part of the effort to reinvent government, unions must also be reinvented.[37] Many state and local unions have faced the need (along with public management) to cope with recurring fiscal crises. And, in a number of cases, unions have been actively involved in achieving results, setting goals, and improving customer service quality.[38] Though the future of public-sector unions is an uncertain one, there is mounting evidence of their ability to change and adapt to new demands and new challenges — the same sorts of demands and challenges that confront public managers.

Developments in Personnel Administration

Over the years, there has clearly been a great deal of ferment and change in the processes of fulfilling government's need for qualified people ("qualified" by whatever criteria). More recently, public personnel administration has become even more susceptible to both internal and external pressures for change and for adaptation to changing values and conditions (for example, the phasing out of the PACE test). In addition, the Carter administration's efforts to reform important aspects of the civil service system have had consequences that merit discussion. Furthermore, the 1980s and 1990s have seen a variety of significant changes with major impacts on public personnel. Five developments illustrate the scope and potential consequences of recent change in personnel management: (1) implementation of the Civil Service Reform Act (CSRA) of 1978; (2) impacts on the civil service of budget cuts enacted since the Reagan presidency; (3) affirmative action and comparable worth efforts in hiring, promoting, and equalizing pay for women and members of minority groups; (4) changing guidelines governing patronage and other partisan activity; and (5) the changes advocated by the Clinton administration, embodied in the NPR report.

THE CIVIL SERVICE REFORM ACT (CSRA) OF 1978

In the course of civil service administration throughout this century, both the advantages and disadvantages of civil service reform became clear. Numerous choices were made that affected personnel management practices. Each time presidential and other commissions examined the national bureaucracy, personnel problems were on their agendas, but, prior to 1978, little in the way of comprehensive change had been brought about. When Jimmy Carter became president, a new effort was begun to alter merit system practices.

The principal targets of the civil service reforms were numerous; each problem had evolved over long periods of time, and solving them posed political as well as managerial challenges. Certainly, one of the most important was the evolution of the merit system from a protection against blatant partisan manipulation to a system that provided what many called excessive job security for employees (competent or not), that made possible virtually automatic salary increases (deserved or not), and that made it difficult for responsible managers to dismiss unproductive employees. This "protected employment system," as it was described by former OPM Director Campbell, was clearly the focus of the Carter reform efforts (see Box 8–4, "The Civil Service Reform Act (CSRA) of 1978"). More to the point for a management-conscious president, existing arrangements made it difficult at best for public managers to direct the operations of their agencies effectively. And there was some interest within the Carter administration in increasing the political responsiveness of top career civil servants.

Other concerns addressed by the reform legislation included (1) the fact that no statute or executive order had ever spelled out the merit principles that were the foundation of the merit system; (2) what, if any, personnel practices were prohibited (for example, management retaliation against whistle-blowers — those disclosing waste, fraud, abuses, or other mismanagement); (3) the status of veterans' preference; (4) the informal — and often haphazard — manner in which employee performance was evaluated; and (5) the lack of a statutory basis for the conduct of labor relations (specifically, collective bargaining) with national government employees.

Unlike the 1883 Pendleton Act, which was devoted almost solely to eliminating patronage practices, the CSRA incorporated a wide variety of complex and interrelated objectives. For example, the design of the SES included the

BOX 8–4   LABOR–MANAGEMENT RELATIONS

The Civil Service Reform Act (CSRA) of 1978

Enacted in October 1978 and effective January 1, 1979, the CSRA made the following changes in the personnel practices of the federal government.[39]

1. Created the Office of Personnel Management (OPM) and the Merit Systems Protection Board (MSPB), replacing the Civil Service Commission.
2. Delegated personnel management authority to agencies, notably regarding performance appraisal.
3. Streamlined the process used to discharge employees.
4. Strengthened procedures to protect whistle-blowers from unlawful reprisals from their agencies.
5. Established a comprehensive statutory framework for conducting labor–management relations.
6. Authorized a merit pay system for middle-level supervisors, based on performance rather than longevity.
7. Established the Senior Executive Service (SES) for top-level career decision makers.
8. Required that objective, job-related, measurable performance evaluation (appraisal) be developed for members of the SES.
9. Enacted both a set of explicit merit principles and a statement of prohibited personnel practices (see Box 8–5, "Provisions of the Civil Service Reform Act [CSRA] of 1978").

following: (1) SES members, drawn primarily from the supergrades (GS-16 through -18), would be able to work more closely and harmoniously with political appointees at the point of contact between the political head of the agency and the careerists (see Chapter 7); (2) the responsiveness of these senior career officials to presidential policy leadership would thus be enhanced; (3) incentives could be developed for greater productivity on the part of senior executives (especially considering that they would sacrifice substantial job security on joining the SES); (4) financial bonuses — and greater acknowledgment of careerists' policy advisory roles[40] — would serve as those incentives; (5) job performance of senior civil servants could be appraised more systematically; and (6) based on those appraisals, decisions about awarding bonuses could be made fairly and objectively.

Similarly, for the merit pay system effective in 1981 for grades GS-13 through GS-15, agencies were required to develop performance appraisal systems that included performance standards and to tie merit pay to performance

BOX 8–5   LABOR–MANAGEMENT RELATIONS

Provisions of the Civil Service Reform Act (CSRA) of 1978

Merit System Principles

Personnel practices and actions in the federal government require:

- Recruitment from all segments of society, and selection and advancement on the basis of ability, knowledge, and skills, under fair and open competition.
- Fair and equitable treatment in all personnel management matters, without regard to politics, race, color, religion, national origin, sex, marital status, age, or handicapping condition, and with proper regard for individual privacy and constitutional rights.
- Equal pay for work of equal value, considering both national and local rates paid by private employers, with incentives and recognition for excellent performance.
- High standards of integrity, conduct, and concern for the public interest.
- Efficient and effective use of the Federal workforce.
- Retention of employees who perform well, correcting the performance of those whose work is inadequate, and separation of those who cannot or will not meet required standards.
- Improved performance through effective education and training.
- Protection of employees from arbitrary action, personal favoritism, or political coercion.
- Protection of employees against reprisal for lawful disclosures of information.

Prohibited Personnel Practices

Officials and employees who are authorized to take personnel actions are prohibited from:

- Discriminating against any employee or applicant.
- Soliciting or considering any recommendation on a person who requests or is being considered for a personnel action unlesss the material is an evaluation of the person's work performance, ability, aptitude, or general qualifications, or character, loyalty, and suitability.
- Using official authority to coerce political actions, to require political contributions, or to retaliate for refusal to do these things.
- Willfully deceiving or obstructing an individual as to his or her right to compete for Federal employment.
- Influencing anyone to withdraw from competition, whether to improve or worsen the prospects of any applicant.
- Granting any special preferential treatment or advantage not authorized by law to a job applicant or employee.
- Appointing, employing, promoting, or advancing relatives in their agencies.
- Taking or failing to take a personnel action as a reprisal against employees who exercise their appeal rights; refuse to engage in political activity; or lawfully disclose violations of law, rule, or regulation, or mismanagement, gross waste of funds, abuse of authority, or a substantial and specific danger to public health or safety.
- Taking or failing to take any other personnel action violating a law, rule, or regulation directly related to merit system principles.

SOURCES: U.S. Civil Service Commission, *Introducing the Civil Service Reform Act* (Washington, D.C.: U.S. Government Printing Office, November 1978), p. 2; reprinted from N. Joseph Cayer, *Managing Human Resources: An Introduction to Public Personnel Administration* (New York: St. Martin's , 1980), p. 32.

on the basis of the appraisal process. Underlying both the SES and merit pay were several assumptions: "Protected employment" would be diluted, performance of middle- and top-level managers would be better evaluated, and pay-for-performance would serve as a positive incentive to those affected. It was hoped that, as a result of these reforms, the overall productivity and effectiveness of national government programs would be enhanced. (Stronger protections for whistle-blowers were designed to achieve the same end.[41])

The early promise of the CSRA gave way instead to considerable frustration. One overriding difficulty, especially in 1981, was the dramatic change in the political and governmental environment that accompanied the transition from the Carter to the Reagan administrations, specifically the PATCO strike, and radical changes at the OPM. Civil Service Reform Act implementation went forward, however, in spite of these and other constraints. But serious difficulties were soon encountered. Some stemmed from the transition from Carter to Reagan; others arose from ongoing conflicts between OPM and the agencies and between Congress and the executive branch; still others resulted from the way that many federal executives believed CSRA would affect their careers.

performance appraisal
a formal process used to document and evaluate an employee's job performance; typically used to reinforce management's assessment of the quality of an individual's work, punish workers who are "below standard," and reward others with bonuses, higher salaries, and promotions.

Specific problems included the following. First, **performance appraisal** suffered from uncertainties about how appraisals would be conducted, how their results would be used, whether OPM would properly monitor and evaluate the new appraisal procedures once they were in operation, and whether factors other than objective performance were the basis for some of the pay adjustments that, in principle, were to be linked to these appraisals. Secondly, problems regarding pay included a salary cap (already noted) on what SES members could earn, controversy over the size of SES salary bonuses and merit pay increases, and a companion dispute over the degree of fairness in awarding SES bonuses. Finally, the design of the SES as a meeting ground for political and career executives came into question. Many careerists, during the early years of the Reagan presidency, objected to what they saw as politically motivated decisions that, in their view, adversely affected them and the programs they managed. Furthermore, "relations between career and political people . . . deteriorated"[42] within an atmosphere of frustration and dissatisfaction. (The Clinton administration was largely able to avoid such conflicts during its first term by recruiting senior-level careerists to help coproduce the NPR.)

One irony regarding the CSRA is that the act may have served as an example for personnel systems in other governments, with greater impacts than those felt in Washington. There is evidence, for example, that civil service reform has been implemented in the governments of twenty-four American states and fourteen other countries at least as fully as it has been in the national government's civil service.[43] Those impacts should be borne in mind, when evaluating the overall effects of civil service reform over the past fifteen to twenty years.

Two other political aspects of national government personnel management should also be mentioned. One is the concern that in the effort to bring about greater responsiveness to political leadership among higher-level civil servants, the CSRA may have gone too far. To paraphrase a number of commentaries made about the changes, achieving greater responsiveness is one thing; gutting the competitive service at the higher grades is quite another.[44] The various steps taken during the Reagan years especially, were cause for concern for many who have defended the merit system over the years. Fewer reservations have been expressed about some of the Clinton administration's personnel initiatives. However, it has been suggested that too much presidential control — even in the name of empowering civil servants — carries with it potentially damaging effects on the civil service as a whole.

The other political dimension has a larger context and perhaps wider-ranging consequences. It has been said, with some justification, that the amount and intensity of criticism aimed at public administrators has reached a level unprecedented in the last hundred years.[45] Those who find this development disturbing (and many do) freely acknowledge that government officials must be held accountable — that, as a nation, we have a legitimate interest in official actions being linked appropriately to established public purposes and policies. On the other hand, the pervasive public habit of scapegoating bureaucracy (see Chapter 1) has become part of our national folklore. It does nothing to promote accountability, and may do a great deal to undermine the morale and self-confidence of conscientious public servants. This denigration (downgrading or deriding) of civil servants has often surfaced in the public utterances of candidates for elective office — including candidates Carter and Reagan, the first time each ran for the presidency, and candidate Clinton (though somewhat less pointedly) at various times during the 1992 campaign. As a result, it is argued, many talented and experienced officials, with a wealth of institutional memory and understanding of public programs, have left government service. Those who replaced them are inevitably less experienced, less informed by past failures and successes, and less familiar with their programmatic and political territory. The net result may well be a government service less prepared to manage programs involving hundreds of billions of dollars or to plan responsibly for policy and program needs ten and twenty years hence. One positive outcome of the 1996 presidential election was the distinct lack of invective directed at civil servants as a group despite negative campaigning aimed at the character of candidates, misuse of taxes, budget priorities, and wasteful public projects.

Downsizing and the Civil Service

Like most other areas of government activity, the civil service felt keenly the effects of initiatives to reduce government spending. Limited entry into the civil service thus has been the rule since the early 1980s. Closely related is the imposition of RIFs (reductions in force) on most domestic agencies (see Chapter 7). The number of positions allocated to each agency was reduced, resulting in net declines in civil service employment of between 10 and 15 percent since the early 1990s (see Table 8–3). A third element mentioned earlier is "bumping" of

TABLE 8–3	National Government Civilian Employment by Function: 1992 and 1998		
Function	1992 Total Employees	1998 Total Employees	Percent Change 1992–1998
Total — all functions	3,046,873	2,765,214	–9.2
Financial administration	137,744	134,202	–2.6
Other government administration	28,966	22,073	–24.2
Judicial and legal	50,768	54,447	+7.3
Police	87,616	100,257	+14.5
Correction	23,818	30,436	+28.2
Highways	4,110	3,598	–12.4
Air transportation	53,937	49,350	–8.5
Water transport and terminals	14,725	14,890	+0.1
Public welfare	10,385	8,872	–14.5
Health	144,339	136,023	–5.7
Hospitals	173,864	161,432	–7.1
Social insurance administration	68,787	67,437	–1.9
Parks and recreation	27,156	24,314	–10.4
Housing and community development	28,006	16,465	–41.2
Natural resources	232,124	185,025	–20.2
National defense and international relations	984,226	738,204	–25.0
Postal service	774,028	856,732	+10.6
Space research and technology	25,339	19,310	–23.7
Other education	13,790	11,303	–18.0
Libraries	4,945	4,376	–11.5
Other and unallocable	158,200	126,468	–20.0

SOURCE: *U.S. Census Annual*, 1992 and 1998.

employees to lower ranks in the career service as part of efforts both to reduce costs and to strengthen agency command structures. Yet another development is increased turnover rates among those remaining in the civil service. As uncertainties increased, individuals often tried to anticipate changes in their agencies by voluntarily seeking other posts. Finally, as noted earlier, pay freezes for many civil servants contributed to each of the phenomena just mentioned, as well as undercutting employee morale. Although the rate of change in these respects has slowed somewhat, the immediate effects on government personnel are obvious. Federal agencies responsible for securing the national defense (Department of Defense) and conducting international affairs (i.e., State Department, Agency for International Development, Immigration and Naturalization Service among others) lost one-fourth of their employees during the 1990s. During the same period of time, the Postal Service gained some 10 percent. Doubtless, many former members of the armed forces "bumped" lower seniority employees, and some were transferred to other agencies, but many civil service workers were permanently "downsized." Moreover, the potential long-range impacts on the civil service are significant if the net effect is to lessen the attractiveness of government employment, damage the management capacities of executive agencies (see Box 8–6, "Budget Cuts and Management Capacities: Much More than Just Dollars"), and reduce the effectiveness and productivity of government programs (for example, could agency understaffing — at all levels of government — be contributing to increases in airline passenger complaints, in environmental pollution, or in juvenile crime?).

BOX 8–6   ETHICAL AND LEADERSHIP CHALLENGES
FOR PUBLIC MANAGERS

Budget Cuts and Management Capacities: Much More than Just Dollars

Environmentalists lobbied for nearly a decade before Congress [in 1988] set aside 35,000 acres of coastal wetlands near Jacksonville, Florida, for the Timucquan Ecological and Historical Preserve. It was supposed to be a model for wetlands preservation. The only problem: the new park's superintendent hasn't been given a staff — or even a boat.

The Department of Veterans Affairs has such a shortage of doctors and nurses that many of its hospitals can accommodate only critical-care patients. Overworked doctors are forced to clean bedpans and administer medication, while patients may wait hours for help in hallways or unmade beds. Only an emergency congressional appropriation [in the spring of 1989] averted the closure of more than 300 clinics and other VA programs.

The Federal Communications Commission, arbiter of advanced telecommunications technologies, still uses 1960s-vintage black rotary telephones at its Washington headquarters.

While attendance at our national parks increased by 62 million people in the period 1980–1988, full-time staff at the National Park Service remained fairly constant in terms of numbers.

At the Federal Aviation Administration (FAA), not only have air traffic controllers been in short supply; the number of FAA inspectors and field maintenance employees has been reduced by about 20 percent. A 1989 General Accounting Office (GAO) study found that, in 1988, less than 40 percent of the operating inspectors received the flight training that the FAA says they must have to perform pilot flight checks, and airworthiness inspectors received less than 50 percent of the training that the FAA said they needed.

Cuts at the Health Care Financing Administration (HCFA) reduced the agency's work force by 20 percent since 1980, at the same time that

(continued)

BOX 8–6   ETHICAL AND LEADERSHIP CHALLENGES
FOR PUBLIC MANAGERS *(continued)*

radical changes in Medicare and Medicaid programs were being made; this has slowed the transition between old and new policies.

The FAA, the Social Security Administration, the Internal Revenue Service (IRS), and HCFA all tackle increasing work loads in data processing and the like on 15- or 20-year-old computers. One defense agency still chugs along with a 22-year-old mainframe. And the U.S. government is the western world's largest buyer of vacuum tubes, the grandfathers of today's microprocessors.

The IRS, even *with* new computers, saw the percentage of yearly tax returns it audits drop by almost 50 percent between 1978 and 1987.

SOURCES: Adapted, with minor revisions, from Mark L. Goldstein, "Hollow Government," *Government Executive,* 21 (October 1989), 12, 16, and 22. Also cited is *Aviation Training: FAA Aviation Safety Inspectors Are Not Receiving Needed Training,* A Report to the Congress of the United States by the Comptroller General, General Accounting Office Report No. GAO/RCED-89-168 (Washington, D.C.: U.S. Government Printing Office, September 14, 1989).

EO 10925 (1961)
issued by President Kennedy, this executive order required for the first time that "affirmative action" guidelines be used to prohibit discrimination in employment by federal agencies and contractors.

1964 Civil Rights Act
landmark legislation prohibiting discrimination by the private sector in both employment and housing.

1972 Equal Employment Opportunity Act
amended Title VII, the Civil Rights Act of 1964, designed to strengthen the authority of the Equal Employment Opportunity Commission (EEOC) to enforce antidiscrimination laws in state and local governments as well as in private organizations with fifteen or more employees.

Equity Pay Act of 1963
prohibited gender-based (or other) discrimination in pay for those engaged in the same type of work.

comparable worth
extended the "equal pay for equal work" principle to develop criteria for compensation based on the intellectual and physical demands of the job, not market determination of its worth.

AFFIRMATIVE ACTION AND COMPARABLE WORTH

In the public service, as elsewhere, there has been emphasis in recent years on hiring and advancement of minorities and women. The rationale behind the affirmative action movement is that some individuals and groups have been unfairly — in many cases, arbitrarily — discriminated against in the past and that seeking to bring them into government service is one effective way to redress old grievances (see Chapter 2). The national government has gone a long way, under executive orders (EO) such as **EO 10925 (1961),** provisions of legislation such as the **1964 Civil Rights Act** and the **1972 Equal Employment Opportunity Act,** to ensure that women and minorities are given at least strong consideration, if not outright preferential treatment, in decisions to hire government employees.

The principle of equal pay for equal work was firmly established by the national **Equity Pay Act of 1963,** requiring an end to any gender-based (or other) discrimination in compensation for individuals engaged in similar work. The issue of **comparable worth,** however, goes beyond that principle. It addresses the question of how to set pay levels for individuals doing work that is different but comparable in value to the employing organization, government, or society at large. Apart from the intrinsic issues, there is a key relationship here to affirmative action since most secretaries, librarians, and nurses are female and lower paid; most managers, engineers, and plumbers are male and higher paid. Some try to justify lower pay for "women's work" on the grounds that, historically, women were not the principal breadwinners; that many younger women were in the workforce only until they married and started a family; or that the forces of labor supply and demand (not gender discrimination) worked to depress compensation levels for nurses, secretaries, telephone operators, teachers, and the like. Others argue that these and similar assumptions — however accurate or inaccurate — represent social stereotypes of women as inherently less valuable workers. Yet another dispute revolves around the methodology that would be used to determine comparability among diverse occupations. And there are vastly differing perceptions of how practical — or useful — the task of comparing is.

Despite the continuing debate over comparable worth, a substantial majority of the states, along with many local governments, have now either enacted statutes containing comparable-worth language, completed studies of the possible consequences of implementing the concept, or both. The national government, on the other hand, has not adopted the concept. In both the Bush and Clinton administrations, no major new steps have been taken to advance the concept in the national government's executive branch; under Clinton, this is at least partly because (as noted earlier) other concerns have come to the forefront, pushing comparable worth (like affirmative action) off center stage in the national government, at least for the time being.

The issues raised by affirmative action and comparable-worth programs are weighty ones. First, if a merit system is viewed as one that goes strictly by the applicant's job-related competence, then affirmative action conflicts with that objective. This has been the basis of many criticisms of such programs. Those who support affirmative action point out, however, that it is entirely appropriate as a remedial effort in light of historic lack of access to jobs suffered by minorities and women. They also point to features such as veterans' preference, along with failure to enforce standards of competence as vigorously after appointment as before, as evidence of imperfection in existing merit practices. The essence of their contention is that denial of access through omission or systematic exclusion of certain groups is best remedied by practicing systematic inclusion through affirmative action. They also claim that this makes the public service more truly representative of different groups in the population and, thus, more responsive to their concerns.

Affirmative action is also said to be needed because of past biases in intelligence (IQ), employment, and promotion testing. That is, it has been alleged that competitive examinations have often been discriminatory above and beyond the *necessary* discrimination (that is, distinction) among the various competencies and skills of those seeking employment or advancement. Advocates of this view argue that testing is based on the experience and training of a white, middle-class population (usually in key management and recruiting positions) and inevitably discriminates unfairly against those whose cultural background, experience and training are dissimilar.

Another major area of controversy regarding affirmative action is the issue of quotas in hiring — setting aside a fixed percentage of all positions or government contracts for members of certain ethnic groups and for women. Court decisions have alternately supported and rejected this practice, though adherence to rigid quota systems is increasingly under fire. Again, the conflict is between those who see systematic inclusion (which is what quotas really amount to) as a remedial device for decades of exclusion for significant numbers of American citizens and those who prefer to staff the public service on the basis of job-related competence and other relatively objective criteria, such as competency, education, and experience.

reverse discrimination
unfavorable actions against white males to achieve affirmative action goals to hire and promote more women and minorities.

The debate over affirmative action, comparable worth, and quotas — indeed the whole area of what many think of as **reverse discrimination** — is likely to continue, regardless of decisions made in legislatures or courts in the immediate future. But what difference has all this furor made? Two generalizations are in order. First, there has been a significant increase in the proportions of minorities and women present in the workforces of national, state, and local governments; to that extent, affirmative action employment programs have succeeded. Second, it is clear that, of the minorities and women in public employment, a substantial majority still tend to occupy the less responsible positions relative to white males, and many are found at lower grade levels of the civil service hierarchy, with correspondingly lower salary or wage levels. (This is a reflection, in part, of the dominance of a generation veterans in upper-level posts.)

Predictably, the picture varies at different levels of government. National government data in 1990 indicated, for example, that women make up more than 43 percent of the total federal civilian workforce, African-Americans hold 16.6 percent of federal civilian jobs, and Hispanics represent 5.4 percent of the federal workforce.[46] But, despite increases in numbers of women and minorities in the federal civil service, they "remain concentrated in lower-echelon jobs."[47] As of 1990, according to one study, women held only 15 percent of the positions in grades GS-13 through -15 (though this was up from 5 percent in 1974 and 10 percent a decade later).[48] And the Merit Systems Protection Board reported in 1992 that women and minorities accounted for only 12 and 9 percent, respectively, of the members of the SES, which suggests that a "glass ceiling" still bars women and minorities from rising to the highest levels of the national civil service.[49]

States and localities present a much more varied picture. There is evidence that white women and minorities of both sexes have made marked gains in government employment generally, but at a slower pace in state and local governments (especially for minorities) than at the national level. Also, as in the case of the national government, white males still predominate in the higher personnel grades and pay levels. Not surprisingly, there is great variation among the states and among the thousands of local governments, as well as among different functional areas. (Note, however, that women and minorities have fared much better in the public sector overall than in the private sector.[50])

Clearly, affirmative action has not done all that its proponents hoped it would; it is questionable that it could have tilted the balance as far as some wanted it to. Furthermore, the outlook for the immediate future is mixed; some developments augur well for affirmative action, and others, such as the passage of **Proposition 209** in California, decidedly do not. In November 1996, the voters of California supported Proposition 209, by a 54–46 percent margin, a referendum abolishing preferential hiring based on gender or race in public hiring, contracting, or education, including admission to state universities. The vote has been widely interpreted as a backlash against affirmative action aimed at blacks, immigrants, women, and other ethnic minorities. The California decision has been upheld by the Federal appeals court and the controversy has spread to other states. In 1998, voters in the state of Washington passed a similar ballot measure repealing affirmative action programs. And, in February 2000, amid considerable controversy, Florida abolished preferential treatment for minorities in contracting, hiring, and admissions to state universities as part of Governor Jeb Bush's "One Florida" initiative.

Proponents of affirmative action point hopefully to numerous court decisions that have sustained various practices, or required government actions, that are consistent with the principle of affirmative action. As one example, the U.S. Supreme Court refused in early 1985 to hear a case brought by fifteen white New York State correctional officers who protested that they were unfairly bumped down a promotion list when the state civil service commission adjusted test results to give more minority candidates passing scores.[51] On the other hand, public administration scholar David Rosenbloom has predicted that affirmative action (at least in the national government) will become a relatively less prominent concern. He notes, among other things, the absence of a strong national consensus supporting affirmative action, along with the rise of new personnel concerns (for example, retrenchment, and productivity[52]); other new concerns, such as sexual harassment, employee empowerment and improving service to "customers," also point to diminished attention to affirmative action. It is doubtful, however, that affirmative action will be thrust aside entirely, especially given its statutory foundations and the growing emphasis on encouraging diversity in the workforce. The ultimate success of state efforts such as Proposition 209 in California to limit federal affirmative actions programs are likely to be decided not by voters but by the federal courts.

> **Proposition 209** ballot initiative in California that repealed all affirmative action and preferential hiring programs for state jobs and admissions to state colleges and universities.

PERSONNEL POLICY AND PARTISANSHIP

The desirability of linking government personnel practices to partisan politics has been a matter of controversy in this nation for nearly the whole of our political history. It is no different now, and two aspects of this issue have loomed large in recent developments in personnel administration.

One revolves around judicial determinations concerning patronage and, in particular, a number of decisions in which various courts have ruled that dismissal of, or other adverse actions against, non-merit-protected employees solely on partisan grounds could be construed as a violation of constitutional rights protected by the First and Fourteenth amendments to the U.S. Constitution. Major cases relevant to this point include *Elrod v. Burns*, 427 U.S. 347 (1976), in which the U.S. Supreme Court ruled that lower-level government workers cannot be fired for partisan reasons; *Hollifield v. McMahan*, 438 F. Supp. 591 (1977), in which a U.S. District Court judge in Tennessee applied the principle to a dismissal of a deputy sheriff after the deputy had openly and actively supported his superior's opponent in an election campaign; *Shakman v. The Democratic Organization of Cook County*, 481 F. Supp. 1315 (1979), in which another district judge in Illinois extended that ruling to include promotions and demotions; *Branti v. Finkel*, 100 Sup. Ct. 1287 (1980), in which the U.S. Supreme Court held that two assistant public defenders in Rockland County, New York, could not be dismissed by their new Democratic boss solely because they were Republicans (thus extending the principle to higher-level officials); and *Rutan v. Republican Party of Illinois*, 110 Sup. Ct. 2729 (1990), in which the U.S. Supreme Court ruled, by a 5–4 margin, that it is a violation of public employees' First Amendment rights to hire, promote, or transfer most public employees based on party affiliation.[53] These rulings do not apply to confidential policy-making jobs, but the courts have not yet determined where to draw the line between these and other posts. And, even though the courts have spoken regarding patronage, such practices are "too entrenched in the American political system to disappear overnight."[54] It is clear that patronage — though often in modified form — is still very much with us.

The other dimension of personnel and partisanship is the issue of whether civil servants should be required to maintain partisan neutrality by virtue of their *being* civil servants. This required neutrality, which was a primary objective of merit reformers in the nineteenth century, was embodied in the Political Activities Act of 1939 (the Hatch Act). This legislation, as amended in 1940 and 1966, prohibited any active participation in political campaigns by national government employees, state and local employees working in any nationally funded program, and employees of private organizations working with community-action programs funded by the Economic Opportunity Act.[55] But, as rights of government employees became a more prominent concern in the 1960s and early 1970s, efforts were made to limit or overturn the Hatch Act. The reasoning behind these efforts was that provisions barring political involvement were said to infringe on rights that could be exercised by others, thus rendering government personnel second-class citizens. The right to vote was not enough, it was argued; government employees should have the right to participate in all aspects of politics.

In a series of court cases in the early 1970s, several state and local versions of the Hatch Act were challenged, some successfully. In 1972, the U.S. District Court for the District of Columbia declared the Hatch Act itself unconstitutional on grounds of vagueness and of First Amendment violations in *National Association of Letter Carriers, AFL-CIO v. United States Civil Service Commission*, 346 F. Supp. 578 (1972). But, in 1973, the Supreme Court reversed that lower court ruling on a 6–3 vote, upholding the act and its constitutionality. After that, efforts centered on persuading Congress to loosen restrictions on government employees' political activities. In the early summer of 1990, Congress enacted a revision of the Hatch Act that would have relaxed many of the restrictions on "political" (meaning, mainly, partisan) activities by national government employees, but President Bush — echoing a position held by Ronald Reagan — vetoed the bill. In 1993, however, Congress again passed repeal of the Hatch Act and, this time, President Clinton signed the bill into law. The effect of this change was to permit national government employees to participate in most aspects of electoral politics in the same manner as any other citizens. The only major restrictions are that federal employees may not run for partisan elective office or solicit campaign contributions from the general public.

THE CLINTON ADMINISTRATION AND PERSONNEL MANAGEMENT

The Report of the National Performance Review, issued in mid-1993, proposed a series of changes that have far-reaching implications for how the national government manages its personnel systems.[56] Specific proposals included: (1) deregulation of personnel policy by phasing out the 10,000-page Federal Personnel Manual (as already noted), together with all agency implementing directives; (2) simplify the existing position classification system by giving more agencies more flexibility in how they classify and pay their employees; (3) permit agencies to design their own performance management and reward systems; and (4) streamline the system for dealing with poor performance, including reducing by one-half the time required to dismiss managers and employees "for cause," that is, for failure to perform their duties in a competent and productive manner. The Clinton administration was intent on both *deregulating and decentralizing* many key aspects of personnel management. What makes such efforts all the more significant is that the fact of the effort, by itself, points the way to new approaches to managing national government employees. The Clinton–Gore team sustained this effort during their second term to bring about fundamental change in managing executive-branch personnel.

Perspectives and Implications

The U.S. civil service has existed for more than a century on a foundation of belief and practice clear in intent and quite consistent in manner of operation. Now, however, all the assumptions underlying past practice are being seriously questioned. The merit system has been modified to accommodate veterans' preference and, more recently, demographic representativeness. At the same time, efforts are under way to breathe new life into the meaning of *merit* by linking performance to compensation and other incentives such as promotion. The Carter administration, as we have seen, sought to achieve a significant degree of change in the merit system in this respect. The Reagan administration undertook other initiatives, designed for the most part to enhance presidential influence over the activities of career civil servants. In terms of the assumptions underlying personnel management, this meant favoring political responsiveness over politically neutral competence, at least to some extent. The resultant uncertainties compounded those associated with civil service reform in the late 1970s. The Bush administration took some steps to ease the "pay crunch" and to reestablish a systemwide point of entry into the national government civil service (with the ACWA examination). The Clinton administration initiated major efforts to reform the personnel system, pointing in directions that are largely new to the national government. Other dimensions of potential change include the impact of future court decisions on patronage practices, backlash against hiring quotas and affirmative action, and more contracting out or privatization of public operations to outside consultants and contractors. State and local government personnel practices are also undergoing change, partly in direct response to initiatives from Washington (including the courts) and partly because of forces at work within their respective jurisdictions.

Recommendations of the 1990 National Commission on the Public Service (the Volcker Commission) bear on the future course of personnel administration as well. The commission recommended, in general, that steps be taken to address the negative perceptions of public service said to exist among many of our citizens, to deal with managerial issues (such as recruitment and retention of public servants), to strengthen education and training for serving in public-sector positions, and to increase pay and benefits for government employees. More specific recommendations were aimed at improving the work environment, reducing hiring of political appointees, increasing access to job openings, and rewarding executive excellence. Some, but by no means all, of these suggestions have been implemented in the federal civil service; whether more of these will be adopted (or even advocated) remains to be seen.[57]

In short, change has been both monumental and fundamental. This kind of turmoil in a central area of public administration has had an effect on quality of job performance and the condition of the public service.[58] The more essential point to consider is the vast uncertainty surrounding public personnel functions, triggered by political pressures from both Democratic and Republican presidents for different sorts of change. As basic concepts and their meanings continue to undergo a long-term process of redefinition and as new concerns command our attention, how public personnel administration will continue to unfold and develop is far from certain.

Summary

Public personnel administration has evolved from a fairly routine function of government to a very controversial one. Personnel practices have varied, reflecting at different times the values of strong executive leadership and political representativeness, on the one hand, and politically neutral competence on the other.

The public aspect reflects the impacts of other political institutions, including, legislative bodies, interest groups, and political parties. The size of government bureaucracies is a matter of concern to both citizens and personnel administrators alike, as is the competence and diversity of employee skills. The greatest increases in size have come in state and local governments, especially for education. Other changes have also occurred — related less to size than to scope of bureaucratic influence — through greater regulation, intergovernmental grant-in-aid activity, and expanded state and local bureaucracies.

Public personnel administration has evolved, at the national level, through a series of stages (from total exclusion of all but the most elite to the broad inclusion of all seeking admittance). These stages relate to changing values about government and administration. In many local governments, the organizational arrangements for personnel management are small, informal, or both. Greater attention to human resource development and professionalism is a relatively recent feature of bureaucracy that has implications for the general conduct of public administration. Similar developments have taken place, varying in extent, in state and local governments that have strong merit systems.

Merit versus patronage is an old debate that is still very much with us. Merit systems emphasize competence related to the job; patronage systems favor political connections and loyalties. Merit offers some continuity and stability in personnel; patronage permits a chief executive to select loyal subordinates. In practice, they often overlap. The formal arrangements of most merit systems are similar. In the national government, over 90 percent of all employees are covered by a merit system of some kind. There is great variation, however, in the extent of merit coverage in state and local governments.

Formal tasks of personnel administration include some traditional and some relatively new functions. Position classification is essential in order to conduct recruitment, administer a broad-gauged entrance examinations, and award equal pay for equal work. Recruitment, examination, and selection all have undergone considerable change. Recruitment has become both more systematic and less restricted. Examination processes are more complex at all levels of government. Achievement-oriented factors, such as education and experience, and ascriptive criteria, such as veterans' preference and demographic representativeness, have played a role in both examination and selection.

Compensation reflects the type of work being done and is comparable to that in the private sector for similar types of jobs. Salary and wage levels in the national government have increased dramatically but have lagged significantly behind those in the private sector for comparable positions, with adverse consequences for the public service. State and local government compensation tends to be lower than that in the national government though there are exceptions. Efforts to achieve pay comparability with private-sector jobs face formidable obstacles.

Public-sector collective bargaining has emerged as a major force in public personnel administration at all levels of government. Within a framework of labor–management relations, what has evolved is a pattern of unified employee organizations created to share control with management over terms and conditions of employment. Although similar to — and patterned after — collective bargaining in the private sector, bargaining in governmental arenas differs in a number of important respects. Various types of employee organizations — most prominently, public-employee unions — have become involved in collective bargaining.

The catalyst for change in public employee organizing was President John F. Kennedy's 1962 executive order permitting national government employees to organize and to bargain collectively with agency employers. State and local experience, though much more varied, has included major union gains in membership, extension of collective bargaining rights in both state and local governments, and greater frequency of public-employee strikes and other job actions. Most work stoppages have occurred in state and local governments. Unlike the situation in the national government, public-sector labor relations in states and localities still lack common legal (and political) definition. A trend has emerged toward comprehensive coverage of all state and local employees, and public managers have had to master new skills in meeting the challenge of collective bargaining.

Collective bargaining in the public sector has diverse impacts, for example, on wages and salaries, service delivery, and employee productivity. General implications of collective bargaining include higher personnel costs; reshaping of the overall personnel function in response to rising labor organization power; the need for public managers to be trained to participate effectively in negotiations with labor representatives, and, more generally, to develop better management practices; and expanded employee rights, solidarity, consciousness, and organizational participation. Developments in public personnel administration include civil service reform, the consequences of budget cuts, affirmative action, attempts to determine comparable worth, changes in patronage rules, and initiatives proposed by the NPR.

The CSRA was an attempt to reform the national government merit system by introducing performance appraisal systems and financial incentives for higher-quality performance and greater productivity. National government budget cuts have been felt in the personnel area in the form of limited entry, reductions in force (RIFs), "bumping" of employees to lower ranks, increased turnover, and pay freezes. Budget cuts generally (and RIFs, pay freezes, and personnel turnover, in particular) have seriously affected the management capacities of many national government agencies. Affirmative action programs have continued to produce gradual increases in the proportions of minorities and women holding responsible government positions. Partisanship, an old issue in personnel administration, has seen some changes recently. Patronage has been challenged successfully in a number of court cases. Efforts to expand the scope of permissible political activity for merit employees, which had been sought by some for a number of years, have succeeded.

Both the NPR and the Winter Commission examined position classification and pay issues at all levels of government. The reports called for significant change, though in somewhat different ways — consolidating (and thus reducing) the number of existing classifications but increasing pay ranges. The Volcker Commission called for numerous steps that would address negative perceptions of the public service, deal with managerial issues, strengthen public-sector education and training, increase pay and benefits, improve the work environment, reduce the number of political appointees hired, increase access to job openings, and reward executive excellence. Finally, the report of the NPR raises the prospect of monumental change in core areas of the national government's personnel management practices.

For several decades, public personnel administration and human resource development has been a dynamic, fluid, even turbulent area of public administration. The outlook is for more of the same. The next phase of personnel development is likely to involve a redefinition of *partnerships*, with more shared-governance arrangements. The role of professionals and the future of bureaucracy remain in flux.

KEY TERMS AND CONCEPTS

diversity
politically neutral competence
public personnel administration (PPA)
human resources development (HRD)
full-time equivalent (FTE) employees
nepotism
Civil Service (Pendleton) Act
egalitarianism
Brownlow Report
Second Hoover Commission
Senior Executive Service (SES)
achievement-oriented criteria
ascriptive criteria
Office of Personnel Management (OPM)
merit pay
General Schedule (GS)
Executive Schedule
position classification
broadbanding
Administrative Careers with America (ACWA)
rule of three
locality pay
collective bargaining

labor–management relations
multilateral bargaining
bilateral bargaining
Executive Order (EO) 10988
Federal Labor Relations Council
Federal Service Impasses Panel
Federal Mediation and Conciliation Service
Civil Service Reform Act of 1978
Federal Labor Relations Authority (FLRA)
impasse procedures
productivity bargaining
Professional Air Traffic Controllers Organization (PATCO)
job action
performance appraisal
EO 10925 (1961)
1964 Civil Rights Act
1972 Equal Employment Opportunity Act
Equity Pay Act of 1963
comparable worth
reverse discrimination
Proposition 209

SUGGESTED READING

Ban, Carolyn, and Norma Riccucci. *Public Personnel Management: Current Concerns, Future Challenges.* Reading, Mass.: Addison-Wesley, 1997.

Cayer, N. Joseph. *Public Personnel Administration in the United States.* 3rd ed. New York: St. Martin's, 1996.

Coleman, Charles J. *Managing Labor Relations in the Public Sector.* San Francisco: Jossey-Bass, 1990.

Dresang, Dennis L. *Public Personnel Management and Public Policy.* 3rd ed. Boston: Longman, 1998.

Farmham, David. *Managing People in the Public Service.* Basingstroke: Macmillian Business, 1996.

Freedman, Anne. *Patronage: An American Tradition.* Chicago: Nelson-Hall, 1993.

Hays, Steven W., and Richard Kearney, eds. *Public Personnel Administration: Problems and Prospects.* 3rd ed. Englewood Cliffs, N.J.: Prentice-Hall, 1995.

Huddleston, Mark, and William Boyer. *The Higher Civil Service in the United States.* Pittsburgh, Penn.: University of Pittsburgh Press, 1996.

Ingraham, Patricia W., and Barbara Romzek, eds. *Rethinking Public Personnel Systems.* San Francisco: Jossey-Bass, 1994.

Ingraham, Patricia W., Barbara Romzek, and Associates, eds. *New Paradigms for Government: Issues for the Changing Public Service.* San Francisco: Jossey-Bass, 1994.

Kearney, Richard C. *Labor Relations in the Public Sector.* 2nd ed. New York: Marcel Dekker, 1992.

Klingner, Donald, and John Nalbandian. *Public Personnel Management.* 4th ed. Englewood Cliffs, N.J.: Prentice-Hall, 1997.

Lewin, David, et al., eds. *Public Sector Labor Relations: Analysis and Readings.* 3rd ed. Lexington, Mass.: Lexington Books, 1988.

Mosher, Frederick C. *Democracy and the Public Service.* 2nd ed. New York: Oxford University Press, 1982.

Rabin, Jack, Thomas Vocino, W. Bartley Hildreth, and Gerald J. Miller, eds. *Handbook of Public Sector Labor Relations.* New York: Marcel Dekker, 1994.

Riley, Dennis D. *Public Personnel Administration.* New York: HarperCollins, 1993.

Risher, Howard, Charles H. Fay, et al. *New Strategies for Public Pay.* San Francisco: Jossey-Bass, 1997.

Rosenbloom, David H., ed. *Centenary Issues of the Pendleton Act of 1883: The Problematic Legacy of Civil Service Reform.* New York: Marcel Dekker, 1983.

Selden, Sally C. *The Promise of Representative Bureaucracy.* Armonk, N.Y.: A.E. Sharpe, 1997.

Shafritz, Jay M., Norma M. Riccucci, David H. Rosenbloom, and Albert C. Hyde. *Personnel Management in Government: Politics and Process.* 4th ed. New York: Marcel Dekker, 1991.

Spengler, Arthur W. *Collective Bargaining and Increased Competition for Resources in Local Government.* Westport, Conn.: Quorum Books, 1999.

Sylvia, Ronald. *Public Personnel Administration.* Belmont, Calif.: Wadsworth, 1994.

Thompson, Frank J., ed. *Classics of Public Personnel Policy.* 2nd ed. Oak Park, Ill.: Moore Publishing, 1990.

ON-LINE RESOURCES:
Public Personnel Administration and Human Resource Development

Administrative Careers with America (ACWA)

http://www.doi.gov/hrm/pmanager/st4k.html

A recruitment source and examination program for federal jobs available through the Office of Personnel Management (OPM).

American Federation of State, County, and Municipal Employees

http://www.afscme.org

Information on managing labor relations from the largest and most influential public employee union.

Commission on Civil Rights

http://www.usccr.gov

The United States Commission on Civil Rights (USCCR) is an independent, bipartisan, fact-finding agency of the executive branch, first established under the Civil Rights Act of 1957. On November 30, 1983, a new commission was established under the Civil Rights Act of 1983 (P.L. 98-183).

Federal Government Jobs

http://www.jobsfed.com

Listing of federal government jobs.

Federal Labor Relations Authority (FLRA)

http://www.flra.gov/index.html

An independent agency responsible for administration of labor management relations programs for 1.9 million federal employees worldwide; also strives to promote stable and constructive labor–management relations that contribute to efficient government.

Federal Mediation and Conciliation Service

http://www.fmcs.gov

Created by Congress in 1947 as an independent agency to promote sound and stable labor–management relations.

FEDWORLD Information Network (U.S. Department of Commerce, National Technical Information Service)

http://www.fedworld.gov

> From its federal job announcement search, you can browse more than 1,500 available U.S. government jobs, updated daily, affording the opportunity to begin a new career that you may not have known about otherwise.

National Commission on Pay Equity

http://www.feminist.com/fairpay/

> The National Committee on Pay Equity (NCPE), founded in 1979, is the national membership coalition of over 180 organizations including labor unions; women's civil rights organizations; religious, professional, educational and legal associations; commission on women; state and local pay equity coalitions; and individual women and men working to eliminate sex- and race-based wage discrimination and to achieve pay equity.

National Labor Management Association

http://www.nlma.org

> The National Labor Management Association (NLMA) is a national membership organization devoted to helping management and labor work together for constructive change.

Society for Human Resource Management (SHRM)

http://www.shrm.org/

> The SHRM provides education and information services, conferences and seminars, government and media representation, on-line services, and publications to more than 130,000 professional and student members throughout the world.

USAJOBS — United States Office of Personnel Management

http://www.usajobs.opm.gov/

> The federal government's official site for jobs and employment information provided by the Office of Personnel Management. To create a résumé for consideration for year 2000 compliance jobs, visit America's Talent Bank and access the job-seeker registration area.

U.S. National Labor Relations Board (NLRB)

http://www.nlrb.gov

> Independent regulatory agency that administers and enforces the National Labor Relations Act and provides useful information on labor unions and issues important to labor unions.

U.S. Office of Personnel Management

http://www.opm/html/topics.htm

Provides overall administration of the federal personnel system and Intergovernmental Personnel Act.

For further information on public personnel administration see:
Bedford/St. Martin's Home Page

http://www.bedfordstmartins.com

Chapter 9

<hr />

Government Budgeting

A billion here, a billion there, and pretty soon you're talking about real money!

Statement attributed to the late U.S. Senator
Everett McKinley Dirksen, Republican of Illinois

The mayor of a financially beleaguered city orders layoffs of some white-collar workers, police and fire personnel, and sanitation workers in a last-ditch effort to balance the budget. The governor of a midwestern state receives a report from the state comptroller that the state's cash accounts are getting dangerously low because of declining tax revenues and rising unemployment compensation and Medicaid costs. The president of the United States, intent on reducing bureaucratic activity, seeks substantial spending cuts — and wins congressional approval by the slimmest of margins. Department heads and bureau chiefs at all levels of government feverishly search for ways to cut back on projected spending levels — a step made necessary by a general fiscal crunch and political demands for more efficient program management. Legislators seek to satisfy their clientele groups by approving program spending, but they must cast a wary eye on a public growing restless with "big government."

In all these examples, *government budgets and budget processes* are at the core of both political and managerial controversies. Budgeting in the public sector is a process central to politics, particularly to administrative politics and the operation of government agencies and programs. It is the major formal mechanism through which necessary resources are obtained, distributed, spent, and monitored. Competition for a greater share of an ever-shrinking fiscal "pie" has always been keen, but never more so than in recent years. The size and shape of individual budgets, and the processes involved in proposing and approving them, are all changing rapidly, with unpredictable consequences for a variety of political interests and government programs.

A number of fiscal and other public policy functions can be served through budgeting, some or all of them simultaneously. At its simplest, a budget can be a device for counting and recording income and expenditures. It may not even be appropriate to label such a document a budget; perhaps *ledger* is more precise. Budgets, however, do include that information. Another function of budgeting is to generate a statement of financial intent constructed on the basis of anticipated income and expenditures.

A closely related function is to indicate programmatic *intent*, showing both preferences and — more important — priorities in deciding what to do with available funds. Budgets should also reflect the mission, or purpose, for a bureaucratic agency's existence. This suggests still another function of budgets, intentional or not: they reflect the political priorities of those who formulate them. In recent decades, the role of the budget in the national government's efforts to manage the economy has increased substantially; that is, many budget decisions are made and evaluated in terms of how they affect general economic growth, as well as specific economic and political interests and concerns.

One other purpose bears mention: controlling the bureaucracy and shaping agency programs. Legislators who cherish control of the purse strings often use that control to influence agency behavior. Ronald Reagan, from the very start of his presidency, used a comprehensive assault on the national government budget as the key to his attempt to reshape the national bureaucracy. Reagan demonstrated convincingly that the most direct way (if not always the easiest politically) to control an agency is to cut — or increase — its budget. Thus, chief executives who seek to direct bureaucratic operations have a strong and continuing interest in budgets and budget making.

The budget of any organization may be read as something of an index to relative distribution of power in the economic and political systems in which the budget was enacted. When we examine how it was made up and what resources were distributed to which participants within that system, power relationships are revealed. This is true whether we are speaking of university decisions to allocate a certain amount for academic scholarships or more faculty or of state government appropriations for education, health care, transportation, or other priorities. Budgets represent decisions to spend money in certain ways in preference to others, and such decisions do not just happen. They are made through a political process in which power and persuasion are crucial to success.

Because the outcomes of budgetary decision making are so important to all participants and beneficiaries, the formal nature of the decision process has long been central to budgetary politics. Throughout much of our history, decisions about public spending could best be characterized as *incremental*, following the model described in Chapter 6. Changes in annual spending from one year (or *biennium* — a two-year period) to the next — and in the policies such spending supported — tended to be gradual. Much of the status quo was simply assumed

entitlements
government programs
(mainly for individuals)
created under legislation
that defines eligibility
standards, but places no
limit on total budget
authority; the level of
outlays is determined
solely by the number of
eligible persons who apply
for authorized benefits,
under existing law.

**mandatory or direct
spending**   a category of
outlays from budget
authority provided in laws
other than appropriations
acts, for entitlements and
budget authority for food
stamps.

discretionary spending
a category of budget
authority that comprises
budgetary resources
(except those provided
to fund direct-spending
programs) in appropria-
tions acts.

**Congressional Budget
Office (CBO)**   created
in 1974; the budget and
financial planning division
of the U.S. Congress. See
**Congressional Budget
and Impoundment
Control Act of 1974.**

deficit   the amount by
which governmental out-
lays exceed governmental
receipts in a fiscal year.

**Gramm–Rudman–Holl-
ings Act**   the informal
title of the Balanced Budget and Emergency Deficit
Control Act of 1985, which
mandated steadily decreasing national government
annual budget deficits
through fiscal year 1991.

to be beyond questioning; how much more should be allocated was a common theme, and a key focus of budget processes.

In recent decades, however, the incremental decision model has had *decreasing* applicability in explaining how budgets are proposed and enacted. In the 1960s, efforts were mounted (though with limited success) to make budgeting more "rational," through reducing the influence of politics as usual and strengthening the role of policy evaluation in long-range planning, in hopes of increasing programmatic effectiveness. The 1970s saw another change: the emergence of legislative formulas as the basis for allocating larger amounts of funds in greater numbers of programs. Spending increased on a formula basis as the number of those eligible for particular government benefits rose (Chapter 4). Such programs have become known as **entitlements,** that is, "legal obligations created through legislation that require the payment of benefits to any person or unit of government that meets the eligibility requirements established by law."[1] Nearly two-thirds of the federal budget is now devoted to such entitlements as Social Security, Medicare, and veterans' benefits. This **mandatory or direct spending** — that is, spending required under existing law — has reduced Congress's ability to influence the overall budget without changing the law that originally authorized the spending. The range of budgetary choices available after all mandatory allocations have been made is termed **discretionary spending;** this now constitutes a far smaller proportion of the total budget than it used to — about one-third. The net effect of these changes has been to drive up overall government spending.

The 1970s also saw the rise of a new congressional budget process that was designed to enhance Congress's ability to monitor expenditures under the direction of its new budget committees (one in each chamber). The new process was also designed to enable Congress to generate independent information concerning revenues, expenditures, and projected surpluses or deficits through the **Congressional Budget Office (CBO)** rather than relying on information furnished by the president's Office of Management and Budget (OMB). Almost inevitably, this new process has meant some increase in conflict between the president and Congress over budgetary matters. The 1980s, in turn, saw rising concern on the part of legislators and the public over continuing annual **deficits** in the national government budget, that is, the difference between what the government collects and what it spends. In 1985, Congress enacted the Emergency Deficit Reduction and Balanced Budget Act, commonly referred to as the **Gramm–Rudman–Hollings Act,** after its Senate sponsors. This act mandated steady reductions in annual budget deficits and, in many ways, became the focus of Congress's budget deliberations. A continuing issue during this period was the question of *which political interests* are best served by a given budgetary approach or emphasis. Both political parties claim credit for efforts to reduce budget deficits, but neither wants to antagonize groups impacted by budget cuts. Incrementalism has not disappeared as a consequence of these changes, but budgetary decision making is far more complex and unpredictable than it was in the past.

We will discuss the impacts and implications of these developments later in this chapter.

Budgetary decisions and decision processes — and the changes in both — have been heavily influenced by their political environments.[2] In recent years, government budget makers have been confronted by growing pressures on revenue sources, calls for balanced budgets, demands for less deficit spending, and citizen resistance to increased taxes, especially at the state and local level. These combined to create pressures on all public budgets, making hard budgetary choices more necessary than ever. Today, government budgeting is widely understood as central to our political life. And it has become the object of a battle among choices that delineate the very role of government in our lives. Whereas, in past years, an underlying public consensus was said to exist about many governmental activities, that consensus has clearly eroded. Since the early 1980s, it has been replaced by a dissensus (or disagreement) reflecting sharp differences and intense conflicts over deficits, taxation, welfare, and military spending. As Wildavsky puts it, "politics is about grand questions: How much, what for, who pays; in sum, what side are you on?"[3] That dissensus was clearly evident during the summer and fall of 1995, following Republican victories in Congress, when considerable time, effort, and energy was spent in negotiations with the president over how to reduce the nation's annual budget deficits. One key development occurred when President Clinton was forced to make spending cuts as part of a deficit-reduction package. At last, after further negotiations at the budget "summit," a new proposal to eliminate the deficit over a seven-year period made its way to Capitol Hill, where it was approved (the third time in six years that such an agreement passed Congress). All this has had major impact on budget making; both the processes and the outcomes of budgetary decisions will continue to be affected in the immediate future. This is especially significant because of the extensive impacts government expenditures have on large segments of society.

Government Budgets and Fiscal Policy

Government budgets are increasingly viewed as instruments for managing national economies. Their impact depends on the relative significance of the public sector in the total economic picture and on the willingness of citizens to accept the authority of governments over the private sector as legitimate. Budgets can be regarded as instruments of **fiscal policy** aimed as "consciously influencing the economic life of a nation."[4] Different governments regard this potential budgetary role quite differently. Similarly, the extent to which national budgets in other countries are treated as tools of fiscal policy varies widely. In many European countries, for instance, the relative share of public resources collected and spent by government is much higher than in the United States (see Figure 9–1). Fiscal policy, as we use the term here, refers to government actions designed to develop and stabilize the private economy; they include: (1) taxation

fiscal policy refers to government actions aimed at development and stabilization of the private economy, including taxation and tax policy, expenditures, and management of the national debt. Monetary and credit controls are also related to fiscal policy.

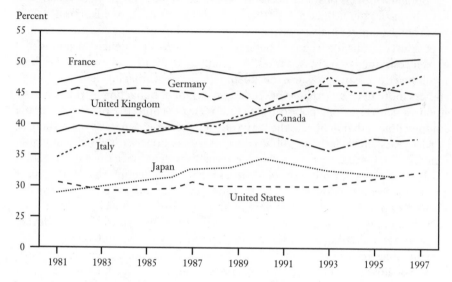

FIGURE 9–1   Revenues as a Percent of Gross Domestic Product (GDP) — Comparison with Other Countries

Source: Organization for Economic Cooperation and Development, calendar year data.

and tax policy, (2) direct budget expenditures, (3) management of the national debt, and (4) indirect tax expenditures. Related to fiscal policy — and, ideally, fully coordinated with it — are monetary and credit controls. We will examine these tools and relate them to the budget process. (Box 9–1, "The Budget: Mastering the Language," provides concise definitions of the basic vocabulary of budgeting at the national level.)

BOX 9–1   BACKGROUND BRIEFING

The Budget: Mastering the Language

The budget is the president's financial plan for the national government. It accounts for how government funds have been raised and spent, and it proposes financial policies for the coming *fiscal* year and beyond.

The budget discusses *receipts* (amounts the government expects to raise in taxes and other fees); *budget authority* (amounts that agencies are allowed to obligate or lend); and *outlays* (amounts actually paid out by the government in cash or checks during the year). Examples of outlays are funds spent to buy equipment or property, to meet the government's liability under a contract, or to pay employees' salaries.

The budget earmarks funds to cover two general kinds of spending. *Mandatory* spending covers *entitlement* programs (such as food stamps, Social Security, and agricultural subsidies) that may be used by anyone who meets eligibility criteria. Mandatory spending may not be limited in the appropriations process. *Discretionary* spending is set annually in the appropriations process.

The budget has a twofold purpose: to establish governmental priorities among programs, and to chart U.S. *fiscal policy,* which is the coordinated use of taxes and expenditures to affect the economy.

Congress adopts its version of the budget in the form of a *budget resolution.* This resolution, which is supposed to be adopted by April 15 of each year, sets Congress's overall goals for taxes and spending, broken down among major budget categories, or *functions* (the president's budget is similarly divided by function). An important step in congressional budgeting is the *reconciliation* procedure, when Congress enacts spending reductions and revenue increases (or both) in order to bring existing law into line with spending targets adopted in its budget resolution. Subsequently, if Congress is unable to pass a budget, or to approve major appropriations bills for executive-branch agencies, it may adopt *continuing resolutions,* which authorize expenditures at the same levels as in the previous fiscal year, until formal action is completed on the budget or appropriations.

An *authorization* is an act of Congress that establishes government programs, defines their scope, and sets a ceiling for how much can be spent on them. Authorizations do not actually spend the money. In the case of authority to enter contractual obligations, however, Congress authorizes the administration to make firm commitments for which funds later must be provided. Congress also occasionally includes mandatory spending requirements in an authorization, in order to ensure program spending at a certain level.

An *appropriation* provides money for programs within the limits established in authorizations. An appropriation may be for a single year, a specified period of years, or an indefinite time, according to the restrictions Congress wishes to place on spending for particular purposes.

Appropriations generally take the form of *budget authority,* which can differ from actual outlays. That is because, in practice, funds actually spent or obligated during a fiscal year may be drawn partly from budget authority conferred in that year, and partly from budget authority conferred in previous years.

Source: Adapted with permission from *Congressional Quarterly Weekly Report,* 43 (February 9, 1985).

FISCAL POLICY TOOLS

taxation   a primary
means by which govern-
ments raise revenues for
public services; taxes can
be collected from individuals and corporations on
income (earned and un-
earned), profits, property
value, sales, and services.

The primary tool of fiscal policy is **taxation,** which has traditionally been viewed simply as a means of raising government revenue. For the past fifty years, however, *taxation and tax policy* have also been used to influence the volume of spending by private citizens and organizations. Raising taxes has at times been a weapon against inflationary spending because it reduces the amount of disposable personal income; conversely, reducing taxes has been viewed as one means of boosting consumer spending. Such policy was relatively clear-cut until the recent wave of worldwide inflation-recession, which seemed to violate the economic principle that either inflation or recession might occur but not both at once. Reducing taxes, for example, to "spend our way out of a recession" works very nicely, assuming that such spending doesn't trigger increased inflation. But, if any significant increase in spending is inflationary, the old rules don't work anymore. The uncertain condition of the national (and world) economy has raised new questions about how to use tax policy as an instrument of economic management.

As with tax policy, there has been a fundamental change in attitude toward government *expenditures.* The traditional view has been that, as governments spent money, the sums expended replaced private-sector spending, representing a "last-resort" action when the private sector could not carry on whatever activities the money paid for. Now, however, the government's spending practices are seen as an essential part of total spending for goods and services and as having major "pump-priming" effect on private-sector expenditures. That is not surprising, considering, for example, that the national government budget exceeds $1.8 trillion in expenditures for fiscal 2001.

Programs funded by these taxes can have a major influence on local communities. For example, governmental decisions to close or not to close several large military installations in the early 1990s carried with them crucial economic implications for regional economies. When these installations were first opened, they pumped millions of new dollars into the local (and state) economies. A multiplier, or *ripple effect*, prevailed — sales and rentals of housing were brisk; retail and wholesale business was up; there was a sharp rise in demand for goods and services of all kinds. This had the effect of increasing tax revenues in all taxing jurisdictions (both state and local) and, in general, strengthening the localities' financial bases because of new jobs created and increased population. The outcry from local politicians and civic leaders, state officials, and members of Congress from the affected areas was ample testimony that they understood what the negative ripple effect would be when the installations were closed. (Despite intense protests, pressures on Congress, and the filing of a lawsuit in the U.S. Supreme Court, the base closures were upheld in 1994.)

A third fiscal policy tool is *management of the national debt.* Sale of government bonds and other obligations took on fiscal policy overtones for the first time during World War II, when the sale of war bonds was touted as another means of holding down consumer spending for scarce goods and services. In selling bonds, "a government changes the composition of privately held assets — converts private assets from money to bonds."[5] This has an indirect impact on the amount and composition of private holdings and on income and spending rates.

Furthermore, in recent years, government borrowing and public debt have become major political issues. When President Reagan took office in 1981, the national debt was just under $1 trillion ($1000 billion); by fiscal 1996, it was over *$5 trillion* — an imposing figure, though some say it should be of less concern because most of the government's creditors are U.S. citizens, banks, and businesses. More important than the size of the debt itself (at least in the short run) is the annual cost of *interest* that must be paid on the difference between how much the government collects and how much it spends. This figure is referred to as the budget deficit. An encouraging result of the deficit-reduction agreements reached by Congress and the Clinton White House in the mid-1990s is that the federal budget deficit as a percentage of **gross national product (GNP)** is lower in the late 1990s than it was in the early 1980s.[6] In light of such figures, political leaders continue to reduce government spending (usually in someone else's district!) in the struggle to balance the national government budget. Both the Congress and President Clinton claimed credit during the 1996 presidential and 1998 Congressional campaigns for fulfilling a 1992 promise to reduce the budget deficit by 40 percent to under $150 billion by FY 1997.

In state and local government, debt management is similarly complex if only because many state constitutions require both state and local governments to operate with *balanced budgets*. Nevertheless, most states and localities have extensive **bonded indebtedness,** meaning that they issue interest-bearing bonds, generally free from federal taxation, to raise funds for specific stated purposes. They must manage the debts they owe to holders of those bonds over the lifetime of the bonds — paying interest on schedule and at the rate stipulated, and redeeming the bonds at agreed-on times. Several larger, older cities (such as New York and Cleveland in the 1970s, Detroit in the early 1980s, and Miami in the 1990s) as well as newer, more affluent jurisdictions, such as Orange County, California, experienced difficulties in meeting their financial obligations. This suggests that problems of debt management may become more severe for all governments in the near future. The problem may become especially acute in the late 1990s as a result of continued devolutions of large federal programs, such as Aid to Families with Dependent Children (AFDC), and reductions in intergovernmental aid (see Chapter 4).

Another less visible fiscal policy tool of increasing importance for all governments is **tax expenditure financing,** the practice of giving favorable tax breaks or creating "loopholes" for certain kinds of spending by individuals, nonprofit institutions, religious organizations, professional sports franchises, and corporate enterprises. For example, the national government permits income tax deductions for interest expenditures on home mortgages, to mention one of the most common. Businesses may receive substantial tax credits if they invest in

gross national product (GNP) the sum of goods and services produced by the economy, including personal consumption, private investments, and government spending.

bonded indebtedness revenue-raising tool for governments to issue notes or promises to pay a certain amount (principal) at a certain time (maturity date) at a particular rate of interest.

tax expenditure financing revenue losses from provisions in the federal, state, or local tax codes that allow a special exclusion, exemption, or deduction from gross income or that provide a special tax credit, preferential rate of tax, or a deferral of tax liability.

purchases of new equipment or hire new workers from designated "empower-ment zones"; the oil industry, in particular, benefits from exemptions related to drilling for new sources of oil and natural gas. Local governments do not collect property taxes on land and buildings owned by colleges, universities, churches or synagogues. In 1997, Bill Clinton proposed tax credits of up to $1,500 for stu-dents attending community colleges and up to $10,000 for college and university expenses. In maintaining such tax incentives for special interests, the govern-ment must balance revenues lost against broader social purposes or probable gains in private-sector expenditures, along with the tax benefits realized by all levels of government as a result of increased private-sector activity.

MONETARY AND CREDIT CONTROLS

Federal Reserve System an independent board that serves as the central bank of the United States. The "Fed" adminis-ters banking, credit, and monetary policies and controls the supply of money available to member banks.

money supply the amount of money available to individuals and institu-tions in society.

Monetary controls are ordinarily exercised in two principal forms by national and state governments. First, the Board of Governors of the **Federal Reserve System** regulates the supply of money released into circulation. Restricting the **money supply** has been used to restrain inflation; increasing the supply, to stim-ulate economic activity. This function of "the Fed" is carried on outside the direct control of the president; he appoints its members but does not have com-mand authority over their decisions.[7] Second, interest rates charged by lending institutions are subject to regulation by the states, and, as we have seen in recent times, the prime lending rates that banks make available to their prime borrow-ers influence business investment, new home construction, and financing of home mortgages. In somewhat different ways, government loan programs (tech-nically different from the controls just described) make a crucial difference in a wide range of activities, such as disaster loans for flood victims and VA or FHA loans for buying or building a house. Loans are controlled in part by the bud-getary process in the form of initial appropriations and yearly expenses to con-tinue operation of loan programs. Even small changes in the cost of borrowing money can have major impacts on business, families, and individuals seeking to provide or upgrade housing, create or expand business, or sell property or assets. Furthermore, loan guarantees have become increasingly important for a broader segment of societal interests.

ECONOMIC COORDINATION

Council of Economic Advisors (CEA) the president's chief advisory and research source for economic advice. Consists of three economists (one appointed as chair) and assists the White House in preparing various economic reports.

Underlying all government activity to influence the private economy is the pub-lic acceptance or *legitimacy*, in principle, of that activity. The national govern-ment's role in this respect gained wide — although far from universal — acceptance during the Great Depression years and afterward, in a period marked particularly by passage of the Employment Act of 1946 to combat the postwar recession. This act made promoting maximum employment, production, and purchasing power an ongoing governmental commitment. In addition, the act established the president's **Council of Economic Advisors (CEA),** discussed in

Chapter 1. These steps were important both in themselves and as indicators of likely governmental responses to subsequent economic crises.

Central economic coordination has come to mean a dominant role for the president both in determining the existence of crisis conditions and in directing governmental responses. One of the most significant steps in this respect during the last thirty years was enactment of the Economic Stabilization Act of 1970, the statutory basis for Richard Nixon's move in August 1971 to impose a ninety-day freeze on prices, rents, wages, and salaries. This intricate and comprehensive program marked "a watershed in economic policy, placing the [national] government *in direct control of the economy*, as distinguished from the more indirect methods utilized in fiscal and monetary policy."[8] Although the president's authority under that specific act lapsed later in the 1970s, a precedent has been set for future chief executives to use.

Even with all these powers at the president's disposal, however, there is still some question as to whether presidential coordination can be truly effective. One influential observer has suggested that although we expect the president to influence the economy significantly, "he lacks the tools to manage its performance in all but the most indirect and crude fashion."[9] Still, the president's role in this area has expanded greatly in the last fifty years.

The Reagan, Bush, and Clinton presidencies gave rise to three important issues concerning the relationship between government activity and the national economy. One is the role of government spending as an economic stimulus. Since the 1930s, prevailing economic doctrines assumed that government played an important role in periods of economic downturn because of its ability to spark demand for goods and services produced in the private economy. Moreover, since the late 1960s, stimulating private-sector activity has been a consistent and deliberate budgetary objective, regardless of economic cycles, and has become a generally accepted part of the national government's overall economic role. President Reagan's determination to limit government spending (without regard, some maintain, to the adverse economic consequences), clearly led to a reassessment of this aspect of government budgeting.

A second issue is the economic impact of continuing budget deficits, which has raised the very real fear that deficits, if left unchecked, will hamper economic recovery and perhaps trigger new cycles of inflation and recession. Closely related is the concern that the government's need to borrow money from private lenders will crowd others seeking credit out of the market. Among President Clinton's major legislative achievements have been the budget deficit agreements of 1995 and 1997, which pledged the executive and Congress to make the cuts necessary to reach a balanced budget by the year 2002. These targets were actually reached two years earlier, in 2000.

The third issue concerns the economy's performance and its impact on government budgets and electoral politics. As unemployment increases, government spending must also rise (for unemployment compensation and other entitlements) at the same time that revenues from sales and income tax receipts usually decrease. Those patterns have always existed. Now, however, instead of the 3 or 4 percent unemployment that existed thirty years ago (constituting what most economists regarded as full employment), contemporary unemployment levels have held fairly steady at 5 to 7 percent. Furthermore, there is reason to believe that these levels are the new norm — that because more people (such as working women) are entering the workforce and because of basic changes in the kinds of jobs available (more lower-paid service positions and fewer industrial jobs). Higher levels of "structural" unemployment resulting from permanent loss of jobs in certain sectors of the economy, such as automobile manufacturing and consumer electronics will be more difficult to deal with. In turn, as a result of larger government payments for unemployment compensation (and perhaps other entitlements) and decreased tax revenue, reducing budget deficits will be more difficult. Regardless of how this problem is addressed, it seems clear that the rules of the game in coping with budget deficits have changed in the context of overall economic and fiscal policy. The consistent economic policies of the Clinton administration, relatively low inflation rates, and a growing economy, helped create over 20 million new jobs from 1992 to 1999. Although they lack direct controls to influence the future direction of the economy, incumbent presidents are nonetheless held accountable for its success or failure.

In sum, we now have not only a "mixed" public and private economy in which both sectors overlap considerably but also the availability set of abroad of economic controls to the national government, with vast potential for decisively influencing virtually every kind of economic activity. At the same time, the kinds of problems confronting government have changed, making economic coordination and stimulation more difficult.

LINKS TO GOVERNMENT BUDGETING

Budgetary decisions are connected to all government attempts to influence the national and regional economies. At the same time, debt management and monetary and credit controls have only incidental relationship to the budgetary process — debt management in that debates over budget allocations may hinge in part on whether adequate revenues are available to finance proposed programs without increasing the debt, and monetary and credit controls in that appropriations are needed to pay expenses of ongoing loan programs. Of much more direct consequence to budgeting are tax policy, expenditures, the power of interest groups to create and maintain tax "loopholes," and economic coordination.

House Ways and Means Committee the primary committee in Congress concerned with taxation and fiscal policy.

Senate Finance Committee the principal Senate committee concerned with revenue generation, taxation, and the operations of the Internal Revenue Service (IRS).

Tax policy obviously influences how much revenue is available for government programs. Tax decisions, however, are normally made outside the direct focus of budget making and involve a different set of participants, both on Capitol Hill — the **House Ways and Means Committee** and the **Senate Finance Committee,** primarily — and in the executive branch. Tax policy, although significant, lacked any direct relation to the national government's budget until the mid-1970s.

Expenditure policy *is* budget making when all is said and done. The effects of spending decisions on national, state, and local economies can be dramatic — as in the case of closing government installations — or hardly visible. But large or small individually, their cumulative consequences act to shape or reshape economic activity in significant ways. In sum, the national government budget is as important for its effects on the nation's economy as for its effects on the operations of government agencies funded through direct budgetary allocations.

The Clinton "investment" strategy, which the president emphasized in his 1992 election campaign, was reflected to some extent in the fiscal year (FY) 1997 budget proposals put forward by the president. The budget included more money for education, environmental protection, job training, technology, and public works. At the same time, only marginal cuts were made in entitlement programs, such as Social Security, Medicare, and Medicaid. All these expenditure categories clearly involve some potential impact on the private economy in either the short or long term and possibly both. *How much* impact and *on whose interests*, however, is another question, one that has always aroused considerable debate whenever any president has presented an annual budget to the Congress.

Finally, economic coordination in the broad sense is tied closely to budget making because the budget is a major instrument of the government's — especially presidential — economic policies. The budget is related to economic coordination not only because it reflects chosen courses of action in existing fiscal policy but also because it can be a major battleground in determining the shape of that policy and, consequently, economic activity in both public and private sectors. This is why the budgetary process is subject to so much political conflict: *control over the content of budgets means the ability to allocate resources to some and not others.* The president has at his disposal other means to use in economic coordination, but the budget remains an instrument of the highest importance.

Foundations of Modern Government Budgeting

Before the Civil War, budgeting was rather informal and routine at all levels of government. The national budget was fairly small, amounting to some $63 million in 1860, though it rose sharply during the Civil War and never returned to its former modest level.[10] The budgetary process was fragmented, with little systematic direction. Beginning with the presidency of Thomas Jefferson (1801–1809), agencies seeking funds had dealt mainly on their own with congressional committees having jurisdiction over their respective operations. The president had no authority to amend agency requests and no institutional means of influencing their formulation. Congress made its appropriations very detailed, both to control executive discretion to transfer funds from one appropriation account to another and to keep spending within the appropriations' limits.[11]

Starting with the Civil War, some important long-term changes began to affect numerous government practices, and the framework of a truly national economy slowly took shape. The war itself was a watershed in national–state relations, as well as in development of the presidency as a predominant force in national politics. During the 1870s and later, three general patterns of government behavior became more prominent, with implications for the rise of the modern budgetary process.

The first of these was growth in the national government's authority to regulate the expanding industrial economy and to exercise the war power and related prerogatives in foreign affairs, in which the president's role especially was enhanced. At the same time, the tax power was used to a greater degree than ever before. The regulatory power represented government response to the industrial revolution and to the emergence of powerful private economic interests. The war power was exercised most visibly in the Civil War and in the Spanish-American War, and U.S. diplomatic involvement was on the rise as well. The tax power was expanded by a constitutional amendment in 1913 permitting a federal graduated income tax.

The second pattern — government involvement in the private economy — meant more than simply regulating the flow of commerce. Starting in 1864, when the National Banking Act created a single, unified banking system as another step toward a national economy, the government's role in financial affairs became more regularized. Equally important, the way was paved for expanded government activity. In this century, this includes not only increasing regulation of private economic enterprise but also participation in planning and managing various public enterprises. Since 1933 and the New Deal era of Franklin Roosevelt, fiscal policy has been the predominant instrument of the national government in influencing the economy, one that presidents of both parties have not hesitated to use when it has suited their economic and political purposes. Because the consequences of these actions reach far beyond the government itself, it is not difficult to see how budgetary processes have grown in importance.

The third pattern was growth in presidential strength and influence, beginning in the last half of the nineteenth century and continuing to the present. The first enthusiastically activist president was Theodore Roosevelt (1901–1909). Others after him, notably his cousin Franklin Roosevelt (1933–1945), made even more dramatic and significant changes in the presidential role. Presidents Truman (1945–1953), Kennedy (1961–1963), Johnson (1963–1969), and Nixon (1969–1974) all actively supported expansion of presidential prerogatives, albeit for widely varying purposes. Dwight Eisenhower (1953–1961) — although not associated with an activist view of the office — presided over a fairly rapid expansion of the role of the executive branch generally, and he did little to roll back changes made before he took office. Action by Congress delegating discretionary authority to the president was a recurring feature of this century. Gerald Ford (1974–1977) and Jimmy Carter (1977–1981) exercised presidential prerogatives a bit more cautiously, in view of the public's negative reaction to Watergate, but the office itself remained very strong. Ronald Reagan (1981–1989), intent on reversing expansion of government's overall role, capitalized on the powers of the presidency in his quest to reduce that role — a major change for a "strong" president. George Bush (1989–1993) was not as strong a president as Ronald Reagan, nor did he pursue as distinct or broad-ranging a policy agenda. President Bush was less decisive in his vision of spending priorities than either President Reagan or Clinton (1993–2001).

Taken together, these three patterns had several important consequences in the development of modern budgetary practice. First, they raised the stakes of budgetary decision making by increasing the scope and economic impact of such decisions, and their effect on political interests as well. Second, they created both the possibility and the necessity of effectively coordinating scattered spending activities of the national government — possibility because of the growing capabilities of the presidential office, and necessity because expenditures were rising and some centralization of control seemed appropriate. Third, they prompted the first stirrings of budgetary reform in the early 1900s. Primary among these was the concept of the **executive budget,** with the chief executive placed in charge of developing and coordinating budget proposals for the entire executive branch prior to their presentation to the legislature.

executive budget
the budget prepared by the chief executive and the central budget office for submission to the legislature for analysis, consideration, review, change, and enactment.

Budget Approaches in the Executive Branch

The growing importance of the executive budget has been a hallmark of American national politics in this century. As the national government budget became an instrument of economic policy, it became steadily more important to have a central budget mechanism that could respond to changing economic conditions and needs. Various efforts at reforming the executive budget have been made. Budget reform, in fact, has been a recurrent theme, stressing, at first, control of budget expenditures, then performance measures aimed at rational procedures to improve management and, more recently, deficit reduction to achieve a balanced federal budget.

LINE-ITEM BUDGETING

The first actions for budget reform were taken at the local level as part of a larger movement for general reform of local government, including the drive to establish the city-manager form of government.[12] By the mid-1920s, most major American cities had adopted some form of budgeting system, in most cases, strengthening the chief executive's budgetary role. At the state level, a strong movement for reform was under way between 1910 and 1920, centering on making "the executive accountable by first giving him authority over the executive branch."[13] By 1920, budget reform had occurred to some extent in forty-four of the then forty-eight states and, by 1929, all the states had central budget offices.

Throughout this same period, action was also being taken at the national level, triggered by President William Howard Taft (1909–1913), whose **Commission on Economy and Efficiency** was established in 1909 and made its final report to the president three years later. That report recommended that a budgetary process be instituted under the direction of the president, a proposal greeted with considerable skepticism by those who feared any such grant of authority to the chief executive. Among these was Woodrow Wilson (1913–1921), who, as president, vetoed legislation in 1920 that would have set up a Bureau of the Budget in the executive branch and a General Accounting Office as an arm of Congress. One year later, President Warren Harding (1921–1923) signed virtually identical legislation into law, and a formalized federal executive budget system was instituted. The 1921 act vested in the president exclusive authority to consolidate agency budget requests and to present an overall recommendation to Congress.

The central purpose in all these developments was *control of expenditures*, with emphasis on accounting for all money spent in public programs. **Line-item budgeting** was the first modern budget concept to gain acceptance, and it remained the predominant approach to budgeting through the 1930s. In this period, budgets were constructed on a *line-item*, or *object-of-expenditure*, basis, indicating very specifically items or services purchased and their costs. The emphasis was on *control* — that is, detailed itemization of expenses, central supervision of purchasing and hiring practices, and close monitoring of agency spending. The focus was on *how much* each agency acquired and spent, with an eye to completeness and honesty in fiscal accounting.

PERFORMANCE BUDGETING

The next broad phase of reform involved a conceptual change and further structural adjustment. Beginning with the New Deal, when management of national programs became centrally important, the line-item budget was partially replaced by performance budgeting. Performance budgeting differed from the previous control orientation in several ways. First, it was directed toward promoting effective management. Second, it dealt not only with the quantity of resources each agency acquired but also with what was done with those resources. Third, it called for redesigning expenditure accounts, developing work and cost measures, and making adjustments in the roles of central budgeters and in their relationships with the agencies.

Performance budgeting demanded a greater degree of centralized coordination and control. In that connection, the Bureau of the Budget (BOB) was transferred from the Treasury Department, where it had been lodged by the Budgeting and Accounting Act of 1921, to the newly established Executive

---

Commission on Economy and Efficiency established in 1909 by President William Howard Taft (1909–1913); recommended that a national budgetary process be instituted under direction of the president.

---

line-item budgeting the earliest approach to modern executive budget making, emphasizing control of expenditures through careful accounting for all money spent in public programs; facilitated central control of purchasing and hiring, and completeness and honesty in fiscal accounting.

---

performance budgeting an approach to modern executive budget making that gained currency in the 1930s and then again in the 1950s, emphasizing not only resources acquired by an agency but also what it did with them; geared to promoting effective management of government programs in a time of growing programmatic complexity.

Office of the President (EOP) in 1939. (The EOP was itself a product of the movement for consolidation of executive control over administrative activities.) Ironically, under performance budgeting procedures, control and planning functions were dispersed to agency heads rather than being retained in BOB. Alleged agency failures to maintain control and to plan adequately for future activities later led to proposals for centralization of these functions within BOB.

During the performance budgeting era, which spanned approximately twenty years (1939-1960), a number of noteworthy developments contributed to more systematic executive budget making. First, during World War II, both presidential powers and the scope of the national budget expanded markedly — roughly eleven times between 1940 and 1946. As in the period after the Civil War, the budget total dropped sharply from its wartime peak but remained substantially higher than prewar levels. Second, enactment of the Employment Act of 1946, discussed previously, signaled government intent to utilize fiscal policy and economic planning to an unprecedented degree. A third development was the report of the **First Hoover Commission** to President Truman in 1949 on improving government management practices. The report made clear that performance budgeting was preferable to line-item budgeting because it indicated more clearly what agencies were actually doing. The report also recommended expansion of BOB's role in budget and management coordination, again emphasizing growing presidential influence in both aspects of administrative operations.

In 1950, Congress passed the Budget and Accounting Procedures Act, which mandated performance budgeting for the entire national government. Aimed at developing workload and unit-cost measures of activities, it appeared to do much more than simply control and record aggregate expenditures. But, as it turned out, although performance budgeting was very good at measuring efficiency of government programs, it did little or nothing to measure effectiveness. "The efficiency of a school district, for instance, might be measured in terms of the cost per student, but the effectiveness might be measured by whether graduates can read and write, are accepted into universities, or obtain and retain well-paying jobs."[14] The difference is between assessing the efficiency of programs in terms of their internal operations and assessing their effectiveness in terms of impacts of program activities, end products, and results. For example, a school board or a group of citizens might wish to evaluate the local high school for *efficiency* by calculating the number of dollars spent per student or dollars per after-school activity, and so forth. But measures of a high school education's *effectiveness* would need to go beyond the question of dollars spent or square feet of space used or hours of time spent in study hall. Such measures would have to address what students actually learned and perhaps evaluate what was learned in light of larger objectives: Was the student college-bound, or on some other track? Was the subject matter relevant to the future needs of society? Thus, measures of efficiency and effectiveness — indeed, the rationales for measuring them at all — are very different and involve different concerns for the public manager.

First Hoover Commission (1947–1949) was chaired by former president Herbert Hoover and tried to reduce the number of federal agencies created during World War II; recommended an expansion of executive budgetary powers.

Planning-Programming-Budgeting: The Rise and Fall of "Rationality"

Planning-programming-budgeting (PPB) was an instrument of executive budgeting designed to alter processes, outcomes, and impacts of government budgeting in significant ways. As the label implies, it was aimed at improving the planning process in advance of program development and before budgetary allocations were made. It was designed to allow budget decisions to be made on the basis of previously formulated plans and was intended to make *programs,* not agencies, the central focus of budget making. It would, proponents promised, make it possible to relate budget decisions to broad national, state, or local goals. In the words of one observer, "the determination of public objectives and programs became the key budget function."[15] Put another way, PPB represented an effort to incorporate *rationality* in budgetary decision making in place of well-entrenched incrementalism. It not only facilitated assessments of agency resources and activities (as under line-item and performance budgeting) but also of the actual external effects of those activities. To accomplish that, it was necessary to create new information systems and, more important, to obtain new and objective information that would demonstrate on a firm factual basis which programs were most likely to achieve their objectives. This required greater attention to program analysis and evaluation (see Chapter 10). The emphasis of PPB was distinctly economic. Implementation depended on the presence in the bureaucracy and in BOB (later OMB) of individuals skilled in *economic analysis —* specifically, cost-benefit analysis of programs. Furthermore, in assessing consequences of budget decisions, advocates of PPB called for examination of their economic impacts on society.

One other aspect of PPB should also be noted. Although there is informed opinion to the contrary, it seems apparent that to make PPB work for the entire executive branch would require centralized control over composition of executive budget proposals, as well as over planning, determination, and evaluation of goals. This, in fact, was one of the arguments made in support of PPB, that it would bring some coherence, consistency, and rationality into a budget process said to be notably lacking in those characteristics. But depending on one's point of view, increased centralization could also be an argument against PPB.

Expectations ran high for PPB in its early stages, during the early and mid-1960s. Some thought it would reform budgeting in the national government so as to bring about greater rationality, less "politics," better and more informed decisions, and so on. But, for a variety of reasons, PPB failed to gain a permanent place in national budget making — perhaps because expectations were inflated or because PPB was flawed or because some of those who were to implement it actively resisted it and others were not sufficiently knowledgeable, experienced in planning and analysis, or motivated to make it work. Most likely, all these explanations have some validity.

There was one other major source of resistance to PPB for much of this period: Congress, especially the appropriations committees. Members of Congress, some of whom had spent years building up their contacts and their understanding and knowledge of agency budgets, were not favorably disposed toward a new budgeting system that, in their view, threatened to disrupt their channels of both information and influence. Even at its peak, budgets were not sent to Congress solely in the PPB format. Agencies and OMB were told to submit budgets in the old agency format as well as the new program format and to indicate where an individual expenditure proposal fit into each. More important, Congress did not change its appropriations practices to accommodate PPB. Also, Congress objected to the implication that it was up to the executive branch, by whatever method, to determine what the nation's programmatic goals were and what programs were needed to achieve those goals. Finally, a Congress in which political rationality and political consequences of spending were at least as important as economic, cost-effectiveness criteria; where simplifying complex budget choices was a way of life; and where consensus and compromise were preferred to direct conflict over choices was not a Congress likely to be very receptive to a budget system stressing economic "rationality."

By the mid-1970s, most budget watchers had concluded that PPB had not worked. Most agreed that PPB had had some impact on national budgeting but had not achieved its primary goal — "to recast [national] budgeting from a repetitive process for financing permanent bureaucracies into an instrument for deciding the purposes and programs of government."[16] Much of the PPB package may have been dismantled, but some components live on: (1) a basic focus on information, (2) concern with the impact of programs, (3) emphasis on goal definition, and (4) a planning perspective. Implementation of PPB went forward in several states and a number of local governments, many of which tried it in the wake of the national government experience. The actual impacts of PPB were a great deal more modest than some early claims for it. In the 1970s, other concerns began to emerge that drew attention away from PPB and toward different issues in the budgetary process.

ZERO-BASE BUDGETING

Activities of government came under increasing pressure in the 1970s for a combination of reasons. One reason was growing public restlessness about particular policy directions, such as the war in Vietnam, civil rights enforcement, and some regulatory activities of the national government. A second reason was the tightening fiscal crunch in which many governments — especially local governments — found themselves, necessitating a more careful choice among competing interests of what would be funded and what would not be. Third, there developed some feeling, reflected in opinion polls, that the public was not getting its money's worth from costly government programs and that a hard look was needed to judge what was working and what wasn't.

Problems of financing activities and evaluating their effectiveness are not confined to government; business and industry have also had to confront these issues. It is no accident that *zero-base budgeting (ZBB)* developed in industry during the same period, when some in government — notably state government — were installing elements of it there. Zero-base budgeting got its start at Texas Instruments, Inc., under the guidance of Peter Pyhrr, who later helped implement it in Georgia during the administration of Governor Jimmy Carter (1971-1975). It is from this base that ZBB was launched in about a dozen other states, numerous industries, some local governments, and the national government.[17]

Zero-base budgeting involved three basic procedural elements within each administrative entity. The first was identification of decision units, the lowest-level entities in a bureaucracy for which budgets are prepared — staffs, branches, programs, functions, even individual appropriations items. Second was analysis of these decision units and formulation of decision packages by an identifiable manager with authority to establish priorities and prepare budgets for all activities within the administrative entity. The analysis began with administrators providing estimates of agency output at various funding levels (for example, 80, 90, 100, and 110 percent of current amounts), and assessing the cost-effectiveness and efficiency of the unit; it then proceeded to formulation of decision packages by each administrator. The third procedural element was ranking of decision packages from highest to lowest priority. Higher-level agency officials next established priorities among all packages from all units, with the probable available funding in mind. The high-priority packages that could be funded within the probable total dollar allocation were then included in the agency budget request, and the others were dropped.

An important aspect of the process was that each manager prepared several different decision packages pertaining to the same set of activities to allow those conducting higher-level reviews to select from alternative sets of proposals for the same program or function. Packages received higher priority as their cost declined, assuming the same set of activities. In practice, ZBB did not project budgetary allocations at "zero" before analysis of activities was begun or reallocate funds on a large scale from some policy areas to others. In theory, it called for reexamining every item in the budget periodically — every one, two, or five years — but, realistically, such a schedule would not be workable because budget makers did not have the authority or the tools to conduct these examinations on a regular basis. Although regarded by some as a rational-comprehensive budgetary tool, the evidence suggests that ZBB was essentially a form of incremental (or *decremental*) budgeting.

RECENT PRESIDENTS AND GOVERNMENT BUDGETS

Led by OMB Director David Stockman, the Reagan administration attempted, early in 1981, to change what it saw as a pattern of "constituency-based" budget decisions, in the interest of creating (and sustaining) a "fiscal revolution" in the national government.[18] Viewing previous budgets as no more than an accumulation of claims on the national treasury made by allegedly greedy special interests, the administration did not hesitate to propose reductions in some strongly supported domestic programs. Also important were the administration's commitments to tax reduction and to balance the budget. These were viewed (according to "supply-side" economic theory) as essential to sparking new, noninflationary expansion of private economic activity, which, it was thought, would result in sustained economic growth and continued reductions in budget deficits. The president persuaded Congress to enact an across-the-board, three-year tax cut with considerable benefit to more affluent taxpayers — which was a continuing source of controversy — on the theory that this would create jobs. Central to "Reaganomics," as this policy was called, was a determination to reduce government spending, especially domestic spending. (Ironically, Bob Dole's 1996 campaign rested on essentially this same premise but was rejected — together with his other proposals — by a majority of voters.)

The "mix," or composition, of the annual budget was altered considerably during the early years of the Reagan presidency. There were major policy and budgetary successes (in that first year, for example, Congress voted to cut spending by $130 billion), which were tarnished only slightly by Stockman's frank admission, late in 1981, that there were few, if any, major differences between supply-side and trickle-down economics.[19] Defense spending was increased substantially; however, in virtually all other functional areas of discretionary domestic spending, budget reductions were vigorously pursued (and achieved). Among the more controversial patterns of budget cutting were efforts to limit health care payments, reduce social services program funding, freeze pay, and reduce pensions for government civilian employees, and cut back levels of national government aid to state and local governments.[20] Adding to the controversy were claims that these expenditure areas were being made to bear a disproportionate share of budget reductions, on the grounds that total nondefense discretionary spending (as opposed to mandatory spending) constitutes as little as 18 percent of the national government's annual budget.[21]

The Bush administration, however, undertook efforts that pointed in somewhat different directions from those of its predecessor. One was fulfilling a campaign pledge of deficit reduction; another was imposition of modest cuts in military spending; a third was a willingness to increase the number of domestic grant programs to states and localities (but not the constant-dollar amounts supporting those grants). Of course, the Bush administration was confronted with the entirely nonroutine expenditures associated with the Persian Gulf War and the savings and loan industry bailout, which cost more than $300 billion in so-called "off-budget" expenses.

The Clinton administration, as noted earlier, sought to emphasize budget priorities in education, job training, technology, and public works. But the president also has been concerned with crime, deficit reduction, drug treatment, the environment, training and better pay for military personnel, and canceling or postponing dozens of military weapons systems. The 1995 budget agreement mandating spending cuts has forced the president to deal with much tighter fiscal constraints than his predessors, so that proposed dollar reductions for Medicare, weapons systems, and public housing (among many others) are becoming more acceptable to budget makers. The president also proposed eliminating or consolidating several hundred grant programs, and making significant reductions in spending from both foreign affairs and agriculture.[22]

At this point, we can review and compare the major approaches of the last seventy years in executive budgeting. Table 9–1 presents key conceptual differences among line-item budgeting, performance budgeting, PPB, ZBB, the Reagan–Bush era, and Clinton eras characterized by top-down, results-oriented budgeting. It is significant that the broader scope of a budget device, the less its chances of full implementation. It is almost certain, however, that the search will go on for other tools that will enhance executive budget control.

The Process of Budget Making

The role of the executive branch, including central budget agencies and the multitude of operating agencies, is far from the whole story of budget making. In American governments, the essential power of the purse is universally vested in the legislative branch; this extends to the authority to levy taxes, determine spending levels, actually appropriate funds, monitor expenditure activities of executive agencies, and establish a wide variety of formulas by which more or less automatic spending decisions are mandated year after year. The rise of the executive budget has sparked frequent, often intense conflict between the two branches of government over definition of spending purposes and control of expenditures. As the budget has grown in importance as a tool of policy formulation, legislative–executive conflict has widened to include that dimension as well. Consequently, the role of legislatures has changed in recent years, serving only to complicate further the intricate interactions that take place in budgetary decision making.

We will examine the essentials of budget making, focusing primary attention on the national government, without overlooking state and local variations. One problem here is that less is known from systematic study about state and local budgeting, although research into that area has increased.[23] Of particular importance are reform of the congressional budget process, begun in 1974, and the emergence of deficit reduction as a top priority, with the Gramm–Rudman–Hollings Act of 1985 and Omnibus Budget Reconciliation Act of 1990 (the **Budget Enforcement Act**) at the center of those efforts. We will discuss essential features of budget making and then review more recent — and crucial — developments.

Budget Enforcement Act the informal title of the Omnibus Budget Reconciliation Act, signed into law on November 5, 1990; an extension of the Gramm–Rudman–Hollings Act requiring that all new spending be offset by either new taxes or reductions in expenditures; provided for a special five-year process for deficit reduction, made permanent changes in the congressional budget process, changed the treatment of Social Security revenues in the U.S. federal budget, and established limits on federal discretionary spending.

TABLE 9–1   Some Differences among Budgetary Concepts

Feature	Line-Item (1921–39)	Performance (1940–64)	PPB (1965–71)	MBO (1972–76)	ZBB (1977–80)	Top-Down Budgeting (1981–92)	Budgeting for Results (1993–Present)
Basic orientation	Control	Management	Planning	Management	Decision making	Control and attainment of a single, system-wide mission	Management
Scope	Inputs	Inputs and outputs	Inputs, outputs, effects, and alternatives	Inputs, outputs, and effects	Alternatives	Mission-specific inputs and mission-specific effects	Inputs and outputs; alternatives as they relate to optional delivery methods
Personnel skills	Accounting	Management	Economics and planning	Managerial "common sense"	Management and planning	Political, coordinative and knowledge relevant to the systemwide mission	Management, planning, and communications
Critical information	Objects of expenditures	Activities of agency	Purposes of agency	Program effectiveness	Purpose of program or agency	Does program or agency further the systemwide mission?	Activities of agency
Policy-making style	Incremental	Incremental	Systemic	Decentralized	Incremental and participatory	Systemic and aggressive	Incremental, participatory, and decentralized
Planning responsibility	Largely absent	Dispersed	Centralized	Comprehensive, but allocated	Decentralized	Centralized	Joint with central budget agency
Role of the budget agency	Fiscal propriety	Efficiency	Policy	Program effectiveness and efficiency	Policy prioritization	Attainment of a single system-wide mission	Assure accountability

SOURCE: From Nicholas Henry, *Public Administration and Public Affairs*, 7th ed., © 1999, p. 244. Adapted by permission of Prentice-Hall, Inc., Englewood Cliffs, N.J.

ESSENTIALS OF THE PROCESS

Nowhere does the fragmented nature of American political decision making have a greater impact on the complexity of the process than in budget making.[24] In addition to institutional conflict between the president and Congress, the House and Senate often treat legislation, including money bills, differently. Committees within the two chambers guard their respective jurisdictions and are sensitive to any perceived "invasion of their turf." In addition, revenue and spending bills are handled by different committees on both sides of Capitol Hill. Tax bills are handled by the House Ways and Means Committee (where all tax bills must originate) and the Senate Finance Committee; appropriations bills are dealt with by the respective appropriations committees. Only since the reforms of the mid-1970s, when Congress created independent (and potentially powerful) budget committees in each chamber, have institutional mechanisms of any sort existed on Capitol Hill for monitoring the relationship over time between revenues and expenditures. In sum, budget making in the national government (as in many states and localities) is characterized by both institutional and political fragmentation, opening the way for influence to be exerted at multiple points during the process — a system that virtually requires compromise as the ultimate basis for most budgetary decisions.

Most governments budget on an annual (twelve-month) or biennial (two-year) basis, though not all funds approved in a given year for expenditure are actually spent in that year. The budget covers a *fiscal year* rather than the calendar year that runs from January 1 to December 31; currently, the national government fiscal year runs from October 1 to September 30. (In state and local governments, the fiscal year begins most commonly on July 1.) Each stage of budget making is predominantly under the auspices of either the executive or legislative branch, though few functions in budgeting are exclusively the responsibility of either one.

Time frames of government budgets involve several elements worth noting. One is that, even though a government as a whole may budget on an annual basis, individual agencies within that government may be permitted an alternative arrangement, such as a three-year budget. Another, more important, element is the distinction between **budget obligations** (also referred to as *budget authority*) and actual outlays of funds. *Obligations* against the budget include orders placed, contracts awarded, services rendered, or other commitments made by government agencies during a given period, all of which will require expenditure of funds (**budget outlays**) during the same or some future period. The outlays themselves are expenditures within a given fiscal year, regardless of when the funds were obligated.[25] The significance of this distinction is that it implies *two separate budgets*, each with its own political and fiscal life. As much as one-third (sometimes more) of annual budget expenditures may support obligations from previous fiscal years. Budget planning and revenue requirements, among other things, are affected by this.

budget obligations orders placed, contracts awarded, services rendered, or other commitments made by government agencies during a given fiscal period that require expenditure of public funds during the same or some future period.

budget outlays agency expenditures during a given fiscal period, fulfilling budget obligations incurred during the same or a previous period.

Government budgets progress in their annual or biennial cycle through five broad stages. In sequence, they are (1) *preparation*, which is almost wholly internal to the executive branch; (2) *authorization*, principally a function of the legislature; (3) *appropriations*, a legislative function; (4) *execution* (implementation), mainly — but by no means entirely — an executive function; and (5) *audit*, carried out by both legislative and executive entities but ordinarily independently of one another. We will examine each stage in some detail, considering not only the essential procedures of each but also important concepts employed at different times. We will focus on the national government for illustrative purposes, although some similarities in the general mechanics can be found in many state and local governments.

OMB AND BUDGET PREPARATION

Preparation of the budget begins when OMB, having made some preliminary economic studies and fiscal projections, sends out a *call for estimates* to all executive agencies. This occurs some fifteen to nineteen months before the fiscal year in question begins — in late spring of the previous calendar year. The call for estimates is a request for agencies to assemble and forward to OMB their projections as to the funding they will need for ongoing and new programs in that fiscal year. This requires heads of agencies and of their subordinate units to develop program and fiscal data that make it possible to formulate an estimate of overall agency needs. This information is sent on to OMB, together with supporting memorandums and analytic studies, especially those relating to proposals for new or expanded programs.

Next, OMB calls on the *budget examiners;* each of 160 examiners is assigned on a continuing basis to an agency or agencies for the purpose of becoming thoroughly acquainted with agency activities and expenditure needs. These examiners, who are, in effect, OMB's field workers, hold hearings with agency representatives on programmatic, management, and budget questions. The agency's representatives normally include unit heads and agency budget officers, although others may be included. Whereas budget examiners work *with* agencies, they work *for* OMB; their job is to probe and question every major expenditure proposal that agency leaders regard as important enough to include in a budget estimate.

When this process is completed, the examiners make their recommendations to OMB. In the meantime, the director of OMB and the president work out general budget policy, major program issues, budgetary ceilings, and other fiscal projections, ultimately developing ceilings for each agency. The examiners' recommendations are incorporated into reviews of each agency's estimates and are often the basis for revision ordered by OMB. After a process that usually takes four to six months, original estimates are generally trimmed, and all agency requests are assembled into a single budget document running to several hundred pages. This becomes the draft of the president's budget message, which is submitted to Capitol Hill shortly after the first of the (calendar) year.

Part of the politics of budget making centers on interactions between each agency and the central budget office (OMB, a state bureau of the budget, or a city finance office). Because the central budget entity speaks and acts for the chief executive whereas operating agencies usually have markedly different priorities, a certain amount of tension between their budget priorities is inevitable. Considerable evidence suggests that deliberate strategies must be followed by agencies seeking to increase their allocations and that the preparation stage is an important opportunity for each to press its case.

AUTHORIZATIONS AND APPROPRIATIONS

The *authorization* stage has historically involved determination of maximum spending levels, or "caps," for each program approved by the legislative branch. This can occur during or apart from the formal budget process, and it is the responsibility of standing committees in each chamber such as the Senate Committee on Banking, Housing, and Urban Affairs, and the House Committee on Foreign Affairs. These permanent subject-matter committees make recommendations to the full chambers for the agencies under their respective jurisdictions. After chamber approval, a bill is normally considered by a conference committee, which irons out differences in the amounts authorized by each chamber. Assuming that agreement is reached (which is almost always the case), the authorization bills are forwarded to the chief executive for approval.

As noted earlier, authorizations may be enacted for expenditures in the same or subsequent years, making this step highly significant in terms of specific authorization provisions. Furthermore, depending on legislative politics, individual programs or agencies may be granted standing authorizations for funding — that is, open-ended authority for fiscal support subject only to yearly appropriations and without the need for reauthorization prior to appropriations action. That status signifies considerable influence in the legislature on the part of the agency or program so favored; it also weakens to some degree the control a chief executive can exercise over such an agency's fiscal and political fortunes.

One other point should be made about the authorization process. The majority of states, and almost all local governments, draw up their budgets without incorporating an authorization stage into their procedures. Thus, as a formal step in determining expenditures, authorization has its greatest role and influence in Congress. This reflects the less formalized budget procedures that exist in many states and localities, as well as the more extensive division of power (between standing committees and the appropriations committees) in Congress.

The *appropriations* stage is one of the most crucial to budget making. Appropriations, as distinct from authorizations, grant the money to spend or the power to incur financial obligations, and the appropriations committees in the two houses (of Congress and most state legislatures) play the major role in this phase of the budgetary process.[26] According to existing rules of procedure, no appropriation may be voted on until after an authorization has been approved for a particular program. But it has been known to happen otherwise. On one occasion, the House appropriated funds for development of the controversial neutron bomb — a weapon said to kill by radiation without destroying neighboring populations or property — before any formal authorization had been made. It was a bomb, some said, that nobody knew we had, and the appropriation had been buried in a $10.4-billion water, power, and energy research appropriation bill. This can work the other way around as well. That is, legislation authorizing a certain level of spending for an agency can include language mandating (ordering) that the agency spend this or that amount of money for specified purposes. As an example, a military authorization bill for weapons systems development may contain a provision directing the Pentagon to spend $125 million on research for medium-range missiles. When that happens, it virtually forces the House and Senate appropriations committees to approve that funding because the agency would be violating the law if it did not spend the money as directed. Not surprisingly, this practice, known as **backdoor financing,** is a source of considerable irritation to appropriations committee members (and many others). More important, backdoor financing eliminates discretionary decision-making control from the appropriations stage and forces anyone wishing to challenge such expenditures to seek to amend the authorization. That is often difficult to do politically; as a result, backdoor financing has had the effect of reducing control over the general level of expenditures.

backdoor financing the practice of eliminating discretionary decision-making control from the appropriations stage of the budgetary process.

One other feature of recent congressional behavior that has major implications for authorization and appropriation processes is the dramatic growth of so-called *entitlement* programs. Entitlement legislation places no limit on the total amount of budget authority for a program; eligibility standards are defined by law, and the level of outlays is determined solely by the number of eligible persons who apply for authorized benefits.[27] Thus, for example, Medicare, Social Security, and many veterans' benefits programs come under the heading of *entitlements.* Furthermore, many entitlements are indexed to the rate of inflation, with benefits rising as the cost of living goes up. The net effect of entitlements, and of indexing, has been to further reduce the year-to-year control Congress might exercise over the rate of growth — and the substantive purposes — of national government spending. Over 60 percent of current annual spending takes the form of entitlements, raising serious issues about controlling spending, and even whether spending is controllable, under existing law.

Backdoor financing and annual "off-budget" accounting procedures tend to mask trends in revenue and expenditure projections. In 1994, the **Bipartisan Commission on Entitlement and Tax Reform** projected that, unless major changes were made, entitlement expenditures, such as Social Security, Medicare, and interest on the national debt, would consume the *entire federal budget* by the year 2012.[28] These dire forecasts were largely ignored by the media, leaders of both political parties, Congress, and the president. Following the 1996 election,

Bipartisan Commission on Entitlement and Tax Reform projected in 1994 that major changes were necessary to prevent entitlement spending from consuming the entire federal budget by the year 2012.

however, President Clinton proposed the creation of yet another commission to study the issues surrounding the drain on federal resources expected from "baby boomers" retiring in the early twenty-first century.

PRESIDENT VERSUS CONGRESS: CONFLICT OVER AUTHORIZATIONS, APPROPRIATIONS, AND FISCAL CONTROL

As a consequence of the fragmentation in national budget making, the ability of any one institutional actor in the process to restrain effectively the growth of national government spending has grown progressively more limited. The political impacts of backdoor spending and entitlement programs include obstacles that must be cleared in order to address the fundamental issue of whether such programs should be continued. These questions obviously engage powerful and well-organized political interests at a very sensitive level. But the crucial point is that, unless a coalition of forces is willing even to raise the issue, thus confronting the collective wrath of those benefiting from the particular expenditure, it is difficult to stem the rise in expenditure levels.

Nowhere was the battle between president and Congress joined more vigorously or more significantly than in the fight over President Nixon's efforts to reduce spending by impounding (withholding) funds after they had been authorized and appropriated by Congress. **Impoundment,** unlike the formal veto power (see Chapter 7) is something of a "super item veto" and is not subject to a congressional override. Nixon was not the first president to impound funds. Indeed, the practice of establishing reserves or of administratively withholding spending authority from some programs dated back at least a century. Impoundment, Nixon-style, was a partisan process: funds for programs that had grown out of the Great Society of the Johnson years were targeted. Members of Congress, among others, condemned this practice in speeches and press releases. Some were moved to file suit against the president, claiming that impoundment was not authorized by the Constitution and that, although precedents existed, these were not constitutionally sanctioned. But Congress, growing increasingly impatient with lengthy court proceedings, acted early in 1974 to halt impoundment through legislation.

The **Congressional Budget and Impoundment Control Act of 1974** abolished an earlier limited authorization for a president to withhold funds. It also sharply curtailed permissible grounds for deferring spending of appropriated funds, required positive action by both House and Senate to sustain an impoundment beyond a period of forty-five days, demanded monthly reports from either the president or comptroller general (head of the General Accounting Office) on any deferred spending, and enabled the comptroller general to go to court for an order to spend impounded funds if a president failed to comply with any of the preceding regulations. These provisions seemingly restored a considerable measure of congressional control over appropriations and expenditures. Gerald Ford's subsequent impoundments were much less obstrusive than

impoundment in the context of the budgetary process, the practice by a chief executive of withholding final spending approval of funds appropriated by the legislature, in a bill already signed into law; may take the form of deferrals or rescissions; presidential authority to impound limited by Congress since 1974.

Congressional Budget and Impoundment Control Act of 1974 changed the congressional budget process and revised timetables for consideration of spending bills; created the Congressional Budget Office.

Richard Nixon's had been; and, in the wake of Watergate, Ford enjoyed high political standing and good support in Congress. With other developments in Congress's budgetary role, impoundment moved off center stage as a key question in legislative–executive relations.

CONGRESS'S NEW BUDGETARY ROLE

In the confrontation between President Nixon and Congress over impoundment, another crucial issue was dealt with: whether Congress had the institutional capacity to monitor its own actions in approving expenditures and to put a brake on rising spending totals. Some observers believe that the 1974 law was at least as important for the new congressional budgetary procedures it instituted as for the restrictions it established on presidential authority to impound funds.

The procedures previously followed (described earlier) left Congress open to the kinds of criticisms Richard Nixon had found effective in justifying greater presidential impoundment authority to control spending: fragmented consideration of and action on the budget, failure to consider financial implications of future expenditure obligations, willingness to enact supplemental appropriations (funds to cover expenses beyond original estimates), and so on.[29] In addition, two other factors have contributed to growing difficulties in maintaining control over, and accountability for, expenditures.

First, very often a subsystem alliance or "Iron Triangle" — consisting of program managers, interested subcommittee chairmen, and outside interest groups — united "to thwart the will of the President and of the Congress as a whole"[30] by effectively controlling the financing and administration of particular programs. Second, whereas, in the past, Congress had routinely cut requests the president made on behalf of the agencies, it gradually came to cut less, and less regularly, than it once had. Appropriations subcommittees, well known for assuming that "there is no budget that can't be cut," were becoming more likely merely to hold the line at the level requested by the president than to assume that cuts would or should be made. Also, many members of Congress displayed less willingness to defer to the judgments of specialized subcommittees and committees, whose spending recommendations were overturned with increasing frequency on the floor of the House and Senate — usually in favor of higher, not lower, amounts.

The combined effect of these changes was considerably higher appropriations levels in legislation passed by Congress. More important, there was a growing realization by observers in and out of Congress that little meaningful legislative control existed over the totality of the budget, with few legislators having any idea what "whole" was the end product of the "parts." The 1974 budget act represented a comprehensive attempt to deal with these problems. The new procedures mandated by the act can be analyzed in five segments.[31]

First, each chamber established a *budget committee* that would consider annual budgets in their entirety. Committee membership, particularly in the House, overlapped with membership on the Appropriations and Ways and Means committees (five from each of those committees serve on the House Budget Committee), thus ensuring some integration of effort among those three key entities.

Second, the act established the *Congressional Budget Office* (CBO), with a professional staff and a director appointed jointly for a four-year term by the Speaker of the House and the president pro tem of the Senate. The CBO was to assist the budget committees and Congress as a whole in analyzing and projecting from budgetary proposals. It was to serve both as a provider of "hard, practical economic and fiscal data from which to draft spending legislation," as the House wanted, and as something of a think tank with a more philosophical approach to spending and an interest in examining national priorities, thus satisfying the Senate. Whether the CBO has succeeded, or could have, in both endeavors is not clear. Some critics in Congress thought that the CBO should have been organized and functioning more rapidly and effectively than they say it was.

Third, the act established a procedure whereby Congress would enact at least two concurrent *budget resolutions* each year, one in the spring and the other in the fall, for purposes of setting maximum spending levels during the appropriations process. The spring resolution was to set targets for spending, revenue, public debt, and the annual surplus or deficit, and the fall resolution was to set the final figures for each.

Fourth, a *new timetable* was put into effect, with the fiscal year beginning on October 1 instead of July 1. Table 9–2 outlines this new congressional budgetary timetable, as it operated (with many problems, complications, and shortcomings) from 1975 to enactment of the Gramm–Rudman–Hollings legislation ten years later.

TABLE 9–2	Original Congressional Budget Timetable, 1975–1985

Action to Be Completed	On or Before
President submits annual budget message to Congress	15 days after Congress meets
Congressional committees make recommendations to budget committees	March 15
Congressional budget office reports to budget committees	April 1
Budget committees report first budget resolution	April 15
Congress passes first budget resolution	May 15
Legislative committees complete reporting of authorizing legislation	May 15
Congress passes all spending bills	Seven days after Labor Day
Congress passes second budget resolution	September 15
Congress passes budget reconciliation bill	September 25
Fiscal year begins	October 1

SOURCE: From Lance T. LeLoup, *Budgetary Politics*, 4th ed. Copyright © 1988 by King's Court Communications, Brunswick, Ohio. Reprinted by permission of King's Court Communications.

Fifth, the act *banned most new backdoor spending* programs, thus extending congressional control over the budget even further. However, because many such programs existed before 1974, backdoor spending has not been eliminated; on the contrary, program costs have increased.

A major factor in the early success of the new procedures was development by the CBO of cost analysis data, relating to proposed legislation, that were seen as objective, straightforward, and timely. These data helped to minimize the "budget-numbers games" that had characterized so much legislative bargaining among the administration, agencies, lobbyists, and Capitol Hill staff. There was some disagreement about CBO's data, but this new situation certainly was an improvement over the previously fluid one, in which whom to believe in forecasting or analysis was itself a major concern.

Another important factor was effective monitoring by both budget committees and the CBO of Congress's revenue and spending actions. Also, the budget committees — through their initial responsibility for projecting total revenues, the annual deficit, and the level of the national debt — could monitor broadgauge effects of individual committee and floor actions and duly inform the members.

Other factors included the severe recession of 1974–1975, which coincided with the backlash (in Congress and in the country) against presidential excesses and provided an opportunity for Congress to assert itself; general public concern over growth of government spending; partisan jockeying during an election year; provisions of the budget act that provided for adequate staff assistance, enforcement mechanisms for various deadlines in the new budget cycle, and structural coordination among key committees; the determined leadership of the House and Senate budget committee chairmen; and a great deal of plain hard work by budget committee members in both chambers.

The budget process encountered rougher going after the late 1970s, however. Many observers believe that, after a few good years, the usual patterns of diffused influence in Congress gradually reasserted themselves; members paid less attention to the need for restraint and more to their geographic and interest-group constituencies. Because the process challenged established practices in one of Congress's most essential functions — allocation of resources — it should come as no surprise that those practices were resistant to change. Also, political conditions prevailing in both House and Senate became increasingly unstable. President Reagan's vigorous pursuit of deep cuts in domestic spending amplified partisan liberal–conservative splits and intensified pressures on most members of Congress for attentiveness to special interests. Heightened tensions in Congress were a reflection, to some degrees, of the changes in the budgetary process in recent years.[32]

Other emerging difficulties in the congressional budget process included an increasing tendency for Congress to ignore — or simply not be able to carry out — a number of the most important functions in the process. One was meeting the chronological deadlines for enacting budget resolutions; beginning in the late 1970s, Congress missed its own deadlines as often as not. There were several reasons for this. For one, members of Congress needed to make judgments about the condition of the economy as part of their budget deliberations, and they sought as much information as possible before doing so. As we saw in Chapter 6, obtaining necessary information can require considerable time. Another reason was that many legislators often tried to postpone the tough political choices involved in budgetary decision making until the last possible moment — an often criticized but entirely understandable tendency. A second recurring problem was inaccurate projections of spending and revenue targets for a given fiscal year (an indication of the difficulty in making such projections eighteen months in advance). A third phenomenon, reflecting both mechanical and inherently political problems, was that several fiscal years began without a budget being enacted into law or, at least, without passage of major appropriations bills. When that happened, Congress simply authorized agency expenditures at the same levels as in the previous fiscal year until action was completed on the budget or on relevant appropriations legislation (this has been called, none too kindly, "government by 'continuing resolution'").[33] This pattern continued as Congress and the Clinton presidency battled to a standstill during 1994–1995.

THE BALANCED BUDGET AND EMERGENCY DEFICIT CONTROL ACT OF 1985 (GRAMM–RUDMAN–HOLLINGS)

Even with a new budget process credited by many observers with improving budget making in Washington, the national government's annual deficits grew larger. Pressures on Congress to take some action mounted accordingly. In December of 1985, Congress passed the Balanced Budget and Emergency Deficit Control Act of 1985, known as Gramm–Rudman–Hollings (GRH), which

> changed the Congressional Budget Act in several significant ways, and mandated a balanced budget by [FY] 1991. To get to a zero deficit in FY 1991, the new act specified reductions [of $36 billion a year] in the deficit beginning with FY 1986. If the appropriations bills failed to achieve the deficit target in any one year, across-the-board spending cuts would be made to eliminate the excess deficit.[34]

Gramm–Rudman–Hollings also provided that these cuts would fall equally on defense and nondefense programs and that the president had authority to suspend the cuts in a recession or during wartime. However, the legislation also provided that Congress could exempt some programs and expenditures from sequestration and, not surprisingly, a number (*quite* a number) of politically sensitive programs were exempted, including Social Security, veterans' compensation and pensions, the Medicaid program, interest on the national debt, Aid to Families with Dependent Children (AFDC), the Supplemental Security Income (SSI) program, food stamps, and child nutrition. The net effect of these exemptions was to remove nearly 75 *percent* of national government spending from the threat of sequestrations under GRH, leaving "program areas such as education, student loans, energy assistance, and defense to bear the brunt of the burden, in the absence of increased revenues."[35] This naturally raised questions about Congress's intentions — not to mention the statute's likely effectiveness!

Gramm–Rudman–Hollings designated the directors of OMB and CBO as key decision makers to determine the deficit outlook each fiscal year, and to recommend whether or not spending cuts would be needed. These cuts, as noted, would be made *only if* Congress failed to meet the specified deficit target before each fiscal year began on October 1. Under such circumstances, however, the president was to have the authority to sequester (impose spending cuts), in keeping with the report of the comptroller general.

In 1986, however, in the case of *Bowsher v. Synar* (106 S. Ct 3181, 92 L Ed. 2d, 583), the U.S. Supreme Court ruled that the role of the comptroller general in the **sequestration** process violated separation of powers — that an official responsible to Congress could not set the guidelines for the president to follow in sequestering funds. Congress remedied that problem in its 1987 amendments to the original bill, authorizing the director of OMB (with advisory recommendations from CBO) to determine whether sequestration would be necessary.

Gramm–Rudman–Hollings made some significant changes in the 1974 Congressional Budget Act by

1. Requiring Congress to approve the size of the deficit in each year's concurrent resolution;
2. Eliminating the second concurrent resolution entirely;
3. Advancing the deadline for congressional action on the concurrent resolution from May 15 to April 15;
4. Changing the deadline for completion of the **reconciliation process** from September 25 to June 15;
5. Placing "off-budget" government corporations "on budget" (thus including the operating surpluses or deficits of such in corporations in deficit-reduction calculations);
6. Placing two Social Security trust funds off budget for the first time; and
7. Incorporating loans and loan guarantees into the concurrent resolution, thus giving official standing to a credit budget (also for the first time).[36]

Reconciliation, referred to in item 4 above, involves making adjustments in existing law to achieve conformity with the annual spending targets adopted in the concurrent resolution. Those adjustments can be spending cuts, revenue boosts, or a combination of the two. The key step, following committee recommendations, is House and Senate action on an omnibus, or all-encompassing, reconciliation bill. When the GRH changes took effect, the timetable of the congressional budget process was also altered, as Table 9–3 indicates.

sequestration the withholding of budgetary resources provided by discretionary or direct spending legislation, following various procedures under the Gramm–Rudman–Hollings Act of 1985 and the Budget Enforcement Act of 1990; the withholding of budget authority, according to an established formula, up to the dollar amount that must be cut in order to meet the deficit-reduction target.

reconciliation process an important step in congressional budgeting, when Congress makes adjustments in existing laws to achieve conformity with annual spending targets adopted in each year's concurrent resolution; these adjustments can take the form of spending reductions, revenue increases, or both.

TABLE 9–3	Revised Congressional Budget Timetable, 1986–1990

Action	To Be Completed By
President submits budget	Monday after January 3
CBO report submitted to Congress	February 15
Committees submit Views and Estimates to budget committees	February 25
Senate Budget Committee reports budget resolution	April 1
Congress passes budget resolution	April 15
House Appropriations Committee reports appropriations bills	June 10
Congress passes reconciliation bill	June 15
House passes all appropriations bills	June 30
Initial economic, revenue, outlay, and deficit projections made by OMB and CBO	August 15
OMB and CBO report tentative contents of sequester order to GAO	August 20
GAO issues deficit and sequester report to the president*	August 25
President issues sequester order	September 1
Fiscal year begins and sequester order takes effect	October 1
OMB and CBO issue revised projections based on subsequent congressional action	October 5
GAO issues revised sequester report to president*	October 10
Final sequester order becomes effective	October 15
GAO issues compliance report on sequester order	November 15

*Role of the GAO in instructing the president to make budget cuts ruled unconstitutional in 1986.
SOURCE: From Lance T. LeLoup, *Budgetary Politics*, 4th ed. Copyright © 1988 by King's Court Communications, Brunswick, Ohio. Reprinted by permission of King's Court Communications.

Unfortunately, this effort was no more successful than the 1974 act. Legislative-executive gridlock on budget issues intensified as timetables were ignored, and deficit-reduction targets were moved back. Congress resisted across-the-board cuts and failed to relinquish control over distribution processes. In 1987, GRH was amended to revise deficit targets downward while postponing the deadline for achieving a balanced budget from FY 1991 to FY 1993. Some saw those decisions as realistic; others wondered if it was going to be possible truly to come to grips with the problem of continuing budget deficits. (It is not heartening to note that — in light of worsening deficits, deep political divisions over what to do about them, and little optimism that workable solutions were at hand — the 1985 deficit-reduction bill was described as "a bad idea whose time has come" by former New Hampshire Republican Senator Warren Rudman — one of the bill's cosponsors![37])

THE BUDGET ENFORCEMENT ACT OF 1990 AND THE OMNIBUS BUDGET RECONCILIATION ACT OF 1993

The Budget Enforcement Act made several changes in the federal budget process by amending both the Congressional Budget Act of 1974 and GRH. The 1990 act amended GRH to work from "baseline" budgets rather than outlays and gave the president much more authority to enforce deficit-reduction targets. The act further revised the GRH deficit-reduction estimates and extended the sequestration process through fiscal year 1995. Further, the 1990 act set limits on discretionary spending for three categories — defense, international, and domestic expenditures — and created a **"pay-as-you-go" (PAYGO)** procedure requiring that increases in direct spending (so-called *uncontrollable* appropriations) be offset by decreases in annual appropriations so that there is no increase in the deficit.[38] This principle formed the basis for congressional–executive-branch budget "summits" in the mid-1990s to compromise conflicting priorities. The 1993 **Omnibus Budget Reconciliation Act** extended the Budget Enforcement Act through FY 1998, established tighter spending limits, limiting discretionary budget authority to FY 1993 levels, and extended PAYGO procedures to a broader range of entitlements. We will see as we conclude this chapter that subsequent events may have served only to force a short-term compromise on deficit reduction targets, without agreement on priorities for long-term role of government in fiscal policy making. At this point, however, we turn to the budget functions of execution and audit to complete the overall discussion of the budget cycle.

"pay-as-you-go" (PAYGO) procedure requiring that spending increases be offset by decreases in annual appropriations so as not to increase the deficit.

Omnibus Budget Reconciliation Act of 1993 extended the provisions of earlier legislation through 1998 and established stricter limits on discretionary spending.

EXECUTION AND AUDITING OF THE BUDGET

Budget *execution* is the process of spending money appropriated by Congress and approved by the president. Money is apportioned from the Treasury, covering three-month periods beginning October 1, January 1, April 1, and July 1. Spending of funds is monitored by an agency's leadership, OMB, standing committees of Congress with jurisdiction over the agencies, and, periodically, the General Accounting Office, the auditing and investigative arm of Congress.

Administrative discretion in spending funds is considerable. Agency personnel, in the course of program operations, may transfer funds from one account to another, reprogram funds for use in different though related ways under established budget authority, and defer spending from one fiscal quarter to the next in order to build up some cash reserves. Administrative conduct is influenced in these respects and others by legislative committees with jurisdiction over the given agency; committee review and clearance is frequently obtained prior to many such spending decisions. Similarly, the president may seek to defer spending of funds as a means of influencing agency or program directions. Congress or the president may also seek to rescind budget authority for funds previously approved for a given fiscal year. Since 1974, any deferral of spending must be reported to Congress by the president in a special message; proposed rescissions (cancellations) must also be transmitted by the president in the same manner. A deferral takes effect unless Congress passes a law overturning it, which the president must sign; for a rescission to take effect, however, both chambers of Congress must approve it within forty-five days of the president's special message.[39]

One other procedural element should be noted, a consequence of the quarterly apportionment arrangement mentioned earlier. Most agencies will try not to spend all their quarterly allotment in that quarter in order to maintain something in reserve — for emergencies, unforeseen expenses, or simply because costs are higher during some parts of the year than others. For example, the National Park Service's expenses in the spring and summer are far greater than during the winter. In the last quarter of the fiscal year, however, this reserve buildup can lead to a strange but widespread practice. Agencies do not want to return money to the Treasury at the end of the year; thus, in the last few weeks, they will attempt to spend all but a small portion of their quarterly allotment plus any reserve accumulated through the first three quarters. The reason for reluctance to return money to the Treasury is that agencies fear being told, when next they go before an appropriations subcommittee, "You didn't need all we gave you last year, so we'll just reduce your appropriation accordingly this year." Whether that would actually happen in every instance is not clear, but the fear is strong enough to produce behavior that is a bit surprising; one might think that agencies would be proud of having demonstrated concern for the taxpayer's dollar. But, most of the time this is not how it works out.[40]

The *audit* stage involves several functions divided among different auditors and carried out during different time periods. Informal audits are ongoing within agencies — they have to be in order to generate fiscal data necessary to demonstrate proper spending of funds and programmatic efficiency. Formal audits are under the direction, at various times, of agency auditors (or of private auditing firms with which agencies contract), of OMB, and of the GAO. In some states, an auditor general or auditor of accounts is responsible, full-time, for maintaining a check on agency expenditures. Also, legislative oversight amounts to an ongoing informal legislative audit, though for somewhat different purposes — for programmatic concerns as well as those of expenditure control.

In recent decades, the focus and purpose of audits have shifted — in some cases, dramatically. The original purpose of auditing was to ensure financial accuracy and propriety; changes came about as budgeting — and management, generally — became more systematic. A *managerial* focus developed hand-in-hand with emphasis on program efficiency. And, in the past decade, *performance* audits have become more common, stressing (as with PPB) program effectiveness and overall agency performance. Unlike PPB, performance auditing has taken firm root in many agencies and is increasingly used by central budget offices in the executive branch to enhance budgetary control by the chief executive.

In summarizing the five stages, we should note that, at any given time, an agency head or budget officer can be giving attention to as many as four fiscal years. By way of illustration, in the late spring of 2000 (the third quarter of fiscal 2000 for the national government), audits of fiscal 1999 were nearing conclusion, expenditures in fiscal 2000 were well under way, budget submissions for fiscal 2001 had already occurred, and preliminary preparation of estimates for fiscal 2002 had begun. With the expansion of the number of actors in the budget process, its complexity has greatly increased. But another factor is also having major impact: the growing need to budget in an era of resource scarcity.

Budgeting and Resource Scarcity

Resources have always been relatively scarce in the sense that there is rarely, if ever, enough to go around to satisfy all the pressures on the public treasury. What is new, since the mid-1970s, is the advent of *absolute* scarcity; declining rates of growth, absolute shrinkage of tax bases (not only in larger, older central cities, where that problem has been evident for years), and rising inflation, coupled with recession, have put governments in a new fiscal squeeze. Getting the most out of existing resources has become a recurring theme, with renewed emphasis on both economy and efficiency, as public agencies adjust to new, harsher realities.[41]

The level of political tension has risen as various interests in the governmental process see all too clearly the possibility of having to defend repeatedly their claims for government support. As long as the total fiscal "pie" was expanding, which was the case for many years, competition for a share of it could be brisk without getting to be cutthroat. Now, however, as the total pie becomes stable or actually decreases in size and costs rise rapidly, the competition greatly intensifies.[42] How much it intensifies depends on the extent of government commitment to costly existing programs, increases in costs, employee demands for wage increases, the condition of the existing fiscal base, political pressures from taxpayers for easing the tax burden, and the like. Thus, hard-pressed cities such as New York, St. Louis, and Cleveland face a much heavier crunch than the expanding states and cities of the West and Southwest, or even the national government. But the differences may be more in degree than in substance; government jurisdictions currently in a more favorable position are well advised to prepare for the fiscal pendulum to swing the other way in their cases as well.

Under these circumstances, controllability of spending becomes a matter of premier importance and political debate. The controllability issue raises questions about government's ability — and the people's resolve — truly to control the purse strings. States, unlike the national government, often have *constitutionally* mandated expenditures, with specific **earmarking** of revenues for designated purposes (such as elementary, secondary, and higher education; road construction and maintenance, or operating game preserves), leaving the legislature without discretion to change them. And, ironically, the decade of the 1970s — when fiscal constraints on government were growing significantly — also saw a

earmarking revenues are "earmarked" for designated purposes (such as elementary, secondary, and higher education, road construction and maintenance, or operating game preserves), leaving the bureaucracy without discretion to change them.

major rise in the proportion of the national budget accounted for by expenditures that are uncontrollable under existing law. Allen Schick has even suggested that, in practice, some 95 percent of the budget is in fact *uncontrollable*.[43] These outlays are uncontrollable in two senses: (1) expenditures are legally mandated unless Congress changes the law; and (2) the level of expenditures is determined by economic and demographic conditions largely *outside* the immediate control of the president and Congress.[44] The welter of entitlements, formula grants, and the like makes efforts to control spending solely through budget devices seem futile. Controllability of the budget must come through nonbudgetary mechanisms (strictly speaking) and the will to use them. (One such approach is improving the productivity and quality of existing programs, which is discussed in detail at the end of Chapter 10.)

Budgeting and the Future: More Questions than Answers

Considering the magnitude of contemporary problems and issues in the budgeting arena and the attention paid to them, one might legitimately wonder why more has not been done to alleviate the worst of the difficulties. It is therefore useful to examine briefly some large-scale dimensions — and questions — concerning budgeting and government spending.

One question worth asking is, Just how high is national government spending? In terms of simple numbers, it would appear to be very high; nearly $1.8 trillion projected by FY 2000 is not small change. That figure, however, does not take inflation into account — that is, it does not reflect the purchasing power of those dollars, as an inflation-adjusted figure *(constant dollars)* would. From FY 1980 to FY 2000, annual outlays (not adjusted for inflation) increased from $591 billion to $1.8 trillion — more than a threefold increase. Measured in constant (1987) dollars, however, the increase in outlays during the same period was only 46 percent (from $832 billion to $1.5 trillion). Projections for the early 2000s indicate an even slower rate of increase in national government outlays, as measured in constant dollars.

Growth in spending, relative to both our nation's population increase and the private economy's growth (measured in terms of the gross national product), has been significant but not necessarily out of proportion. In FY 1970, national government outlays represented just under 20 percent of the gross national product; these rose to nearly 25 percent in FY 1983, then dropped to just under 22 percent in FY 1995. Also, it should be kept in mind that between 1950 and 1997, the population of the United States increased by 78 percent — from 151 million to 270 million people. Even if national government expenditures (in constant dollars) had increased only in exact proportion to the population growth during that same period, the net increase would be substantial — and, indeed, it has been just that. Governments in other advanced industrialized countries collect and spend far more as a percentage of their gross national products (GNPs) (see Figure 9–1 on page 342).

Another, crucial dimension of increased government expenditure is the extent to which so-called *uncontrollables* have influenced the increases. Entitlement payments for individuals have doubled from 30 percent of total outlays in FY 1969 to 60 percent in FY 1998.

Out of these figures comes an important reality: *The performance of the private economy is critical to the condition of the national budget.* This is, of course, true on the revenue side, because a robust economy generates more tax dollars at the same tax rates that a sluggish economy does. It is also true on the expenditure side, however, because, during periods of slow economic growth, tax collections decline, payments to individuals increase, thus putting more pressure on a government treasury already suffering from decreased revenues. The recession of the early 1980s made it more difficult to move toward a balanced budget; slow growth in the GNP during most years since then has not eased the situation.

One should recall, too, that there was a sizable reduction in income taxes in 1981. It has been estimated that, in the first three years (combined) after that tax cut, $135 billion that might have helped reduce budget deficits were not collected — good news for the individual and corporate taxpayer, but bad news for deficit reduction! Congress, in fact, took some potentially unpopular steps to curb the deficit, raising selected taxes (despite resistance by the Reagan administration) in 1982, 1983, and 1984. It has been suggested that increased revenues from these taxes have had the effect of lowering annual deficits from what they would have been otherwise by about $75 billion per year, from FY 1986 onward.[45]

"No new taxes," in turn, became a watchword of the Bush campaign for the presidency in 1988 — a pledge that took on a somewhat hollow ring for many Bush supporters when, in June 1990, he indicated publicly that, as part of high-level negotiations between Democrats and Republicans (over the FY 1991 budget), tax increases were one of many possibilities up for discussion in the negotiations. Some of the president's detractors were quick to point out that they had described the original pledge of no new taxes as ill advised when it was made. The larger point is that, in the absence of stronger economic performance in the private sector, increased taxes combined with spending restraint may be one of the best options available to combat chronic budget deficits. One difficulty, of course, is that, while we as a nation have long resisted "taxation without representation," lately many of us seem to be almost equally unhappy about the prospect of taxation *with* representation! Another difficulty is that cutting spending continues to have broad popular appeal — even if, under present law, most of the national government's annual expenditures are beyond reach unless entitlements are cut. However, it is increasingly apparent that, if the president and a majority of Congress agree to change present law, no entitlement is guaranteed, and no expenditure is actually uncontrollable.

PROBLEMS AND PROSPECTS

The budget process continues to be a center of attention in the nation's capitol, and in many states and localities, as well. Five examples suggest the kinds of problems and prospects that are still with us. Two are focused on deficit-reduction efforts; a third pertains to changes we could make that are designed to place stronger curbs on the growth of public expenditures; the fourth raises questions about the effects of budgetary pressures on Congress and the executive branch; and the last example suggests another, broader aspect of recent budget efforts.

Under the budget-reductions statutes of 1985, 1990, and 1993, *sequestration* is mandated if Congress fails to achieve the deficit target for a given year. That seems straightforward enough, but it has turned out not to be. In 1987, efforts were made to meet the deficit target by backdating expenditures from one year to the previous one, selling major national government assets, and delaying some individual purchases from September 30 to October 1 (so that associated costs would be reflected on the next fiscal year's ledger). Another issue has surfaced concerning calculation of the deficit itself, with accusations being heard that some are engaging in budget gimmickry to arrive at the designated deficit targets, that others are using "blue smoke and mirrors," and so on. Such accusations hurled back and forth between the White House and the Capitol, between Democrats and Republicans, have had the effect of increasing mistrust among large numbers of key participants in the budget process.

A related issue that surfaced in 1989 and 1990 was the Bush administration's deficit projections incorporating, on the "plus" side, the substantial and growing surpluses in the main trust fund of the Social Security system. Those surpluses are the result of boosts in Social Security taxes; they are deliberate, and designed to create — over a period of many years — a reserve in the system sufficient to meet the system's payout obligations when especially large numbers of American workers begin retiring (about the year 2012). The administration was roundly criticized for including such trust-fund surpluses in its calculations; indeed, the whole issue of calculating surpluses and deficits in subparts of the overall budget was raised by this practice. The major contention was that incorporating trust-fund surpluses into calculations about the budget deficit gave a misleading, if not false, impression concerning existing realities. The Bush administration came under increasing pressure regarding such calculations, which perhaps contributed to increased willingness to negotiate about future efforts to combat the deficit in a bipartisan manner.

The third issue, which has generated considerable interest in some quarters, is the possibility of strengthening the chief executive's authority to restrain expenditures selectively. Presidents Ronald Reagan, George Bush, and Bill Clinton advanced proposals dealing with the nation's continuing ability to control government spending. Presidents Reagan and Bush actively supported a constitutional amendment that would require the national government to maintain a balanced budget. Presidents Reagan and Bush also advocated a constitutional amendment or legislation that would enable the president to exercise a *line-item veto* over appropriations (see Chapter 7) — a proposal that also was part of the 1994 Republican *Contract with America*. It remains to be seen whether (and how) this power, if determined by the Supreme Court not to violate the Constitution, and made available to presidents in the future, will be used to eliminate wasteful and unnecessary spending or to promote the interest of the political party in power.

A fourth issue is the effect of sustained budgetary pressures on Congress and its members and on executive-branch personnel. The late political scientist Aaron Wildavsky noted that there is a great deal more uncertainty in agency and congressional operations when the budget process calls for involvement not only in annual budget deliberations (the usual time cycle for such decision making) but also in virtually continuous revision in dollar amounts available to the national government's executive-branch agencies.[46] There is one other implication of continuous budgetary revision: the likelihood that budget making will command more and more of the attention of government decision makers, possibly crowding off the public agenda other issues and concerns that merit attention as well. Some say that this is exactly what has been happening in Washington as concern about budgets and deficits becomes ever greater. The NPR recommended a *biennial* (two-year) *budget*, eliminating the need for Congressional and White House staff to review budget proposals annually. As of late 1996, Congress had not acted on this recommendation.

Finally, we come to the phenomenon sometimes labeled **summitry** in national government budget making: the practice of initiating negotiations among leaders of Congress and the White House involving top Democrats meeting with top Republicans (usually away from public view), in efforts to confront more effectively the seemingly intractable budget (and budget deficit) challenges of the past two decades. Summitry did not happen overnight; it represents the culmination of a series of events, dating back nearly twenty years. First (it is said), the president's budget message ceased to serve as Congress's starting point in budget deliberations. Then, Congress's own procedures mandated under the 1974 legislation, failed to halt the growth of national government expenditures, producing additional frustration at both ends of Pennsylvania Avenue (the Capitol and the White House). A summit held in 1989 succeeded only in producing an agreement no one seemed to like and sowed seeds of further partisan mistrust; neither Republicans nor Democrats wanted to take the blame for failing to deal with the deficit.

If all this sounds like high-level international diplomacy, there is a great deal in these processes that resembles it. The significant point is that we seem to have reached a condition of near chaos in our budgetary decision making, with so many pressures applied on behalf of so many interests from so many different directions that it appears as if summitry may be the only way to deal with the root causes of our difficulties. In terms of some of the perspectives we discussed in Chapter 5, it might be said that the budgetary process has been burdened with

summitry in national government budget making, the practice of initiating negotiations among leaders of Congress and the White House, involving top Democrats meeting with top Republicans (usually away from public view), in efforts to confront more effectively the seemingly intractable budget (and budget deficit) challenges of the past two decades.

the consequences of a great deal of long-term decentralized participation. It can be argued that we have now reached the point at which the need for central direction (summitry), to restore a degree of order essential to decision making, has become so great that only at the highest levels of government can individuals holding sufficient influence in the process come together with any hope of resolving what needs to be resolved for the system to function.

Clearly, the nature of budgeting has changed in the past thirty years; it is equally clear that change has not occurred in a social or political vacuum. As Allen Schick has observed: "The budget cannot make order out of chaos, it cannot bring concord where there is unlimited strife. Where there is [political] instability . . . [budget] issues become symbols of larger, unresolvable political conflicts."[47] That view is consistent with the position taken at the outset of this chapter, namely, that government budgets reflect the political preferences and priorities of those who make them — and, by implication, of the citizenry at large. Where those preferences and priorities are very much in turmoil, as they have been in recent decades, it is not surprising that the politics of government budgeting is similarly turbulent. It appears certain that we face continuing political and fiscal conflict as we grope for a new national consensus on the proper role of public spending.

Summary

The budgetary process is central to resource allocation in the political system. The nature of decision making has long been an issue of considerable importance, with political influence, policy control, and rationality as key variables. The scope of government spending and its impacts on society have dramatically expanded in recent decades, with new practices and new concerns emerging since the 1970s.

Budgets are tools used by governments to influence the course of private-sector economic activity. The chief instruments related to budgeting include taxing and spending patterns, management of debt, monetary and credit controls, and economic coordination. Such uses of the budget are of relatively recent vintage, having developed fully only in the last fifty years. Accompanying these changes has been a marked increase in both the role of the national government and the influence of the president in budget and policy formulation. The executive budget has been central to all this, while Congress maintains control over public purse strings.

Budget formulation in the executive branch has been characterized at different times by various orientations and emphases. Line-item budgeting stressed control of, and accountability for, expenditures. Performance budgeting emphasized managerial coordination and control, focusing on program efficiency. Planning-programming-budgeting (PPB) was designed to forge links between planning and budgeting to introduce a greater degree of decisional rationality into the process. However, PPB largely failed to accomplish its purposes. Zero-base budgeting (ZBB) provided for ranking packages of services, assessing impacts of various levels of services, and establishing orders of priority for funding within given revenue constraints.

The process of budget making is highly fragmented in many American governments and includes choices as to annual or multiyear budgeting, as well as current and future obligations. Budget preparation focuses on the roles of agencies and a central budget office (the latter usually serving the chief executive) in assembling executive budget proposals to the legislature. Authorizations are legislative determinations, first, of programs themselves, and second, of maximum spending levels. Appropriations allocate actual funding or obligations, and normally must follow — and be governed by — authorizations. However, a recent tendency has emerged toward backdoor spending authority and entitlement programs that remain in force unless deliberate action is taken to change their provisions. This has simultaneously weakened controls over spending and contributed to rapidly rising expenditures, at least in the national government budget.

The 1970s saw a concerted effort in the national government to apply restraints to the rise in spending. First, President Nixon engaged in the practice of impoundment, on a wider scale than most previous presidents; subsequently, Congress legislated a congressional budget process. In the mid-1980s, Congress passed the Gramm–Rudman–Hollings Act in an effort to deal with rising annual budget deficits. Deficit problems have still not been completely overcome, but the Omnibus Budget Reconciliation Act of 1993 established limits on discretionary spending through fiscal 1998 to achieve deficit-reduction targets.

Budgeting in an era of resource scarcity is a harsh new reality. Rising costs of government have combined with stabilizing or even shrinking resource bases to create a serious fiscal squeeze for many governments. Among the consequences are increasing importance of budgetary decisions, increasing demands for controllability of expenditures, and such emerging practices as PAYGO, sequestration, and summitry. Important issues, including deficits and chief executive powers, continue to be associated with budgets and budget making. A consensus on the appropriate government role in fiscal decision-making has yet to be achieved.

KEY TERMS AND CONCEPTS

entitlements	fiscal policy
mandatory spending	taxation
discretionary spending	gross national product (GNP)
Congressional Budget Office (CBO)	bonded indebtedness
deficit	tax expenditure financing
Gramm–Rudman–Hollings Act	Federal Reserve System

KEY TERMS AND CONCEPTS *(continued)*

money supply	budget outlays
Council of Economic Advisors (CEA)	backdoor financing
	Bipartisan Commission on Entitlement and Tax Reform
House Ways and Means Committee	impoundment
Senate Finance Committee	Congressional Budget and Impoundment Control Act of 1974
executive budget	
Commission on Economy and Efficiency	sequestration
	reconciliation process
line-item budgeting	"pay-as-you-go" (PAYGO)
performance budgeting	Omnibus Budget Reconciliation Act
First Hoover Commission	earmarking
Budget Enforcement Act	summitry
budget obligations	

SUGGESTED READING

Axelrod, Donald. *Budgeting for Modern Government.* 2nd ed. New York: St. Martin's, 1995.

Franklin, Daniel P. *Making Ends Meet: Congressional Budgeting in the Age of Deficits.* Washington, D.C.: Congressional Quarterly Press, 1992.

Hyde, Albert C., and Jay M. Shafritz. *Government Budgeting: Theory, Process, Politics.* Pacific Grove, Calif.: Brooks/Cole, 1992.

Johnson, Ronald W., and Robert D. Lee, Jr. *Public Budgeting Systems.* 6th ed. Rockville, Md.: Aspen Publishing, 1998.

Jones, Vernon D. *Downsizing the Federal Government.* Armonk, N.Y.: M.E. Sharpe, 1997.

Kettl, Donald F. *Deficit Politics: Public Budgeting in Institutional and Historical Context.* New York: Macmillan, 1992.

Kettl, Donald F., and John DiIulio Jr. *Cutting Government.* Washington, D.C.: The Brookings Institution, 1995.

Koven, Steven G. *Public Budgeting in the United States: The Cultural and Ideological Setting.* Baltimore, Md.: Georgetown University Press, 2000.

Light, Paul. *Thickening Government.* Washington, D.C.: The Brookings Institution, 1995.

Mikesell, John L. *Fiscal Administration: Analysis and Applications for the Public Sector.* Orlando, Fla.: Harcourt, Brace, Jovanovich, 1998.

Oleszek, Walter J. *Congressional Procedures and the Policy Process.* 4th ed. Washington, D.C.: CQ Press, 1988.

Rabin, Jack, ed. *Handbook of Public Budgeting.* New York: Marcel Dekker, 1992.

Reischauer, Robert D., and Henry J. Aaron. *Setting National Priorities.* Washington, D.C.: The Brookings Institution, 1998.

Schick, Allen. *The Federal Budget.* Washington, D.C.: The Brookings Institution, 1994.

Wildavsky, Aaron, and Naomi Caiden. *The New Politics of the Budgetary Process.* 4th ed. New York: Longman, 2001.

ON-LINE RESOURCES:
Government Budgeting

Center on Budget and Policy Priorities

http://www.cbpp.org/

The Center on Budget and Policy Priorities is a nonpartisan research organization and policy institute that conducts research and analysis on a range of government policies and programs, with an emphasis on those affecting low- and moderate-income people.

Citizen's Guide to the Federal Budget

http://cher.eda.doc.gov/BudgetFY97/guidetoc.html

Designed to give citizens a walking tour of the federal budget. Outlines how the government raises revenues and spends money, how the president and Congress enact the budget, why the budget deficit and federal debt are problems, and what the president hopes to accomplish with the budget.

Congressional Budget Office

http://www.cbo.gov/

Budget and financial management arm of Congress.

Federal Reserve Board

http://www.bog.frb.red.us

Policy and regulatory information regarding the Federal Reserve System, including monetary, credit, and banking regulations.

Government Finance Officers Association (GOFOA)

http://www.financenet.gov/gfoa.htm

The Government Finance Officers Association of the United States and Canada is the premier association of public-sector finance professionals and is dedicated to providing high-quality support to state and local government finance officials.

National Association of State Budget Officers (NASBO)

http://www.nasbo.org

The National Association of State Budget Officers serves as the professional membership organization for state finance officers. NASBO is the instrument through which the states collectively are advancing state budget practices. As the chief financial advisors to our nation's governors, NASBO members are active participants in public policy discussions at the state level; this site has excellent links to other substantive policy areas in state government.

For further information on government budgeting see: Bedford/ St. Martin's Home Page

http://www.bedfordstmartins.com

Chapter 10

Public Policy and Management

Our goal is to make the entire federal government both less expensive and more efficient, and to change the culture of our national bureaucracy away from complacency and entitlement toward initiative and empowerment. We intend to redesign, to reinvent, to reinvigorate the entire national government.

President Bill Clinton, March 1993

To speak of government policy in areas such as agriculture, criminal justice, environmental quality, foreign affairs, health, transportation, or land-use planning conveys an impression of well-defined purposes — carefully mapped out, the necessary resources marshaled and at the ready, with consistent support through the political process. But reality is often very different from this conception.

In our complex and fragmented system, there is no single political majority capable of determining policy in every instance. Congressional voting coalitions are usually temporary, changing from one issue to the next; presidential election majorities, if they exist at all, are often fashioned out of very diverse groups in the population, each with policy interests that conflict with others; court rulings may not coincide with public sentiment; administrative agencies are not permanently tied to any one political coalition. The combined impact of these institutions and a very heterogeneous population on the formulation, implementation, and evaluation of public policy tends to blur rather than clarify policy objectives and content. Instead of being clear and unmistakable government commitments, many policies are mixed bags of programs that represent a variety of past actions and declarations, ad hoc responses to contemporary situations, and considerable uncertainty about future policy directions.

Yet there are strong expectations that public programs will be well managed — that they represent the culmination of deliberate efforts to plan, design, fund, and operate sets of activities appropriately directed toward accomplishing agreed-on objectives. There is the further expectation that managers and others will be capable of evaluating the actual achievements of government programs. For, in a real sense, programs are the means through which broader policy goals are to be fulfilled, if at all. Thus, although it may be difficult to identify or rationalize all aspects of a given policy, managers must focus on discrete tasks involved in organizing and operating programs. This is necessary despite the ever-present swirl of political controversy that frequently surrounds much of what governments try to accomplish.

In these endeavors, a particular bureau in the administrative process, and the individuals within a bureau (as well as government contractors) come together in the common effort to achieve policy goals. Managing public programs, individually and as they affect the course of public policies, involves major concerns discussed in previous chapters: executive and managerial leadership, organization structure, motivation, decision making, personnel selection, and budgeting. All these have a bearing on the roles of bureaucracy and the ultimate success or failure of government problem solving. And with growing sophistication in our capacity to analyze public programs has come a greater potential for more intelligent, more "rational" conduct of public management processes. Nonetheless, policies are still applied through a complicated and fragmented political process that is anything but rational.

In this chapter, we will examine the nature of public policies; the policy-making processes, particularly as they involve administrative entities; program management, planning and analysis; implementation, including how some policy directions are altered in the course of implementing individual programs; how programs are (or could be) evaluated and how those evaluations are used; and the challenges of improving productivity, quality, and customer service. Our ultimate purpose is to understand how public policies evolve as they do, the role of administrative politics in this process, and the operational realities — including the problems — of managing public programs to achieve policy goals.

The Changing Nature of Public Policies

public policy   (1) the organizing framework of purposes and rationales for government programs that deal with specified societal problems; (2) the complex of programs enacted and implemented by government.

What precisely is **public policy**? It can be defined as *the organizing framework of purposes and rationales for government programs that deal with specified societal problems.* Many people regard public policies as deliberate responses to problems and needs systematically identified by some legitimate means. It is commonly assumed that government policies are intended to solve — or at least cope with — major social and economic problems. There is typically some disparity, however, between the perception of the average citizen about policy processes and outcomes, and the realities of policy making.

Let us consider some of the most common popular assumptions about government policy. First, some people believe that governments have clearly defined policies, well thought out in advance, on all or most major issues and problems.

Second, many believe these policies are established through some kind of rational choice made by political leaders. Third, some think — logically enough — that everything that is done to address a problem or issue follows those policies. Fourth, it is often assumed that the policies of government are clearly perceived and understood by citizens. And fifth, many believe that government policies are widely agreed on and supported — otherwise, how could they remain in force? As appealing or logical as these ideas might be, *not one of them is entirely true.*

Public policies are generally *not* clearly defined in the sense that all major problems are anticipated and the machinery of government geared up to meet them before they get out of hand. That would require the kind of centralized leadership inconsistent with the Constitution and resisted by most of us. Some processes designed to foresee future developments and prepare for them have not accomplished all that they were intended to, and "circumstances beyond our control" often prevail. With the exception of threats to national security and major natural disasters, it is unusual to have a consistent policy for dealing with a specific problem. As a practical matter, governments could not possibly have pre-determined policies on all issues. Thus, policies tend to be less consistent and coherent than many might like. Moreover, policies are more often the product of *responses to particular circumstances* or problems rather than the result of deliberate actions. They frequently result from ad hoc decisions made at many levels, at different times, by officials and others who see only some parts of the overall problem. Rational policy choice implies a decision-making capacity largely lacking in our noncentralized government institutions. The diffuse intergovernmental substructure of 87,000 governments further weakens the capacity for centrally coordinated actions.

Because of this size and diversity, many government activities do not follow official policy directions or support publicly stated goals. Political party platforms, pronouncements by top executives, state and local initiatives and referenda, even resolutions of Congress, are often a better reflection of intent than of reality in policy making. What actually takes place may well differ from official definitions of what was supposed to occur. Many policies are not clearly perceived or understood by the general population. We tend to pay attention to government activity that is likely to have a tangible impact on our lives but, otherwise, it is unusual for large numbers of people to comprehend the intricacies of public policy. A good example is foreign policy. Different ethnic and nationality groups are sensitive to even small changes in what this nation does or contemplates doing regarding their mother countries, but most citizens have only a generalized awareness of our overall foreign policy. Many domestic policies are also understood only in broad outline. In short, it is not accurate to assume that most Americans are knowledgeable in detail about individual policies.

Finally, it is not true that there is widespread, *active support* for existing public policies, although most have at least *passive backing.* Policy directions that offend basic values of large numbers of people are not likely to be sustained for very long without at least being challenged. Examples of sharp public reaction to disputed policies include opposition to the 1973 Supreme Court ruling on abortion, challenges to hiring preferences and "quotas" for affirmative action, resistance to the Supreme Court ban on prayers in the public schools, and expressions of public distaste for some forms of health and safety regulation. In one sense, policies that exist without widespread challenge may be taken as a barometer of public feeling about what is acceptable. Few policies survive that offend either powerful political interests or large numbers of ordinary citizens, or both. In sum, although support for what government does is not necessarily enthusiastic, policies have to have a certain amount of *acceptability*. Moreover, the most acceptable policies may not be the most effective, and the most effective policies may not be acceptable to a majority or a strong minority. Some compromise is often necessary to implement most public policies.

It makes a difference *which* situations are defined as problems, *who* defines them, and *why* they deserve attention in the policy arena. Unequal access to health care, for example, was part of the American scene for decades before President Clinton identified it as a high-priority problem in 1993. Nuclear waste disposal, crime control, job training, and welfare to "workfare" reform are other examples of issue areas that were defined as policy problems long before any action was taken. Also, policy initiative can come from many parts of the body politic — the president, Congress, interest groups, the mass media, state or local government, and so on. Perhaps the only policymaker prohibited in theory from initiating policy changes on its own is the judiciary. Chief executives are usually in the best position to take the initiative, but they have no monopoly on attempting to raise issues for public and governmental attention. Furthermore, most policy changes come about slowly; it is far easier to resist change than to bring it about. American government tends to move in evolutionary fashion; incrementalism has generally been the order of the day. Finally, many policy actions are more symbolic than real. *Symbolism* is not without value in politics, but it should be understood for what it is and not confused with substantive change.[1] State laws punishing desecration of the American flag, legalizing moments of silence to counter federal decisions banning school prayer, state flags bearing Confederate symbols, and calls for a balanced federal budget amendment to the U.S. Constitution are largely symbolic.

symbolic actions
proposals for policy changes that serve some limited political purpose, but do not threaten the current situation.

Because most citizens are unfamiliar with the details of policy, **symbolic actions** are often sufficient to satisfy calls for change without threatening the status quo. The passing of public attention from an issue often signals a slowdown in dealing with it, even if many in government would prefer to move more rapidly. Organized group support and opposition make a major difference in how substantive — or simply cosmetic — policy changes are.

Public policies, then, tend to be haphazard, not widely understood or actively supported, and often inconsistently applied. Not all situations in society that might be classified as problem areas are, in fact, defined as such. Sometimes, an unspoken policy exists to take no action on a problem; the decision *not* to act can be just as significant as a stated government policy to those interests that benefit from the status quo. And when changes in policy do occur, they tend to be rather slow and unfocused. That any coherent policies exist is often a surprise.

TYPES OF POLICIES

There is great variety in the kinds of policies pursued by government entities. These can be distinguished on the basis of their essential rationales, their impacts on society, and the respective roles played by administrative agencies in each. Major policy types include distributive, redistributive, regulatory, self-regulatory and, its logical extension, privatization.[2]

Distributive policies deliver large-scale services or benefits to certain individuals or groups in the population. Examples are loans and loan guarantees provided by the national government to cover private-sector losses, such as those by the saving and loan industry in the late 1980s and Chrysler Corporation in the early 1980s; agricultural price supports, tax deductions for interest paid on home mortgages; loans for college students; and government contracts. These involve policy subsystems or "iron triangles" (see Chapter 3) on almost an ad hoc basis, with direct beneficiaries who do not pay direct costs. Bureaucracies are often, but not always, involved in both the enactment of such policies and their implementation.

Redistributive policies "involve deliberate efforts by the government to shift the allocation of wealth, income, property, or rights among broad classes or groups" within the population.[3] They are often the source of intense controversy in the political arena and, significantly, that controversy usually affects the execution of a policy as well as its initial adoption. Thus, redistributive policies, such as affirmative action, the graduated income tax, Medicare for the elderly, and Aid to Families with Dependent Children (AFDC), were all subject to intense debate and conflict during legislative deliberations and have all attracted continuing attention from supporters and opponents. This type of policy is most sensitive politically and thus most susceptible to political pressures. Policies such as the graduated income tax have lost much of their redistributive character as a result of changes (exemptions, lower tax rates, income shelters, and similar loopholes) made in the basic law — some of which were proposed by the agency responsible for its administration! Redistributive policies, because of the level of controversy they generate, almost inevitably draw bureaucracies directly into the policy process, even though many would prefer to remain on the sidelines. In other instances, agencies with jurisdiction over redistributive policies have taken the lead in maintaining their essential character.

Regulatory policies promote restrictions on the freedom to act of those subject to the regulations. The most prominent such policies pertain to business activities — for example, advertising practices, pollution control, natural-gas pricing practices, and product safety. Other regulatory policies are also in effect in areas such as civil rights, job safety, and local government zoning ordinances. These are usually the product of conflict between competing forces — such as

distributive policies
policy actions such as subsidies or tax deductions that deliver widespread benefits to individuals or groups who often do not bear the costs.

redistributive policies
deliberate efforts by governments to shift the allocation of valued goods in society from one group to another; highly controversial and often accompanied by bitter political conflicts.

regulatory policies
establish restrictions on the behavior of those subject to the regulations, aim to protect certain groups, range broadly in scope, and are often enforced against businesses.

producer and consumer — each of which seeks to control the behavior of the other to some degree. Thus, regulatory policies involve greater tension among relevant actors and usually incorporate a larger role for bureaucracies. The regulative actions of government have increased substantially in recent years (see Chapter 11).

Self-regulatory policies represent a variation on regulation in that policy changes are often sought by those being regulated as a means of *protecting or promoting their own economic interests.* The leading example is licensing of professions and occupations, such as law, medicine, real estate, and taxi driving. Normally (especially in the case of professions), a legislative body enacts a licensing law, providing for enforcement by a board dominated by the licensed group. Other bureaucracies, and most other interests, typically take little interest in this kind of policy.

Bureaucratic agencies play somewhat different roles in each type of policy. As already implied, their roles may also vary within a given policy category, as is the case in redistributive policy. Subsystems exert considerable influence in the formation and implementation of distributive policies, although in a highly individualized manner. Depending on the kind of policy at issue, bureaus and their allies may be more or less involved; degree of involvement hinges primarily on the extent to which formal responsibilities are assigned to a given agency. Self-regulation only sporadically engages the attention of agencies outside a specific profession or occupation (although some subsystem politics is involved). Proposals to reinvent government criticized the limited range of policy options available to public managers and recommended a greater number of choices, such as competition, coproduction of services, community ownership, entrepreneurism, and diversion of public resources to the market-driven private sector.[4]

The competing demands of diverse interest groups (subsystems) force elected officials to reconcile multiple, vague, and often conflicting demands. Under such conditions, the temptation to distribute resources *broadly* rather than to *target* high-priority problems is always present. Governments are unique entities that serve broader social interests and lack the opportunity — or obligation — to "sell" their products or services at costs suited to prevailing markets. Concerns about equality, fairness, special interests, and redistribution of public resources *inhibit* but do not *prohibit* a public agency from applying market-based, entrepreneurial, or "for-profit" approaches such as deregulation, privatization, or **contracting out** to private firms. Thousands of communities are contracting for services; for instance, over 3,000 (among them San Jose, Phoenix, Memphis, Boston, and Omaha) have contracted out trash removal. Other services range from utility billing, voter registration, and street lighting to ambulance services, prison operation, golf course maintenance, firefighting services, and street maintenance.[5] Given the selective nature of political decision making, legitimate concerns have been raised about just *how much* authority can be delegated from the public to the private sector. Despite the risk that scarce resources will be misused, the *new boundaries of public and private administrative*

self-regulatory policies protective regulations that either advantage certain professions or classes, or remove from the government the power to regulate.

contracting out a practice under which private-sector contractors provide designated goods or services to governments, or to individual agencies, for an agreed-upon fee; an example both of a "twilight zone" between public and private sectors, and of public-sector responses to growing fiscal stress; services contracted for include trash collection and fire protection.

relationships are being drawn on a case-by-case basis, involving a broader range of policy areas and greater numbers of governments.

In sum, the part played by administrative entities in a given policy area or process can depend to a considerable extent on the type of policy, its specific issue content, local political constituencies, and its impact on subsystem support networks. Elected politicians, affected interests, and agency officials share common policy-making responsibilities. The long-term trend has been toward more partnerships and "shared-government" policy making, with active participation from private, as well as public, stakeholders.[6] Note that contracting out and privatization are obvious examples of shared governance, which promises to continue growing in large part in response to intensifed fiscal stress.

The Policy-Making Process

The policy-making process involves all the demands, pressures, conflicts, negotiations, and compromises, and formal and informal decisions that result in the pursuit and adoption of particular objectives and strategies through actions of government. This is a broad definition, and deliberately so, for making policy is not the exclusive province of any one branch or level of government.

Various authors have noted the intricate and complex nature of policy making.[7] As mentioned above, it is characterized by a lack of centralized direction; focus on interactions of national, state, and local governments; and involvement of private interests pressing government to respond to their specialized concerns. It is very loosely coordinated, highly competitive, fragmented and specialized (like budgeting), and largely incremental. Thus, the policy process is not a smoothly functioning, ongoing sequence with one phase predictably following another. Rather, it responds to pressures placed on it at many points along the way, so that policy usually reflects the influence of diverse political forces.

Where administrative agencies play a central role in the policy process, policy making is best described as occurring in four stages.[8] The first is a *legislative stage* involving both Congress and the president (and often agency administrators), in which basic legislation is drawn up, considered, and approved as law. In the second and third stages, which are primarily *administrative*, the agency writes detailed regulations and rules governing application of the law; this is followed by actual implementation. The fourth is a *review* stage, by the courts or Congress or perhaps both, during which modifications of existing policy are possible for legal, substantive, or political reasons. These stages are part of continuous policy *cycles*, during which policies are defined and redefined, with incremental adjustments made to accommodate major interests.

The legislative stage normally centers on actions of the chief executive (the president, governors, or mayors) and of key legislators on Capitol Hill (and on their counterparts in state and local governments). But the role of higher-level administrators (both political appointees and senior career officials) in formulating and proposing new policy options can also be very important. For example, agency personnel — usually in responsible positions — may perceive a need to modify legislative authorizations in order to smooth out implementation difficulties. They may wish to initiate a new activity to fulfill their own policy objectives. Or they may propose curtailing part of a program in order to concentrate attention, energies, and resources on matters of higher priority to them. In all such cases, their proposals must wend their way through the usual legislative process, and administrators must call on legislative (and executive) allies to ensure a proper hearing for their ideas. The main point, however, is that administrators are regular participants at this stage of the policy cycle, not merely passive observers.

Administrative involvement in subsequent stages of the policy process can assume a variety of forms. These include rule making, adjudication, law enforcement, and program operations. *Rule making*, a quasi-legislative power delegated to agencies by Congress, represents authority to enact "an agency statement of general applicability and future effect that concerns the rights of private parties and has the force and effect of law."[9] Rules may serve different functions — elaborating on general statutory provisions, defining terms (such as *small business*, *discriminate*, or *safe speed*), indicating probable agency behavior in particular matters. Agencies well known for their rule-making decisions include the **Federal Trade Commission (FTC),** the **Occupational Safety and Health Administration (OSHA),** and the Department of Transportation (DOT).

Adjudication, unlike rule making, is a quasi-judicial function involving the application of current laws or regulations to particular situations by case-to-case decision making. The scope of such actions is much narrower than that of rule making but, collectively, they can have great impact on policy as a whole. Agencies that engage in adjudication include the **National Labor Relations Board (NLRB),** which has used the process in settling unfair labor practices cases since its creation in 1935; the Social Security Administration (SSA), which became a separate clientele-based agency in 1995, in determining eligibility for benefits; and the **Internal Revenue Service (IRS).** Adjudication is an adaptation of, and a substitute for, possible formal proceedings in a court of law — particularly in the case of the NLRB and the IRS.

Law enforcement refers to securing compliance with existing statutes and rules (and not necessarily to police functions) and, more specifically, to the enthusiasm an agency brings to the task of implementing legislative authorizations. By exercising administrative discretion, an agency may influence the policy process by countless kinds of action — or inaction. Another factor is the techniques of enforcement available to an agency. For example, in the early 1960s, a **Justice Department** task force on voting rights of black Southerners might have wanted to file suit on behalf of blacks denied an opportunity to register, but the 1957 and 1960 Civil Rights Acts did not confer that power on the Justice Department. A plaintiff had to shoulder the legal burden — particularly the costs — if a case was to reach the courts. Not until the 1964 Civil Rights Act did the Justice Depart-

Federal Trade Commission (FTC) independent regulatory commission charged with enforcing antitrust acts to protect consumers against unfair trade practices.

Occupational Safety and Health Administration (OSHA) the mission of OSHA is to save lives, prevent injuries, and protect the health of America's workers, under provisions of the Occupational Safety and Health Act of 1970.

National Labor Relations Board (NLRB) independent federal agency created in 1935 to enforce the National Labor Relations Act; conducts secret-ballot elections to determine whether employees want union representation, and investigates allegedly unfair labor practices by employers and unions.

Internal Revenue Service (IRS) responsible for administration of federal tax policy and collection of revenue from individuals and corporations.

Justice Department cabinet-level executive agency responsible for the enforcement of federal law.

ment acquire the ability to act on behalf of aggrieved citizens claiming improper denial of voting rights (Justice Department attorneys themselves sought that authority at the legislative stage!). Even then, another year passed before the Voting Rights Act broadened national authority to register voters directly in areas where fewer than half of those eligible were registered.

Program operations — including the actual administration of loans, grants, insurance, purchasing, services, or construction activities — constitute a large part of agencies' impacts on the policy process. Again, discretion is vital; out of thousands of small-scale decisions come large-scale policies. Later in this chapter, we will look in more detail at program implementation and the politics involved in it.

One further aspect of policy making deserves mention: the extensive impact of intergovernmental relations and policy development. As we discussed in Chapter 4, many facets of both program funding and administration are closely tied either to intergovernmental collaboration or competition, or to parallel activities of some kind, as in the case of environmental policy. This serves to complicate both policy making and any effort to trace the roots of a particular policy direction. Legislative and administrative mechanisms at each level of government are fairly complex, affording numerous opportunities for interested parties to have some say in the policy-making process. Slight alterations in policy are possible each time influence is exerted, and their cumulative effects at the same level of government can be significant. It is not difficult to imagine what multiplying these patterns by three (or more) levels of government can do to the shape of policy. Intergovernmental dimensions, then, constitute an important contributing factor in the overall implementation of policy.[10] Private firms that bid to supply a government with a service or product, or contract with governments to provide direct services, are increasingly concerned with intergovernmental policy making and operations.

In sum, the policy-making process helps account for the disjointed nature of most public policies. Multiple opportunities for exerting influence and an absence of centralized direction characterize many phases of policy making, producing policies that look (accurately) as though they were arrived at from many directions at once. It is not difficult for a chief executive, for example, to define a formal policy intention, but it is another matter altogether to put it into effect. On one occasion, John F. Kennedy signed a bill into law, then turned to his aides and remarked: "We have made the law. Now it remains to be seen whether we can get our government to do it."[11]

From the earlier discussion regarding myths about public policy, it is clear that policy refers to intentions and symbols as well as actual *results* of governmental activity. We must be careful, therefore, about the sense in which the term is used. Results, however, are normally sought and evaluated in the context of specific government programs rather than broad policies. Programs, in turn, can be further divided into projects dependent for their completion on individual performance on the job. The linkage between policies, programs, projects, and individual performance is an important one. Policies are put into effect only to the degree that program objectives related to them are met; programs are, in turn, the sum totals of supporting projects; and each project represents the labors of individuals within the responsible agencies. Discussion of public policy, in a *management* sense, must focus, then, on programs and projects, the essential building blocks of what government does. Although there are some differences between the two in terms of organizing and directing them, we will emphasize a number of management concerns common to both:

1. Planning and analysis,
2. Implementation,
3. Evaluation,
4. Productivity and measurement of results,
5. Total quality management, and
6. Meeting customer service standards.

These are linked conceptually; to the extent that they are linked in practice, they greatly enhance program management and effectiveness.

Planning and Analysis

Just as governmental and political goals need to be clearly defined, as discussed in Chapter 6, individual program or project goals do also. Ideally, goals at this level should be clearly *operationalized* — that is, formulated in specific and tangible terms related to the general mission or purpose of the agency. **Planning and analysis** — even though they are carried out imperfectly much of the time — are essential elements of the goal definition process.

planning and analysis the process of deliberately defining and choosing operational goals of an organization, analyzing alternative choices for resource distribution, and choosing methods to achieve those goals over a specified time period; increasingly important tools for public management.

All organizations function according to some type of basic plans, but program administrators must both promote planning by others in their organizations and weave "various plans together into a common purpose pattern. In essence, . . . *administrative planning* is purposeful action to develop purposefulness."[12] The keys to planning are to be found in accurate forecasts of future need, goal definition, means–ends linkages, and the kind of coordination and direction supplied by the organization's administrator. (Note the heavily rationalistic flavor of the first three "keys.")

operational goal a specific and measurable goal for organizational attainment.

Complicating the planning process is the fact that goals exist at different conceptual levels within any public agency or organization. Ideally, then, linkages should be forged among different types of goals. Also, the interrelationships among goals, plans, programs, and projects are important. For example, one official *goal* of the United States government is to increase the educational attainment level of the American people. An **operational goal** is the achievement of a certain minimum reading level for every American aged eighteen or older. One *plan* for achieving this operational goal includes educational assistance to urban high-risk areas. A *program* is distributing loans and grants to eligible students. A *project* was the proposal by the Clinton administration to provide computers and wire every schoolroom in America to the Internet by the year 2000.

Administrators at all levels of bureaucracy must operate within this complex web of objectives and arrangements and, in particular, must successfully organize activities addressed to meeting the goals of the administrative unit (for example, processing unemployment checks, monitoring eligibility rolls, and serving related clientele needs). The recipients of job placement services, for example, might not share the goal of limiting benefits or the program efficiency concerns of senior program administrators.

Public managers are encouraged to use **strategic planning** to determine a course of action, beginning with preliminary consideration of goals. Essential steps are identifying desired outcomes, assessing environmental constraints, determining the appropriate mix of public and private responsibility for program management, establishing performance expectations, and assessing probabilities of achieving desired outcomes.[13] Depending on the results of such deliberations, goals can be selected, and perhaps modified, by those involved. The point is, however, that, in one form or another, this must be done early in the life cycle of a project or program, and periodically throughout its existence, to make any sense out of varied support activities. For example, it would be considered careless policy making to spend public funds for "improving education" without a clear idea of specific project goals — remedial reading instruction, additional equipment and materials, more counseling services, or better testing methods and devices. These are demonstrably related to the broader program goal of "improving education," which, in turn, may be part of an urban policy designed to "improve the quality of urban life."

That these imperatives exist in an organization does not guarantee that planning will be undertaken or that it will serve its purpose if it is undertaken. Other factors may interfere with agency planning processes. These include "a threatening political environment, an unrecognized or unacknowledged intraorganizational conflict, a lack of trust or communication [among] planning participants, and conflicting perceptions of the goals, values, and norms of the organization."[14] An important task for public managers is to ensure that these potential obstacles to effective planning are recognized and dealt with in a timely way.

One further point should be made. As noted in Chapter 6, goals are not simply "there" to start with. They must be arrived at in deliberate fashion and can reflect varying combinations of substantive and political judgments about the need to pursue them. More important in an operating sense, program and project managers are not ordinarily official goal setters (as noted in Chapter 1). They may not even dominate the process, though they do usually contribute to shaping formally adopted goals. Thus, goal definition for the middle-level manager is a *shared* process, one in which the most influential voices are often those outside the agency. Senior police officials must be sensitive to the needs of the community in deploying officers to prevent crime; a school superintendent must

strategic planning
a process used by an organization to formulate a mission statement, consider environmental opportunities, threats, strengths, and weaknesses, identify areas for strategic action, conduct *cost-benefit analysis* to evaluate and select actions, draw up implementation plans, and incorporate *operational goals* into annual budgets.

heed the wishes of the school board; the senior managers of a municipal airport must be sensitive to city commissioners' preferences. Yet an effort to delineate goals must be made *inside* the agency as well.[15]

APPROACHES TO ANALYSIS

As suggested above, planning leads directly to processes of analysis — of examining alternative options (however systematically) and attempting to identify and compare the potential outcomes. To the extent that planning produces or represents consensus among key individuals regarding appropriate program directions, formal plans can serve as a guiding standard for subsequent analysis and choice. If, however, significant dissent from adopted plans persists (which often happens), that dissension can complicate analysis by extending political conflict into analytic processes themselves.

Agency performance frequently depends on the quality of prior analysis regarding projected impacts of activities on the problem at hand. Politically, the old adage "Good government is good politics" has never been more true if good government is taken to mean better performance. For agencies with strong political backing, a solid foundation of objective program analysis adds substance to strength. For weak agencies, careful and thorough analysis of their options before selecting the most appropriate one(s) might make the difference between organizational vitality and decay.

The purpose of analysis is to facilitate sound decisions by establishing relevant facts about a situation before attempting to change it in some way and by determining, if possible, the respective consequences of different courses of action. The nature of a given problem is not always clear — for example, in education, poverty, crime control, or energy — and analysis can help sharpen the focus of decision makers as they consider various objectives and options. Analysis is also crucial to improving public management as a key aid to appropriate use of scarce resources and targeting of programs. Several kinds of analysis might be used; we will review each one briefly.

policy analysis the systematic investigation of alternative policy options and the assembly and integration of evidence for and against each; emphasizes explaining the nature of policy problems, and how public policies are put into effect.

Policy analysis can be defined as "the systematic investigation of alternative policy options and the assembly and integration of the evidence for and against each option."[16] Activities suggested by such a definition have long been a part of the government process, but only in the past four decades has a distinct analysis function become formally associated with public decision making. A key emphasis is on explaining the nature of problems, and how policies addressed to those problems are put into effect. An equally legitimate function, however, is to improve processes of policy making as well as policy content. In its broadest sense, policy analysis makes it possible to investigate policy outcomes in interrelated fields, to examine in depth the causes of societal and other problems, and to establish cause-and-effect relationships among problems, the contexts in which they occur, and potential solutions to them. Program or project managers generally concentrate on analyzing considerations most relevant to their immediate responsibilities.

Because problems vary widely in their scope and complexity, policy analysis needs to be flexible enough to permit selection of analytical approaches and techniques appropriate to the particular problem under study.[17] One proposal (among many others) for dealing with this dimension of policy analysis suggests four types of analysis suitable to four different sets of circumstances.[18] These are (1) *issue analysis*, where there is a relatively specific policy choice (for example, whether a particular group of businesses or industries should receive a tax reduction) and a highly politicized environment of decision making; (2) *program analysis*, involving both design and evaluation of a particular program (for example, a manpower-training program); (3) *multiprogram analysis*, in which decisions must be made concerning resource allocation among programs dealing with the same problem (for instance, different manpower-training programs); and (4) *strategic analysis*, where the policy problem is very large (for example, an economic development strategy for a depressed region).

At the programmatic level, the process of analysis and the analyses resulting from it should meet most of the following criteria.[19] First, they should clearly define issues and problems being addressed, including identifying clientele groups and their future size, specifying appropriate evaluation criteria, and providing estimates of future need. Second, they should present alternatives in a form specific enough to be evaluated. Third, in considering each alternative, accurate cost estimates should be provided. These should include direct and indirect costs (for example, employee benefits as well as salaries), costs incurred by other agencies (such as higher jail and court costs stemming from an increased police force), and documentation that demonstrates solid grounding for current and future costs. Fourth, program analyses should carefully estimate program effectiveness by ensuring that evaluation criteria are themselves comprehensive, by using multiple measures of effectiveness, and by ensuring that data adequate to measure both present and future circumstances can be employed in assessing program results. Fifth, analyses should openly acknowledge any uncertainty in basic assumptions and program data — that is, the probability of inaccuracies and the likely consequences of error. Sixth, the time period of the program (or project) should be identified, with a clear statement of whether enough time is allowed to provide a fair comparison among alternatives. Finally, an analysis should contain recommendations based on substantive data rather than on unsubstantiated information, should discuss any anticipated difficulties in implementation, and should document all relevant assumptions. (See Box 10-1, "Steps in the Standard-Form Policy Analysis.")

Policy analysis faces some obstacles, however. For one thing, it is not always clear what kind of analysis can be done and what uses can (or should) be made of the results when negotiation and bargaining among competing political forces are the most common means of carving out policy. Another difficulty is

BOX 10–1   PRODUCTIVITY AND SERVICE QUALITY IMPROVEMENT

Steps in the Standard-Form Policy Analysis

1. Define the problem.
2. Establish criteria for problem resolution.
3. Propose alternatives.
4. Collect data relevant to the problem.
5. Analyze the likely consequences of each alternative.
6. Evaluate the trade-offs.
7. Select an alternative.

limitations on the applicability of various analytical techniques used, depending on the kind of problem at hand.[20] That there are any limitations at all is unfortunate because the aim of analysis is essentially to facilitate the targeting, design, and operation of programs in the most effective and efficient ways possible. But even the most rigorous, sophisticated techniques are not always appropriate. For example, decision tools rooted in mathematics and economics are used to best effect where problem definition is straightforward, where there is "a convenient method of quantifying the problem (usually in terms of probability or monetary units), and where there is some function or set of functions (such as time, profit, payoff, or expected value) to be maximized or minimized."[21] In contrast, if a problem involves questions and issues not measurable in economic or quantitative terms, these decision tools are less appropriate.

ANALYTICAL TOOLS

Because analytical tools are widely used in dealing with quantifiable problems, some discussion of them is in order. Perhaps the broadest approach is *systems analysis*. This approach is usable (in principle) for integrating how all elements of political, social, economic, or administrative systems might affect and be affected by a given project or program (see the discussion of systems theory in Chapter 5). Managers utilizing systems analysis need to understand the nature of *interrelated* systems, carefully measure objectives and performance, and analyze the *external* social environment, available resources, system components, and how processes *internal* to the system can be better managed. The overriding objective of systems analysis is to produce greater rationality in management decision making, and efficiency and effectiveness in actual program operations. In terms of the discussion of decision making in Chapter 6, systems analysis is devoted to the rational approach. The comments made there about seeking comprehensiveness, coping with information needs, and maximizing return on a given investment of resources also apply here.

Perhaps the greatest advantage of systems analysis is its potential for bringing some order in decision making out of the seeming confusion and discord prevalent in the policy process at large.[22] A companion strength is that it permits a broader view of constraints and consequences relating to an individual program. A weakness, besides those associated with rational decision making, is the possibility that trying to achieve rationality within a single system will cause decision makers to ignore other interdependent systems that might also be relevant. An example would be an effort to analyze political factors influencing grants-in-aid to states and localities without also analyzing the nation's economy, which provides the tax base for raising revenues. A greater weakness, from a practical standpoint, is that systems analysis can generate such a staggering workload that decision makers have little chance of coping with it while still reaching a decision.

Cost-benefit analysis measures relative gains and losses resulting from alternative policy or program options. Usually implying quantitative measures and assuming objectivity, it can assist decision makers and program managers in determining the most beneficial path of action to follow. A cost-benefit analysis seeks to identify the actions with the most desirable ratio of benefit to cost. Given adequate information, cost-benefit analysis can be useful in narrowing a range of choices to those most likely to yield desired gains for an affordable cost. An example of cost-benefit analysis might involve a decision on whether a dam should be built in an uninhabited area.[23] Benefits (new jobs, new business, reduced flooding) and costs (construction expenses, environmental damage, foreclosed options for other uses of the land) are calculated, as well as the ratio between them. The same technique can be used to measure alternative benefits from other uses of the same funds and the related effects of constructing the dam (for example, on residential and tourist patterns in adjoining areas). Such an analysis might be useful both in advance of the project and as an evaluative instrument after the fact.

Operations research (OR) actually represents a collection of specific decision-making techniques using systems theory, modeling, and quantitative methods to ascertain how best to utilize available resources. The greatest value of OR lies in solving problems of efficiency — such as scheduling bus stops, managing aircraft in a holding pattern, or processing military recruits — rather than in helping to select particular alternatives. After policy choices have been made, OR makes use of mathematical techniques such as linear programming for reaching the optimal solution. Where "routine" administrative problems repeat themselves, OR can be especially valuable.

operations research (OR) a set of specific decision-making and analytical tools used in systems theory, modeling, and quantitative research to determine how best to utilize resources.

In sum, analysis is a key managerial activity. As noted earlier, knowledge is power in administrative politics, and analysis greatly enhances a manager's ability to obtain, organize, and apply relevant information in the course of choosing desirable program options.

Program Implementation

In speaking of implementation, we adopt Charles O. Jones's definition of the term, as well as his elaboration of it:

> Let us say simply that implementation is that *set of activities directed toward putting a program into effect*. Three activities, in particular, are significant: (1) *organization* — the establishment or rearrangement of resources, units, and methods for putting a program into effect; (2) *interpretation* — the translation of program language (often contained in a statute) into acceptable and feasible plans and directives; and (3) *application* — the routine provision of services, payments, or other agreed-upon program objectives or instruments.[24]

By transforming legislative language into clear administrative guidelines, by developing necessary arrangements and routines, and by actually furnishing mandated services, programs are carried out and, ultimately, policies are implemented.

All that sounds rather routine. Citizens expect program implementation to be relatively easy under normal conditions. We therefore seek to explain programmatic failures in terms of conflict, extraordinary events, or unexpected circumstances that develop in the course of implementation. However, failure to implement programs in accord with our expectations can often be attributed to less dramatic factors. For example, the difficulties that were encountered in putting into effect a much-heralded job training program of the U.S. Economic Development Administration (EDA) in Oakland, California, that was designed to provide permanent employment to minorities through economic development:

> The evils that afflicted the EDA program in Oakland were of a prosaic and everyday character. Agreements had to be *maintained* after they were reached. Numerous approvals and clearances had to be obtained from a variety of participants. . . . These perfectly *ordinary circumstances present serious obstacles to implementation*. . . . If one is always looking for unusual circumstances and dramatic events, he cannot appreciate *how difficult it is to make the ordinary happen*.[25]

program implementation a general political and governmental process of carrying out programs in order to fulfill specified policy objectives; a responsibility chiefly of administrative agencies, under chief executive and/or legislative guidance; also, the activities directed toward putting a policy into effect.

Thus, few things can be taken for granted in implementation, least of all that participants in a program will automatically fall into line in trying to make it work. Not that they harbor devious motives; it is simply a case of cooperation having to be induced on a routine basis rather than being assumed. Virtually everyone participating in program management has other responsibilities, causing some distractions among even the most conscientious individuals. In sum, a concerted effort is required to manage minimal aspects of **program implementation.** It is no wonder, then, that so many programs (and policies) are said to be only partially implemented — contrary to legislative mandates, executive orders, and public expectations. The essential point, however, is this: Failures in implementation are traceable far more often to these rather unexciting obstacles than to anything more dramatic.

DYNAMICS OF IMPLEMENTATION

On occasion, it is necessary to create a separate organizational unit to implement a new program or to pursue a different policy direction. This can happen in several ways. One is creation of a totally new agency, such as the U.S. Department of Veterans Affairs. Another is consolidating, upgrading, or dividing existing agencies, such as separating the Social Security Administration from the Department of Health and Human Services. More often, programs are assigned to existing agencies, which must still interpret and apply the laws and develop appropriate implementation methods.[26] In most legislation, Congress's intentions regarding program implementation are stated very broadly, such as: to carry out a program in a "reasonable" manner or "in the public interest, convenience, and necessity."[27] Thus, the responsible agency has discretion in developing operating guidelines and substantive details. This can result in a key agency role in shaping legislated programs and possibly *modifying* congressional intent. Political pressure on agencies responsible for implementing congressional directives is both real and constant. If it is true that "programs often reflect an attainable consensus rather than a substantive conviction,"[28] it follows that, if the political consensus changes in the course of implementing a law, chances are good that its implementation will also be modified to accommodate the change.

Because legislative language is so often vague, interpreting legislative intent can present pitfalls for an agency. Legislators themselves frequently cannot comprehend all the implications of their enactments. Without clear guidance, an agency may be left to fend for itself in the political arena and — worse — be caught up in disputes over just what the legislature meant in the first place! Not only is it difficult to make interpretations of initial legislative intent, it is also a tricky business to keep abreast of *changing* intent after passage of the original law (and in the absence of formal amendments to it). That can happen as committee memberships change, new interests surface, and the like.

Many times, authorizing legislation represents the best available compromise among competing forces. Under those circumstances, it is nearly certain that conflicts avoided or diluted in the course of formulating a law will crop up in the processes of interpreting and implementing it. Such controversy is not likely to do the responsible agency any good in the political process. Thus, interpretation, although necessary, has many potential pitfalls for the administrator.

Application of legislation follows from its interpretation by an agency and usually represents a further series of accommodations. Applying a law is complicated by the likelihood that other agencies also have an interest in the policy area and may well have programs of their own, by difficulties in determining optimum methods for carrying out legislative intent, and even by continuing uncertainty about the nature of a problem or program goals. Many programs are put into operation without full appreciation of a problem's dimensions; political needs to "do something" can outweigh careful and thorough consideration of what is to be done. One example of this phenomenon was the federal funding made available to state and local law enforcement agencies through the U.S. Law Enforcement Assistance Administration (LEAA). Public concern about rising crime rates in the 1960s prompted Congress to allocate funds for more (and presumably better) crime-fighting hardware, police officer training, and so on. But in retrospect, although there have been some improvements in fighting crime, it is not clear that LEAA did what it was supposed to — partly because there is less than universal agreement on just what that was and partly because the problem of crime has many more facets to it than the ability of the police to control it.[29] Frustration over the failure of crime control policies led to an equally ambitious $30 billion crime bill, enacted in mid-1994. Whether this effort will be more successful than its predecessors remains to be seen. Similar obstacles have hampered application of other policies and programs as well.

It is necessary, then, for agencies to determine the limits to which they can go in enforcing a policy. Usually, informal understandings are reached between *program managers* and persons or groups outside the agency about what will and will not be done. One danger here, of course, is *co-optation* of the program by external forces. Depending on the balance of forces, programs may be more or less vigorously pursued; the more controversial a program, the more likely it is that there will be resistance to it.

Support for an individual program is also affected by other programs an agency is responsible for managing and the order of priority among them within the agency. Other factors affecting program application are the values and preferences of agency personnel concerning individual programs, as well as their own roles and functions. An example that illustrates these points is the response of the EDA, particularly its Seattle regional office serving the San Francisco-Oakland area, when the head of the agency formulated a program for promoting minority hiring in Oakland. An Oakland task force was also established, bypassing normal organizational channels. Many in EDA felt more comfortable working with its traditional concern, which was rural economic development. After the person who had set up the Oakland program and task force departed from EDA, the project was treated with far less urgency by EDA, a reflection of its reduced standing in the eyes of most EDA employees working with it.[30]

program evaluation and review technique (PERT) a management technique of program implementation in which the sequence of steps for carrying out a project or program is mapped out in advance; involves choosing necessary activities and estimating time and other resources required.

APPROACHES TO IMPLEMENTATION

There are numerous program management approaches that might be used in carrying on agency activities. Until the mid-twentieth century, little attention was paid to this aspect of administration. It was apparently assumed that, once a program was in place, with adequate funding and political support, writing operating rules and regulations and actual administering the program followed routinely. However, specific management approaches that apply to tasks of program operation have evolved since World War II. We will examine two of the most important: the **program evaluation and review technique (PERT)**, which can include a related device known as the **critical path method (CPM),** and **management by objectives (MBO).**

The analytical tool known as PERT is founded on the belief that it is necessary to map out a sequence of steps in carrying out a program, or a project within a program. The steps involved normally include (1) deciding to address a given problem; (2) choosing activities necessary to deal with all relevant aspects of the problem; and (3) drawing up estimates of the time and other resources required, including minimum, maximum, and most likely amounts.[31] These help the administrator determine what needs to be done and — more important — in what order, as well as time and other resource constraints for completion of various steps in a process, or projects within a program. Ideally, a PERT chart should indicate how various processes are related to one another in terms of their respective timetables, sequence of execution, and relative resource consumption. The critical point of the PERT analysis is that at least some of these steps can logically be taken only *after* other steps have been completed. A clear implication of PERT is its potential for assisting program managers in their coordinative roles, discussed in Chapters 5 and 7.

A PERT chart can also be useful in calculating not only the time, funding, personnel, and materials that will be necessary, but also how much extra of each the agency will have as a cushion against unforeseen difficulties. For this reason, PERT charts are often used to calculate probable resource requirements for alternative paths of action. Such charts enable a program manager to see which path of action represents the best choice in terms of having margins of safety, as well as evaluating alternative paths. The path with the smallest margins of extra resources with which to complete all assigned program activities is the *critical path* because any breakdown in program management, for whatever reason, becomes critical in determining the program success or failure. Advance knowledge of such possibilities is clearly in the best interests of the manager, the program, and the agency.

Despite increasing sophistication in methods such as PERT and CPM, there remains a large component of human calculation in determining optimum paths of action. Activities are interdependent and must therefore be planned with an eye to step-by-step execution, but there are no assurances that calculations will be accurate. "Best estimates" are often the most reliable data available in projecting into the future. These can be very educated guesses, it is true, but there are risks in placing too much stock in them. Even so, a best estimate is often all a program manager has to go on.

A second major approach to implementing a program or policy is management by objectives. First outlined explicitly nearly fifty years ago,[32] MBO has been put into practice in national and state governments as a fairly flexible approach to defining long- and short-term agency objectives and to keeping a record of actual program results and (perhaps) effectiveness. It is another in a succession of efforts to achieve improved governmental effectiveness and is

critical path method (CPM)   a management approach to program implementation (related to PERT) in which a manager attempts to assess the resource needs of different paths of action, and to identify the path with the smallest margin of extra resources needed to complete all assigned program activities (the "critical path").

management by objectives (MBO)   a management technique designed to facilitate goal and priority setting, development of plans, resource allocation, monitoring progress toward goals, evaluating results, and generating and implementing improvements in performance.

related in some respects to performance budgeting, PPB, and other movements toward "better management." Management by objectives is more effective when integrated into other management approaches than when used alone.

Some important features of MBO include setting objectives, tracking progress, and evaluating results, along with the potential to make objectives explicit, to recognize the multiple-objective nature of administration, to identify conflicting objectives and deal with them, to provide opportunities for employee involvement in defining organization objectives, and to provide for feedback and measurement of organizational accomplishment.[33] Some have suggested that MBO makes it possible to pinpoint conflicting objectives before efforts are begun to pursue them.

Involvement of employees in *participative management* has been regarded by some as one of MBO's most important elements; this aspect has been described as fostering employee commitment to organization objectives, as well as employee participation in determining objectives.[34] At the same time, there is evidence that MBO can shift power *upward* in an organization by forcing information upward (especially bad news about program performance).[35] Thus an effective MBO system could alter somewhat the relationship between managers and their subordinates, for two reasons: (1) it is harder for subordinates to shield from their superiors that something is awry in program activities (for which the subordinates might be held accountable), and (2) early information about program difficulties is very useful to agency managers if they are to succeed in correcting the problems.

As with other approaches to improving management, there are obstacles to MBO's full realization (some of which we discussed earlier in reference to goals). Management guru Peter Drucker has noted that agencies often have ambiguous goals that are difficult to make operational.[36] Another dimension is that an organization's stated objectives may not be the real ones. Furthermore, there are "no commonly accepted standards for monitoring performance or measuring achievements of many public objectives."[37]

If, however, objectives can be defined in operational terms, MBO can be a useful management instrument. Although its application in the national government already appears to have waned somewhat, its residual effects seem destined to become part of the foundation for further management developments. For one thing, MBO may have value in helping decision makers choose which programs to delay or eliminate. In a time of great concern about priority setting and "less government," MBO may prove a harbinger of things to come.

PROBLEMS AND POLITICS OF IMPLEMENTATION

Despite the availability of numerous approaches to implementation, problems common to many managerial situations persist. It is appropriate to treat briefly three of the most important ones.

First, management *control* is a continuing challenge. This has two dimensions: one relating to management's ability to secure subordinates' cooperation in program activities and one concerning the agency's ability to cope with specific situations and with the surrounding environment. The more pressing of the two, from a manager's standpoint, is the former. Control of staffing, allocation of fiscal resources, designation of work assignments, and delegating discretionary authority are potentially useful devices for enhancing managerial efficiency. Even these, however, do not guarantee effective direction of internal activities.

Related to management control is the challenge of developing harmonious, productive, and beneficial *working relationships* within an agency. The lessons of the human relations school of organization theory and of organizational humanism, and concerns about effective leadership (see Chapters 5 and 7, respectively), enter into the organizational life of both manager and employee in this regard. Of central importance are vertical (leader–follower) and horizontal (teamwork and peer-group) relationships in all their forms. Meeting ego needs, regularizing on-the-job recognition for excellence, developing opportunities for employee independence or creativity, and facilitating communication among employees represent possible ways of creating and maintaining the kinds of relationships sought. Managers must be alert to all the possibilities.

A recurrent problem associated in the public mind with bureaucracy, namely, resistance to change, is indeed an operating problem of some importance. (See Box 10–2, "Resistance to Change: One Example.") Any time an organization is called on to undertake a task, the potential for change is present. Pressures for change can be real and direct, prompting employee reluctance to go along. The *conserver* in Anthony Downs's typology of bureaucrats may not be the only one within an agency to exhibit a degree of conservatism; others of every type and description may at times resist change and even the prospect of change. Overcoming such resistance is often a delicate managerial task. It is made more complicated by the fact that managers themselves may fear "upsetting the applecart" in their existing situation. Much of the time (though not always), this is due to a survival instinct that can be difficult for outsiders to understand. Nonetheless, the problem is real. It can, for example, hamper development of new activities, adaptation of existing operations to new circumstances or challenges, and maintenance of sufficient flexibility to meet emergencies. Moreover, in the new "deregulated" and competitive environment, more bureaucrats are expected at least to think like entrepreneurs, to raise rather than just spend revenue. Whatever the causes, costs of resisting change can be substantial, and constant effort is necessary to gain and maintain support for many kinds of change in administrative behavior.

In the midst of criticism concerning the failure of programs to live up to their promise, a little-noticed aspect of implementation deserves attention: the real possibility that agency implementation of a law may entail actually changing its purpose(s) in order to satisfy shifting political demands. If the legislative

BOX 10–2   PRODUCTIVITY AND SERVICE QUALITY IMPROVEMENT

Resistance to Change: One Example

Inglewood, California, has used one-man refuse trucks for more than a decade at significantly reduced cost and with fewer injuries and greater satisfaction for personnel.

Informed of the one-man trucks, the sanitation director in an eastern city using four men to a truck said he did not believe it. Having confirmed that they were in use, he opined that Inglewood's streets and contours were different from his city's. Convinced that conditions in both places were generally the same, he lamented that his constituents would never accept the lower level of service. Persuaded that the levels of service were equal, he explained that the sanitation men would not accept a faster pace and harder work conditions. Told that the Inglewood sanitation men prefer the system because they set their own pace and suffer fewer injuries caused by careless coworkers, the director prophesied that the city council would never agree to such a large cutback in manpower. Informed of Inglewood's career development plan to move sanitation men into other city departments, the director pointed out he was responsible only for sanitation.

SOURCE: *Improving Productivity in State and Local Government* (New York: Committee for Economic Development, March 1976), p. 46.

coalition that was strong enough to pass a law does not continue to support the agency in charge of implementation, it may turn out, on later examination, that effects of the law were different from those envisioned for it. It is not uncommon for those who failed to "carry the day" in the legislative struggle to recover some of their losses by applying pressure on administrative agencies, thus altering the nature of the program that the majority thought it was adopting. Sometimes administrators are willing allies in this effort, sometimes not. Either way, the outcome is the same: substantive modification of programs or policies.

Consider the following case history. Title I of the Elementary and Secondary Education Act of 1965 greatly increased the national government's presence in many phases of education nationwide, most of all in funding local school districts and, to a lesser extent, state education agencies.[38] Title I of ESEA "dictated the use of massive [national] funds for the general purpose of upgrading the education of children who were culturally and economically disadvantaged," while leaving considerable discretion in the hands of local education agencies to develop local programs for achieving that goal.[39] "If there was a single theme characterizing the diverse elements of the 1965 . . . Act, it was that of reform . . . ESEA was the first step toward a new face for American education."[40] The key emphasis of Title I was infusion of aid to school districts in which there were large numbers of poor children, with the idea that education could contribute to ending poverty for these students, at least in their adult years. The national government's prevailing political focus in the mid-1960s was on combating poverty, and educational aid allocated as special-purpose funding was viewed by many as essential to the antipoverty effort.

There were, however, other purposes of Title I that, although they did not conflict with aid to disadvantaged students, made it more difficult to determine what the central purpose of Title I really was. These included raising achievement levels, pacifying the ghettos, building bridges to private (sectarian) schools, and providing fiscal relief to school districts.[41] Depending on which of these was to receive the greatest emphasis in Title I implementation, it would be possible to draw varying conclusions about whether the purpose of Title I was, in fact, being fulfilled.

The point to be made here, however, does not concern evaluations of Title I implementation; we shall deal with that subject shortly. Rather, it is that actual congressional intent — as distinguished from the legislation's stated purpose — may have changed during the first decade of the law's operation (1965–1975), until the only form of aid to education that could gain majority support in Congress was general-purpose, not special-purpose, aid. As the political scene changed in the late 1960s and early 1970s, support for Title I in its original, legislated form apparently changed also. As a result, funding under Title I came increasingly to be general-purpose aid. This matched long-standing preferences of traditional bureaucrats in the Office of Education. But, more significantly, Congress itself, in effect, broadened Title I aid categories to include general-purpose aid. What the most powerful education subsystems wanted, they got — and poverty-related education aid was not their highest priority. Redirecting implementation of a law can also occur when a new chief executive regards it as sufficiently important to do so.

Program Evaluation

In recent years, evaluation of programs has become a central concern to virtually all administrative policymakers, most political executives, legislators, and the public. Whether a program is accomplishing what it was designed to do is a key question for managers; it also affects future planning of program efforts as the policy cycle is repeated in a continuous cycle of policy formulation and revision (see Figure 10–1).

Only since the early 1970s has widespread interest developed among public managers in *systematic* rather than intuitive evaluation procedures. The latter have been in use for some time — by political superiors, clienteles, the mass media, and academics, among others. As used here, *evaluation* can be defined as systematic measures and comparisons to provide specific information on program results to senior officials for use in policy or management decisions.[42] This

FIGURE 10–1   The Plan-Do-Study-Act Cycle

Act on What Was Learned
• Improve ~ Test ~ Monitor ~ Improve
• Make recommendations
• Test effect of recommendations

Plan a Change or Test
• Define the problem
• Suggest possible causes

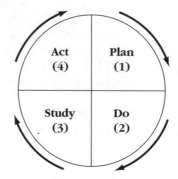

**Observe the Effects
of the Change or Test**
• Summarize data

**Carry Out the Change
or Test, Preferably
on a Small Scale**
• Collect data

SOURCE: Michael E. Milakovich, "Creating a Total Quality Healthcare Environment," *Healthcare Management Review,* 16 (Spring 1991), p. 16.

definition suggests that evaluation can be used in both policy-related and programmatic decision making. In the former, evaluation can be a useful device for identifying, documenting, and clarifying the most important objectives of a project, program, or agency; it can also be used to develop measures for success that can be incorporated into management processes. At the programmatic level, evaluations can help managers continuously monitor resources spent, activities under way, and actual performance compared to performance standards.[43] All these efforts can — and should be designed "so as to enable us to learn the true efficacy [effectiveness] of the supposed good."[44]

program evaluation
the systematic examination of government actions, policies, or programs to determine their success or failure; used to gain knowledge of program impacts, establish accountability, and influence continuation or termination of government activities.

Program evaluation can be used for three purposes: (1) to learn about a program's operations and effects, (2) to fix accountability of those responsible for program implementation, and (3) to influence the responses of those in the program's external political environment. Most agency managers fail to take full advantage of these possibilities, however, by beginning their evaluation programs too late, assigning evaluation responsibilities to staffs that lack the requisite skills, or yielding to temptations to distort or suppress unfavorable evaluation findings. Thus, simply understanding the mechanics of conducting evaluations is not enough; managers must be aware of the potential pitfalls and take steps to avoid them.

EVALUATION PROCEDURES

Evaluation requires certain preconditions and a series of steps. The most important preconditions are, first, an understanding of the problem toward which a government program or policy was directed and, second, clarity of goals that the program or policy was designed to achieve. It makes no sense to evaluate in a vacuum — that is, without some conception of what was supposed to be accomplished. Evaluation deliberately related to program goals has grown out of recent developments in the budgeting process, where cost-efficiency criteria told little about what an enterprise was actually doing. Performance budgeting, too, fell short in this regard, though not by as much. For example, a study of per-capita expenditures in a governmental program might tell us something about political influence and governmental commitment but not much about the effects of money being spent. Only with increasing concern for program impact and effectiveness could the process of evaluation as a distinct function really come into its own.[45]

Steps to be taken in an evaluation include at least the following.[46] First, there must be *specification* of what is to be evaluated, regardless of how narrow and precise or broad and diffuse the object of evaluation is. A nationwide program to immunize children against measles and one to reduce illiteracy among poor adults can both be specified for purposes of evaluation. The second step is measurement of the object of evaluation by *collecting data* that demonstrate the performance and effect of the program or policy. There are several possibilities, ranging from highly systematic, empirical data and methods to casual, on-the-scene observations by untrained observers. The third step is *analysis*, which can vary in the rigor with which it is carried out. How each of these steps is defined and executed affects the final evaluation product.

In order to make a coherent and rational evaluation of program or policy effectiveness, a clear cause-and-effect relationship has to be established between given actions by an agency and demonstrated impacts on a societal problem. For example, FBI crime data indicated that, during the coldest months of a recent winter, the number of crimes usually committed out-of-doors — muggings, assaults, and so on — dropped dramatically. Some might have argued that this was due to beefed-up police patrols or to larger law enforcement expenditures. Yet the bitter cold weather seems to have played a bigger part than either of these. The crux of the matter, however, is that, if police patrols *had* been beefed up or if expenditures *had* been up sharply, it might have been easy — and politically profitable — to conclude that these factors, not the weather, *caused* the drop in crime. That an intended result materializes is no guarantee that the relevant program caused it to occur. Certainly, there is a chance that a cause-and-effect relationship does exist, but it is useful to confirm that.

Designing a program evaluation is a complex task, with several different evaluation designs possible.[47] It is important to tailor a design to the particular program being evaluated so that the results can be relied on. Programs as diverse as manned space exploration, school lunches, garbage collection, and downtown redevelopment require varied evaluation schemes appropriate to their respective objectives, modes of operation, and units of measurement. In all cases, however, the question that evaluators would ideally ask is, "What actually happened, compared to what would have happened had the program not existed and everything else had been exactly the same?" Five evaluation designs are commonly used (though there are others), each of which lends itself to specific techniques.

before-versus-after studies evaluation and comparison of results before and after program implementation to determine what results, if any, were achieved.

Before-versus-after studies compare program results at some appropriate time after implementation, compared with conditions as they were just before the program got under way. It is especially useful when time and personnel available to conduct the evaluation are in short supply and when the program is short-term and narrow in scope. One drawback is that it is difficult, using this method, to be sure that any improvements are, in fact, due to the program's operation (recall the example of fewer crimes in cold weather).

time-trend projection the comparison of pre-program data with actual postprogram data.

Time-trend projection of preprogram data versus actual postprogram data compares results with preprogram projections. This method can be used to measure various kinds of trends as they are affected by a program. An example might be a local volunteer-sponsored newspaper recycling effort that gives way to a municipal recycling program. Data can be gathered on tons of newspaper collected over a period of years before municipal recycling, and projections made concerning the likely increase in tonnage without the program change. Later, comparisons of actual tonnage to those projections can shed light on actual program impact.

Comparisons with jurisdiction or population segments not served by the program have the advantage of controlling for nonprogrammatic factors. That is, by comparison with other jurisdictions, or with parts of the internal population not served by the program, it is possible to determine whether any change was due to the program. An example is the State of Connecticut's strict highway speed enforcement program. One criterion for evaluating the program was its effectiveness in reducing the number of traffic fatalities per 100,000 population. Initial data indicated a decline in traffic deaths, starting at about the time the enforcement program went into effect. But could evaluators be sure that the decline was not due to other factors — safer cars, more advertising stressing careful driving, gas shortages? To answer that, Connecticut's highway death rate was compared to those in neighboring states in which no new enforcement program had gone into effect, and it was found that the fatality rate had indeed declined relative to the statistics for the other states. Thus, it was evident that some factor unique to Connecticut — a reasonable inference being the speed enforcement program — had accounted for reducing traffic deaths.

Many evaluation techniques compare planned versus actual performance and measure postprogram data against targets set in prior years, whether before or during program implementation. This is a more general device, one used by many state and local governments to compare performance of a program to implied rather than explicit targets. For example, one state found that its guaranteed student loans were being used by far more middle-income families than those with lower incomes. It's not that the former were ineligible — but simply that the general need for student aid was assumed to be greater among the latter. (Perhaps it was, but that apparently was not a determining factor in patterns of use.) Ideally, this method should be used to supplement one or more of the other four techniques.

Controlled experimentation, one of the most complex and costly methods of evaluation, involves comparing preselected, similar groups of people, some served by the program and some not (or served in different ways). Most important, here, is seeking to ensure that the two groups are as similar as possible, except for their participation (or nonparticipation) in the program. This can be accomplished either by deliberately matching individuals having similar characteristics and subsequently placing them in the different groups, or by random selection (randomization) of members in both groups. The experimental and control groups (for example, individuals involved and not involved in manpower training or alcohol abuse treatment programs) would be subjected to performance measures of their relevant behaviors before and after program implementation.[48] If the experimental group showed substantially greater improvement, this would provide strong evidence that the program was responsible. This method can be used in combination with time-trend projections and jurisdictional comparisons but much greater precision is required — principally by seeking close similarity between the two groups or populations being studied.

controlled experimentation involves comparisons of two groups of similar people, one served by the program and another (control group) not served, or served differently; the most expensive and least practiced form of evaluation.

PROBLEMS AND POLITICS OF EVALUATION

If the purpose of evaluation is to assess program performance and accomplishment objectively, it is evident that there are numerous difficulties involved. Some concern problems of performance measurement — the nature of evaluation data, criteria of evaluation, information quality, and the like. Others pertain to political factors that can be injected into an evaluation process, changing the nature — even the very purpose — of a program evaluation. These difficulties often overlap, compounding the existing problems.

A central problem in evaluating public programs is considerable uncertainty about the reliability of performance indicators. Available indicators of accomplishment that have been used extensively are widely regarded as inadequate. It has been difficult to develop measures with enough objective precision to produce meaningful evaluative results. In part, this is a matter of deficiencies in obtaining necessary information although, in recent years, more sophisticated management information systems have been designed and put into operation. Improved information capability should enhance the total process of evaluation as an objective function of public administration.

Another dimension of the problem of performance indicators is the fact that the same data can often be manipulated and interpreted in different ways to produce different results. For example, educational information is quite confusing — few can be certain how well our educational systems function. Yet we have hundreds of studies of educational attainment, test scores, measures of test validity, and a great deal more. What does it all mean? A dozen different experts might give a dozen different answers. Thus, improving evaluation instruments remains very much on our agenda of unfinished business.

A third factor is whether there are major disparities between a program's official goals and those of the program's key implementers. This seems to have occurred to some extent in the case of ESEA. One of the harshest evaluations of Title I implementation accused the Office of Education of not fulfilling the mandates of Title I — specifically, of not ensuring that money intended for educating poor schoolchildren was actually being spent by state and local school officials for that purpose. The problem, according to one observer, was that the reformers and implementers were different people and that the Office of Education staff did not regard itself as investigation-oriented and was not inclined to monitor state agencies in their expenditure of Title I funds.[49]

One other problem is the *time frame* in which programs operate and how much time is required before a meaningful appraisal of program results can be made. Because no program works perfectly, it is natural for those in charge to seek more time than others might want them to in order to correct shortcomings and produce positive results (another instance in which political considerations overlap). But, even in purely objective terms, required time frames of different programs vary. And reasonable time requirements have to be taken into account — assuming that "reasonable" can be satisfactorily defined.

The "politics of evaluation" raises different kinds of issues, although they are not unrelated to those already discussed. Evaluations are used in the most general sense to determine whether there is justification for continuing a program to the same extent, in the same manner, and for the same cost. But *justification* is a tricky term, and it raises a fundamental issue in the evaluation process. On the one hand, evaluation, in an ideal sense, is designed to be value-free and objective; on the other, *justification* is a value-loaded term because, in order to justify something, a context of values must be present. That is, nothing is ever simply justified; it is only justified in terms of something else. Thus, an evaluation to determine whether a program is justified necessarily becomes bound up with different sets of values about what constitutes adequate justification.

The usual pattern seems to be that evaluations by those in charge of a program or policy are more favorable to its continuation in substantially the same form than are evaluations carried out by independent third parties, especially those who are skeptical. It is not unduly cynical to suggest that an agency will almost always be kinder in judging its own data than will others who do not have the same stake in the agency's activities and that the agency will adopt the time frame most likely to produce the intended program effect and that it will try to ignore other variables that could also have produced the desired effect(s).[50] Because program survival may depend on whether evaluations are positive or negative, a process that many see as value-free and therefore politically neutral is, like so many other things in public administration, weighted down with political implications. That is why internal evaluations so often point up program successes, whereas external evaluations tend to emphasize deficiencies and ways to improve program management.

Perhaps the mix of factors frustrating truly objective evaluations can best be summed up by the following description of Title I evaluation by the Office of Education:

> Since the beginning of the program, evaluation has been high on the list of rhetorical priorities, but low on the list of actual USOE priorities. The reasons for this are many. They include fear of upsetting the [national]–state balance, recognition of [the fact] that little expertise exists at the state and local levels to evaluate a broad-scale reform program, and fear of disclosing failure. No administrator is anxious to show that his [or her] program is not working.[51]

There is another important dimension to evaluation: the uses made of evaluation results. Even when evaluations produce entirely objective data (which, as noted earlier, is infrequent), there is no assurance that they will become the basis of efforts to bring about significant change — whether in program goals, in the way program activities are carried out, or in ultimate performance. Concentrated and effective political support for or against a given program can render evaluations of that program virtually irrelevant, whether those evaluations are favorable or unfavorable.

This point is illustrated by the national government's housing program (particularly public housing), which has consistently fallen far short of its projected goals, according to a number of separate evaluations. A national goal, established in 1949, was construction of 810,000 housing units for low-income families over a period of six years — nearly 50 years later, that number has still not been reached! Regardless of the many criticisms of these efforts, those who favor the housing program have not generated the necessary political support for reaching its goals. The interests served by building low-income public housing (the urban poor, primarily) are severely outweighed by the influence of other interests for whom public housing is a low priority — bankers, contractors, real estate brokers, and the great majority of the population that is not low-income. Criticism of the program's alleged failures did not sway its opponents, and the program has continued as merely a shadow of what it was supposed to be.[52]

Several concluding observations about evaluation are in order. First, despite the aura of value neutrality that frequently is associated with evaluation, its true significance may lie in its having caused public managers and others to focus "on the fundamental value choices that are inherent in the decision to initiate or terminate a policy, or to increase or reduce funding for a program."[53] This would indicate both how important and how difficult it is to conduct evaluations with a high degree of impartiality. Second, as psychologist Donald Campbell suggested, one way to reduce the political "liability of honest evaluation" would be to "shift from . . . advocacy of a specific reform [program] to . . . advocacy of the *seriousness of the problem* [that the program is designed to address], and hence to the advocacy of persistence in alternative . . . efforts *should the first one fail.*"[54] Campbell continued:

> The political stance would become: "This is a serious problem. We propose to initiate Policy A on an experimental basis. If after five years there has been no significant improvement, we will shift to Policy B." By making explicit that a given . . . solution was only one of several that the administrator . . . could in good conscience advocate, and by having ready a plausible alternative, the administrator could afford honest evaluation of outcomes. Negative results, a failure of the first program, would not jeopardize [his or her] job, for [the] job would be to *keep after the problem* until something was found that worked.[55]

Although government fiscal constraints might make it more difficult, in some respects, to proceed in this manner, more dispassionate and sound evaluations might well result from taking such an approach. Third, in recent years the U.S. **General Accounting Office (GAO)** has conducted an increasing number of systematic reviews and evaluations of national government programs. The GAO has an established reputation for professionalism, political neutrality, and conducting objective evaluations. Finally, "evaluation is likely to lead to better program performance only if the program design meets three key conditions: (1) program objectives are well defined, (2) program objectives are plausible, and (3) intended use of information is well defined."[56] That is, if we are to evaluate public programs properly, those programs must have had the *capacity to be evaluated* built into them from the outset. (This caveat brings us full circle — back to program planning and design as a key building block of all program operations and management.) As evaluation continues to grow in significance, our sophistication in designing, conducting, and interpreting evaluations will have to keep pace.[57]

General Accounting Office (GAO) the investigative arm of Congress that helps Congress oversee federal programs and operations to assure accountability to the American people through a variety of activities including financial audits, program reviews, investigations, legal support, and policy/program analyses.

Government Productivity and Measurement of Results

Within an economic framework of scarce resources and downsizing, making optimum use of public resources is a primary concern; thus, the productivity of government programs has taken on increasing political, economic, and social significance. Links between productivity and other aspects of management — such as efficiency, goal setting, and strategic planning — have also been stressed. A brief look at key elements of productivity will indicate where scholarly observers and others have placed the most emphasis.[58]

Productivity and efforts to achieve it are lineal descendants of concern for efficiency in government, yet they encompass a broader area. **Productivity,** unlike its forerunner, focuses on both efficient use of governmental resources and actual impacts of what government does — that is, on efficiency (of programs) and effectiveness (of results). It springs also from efforts to identify specific program objectives and to measure progress toward achieving them. The task is made more difficult by the fact that measures available to public managers for effectively monitoring programs are less precise than we might like. In addition, measures of public productivity are not as simple as those employed in the private sector. There is no bottom line profit-loss measure of results in most public agencies. Much of what government tries to do involves *preventing* various social ills — crimes, disease, teen pregnancy, destruction by fire of lives and property. How does one measure the productivity of such functions? There is no easy answer. Yet it has been possible to develop some useful measures for assessing the productivity of individual programs in conjunction with other emphases in program analysis and evaluation.

The first approach deals with programs in which output is easily measurable — for example, tons of refuse collected per sanitation truck shift, where the goal is reducing the unit cost while improving responsiveness. Routine urban functions like upkeep of park facilities, repair of potholes, and maintenance of sanitation vehicles lend themselves to unit-cost measurement of productivity.

The second approach concerns programs or functions in which output is harder to measure — for example, provision of police or fire protection or administration of federal unemployment or public assistance programs. Here the intent is to improve deployment of resources by assessing probable needs so as to ensure that resources will be available when and where they are needed most. This approach can also be usefully employed in sanitation departments, rescue services, and civil defense offices. State governments can use productivity measures to assess the impact of programs in corrections, education, health care, and transportation.

But efforts to improve productivity, however measured, may encounter obstacles. Table 10–1 lists common problems at the local level, with possible ways to overcome them. Two general approaches to solving productivity problems have been used. One stresses improving organizational and processing procedures, particularly through imaginative use of information technology (IT), such as computers, LANs (linked area networks), and management information systems. Government agencies extensively involved in provision of social services, with attendant recordkeeping needs, may find this technology especially beneficial for increasing cost efficiency in a wide variety of programs. For instance, federal welfare and supplemental Social Security benefits have been available since mid-1994 at automated teller machines (ATMs). In addition, by 1999, electronic delivery and direct deposit of monthly checks is expected to cover nearly all 34 million recipients of Social Security benefits, reducing fraud and saving nearly $200 million annually.[59] Computer and software applications

productivity the measurable relationship between the results produced and the resources required for production; a quantitative measure of the efficiency of an organization.

TABLE 10–1	Some Common Problems of Low Productivity in Local Government and Suggestions for Corrective Action	
Problem	*Possible Corrective Action*	*Illustrative Examples*
Sufficient work not available or work-loads unbalanced	Reallocate manpower	Housing complaint bureau schedules revised and temporary help employed during peak winter season
	Change work schedules	Mechanics rescheduled to second shift when equipment is not in use
	Reduce crew size	Collection crew size reduced from 4 to 3 men
Lack of equipment or materials	Improve inventory control system	Inventory reorder points revised to reduce stock-out occurrences
	Improve distribution system	Asphalt deliveries expedited to eliminate paving crew delays
	Improve equipment maintenance	Preventive maintenance program instituted
	Reevaluate equipment requirements	Obsolete collection trucks replaced
Self-imposed idle time or slow work pace	Train supervisors	Road maintenance foremen trained in work scheduling, dispatching, and quality-control techniques
	Use performance standards	"Flat rate" manual standards adopted to measure auto mechanics' performance
	Schedule more work	Park maintenance crews mobilized and work scheduling system installed
Too much time spent on non-productive activities	Reduce excessive travel time	Permit expiration dates changed to reduce travel time of health inspectors
Excessive manual effort required	Reevaluate job description and task assignments	Building inspectors trained to handle multiple inspections
	Mechanize repetitive tasks	Automatic change and toll collection machines installed and toll collector staffing reduced
Response or processing slow	Combine tasks or functions	Voucher processing and account posting combined to speed vendor payments
	Automate process	Computerized birth record storage and retrieval system installed
	Improve dispatching procedures	Fire alarm patterns analyzed and equipment response policies revised
	Revise deployment practices	Police patrol zones redefined to improve response time
	Adopt project management techniques	Project control system installed to reduce construction cycle

SOURCE: From *So, Mr. Mayor, You Want to Improve Productivity. . . .* Washington, D.C.: National Commission on Productivity and Work Quality, 1974.

can make a noticeable difference in areas such as large education systems, unemployment compensation and retraining, welfare programs, monitoring of capital construction programs, procurement of goods and services, and payments to those who provide goods and services to a government or an individual agency. The other approach calls for development and application of new technological devices that could result in more efficient use of human resources — for example, polymerized water for better and less expensive firefighting. Current efforts along these lines are still relatively limited, but the possibilities are impressive: improved techniques for combating air and water pollution, construction of low-cost modular housing, use of closed-circuit television for simple medical tests of government employees or prisoners, and many others. It must be emphasized, however, that computerization and technology are viewed more often as capital investments than as techniques for improving productivity. Other productivity-enhancing techniques are human resource training, upgrading of methods (or software), and computer and information-processing training.

Measurement of performance and results has been a persistent concern for all executive agencies at all levels of government. The idea has received high-level attention in the Clinton administration.[60] The **Government Performance and Results Act (GPRA)** of 1993 is one step that the federal government has taken to shift the focus of government officials from program "inputs" to program execution and measurement of results. To bring about this shift in focus, GPRA sets out requirements for defining long-term general goals, setting specific annual performance targets derived from general policy goals, and annual reporting of actual performance compared to the targets. (Notice the similarity between these standards and those of management by objectives, described earlier.) As federal managers are held more accountable for achieving measurable results, they are also given more discretion in how to manage programs for optimum outcomes. The legislation established various performance and budgeting concepts and called for implementation of performance measurement in all federal agencies by fiscal year 1999. Two sets of pilot projects have been in existence to test and demonstrate annual performance plans, strengthen program performance reporting, and encourage managerial accountability and flexibility. Full-scale governmentwide implementation of strategic planning, annual program goal setting, and annual program reporting of expenditures began for all federal agencies in 1997. These tests will be evaluated with the goal of optimizing resources ultimately allocated for results. The legislation is characterized by the policy-making principles noted in Table 10–2.

With the full implementation of GPRA, it is anticipated that much greater emphasis will be placed on the execution of results measurement programs (outcomes, outputs, and results) than on traditional policy analysis. This could lead to "demonstration" projects in states and local governments, as well as more effective use of expenditures because ineffective programs will be either improved or terminated. Much of its success will depend on the skill of senior managers in implementing management and evaluation systems. Not unlike

Government Performance and Results Act (GPRA) commonly called the Results Act, requires federal managers to plan and measure performance in new ways.

TABLE 10–2	Principles of the Government Results and Performance Act of 1993

1. Defining an agency's mission and setting general goals and objectives are inherently viewed as budget and policy issues that involve broad groups of agency, congressional, and public stakeholders.
2. Annual performance goals should correspond to requests for program resources and be linked to budget requests.
3. There should be emphasis on agencies' identification of performance measures, so that performance goals can be properly set.
4. With implementation ultimately an executive agency responsibility, administrators must take a leadership and coordinative role during the pilot phase, in preparation for full-scale implementation.
5. Agencies will have substantial discretion in defining annual goals and performance measures.
6. Prescriptive directives or guidance, such as "how-to" instructions from the Office of Management and Budget, will be limited.
7. Implementation should be limited to existing agency resources as much as possible and should apply existing systems and processes.
8. Use of the pilot phase (1994–1996) as a "lessons learned" opportunity to identify and resolve problems.

ZBB, PERT-CPM, and MBO before it, the shear scope of the GPRA — with its "detached" mechanistic approaches to decision making and results measurement — may "misinform as much as . . . inform, if users are unaware of the subtle limitations of measurement systems."[61]

Productivity and results measurement concerns will continue to grow in importance, if for no other reason than public awareness of the limited resources available to successfully implement public policies. It is becoming more widely accepted in government and elsewhere that, increasingly, we may have to make do with what we have. The promise of efforts toward greater productivity lies in the fact that technology has not yet been fully applied to this area, and there is a growing track record of successes, which should encourage similar efforts elsewhere.[62]

Total Quality Management

Reflecting a long-term trend toward participatory (Theory Z) management in American society, *total quality management (TQM)* is based on the idea that the greater the involvement that individual employees (or teams of "empowered" employees) have in determining and implementing organizational goals, the more committed they will be to achieving those goals. By providing incentives to increase the success of the whole enterprise, TQM encourages organizationwide commitment, teamwork, and better-quality results. A management system developed in private industry and based on *statistical process control (SPC)* techniques, TQM is aimed at satisfying customer expectations by continuously working across the organization to improve internal and external processes. Over 5,000 companies and hundreds of governments in the United States now practice some form of TQM, encouraging teamwork and active employee participation; utilizing problem-solving techniques such as brainstorming, quality circles, or Pareto analysis; and employing statistical process control methods.[63] Key elements of a typical TQM system include the following:

- Top-level support and commitment
- Focus on customer satisfaction
- Written productivity and quality goals and an annual improvement plan
- Productivity and quality measures and standards that are consistent with agency goals
- Use of the improvement plan and measurement system to hold managers and employees accountable
- Employee involvement in productivity and quality improvement efforts
- Rewards for quality and productivity achievement
- Training in methods for improving productivity and quality
- Retraining and out-placement for any employees who might be negatively affected by improvement efforts
- Reducing barriers to productivity and quality improvement

Public managers realize that performance measurement alone does not necessarily lead to quality improvement. Likewise, merely training employees in the use of quality techniques and tools, without guidance on how to *apply* them to their specific environments, does not guarantee improved quality service or better results. All the elements described above are *necessary* but are *insufficient* by themselves to continuously improve management systems and customer service. Structural as well as attitudinal barriers must be overcome to sustain any total quality improvement effort.

Total quality management is based on *internal* regulation and worker self-management commonly known as *empowerment;* its strategies are designed to reduce internal competition, foster teamwork, improve decision-making processes, and reduce costs. In the competitive manufacturing sector, these techniques have produced remarkable gains in quality, productivity, and competitive position. In public administration, TQM has communicated an attitude that stresses extended customer satisfaction, encourages employees to examine relationships between existing management processes, improves internal agency communications, and responds to valid customer demands. In exchange for the authority to make decisions at the point of customer contact, all empowered employees must be thoroughly trained, and results (at least until new systems are in place) must be carefully monitored. The importance of training in TQM — as in government generally — is often overlooked. A 1989 Task Force of the National Commission on Public Service found that the federal government spends only 0.8 percent of its total payroll on training. In contrast, corporations such as Hewlett-Packard, Motorola, and IBM spend almost four times as much (an average of 3 percent) on employee training. Governments at all levels will find it increasingly necessary to fund training for quality improvement, especially for lower-ranking employees, who have the most direct contact with citizens/customers/taxpayers.

Despite resistance, TQM is being used extensively to improve a wide range of federal executive agencies, public utilities, and state and local governments. One observer has argued, however, that "pure" quality initiatives are ill suited to public-sector organizations, citing four key limitations: (1) defining the customers of government is ambiguous; (2) public administrators are service- rather than product-oriented; (3) public agencies are input- rather than output-oriented; and (4) politics works against long-term leadership and constancy of mission.[64] Others have suggested that political leadership is necessary to achieve any change, and that governments are primarily service organizations that can (and must) respond to customers.[65] Nonetheless, since 1988, OMB has provided leadership for a joint public- and private-sector quality improvement effort, designating TQM as the official management improvement system for all federal executive agencies.

Application of quality improvement techniques by state and local agencies responds to citizen demands for better service quality, improves government's ability to effectively solve public problems, and provides a promising model for future "customer-responsive" public management practices. Although too numerous to describe in detail, many other public agencies, nonprofit organizations, and service organizations are involved as well. Arkansas, Florida, Minnesota, North Carolina, New York, and Vermont have established state quality awards patterned after the federal government's **Malcolm Baldrige National Quality Awards**, and many other states and localities have launched quality improvement efforts.

Malcolm Baldrige National Quality Awards created by Public Law 100–107, and signed into law on August 20, 1987; led to the creation of a new public–private partnership. Principal support for the program comes from the Foundation for the Malcolm Baldrige National Quality Awards.

Reflecting our federal system of diverse, decentralized, and divided authority, specific projects and strategies to implement total quality management and productivity improvement differ substantially from county to county. Considerable progress has been made, however, since the late 1980s. The federal government has implemented TQM, with over two-thirds of all agencies participating; state initiatives date from the early 1990s, with over one-half involved;[66] and about one-fourth of local governments (cities over 25,000) report customer service, quality improvement, or employee empowerment in at least one function.[67]

Initiatives have been established to promote a political environment for better customer service in such diverse areas as Hampton, Virginia (see Box 5–1, "Hampton, Virginia, Case Study."); Lauderhill, Florida; Jackson, Michigan; Maricopa County, Arizona; Erie, Pennsylvania; the Port Authority of New York and

New Jersey (Kennedy, La Guardia, and Newark Airports); Salt Lake City, Utah, and Sunnyvale, California. Local governments are adopting a *process approach* to improving common areas such as personnel administration, recordkeeping, vehicle maintenance, and community development. Cities and counties are **benchmarking** the best practices of leaders in various processes. In this way, management improvements are being made, and standards set, on the basis of experience in other, similar jurisdictions. Public agencies are learning from each other how best to respond to the needs of all their customers.

benchmarking a quality and productivity improvement methodology which examines those organizations that are best at performing a certain process or set of processes (for example, employee relations) and then transplanting the methods into one's own organization.

The Emerging Customer Service Focus in Government

Responding to demands for improved service from citizens, clients, constituents, or taxpayers — all the "customers" of government — is a continuing challenge facing all public organizations. Implementing policies which include meeting standards for customer-driven service quality requires changes in existing organizational structures, closer customer–supplier relationships, an empowered and self-directed workforce, and better measurement of results. All public services — but especially those receiving a substantial share of revenues directly from user fees, tolls, or service charges — must provide the training, leadership, and resources necessary to initiate customer-driven Total Quality Service (TQS).[68] Above all else, responsiveness to a wide range of customers necessitates an attitudinal change. Senior public officials are increasingly aware that traditional productivity enhancement efforts alone do not improve customer satisfaction. The challenge for public managers is to motivate employees toward higher levels of performance while continually lowering costs and improving areas *defined by customers* as needing improvement. Not unlike TQM in private industry, TQS is a theory-based strategic option that allows public managers to reward truly exceptional individual performance, yet increase the capacity for organizationwide cooperation and continuous process improvement.

Despite persistent calls for reform, few governments have thus far succeeded in simultaneously improving service quality, increasing productivity, and reducing costs. In recent years, more and more emphasis has been placed on productivity improvement strategies variously known as total quality management (TQM), continuous quality improvement (CQI), and customer service quality improvement (CSQI) to achieve closer customer–taxpayer–provider–supplier relationships. All generally incorporate the following principles:

1. Commitment to meeting customer-driven quality standards;
2. Employee participation, or empowerment, to make decisions at the point closest to the customer;
3. Actions based on data, facts, outcome measures, results, and statistical analysis;

4. Commitment to process and continuous quality improvements; and
5. Organizational changes and teamwork to encourage implementation of the above elements.

To sustain a long-term public service quality improvement initiative, these basic changes, coupled with new attitudes and management practices, are needed. Three "blue-ribbon" National Commissions have recommended similar reforms and have focused on leadership at the local, state, and federal government levels.[69] The National Performance Review offered specific recommendations for decentralizing decision making, *putting customers first*, empowering employees, and simultaneously allowing for greater efficiency in budgeting, personnel, procurement, and empowerment of states and local governments. There is now a clear national strategy for applying total quality and customer service principles to improve the operations of all public agencies. It remains to be seen, however, whether individual public administrators respond to challenges of customer service or continue to use obsolete productivity methods.

ESTABLISHING CUSTOMER SERVICE STANDARDS

In other sectors of the American economy, reliance on individual productivity measures over total system and process improvement approaches has been linked to declines in both service quality and employee productivity. Some public agencies have discarded approaches that emphasize individual productivity and replaced them with newer, customer-driven, system-focused strategies that promote teamwork, improve internal processes, reduce costs, and meet customer standards. Various strategies can achieve results without the need for additional long-term resources by changing the relationships between existing management systems, enhancing the capacity for individual agencywide cooperation, and continuously improving processes.

What differentiates current customer service quality efforts from past attempts to achieve results? Past public-sector efforts stressed *externally* imposed methods of goal setting, decision making, individual performance appraisal, inspection, and program evaluation to achieve public priorities. Although methodologically sophisticated, these efforts used techniques such as ranking employees for pay purposes, merit increases, and bonuses to increase output from individuals, which motivated some employees, but neglected customer service, teamwork, and measurement of results. Applications of such techniques have not eliminated complaints of inefficient or ineffective services, wasted resources, or lack of responsiveness by public employees.

Achieving customer service quality without increasing costs in the long term (higher taxes or user fees) is difficult (but not impossible) in the public sector because of the role played by elected politicians as the final decision makers and because of the complex relationships among elected officials and the appointed public administrators who actually implement decisions. The two groups live in separate (but often overlapping) worlds of public accountability, leadership, special interests, and policy making. They must collaborate to achieve customer-driven service quality improvement.

Since September 1994, more than 200 federal agencies have been asking their customers what they wanted and how *they* judged good service. These surveys, focus groups, and opinions have been used to establish **customer service standards** for all federal agencies. President Clinton issued Executive Order 12862, "Setting Customer Service Standards," which required all agencies to publish customer service standards by Sepember 15, 1995, to:

customer service standards explicit standards of service quality published by federal agencies and part of the reinventing government initiative.

- Identify customers who are, or should be, served by the agency;
- Survey customers to determine the kind and quality of service they want and their level of satisfaction with existing services;
- Post service standards and measure results against them;
- Benchmark customer service standards against the "best in business";
- Survey front-line employees on barriers to, and ideas for, matching the best in business;
- Provide customers with choices in both the sources of service and the means of delivery;
- Make information, services, and complaint systems easily accessible; and
- Provide means to address customer complaints.

All agencies have complied, and the specifics of these standards are being worked out on an agency-by-agency basis. More importantly, the precedent has been set that *customers matter*, and some agencies have already achieved the goal of providing service that meets or exceeds the best in the business. (See Box 10–3, "Customer Service Standards: Social Security Administration.")

BOX 10–3   PRODUCTIVITY AND SERVICE QUALITY IMPROVEMENT

Customer Service Standards: Social Security Administration

As part of its participation in the National Performance Review, the Social Security Administration will publish nationally, and post in each of its offices, these performance standards:

- You will be treated with courtesy every time you contact us.
- We will tell you what benefits you qualify for and give you the information you need to use our programs.
- We will refer you to other programs that may help you.
- You will reach us the first time you try our 800 number.

Even President Clinton was surprised on May 3, 1995, when Dalbar Financial Services, Inc., of Boston, Massachusetts, recognized the Social Security Administration (SSA) as the best 800-number customer service provider in North America.[70] This prestigious *independent* business-service ranking rates all organizations it surveys for attitude, helpfulness, knowledge, and the time it takes to reach a personal representative. The Social Security Administration was rated first for being "courteous, knowledgeable, and efficient." As a result, some private-sector companies that rely on 800 numbers for customer service are asking SSA for ideas. This is clearly not an isolated instance, as many other agencies are working to attain higher-performance customer service standards.

THE POLITICS OF SERVICE QUALITY IMPROVEMENT

Failure of traditional policy analysis, evaluation, and productivity improvement approaches have led many to recommend shifting public responsibilities to the private sector. Although always an option, simply divesting public-sector functions, via privatization or contracting out, without structural changes is unlikely to achieve public service quality improvement. The diverse constituencies of governments increase the importance of improving the quality of services *from a customer perspective*.

Moreover, partisan, competitive political processes forces elected representatives to focus on immediate political decisions rather than long-term professional-administrative values such as efficient use of resources and increased productivity. There are always some exceptions, but annual budget cycles tend to reinforce a short-term perspective. Instead of responding with innovative solutions, elected officials often *claim* to be frustrated by bureaucratic resistance. At the same time, some avoid political accountability for results by *blaming* public employees or prior administrations for failure to improve conditions.

Appointed public managers have typically operated in a noncompetitive, "monopolistic" environment with far less control than their private-sector counterparts in staffing, defining missions, and controlling markets. Most are not required to run for reelection or raise revenue and have largely been protected from being fired by civil service rules. One of the conditions of becoming more **results-oriented** is to allow individual public managers more discretionary authority in removing employees who do not perform. Still, many bureaucrats are aware of the limitations of current public management practices but claim to be powerless to change them without political approval.

This **"blame and claim" strategy** has become a vicious circle, with no winners and too many losers, especially taxpayers and recipients of wasteful and inefficiently managed government programs. The results have been frustrating for both politicians and administrators, prompting further loss of public confidence in the ability of government to deal with basic social issues, as well as calls for abolishing government programs altogether.

results-oriented government programs that focus on performance in exchange for granting greater discretionary decision-making power to managers.

"blame and claim" strategy situation where politicians "blame" bureaucrats and bureaucrats "claim" not to have the authority to act.

Until now, neither side was willing to examine organizational structures and take the bold steps necessary to change existing public management processes and strategies. The issue has too often been framed in *ideological terms* rather than as how best to resolve a specific set of problems. Some argue that the efficiency of government is inherently limited by democratic values and that, given the choice, most citizens would prefer private alternatives or smaller, more expensive, local governments. Whether governmental institutions can be *improved* or should be *dismantled* and replaced by private institutions is part of this debate. Most advocates of privatization typically ignore the loss of accountability, benefits to special interests, the need for closer monitoring, and the corruption that accompanies many such efforts. Maintaining some degree of government inefficiency, overlapping functions, and checks and balances reminds us that "the responsibility for providing services — determining their scope, level, and the conditions under which they are delivered — should remain in the hands of government officials committed to *the public interest*."[71] Rather than replacing government with private-sector alternatives, most Americans want government that "delivers more and costs less." This strategy seems to have been supported by the results of the 1996 presidential and 1998 congressional elections.

In government, decisions are more complex, greater numbers of interests are affected, rewards tend to be less immediate, and leadership is less stable. Compared with management of the private sector, where competition, standardization, and markets dominate decision-making processes, many governments do lag behind. In the past, when governments have tried to become more efficient, elected legislatures have tended to reduce their budgets (see Chapter 9). Attitudes are changing as the recommendations of the National Performance Review are implemented. Among the bolder recommendations of the NPR (yet to be enacted by Congress) is to streamline the federal budget process by eliminating thousands of regulations, empowering states and local governments, and moving to a biennial (two-year) budget and appropriations cycle.[72] To lessen the fiscal impact of reinventing government, agencies are encouraged to become more *results-oriented*, as opposed to *inputs*-oriented. Program managers who achieve measurable targets would be allowed to keep a portion of the "profits" and distribute them by way of a predetermined formula. Details have yet to be worked out, but the **"gain-sharing"** principle has been accepted and recommended by the National Performance Review. While there appear to be more "incentives" to becoming results-oriented and customer-focused, there is still no equivalent to the "bottom line" for determining customer satisfaction in the public sector.

"gain-sharing" analogous to "profit-sharing" in the private sector, allows public agencies to share a portion of the savings accrued from implementing productivity improvements.

Summary

Public policy making is a highly diffuse series of interrelated processes, involving a multitude of actors inside and outside of government. Program management is expected to be of good quality, leading to the achievement of program and policy goals. The way in which policies and programs are managed affects virtually every facet of the administrative process. Policies differ in their rationales, broad impacts, and administrative components; major policy types have been described as distributive, redistributive, regulatory, self-regulatory, and privatization. The policy-making process is complex, loosely coordinated, highly competitive, disjointed, fragmented, specialized, and largely incremental, resulting in a great deal of inconsistency in the policies adopted and sometimes outright contradictions.

Policy making occurs in four stages: (1) drafting and enactment of basic legislation; (2) writing of rules and regulations; (3) implementation of the law; and (4) oversight of application and implementation, involving Congress, the courts, or both. Problems and demands are constantly defined and redefined in the policy process, suggesting a policy cycle that repeats these four stages more than once. Direct administrative involvement can take the form of rule making, adjudication, law enforcement, and program operations. Intergovernmental relations and contracting out also figure prominently in the making of public policy.

Policies, programs, projects, and performance measurement are systemically interrelated, all contributing to the results of government operations. Programs and projects are the building blocks of policy and, from a management standpoint, require particular attention in six areas: planning and analysis, implementation, evaluation, productivity, total quality management, and improving customer service.

Planning is essential for meaningful definition of program goals. The planning process calls for substantive, administrative, and political skills on the part of top management; a major challenge is to develop purposefulness in agency operations. Analysis is equally essential as a decision tool. Both informal and formal techniques abound; the latter have assumed a larger role in recent years. Among the more prominent formal analytic techniques are policy analysis, cost-benefit analysis, and operations research.

Implementation refers to activities directed toward putting a program into effect. It is necessary for agencies to organize, interpret, and apply programmatic or policy directives contained in the authorizing legislation. Controversy over legislative intent can make interpretation a difficult task. In addition, program application often takes place through a series of compromises. Other factors affecting application include informal limits on an agency's activities, controversy surrounding a given program or activity, agency priorities in relation to its other responsibilities, and values and preferences of agency personnel concerning individual programs and their own general role and function.

In order to determine actual programmatic results, it is necessary to specify what is to be evaluated, measure the object of evaluation by collecting useful data, and analyze the data. A cause-and-effect relationship must be established between specific program activities and apparent results. Methods of evaluation vary widely, from institutionalized procedures and informal evaluation devices to more formalized techniques. The rigor of evaluation methods and the uses made of the results will determine the value and impact of the evaluation process. A central problem in evaluating public programs is lack of adequate indicators of performance. Other difficulties include defining problems, identifying specific goals, dealing with disparities between official goals and those of key implementers, and defining the time frame necessary to give the program a chance to work. Evaluations are designed fundamentally to show whether a policy should be continued in much the same form as before. In theory, evaluation should be objective and value-free. Political factors can affect the uses made of evaluations. A focus on problems, not programs, may reduce the political costs of honest program evaluations.

Concern for government productivity and alternative sources of delivering services is on the rise. There are several approaches to measuring productivity and to improving productivity levels. Under conditions of limited resources (of all kinds), productivity in government and elsewhere will continue to be important.

Various strategies and tactics have been devised for conscientious managers who want to improve their administrative operations and their responsiveness to customers. Total quality management (TQM) is a systemwide strategy used by thousands of governments for improving processes and achieving agency goals. Customer service is becoming an important productivity improvement strategy in many governments. Federal agencies have set standards for customer service that can be used by citizens to evaluate the quality of service received.

KEY TERMS AND CONCEPTS

public policy	National Labor Relations Board
symbolic actions	(NLRB)
distributive policies	Internal Revenue Service (IRS)
redistributive policies	Justice Department
regulatory policies	planning and analysis
self-regulatory policies	operational goal
contracting out	strategic planning
Federal Trade Commission (FTC)	policy analysis
Occupational Safety and Health	
Administration (OSHA)	

KEY TERMS AND CONCEPTS *(continued)*

operations research (OR)	productivity
program implementation	Government Performance and
program evaluation and review	Results Act (GPRA)
technique (PERT)	Malcolm Baldrige National Quality
critical path method (CPM)	Awards
management by objectives (MBO)	benchmarking
program evaluation	customer service standards
before-versus-after studies	results-oriented
time-trend projection	"blame and claim" strategy
controlled experimentation	"gain-sharing"
General Accounting Office (GAO)	

SUGGESTED READING

Banovetz, James M., ed. *Managing Local Government: Cases in Decision Making.* Washington, D.C.: International City Management Association, 1990.

Barzelay, Michael. *Breaking Through Bureaucracy: A New Vision for Managing in Government.* Berkeley: University of California Press, 1992.

DiIulio, John J., Jr., Gerald Garvey, and Donald F. Kettl. *Improving Government Performance: An Owner's Manual.* Washington, D.C.: Brookings Institution, 1993.

Holzer, Marc, ed. *Public Productivity Handbook.* New York: Marcel Dekker, 1992.

Lee, Dalton S., and N. Joseph Cayer. *Supervision for Success in Government: A Practical Guide for First Line Managers.* San Francisco: Jossey-Bass, 1994.

Levin, Martin A., and Mary Bryna Sanger. *Making Government Work: How Entrepreneurial Executives Turn Bright Ideas into Real Results.* San Francisco: Jossey-Bass, 1994.

Meier, Kenneth J., and Jeffrey L. Brudney. *Applied Statistics for Public Adminstration.* 4th ed. Fort Worth, Tex: Harcourt Brace Jovanovich, 1997.

Nathan, Richard. *Turning Promises into Performance: The Management Challenge of Implementing Workfare.* New York: Columbia University Press, 1993.

Neiman, Max. *Defending Government: How Big Government Works.* Upper Saddle River, N.J.: Prentice-Hall, 2000.

Newell, Charldean, ed. *The Effective Local Government Manager.* 2nd ed. Washington, D.C.: International City/County Management Association, 1993.

Palumbo, Dennis J. *Public Policy in America: Government in Action.* 2nd ed. Orlando, Fla.: Harcourt, Brace, 1994.

Pressman, Jeffrey L., and Aaron Wildavsky. *Implementation.* 3rd ed. Berkeley: University of California Press, 1984.

Rainey, Hal G. *Understanding and Managing Public Organizations.* 2nd ed. San Francisco: Jossey-Bass, 1996.

Schwarz, Roger M. *The Skilled Facilitator: Practical Wisdom for Developing Effective Groups.* San Francisco: Jossey-Bass, 1994.

Sylvia, Ronald, Kathleen Sylvia, and Elizabeth Gunn. *Program Planning and Evaluation for the Public Manager.* Prospect Heights, Ill.: Waveland Press, 1997.

Thompson, Frank J., ed. *Revitalizing the State and Local Public Service: Strengthening Performance, Accountability and Citizen Confidence.* San Francisco: Jossey-Bass, 1993.

Vasu, Michael L., Debra W. Stewart, and G. David Garson. *Organizational Behavior and Public Management.* 2nd ed., revised and expanded. New York: Marcel Dekker, 1990.

ON-LINE RESOURCES:
Public Policy and Management

American Enterprise Institute

http://www.aei.org/.

Conservative Washington think tank.

American Society for Quality

http://www.asq.org/

Association applying, promoting, and providing *quality* related activities, education, and services to several types of organizations, including governments.

Association for Public Policy Analysis and Management

http://qsilver.queensu.ca/appam/

For graduate and undergraduate public policy programs, research institutions, and individuals in the public policy and management field.

Benchmarking

http://www.ibc.apqc.org

International Benchmarking Clearinghouse contains information about the best practices, networking opportunities, and benchmarking resources to discover, research, understand, and implement emerging and effective improvement methods.

Brookings Institution

http://www.brook.edu/

A private nonprofit organization that seeks to improve the performance of American institutions, effectiveness of government programs, and the quality of U.S. public policy.

Center for Rural Studies

http://www.crs.com

A nonprofit, fee-for-service research organization that addresses social, economic, and resource-based problems of rural communities.

Government Performance and Results Act Resource Center

http://www.opm.gov/gpra/index.htm

An invaluable collection of resources, tools, and guidance is available through this Web site to assist in implementing the Results Act.

Information and Referral Resource Network — IR-NET

http://www.ir-net.com/

Lists agencies providing information and referral, social service, health care, counseling, mental health, child care, domestic violence, drug abuse, alcohol abuse, welfare programs, and substance abuse.

Innovations in American Government

http://www.ksg.harvard.edu/innovations/

Comprehensive awards and recognition program funded by the foundation and administered by the Kennedy School of Government at Harvard University.

Library of Congress

http://lcweb.loc.gov/

Official federal government Web site includes on-line catalogues, collections, and specialized research.

Malcolm Baldrige National Quality Awards (MBQA)

http://www.quality.nist.gov/

Created by Public Law 100–107, signed into law on August 20, 1987. The award program led to the creation of a new public–private partnership. Principal support for the program comes from the Foundation for the Malcolm Baldrige National Quality Awards, established in 1988.

National Aeronautics and Space Administration (NASA) Project Management Resource Lists

http://www.hq.nasa.gov/office/hqlibrary/ppm/ppmbib.htm

Excellent bibliographies on a wide range of government productivity improvement issues; frequently updated.

National Center for Policy Analysis

http://www.ncpa.org/

Research institute that seeks innovative private-sector solutions to public policy problems; includes analysis of current international and domestic issues.

National Center for Public Productivity

http://www.andromeda.rutgers.edu/~ncpp/ncpp.html

A research and public-service organization devoted to improving productivity in the public sector. Founded in 1975, the center is the only productivity center in the United States devoted to public-sector productivity improvement whose mission is to assist federal, state, local, and not-for-profit agencies in further improving their capacity to provide quality services.

Policy Analysis

http://www.policy.com/news/index.html

Policy.com is a comprehensive policy news and information service.

Public Policy and Administration Links

http://www.wmich.edu/spaa/dicker/links.html

Western Michigan professor's links to policy areas such as criminal justice links including police departments; government links including agencies, organizations, research and data; public policy and policy analysis links; public administration links; and software sources.

Public Sector Continuous Improvement Site

http://www.deming.eng.clemson.edu/

The Department of Industrial Engineering at Clemson University provides this service in support of worldwide efforts in quality improvement and education in quality.

State Quality Awards

http://www.qualitydigest.com/html/state1.html

Listing of all state quality awards.

Urban Institute

http://www.urban.org/

The Urban Institute investigates social and economic problems confronting the nation and analyzes efforts to solve these problems.

U.S. General Accounting Office (GAO)

http://www.gao.gov/

The investigative arm of Congress that helps Congress oversee federal programs and operations to ensure accountability to the American people through a variety of activities, including financial audits, program reviews, investigations, legal support, and policy/program analyses. GAO is dedicated to good government through its commitment to the values of *accountability*, *integrity*, and *reliability*.

For further information on public policy and management see:
Bedford/St. Martin's Home Page

http://www.bedfordstmartins.com

Chapter 11

Government Regulation
and Administrative Law

> No *law is stronger than is the public sentiment where it is to
> be enforced.*
>
> Abraham Lincoln (1809–1865), letter to John J. Crittenden,
> 22 December 1859

Regulating various aspects of business and society is a long-standing and increasingly controversial aspect of government, especially at the national level. As suggested in Chapters 9 and 10, much of what the national government does has an impact on individual citizens, private corporations and other business enterprises, agricultural producers and marketers, labor unions, and state and local governments. But some functions are explicitly *regulative* in nature, setting and enforcing the rules for many private — especially economic — activities.

As we shall see in this chapter, the first national regulatory efforts in the late 1800s were aimed at punishment for, and then prevention of, abuses in the marketplace — antitrust violations and price gouging, for example. In this century, government regulation has become more extensive, focusing not only on *preventing* certain kinds of practices but also on *requiring* that certain operating standards and requirements be met. For example, before new products can be put on the market, they must be shown to meet the safety standards for the intended purposes. Examples of operating standards include accuracy in information supplied to consumers — the truth-in-packaging or truth-in-lending requirements enacted mainly in the 1970s.

Since 1960, more than a dozen new regulatory agencies in the national government have been created, with scores of new regulatory statutes. Regulatory actions touch virtually every part of our lives — our transportation (air bags, seat belts, aircraft maintainence and safety standards, freight rates), the food we eat, what can or cannot go into our beverages (for example, saccharin and aspartame), medications that may be used to treat disease, air and water quality standards, consumer health and working conditions, and the like. In addition, many of the post-1970 regulations have been of a different type from most previous ones. There are significant differences between "traditional" regulations — which emphasize price control and service enhancement — and "new" regulations — which are designed to prevent harm from a process, a product, or their side effects.[1] New regulations incorporate *social* as well as economic goals into the regulatory process, and they are much farther-reaching in their effect. (We will deal more fully with this distinction later in this chapter.)

Some government actions that are seemingly unrelated to regulating private lives, in fact, do so. These include local building codes and zoning laws; housing loan programs with minimum income requirements, effectively cutting off many poorer citizens from a chance to buy homes; school desegregation guidelines; equal employment opportunity requirements, housing, and education; nursing home inspections; minimum-wage laws; workplace hygiene and safety requirements; and tax policies at all levels of government. National and state energy policies touch many areas of our lives — automobile travel, home insulation, energy conservation, and so on. State and local regulation of public utilities directly affects consumers' utility rates.

The whole subject of government regulation in a "free-enterprise" economy can be highly complicated. Some contend that the most effective regulator is **free-market competition** among those seeking to attract the buying public. They argue that **government regulation,** by interfering with the marketplace, works to the disadvantage of both consumers and producers. Advocates of government regulation, however, see greater need to monitor and guide the course of competition; they believe that a completely unrestrained market will lead to **monopolistic practices,** higher costs, and lower-quality goods and services. In the twentieth century, the national government tried increasingly to strike a balance between regulating producers and permitting, indeed encouraging, competition in the marketplace, supporting both the right of consumers to purchase products that meet certain standards of safety and effectiveness and the right of producers to make a decent profit.

Regulatory activities are conducted by a wide variety of government entities. The earliest regulatory bodies — the **independent regulatory boards and commissions** of the national government — first appeared in the late 1800s and have expanded their numbers and activities in this century. Independent regulatory bodies are similar to other administrative entities in operating under delegated legislative authority, exhibiting functional overlap, and being influenced by political considerations. They differ in the kind of work for which they are legally responsible and in structural design. More recently, regulation has been an increasing responsibility of administrative bodies housed within cabinet departments or standing independent of any other administrative "home." We will discuss their origins, both societal and political; analyze the formal and polit-

free-market competition basis of U.S. and other free-enterprise economic systems where the means of production and distribution of goods and services are owned by private corporations or individuals, and the government role in the economy is minimal.

government regulation government activity designed to monitor and guide private economic competition; specific actions (characterized as economic regulation) have included placing limits on producers' prices and practices, and promoting commerce through grants or subsidies; other actions emerging more recently (termed social regulation) have included regulating conditions under which goods and services are produced and attempting to minimize product hazards and risks to consumers.

monopolistic practices a situation in which a certain company or group of companies controls the production and distribution system of that market to exclude all other competitors.

independent regulatory boards and commissions delegated authority by Congress to enforce both executive and judicial authority in the application of government regulations.

ical setting in which they operate, and with what consequences; and discuss some of the most volatile issues concerning government regulation in the past thirty-five years.

We will also discuss a related — and increasingly important — area of public administration: **administrative law.** "Administrative law is law governing the legal authority of administrators to do anything that affects private rights and obligations. It limits not only scope of authority, but also *the manner in which that authority is exercised.*"[2] All public administrators are governed in their operations by this body of law, as well as by legislative and chief-executive directives; but administrative law is particularly significant in the regulatory process because the latter bears directly on "private rights and obligations." Viewing the relationship between regulation and administrative law another way, we might say that regulation involves certain kinds of constraints that government places on private citizens, groups, and institutions, whereas administrative law is concerned with the constraints government places on itself. After discussing government regulation, we will take up administrative law and attempt to place the relationship between the two in its proper perspective.

administrative law an important body of American law pertaining to the legal authority of public administrative entities to perform their duties, and to the limits necessary to control those agencies; administrative law has been created both by judicial decisions (especially in the national government courts) and by statute (principally in the form of Administrative Procedure Acts, enacted by both national and state governments).

A word is in order concerning the terminology to be used in this chapter; this is especially important because of the number and variety of government entities currently engaged in some form of regulation. The term *regulatory agency* will refer to a regulatory body headed by a single individual (most commonly a director or administrator); a *regulatory commission* is headed by a group of commissioners (or, sometimes, board members); the term **regulatory body** will refer to both kinds of structures. These terms are consistent with the formal titles of such entities. For example, the Environmental Protection *Agency* (EPA) is headed by a single administrator — unlike the the Federal Communications *Commission* (FCC).[3] These usages will help us understand some of the differences among different types of regulators, in their operations as well as their formal structures.

regulatory body refers to all types of dependent and independent regulatory boards, commissions, law enforcement agencies, and executive departments with regulatory authority.

The Rise of Government Regulation

Historically, government regulatory activities have taken one of two forms: (1) putting certain limits on prices and practices of those who produce commercial goods, and (2) promoting commerce through grants or subsidies, on the theory that such payments are a public investment that will yield greater returns for the consuming public in the form of better goods and services. A prime example is airline subsidies. The first of these has a longer history than the second.

Regulation of interstate commerce under Congress's direction was a constitutional power of the national government (in Article I, Section 8) right from the start. Yet, for virtually all of our first century as a nation, responsibility fell to the states to carry on most of whatever regulation existed — for example, transportation tolls on and across rivers, prices farmers had to pay to grist mills and cotton gins, water rates, and railroad fares. In the post–Civil War period of industrialization, the national government gradually assumed more responsibility for both controlling and promoting commerce although the states still played an important role in developing and testing ways of controlling prices and commercial practices. As the emerging national economy grew and flourished, however, pressure began to mount for the national government to enter more extensively into the regulatory arena. This pressure stemmed from strong demands that the abusive practices of the railroad industry, in particular, be brought under control. State regulatory agencies, some of which were quite active, lacked jurisdiction to deal with enterprises (such as rail companies) that crossed state lines. Beginning with the New Deal, the national government came to exercise primary responsibility for both controlling and promoting economic activity. Although the states are still primary regulators of a few industries, such as insurance, and secondary regulators of industries such as banking, Washington is now the center of regulatory activity.

Making government policy has been regarded as a *legislative power* under the Constitution. Yet Congress and most state and local legislatures have found it difficult to write all the varied and detailed provisions that are necessarily part of governing a dynamic and complex society. There are two dimensions of the problem for a legislative body. First, most legislatures lack the time and technical expertise required to establish detailed rules and regulations on such complex subjects as nuclear energy, monetary policy, air safety, or exploration for, and marketing of, natural gas. As these and other areas of policy became important, it was increasingly necessary to create regulatory bodies able to deal with them. Second, even if legislatures had the time and skills, a large, collective decision-making body lacks the flexibility needed to adjust existing rules and regulations to changing conditions, again justifying creation of other entities to concentrate on each area.

Thus, even in the nineteenth century in the national government, it was apparent that it would be necessary to delegate authority to administrative agencies, with Congress monitoring their operations and adjusting their legislation but doing little actual regulation. This pattern has been followed in the twentieth century as well, at all levels of government. In a very real sense, then, regulation emerges as the outcome of legislative delegation of authority. Thus, any strengths or weaknesses of regulatory agencies and processes can be attributed, in the first instance, to actions of local, state, and national legislatures.

The first major institutional development in the national government was the creation in 1887 of the Interstate Commerce Commission (ICC) in response to public disenchantment with the railroads, especially in the Mississippi Valley and the West. Unlike the eastern portion of the country, where numerous rail lines were engaged in vigorous competition, the nation's midsection and expanding West were served by a small number of railroads that were able to engage in monopolistic practices. Establishment of the ICC signaled a clear change from the prevailing notion of governmental action taken to punish unlawful acts after they had occurred. This was the first step in *preventing* such acts from occurring and doing so by laying down rules that applied to a class of industries and actions, relieving the government of the need to proceed on the previous case-by-case basis in the courts.

Public pressure for controlling industry became stronger in the late 1800s and early 1900s, led by men such as James Weaver of the Greenback Party in the 1888 presidential election and, especially, William Jennings Bryan. The great trustbuster, Theodore Roosevelt, was followed in the White House by Woodrow Wilson; both men favored government measures to maintain economic competition and fair trade practices. In response to the stock market crash of 1929 and the other economic woes of the Great Depression, Franklin Roosevelt opened the way for even more stringent and far-reaching regulation. These individuals and their allies, and the policies they promoted, led to a significant increase in the scope of national government regulation.

The **Sherman Antitrust Act** of 1890 made it illegal to conspire to fix fares, rates, and prices or to monopolize an industry. Although enforcement mechanisms were not provided for in the original act, in 1903, the Antitrust Division of the Justice Department (which is not an independent regulatory agency) was created to direct enforcement of the Sherman Act. This proved difficult because of unclear language in the law and lack of authority delegated to the division. The result was increasing reliance on the courts to interpret legislative language and, some maintained, an inappropriate and perhaps excessive involvement of the courts in direct policy making. With delegation of authority to the ICC as a precedent, Congress attempted to solve the problem by creating another independent regulatory agency modeled after the ICC. In 1914, the Federal Trade Commission (FTC) was established to assist in antitrust enforcement, principally by interpreting and enforcing provisions of the **Clayton Act,** which had been passed the same year and which prohibited price discrimination if the purpose or effect of such discrimination was to lessen competition or to create a monopoly.[4] The FTC's involvement eased the burden on the courts although it did not remove it entirely; the commission has been active continually over the years in settling antitrust questions. The FTC was also given responsibility for controlling deceptive trade practices but, until 1938, this was not a primary function.

Subsequently, other entities modeled after the ICC and FTC were also established. The Federal Power Commission (FPC) was created in 1920 to regulate interstate sale of wholesale electric energy and the transportation and sale, along with rates, of natural gas; in 1977 the FPC was reorganized as the Federal Energy Regulatory Commission (FERC) and made part of the newly created Department of Energy. The Federal Communications Commission (FCC), established in 1934, regulates civilian radio and television communication (except for rates), as well as interstate and international communications by wire, cable, and radio (including rates). The FCC assigns frequencies and licenses operators of radio and television stations and has become increasingly involved in issues concerning cable television franchises and pay television. The

Sherman Antitrust Act first major antitrust legislation, passed in 1890, which made it illegal to fix prices or to monopolize an industry.

Clayton Act prohibits price discrimination to eliminate competition or create a monopoly.

Securities and Exchange Commission (SEC) responsible for regulation of stocks, securities, and investments.

Securities and Exchange Commission (SEC), also founded in 1934, was one means used by the government to try to prevent a repetition of the 1929 stock market crash. The Civil Aeronautics Board (CAB) was created in 1938 to regulate airline passenger fares and freight rates, promote and subsidize air transportation, and award passenger service routes to commercial airlines. The CAB was disestablished on January 1, 1985 — the first major regulatory agency to close its doors permanently — and its functional responsibilities were divided among the FAA (Federal Aviation Administration), the DOT (Department of Transportation), and the NTSB (National Transportation Safety Board).

There are other, similarly organized commissions. Also, as government activity generally has increased, regulative functions have come to be exercised by other types of agencies as well. It is possible to play "Washington alphabet soup" with the EPA, FAA, OSHA (Occupational Safety and Health Administration), and FDA (Food and Drug Administration), to name only a few (see Table 11–1). Important areas of regulatory responsibility are under these entities' jurisdictions.

Mention also should be made of state regulatory agencies, many of which are patterned after those at the national level, and local regulatory activities that have an impact on certain local economic enterprises.[5] As noted previously, states have primary responsibility for regulating insurance and are involved secondarily in regulation of banks. States also examine and license physicians, insurance agents,

TABLE 11-1   Selected Major U.S. Regulatory Bodies*

Federal Reserve Board (FRB)
Founded in 1913. Makes and administers credit and monetary policy, and regulates commercial banks in the Federal Reserve System.
Budget: $177 million[1]   Personnel: 1,655[2]

Federal Trade Commission (FTC)
Founded in 1914. Regulates business competition, including some antitrust enforcement, and acts to prevent unfair and deceptive trade practices.
Budget: $35 million   Personnel: 652

Food and Drug Administration (FDA)
Founded in 1930. Located in HHS; conducts testing and evaluation programs — and sets standards of safety/efficacy — for foods, food additives and colorings, over-the-counter drugs, and medical devices; certifies some products for marketing; and conducts research in other areas such as radiological health, veterinary medicine, and the effects of toxic chemical substances.
Budget: $881 million   Personnel: 8,487

Federal Communications Commission (FCC)
Founded in 1934. Regulates interstate and international radio, television, cable television, telephone, telegraph, and satellite communications; licenses U.S. radio and television stations.
Budget: $70 million   Personnel: 1,753

(continued)

TABLE 11-1   Selected Major U.S. Regulatory Bodies *(continued)*

U.S. International Trade Commission (USITC)
Founded in 1916. Renamed in 1974. Advises the president as to potential economic effect on domestic industry and consumers of modifications to trade barriers. It investigates the impact of increased imports on domestic industries, unfair practice, and imports of agricultural products that interfere with U.S. Department of Agriculture programs.

Budget: $42 million   Personnel: 383

Securities and Exchange Commission (SEC)
Founded in 1934. Regulates issuance and exchanges of stocks and securities; also regulates investment and holding companies.

Budget: $307 million   Personnel: 2,797

National Labor Relations Board (NLRB)
Founded in 1935. Conducts elections to determine labor union representation: prevents and remedies unfair labor practices.

Budget: $181 million   Personnel: 2,040

Equal Employment Opportunity Commission (EEOC)
Founded in 1964. Investigates and rules on charges of racial and other arbitrary discrimination by employers and unions, in all aspects of employment.

Budget: $268 million   Personnel: 3,022

Environmental Protection Agency (EPA)
Founded in 1970. Issues and enforces pollution control standards regarding air, water, solid waste, pesticides, radiation, and toxic substances.

Budget: $915 million   Personnel: 13,015

Occupational Safety and Health Administration (OSHA)
Founded in 1970. Located in Department of Labor; develops safety and health standards for private business and industry; monitors compliance and proposes penalties for noncompliance.

Budget: $341 million   Personnel: 2,415

Consumer Product Safety Commission (CPSC)
Founded in 1972. Develops and enforces uniform safety standards for consumer products, and can recall hazardous products.

Budget: $43 million   Personnel: 487

Nuclear Regulatory Commission (NRC)
Founded in 1975. Issues licenses for nuclear power plant construction and operation, and monitors safety aspects of plant operations.

Budget: $475 million   Personnel: 3,077

---

*Budget figures shown represent net budget authority; personnel figures represent full-time equivalent employees (1996 estimate). The Federal Reserve Board has no budget authority; its activities are financed through assessments paid by Federal Reserve System member banks.

[1]Estimated fiscal year 1997 budgets; 1995 figure given for EPA.

[2]Personnel figures are estimated 1997 figures; 1995 figure given for EPA.

SOURCE: *Budget of the United States Government, 1997. Appendix* (Washington, D.C.: U.S. Government Printing Office, 1996). //www.doc.gov/budget FY97/index.html

funeral homes, and real estate agents and certify those qualified to practice medicine and law. In highly technical and professional fields, such as medicine and law, the respective professional associations have key roles in setting state standards for entry into the professions. Indeed, in some instances, formal state decisions amount merely to ratifying standard-setting actions taken by professional associations (the *self-regulatory* category of public policy noted in Chapter 10).

Other state entities also have regulative impact. As noted earlier, public utility commissions have a great deal to do with setting intrastate retail rates for electricity and natural gas, and some also have investigative capacities. State commerce commissions regulate commercial activity occurring entirely within state boundaries and can have a substantial influence on shipping rates and other shipping practices. Liquor control boards (in some states, there are state-run "package stores" or liquor outlets), recreation departments, and environmental protection agencies are further examples of state entities that affect private economic enterprise. These can all act on their own authority and initiative without being subject to decisions made at the national level. In some areas of regulation, however, state and national agencies have collaborated on standard setting, accounting systems, and the like, contributing to the patterns of specialized intergovernmental contacts discussed in Chapter 4. Examples include cooperation prior to the mid-1960s between the ICC, FDA, FCC, and FTC and their respective state counterparts[6] and, in more recent times, between state and national EPAs.

At the local level, regulation of business activities most often involves granting licenses for operating taxis and establishments such as hotels, restaurants, and taverns. Other kinds of local regulative activities, however, can be very significant, such as housing and building codes, zoning ordinances, and transportation planning. There has been little research on local government regulatory impacts, which may be an unfair reflection on their scope and importance.

The New Social Regulation

The distinction between economic (old) and social (new) regulation (Table 11–2) merits further examination. That distinction has been described thus:

> While all regulation is essentially "social" in that it affects human welfare, [there are] some very significant differences. The old-style economic regulation typically *focuses on markets, rates, and the obligation to serve*. . . . On the other hand, the new-style social regulation *affects the conditions under which goods and services are produced,* and *the physical characteristics of products that are manufactured.* . . . The new-style regulation also extends to far more industries and ultimately affects far more consumers than the old-style regulation, which tends to be confined to specific sectors [of the private economy]. Whereas the effects of CAB regulation [were] largely limited to air carriers (including their stockholders and employees) and air passengers, the regulations of OSHA apply to every employer engaged in a business affecting commerce.[7]

TABLE 11-2	Selected Regulatory Bodies Engaging in "Old" and "New" Regulation*

Old

Federal Communications Commission
Federal Reserve Board
Securities and Exchange Commission

New

Consumer Product Safety Commission
Environmental Protection Agency
Equal Employment Opportunity Commission
Federal Trade Commission
Food and Drug Administration
International Trade Commission
National Labor Relations Board
Nuclear Regulatory Commission
Occupational Safety and Health Administration

*Agencies listed here are those appearing in Table 11–1, classified according to their principal responsibilities.
SOURCE: From Lawrence J. White, *Reforming Regulation: Process and Problems,* © 1981, pp. 32–33, 36–39. Adapted by permission of Prentice-Hall, Inc., Englewood Cliffs, N.J.

As of the early 1960s, the national government had significant economic regulatory responsibilities in just four areas: antitrust, financial institutions, transportation, and communications.

In each of these areas, the policy objective was to prevent or mitigate the economic damage associated with provision of goods or services, typically within a single industry. Thus, while regulatory agencies might possess broad-ranging discretionary authority to influence actions within a specific industrial sector, their standards and guidelines generally did not affect the economy as a whole.[8]

How can we account for so drastic a shift in both the substance and the processes of government regulation? One explanation is that, in the late 1950s, there was increased public concern about perceived threats to human life, such as carcinogens (cancer-causing materials such as air pollution and asbestos), and about how pollutants affected ecosystems. This resulted in a series of **social regulatory initiatives** that thrust government into new areas of health, environmental protection, and safety regulation. These initiatives were backed by the growing environmental and consumer movements, as well as "the activities of other specialized interest groups mobilized at least in part by *heightened awareness of risks.*"[9] Thus, social regulation (unlike economic regulation) centrally addresses minimizing — or at least reducing — "public involuntary and occasionally even voluntary exposure to risk."[10] Congressional response to these public and scientific

social regulatory initiatives government actions in the late 1960s and early 1970s to regulate new social areas involving individual health, environmental protection, and public safety; resulted in the creation of several regulatory bodies.

pressures has taken several forms: delegation of broad discretionary powers to regulatory agencies (as with the Clean Air and Clean Water Acts); defining and dealing with problems in narrower terms (for example, regulation of potentially hazardous chemicals); and enlarging Congress's own "role in determining how the goals of regulation will be attained."[11] (Note again the importance of the role of Congress, and the significance of legislative delegation of authority as the basis for regulatory activity.) Some of these initiatives contributed to the emergence of intergovernmental regulation, discussed in Chapter 4.

Dealing with the problem of risk, however, has not been easy. A fundamental difficulty has been *how to determine* the degree of risk involved in use of, or exposure to, a product or substance (such as alcohol, aspartame, saccharin, caffeine, or tobacco), and at what point a level of product risk becomes unacceptable (as a *general* standard). Compounding the problem are the high economic stakes involved in risk assessment; a finding of risk has come to carry with it the real possibility of a product being banned or otherwise restricted in the marketplace. Furthermore, the need for technical expertise — and for *agreed-on criteria* — in defining risk was joined to the issues mentioned above. Because of the economic stakes involved, however, little agreement has been reached on risk criteria. (Failure to reach agreement has not kept government regulators from defining — and applying — such criteria, even though they have remained a focal point of impassioned debate.) Finally, with expert opinion looming ever larger in disputes over just how much risk a given product or substance entails, the spectacle of "dueling experts" (in public debates, legislative testimony, agency reports, and the like) has become more frequent. Thus, the stature of experts and of their knowledge became a subissue within the larger context of regulatory politics (see Chapter 3). (These issues emerged in connection with regulating products that many of us voluntarily use. The question of *involuntary* exposure to products such as hazardous chemicals, second-hand smoke from tobacco products, automotive exhaust, or toxic wastes only compounded the matter, especially with regard to the potential urgency of making new regulations and rules for risk reduction.) In sum, as even the most casual observer of recent American politics can testify, considerable tension has characterized the regulatory arena, most of it centering on the new focus — and style — of regulating private economic activity.

Why Government Regulation Has Developed: Other Perspectives

The extent of regulatory activity prompts us to ask what other factors account for its development. One way to explain it is a scenario of deliberate decisions by bureaucrats and their political allies to expand their sphere of influence over private-sector activities. Although this scenario may have occurred in a few instances, it is not a generally applicable explanation. More important is the growth of red tape as government has responded to pressures for dealing with a broader range of societal problems or meeting specific social objectives.[12] The average citizen, confronted with nuisances (such as noise pollution) and outright menaces (such as toxic wastes), reacts by saying, "There ought to be a law. . . ." If enough organized opinion exists, pressure can be brought to bear on government to enact such laws. Regulations have become more widespread in just this way, focused particularly on two worthy social purposes: *demonstrating compassion* for the individual and *ensuring representativeness and fairness* in governing processes.

Motives of compassion have led, first, to rules and regulations aimed at protecting people from each other — governing relations between buyers and sellers, employers and employees, universities and students, tenants and landlords, or lenders and borrowers. Government has also been asked to alleviate various kinds of human distress — through Supplemental Security Income (SSI) payments; aid to the disabled, the handicapped, and the elderly; aid to the poor; disaster relief; toxic waste cleanup; and unemployment compensation. In all such cases, rules and regulations accompany basic legislation to make it possible to administer such programs fairly and equitably. The national government, in particular, has acted to prevent major disruptions in national (and international) economic and political systems — stepping in to mediate labor–management disputes in vital industries (such as President Clinton's intervention in the American Airlines strike in November 1993), attempting to bring inflation under control, protecting supplies of vital natural resources, or resolving international conflicts that menace the peace. It is, of course, expedient politically for leaders to respond to pleas for governmental assistance, but that only increases the proliferation of rules and regulations accompanying government action.

Regulations also stem from efforts to increase public representativeness in government decision-making processes as one way to maintain popular control and equitable treatment. Provisions of the **Administrative Procedure Act of 1946** require procedural fairness in administrative agency operations (including detailed guidelines for advance notice and public participation in many aspects of administrative decision making). A maze of rules is designed to minimize dishonesty and corruption in public affairs (watchdogs who watch watchdogs watching watchdogs). Also, America's tax laws reflect a desire that citizens receive a "fair shake" from their government. Yet all such protections involve lengthy and complex elaboration in substantive and procedural rules, which add still further to the tangle of red tape.

It would seem, in short, that regulation has been fostered by a willingness — a desire — to have government protect individuals, groups, and society at large from many ills and evils. In virtually all cases, no *intent* to create red tape has existed, but it has inevitably accompanied each effort. The rise of **protective regulation** might well be explained, in sum, in the words of the comic strip possum, Pogo: "We have met the enemy, and he is us!"

Administrative Procedure Act of 1946
a law upon which all federal administrative procedures are based.

protective regulation
advantages certain groups or individuals by granting special access or licenses; used with professionals.

The Clinton administration, as part of its overall effort to reinvent government and streamline many aspects of the national government's regulatory activity, has put a high priority on reducing "regulatory overkill." Although a large part of this focus on regulatory restructuring is directed toward cutting internal agency regulations (that is, regulations that national government administrators must follow), there is no mistaking the administration's concern about regulations that affect private citizens and organizations. According to the National Performance Review, as of September 1996, 55 percent of the existing 86,000 pages of federal regulations had been either eliminated (16,000 pages) or revised (31,000). Teams of "reinventors" were working on clarifying and simplifying the remaining 39,000 pages of regulations.[13] The NPR has emphasized an awareness of the content, administrative burdens, and costs involved, and has signaled a clear intent to cut back "unnecessary" regulation, in all respects.

Structures and Procedures of Regulatory Bodies

The national government's regulatory bodies have certain features in common with other administrative entities but differ in important respects. One similarity (already noted) is that all administrative entities operate under authority delegated by Congress, and they must therefore be aware of congressional sentiment about their operations. On occasion, Congress as a whole has been persuaded to restrict regulatory activities in some way, as was the case with the FTC more than once in the past twenty years. A second similarity is that there can be functional overlap among regulatory bodies, just as with other entities. For example, during the controversy over cigarette smoking and public health in the mid-1960s, one question was whether allegedly deceptive radio and television advertising of cigarettes was properly under the jurisdiction of the FTC, which is responsible for controlling deceptive trade practices, or the FCC, which generally regulates radio and television advertising.[14] A third similarity is that politics is as important in the regulatory process as in other aspects of public administration — maybe more important. Although the design of government regulation seems to assume some separation between regulation and "politics," in truth, interested groups and individuals expend considerable effort to influence regulatory activity. Close ties usually link clientele groups and so-called **dependent regulatory agencies (DRAs)** — agencies charged with regulating economic activity but housed within an existing cabinet department or other executive structure. Examples include the National Highway Traffic Safety Administration (NHTSA) in the Department of Transportation, the Agricultural Marketing Service in the Department of Agriculture, and the FDA in Health and Human Services. But, regardless of organizational form, regulatory politics — the quest for leverage and influence in the making of regulatory decisions — is a very real phenomenon.

dependent regulatory agencies (DRAs) subdivisions of other executive agencies.

REGULATORY STRUCTURES

Regulation was initially to be a function conducted by administrative boards and commissions with greater independence — in particular, independence from control by the president. That being the case, the structuring of those entities was a matter of some importance. As regulatory activities spread to the executive branch, however, those activities did not have the effect of altering the structure of *existing* entities (most of which were, and are, agencies with a single head). Thus, questions of organizational structure are now less significant than they once were. The scope of regulation that is undertaken, the types of regulations issued and enforced, and the impacts of those regulations are often at least as great for executive-branch regulators as for the older, independent regulatory boards and commissions.

There *are* some structural differences between DRAs and independent regulatory boards and commissions (IRCs). First, IRCs have plural — not individual — leadership; a *collective* decision-making process exists from the start. Second, board members or commissioners do *not* serve "at the pleasure of the president" as do cabinet secretaries and other political appointees, and presidential powers to remove them are sharply curtailed. Their terms of office are fixed and are often quite long — for example, the fourteen-year terms of Federal Reserve Board members. Also, terms of office are staggered — that is, every year or every other year, only one member's term expires. Thus, no president is able to bring about drastic shifts in policy by appointing several board members at once, nor is policy within the agency likely to change abruptly because of membership turnover. Third, each commission or board has an odd number of members, ranging from five to eleven, and decisions are reached by a majority vote. Finally, there must be a nearly even partisan balance among the members — a five-member board must be three to two Republican or Democratic, a seven-member commission must be four to three one way or the other, and so on.

The combined effect of these provisions is — or was intended to be — that these entities were better insulated from political manipulation than others in the executive branch. In particular, it was deemed centrally important to prevent *presidential* interference with regulatory processes and to make the regulators answerable to Congress. The effectiveness of political insulation can be questioned, however. Decisions clearly favoring some interests over others are not uncommon, although most decisions have substantive as well as political roots. The larger purpose behind organizing the boards and commissions in this manner is to protect the public interest in preference — and sometimes in opposition — to private economic interests. But where and how to draw the line between them is frequently decided through the political process rather than as a result of clearly defined boundaries.

Does regulatory structure make any real difference in the operations of regulatory bodies? Surprisingly, existing opinion on that question consists mainly of

444 Part III: The Core Functions of Public Management

impressions and conventional wisdom; it is not based on careful research, of which there is very little. When comparing DRAs with IRCs, there is no hard evidence that structure affects regulatory policy making. However, a 1980 study of twenty-three regulatory bodies (divided about equally between DRAs and IRCs) indicated that DRAs (1) have political environments much more supportive of regulation than do IRCs; (2) are usually designed to regulate *in the interests of* those regulated (which might explain the degree of support for regulation); (3) usually have other, nonregulatory functions that lead to their having larger workforces, larger budgets, and greater geographic decentralization; and (4) operate with more discretion and can make greater use of their rule-making powers.[15] It is perhaps significant that DRAs, such as the FDA and the NHTSA, generated political controversy during the 1980s, as did IRCs, such as the FTC and the Consumer Product Safety Commission. Some DRAs, in other words, may be less inclined than in the past to regulate only in the interests of those regulated.

It should be noted, too, that regulatory structure seems not to matter on those occasions when either Congress or the president (or the courts, for that matter) attempts to impose restraints on regulatory bodies that may have acted unacceptably or illegally. As we shall see later in this chapter, different regulatory bodies are subject to the same sorts of constraints, regardless of structure. In much the same way, the procedures followed by diverse entities have become increasingly uniform. To these we now turn.

REGULATORY PROCEDURES

Procedures used by regulatory bodies fall into two broad categories: **rule making** and **adjudication** proceedings. Regulators are empowered under the 1946 Administrative Procedure Act to engage in rule making, a *quasi-legislative* action involving the issuance of formal rules that cover a general class of activities. It has about the same effect as a law passed by Congress or another legislature. For example, a rule issued by the Department of Transportation might limit the width of tractor-trailers on interstate highways or require lower shipping rates for products made from virgin materials than for those made from recycled material (as in the case of many paper products). Rules apply to all individual operators, shippers, and others who come under their provisions. Rule making is less formal than adjudication, rules apply uniformly, and all cases within a given category are affected.

The rule-making process (see Figure 11–1) calls for regulators to issue notice of *proposed* rules relevant to administration of any given statute, with a period of public comment lasting at least thirty days (and often longer).[16] The notice of proposed rule making is published in the *Federal Register*, the government's official medium for disseminating information to the public concerning implementation of a statute. Written comments can be submitted by interested parties and, if deemed appropriate, oral presentations can also be made. Although legis-

rule making a quasi-legislative power delegated to agencies by Congress; a rule issued under this authority represents an agency statement of general applicability and future effect that concerns the rights of private parties and has the force and effect of law.

adjudication a quasi-judicial power delegated to agencies by Congress, under which agencies apply existing laws or rules to particular situations, in case-by-case decision making; related term: *adjudicatory proceeding*.

Federal Register a listing of all proposed and active federal regulations.

FIGURE 11-1   **The Rule-Making Process**

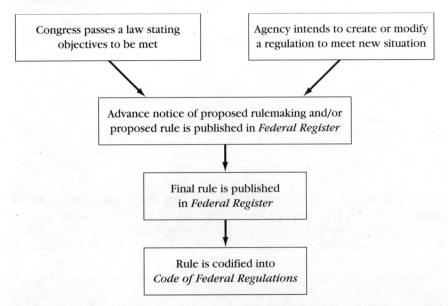

SOURCE: *The Federal Register: What It Is and How to Use It* (Washington, D.C.: Office of the Federal Register, National Archives and Records Service, General Services Administration, 1980), p. 91.

lation can specify a deadline for publishing proposed rules and regulations, these deadlines are not always met. Considerable time can elapse between the effective date of a law and proposed rules and, again, between public comment and issuance of a final rule published in the **Code of Federal Regulations** — sometimes as long as seven years!

Several important points should be made about this process. First, it is almost always the *organized* public — clientele groups and other interest groups — that responds to opportunities for public comment; very few average citizens pay close attention to proposed rules (or anything else) in the *Federal Register*. Thus, the version of public opinion rendered in public comments is not likely to truly represent general popular sentiment. Second, regulators vary in their responsiveness to public comment. The right to comment does not by itself confer influence over ultimate action, and more powerful groups can expect to have their views heeded more closely than those of others. Perhaps most important, however, that the general public *can* become involved in rule-making processes means that regulators must be mindful of public feeling and must try to anticipate public reactions.

In adjudicatory proceedings, rulings are made on a *case-by-case basis* and procedural requirements somewhat resemble those observed in a court of law. In a majority of cases, there is no formal proceeding before the decision. The

Code of Federal Regulations   source of all laws that authorize regulatory agency actions.

regulators routinely settle such questions as whether to renew FCC radio station licenses. In such instances, a regulator is likely to follow informal precedents set in earlier rulings involving similar circumstances, although regulatory precedents do not carry the same legal force as court precedents do in judicial decision making.

Sometimes, however, adjudicatory proceedings are quite formalized. This usually occurs during a class action, when major interests are affected involving thousands of people or millions of dollars or when a case is contested or when there is no applicable precedent. Under such circumstances, the rules followed represent an adaptation of courtroom procedures and congressional hearing requirements, including formal rules governing attorneys, evidence, testimony, and witnesses. Some groups make use of a public counsel, much like a public defender, who argues the consumer's point of view at public hearings. A much more common figure in adjudicatory proceedings is the **administrative law judge** — formerly known as the hearing examiner — who acts for commissioners or board members in conducting public hearings, taking testimony, and then writing a preliminary recommendation, which is the basic factual summary presented to the regulatory body. This procedure is designed to keep cases from going to court and greatly reduces the time it takes to reach a decision.

Administrative law judges, now numbering well over 1,100 in 30 different departments, are among the most highly specialized national employees. They are career employees assigned to regulatory bodies who occupy a unique niche in the public service; yet they are independent of their nominal superiors and have a degree of job security unusual even among merit employees. The nature of adjudication requires this; they are expected to avoid being arbitrary and unfair while exercising sufficient freedom to write recommendations on the basis of information received and interpretation of those data.[17] Although their recommendations do not carry final authority and can be appealed to the regulatory entity, administrative law judges enjoy considerable prestige, and their recommendations are commonly accepted.

Apart from rule making and adjudicatory procedures, regulators frequently attempt to resolve disputes or disagreements by encouraging informal, voluntary compliance with regulatory requirements. The Federal Trade Commission, for example, employs three principal devices to secure voluntary cooperation. The first is issuance of an **advisory opinion,** indicating clearly how the FTC would decide a particular question if it were to formally come before the commission. Regulatory bodies, unlike courts, are permitted to issue such opinions on questions that might, but have not yet, come before them. The second is convening of a *trade practices conference,* to which all or most members of an industry are invited for a general airing of their regulatory problems and, it is hoped, for promoting better understanding on all sides of the problems discussed. The third is a **consent order,** representing an agreement voluntarily reached between the FTC and an industry before, or possibly during, an adjudicatory proceeding. (It is sometimes said that consent orders constitute a promise by an industry to stop

administrative law judge member of the executive branch who performs quasi-judicial functions.

advisory opinion one means used by some U.S. regulatory entities to secure voluntary compliance with regulatory requirements; involves issuance of a memorandum indicating how the entity (for example, the FTC) would decide an issue if it were presented formally.

consent order one means used by some U.S. regulatory entities to secure voluntary compliance with regulatory requirements; involves a formal agreement between the entity and an industry or industries, in which the latter agree to cease a practice in return for the entity's dropping punitive actions aimed at the practice.

doing something it hasn't admitted doing in the first place![18]) Without devices such as these, regulatory bodies would have an even more difficult time keeping up with their caseloads than they do now.

The Politics of Regulation

Regulatory politics is only rarely the partisan politics of Democrats and Republicans. Rather, it is the politics of *privilege*, in terms of those with a stake in regulatory policies gaining preferred access to decision makers; and, to a lesser extent, of *patronage*, in the appointment of commissioners, board members, legal counsels, and staff personnel.[19] This is especially true of IRCs but (in the case of patronage) much less true of DRAs. It is also a many-sided game played by the regulators themselves, who are sensitive to pressures placed on them and who are aware that reappointment may depend on political forces; by executives and legislators, because businesses, industries, and labor unions subject to regulation are important constituents; and by those regulated, who cannot afford not to play. Thirty years ago, the only ones who seemed to be excluded were consumers, although that has changed decisively; now consumers play the game hard, and well.

Regulatory politics for both IRCs and DRAs is also characterized by issues of *distribution, quality, and price*. An excellent example is the burgeoning cable television industry. Communications regulators must answer a host of questions as cable television expands into more and more markets. Among the most important questions are: Which communities will be granted cable TV service to begin with? What criteria will be used in evaluating franchise applications, and how will those criteria be determined? What requirements (if any) will be imposed concerning picture quality provided and service available? How many channels will the cable system offer, and which ones? What prices will be charged, and how many price packages will be offered? Although this is one of the most complex regulatory areas, similar issues arise in almost every other regulatory sphere.

The politics of regulation in the national government merits further discussion. A leading study of the FCC suggests that in addition to Congress, there are five major institutional influences on broadcast regulatory policy: the FCC itself, the broadcasting industry, citizens' groups, the courts, and the White House.[20] It is another indication of the nature of regulatory politics, however, that, in the study cited, the focal point of the discussion was Congress.[21] The relative strength of these participants in broadcast regulation, their respective abilities to make Congress act, and the rules Congress writes for the FCC and the courts (regarding access to judicial review of FCC decisions) all play a part in shaping broadcast policy. Regulatory policies in other areas result from similar configurations of institutions and power.

The political environment of regulation includes many of the same features that apply to all other administrative agencies: legislative oversight by committees of Congress; appropriations concerns centering on the appropriations committees, OMB, and the budget committees; an increasing focus on potential effects of budget cuts and deficit reduction; and attention to a political clientele — which, for a regulatory body, is frequently *the very industry or industries it is responsible for regulating*. One example of this kind of relationship involves the FDA and the pharmaceuticals industry. In addition, business and corporate interests generally have their own partisan leanings. It follows that there might well be partisan undercurrents in regulatory politics, depending in part on which party holds the White House.

Furthermore, the degree of *independence* possessed by an agency may fall short of that apparently conferred on it: as already noted, the president, Congress, and powerful economic interests frequently interact with a regulatory agency, thereby affecting what it does. Critics of regulatory agencies have charged that they often are more effective in protecting the industries they are supposed to regulate than they are in regulating them — a charge not without some foundation. At the same time, however, another set of criticisms has begun to be heard, accusing some regulatory bodies of going too far in the exercise of their discretionary authority. Thus, regulatory agencies are increasingly caught in a squeeze.

INDEPENDENCE FROM THE PRESIDENT

Regulatory *agencies* operate in much the same relationship to the president or governor that other agencies do: political appointees head the overall (cabinet-level) department, but career employees direct the work of the regulatory entity itself. On the other hand, regulatory boards and commissions are designed to answer to Congress's direction and to be shielded from presidential influence. Commissioners cannot be fired by the president; staggered terms inhibit presidential ability to "sweep out the old and bring in the new"; and partisanship in the agencies' makeup is limited by law. At the same time, a president who serves two full terms — or even part of a second term, as in the case of Richard Nixon, Ronald Reagan, and Bill Clinton — can have a powerful impact on agency composition and, therefore, policy directions. Former President Nixon, during five and one-half years in the White House, appointed or reappointed the *full* membership of *eight* regulatory entities, including the FCC, CAB, FPC, and SEC, and most of the members of all other regulatory bodies.

Jimmy Carter sought to bring regulatory bodies under tighter control and direction. In March 1978, Carter issued Executive Order 12044, designed to improve regulations in a number of ways: simplicity and clarity of the rules themselves, improved public access during rule making, and more publicity about "significant regulations under development or review." The executive order also sought more control by regulatory entity heads, some of whom were directly accountable to Carter.[22] Ronald Reagan, of course, went much further in an effort to slow regulatory growth by suspending, postponing, or canceling numerous rules and regulations while they were still in the proposal stage. (We will discuss the Reagan regulatory initiatives later in this chapter.) As public concern about overregulation has increased, recent presidents — and Congress, too, as we will see — have moved against individual regulators with some success.

One other aspect of presidential influence, in the realm of appointing and reappointing board or commission members, deserves mention. The most common practice is for presidents to avoid, if possible, any appointment that will generate controversy. The most convenient method is to allow leaders of regulated industries an informal voice in the selection process. Not all presidents give equal weight to these informal recommendations, but rare indeed is the president who goes ahead with an appointment that is publicly and vigorously opposed by a regulated industry.

There are two reasons for this presidential deference to industries. First, all presidents — regardless of political party — count on significant support from business and industrial leaders, and it is common courtesy to his supporters for a president to touch base on a matter of considerable interest to them. Second, a president runs the risk of shaking business confidence and, in the long run, continued economic vitality by setting himself in perpetual opposition to Wall Street and to the nation's business and financial communities. As a result, most presidents take care to keep their fences mended with business and industry. What effect that has on a process of regulation designed to be objective and detached is another matter, but the president's political needs may account for some of the gap between promise and performance of regulatory bodies.

Under the Reagan administration, another tool of presidential control was used to strengthen the president's ability to direct the general emphasis of regulatory activity, if not specific rules themselves. The Office of Management and Budget (OMB) was authorized, by a series of executive orders, to review proposed regulatory rules and to influence their content substantively if OMB deemed it appropriate to do so. In one such case in 1987, OMB was accused of blocking parts of a so-called workers' right-to-know regulation that had been issued by OSHA. In the ensuing controversy, OMB was also accused of singling out health and safety regulations for more drastic paperwork reduction, compared to some other regulations, under provisions of the Paperwork Reduction Act of 1980.[23] The Clinton administration has taken another approach to reducing the scope of regulation by proposing frequent consultation and negotiation involving OMB and agencies of the national government regarding the regulatory process. This is far different from the pattern followed during the Reagan presidency, which emphasized a more centralized mode of operation, with OMB "directing traffic" in a much more systematic way. This is also consistent with the broader approach followed by Clinton and Gore in their efforts to bring about far-reaching change in governmental activities.

INDEPENDENCE FROM CONGRESS

From the standpoint of Congress as a whole, regulatory bodies have a great deal of independence. After an entity is established and the processes of regulation are begun, the main contact members of Congress collectively have with it is in considering its annual appropriations. Congress does exercise considerable influence, however, through committee oversight of regulatory bodies, especially if complaints have been received about the activities of a given regulator. Because the regulators operate under delegated legislative authority, it is the prerogative of Congress to review and possibly modify the authority that was granted, and regulatory entities are cautious about offending powerful interests in Congress that could trigger committee action "to rein them in." This does not happen often, but the possibility does exist.

At times, Congress's interaction with, and influence over, a regulator is direct and forceful. An example involving the FTC illustrates this point: In the 1960s, at the beginning of the continuing controversy over the health hazards involved in smoking cigarettes, a conflict which foreshadowed more recent lawsuits by states against tobacco companies over the health risks associated with smoking and the medical costs to treat victims of smoke-related diseases, several regulatory entities — among them the FTC — tried to counter tobacco advertising that depicted smoking in a very favorable light. However, current controversies over the health hazards posed by secondhand smoke, restrictions on cigarette advertising, and treatment of nicotine as an addictive drug, indicate that public pressure on the tobacco industry has intensified, and Congress may have responded to that pressure in more decisive terms than it did forty years ago.

With the cigarette conflict in mind, we can ask if regulatory bodies are truly independent of Congress. The answer is no, but a word of caution is in order. Although regulatory bodies were never designed to be *completely* independent, they can gain some measure of independence if their political support is strong enough — including congressional support. An "essential characteristic of independent regulatory commissions [and DRAs] is their need of political support and leadership for successful regulation in the public interest."[24] An entity that is truly an "independent operator" is the exception rather than the rule because neither Congress nor industry is likely to consent willingly to such autonomy. Regulators that try to act independently find themselves reined in by congressional committees or Congress as a whole far more often than they are turned loose. It is the nature of the game, depending on the balance of political forces at work. But there is almost always a balance of some kind, and regulators have to adapt to this, ensuring (if possible) that their support is always stronger than their opposition.

The question of independence from the president and from Congress has no final answer. William Cary, onetime chairman of the Securities and Exchange Commission, once described regulatory entities as "stepchildren whose custody is contested by both Congress and the Executive, but without very much affection from either one."[25] That sounds as though regulatory bodies are caught in a crossfire between the White House and Capitol Hill, which is a frequent situation. If neither the president nor Congress regularly lends support and if support is still needed, a dilemma develops from which one escape seems most promising. Regulators can try to reach acceptable operating understandings with the industries they regulate, in exchange for their support — which poses a whole new set of problems for regulators' independence.

INDEPENDENCE FROM THOSE REGULATED

Among the most intense criticisms of regulatory bodies has been the charge that they are "owned," unduly influenced, or have been co-opted by the industries they are supposed to regulate. The most devastating critiques probably were those of "Nader's Raiders" — a group associated with consumer advocate and 2000 Green Party presidential candidate Ralph Nader — aimed at such venerable agencies as the ICC and (ironically) the FTC. Charges of lack of experience on the part of regulators, unfamiliarity with problems of particular industries, political cronyism in appointments, and lack of initiative and vigor in pursuing violators of regulatory requirements were the most common ones. A companion theme has been that regulators often were first actively involved in affairs of industry, then came to serve in regulatory entities, and subsequently returned to those *same* industries (for example, industrial chemicals, broadcasting, or transportation, among others — the proverbial revolving door). The central theme underlying such allegations was that regulatory bodies do more to protect and promote "their" industries than to regulate industry in the public interest.

The fact remains, however, that those serving on regulatory bodies can never be expected to isolate themselves personally from those with whom they deal. On the contrary, some interaction is considered necessary in order that those working for the regulatory body understand fully the workings of the regulated industry. How to maintain that interaction and still keep an acceptable degree of detachment and objectivity is the central question.

Regulators have all kinds of direct social and professional involvement with individuals in the industries they regulate. Frequently, contact occurs in private, informal rule-making and adjudicatory proceedings, where problems can be addressed without all the trappings of a formal regulatory action. Just what comes out of such meetings in terms of protection of the public interest is not easy to determine (if the public interest itself can be defined), and the private nature of the conferences is one irritant to observers such as Nader and the public-interest lobbying group *Common Cause*.

Also, regulators routinely attend industry conferences, where they are frequently the main speakers, and friendly conversation during the social hour is not at all out of place under such congenial circumstances. Then there are private chats in offices, out-of-town visits to companies by regulatory officials, and luncheons and dinners at which regulators and industry representatives are part of a larger social gathering.

Three aspects of these relationships should be emphasized. First, these social and professional contacts are routine occurrences not inconsistent with the job of regulation. Second, private industries have a legitimate economic self-interest to uphold, and industry executives fear that, if they do nothing to present their cases to government regulators, their competitors will. Third, out-and-out industry pressure on a regulator is rare — bribery appears to be almost nonexistent, as are blatant attempts to intimidate or otherwise pressure regulatory officials. Direct exchanges of views, combined with the indirect pressure that can be placed on an entity through the president and Congress, are usually enough to ensure industries a fair hearing.

That regulatory bodies and their members are expected to be expert as well as detached raises yet another question: How does one become knowledgeable about an industry without also coming to share that industry's values and outlooks? Appointees to regulatory positions often come from industry backgrounds, a natural training ground for acquiring relevant expertise but also a likely place to adopt perspectives favorable to industry interests. Also, as noted earlier, a revolving-door pattern has emerged — regulators can often expect to go to work, or go back to work, for a regulated industry when their terms expire. Other appointees have backgrounds that hardly equip them to deal with the industries — some are named as political favors, others simply because they are noncontroversial appointees (or sometimes for both reasons). In either instance, the industry has an advantage; individual regulators are likely to be sympathetic to — or else largely ignorant of — the industry's problems and are consequently reluctant to intervene in industry affairs. (In the past, there has been a more difficult problem with respect to IRCs than DRAs.)

Sometimes, an industry maverick is named to a regulatory body, someone who does not share the predominant economic or social outlook of the industry even though he or she has been a part of it. But such appointments are exceptions to the rule. The pattern of appointing people with industry backgrounds is so well entrenched that it is considered news when someone is rejected by the Senate for that reason. Thus, the need for both expertise and detachment in regulatory entities clearly presents a problem not easily solved.

Consumers, Consumerism, and Regulation

The consumer movement has had significant impact on government regulatory activity. Before the rise of consumerism, almost all major economic interest groups represented manufacturers or producers — those involved in the assembly, growing, processing, shipping, and selling products in the marketplace. These groups naturally sought to shape market regulation in favor of producer needs and preferences. Customers or consumers were largely unrepresented in any organized fashion. However, major conflicts over cigarettes and public health, and over automotive safety, began to change that situation in the 1960s.

Leaders of the budding consumer movement looked to regulatory entities and other administrative bodies to promote and protect consumer interests. They apparently placed little faith in Congress, reasoning that legislators would be far more likely to respond to producers' wishes than to contrary pressures applied by consumer groups. Rightly or wrongly, they chose to make use of administrative weapons in fighting their political battles, which, of course, brought them into conflict with both producers and Congress. Advocates of change, such as the Nader organizations, saw, in addition, a need to reform administrative regulation in order to maximize consumer gains. Not all consumer groups agreed with that view, but they generally supported efforts for reform.

There is little question that consumerism changed the face of government regulation, both because of new political pressures applied and because of primary reliance on regulatory agencies. Several studies of consumer protection in the early 1970s noted that administrative processes were key targets in the growth of consumer protection policy and that "consumer measures [such as tobacco warning labels] depended heavily on the power of administrative agencies to make public policy."[26] Pressure was placed on Congress — with some success — not only to respond directly to consumer demands but also to increase access to regulators and to the courts for redress of consumer grievances. Congress's record in these respects is mixed, but even that represents an improvement over the past, when consumer groups were much weaker and less organized and could point to only a handful of gains over long periods of time.

The Nader phenomenon and the rise of consumerism are not unrelated. There is informed opinion that, without the Nader organizations — their expertise, full-time commitment, and vigorous criticism of both corporate power and regulatory efforts — the consumer movement would not have enjoyed the influence it has. By awakening consciousness of consumer interests among the general public, Nader and others strengthened, perhaps created, a constituency with sufficient political power to contest the influence of long-established producer groups. Consumer pressure clearly accounted for much of the increase in government regulation during the past thirty years, as well as for increased political conflict over regulation.

More recently, however, the pendulum has swung the other way; there seems to be more resentment of, rather than sustained support for, distinctly consumer-oriented regulation. Congress and Presidents Reagan and Bush seemed more sympathetic to producers than their predecessors had been. President Clinton's position on the general question of government regulation has appeared to differ in important respects from the positions of Reagan and Bush, but the Clinton administration has clearly moved cautiously in undertaking new regulatory initiatives, focusing efforts on eliminating regulations or simplifying existing "necessary" ones. More important, perhaps, is the fact that public opinion is shifting on the question of what constitutes *appropriate* government regulation.

Illustrative of the interplay between regulators and public sentiment (and of the difficulties confronting conscientious regulators) is the case of the FDA. During the 1960s and 1970s, this agency acted frequently to ban various products and substances said to endanger human health because they were unsafe, ineffective, or both. Food and Drug Administration officials said, more than once, that the agency, under existing legislation, had no choice but to remove a product from the market when its potential disease-causing properties were demonstrated under controlled laboratory conditions. This was an especially important position politically in the controversy over the FDA's proposal to ban saccharin, which, in a number of Canadian tests, had been linked to cancer, first in laboratory rats and then in human males.

The FDA's stand caused a powerful coalition to question the basic law requiring FDA action against carcinogens (substances linked to cancer). Key elements in that coalition were food companies, manufacturers of soft drinks (including diet soft drinks), and, perhaps most important, an aroused group of citizens — for example, diabetics — who, for various reasons, needed or wanted sugar-free beverages available. Pressure was applied on both sides of the issue, with some arguing that suspected carcinogens should be banned as required by law, regardless of public outcry, and others arguing that it was time to update 1958 legislation requiring FDA action, to permit the FDA to examine potential benefits in relation to the cancer risk.[27] Any time an agency receives *70,000* angry letters over a single issue, there is reason for it to reconsider its decision, which the FDA did. Its course of action has been affected, however, more by congressional pressure for a delay in banning saccharin than by either direct industry or public pressure. The latter has to be translated into congressional action to be truly effective. The proposed saccharin ban and public reaction to it were not the only episodes in which the general public has been critical of regulatory action.

Another recent controversy involved the regulations mandating both driver- and passenger-side air bags on all new automobiles, ostensibly as a safety measure. Air bags increased the costs of cars by as much as $500 and were never intended to be used without seat belts. It has been known for some time that improperly installed child restraint seats (also required by some states) can severely injure or kill infants when air bags inflate, even in relatively minor accidents. However, many consumers were unaware of the dangers that rapidly inflating air bags could pose to children or small adults. After over fifty people had been killed in minor accidents, public response was so intense that, in November 1996, the NHTSA reversed its policy to allow individual car owners to voluntarily disconnect the air bags, pending installation in 1999 of so-called smart air bags, with sensors that adjust to a person's height and weight. These episodes of forced regulation without exhaustive testing for the dangers of "safety" equipment, and subsequent reversals of policy a few years later, do little to inspire public confidence in regulatory processes.

Still another issue highlighting growing public frustration and disenchantment with regulation was the controversy over Laetrile as a treatment for cancer patients. Laetrile — a substance extracted from apricot pits and said by some to be effective as a cancer treatment — has not been an approved drug on the FDA lists. Yet, during the late 1970s, demands became more insistent that those who wanted to be treated with Laetrile should have the chance, FDA approval or not, with some arguing that this was an issue of freedom versus government control. The respective points of view have been summed up as follows:

> Freedom is the issue. The American people should be allowed to make their own decisions. They shouldn't have the bureaucrats in Washington, D.C., trying to decide for them what's good and what's bad — as long as it's safe. . . . The FDA is typical of what you get in regulatory agencies — a very protective mentality in bureaucrats who want to protect their own jobs and their own positions. It's easier for them to say "No" to a product — Laetrile or anything else — than it is to say "Yes." . . . The simple fact is that stringent drug regulation for society as a whole limits therapeutic choice by the individual physician who is better able to judge the risks and benefits for the individual patient. I think the whole argument centers on FDA's intervention on the basis of a product's efficacy. . . . I agree that no one should be allowed to defraud the public, but you don't need to rely on the FDA. . . . The real question is: Should the government be protecting you from yourself?[28]

And, on the other side of the Laetrile/FDA question:

> I believe in a society that protects the consumer from the unscrupulous vendor. There was a time in America when we gave free rein to the philosophy of caveat emptor: let the buyer beware. We abandoned that a couple of generations ago, and now we have all kinds of consumer protections built into our society.[29]

> Instead of freedom of choice, it could be freedom of the industry to defraud the consumer. With the tremendous number of drugs available, it is not possible for the physician and the consumer to really have the information necessary upon which to base an informed judgment in regard to the safety and effectiveness [of a drug].[30]

Even though such disputes continue to be with us, government regulators continue to follow the statutory directives of Congress, as the following actions, paraphrased from newspaper accounts, indicate.

Item: In August 1987, the Labor Department extended "right-to-know" regulations, requiring companies to tell workers about hazardous chemicals and other toxic substances present in the workplace, to 18 million workers at more than 3.5 million work sites. Occupational Safety and Health Administration (OSHA) officials predicted that the regulations would reduce the number of chemical-related injuries, illnesses, and deaths by 20 percent in nonmanufacturing industries.[31]

Item: The EPA announced that a review of 150 groundwater studies over the period 1978–1988 had identified seventy-four chemicals in the groundwater of thirty-eight states. Most of the chemicals were thought to be residues of pesticides used in agriculture. The EPA was careful to say that the extent of the pollution, and the danger that it might pose, had not been clearly established.[32]

Item: The Securities and Exchange Commission decided, in mid-1989, to offer cash rewards to individuals who provide information that leads to the conviction of so-called inside traders on securities (stocks and bonds) markets.[33]

Item: In 1990, the Secretary of Labor, in announcing mandatory safety-belt use for all private-industry employees who drive or ride in motor vehicles on the job, estimated that, each year, the rules would save almost 700 lives and prevent as many as 32,000 lost-time injuries on the job. The secretary also estimated that the original safety-belt rule issued in 1984 had saved more than 20,000 lives between 1984 and mid-1990.[34]

Item: In late 1990, the ICC voted unanimously to ban smoking on all regularly scheduled interstate buses in the United States. The rule affected passengers served by some 300 bus companies; the number of passengers served was approximately 24 million in 1990.[35]

Item: In late 1993, the Agriculture Department proposed (for the second time) new rules requiring information on safe handling, thawing, cooking, and storing of raw meat and poultry. The department did so in the midst of pressure from three directions: from Congress for not moving quickly enough to improve meat inspections, from the meat industry for reissuing rules that had previously been struck down by a federal judge, and from Vice President Gore's reinventing government team, which sought to transfer meat and poultry inspection from the Department to the FDA. These actions were sparked by the deaths of three children and the hospitalization of forty other people in the state of Washington in January 1993 after they ate undercooked hamburger meat at a fast-food restaurant.[36]

Item: One intended purpose of the 1990 Americans with Disabilities Act (ADA) was to provide jobs and eliminate architectural impediments for the disabled. Regulations require employers to make reasonable accommodation for otherwise qualified persons who are physically handicapped or in wheelchairs. However, studies show that the proportion of those disabled and in the workplace have actually *declined* since the ADA was passed, despite the regulations and benefit programs available to disabled persons.[37]

Item: Despite the evidence of increased use of drugs by teenagers, the voters of California and Arizona approved statewide initiatives in November 1996 to legalize the medical use of marijuana for treatment of glaucoma. In effect, the voters of these states increased the potential availability of marijuana without waiting for the FDA, or any other regulatory body, to approve its expanded use for treatment of eye disease. For many, the issue was not protection from harmful effects of drugs but, rather, the freedom to use an otherwise controlled substance for personal medical reasons.

Whether such activity is regarded by most of us as being in our best interest seems to be at the core of current controversies surrounding government regulation. Clearly, not all consumers share the values and objectives of consumer groups; these conflicting views contribute to the squeeze on regulatory agencies and others, such as the Department of Transportation, FDA, and NTSB, that are increasingly active in regulation. It has been well known for some time, for example, that many people do not use their auto seat belts, despite impressive statistical evidence that use of seat belts can greatly reduce risk to life and limb. Although the proportion of seat-belt users is increasing, many people resent having to pay for safety and for mandatory pollution-control devices on their automobiles. An auto ignition–seat-belt interlock system, which would have forced all drivers to "buckle up" before starting their cars, was defeated rather handily in Congress once the public's negative sentiments became evident. That could happen again — with regard to auto safety, the effectiveness of medicines, the safety of food products, and other areas.

Most of us, given the *abstract* choice between clean and polluted air, pure and impure food and drugs, safe and unsafe cars, and so on, would clearly select the former. But how to ensure and maintain such conditions without imposing excessive compliance costs or changes in personal lifestyles is what most controversies are all about. And what may be happening is simply a shift in prevailing political views about what constitutes *appropriate* regulation of particular products. Perhaps the best way to view such controversies is as cyclical processes, with the tide of public opinion ebbing and flowing on behalf of vigorous government regulation.

Government Regulation of Tobacco Products

The use of tobacco products is one of the most controversial issues in public policy today. The debate centers on how to regulate a product that is unhealthy when used as intended, but remains legal for people over the age of eighteen. The policy debate is about when, how, and under what circumstances the state can regulate personal choice, and it relates to several questions: Under what circumstances can government limit individual freedoms to protect citizens from their personal lifestyle? What is the role of the federal, state, and local governments in regulating the use of tobacco? What is the relationship between government intervention to protect public health and a person's individual liberties?

Federal activity to regulate smoking has had a mixed history. Antismoking legislation was first enacted in the late nineteenth century in response to the fire hazards and the morality of smoking. Opposition to smoking on moral grounds was swept aside because of the economic benefits in the form of cigarette taxes to the states associated with tobacco production and consumption.[38] By 1927, all states had repealed such statutes; political action did not begin again until the 1960s and did not gain momentum until the 1980s. Most of the legislative debate in the 1970s and 1980s at the state level centered around personal freedom issues. The tobacco industry emphasized individual rights as their defense, however, as scientific evidence of harmful effects of tobacco grew, legislative activity also grew on state and federal levels. Along with providing tobacco farmers with subsidies, Congress has limited federal regulation of tobacco products because of industry lobbying pressure.[39] At the same time the surgeon general spoke out against smoking as a health hazard. In response to the 1964 *Surgeon General's Report* on smoking, Congress enacted the Cigarette Labeling and Advertising Act in 1965, which required health warnings on all cigarette packages. In 1967 the Federal Communications Commission (FCC) ruled that the "Fairness Doctrine" be applied to cigarette commercials. As a result, all broadcasters who carried cigarette advertising were required to provide equal time to warn the public about cigarettes. In 1969, all cigarette ads were banned from TV and radio with the passage of the Public Cigarette Smoking Act. Between 1972 and 1986 many laws were passed that required warnings to be placed on the packages of cigarettes and smokeless tobacco products, and in 1989, Congress voted to ban cigarettes on airplane flights of less than six hours.

In the 1990s the debate shifted toward the effects of smoking on children. Antismoking forces embraced this as an effective strategy because of its political attractiveness to legislators and because it is difficult for the tobacco industry to publicly oppose restriction on youth access to tobacco products. In 1992 the federal government enacted the Alcohol, Drug, and Mental Health Agency Reorganization Act, known as the *Synar Amendment*, requiring states to enact and enforce laws against the sale and distribution of tobacco products to individuals under the age of eighteen. All states have now enacted youth access restrictions to comply with the *Synar Amendment*. In 1994 Congress passed the Pro Children Act, which prohibited smoking in indoor facilities that are routinely used for the delivery of certain services to children, including schools, libraries, day care, health care, and early childhood development centers.[40] On February 25, 1994, the Food and Drug Administration (FDA) announced that it was considering regulating tobacco products under the authority of the Federal Food, Drug, and Cosmetic Act. To receive this authority the FDA would have to find that "tobacco products were drug-delivery devices for nicotine and determine whether the products were intended to affect the structure or function of the body."[41] The FDA investigated this as well as the effects of advertising and marketing by the tobacco industry on children and adolescents. On August 10, 1995, President Clinton announced that the agency's evidence and analysis supported a finding that the nicotine in cigarettes and smokeless tobacco products is a drug and that cigarettes are a drug-delivery device under the terms of the act. Citing evidence that smoking begins in childhood as a "pediatric disease," the FDA proposed a regulatory program that would reduce the use of cigarettes and smokeless tobacco by young people by limiting its advertising and sale.

In April 1997, the tobacco industry appealed the decision to the U.S. District Court in Greensboro, North Carolina, but it was upheld. The court ruled that the FDA does have jurisdiction under the Food, Drug, and Cosmetic Act to regulate nicotine-containing cigarettes and smokeless tobacco. It also upheld the restrictions that prohibited the sale of these products to people under the age of eighteen and required that retailers check for proof of age for people under the age of twenty-seven. However, the ruling invalidated the restrictions that the FDA put on advertising and promotion of cigarettes, finding that the agency exceeded its statutory authority. Both sides appealed this ruling. In August 1998, a three-judge panel of the U.S. Court of Appeals in Richmond, Virginia, ruled that the FDA lacks the jurisdiction to regulate tobacco products. Their decision was based on evidence that Congress did not intend the Food, Drug, and Cosmetic Act to be applied to tobacco products. This resulted in the repeal of the restrictions that restricted the sale and distribution of cigarettes to children and adolescents.

Much has changed in the tobacco industry since April 14, 1994, when representatives from seven of the leading tobacco companies stood before Congress and swore that nicotine was not an addictive substance. The tobacco industry has since admitted that tobacco is an addictive and dangerous substance that was marketed aggressively to minors.[42] As a result the tobacco industry agreed to a settlement of $246 billion with forty-six states in November of 1998. This deal settled all state lawsuits pending against the industry. The settlement will pour billions into state treasuries over the next twenty-five years and provide about $1.5 billion for research and advertising against underage tobacco use. Another result will be the rising cost of cigarettes. The increase should be about 40 cents per pack by 2003. Another positive outcome of the settlement was the acceptance of the FDA's limited power to regulate the tobacco industry. Most power of regulation will be at the state and local levels. As a result, the number of ordinances restricting smoking have increased. Over five hundred counties or cities have enacted antismoking ordinances. Most antismoking laws have targeted teenagers. At least thirty cities have outlawed the use of cigarette vending machines and others require the machines to be placed in view of an employee. In addition to federal advertising regulations, several localities have restricted advertising for tobacco products. This includes banning ads on mass transit systems and on publicly visible billboards. The settlement also calls for tobacco companies to open a Web site that includes all documents produced in state and other smoking and health-related lawsuits. Since July 1999, the distribution and sale of apparel and merchandise with brand-name tobacco logos is banned. The settlement also bans payment to promote tobacco products in movies, television shows, theater productions, live or recorded music performances, videos, and video games. For events with a significant youth audience or where the participants are underage, brand-name sponsorship is also prohibited. To ensure the enforcement of the settlements terms the courts have jurisdiction for implementation and enforcement. If the tobacco industry violates any of the agreements the courts may order monetary, civil contempt, or criminal sanctions to enforce compliance. State attorneys general have access to company documents, records, and personnel to enforce the agreement.

There are many debates on how different states will spend the money from the tobacco settlement. The mayor of Los Angeles said recently that he wants to improve sidewalks and crosswalks. In Connecticut, the governor would use large shares to cut property taxes, buy school computers, and maintain state university tuition rates. In North Dakota there is a proposal to build a new morgue. Governors and lawmakers say that they are skeptical about pouring millions into untried programs designed to cut smoking rates. Some say that because of a nation wide antismoking campaign the programs are not needed. Others say that the money should be spent like any other state funds used for a wide variety of purposes. The National Conference of State Legislatures said that more than four hundred bills have been introduced around the country proposing how the money should be spent. Only four states have pledged to fund tobacco control programs beyond a minimum level. There have been many federal proposals mandating that an arbitrary percentage of the settlement go to programs aimed at reducing smoking. The states feel that they should not be required to spend a significant portion of the settlement on smoking reduction and prevention. The reason is that many states have already committed funds to these types of programs, and mandating spending on certain types of programs will limit the state's ability to fund other critical programs, such as expanding health care benefits to low-income children. Many states are in the process of enacting legislation to direct the placement of the funds.

Despite many of the positive outcomes, the tobacco settlement is under attack from many health groups who say that it is a disaster. The tobacco industry has fought back by spending millions of dollars lobbying, making substantial contributions to the Republican Party, and launching a $40 million advertising campaign.[43] In the 1997–1998 elections, the industry contributed at least $5.3 million in individual, PAC, and soft money to federal candidates and parties. Because of the tobacco industry's power through lobbying and campaign contributions, the settlement also prohibits the industry from opposing proposed state or local laws that are intended to limit youth access and consumption of tobacco products. The industry must require its lobbyists to certify in writing that they have reviewed and will fully comply with settlement terms, including disclosure of financial contributions regarding lobbyists' activities and new corporate culture principles.

Tobacco control advocates, the state attorneys general, FDA, FCC, and individual cases have brought a wide range of force down upon the tobacco industry. For over thirty years the tobacco industry went unchecked in their marketing abuses and indifference toward public health concerns. Because of these actions by the tobacco industry, there has been an emerging movement by the public and mass media to expose the industry's wrongdoing. This led Congress to hold hearings in the subcommittee on nicotine and product regulation and publish a report by former FDA head David Kessler focusing on regulation of tobacco products. Some of the policy recommendations include: (1) Congress should repeal the federal law that precludes state and local governments from regulating tobacco advertisement occurring entirely within a state's borders; (2) communities should work toward smoke-free environments and receive assistance from state and local public health agencies to develop ordinances and implementation strategies: (3) the National Cancer Institute should be active in designing, promoting, and evaluating tobacco control strategies; (4) the Center for Disease Control and Prevention should provide sufficient funds to ensure statewide, community-based tobacco use prevention and control programs; (5) the industry should be subject to penalties if youth tobacco use fails to drop 15 percent in two years, 30 percent in five years, 50 percent in seven years, and 60 percent in ten years.[44]

The subcommittee applauded the work of the antitobacco groups and the coverage of the mass media to expose the tobacco industry's fraud, deceit, conspiracy, and corruption. The media's effect can be seen in opinion polls that show dramatic increases in public recognition of tobacco as an addictive drug, public belief that tobacco companies deliberately target youth in their ads, and public support for criminal prosecution of tobacco executives for lying to Congress. The media coverage of the tobacco industry and its effects on public health benefit in changing peoples' attitudes toward tobacco use and behavior. The Academy Award–nominated film *The Insider* is an example of just how powerful the media can be in delivering the antitobacco message.

No matter how successful the antismoking campaign is in lowering cigarette consumption and putting the tobacco industry on the defensive, the industry remains a strong and relentless opponent. In March 2000, the U.S. Supreme Court ruled against the Clinton administration's policies to control how cigarettes are marketed. In a 5–4 decision, the Court ruled that under federal law the FDA lacks the power to regulate the tobacco industry. The issue of the relationship between the right of the government to protect public health and the equally powerful right of a person to decide to live their life without government interference is still in debate. Nonetheless, antismoking advocates have come a long way in reducing the public's exposure to cigarettes and the harms of tobacco.

Administrative Law

As discussed in previous chapters (especially Chapters 1 and 3), public administration developed on an ever-larger scale, beginning about 100 years ago. In many ways (although certainly not all), that growth was traceable to the need "to get a certain kind of twentieth-century job done: the regulation of huge, complex, rapidly changing enterprises."[45] The doctrine of separation of powers, so central to our governmental scheme, seemed in this context to be something of a barrier to meeting contemporary needs. That doctrine, in the past as in the present, is designed

> not to promote efficiency but rather to promote liberty. While certain kinds of liberty may be served by separation of powers, speed and efficiency are not served, and it is *precisely speed and efficiency that [are] required* for the governance of a great many things in the twentieth [and twenty-first] century.[46]

The shift in the U.S. economy from large-scale manufacturing to smaller, less centralized businesses, high-tech firms, and service industries has contributed to the reversal of public attitudes about regulation.

Thus, as a perceived need grew for greater governmental efficiency, the administrative apparatus of all government grew with it. As an offshoot of that growth, concern rose for establishing safeguards in the administrative system for the rights and liberties of those touched by the system — meaning virtually all of us, but especially those in direct contact (or conflict) with public administrators.

THE NATURE OF ADMINISTRATIVE LAW

As noted earlier, administrative law pertains to *the legal authority of public administrative agencies to perform their duties, and also to "the limits necessary to control [those agencies]."*[47] It should be noted, however, that administrative law is not clearly or neatly separated from other areas of the law. Rather, there is a distinctive focus to this legal area that sets it apart conceptually from other areas. The principal foci of administrative law, giving it a separate identity as an emergent field, are (1) the rules and regulations set out by administrative agencies, and (2) the law concerning the powers and procedures of those agencies across a whole host of administrative operations.[48]

We have already considered some aspects of administrative activity that involve administrative law — for example, the discussion of red tape earlier in this chapter; the various types of operations in which agencies can engage (Chapter 10); and certain aspects of public employee protections (Chapter 8). Many criticisms of regulations that are designed to achieve fairness in administrative operations are direct references to the growth of administrative law; various approaches to achieving fairness (which we will consider shortly) are themselves examples of how law, administration, and politics come together in a multitude of circumstances in support of **procedural fairness** or, more accurately, **procedural due process.**

procedural fairness
assures fairness in the adjudication process.

procedural due process
legal term that refers to the legal rules governing a specific case.

Administrative law expert Kenneth Warren has suggested a number of "vital administrative law questions" that, he contends, shed light on the scope and nature of the subject. Among these are the following: (1) How much power should be delegated to administrative agencies? (2) How much administrative discretion is too much? (Note the political power implications inherent in that question!) (3) What constitutes arbitrary and capricious agency decisions? (4) What are the components of a fair hearing? (5) How much official immunity should be extended to governmental administrators (that is, immunity from being sued by citizens and organizations for actions taken as part of their official duties)? (6) How can administrative abuses be effectively checked? (Note the possible links to issues such as whistle-blowing, discussed in Chapter 8, and to a variety of concerns affecting democratic administration, noted in Chapter 2.) (7) What role should the courts play in the review of agency decisions? and (8) What should be done to control the regulators (watchdogs watching watchdogs!)?[49]

Complicating the process of answering such questions are several difficult challenges. First, of course, is the probability that the precise meaning of an individual protection or procedural guarantee may vary from situation to situation. Second, answers to any one of these questions — even if they are *definitive* — may help to shape (or be shaped by) responses to other questions. Third, courts and judges have made a significant contribution to the incremental rise of administrative law in that they have been asked, via judicial decisions, to define precisely how due process requirements can be applied to administrative procedure. This is not to say that legislatures have stood idly by as this body of law has evolved. Indeed, administrative procedure acts (both state and national) have given added meaning to due process, as have the everyday actions of thousands of public administrators. Out of all these steps in the evolution of administrative law have come a number of distinct and identifiable patterns of protection for the individual who comes into contact with the public administrative system. We shall consider, in turn, key provisions governing the general rule-making process, provisions governing the process of administrative adjudication, authority for (and restrictions on) administrative discretion, and some of the most important court decisions, which constitute significant guideposts in administrative law.

RULE MAKING AND ADMINISTRATIVE LAW

As noted in Chapter 10, rule making involves administrative issuance of statements and other guidelines that have *general applicability* — that is, they set out enforceable standards that affect a category or classification of enterprises or activities. Rule making, especially if it occurs informally, is constrained by far fewer procedural restrictions than is administrative adjudication, whether these restrictions arise from statutes or from judicial decisions.[50] Among the requirements that apply to rule making are the following. First, *public participation* is considered essential in rule making. In order to make that possible, public notice of proposed rule making is required almost universally. Administrative procedure acts that may be largely silent on rule making nevertheless include this provision. (There are some circumstances in which prior notice may not be required.[51]) Another provision relating to public participation concerns the opportunity to present views — that is, access to the process for interested outside parties who wish to enter their view into the record (however formally or informally that record may be kept). Presentation can take the form of filing petitions, consulting informally, or becoming involved in several varieties of hearings. A second requirement designed to promote fair procedure in rule making is postponing effective dates of newly issued rules while publicizing the content of what has been decided; a third requirement (not always found) is judicial review of proposed or actual rules.

Administrative entities are authorized to make three kinds of rules: substantive, procedural, and interpretative.[52] *Substantive rules* apply to, or direct, law or policy — for example, Nuclear Regulatory Commission rules that set safety regulations for nuclear power plants or Federal Trade Commission rules governing TV advertising directed at children. *Procedural rules* embody requirements for an agency's organization, procedures, or practices. These may be imposed by an administrative procedure act but may also be issued — or perhaps supplemented — by agencies themselves (in the latter case, agencies are bound to honor their own rules in the same way they follow those set by statute). *Interpretative rules* are an agency's views of the meanings of its regulations or of the statutes it administers. Interpretative rules are analogous to advisory opinions that might be issued by a regulatory (or other) entity; that is, they give some indication of how an administrator perceives or understands existing law. One familiar example of an interpretative rule is the advice that a taxpayer might receive from the Internal Revenue Service about permissible deductions in the course of preparing his or her tax return. Occasionally, a dispute may arise over whether a particular rule is substantive, procedural, or interpretative. Such disputes are normally resolved by the courts, with both the government agency and the affected individuals bound by the results.

ADMINISTRATIVE ADJUDICATION AND ADMINISTRATIVE LAW

To adjudicate means to exercise judicial authority, broadly defined. When administrative agencies engage in adjudication, they act in the manner of a court — that is, settling "controversies among named parties, and [determining] legal rights and obligations of the parties on the points in dispute."[53] Courts have historically gone to greater lengths to ensure procedural fairness to individuals than to the public at large; this is one of the main reasons why administrative adjudication is the focus of so much administrative law. Adjudication may occur either formally or informally. Formal procedures entail at least three essential due-process guarantees born in constitutional law and embodied (at the national level) in the Administrative Procedure Act of 1946: fair notice, an opportunity to be heard, and a decision rendered by an impartial decision maker.[54] Other due-process requirements that usually must be met include the individual's right to counsel, the right to present evidence, and the right to cross-examine. Informal adjudication (the more common of the two) may be conducted on the basis of mutual consent of the parties; thus, it can take many forms, and it generally operates within looser constraints, as noted earlier.

A wide range of issues have been disputed and resolved by the courts regarding adjudication (especially the formal variety). In particular, the nature of the hearing itself is often at issue. Potential questions abound: (1) Is a hearing required and, if so, at what point in an administrative action? (2) What kind of hearing is required? (3) What sorts of evidence can be presented? (4) How will the presiding officer (usually an administrative law judge) evaluate the evidence presented, and how will he or she weigh the evidence in determining the outcome? The way such questions are answered is central to procedural due process, which, in turn, is at the heart of administrative adjudication and all its attendant rules.

ADMINISTRATIVE DISCRETION AND ADMINISTRATIVE LAW

Much has already been said in this book about *administrative discretion* — the reasons for it, some disputes about it (see Chapter 3, especially), and some of its consequences, direct and indirect. We have already commented on factors that have contributed to increased discretion (legislative delegations of authority to administrative entities, professional expertise of administrators, and political support from organized groups). In this context, however, the central question pertaining to administrative discretion is how to balance what have been called *administrative imperatives*, such as expertise, flexibility, and efficiency, and *judicial imperatives*, such as due process, equal protection, and substantial justice.[55] Many conflicts manifested in administrative law have revolved around concerns that administrative *arbitrariness* might result from the flexibility enjoyed by administrators acting in pursuit of efficiency. Consistent with this line of reasoning, those mindful of the judicial imperatives look to responsible administrators, executive and legislative oversight of bureaucracy, and judicial remedies as safeguards of the life, liberty, and property of individuals affected by administrative actions. We will conclude this section by examining several cases that simultaneously illustrate some of the most difficult problems addressed in administrative law and indicate why judicial review — as a check on administrative discretion — can be of major significance.

SELECTED CASES AND RULINGS IN ADMINISTRATIVE LAW[56]

Before passage of the Administrative Procedure Act in 1946, the U.S. Supreme Court handed down several major rulings dealing with substantive and procedural fairness in administrative actions. Among the best known of these early cases was *Morgan v. U.S.* (304 U.S. 1, 1938), one of a series of cases in which the Court "conveyed the clear message [that] public agencies needed to improve their hearing procedures to make them more consistent with constitutional due process standards."[57] Morgan, a stockyard operator, argued that the secretary of agriculture had violated his (Morgan's) due-process rights by setting the maximum rate Morgan could charge in his business without a hearing.[58] Congress, in legislation enacted in 1921, had delegated considerable discretion to the secretary for setting maximum and reasonable rates for meatpackers and stockyards. However, it also had required a "full hearing" for stockyard operators — a hearing that Morgan claimed had never been held. The Court ruled in Morgan's favor and, in its opinion, elaborated on what constituted, in its judgment, a "fair hearing" (the opportunity for individuals to know the claims against them, the right to present evidence on their own behalf and to counter evidence presented against them, and the like). The ruling in this case served as something of a prototype for many of the provisions regarding fair hearings that were included in the Administrative Procedure Act passed by Congress eight years later.

Another landmark decision came in the case of *Goldberg v. Kelly* (397 U.S. 254, 1970). Goldberg, as director of the New York State Department of Social Services, was sued by Kelly and other Aid to Families with Dependent Children (AFDC) recipients after the department had terminated their welfare payments. The department maintained that the recipients' due-process rights were protected by the combination of a pretermination review and a posttermination fair hearing; Kelly and the others argued that a hearing before benefits were terminated was an essential element of due process in these circumstances. One central issue, then, was whether a pretermination hearing was necessary for the state to meet recipients' due-process requirements. Another issue, not as obvious, was whether the welfare benefits in question were rights (and as such procedurally protected by constitutional standards) or privileges (and thus not afforded the same protections — such as a fair hearing). In the Goldberg case, the Court actually tried to establish a somewhat different basis for deciding whether a hearing was needed, arguing that the right to a hearing should depend "on the extent to which a person might be expected to suffer a 'grievous loss,'"[59] not on whether a right or a privilege had been provided or denied. The Court ruled in favor of Kelly, holding that the recipients must have timely and adequate notice of the termination of benefits and that the decision to terminate must be based entirely on rules and evidence introduced at the pretermination hearing.

Numerous other cases, covering a wide variety of issues, circumstances, and procedural questions, have come before the Court. A sampling of cases will suggest just how broad the range of concerns has been. In *Bi-Metallic Investment Company v. State Board of Equalization of Colorado* (239 U.S. 441, 1915), the Supreme Court ruled that it does not violate the due-process clause of the Fourteenth Amendment for a governmental body to take a general rule-making action (in this case, raising the property tax in the city of Denver) without giving each individual an opportunity to dispute the action. In *Energy Reserves Group, Inc. v. U.S. Department of Energy* (589 F. 2d 1082 (Temp. Emer. Ct. App., 1978), the Court held that it is not necessary for an agency to use the notice-and-comment provisions of the Administrative Procedure Act before it publishes a proposed rule as long as that rule only interprets existing law rather than formulating new law. The case of *Federal Crop Insurance Corporation v. Merrill* (332 U.S.380, 1947) illustrates how the principle known as *estoppel* can be applied in administrative law. Estoppel may be defined as the act of being stopped from proving or presenting something in court because of something the party involved did previously that contradicts their present position. In this case, Merrill, a farmer, had asked an agent of the Federal Crop Insurance Corporation (FCIC) if spring wheat planted on land that had grown winter wheat was insurable under the Federal Crop Insurance Act. After the agent assured him that it was, Merrill planted spring wheat, which was then destroyed by drought. When Merrill applied for payment, the FCIC refused on the grounds that its regulations prohibited the insuring of reseeded crops. Merrill, claiming that he had been misled by the government, filed suit. The issue before the court was this: Is a governmental agency prohibited (estopped) from relying on written regulations as a defense when a claimant relies on a verbal statement that turns out to be incorrect? In this case, the Court held that, where terms and conditions for creating governmental liability are defined in explicit language in a statute, there is no liability for which a claimant may collect damages — even if both the claimant and the FCIC were ignorant of such a restriction! The Court, in effect, put its weight behind the *explicit* (written) *nature* of the regulation as the guiding standard to be followed — and to be used in case of legal challenge.

ADMINISTRATIVE LAW AND GOVERNMENT REGULATION

The field of administrative law encompasses considerably more than government regulation, narrowly defined. Agencies of all kinds and at all levels of government are subject to rulings of the courts and to provisions of administrative procedure acts regarding many aspects of their operations. Nevertheless, it is government's regulatory activities that are at the heart of administrative law precisely because regulation sits at the crossroads between government power and private behavior. It should be no surprise that administrative law grew initially because of the expansion of government regulation. Ironically, however, even if regulation should not continue to expand (a prospect discussed in the concluding section of this chapter), administrative law is likely to become more extensive in its scope and reach. The same forces that would urge reforms in, if not a slowdown of, government regulation would also be likely to support *expanding* an area of American law that places at least procedural (and sometimes substantive) restraints on the actions government agencies can take relative to our nation's citizens.[60]

The Future of Government Regulation

Regulatory reform has been a recurring theme over the years, with every president since John F. Kennedy paying at least some public attention to the subject. Studies undertaken at presidential request, as well as other proposals, have become part of the reform literature.[61] Presidents Ford, Carter, Reagan, and

Clinton made regulatory reform a high-priority matter, and the issue took on greater urgency in and out of government.

Complicating regulatory reform, however, is the wide variety of motives, assumptions, and policy objectives that have given rise to reform efforts. More effective (and more *cost-effective*) regulation of the private sector is one potential goal. Another is enhancing regulatory accountability to the president; a third is increasing accountability to Congress.[62] Yet another is ending existing fragmentation in substantive areas of regulatory responsibility (for example, transportation); still another is *separating* responsibilities that can conflict, for example, *regulation* of an industry versus *promotion* of that industry's products. (Note that it would be both logically and politically difficult to pursue all these, or even particular combinations, simultaneously.) At various times in the past thirty years, reform proposals have been put forward that embodied one or more of these emphases.[63]

deregulation strategy to reduce or remove regulations in a particular sector.

Finally, of course, there is the policy option of pursuing **deregulation** — of reducing the national government's overall regulatory presence. Though this last goal was most clearly identified with the Reagan administration, it was not Ronald Reagan's only regulation-related objective. Nor was he the first president to seek deregulation. Under Jimmy Carter, major steps were taken (especially in trucking and in rail and air transportation) to reduce regulatory activity and power.[64]

Ronald Reagan came to office ideologically committed to "regulatory relief" for American business. In the context of the values and objectives noted above, his program was founded on a combination of deregulation and increased presidential control, with apparent attention to more cost-effective regulation as well. Although here, as elsewhere, the president did not achieve all he sought, the impacts of his actions will continue to be felt for some time.

That is especially true with regard to budget and personnel reductions affecting regulatory bodies. These merit brief attention because of the impacts these reductions had — and continue to have — on the capacity of regulators to carry out their statutory responsibilities.[65] With the exception of a few regulatory bodies, the 1980s saw deep reductions (in both dollars and personnel) in regulatory budgets. Some came in for particularly severe cuts. Examples include the ICC's 50 percent workforce reduction between fiscal years 1982 and 1986 (followed by disestablishment in 1995), and the FTC's 30 percent personnel cut. More specifically, comparing FY 1995 and FY 1997, only half of the twelve regulatory bodies included in Table 11–1 received funding increases; only two of the twelve (OSHA and the CPSC) added personnel, and another (the ICC) was eliminated. It should be remembered, however, that the figures used as the basis for this assessment are in current dollars; measured in constant dollars (that is, controlling for inflation), most regulators continue to lag behind 1980s funding levels. In short, the harsh treatment of regulators under Ronald Reagan (especially) in his first term has not improved under either George Bush or Bill Clinton. Clinton targeted some regulatory bodies for further cuts while boosting the budgets and responsibilities of others, particularly the Occupational Health and Safety Commission (OSHA) and Consumer Product Safety Commission (CPSC).

As always, however, all may not be what it seems in the debate over necessary and unnecessary regulation. For one thing, it is not uncommon to find some businesses that regard regulation as advantageous to their interests and, therefore, wish to remain regulated. Two examples are various segments of the trucking industry, including the teamsters union (even though the ICC is history and a deregulation bill is now law) and the communications industry, particularly with reference to regulation of new video technologies.[66] Another unexpected twist is a regulatory commission wishing to ease the regulatory burden and willing to go much further than the Congress — witness the FCC, which will decide in the next few years the future course of those same video technologies over which many broadcasters want the agency to retain a measure of control. The coming communications revolution — especially the likely emergence of the so-called **information superhighway** (use of cable television for access to the World Wide Web and Internet) for creating interactive communication for homes, schools, and businesses — poses serious questions regarding regulation of at least this aspect of American life.

information superhighway   nickname for the World Wide Web.

Predictably, strong movement toward deregulation opened up new issues concerning the *impacts* of deregulation. It is impossible to generalize about the impacts, simply because so many fields of economic activity (air, rail, and highway transport; communications; securities trading; and savings and loans institutions, to name only a few prominent areas) have been affected by deregulation and, in some cases, in markedly different ways. Taking airline transportation as just one example, there are indications that deregulation — regardless of the benefits claimed for it — has been a mixed blessing. Some claim that, because of deregulation, air fares have come down (others dissent from that view); some claim that competition among air transport companies has improved (again, not everyone agrees); there are real concerns about air safety in the wake of deregulation (based on cutbacks in air traffic control and safety inspections and the like). It is not surprising if an observer comes away from a review of such commentaries a bit bewildered. Expert observers of just this one area of economic activity disagree as to the effects of deregulation.

More recently, efforts have gained momentum in the direction of **reregulation,** thus reversing the direction set by the Reagan and Bush administrations. Here, again, a key focus is on the airlines, with various government efforts addressing concerns about the safety of start-up airlines, provision of air service to smaller communities, frequency of late arrivals (amid a good deal of publicity about that matter), lack of FAA inspections, transportation of hazardous materials in commercial passenger aircraft, and frequency of passenger complaints about lost luggage. Congress showed a willingness to respond to consumer pressures when, in 1992, it overrode George Bush's veto of a cable-TV regulatory measure (the only Bush veto that Congress successfully overrode); in mid-1993, it enacted legislation regulating the charges that cable companies can levy for

reregulation   decision by Congress or an administrative agency to stregthen or reestablish government regulatory requirements.

cable service. As previously indicated, in 1994, the FDA signaled its clear intention to bring cigarettes under direct federal regulation if it could be proved that the tobacco industry had deliberately manipulated cigarette nicotine levels, knowing that, at certain levels, nicotine can become addictive. Other regulatory debates have also surfaced — for example, the possibility that lack of sufficient staff to enforce FAA regulations may have contributed to commercial aviation disasters, and the possible expansion of the FDA's role in food inspection, given the recent fatalities due to *E. coli* bacteria poisoning and the animal fecal material allegedly found in some beef products. Reregulation has already been proposed in other areas as well.

Plainly, continuing debate over government regulation is inevitable in the years ahead. With regulatory activity strongly supported by some as a means of ensuring fairness and equity in the marketplace — as well as safety and good product quality — while opposed with equal vigor by others on the grounds that it constitutes unwarranted interference and a potential threat to individual economic and social freedoms, any conflict is bound to be intense. Regulation continues to be at a crossroads. Much more is at stake than a rule here or a regulation there — the nature of our economy and government's relation to it are also at issue.

Summary

Government regulatory activity dates back to the late 1800s. Both independent regulatory boards and commissions, as well as other government entities, engage in regulation that, in recent decades has become broader in scope and more controversial. Regulation is a mix of two principal approaches: regulating producers and encouraging competition in the marketplace. The focal point of regulatory activity has shifted steadily over time from the states to the national government. Both Congress and state legislatures have increasingly delegated legislative authority for regulation to entities created specifically as regulatory bodies. Several federal regulatory boards and commissions were established in the period 1887–1938.

State and local regulation is not unimportant. In addition to regulating insurance and banking, state agencies examine and license physicians, lawyers, insurance agents, real estate agents, and so on. Other examples include commerce commissions, liquor control boards, and recreation departments. Local regulation consists primarily of licensing certain businesses and setting and enforcing various regulative codes.

Economic "old" regulation focuses on markets, rates, and the obligation to serve. Social "new" regulation affects the conditions under which goods and services are produced and the physical characteristics of the products manufactured. Social regulation also differs from economic regulation in the wider scope of its impacts. Social regulation arose out of a concern for reducing involuntary (and voluntary) public exposure to risk.

Government regulations have developed in large part as a result of decisions designed to protect individuals and to maintain representativeness and fairness in governing. A by-product of the growth of the regulatory bureaucracy has been a mounting tangle of red tape. The Clinton administration, however, has undertaken major initiatives to redefine the scope and manner of regulation, with emphasis on reducing the number of regulations and the degree of difficulty associated with compliance.

Regulatory procedures fall into two categories: rule making and adjudicatory authority. Rule-making procedures involve publication of proposed changes in rules, a period of public comment, issuance of final rules, and codification in the Code of Federal Regulations. The number of new or revised rules increased substantially in the 1970s. The increase in regulatory decisions, particularly in adjudication, has meant a substantial increase in the importance of administrative law judges. The growth of administrative law itself has been a major phenomenon of the regulatory process.

Regulatory politics is not usually partisan. Rather, it is the politics of privilege and patronage, of product distribution, quality, and price. For regulators, constituency support can create an awkward and sensitive problem: Regulators are likely to find such support among those in the industries they regulate.

The independence of regulatory bodies from the president is far from absolute, though structural features do shield members from some presidential influence. Presidential appointment power, with Senate consent, is substantial, and other forms of White House intervention are not unknown. In recent years, the Clinton administration has tried to encourage more consultation and negotiation — between regulators and those regulated and between the chief executive and government regulators.

Independence from Congress is limited, although regulators have more to do with individual committees than with Congress as a whole. However, they occasionally become more involved with the whole Congress, and with committees, if there is adverse public or industry reaction to proposed actions. The question of independence seems to have an ironic answer: Regulators are independent to the extent that they have adequate political support to ensure freedom of action.

Regulators are in frequent contact with industry leaders, both professionally and socially. Industries have a legitimate self-interest to uphold, but direct pressure on regulators is the exception, not the rule. Another problem is that individuals having the kind of expertise needed and sought by regulatory bodies often received their training and experience in the regulated industries themselves and, thus, bring with them a natural "industry slant" on problems and needs. An alternative is to appoint someone with no expertise, which breeds another kind of problem.

Consumerism has had a major impact on government regulation. Beginning with concern for the health hazards of cigarette smoking and for auto safety, the consumer movement has grown to a point of considerable political influence. Consumer leaders have relied more on administrative regulators than on

Congress for registering consumer gains, while attempting to reshape regulation itself.

Administrative law has expanded in response to a growing governmental administrative apparatus. Administrative law pertains to the authority needed by administrative entities to perform their duties and to the limits necessary to control their activities. The field focuses on the rules and regulations issued by administrative entities and on administrative powers and procedures; the field brings law, administration, and politics together. National and state administrative procedure acts have given meaning to procedural due process.

Rule making is governed by requirements of public participation (including prior notice and opportunity for the public to present its views), publication of rules, and judicial review of proposed or actual rules. Rules themselves can be substantive, procedural, or interpretative. Adjudication involves settling controversies between contending parties and determining legal rights and obligations. Formal adjudication entails fair notice, opportunity to be heard, and a decision rendered by an impartial arbiter. Informal adjudication is far more common, often occurring on the basis of mutual consent within looser constraints. Legal issues surrounding the exercise of administrative discretion center on how to balance administrative and judicial imperatives; a central concern is bureaucratic arbitrariness.

Regulatory reform can be addressed to a variety of objectives that are not necessarily consistent with one another. Under recent presidents, deregulation has assumed greater importance. Regulatory relief involves reviews of existing rules, a slowdown in issuing major new regulations, relaxing enforcement of existing rules, and making significant reductions in regulatory budgets and personnel. Ironically perhaps, not all industries wish to be deregulated, and not all regulators have sought to retain their authority. Debates over government regulation are likely to continue well into the future.

KEY TERMS AND CONCEPTS

free-market competition	Sherman Antitrust Act
government regulation	Clayton Act
monopolistic practices	Securities and Exchange Commission (SEC)
independent regulatory boards and commissions	social regulatory initiatives
administrative law	Administrative Procedure Act of 1946
regulatory body	

protective regulation
dependent regulatory agencies
    (DRAs)
rule making
adjudication
Federal Register
Code of Federal Regulations
administrative law judge

advisory opinion
consent order
procedural fairness
procedural due process
deregulation
information superhighway
reregulation

SUGGESTED READING

Carter, Leif, and Christine Harrington. *Administrative Law and Politics.* New York: HarperCollins, 1991.

Cooper, Phillip J. *Public Law and Public Administration.* 2nd ed. Englewood Cliffs, N.J.: Prentice-Hall, 1988.

Fritschler, A. Lee, and James M. Hoefler. *Smoking and Politics: Policy Making and the Federal Bureaucracy.* 5th ed. Upper Saddle River, N.J.: Prentice-Hall, 1996.

Harris, Richard A., and Sidney M. Milkis. *The Politics of Regulatory Change: A Tale of Two Agencies.* New York: Oxford University Press, 1989.

John, DeWitt. *Civic Environmentalism: Alternatives to Regulation in States and Communities.* Washington, D.C.: Congressional Quarterly Press, 1993.

Kettl, Donald F. *Leadership at the Fed.* New Haven, Conn.: Yale University Press, 1986.

Landy, Marc K., Marc J. Roberts, and Stephen R. Thomas. *The Environmental Protection Agency: From Nixon to Clinton.* Expanded ed. New York: Oxford University Press, 1994.

Meier, Kenneth J. *Regulation: Politics, Bureaucracy, and Economics.* New York: St. Martin's, 1985.

Rosenbloom, David H., and Richard D. Schwartz, eds. *Handbook of Regulation and Administrative Law.* New York: Marcel Dekker, 1994.

Strauss, Peter L., Todd Rakoff, and W. A. Gellhorn, eds. *Gellhorn and Byse's Administrative Law: Cases and Comments.* Westbury, N.Y.: Foundation Press, 1995.

Tolchin, Susan J., and Martin Tolchin. *Dismantling America: The Rush to Deregulate.* Boston: Houghton Mifflin, 1983.

Warren, Kenneth F. *Administrative Law in the Political System.* 3rd ed. Upper Saddle River, N.J.: Prentice-Hall, 1997.

ON-LINE RESOURCES:
Government Regulation and Administrative Law

Administrative Law Index

http://www.law.indiana.edu/law/v-lib/

> The virtual law library at the Indiana University School of Law provides a good starting place for information on administrative law as well as links to other research tools and comprehensive sites.

Code of Federal Regulations

http://www.gpo.gov/nara/cfr/index.html

> The National Archives and Records Administration has designed this site to provide the public with enhanced access to government information; the site is divided into fifty titles that represent broad areas subject to federal regulation.

Disability Rights Education and Defense Fund, Inc. (DREDF)

http://www.dredf.org/

> Founded in 1979 by people with disabilities and parents of children with disabilities, the Disability Rights Education and Defense Fund, Inc. (DREDF) is a national law and policy center dedicated to protecting and advancing the civil rights of people with disabilities through legislation, litigation, advocacy, and technical assistance.

Environmental Protection Agency (EPA)

http://www.epa.gov

> The mission of the EPA is to protect human health and to safeguard the natural environment — air, water, and land — upon which life depends.

Equal Employment Opportunity Commission (EEOC)

http://eeoc.gov

> Updates current legal issues and regulations on employment discrimination and labor unions.

Federal Communications Commission (FCC)

http://www.fcc.gov

> The FCC offers information on legislation, technological advancements, and media systems.

Federal Register

http://www.federalregister.com

Complete listing of proposed and active federal regulations is available on this site.

Federal Trade Commission (FTC)

http://www.ftc.gov

Independent regulatory commission responsible for enforcement of anti-trust laws such as the Sherman and Clayton Acts that prevent unfair trade practices.

FEDWORLD Information Network (U.S. Department of Commerce, National Technical Information Service)

http://www.fedworld.gov/

FEDWORLD enables users to find useful federal sites for everyday needs. It is one of the premier government Web sites, serving as a jumping-off place to all other government divisions.

Food and Drug Administration (FDA)

http://www.fda.gov

This site offers a wealth of information on the mission of the FDA and its role in maintaining health and safety standards, food and drug testing, and assessment.

Food and Drug Administration Backgrounder

http://www.fda.gov/opacom/backgrounders/tobacco.html

Summary of U.S. Court of Appeals for the Fourth Circuit ruling on the FDA's jurisdiction over, and regulation of, cigarettes and smokeless tobacco.

Nuclear Regulatory Commission

http://www.nrc.gov

Information on nuclear power plant safety, regulations, operations, and construction.

Office of Administrative Law Judges

http://www.oalj.dol.gov

New regulations on recent regulatory developments of particular importance to adjudication proceedings before administrative law judges.

Policy News and Information Services

http://www.policy.com/reports/tobacco

Focuses on the current status of the tobacco settlement and examines the bipartisan National Tobacco Policy and Youth Smoking Reduction Act organized by Senator John McCain.

Securities and Exchange Commission (SEC)

http://www.sec.gov

Information on what the SEC does, including regulation of stock brokers, securities exchanges, and investments.

Supreme Court Cases

http://www.findlaw.com/casecode/supreme.html

This Web site is useful for exploring cases settled by the Supreme Court and also contains news from the federal courts and constitutional law message boards.

U.S. International Trade Commission (USITC)

http://www.usitc.gov

This Web site offers voluminous information about trade barriers, imports and exports, unfair trade practices and policies, and regulations.

For further information on government regulation see: Bedford/ St. Martin's Home Page

http://www.bedfordstmartins.com

Chapter 12

Conclusion: Public Administration in a Time of Rapid Social Change

> *Never before has man had such capacity to control his own envi-*
> *ronment, to end thirst and hunger, to conquer poverty and disease,*
> *to banish illiteracy and massive human misery. We have the power*
> *to make this the best generation of mankind in the history of the*
> *world — or to make it the last.*

John F. Kennedy (1917–1963), United Nations address,
New York City, 20 September 1963

Our examination of public administration in the United States is now completed. From treatment of various topics in the text — values, intergovernmental relations, organization theory, entrepreneurial government, leadership, personnel and budgeting, service quality and productivity, government regulation, and the rest — several impressions have emerged clearly. Most important is that the current state of public administration is characterized by considerable uncertainty and rapid change, accompanied by dramatic developments in and out of the field affecting what it presently is and does, and its likely future shape.

Another impression is that although it is desirable to maintain various features of governmental and administrative practice — such as efficiency, accountability, ethical standards, participation, and strong leadership — it is difficult if not impossible to achieve all or even most of them *simultaneously*. The conservative quest for accountability, efficiency, and effectiveness often conflicts with more liberal social goals, such as promoting diversity, redistributing resources, and expanding participation. This poses difficult questions for us. On which feature(s) do we place greatest value? Which are we willing to forego in order to achieve another? Who benefits and who loses from choosing one over another? In short, intricate and perplexing questions abound — questions for which there are no easy answers.

In this concluding chapter we will discuss how public administration interacts within the context of citizen frustration and continuing uncertainty about the future. We first consider the social and governmental environment, then the growing dissatisfaction with certain practices of governmental administration, review evolving issues and challenges in its study and teaching, and conclude by noting several continuing features — and questions — in the field. Throughout this discussion several themes will be evident: (1) the presence of numerous paradoxes in public administration; (2) tensions existing among these paradoxes, and the challenge of dealing with them; and (3) the accelerating pace of change in administrative theory and practice.

The Social and Governmental Environment

For the past forty years, social and political struggles have taken new forms in the country, imposing continuous pressures on our values and institutions. Rising social tension and value conflicts stem from our resolve to foster goals such as social diversity while maintaining economic freedom and independence. Societal relations directly affect political interests and competition. If those relations are tense and combative, as they have been recently, that will be reflected in political values and procedures, including those in administration. The national government "has become a microcosm of the conflicts and differences that pervade society. . . . As government [at all levels] becomes coextensive with society in composition and function, it experiences the disorganization . . . of society itself."[1]

There is much more to the social and governmental environment than simply promoting diversity, however. Recent turbulence surrounding public administration has resulted from a host of changes, paradoxes, and conflicts. Chief among them is *rapid social change*, not only in population growth, immigration patterns (for example, increasing numbers of Asian, Caribbean, and Latino immigrants), and geographic distribution, but also in economic instruments, evolving governmental roles, and technological innovations. Our capacity for economic growth is seriously hampered by dependence on imported goods and raw materials — chiefly automobiles and oil, but also metals from other countries — as well as limits resulting from depletion of our natural resources. Directly related to this is the loss of income and jobs from our products being less competitive in world markets. Decreasing math, reading, and science scores of American students are also serious social issues with economic consequences. And politically, we as a nation continue to search for greater consensus about the direction in which we should try to move. In the past twenty-five years, we have elected or reelected four different presidents (two Democrats and two Republicans) — each with vastly different visions of the nation's life and needs, each with a sharply different policy priorities.

Another factor is the **knowledge explosion**, spread of technology, and growth in the use of the Internet, which carries with it increasing potential for very different kinds of human interactions — both positive and negative.

knowledge explosion
a social phenomenon of the past forty years, particularly in Western industrial nations, creating new technologies and vast new areas of research and education; examples include biogenetic engineering, space exploration, mass communications, nuclear technology, mass production, and energy research.

Growth of knowledge, science, and **technological change** are closely linked with changes in the nature of society and in human capabilities, values, and behavior. As one example, scientific explanations about the origins of the universe and of life on this planet may profoundly affect traditional religious beliefs; new wireless communications linkages permit direct citizen-to-citizen contacts across international borders; as another example, consider the implications of unlocking the mysteries of human genetics. If these were once the stuff of dreams or science fiction, they are no longer.

Such developments have an ironic twist. We have had faith for decades that expanding our knowledge would make our world both safer and more predictable, and that science would help us answer age-old questions with much more precision and certainty. Yet we have found just the opposite: the more we have learned, the *less certain* everything seems. Many people are disturbed by all this uncertainty, and it is possible that expanded knowledge contributes to social instability, with many seeking to return (in effect) to "the good old days" that many remember as a less unnerving past. One indication of this is the phenomenon of religious revivalism, or **fundamentalism,** among growing numbers of Christians, Jews, and Muslims in many countries of the world.

The present social and governmental environment threatens long-standing safety nets for many millions of low-income, disadvantaged, and elderly Americans. Debates over the future of welfare, Medicare, and Social Security reflect a new "fend-for-yourself" attitude in dealing with social problems. A direct link exists between this emphasis and public administration, because government is involved with virtually every major challenge and opportunity, from disaster relief, to eliminating crime, race or sex discrimination, protecting retirement plans, or rescuing a bankrupt savings and loan. This continues despite the fact that many problems cannot be fully resolved, only temporarily coped with until the next crisis develops. In some cases, demands on bureaucracy to solve problems may be unrealistic.

The cost of entitlements (over 60 percent of the federal budget) is creating "intergenerational conflict" between younger workers, baby boomers, and older retirees. When Social Security was passed in 1935, there were forty workers for every one retiree. We are now approaching a 3-to-1 ratio and political movements are gaining strength to "redistribute" more government programs from the elderly to younger workers, students, and parents of young children.

Nevertheless, in terms of a balance between public and private sectors in dealing with society's problems, the public (governmental) side of the scale received greater weight (at least until the late 1970s). Furthermore, "as the range of public problems and programs broadens, and as knowledge relevant to each grows and deepens, it becomes less and less possible for politically elected representatives to get a handle on more than a few of the significant issues."[2] Thus, the role of expert administrators to whom responsibility for program management is delegated becomes ever larger (although not unlimited, by any means).

technological change
rapidly emerging patterns of change (related in part to the knowledge explosion) in communication, medical, and transportation technologies, among others, with significant implications both for the societal challenges confronting government and for the means and resources increasingly available to government for conducting public affairs.

fundamentalism
the practice of certain religious groups that adhere to strict beliefs and literal interpretation of a set of basic religious principles.

chronic fiscal stress
a condition confronting increasing numbers of governments and public agencies, resulting from a combination of economic inflation, declining productivity, slower economic growth, and taxpayer resistance to a larger tax burden.

One other aspect of the immediate social and governmental environment of public administration — with enormous significance for the future conduct of government generally — is the advent of **chronic fiscal stress**. As inflation combined with declining productivity to slow economic growth in the private sector, the revenue base of government at all levels shrank. Consequently, administrative agencies and government units, by the hundreds, faced deep cutbacks in funding, personnel, and the levels of services. (Deficit reduction and budget agreements between President Clinton and Congress had the same effect on the national government.) The unwillingness of taxpayers to assume additional tax burdens has only compounded the problem for government officials. This has obvious financial implications for budget making but also directly affects personnel management, labor relations, and the push for greater efficiency, effectiveness, service quality, productivity, and accountability in public management.

The central difficulty, however, is the need for us to adjust our assumptions about economic growth as the foundation for continued governmental growth. Agencies, their administrators, and their clienteles, accustomed to successive increases in operating budgets and the programmatic benefits they could provide, have been rudely jolted by new economic and political realities. Explicit (and increasing) attention is now being paid, at all levels of government, to the need for "doing more with less" — even though there is mounting evidence that in many places, doing *less with less* is the emerging reality (see Box 12–1, "You Get What You Pay for — If You *Pay* or If You *Don't*," for one example). The present environment in this respect has bred increasing hostility toward "big government" — out of economic necessity, if not always due to direct public animosity. The long-term consequences of this change may prove to be both permanent and fundamental in their impact on government, and on administrative operations in particular.

All this is occurring in the context of more fundamental value changes in society. A wide range of beliefs and institutions is under attack from new and competing ideologies. Central to change at this basic level is *decline of respect for authority;* traditional sources and centers of authority — including parents, teachers, religious leaders, politicians, and judges — exert diminishing influence on greater numbers of young people. Decline of authority suggests changing institutional patterns. The ability of government to govern may well be compromised, to say nothing of how other institutions, such as courts, churches, universities, and businesses, will be affected. Current (and growing) unrest and the rise of organized crime within the newly independent republics of the former Soviet Union illustrate the decline of authority within that crumbling authoritarian system. Other societies are experiencing similar breakdowns.

Social and Governmental Paradoxes

Contributing still further to uncertainty in public administration is a series of paradoxical developments, some within this country alone and others worldwide

BOX 12-1 ETHICAL AND LEADERSHIP CHALLENGES FOR PUBLIC MANAGERS

You Get What You Pay For — If You Pay or If You *Don't*

The Colorado Tourism Board, no longer supported by tax dollars, is working with a skeleton staff of three [compared to the fifteen people formerly employed in the Board's Denver headquarters] and a shoestring budget, to service the flood of would-be visitors telephoning for information. Even when they answer the calls of potential tourists, the Tourism Board has *no information to send them.*

Colorado voters, in November 1993, abolished the state's 0.1 percent tourism-promotion tax. Without the $11 million annually the tax provided for advertising and promotion, the Tourism Board was forced to pare its staff and was unable to print the 2.5 million state maps and large, full-color vacation guides that it sent to callers in previous years.

Two or three callers each day are so angry they hang up on the board staffers. Some of the angriest are Colorado residents who want information for out-of-state friends and relatives. As one staff member noted, "Some of these are *the same people who voted against the tourism tax,* and now they can't believe they can't get information."

SOURCE: Adapted from a Scripps-Howard news service story appearing in the *Bloomington-Normal* (Ill.) *Pantagraph,* April 3, 1994, p. B-3 (emphasis added).

in their scope. First, as noted in Chapter 1, there is a blurring of distinctions between public and private sectors in the United States, contrary to the popular belief that they are separate and distinct. Every important program to raise income, employment, and productivity; relieve social distress; correct abuses; guarantee health care and social security; and protect rights has "entailed the creation of new and complex arrangements in which the distinction between public and private has become more blurred."[3] Examples are numerous: Amtrak, the Corporation for Public Broadcasting, and the Legal Services Corporation, at the national level; community action agencies and health systems agencies (both bridging public–private and intergovernmental boundaries); and quasi-public organizations established to work with government in public programs such as Medicare, Medicaid, and community development. As indicated, the influence of these public and private partnerships has grown considerably, and will likely continue in an entrepreneurial and market-driven environment.

Second, we are confronted by a **revolution of rising expectations,** which still dominates politics in developing nations and many portions of our own population. At the same time, an appeal has gone up from others for a lowering of our expectations. Both refer to expectations about economic development, higher productivity, more leisure time, acquisition of material possessions, and

revolution of rising expectations a social phenomenon of the period since World War II, affecting many nations, in which people who have been relatively poor have sought to increase their level of prosperity both as individuals and as groups; related in part to faith in technological and social advances.

increased standards of living. In this country, rising expectations and many governmental responses to them in the past thirty years have centered on poor and middle-income Americans, who have by no means given up their aspirations to the "good life." The countertrend toward breaking the dependence on government and on *lesser* expectations reflects an economic realism about the loss of real income for the past twenty years, concern for environmental quality, finite resources, population stabilization rather than growth, and quality of life as opposed to standard of living. Ideological and political controversies over the ill-fated Republican *Contract with America*, "economy versus ecology," reinvention, welfare to "workfare," the future of Social Security, Medicare, and Medicaid, among others, illustrate this paradox.

Third, a paradox exists between continuing emphasis on industrialization (closely linked to economic development and rising expectations) and the emergence of what has been called the "postindustrial society." **Postindustrialism** refers to a socioeconomic order in which there is a relative decline in importance of production, land, and labor as economic forces, and a relative upsurge in importance of knowledge, information, new technologies, rendering of services (as opposed to production of goods), and available leisure time. Implications for government and administration are immense: changes in revenue patterns, educational and service needs, information technologies and capabilities, political demands, and so on. Elements of postindustrial society have become a part of the fabric of social and economic life, and therefore of the complex forces pressing on business, industry, and government. This paradox is complicated further by an emerging emphasis on *reindustrialization*, that is, on upgrading and modernizing industry as our aging physical plant and production capacity fall behind those of other nations.

Fourth, forces of *nationalism* still run strong in many parts of the world, while conflicting currents of so-called postnationalism have arisen and are gaining strength. In some of the older nation-states, nationalism — identity with a national unit of government, patriotism, observance of duties of citizenship, pride in one's country — seems to be in decline. Postnational cynicism toward patriotism and political symbols such as anthems and flags, and growing alienation from government institutions all mark this decline. Postnationalism could mean one of two things. It could mean an awakening of feeling for "community," for organizing political arrangements that would eliminate trade barriers and strengthen international bonds of cooperation and respect (such as the European Community and the North American Free Trade Agreement). However, it also could suggest a trend toward emphasizing individual group identities within nations at the expense of established political entities. Tribalism in many African nations, the reemergence of National Socialism in Germany, the Quebec separatist movement, language rivalries in Belgium, and ethnic tensions in the former Soviet Union are examples of the latter.

A fifth paradox involves tendencies toward *violence, nonviolence, and terrorism.* Violence is no stranger to world affairs or to our own domestic scene. Huge

postindustrialism a social and economic phenomenon emerging in many previously industrialized nations; characterized by a relative decline in the importance of production, labor, and durable goods, and an increase in the importance of knowledge, new technologies, the provision of services, and leisure time.

stockpiles of nuclear weapons in the United States and former Soviet Union, with the prospect of other countries such as Iraq, Libya, North Korea, and Pakistan joining the "nuclear club," create potential for worldwide holocaust. Nonnuclear conflicts exist between or within nations such as the former Yugoslavia, reminding us of how far we are from a world order characterized by the peaceful rule of law. On the other hand, rising sentiment exists for nonviolent resolution of disputes, with considerable organizational sophistication in some instances — the United Nations and its complex of organizations is the best-known example. Martin Luther King, Jr. patterned his nonviolent civil rights movement after the example of Mohandas Gandhi, leader of India's independence movement against Britain in the 1940s; the antiwar movement that tried to stop our involvement in Vietnam during the late 1960s and early 1970s was generally (although not entirely) nonviolent; and growing opposition to nuclear weapons (largely nonviolent) surfaced in the 1980s. Another irony is present, in that some revolutionary movements use violence as a means to promote their "peaceful" aims. Bombings by revolutionary and separatist groups continue in Northern Ireland, Great Britain, Spain, Japan, and France despite countermeasures to secure public places such as airports, railroads, and subway stations.

Sixth, as noted in Chapter 2, the value of *limited government and deregulation* of public authority continues to exert a hold on our thinking in this country, yet many government programs and activities seem to conflict with it. Government regulation is a prime example. To the extent that we look to government to protect us from market abuses and related ills, we create the potential for government to regulate more than economic behavior. *How limited* we want our government to be will continue to be an issue in politics and administration for the foreseeable future. The reemergence of neoconservatism, the Republican sweep of congressional elections in 1994, and the enactment by Congress of seven of the ten proposals in the *Contract with America* further reinforce the popularity of this restrictive view of government. On the other hand, President Clinton's defeat of Republican Bob Dole in 1996, Republican losses in congressional races in 1998 followed by House Speaker Newt Gingrich's resignation, and Clinton's survival of the Republican impeachment attempt in 1999, all make it difficult to predict how voters will respond in the future.

Seventh, a paradox similar to the one just noted exists in the tendencies of many people to regard government (and bureaucracy, more specifically) with hostility at the same time that they want public agencies to satisfy their demands. Parallel to the emerging "fend-for-yourself" view of government entitlements, a prevailing attitude appears to be one of "I want mine" from government, while not respecting or trusting government institutions very much. More generally, many have come to demand less government in the abstract, while still looking to government officials for protection from dangers that are all too tangible. It takes more government (and bureaucracy), not less, to protect the public against natural and man-made disasters such as toxic waste, nuclear accidents, or potentially unsafe modes of transportation. Another aspect of this "hostile dependence" is criticism and calls for restraining bureaucratic program growth by individuals who refer to programs that benefit *others*, and rarely to those programs that benefit them. The less government there is, the more we like it, until a natural or man-made disaster overwhelms us and we ask: where is Uncle Sam when *I need help?*

Finally, multiple meanings of representation and representative pose an important paradox. Throughout our discussion we have referred to the calls for *representativeness* as calls to include in decision-making processes those whose interests are affected by decisions made, especially those previously excluded. An older, more traditional meaning of representation refers to **"overhead democracy"** — a representative process.[4] Old and new meanings of representation have collided in theory and practice during the past three decades, and no slackening of the conflict between them is in sight. Ultimately, it is a conflict between concepts stressing, respectively, majoritarian and minoritarian political representation — that is, generalized majority rule versus systematic inclusion of diverse social, political, and economic minorities.

"overhead democracy" majority control through political representatives who supervise administrative officers responsible and loyal to their superiors for carrying out the directions of the elected representatives.

These paradoxes have a number of aspects in common. Where our values have changed — for example, nationalism and postnationalism — it is impossible to pinpoint just when the emphasis shifted from one to the other or, for that matter, just how far it has moved. Also, divergent tendencies present in all the paradoxes are related to one another in some instances — for example, in antipoverty programs where rising expectations, public/private overlap, and postnationalism come together; or in the highway program, where many people want no limits on auto travel but worry about air pollution and, most of all, do not want highways built through their neighborhoods; or in the quest for access to quality health care, which everyone wants, but no one wants to pay for.

Most important, these paradoxes have crucial implications for public administration as a whole. Administration is the machinery government uses to deal with general social problems and consequently it is located in or between the paradoxes that exist in the surrounding society. Whatever social or economic forces and turbulence exist will influence government attempts to act, to restrain, or to change policy direction. Because of public expectations that government *will* act, administrative agencies and personnel must do so, even when choices are unclear, consequences are only dimly perceived, and political pressures arising from these paradoxes are troublesome and unyielding.

In sum, the existing environment, with its turbulence and paradoxes, poses many challenges to public administration. Because the outlook is for even more societal complexity in the future, the prognosis for public administration is that it will experience continued pressures — for improved service delivery, adaptation to new needs and challenges, and political responsiveness to varied (and often conflicting) interests.

Ferment and Change in Public Administration: Concepts and Practices

This discussion of public administration will cover some of the same ground explored in earlier chapters. However, it is appropriate here to reexamine the contours of change in the context of what it may portend for the future.

First, the architecture of bureaucracy has changed considerably in the past quarter-century. The command- and control-oriented Weberian bureaucratic hierarchy, with its emphasis upon formal structure, secrecy, routinization, and efficiency in its narrow sense, is rapidly becoming obsolete. It is especially inadequate for organizations — public, private, and nonprofit — operating within a rapidly changing environment, facing increasing complexity in their programs, and staffed heavily with highly professional or scientific personnel. Such organizations, in order to maintain needed flexibility, creativity, and innovativeness, must be structured around projects or problems to be solved rather than as permanent hierarchies. A "core" staff will remain for various administrative purposes, such as record keeping, financial auditing, and performance evaluation, and for fixing final responsibility, but work processes are being organized around fast-response teams. Decisions will be made collegially through the pooling of the perspectives and techniques of various specialists. Leadership will become increasingly stimulative and collaborative rather than directive. This assessment is in keeping with the discussion of alternative forms of organization in Chapter 5.

A dramatic change in Weberian practices as well as structures is already detectable. Among its most basic functions were orderliness, predictability, and control, each of which has been profoundly affected by contemporary turbulence in and around public administration. Another irony is evident: many people longing for bureaucratic predictability are among the harshest critics of **"overhead bureaucracy,"** which highly values increased citizen participation and greater sensitivity to bureaucracy's "customers," imperatives that have further reduced predictability. The control function has been redefined a number of ways (including a shift in emphasis toward *greater accountability for results* rather than simply more control). Much more complex and elaborate leader–follower relations have been prescribed by the human relations school, organizational humanists, scholars of leadership, and advocates of organization development, who emphasize democratic leadership and employee participation. Also, the control function is disrupted by subsystem politics, discussed in Chapter 3, wherein administrators develop foundations of power outside traditional vertical bureaucratic channels of command and responsibility.

Finally, *official secrecy*, which Weber saw as a protection for bureaucrats, has been diminished considerably by efforts to increase public access to records and decision processes — what one observer calls "watchdogging functions."[5] Such functions have expanded significantly in the past two decades. The National Performance Review estimated that as many as one-third of all federal employees

"overhead bureaucracy" increased costs of administering government programs imposed by mandates to include those affected by policy-making decisions; program efficiency tends to decrease as participation increases.

serve as "inspectors" checking the work of the other two-thirds. The seemingly permanent movement away from Weberian formalism toward much less structured, decentralized, and more diversified bureaucratic forms also indicates that Weber's influence lingers, but decreasingly.

Other major changes are occurring. First is a far wider range of participation and demands for new forms, including the Internet and World Wide Web, of interacting with government. From what is usually known as the liberal side of the political spectrum came calls for *greater internal participation* or **empowerment** in decision making by agency employees and external participation by affected clienteles. In the 1990s, however, both of these themes have been taken up by others whose politics are decidedly not liberal — including President Clinton. But participation has two other dimensions as well. One is devolution (transfer) of federal programs to states and local governments, advocated by many political conservatives, and more recently espoused by high-level Clinton administration appointees, including the former director of the Office of Management and Budget and Federal Reserve Board members.[6] The Clinton administration responded with proposals to consolidate 107 health service grants into six "performance partnerships" and eleven consolidated (block) grants, giving states and local governments more program authority. As described in Chapter 4, federal block grants began a major effort to shift responsibility for important social programs to state governments. The potential long-term significance of this shift is immense, politically and administratively. Persistent demands for greater participation and for devolution reflect a distrust of bigness and represent an attempt to gain control of decisions affecting clienteles and interest groups.

The other dimension of participation is *structural* in nature but reflects the same impulse for greater popular control over government. Regional associations of governments, special purpose districts, economic development commissions, and community action organizations have sprung up, partly at the behest of national planners but also in response to local involvement. Elements of both participation and devolution, as well as specific administrative and economic considerations, have played a part in developing such organizations. The point here is that various steps already have been taken to translate existing preferences for participation and devolution into organizational reality (for example, community councils and citizen action groups of various kinds).

A second significant change has been further development of management science techniques that have contributed to more sophisticated and systematic administration. One dimension involves the growing use of *quantitative methods, information technology, and computers* — in short, management science. Others include project management, a package of techniques designed to move individual projects along paths set out for them; "business process reengineering," a technique emphasizing parallel rather than sequential processing, the wide availability of procedural information, rapid paperless information logging, and automation;[7] and the practice of contracting out, under which private contractors or independent consultants provide designated goods or services to govern-

---

empowerment
an approach to citizen participation or management that stresses extended customer satisfaction, examines relationships among existing management processes, seeks to improve internal agency communications, and responds to valid customer demands; in exchange for the authority to make decisions at the point of customer contact, all "empowered" employees must be thoroughly trained, and the results must be carefully monitored.

ment agencies for an agreed-upon fee. (Note, also, that trends toward more participation and more systematic management methods may conflict, but that has not prevented many governments from pursuing both!)

A third development is public employee unionization and collective bargaining, treated in Chapter 8. Underlying this development is a concern for job security coupled with the rise of a service-oriented economy (postindustrial), with a larger proportion of "knowledge workers" engaged in public employment. Also, general social and economic pressures have contributed to relaxation of laws and regulations restraining public-sector unionization. These developments directly impact public personnel management, but also have an impact on government's role in economic and social affairs and the status and nature of government itself as an employer. As noted earlier, these may be changing again, this time in different directions. Public-sector union membership (described in Chapter 8) has stabilized at about 44 percent, while the percentage of union members in private service and manufacturing firms has declined to under 10 percent of the total workforce. This huge and growing disparity between the percentages of nonunionized workers in the private and public sectors foreshadows major political conflict ahead.

A fourth development is emphasis on budgets, results, evaluation, customer service, and employee productivity, treated in Chapters 9 and 10. Efforts to improve our capabilities are going forward in these areas, and some results are encouraging. One problem, however, deserves mention here, in addition to those treated earlier. That is whether unionization and collective bargaining in the public sector will help or hinder efforts to reduce expenditures, increase productivity, and improve job performance. The latter issue will hinge on the level of trust or distrust between unions and management and whether union leaders and members are as concerned about these challenges as are employers. Plainly, the increasing disparity between the public and private sector union membership will draw critical attention, especially from conservatives and others who perceive government as bloated, self-serving, and unresponsive to change.

A fifth development concerns the growing pressures on government spending, at all levels, with many serious budgetary constraints: extensive reductions in public funding, deep cuts in personnel and in services rendered, substantial boosts in "pay-as-you-go" financing for programs that remain in operation, and so on. There is substantial public frustration evident regarding the proper role and desirability of government expenditures across a wide range of program areas at all levels of government — not to mention continued taxpayer resistance to proposed increases in government revenues. State and local governments, especially, have been hard pressed to raise new revenues. Moreover, in many government jurisdictions, election outcomes have been heavily influenced by which of the candidates was able to strike more of an antitax pose before the electorate. With the national (and international) economies more difficult to manage and predict, issues concerning government revenue have, if anything, become more complex and challenging than in the decades immediately past.

Finally, we should note other developments as well. Continuing specialization and professionalization raise the challenge of bridging gaps among specialists in different professions. Executive reorganization promises to receive wider use in years ahead. More states permit their governors to submit package proposals to their legislatures, and recent presidents (for example, Bill Clinton, Jimmy Carter, and Ronald Reagan — all former governors) stressed reorganization as a policy instrument. Continuing unrest — and potentially major change — in fiscal federalism will affect state and local administration in thousands of program areas. Finally, public administration will be affected by efforts to **debureaucratize** organizational life in the public service — by downsizing agency personnel, deemphasizing credentials of public servants, broadening decision making, decreasing rigidities, and increasing lateral communication within bureaucracies — especially to the extent that recommendations of the National Partnership for Reinventing Government (NPRG) are accepted by Congress and put into practice in the federal bureaucracy.

debureaucratize
strategy to decentralize and deregulate the public sector by reductions in force, promoting greater flexibility in personnel decisions, and increasing result-oriented incentives to reduce "overhead" costs.

Paradoxes in Concept and Practice

Just as there are paradoxes in the environment surrounding public administration, there are paradoxes in its concepts and practices. One broad paradox revolves around impacts of participation in administrative decision making by divergent — and frequently conflicting — groups. These include program clienteles, public employee unions, and agency personnel seeking to participate in management consistent with their own organizational values. All three kinds of participation offer potential opposition to the values of rationality, professionalism, leadership, and accountability.

Participation can conflict with rationality because the former is based on *political inclusion of new and varied interests*, whereas the latter presumes to objectively identify the *most advantageous courses of action* without regard to particular political interests or impacts on them. Furthermore, participation can conflict with professionalism because, as noted earlier, its advocates seek to have decisions framed in terms of their impacts on those affected rather than on the basis of what professionals think is best for the people. One way out of this dilemma is negotiation and political mediation by a respected third-party not clearly identified with either side of the issue. However, participation can also conflict with traditional forms of leadership by acting as a constraint on leaders' ability to set the direction of organizations or political systems. Participation is a potential counterweight to what leaders desire, although it also can be a source of leadership support. It comes down to a question of what views and interests are added to the decision-making process by expanding participation.

Finally, participation can conflict with accountability. Considering that the former is specifically designed to promote the latter, how can this statement be justified? The answer is this: by increasing participation in decision making, it becomes more difficult to pinpoint just who was responsible for initiating and enforcing a decision, and therefore to hold those persons accountable for their actions. A skillful leader may be able to guide a participatory decision-making system along lines he or she prefers, with no one the wiser; such a technique camouflages where responsibility for a given decision really lies. Thus, although intended to promote accountability, participation has the potential for doing precisely the opposite.

Recalling the discussion of *scientific management* in Chapter 5, emphasis on participation reflects a strong faith in process leading to "correct" (optimum, appropriate) results. Americans have a reputation for being pragmatic people with concern for how things are done. Yet this discussion of participation points up an important lesson in and out of public administration. Programs that are efficient are not always effective. Casually assuming a relationship between "doing it the right way" and getting the desired results can be risky. It may be necessary to examine precisely what is produced via particular steps to determine whether that is the way participants or clienteles wish to continue operating. Concern with consequences, as opposed to simply "perfecting the machinery," is growing — though it is to be hoped that we will not end up ignoring means and concentrating only on results (in participative-management terms, or in any other respect).

A second paradox involves contradictory tendencies toward centralization and decentralization, with the latter preferred by many Americans. Moving away from centralization has looked increasingly attractive (at least in the abstract) to millions of citizens, and appeals to this popular preference have become more common as a basis for government action. Yet many factors in the social and economic environment still illustrate the need for well-coordinated (centralized) responses to shared problems — for example, whether one state's garbage can be taken to (and dumped in) another state's landfills, how education standards in one state might impact the emerging workforce elsewhere in the country, or how economic development policies in individual states or localities might impact national economic growth. In short, geographic interdependence — within this nation and between our country and others — has increased recently, and such **global interdependence** requires some degree of centralization in public (as well as private) policy. With public support for greater decentralization, the challenge for officials confronted by policy problems stemming from global interdependence has been to move in both directions at the same time — no easy task! Interestingly, this paradox has sparked renewed attention to federalist-style arrangements in both public and private organizations, in which some functions are delegated to a general unit or level, while others are assigned to smaller (often neighborhood, community, or citizen) organizations.[8]

Another paradox is the need for better communication among diverse professionals, in the face of continued emphasis on professional specialization. It is not merely a matter of teams of professionals being assembled to work on specific projects. Rather, problems in today's society are so complex and have so

global interdependence the growing web of interrelationships—in social, economic, cultural, political, technological, institutional, and policy respects—among nations and peoples around the world; particularly significant as it relates to our abilities to communicate globally, and to the speed with which challenges found in one part of the world become a part of the governing environment in other locales.

many dimensions that professionals from different fields must learn to work together to alleviate them. Growing professional *inter*dependence, in short, will characterize public administration in the future much more than in the past — perhaps in part due to pressures for cutting back on the numbers of government employees, as well as the increasing complexity and interrelatedness of many policy challenges such as crime control, health care reform, and environmental protection.

Another dimension of diversity, of course, is demographic diversity in the workforce itself. This involves both the challenge of attracting a more diverse cross section of the population to government service, and harnessing their energies in a common effort to strengthen service provision and program management.

Some other general comments should be made. First, those who advocate greater competition, entrepreneurism, and market orientation in organizational life see emphasis on careerism in the public service as an impediment to those goals. This view is based on the assumption that careerism limits one's options for doing innovative work or otherwise "taking risks" because of real or imagined potential for harming one's career aspirations. A related implication is conflict between individual talents such as creativity, initiative, innovation, and experimentation on the one hand, and efficient, coordinated (often controlling and incremental) organizational leadership on the other. Obviously, that would depend on situational factors, primarily on whether tasks and leadership of an organization are conducive to allowing, or encouraging, innovation by group members. There is little question, however, that leaders often regard themselves as custodians of the organization's mission, thus discouraging both subordinates' participation and creativity. In many cases, the pattern appears to be one of conflict between central, control-oriented, incremental, directive leadership and flexible, creative, innovative, and participative organizational operation.

Second, administrative discretion has become an issue and is likely to remain one for some time. Plainly, discretionary actions by public administration professionals may not promote representational qualities; nevertheless, discretion does not necessarily interfere with achieving accountability. We might legitimately try to achieve one or both, but they must be understood properly as separate and distinct features of administrative politics in order to pursue either of them sensibly.

Finally, it would appear that as a nation we are uncertain about how to achieve accountability. The design of our political system stresses accountability to the people through a complex, interrelated web of institutional channels. However, current efforts seem to focus on making all of government accountable to all of the people, *all* of the time. It is difficult to see how that can be done. Direct accountability to the people is an appealing idea, but it may also be said that if officials are accountable to everybody, they are accountable to nobody! It requires careful structuring of mechanisms of accountability to maximize the chances of attaining it. Can we, then, rely on a single mechanism? Probably not; that would result in too much power in too few hands. The next best thing would seem to be a variety of mechanisms, each acting as a channel for public control but also held to account for what it does. There is a label for such a complex mechanism of multiple accountability: *checks and balances*. We may simply need to gain better control over them — again — in order to ensure accountability to public preferences and interests.

Ferment and Change in Public Administration as a Field of Study

Given the wide-ranging change in concepts and practices of public administration, it is not surprising that the academic field of study known by the same name is subject to considerable turbulence as well. Some of these areas were discussed previously, particularly in Chapter 1, but we will deal with them as interrelated factors helping to shape the future of the discipline.

First, movement away from political science — its ancestral home, so to speak — has characterized much of public administration and its academic professionals. Developments in both fields after World War II led to increasingly divergent emphases, with political science stressing behavioral research of a type that many in public administration found uncongenial to their work. The latter was often treated as an academic "second-class citizen," giving rise to pressure for separation in the form of interdisciplinary programs in public administration and growing numbers of independent programs and departments. Yet postbehavioral changes in political science raise the possibility that the two may be able to draw somewhat closer together. The emergence of "public policy" as a distinct and legitimate field of study has helped to bridge the methodological gap between the rival disciplines.

Second, some schools of management and business administration have inaugurated distinct public-sector management portions of their course offerings, recognizing both the growing importance of education in public-sector-related fields for business graduates and the intentions of larger numbers of their students to work in the public sector upon graduation. Public administration, however, has never been — nor will it ever be — merely a branch of business administration. Efforts to develop joint business and public policy degrees based on the "best practices" of both public and private management hold promise for preparing future careerists.

Third, schools, programs, and institutes of public administration have proliferated in the past thirty-five years, with a number of distinctive features. They are generally separate from political science departments, as already implied. They tend to be graduate-level rather than undergraduate programs, building on a base of a good general education. And they clearly reflect a flexible, heterogeneous approach to the subject matter taught. Labels such as "public administration," "public policy," "public affairs," "management," and "management science" abound.

Also, organizational humanism and organizational development have continued to exert an influence in public administration. Organizational humanism, stressing increased self-realization and greater organizational democracy, has found some response within public administration, especially in organizations with less structured tasks permitting greater creativity and initiative. Organizational development has evolved from early emphasis on hardware and systems — with less concern for interpersonal relations — to a more widely supported focus on human components of the organization and concern for normative organizational goals and values (what should be done). Although both approaches have had only limited impact in the great majority of public (and private) organizations, their influence seems to be on the rise.

The rise in the study and application of quality and productivity improvement systems, such as total quality management, has similarly had a substantial impact on public administration as a field of study. The scholarly community has been paying much greater attention in the past decade to team building, customer service quality, the roles of leadership, and the like — and it seems likely that this attention will continue. Along the same lines, there can be little doubt that themes such as reinventing government, empowerment, and simplifying both regulations and procedures have made their way into the classroom and into relevant academic literature. The recommendations of various commissions examining government operations — such as the Grace Commission, the Volcker Commission, and the Winter Commission (which focused on state and local management) — have become a part of the field of study, as have numerous reactions to those recommendations, reflecting myriad perspectives.[9]

Furthermore, the teaching of administrative ethics has assumed a more prominent place in the study of public administration.[10] Bureaucrats have both the need and the opportunity to make *value choices* affecting the lives of others in the course of discharging their responsibilities. Moral and ethical questions abound — occupational safety and health programs, affirmative action policies, nuclear safety, or (on an individualized level) temptations to engage in improper or outright corrupt behavior. There has been, therefore, a resurgence of interest in ethics in public administration curricula. Part of the vitality of this area lies in the growing recognition among academics of both the complexity of the subject and the diversity of possible approaches to it (see Chapter 6). Attention to ethical issues, to maintaining ethical standards, and to ethics education and training is certain to continue in the future.

Finally, the very nature of the academic field, and of the subject matter that it comprises, remains an unsettled question. One observer, discussing constitutional separation of powers and administrative theory, has noted three separate approaches to public administration: a "managerial" approach most closely associated with the chief executive, a "political" approach geared to legislative concerns, and a "legal" approach associated with the judiciary.[11] Another observer has described the situation this way: "Students of public administration will probably never agree on the proper blend for the elements of their discipline.

What degree of prominence should be given to the study of management, politics, social psychology, economics, or law?"[12] In light of these divergent tendencies, it appears unlikely that any "*single* school or philosophy, academic discipline, or type of methodology — or combination of these — would . . . persuade public administration to march under its banner."[13] This may not be altogether a bad thing. A complex, swiftly changing world may be better addressed by a curriculum that contains many facets, perspectives, interests, and methodologies: one which is eclectic, experimental, and open-ended.

A number of other observations merit inclusion here in assessing the academic field of public administration. One of its most important functions has been professional training — in programs that offer a master of public administration or public affairs (MPA) degree — of those who go on to take administrative positions at all three levels of government. Some observers are concerned about the kind of training available, stressing particularly that programs should not turn out narrowly specialized individuals who "can't see past the end of their noses." The late Frederick Mosher advocated well-trained professionals "who also have perspective on themselves and their work, and on social and political contexts in which they will find themselves working." Further, he noted that universities are "equipped to open the students' minds to the broader value questions of the society and of their professions' roles in that society."[14] Mosher and others have argued for a generalist preparation, rather than narrow professional specialization, which limits the level of knowledge about the society and the culture in which public administrators live and apply their skills.

The academic discipline of public administration appears to be in flux. There is a need to teach courses with an *applied* focus with less emphasis on pure theory. If rapid change, diversity, and uncertainty characterize the discipline now, they will be ever more characteristic of it in the years ahead. Of course, that is true of the practical side of the field as well.

Further Thoughts and Observations

In this closing section, we will take the opportunity to add a few comments that seem important in the overall scheme of things in public administration. They are intended to supplement what has been said earlier in this chapter and to point out other significant areas in the field.

First, we must bear in mind the increasing importance of managing public programs. More to the point, those of us not engaged in managerial activities in the public sector should recognize how crucial it is that we appreciate the complexities *unique to* public-sector management (see Box 2–1, "The Public Manager: An Overview," p. 49). It is easy enough to criticize what is done or not done by public administrators; we would find, however, that things look very different from the manager's perspective. Bureaucratic ways of doing things may not be entirely understandable to the outside observer, but (as noted in Chapter 7) they may be politically justifiable in terms of bureaucracy's continued needs and responsibilities. This is not to excuse shortcomings, or worse, in administrative behavior — it is only to suggest that we should not be too quick in passing judgment or too harsh in our assessments regarding bureaucratic actions. Public administrators are indeed engaged in honorable work. (It may even be true that public administrators are appreciated by the public more than has been supposed — see Box 12–2, "Contest Names Favorite Bureaucrat".) The challenge is to *reinvigorate* the profession by persuading aspiring students as well as mid-careerists that there is value to the public service, that it is not all negative. Equally important is *reinspiring* all citizens with an appreciation of the bureaucracy as an organic whole that is capable of responding to its environment, and convincing students and midcareerists that they can change it.

BOX 12–2   ETHICAL AND LEADERSHIP CHALLENGES FOR PUBLIC MANAGERS

Contest Names Favorite Bureaucrat

KNOXVILLE, Tenn. (AP) — A contest to determine the nation's "favorite bureaucrat" found the winner not in a haven of officialdom like Washington, D.C., but in rural Tennessee.

It wasn't an easy search.

Matthew Lesko, a best-selling writer and governmental information access expert, spent a year promoting a contest called "My Favorite Bureaucrat."

The idea was to get nominations from ordinary folks who had been helped in some special way by a public servant. The best nominating letter would win $5,000 and the bureaucrat would get a trophy.

But after six months, he had received only one nomination — and that was from another bureaucrat nominating her boss.

Lesko's predicament, however, brought true publicity to the contest. "Bureaucrats may deserve their bad reputation, after all," wrote *The Wall Street Journal.*

Lesko's Information USA Inc. then was flooded with nominations. More than 1,100 entries poured into the office, staff members said.

He heard about a bureaucrat who helped a woman with cancer get medical attention, one who helped find a father missing for 20 years, another who gave $5,000 in free tax advice, and one who gave free legal help to press a grandmother's sexual harassment charge.

And then he read the letter from small businessowner Charles "Frosty" Kimbrough of Morristown, Tenn. This was it, Lesko thought.

"I have been in business on my own for seven years," wrote Kimbrough. "I've had a lot of ups and downs, and at times was ready to give it up."

Then last year, Kimbrough wrote, he met Richard McKinney, a consultant at the Small Business Development Center at Walters State Community College. The center is partially funded by the federal Small Business Administration.

With McKinney's help, "it's been a great year. My income doubled and I'm more confident about the future of my business," Kimbrough wrote.

Kimbrough's company makes picnic tables and cooking grills. His workforce is himself, his wife, and sometimes another worker or two.

McKinney helped Kimbrough get on a bidding list with the state parks system, figure his costs, get credit extensions with his suppliers and locate materials, and showed his wife, how to do the books.

"All I had was just a big question mark, you know?" Kimbrough said in a recent interview. "I've never been able to pay anybody to help me like he has."

And when Kimbrough was hurt just as he tried to meet his first big state contract deadline, McKinney helped paint grills on his own time to get the order out.

"He needed business and I helped bid the stuff. I felt that in order for him to succeed and get other state orders, he had to deliver on time," McKinney said.

SOURCE: Adapted with permission from an Associated Press wire-service report, appearing in the *Bloomington-Normal* (Ill.) *Pantagraph* (July 2, 1990).

At the same time, we must pay more attention than we have recently to controlling bureaucratic waste, fraud, and mismanagement. Recently these concerns have become more of a political issue, frequently (though far from exclusively) involving defense spending. Both the OMB and the General Accounting Office (GAO) have taken numerous steps to combat waste, fraud, and abuse. These have included investigations of allegedly lax accounting procedures; reports on government waste in areas such as Pentagon procurement contracts, Medicaid and Medicare fraud, and spare-parts disposal practices; and establishing a toll-free "hot line" to report incidents of possible waste and mismanagement. One potentially significant development in this area is that increasing attention is being paid to financial accounting as one means of combating waste, mismanagement, and fraud.[15] Courses in this subject are finding their way into MPA curricula.

Two cautionary words are in order here. First, we should not put too much faith in sophisticated management techniques as remedies for these problems, because such techniques can be used to commit wasteful or fraudulent acts as well as to control them. We may instead need to *rediscover and revitalize* traditional practices such as financial auditing if we are to move effectively against these challenges. Second, we should be discriminating in our judgments, in the best sense of the phrase, about bureaucrats' behavior — taking care not to condemn the many because of the actions of a few. Nonetheless, renewed concern over these matters is entirely appropriate, especially at the state and local government levels, where opportunities still exist for politically inspired graft and corruption.

In a larger sense, we should not dwell so much on problems and weaknesses of bureaucracy as a form of organization that we overlook its strengths.[16] One is bureaucracy's very orderliness (at least potentially), which is so often denounced as inflexibility; if the alternative is patronage, nepotism, capricious judgment, or chaos (which it often was in Max Weber's time), that is a plus. Another is the system of legal guarantees against arbitrariness that governs so much administrative activity; still another is the "commitment of bureaucracy to democratic decision making — and the processes of consultation, negotiation, and accommodation" where it is clear that "broad and complex tasks require broad and complex organizations"[17] — a recognition of bureaucracy's appropriateness to many (though of course not all) organizational activities. Furthermore, if the rise of bureaucracy was originally tied to the increasing complexity of society, the outlook in these complex times is at least for survival of this form of organization, if not its further expansion.

There are other areas of concern. First, it is likely that there will be *continued pervasive ambiguity* concerning goals in politics and administration, as well as performance. Efforts to define our goals will probably continue, but goals in our pluralist democratic society will also continue to be only partially agreed upon (at best). With goals vaguely defined or even in conflict, measuring performance against common goals is, of course, impossible. Nevertheless, developing improved performance indicators within specific programs and projects will yield some benefits incrementally in the form of improved planning and direction of those programs.

Second, the role and scope of government regulation continue to be in flux. This has several aspects. One is the movement toward deregulation, though how fast, how far, and in how many areas of economic activity are questions still to be answered. (As noted in Chapter 11, the possibility of reregulation has also emerged from this policy debate.) Another aspect is the red-tape concern discussed previously; demands for protection and risk reduction in our daily lives account for a large part of regulatory growth. A serious issue here is how far we as a nation should go in reducing risks and ensuring public health and safety. Most agree that it is unrealistic to strive for a "no-risk" society, and that such an endeavor is not only futile but may be detrimental to other functions in society (such as private-sector productivity). There is precedent for pursuing at least one alternative approach: using government agency performance as a basis for comparison with (a "yardstick" against which to measure) private-sector performance. A memorable case in point was (and is) the Tennessee Valley Authority (TVA), which for over sixty years has marketed electric power in seven midsouth states at rates noticeably lower than those charged by private power companies elsewhere (this is still true, despite substantial TVA rate increases since the 1970s). Another issue concerns the calls for use of cost-benefit analysis in evaluating proposed (and operative) regulations. The question here is whether such analysis can be truly neutral. If so, it could add a useful dimension to processes of drafting and enforcing regulations. If not, however, it is likely that insisting on its use would continue to generate substantial controversy among contending forces in government regulation, because of disagreements over whether dollar costs should be regarded as the sole — or even the primary — consideration in evaluating the effectiveness of regulations. Such controversies could thus make it much more difficult to sensibly reform government regulation while maintaining regulatory effectiveness.[18]

There is one final regulatory issue. It is clear that sentiment has been growing for wholesale reduction of government regulations of all kinds. At the same time, perhaps not enough attention has been paid to the consequences of that course of action.[19] There even appears to be some feeling that almost anything government does is "regulation." That perception is not accurate, of course; but in a democracy, what the citizens believe to be the case may be more important in some instances than the objective reality. This, then, will also influence the future course of government regulation.

Managing public personnel is another area of significant change and challenge. At least three issues are central in this regard. One is the question of maintaining the partisan and policy neutrality of the civil service, versus enhancing the political responsiveness (if not outright loyalty) to the chief executive that exists among administrative personnel. As noted in Chapter 8, this has been a recurring issue in our political history, and it has surfaced again in the past twenty years. In that time the Office of Personnel Management (OPM), under three presidents, has taken various actions that affected (among other things) Senior Executive Service staffing, performance appraisal, pay caps, phasing out of the PACE exam, budget reductions for personnel functions, and (most recently) streamlining of federal personnel procedures. On the other hand, there were many who took issue with at least some of OPM's initiatives, due to disagreement with general administration policies or with specific personnel actions, or both. Controversies over OPM personnel policies were especially acute under President Reagan, but since then have receded in both visibility and intensity. Under the Clinton administration, OPM occupied a less prominent position, instead focusing on more of a support role in crafting Clinton–Gore personnel initiatives.

A second basic personnel concern is related to what motivates public servants. Specifically, even though financial bonuses and merit pay have been established in the national civil service (with parallel systems in about half of the states), there is some question as to whether monetary incentives — so crucial to recent reform initiatives — are in fact the most effective motivators of senior career executives (recall Chapter 5, and the discussion of motivation in the organizational humanism school of organization theory). These theoretical formulations have recently been given support; from several sources has come evidence that interesting work, job satisfaction, personal and group recognition, and a sense of group recognition are as important as limited financial incentives. To the extent that is so, it suggests that bonuses and pay-for-performance may have been misdirected. It may also help explain why these financial incentive plans (at least for a time) failed to slow the exodus of veteran senior executives from the national civil service (they could even have accelerated that trend)[20]

Closely related to the preceding concerns (as we saw in Chapter 8) is a growing morale problem, especially (but not exclusively) in the national civil and military services. After many years of various politicians (and the public) "taking potshots" at public servants, these individuals have now experienced even more severe buffeting about (for example, reductions in force during the 1980s and 1990s), which has introduced more uncertainty into the national civil and military services than has existed for a century.[21] The Clinton administration itself has sent "conflicting signals" to the bureaucracy, thus adding to the uncertainty. On the one hand, Vice President Gore's National Performance Review called for streamlined procedures and other steps designed to increase "empowerment" of federal civil servants. But on the other hand, Bill Clinton made it clear that more personnel cutbacks were necessary to "reform" bureaucratic operations. (And recall President Clinton's remark, noted in Chapter 1, in which he called for rewarding the people and ideas that work, and *getting rid of* those that do not.) In these and other respects, there is much about which to be concerned in contemporary personnel management.[22]

There also is growing interest in (and possibly changing perspectives on) administrative discretion. The literature on public administration has tended to reflect the position that perhaps discretion should not be hemmed in — that we should attempt instead to legitimize (in Woodrow Wilson's words) "the exercise of large and unhampered" administrative discretion with the expectation that public servants will act in the public interest. This may be a fleeting hope; one observer has suggested, for example, that "there are numerous ways to check agency power at the national government level . . . [and] bureaucrats typically face many of these checks simultaneously; the degree of freedom to make policy enjoyed by an agency is always limited to one degree or another. Autonomy may ebb and flow with time, but it is *rarely if ever absolute.*"[23] The public's view of administrative discretion would obviously be more favorable if it were perceived that civil servants acted most often in the broad public interest.

Something else to be borne in mind — as we refine our theories of organization, leadership, and management control — is that there are limits on how widely such theories can be applied. The nature of work, workers, and organizations affect applicability of theories (such as organizational humanism), leadership styles, and methods of management control (see Chapters 5, 7, and 10, respectively). These limitations must be respected to avoid problems resulting from wholesale acceptance of any one theory or combination of theories.

Also, there is some irony in current pursuit of greater efficiency, rationality, and productivity — three major elements in Frederick Taylor's theory of scientific management. This is not to say we have returned to his concepts with nothing else changed. However, we may find these norms more attractive now due to growing constraints on our resources, financial and otherwise. It should be noted that the appeal of these values has also permeated the study of public administration. The "public management approach has for some time been characterized by 'a strong philosophical link' with a scientific management tradition."[24]

Furthermore, some favorite terms and concepts we apply to public administration may require rethinking. We tend to speak of a leader, while we should be concerned instead with the *relationship* of leaders to their respective organization units — in terms of that which is led. In the same way, we may need to speak of politicians and administrators who are *accountable to*, not just accountable; *responsive to*, not simply responsive; bureaucracies efficient at, not merely efficient; and organizations *productive in terms of*, not just productive. We must bear in mind that these values are most important as means of achieving other, higher ends — not as ends in themselves. Yet all too often we treat them as the latter. For example, why is it important to be efficient? Is it always desirable? The norm of efficiency is not a truly neutral standard; one cannot always be efficient at something, and values are almost always involved. Further, is efficiency (or anything else) to be pursued in all cases, even at the expense of other desired ends? These are troubling considerations, and they should serve as reminders that we need to think clearly about our own assumptions. Clear thinking is especially necessary in turbulent times.

The political environment of public administration has changed dramatically, as discussed previously. But certain contemporary elements of that change — and particular disputes that have surfaced in the contemporary environment — deserve mention as we close. First, emphasis on both effectiveness and accountability of administrative agencies has led to numerous adjustments in their relationships to other institutions in the political system — and companion emphases on reinventing government, customer service standards, employee "empowerment," and measurement of results have only reinforced this trend. Among the areas affected by these changes are the politics of structure, bureaucratic neutrality versus advocacy, the significance of "overhead" control of administration (president and Congress as a whole, versus subsystems, as well as conflicts between president and Congress), altered budget procedures involving

Congress and the president, "fend-for-yourself" federalism and "devolved" intergovernmental relations, and new initiatives in public personnel administration. All these, significantly, were controversial issue areas in the national government during the 1970s, and have become more significant in the Reagan–Bush as well as the Clinton presidencies.

These conflicts have spawned related debates over the very nature of the changes being proposed in the early and mid-1990s. For one, the effort to reinvent government has itself been criticized, on various grounds. For example, in their best-selling book *Reinventing Government*, David Osborne and Ted Gaebler recounted numerous anecdotes and drew large-scale conclusions from those anecdotes, but failed to identify meaningful empirical patterns of administrative behavior that might more properly be used as a justification for large-scale governmental reform.[25] Accepting without question the underlying assumptions of reinventing government means willingly adopting the "entrepreneurial" paradigm (approach) as a substitute for the "administrative management" paradigm that has been in use for more than a century — with consequences that are impossible to predict.[26] One other salient point that has been raised is simply that presidential efforts to reform the bureaucracy often seem to overlook the "joint custody" nature of American public agencies — a custodial responsibility that is shared between the chief executive and the legislature. Thus, unilateral efforts to impose new systems and procedures often run afoul of legislative prerogatives — not to mention legislative preferences.[27]

Furthermore, there is some tension between the concept of the individual as "customer" of government agencies/services, on the one hand, and as "citizen" of the republic, on the other. The former clearly implies that service provision is a primary concern of government, and "serving the 'customer'" must necessarily be a high priority for all those involved in that endeavor — including legislators and chief executives as well as administrators themselves. The latter, by contrast, suggests a very different relationship between the individual and his or her government, one in which the citizen is an integral part of the governmental system, and not only a consumer of government services.[28]

A related concern also exists, namely, the contrast between "public"-oriented versus "private"-oriented conceptions of government. If government, acting in an "entrepreneurial" manner, simply serves "customers," then what is its unique role as distinct from the activities — and purposes — of private-sector businesses? Now, this question is deliberately overstated — and the phrasing is deliberately provocative. Few if any of those advocating higher quality in the provision of public services, or arguing the need for reinventing government, would quarrel for a moment with the conceptions of citizenship that are at the foundation of the republic, nor would they hesitate to defend the basic political relationships that are defined in the Constitution and our subsequent governmental history. But the point is this: what we choose to emphasize about our governmental processes reflects what we think is important, at the moment, about government, and it may influence our thinking in the years ahead as well.

In other words, we could end up moving in a direction that causes us — intentionally or not — to redefine what sort of broader governmental system we will have. In short, if we focus so heavily on "reinvention," productivity improvement, "quality," or "empowerment" that we lose sight of some of the basic assumptions and concepts underlying the political system, we may have made some useful short-term gains, but in the process we might trade off (or trade in) more fundamental notions of who we are as a polity.

Put somewhat differently, citizens have both rights *and* responsibilities; customers, on the other hand, because they are purchasing a good or service on the open market, have few if any of the latter. Perhaps the rise of the customer is a sign of the times in this nation, where more attention has been paid to *individual* rights and liability issues in recent decades. Some say that this has occurred at the expense of proper attention to *collective* responsibilities. But another implication of this is that only as we exercise responsible citizenship will we be in a position to improve the quality of government services available to them (us) as customers.

One other aspect of the tension between citizen and customer concepts is that it seems to parallel some of the existing tension between concepts reflecting political science and public administration approaches to government. For there can be no doubt that providing highest-quality and lowest-cost services to those who want and need them is a major responsibility of government today. Not even the most avid "political" observer of modern American government can afford to overlook the complexity of both public demand and public services as these affect what government does, and what it is asked to do. Nevertheless, the larger point here is that we would do well to keep all relevant conceptions of government in mind, especially as we make whatever efforts we choose to make to strengthen government performance in ways that are both meaningful and enduring.

The second dimension of the political environment is the presidency, especially the extent of recent presidential efforts to change the direction of government. A significant legacy of the Clinton years (with continuing impact on the national executive branch) has been the ongoing effort to reduce the sheer size of the public sector — in personnel, budgets, regulatory authority, and general scope. Both the Bush and Clinton administrations placed considerable emphasis on budget deficit reduction and, with the success of these efforts, has come the ironic dilemma of deciding how to best spent the budget *surplus* projected for the early twenty-first century.

There has been no shortage of recommendations regarding ways that the president could allocate this surplus or quicken the pace of reform. One observer has suggested that presidents must "continuously prioritize effective management" (and that members of Congress should loosen their control over federal agency managers — though we should note carefully the implications of such changes regarding the "joint custody" arrangement referred to earlier)[29] Another has suggested that presidents would do well to monitor OMB for mismanagement, clearly implying that OMB itself might be a source of some presidential difficulties.[30] Also, persistent calls for more contracting out, privatization, and deregulation of the public sector continue to be heard, and (as noted in Chapter 10) various efforts have already succeeded in that direction. Numerous factors will affect whether that trend continues, although questions about it are more likely to center on the extent to which we should privatize and deregulate, rather than on whether we should do so at all.

Several other political dimensions also stand out. For example, the federal courts are now deeply involved in many substantive aspects of public administration. Most important, perhaps, are federalism and intergovernmental relations, affirmative action, labor relations, and government regulation; but in case after case, across the board, court decisions shape both the environment and the content of administrative decision making. Public administration is not alone in that, but the impacts on its future will be substantial.

Another aspect of uncertainty in public administration was highlighted by outgoing EPA Administrator William Ruckelshaus, almost two decades ago. In a press interview Ruckelshaus, a Republican, noted that, in his view, constant attacks by environmental groups on the EPA carried with them the risk of destroying the agency's ability to function. In his words:

> The cumulative effect of [the attacks] is to cause the essential trust of the society to be so eroded it [EPA] can't function. . . . When you don't distinguish between individuals with whom you disagree, or policies with which you disagree, and the agencies themselves . . . you risk destroying the very institutions whose success is necessary for your essential goals to be achieved.[31]

Ruckelshaus's point, though addressed to environmentalists, applies to virtually every active group of citizens — and to any administrative agency — at all levels of government, from local police departments to the White House. In a turbulent and tense political atmosphere, many sincere (and often impatient) citizens might do well to consider his advice. There is another implication as well: such attacks foster an atmosphere of **public cynicism and distrust,** making it far more difficult for administrative agencies to retain the capacity to respond when we do call upon them! And we surely will continue to do so, to deal both with largescale public problems and with occasional crises, such as earthquakes, civil disorders, hurricanes, floods, or public health emergencies.

public cynicism and distrust negative public opinion about politics and government reflected in opinion polls and low voter turnouts.

Another point worth bearing in mind pertains to that same impatience about governmental action (or inaction) in the context of our basic (and limited) governmental system. As we discussed in Chapter 2, those who framed our Constitution sought generally to place limits on what government is able to do, without diluting its essential ability to govern. The founding fathers did not want government to be too efficient or adventurous. "Overall, the government was designed to be responsive slowly to relatively long-term demands and to require the development of relatively broad agreement among the electorate prior to taking action."[32] In other words, for government agencies to operate not under pressure would require time and broad popular support — both of which often seem to be lacking in controversial policy areas, such as gun control, police–minority relations, and sex education in public schools. Our impatience with government action seems to be directly related to the extent and the depth of policy disagreements dividing the nation. Once again, as noted earlier in this chapter, public administration is squarely in the middle of popular discontent, reflecting the disorganization (and policy differences) present in society itself.

There are three other matters to consider. For over thirty years we have been experiencing a crisis of confidence — indeed, a **"crisis of legitimacy"**[33] — regarding government and its actions. More recently, certain new assumptions or premises appear to be gaining currency in shaping (and perhaps reflecting) popular perceptions of government. These have been expressed as follows: (1) public programs are counterproductive to the social and economic well-being of the country; (2) the public no longer expects public programs to work, and is increasingly unwilling to spend additional funds on them; (3) public programs are better administered at the state and local level — further, many functions should be taken over by private organizations and voluntary community efforts; (4) national government program managers are becoming less important, with fewer needed; and (5) public managers are already overpaid, and any system of reward or penalties in the public sector will be abused.[34] Such thinking may be fashionable, but it can also be highly dysfunctional (not to mention inaccurate). Diminished public trust does not bode well for maintenance of either democratic processes or effective government. As conservative an individual as syndicated columnist George F. Will warned more than a decade ago against "indiscriminate skepticism about the competence, even the motives, of government" and against thinking that "government cannot do anything right anyway."[35] That caveat is not for conservatives only; many individuals of all political persuasions have fallen prey to this crisis of confidence.[36]

One symptom (perhaps a result) of this crisis of confidence has been public pressure to enact sunshine and sunset laws, discussed in Chapter 2. These apply more to legislative than to administrative entities, but they affect the latter as well. Yet one of the unintended impacts of the "open government" laws may have been to make compromise and accommodation harder to achieve, among contending forces. In the words of one observer:

> Representative democracy rests upon our ability to create a consensus. This requires that the system be open to compromise (a dirty word in America) and bargaining. Without these, we either reach no decision or we impose a decision. The former leads to deadlock, the latter to authoritarianism. What has been lost by "opening the doors" [meetings] is the decision makers' ability to make concessions, and to reach an accommodation, with dignity and decency. Now that the interest groups are all watching, no one can afford to make "public" policy; rather, they must yield to the pressures that are sometimes very narrow.[37]

Ironically, this dark mood of mistrust is if anything unwarranted. Scholarly studies of public opinion, both of recent vintage and earlier, have indicated that the

"crisis of legitimacy"
a political condition under which government officials are perceived to lack the legal authority and right to make binding decisions for the people.

public's voice is heard by those in government — including those in bureaucracy — if that voice is clear in what it is saying and forceful in its expression. The "voice of the people" is really many voices, saying many things — about particular policies, the effectiveness of government activities generally, public ethics, and much more. Yet it has been demonstrated that when public opinion is generally united on a position and feelings run strong on the matter, government's response is nearly always in the direction desired by the majority. Thus, perhaps we can afford a somewhat more optimistic view of governmental responsiveness to majority preferences than many seem to hold at this point. As one knowledgeable observer has put it: "In the long run, the public almost always gets its way."[38]

What, then, is the prognosis for public administration? Without question it will continue to be a focal point of concern, with controversy encompassing virtually every major policy area and every political interest with a stake in administrative operations. In the words of political scientist Carl Friedrich, public administration is "the core of modern government." Clearly, then, public administration "is and will be a focal area for change and transformation in society generally."[39] The only certainty in all this is the uncertain directions public administration will take.

One final matter remains, related in part to the level of public confidence in what government does. In this era of rampant downsizing and deregulation, how might we judge the worth of government expenditures? James Joseph, a retired Undersecretary of the Interior, offered five criteria (standards), derived from an appropriate source, the preamble to the Constitution. The criteria are, simply, the degree to which a government project contributes to the sense of equity, community, utility, security, and quality of life in America.[40]

Clearly, we have been forced in recent years to consider ever larger questions about the role and activities of government — and not only concerns about how high government expenditures will be. In light of that, these sorts of criteria might well be useful as we continue to sort out what kind of government we expect and need in the years ahead. An integral part of that debate will be the role of public administration in securing the quality and equality of community life for the society we want to create in the future.

KEY TERMS AND CONCEPTS

knowledge explosion	"overhead bureaucracy"
technological change	empowerment
fundamentalism	debureaucratize
chronic fiscal stress	global interdependence
revolution of rising expectations	public cynicism and distrust
postindustrialism	"crisis of legitimacy"
"overhead democracy"	

SUGGESTED READING

Beneveniste, Guy. *The Twenty-First Century Organization: Analyzing Current Trends — Imagining the Future.* San Francisco: Jossey-Bass, 1994.

Bozeman, Barry. *All Organizations Are Public.* San Francisco: Jossey-Bass, 1987.

DiIulio, John J., Jr., ed. *Deregulating the Public Service: Can Government Be Improved?* Washington, D.C.: The Brookings Institution, 1994.

Etzioni, Amitai. *Public Policy in a New Key.* New Brunswick, N.J.: Transaction Publishers, 1992.

Farazmand, Ali, ed. *Handbook of Bureaucracy.* New York: Marcel Dekker, 1994.

Fry, Brian R. *Mastering Public Administration: From Max Weber to Dwight Waldo.* Chatham, N.J.: Chatham House, 1989.

Hill, Larry B., ed. *The State of Public Bureaucracy.* Armonk, N.Y.: M. E. Sharpe, 1992.

Kettl, Donald F. *Sharing Power: Public Governance and Private Markets.* Washington, D.C.: The Brookings Institution, 1993.

Lynn, Naomi B., and Aaron Wildavsky, eds. *Public Administration: The State of the Discipline.* Chatham, N.J.: Chatham House, 1990.

Martin, Daniel W. *The Guide to the Foundations of Public Administration.* New York: Marcel Dekker, 1989.

Ostrom, Vincent. *The Intellectual Crisis in American Public Administration.* 2nd ed. University, Ala.: University of Alabama Press, 1989.

Peters, B. Guy. *The Future of Governing.* Lawrence: University Press of Kansas, 1996.

Rivlin, Alice. *Reviving the American Dream: The Economy, the States, and the Federal Government.* Washington, D.C.: The Brookings Institution, 1992.

Thomas, Camaron J. *Managers: Part of the Problem?* Westport, Conn.: Quorum Books, 1999.

Thompson, Frank J., ed. *Revitalizing the State and Local Public Service: Strengthening Performance, Accountability and Citizen Confidence.* San Francisco: Jossey-Bass, 1993.

Waldo, Dwight. *The Administrative State.* 2nd ed. New York: Holmes & Meier, 1984.

Wamsley, Gary L., et al. *Refounding Public Administration.* Newbury Park, Calif.: Sage, 1990.

Wilson, James Q. *Bureaucracy: What Government Agencies Do and Why They Do It.* New York: Basic Books, 1989.

Appendix

Professional Associations for Information and Job Opportunities, and Public Administration Journals for Research

Professional Organizations and Internet Job-Search Links

Like all other professions, public administration has a number of affiliated and specialized groups concerned with technical areas within the discipline. These range from civil engineering to law enforcement, to housing, state government, and welfare administration. Most of these groups have Web sites, publish journals or newsletters, and advertise for jobs. They can be a rich resource for students seeking initial job appointments or for midcareerists seeking new jobs. The names, addresses, and Web sites (when available) of selected academic, professional, and public interest organizations, as well as selected job-search links, are listed alphabetically.

Academy for State and Local
Government
444 N. Capitol St., NW, Ste. 349
Washington, DC 20001

Alliance for Redesigning Government
1120 C St., NW, Ste. 850
Washington, DC 20005
http://www.alliance.napawash.org/alliancelindex.html

American Association of School
Administrators
1801 N. Moore St.
Arlington, VA 22209
http://www.aasa.org

American Correctional Association
4380 Forbes Blvd.
Lanham, MD 20706-4322
http://www.corrections.com/aca

American Management Association
1601 Broadway
New York, NY 10019-7420
http://www.amanet.org/usindex.htm

American Planning Association
1776 Massachusetts Ave., NW,
    Ste. 400
Washington, DC 20036
http://www.planning.org

American Political Science
Association
1527 New Hampshire Ave., NW
Washington, DC 20036
http://www.apsanet.org
Foremost international association
    of academic political scientists;
    publishes newsletter with job
    listings.

American Productivity and Quality
Center
123 N. Post Oak Ln.
Houston, TX 77024
http://www.apqc.org
Job listings on Web site.

American Public Transit Association
1201 New York Ave., NW
Washington, DC 20005
http://www.apta.com

American Public Welfare Association
810 First St., NE, Ste. 500
Washington, DC 20002-4267
http://www.apwa.org

American Public Works Association
2345 Grand Blvd., Ste. 500
Kansas City, MO 64108
http://www.pubworks.org

American Society for Public Administration — The Recruiter On-Line
1120 G St., NW, Ste. 700
Washington, DC 20005-3885
http://www.aspanet.org/recruiter/
recruit.htm
Job listings also on-line in *PA TIMES*
    Newsletter (see Journals for
    Research section).

Association of Government
Accountants
2200 Mt. Vernon Ave.
Alexandria, VA 22301
http://www.rutgers.edu/accounting/
raw/aga

Brookings Institution
1775 Massachusetts Ave., NW
Washington, DC 20036
http://www.brook.edu

Canadian Association of Programs
in Public Administration
http://leroy.cc.uregina.ca/~rasmussk/

The Cato Institute
1000 Massachusetts Ave., NW
Washington, DC 20001-5403
http://www.cato.org/

Center for Community Change
1000 Wisconsin Ave., NW
Washington, DC 20007
http://www.ncl.org/anr/partners/
ccomch.htm

Center on Budget and Policy
Priorities
777 N. Capitol St., NE, Ste. 705
Washington, DC 20002
http://www.igc.apc.org/handsnet/hn.
community/profiles/cbpp.html

Committee for Economic
Development
2000 L St., NW, Ste. 700
Washington, DC 20036
http://www.bcer.org/orgs/ced.htm

Common Cause
1256 Connecticut Ave., NW, Ste. 600
Washington, DC 20036
http://www.commoncause.org

Conference Board
845 Third Ave.
New York, NY 10022-6679
http://www.tc-indicators.org

Conference of Minority Public
Administrators (COMPA)
PO Box 3010
Fort Worth, TX 76113
http://www.compa.org

Congressional Quarterly Service
1735 K St., NW
Washington, DC 20006
http://www.cq.com/

Council for Excellence in
Government
1620 L St., NW, Ste. 850
Washington, DC 20036
http://www.excelgov.org/

Council of State Community
Development Agencies
Hall of the States
444 N. Capitol St., Room 251
Washington, DC 20001
http://www.sso.org/coscda/overview.htm

Council of State Governments
PO Box 11910
Lexington, KY 40578-1910
http://www.csg.org/

Employment Resources on the
Internet
http://www.jobbroadcasting.com/
insight/jobs/toc.html

Freedom of Information Center
127 Neff Annex
University of Missouri
Columbia, MO 65211
http://www.missouri.edu/~foiwww/
index8.html

Government Finance Officers
Association
(formerly the Municipal Finance
Officers Association)
180 N. Michigan Ave., Ste. 800
Chicago, IL 60601
http://www.gfoa.org

Government Management
Information Sciences
Headquarters
PO Box 421
Kennesaw, GA 30144-0421
http://www.co.catawba.nc.us/gmis/
gmis.htm

Governmental Research Association
24 Providence St.
Boston, MA 02108
http://www.caltax.org/gralist.htm

Institute of Public Administration
55 W. 44th St.
New York, NY 10036

Inter-Governmental Network
7910 Woodmont Ave., Ste. 1430
Bethesda, MD 20814

International Association of Chiefs of
Police
515 N. Washington St.
Alexandria, VA 22314
http://www.www.erols.com/de13047/

International Association of Fire
Chiefs
1329 Eighteenth St., NW
Washington, DC 20036
http://www.ichiefs.org

International City/County
Management Association
1120 G St., NW
Washington, DC 20005
http://www.icma.org

International Institute of Municipal
Clerks
160 N. Altadena Dr.
Pasadena, CA 91107
http://www.financenet.gov/financenet/
state/iimc/iimc.htm

International Personnel Management
Association
1617 Duke St.
Alexandria, VA 22314
http://www.ipma-hr.org

Internet Job-Hunting Sites — Public
Policy and Administration
http://www.uww.edu/StdRsces/career/
jobsearc/d12-165.htm

Jobs in Government
http://jobsingovernment.com

Labor–Management Relations Service
1620 I St., NW, 4th Floor
Washington, DC 20006

Local Government Job Net
http://www.lgi.org/p14.htm

National Academy of Public
Administration
1120 G St., NW, Ste. 850
Washington, DC 20005
http://www.napawash.org/napa/index.
html

National Assembly of State Arts
Agencies
1029 Vermont Ave., NW, 2nd Floor
Washington, DC 20005
http://www.nasaa-arts.org

National Association for the
Advancement of Colored People
(NAACP)
Washington Bureau
1025 Vermont Ave., NW, Ste. 1120
Washington, DC 20005
http://solar.rtd.utk.edu/ccsi/csusa/law/
naacp.html

National Association of Counties
440 First St.
Washington, DC 20001
http://www.naco.org/naco/index.htm

National Association of Housing and
Redevelopment Officials
630 I St., NW
Washington, DC 20001-3736
http://www.nahro.org/

National Association of Regional
Councils
1700 K St., NW
Washington, DC 20036
http://narc.org/narc/

National Association of Schools of
Public Affairs and Administration
1120 G St., NW, Ste. 730
Washington, DC 20005
http://www.apsanet.org/related/
naspaa.html

National Association of State
Directors of Administration and
General Services
167 W. Main St., Ste. 600
Lexington, KY 40507-1324
http://www.nasdags.org

National Association of State
Information Resource Executives
167 W. Main St., Ste. 600
Lexington, KY 40507-1324
http://www.nasire.org

National Association of Towns and
Townships
1522 K St., NW, Ste. 780
Washington, DC 20005
http://sso.org/natat/natat.htm

National Center for Public
Productivity
445 W. 59th St.
New York, NY 10019
http://www.newark.rutgers.edu/~ncpp/
ncpp.html

National Civic League
1445 Market St., Ste. 300
Denver, CO 80202-1728
http://www.ncl.org/ncl

National Conference of State
Legislators
1560 Broadway, Ste. 700
Denver, CO 80202
http://www.ncsl.org/

National Electronic Commerce
Coordinating Council (NECCC)
444 N. Capitol St., NW, Ste. 234
Washington, DC 20001
http://ec3.org/

National Employment Bulletin
for Jobs in Management and
Business
http://www.graduatejobs.com/business.
html

National Governors Association
Hall of the States
444 N. Capitol St., Ste. 250
Washington, DC 20001
http://www.nga.org/

National Institute of Governmental
Purchasing
11800 Sunrise Valley Dr., Ste. 1050
Reston, VA 22091-5303
http://www.iog.unc.edu/purchase/orgs.
htm#nigp

National Institute of Public
Management
1612 K St., NW
Washington, DC 20006

National League of Cities
1301 Pennsylvania Ave., NW
Washington, DC 20004
http://www.nlc.org

National Public Employer Labor
Relations Association
1620 I St., NW
Washington, DC 20006
http://www.npelra.org

National Recreation and Park
Association
22377 Belmont Ridge Rd.
Ashburn, VA 20148
http://www.nrpa.org/

National Society for Human
Resource Management
(formerly the American Society for
Personnel Administration)
606 N. Washington St.
Alexandria, VA 22314

National Society for Internships and
Experiential Education
(formerly the National Center for
Public Service Internship Programs)
122 St. Mary's St.
Raleigh, NC 27605

National States Geographic
Information Council
Administrative Offices
45 Lyme Rd., Ste. 304
Hanover, NH 03755
http://www.geo.drake.edu/nsgic

Opportunities in Public Affairs
http://www.opajobs.com/

Policy Studies Organization
University of Illinois
702 S. Wright St.
Urbana, IL 61801
http://www.apsanet.org/related/pso.html

Public Administration Service
1497 Chain Bridge Rd
McLean, VA 22101

Public Sector Network
(formerly the Public Sector
Improvement Network)
611 E. Wisconsin Ave., PO Box 3005
Milwaukee, WI 53201

Public Service Research Foundation
8330 Old Courthouse Rd., Ste. 600
Vienna, VA 22180
http://www.psrf.org/

Public Technology, Inc.
1301 Pennsylvania Ave., NW, Ste. 800
Washington, DC 20004
http://pti.nw.dc.us/

Rand Corporation
1700 Main St.
Santa Monica, CA 90406
http://www.rand.org/

Society of Government Meeting
Professionals (SGMP)
6 Clouser Rd.
Mechanicsburg, PA 17055
http://www.sgmp.org/home.htm

Tax Foundation
1250 H St., NW, Ste. 750
Washington, DC 20005
http://www.taxfoundation.org

United States Conference of Mayors
1620 1 St., NW, 4th Floor
Washington, DC 20006
http://www.mayors.org/uscm/home.
html

Urban Institute
2100 M St., NW, 4th Floor
Washington, DC 20006
http://www.urban.org/

USA Jobs
http://www.usajobs.opm.gov

Women Executives in State
Government
1225 New York Ave., NW, Ste. 350
Washington, DC 20005
http://www.wesg.org

Yahoo! Government
http://dir.yahoo.com/Government/
USGovernment/Employment/

Journals for Research

The following list identifies selected journals that are relevant to various subfields of public administration. They cover a broad spectrum of specialized areas in the "core" areas of the discipline such as budget and financial administration, personnel, public policy, and regulations as well as other adjacent fields of study. They are listed alphabetically, with addresses and Web sites when available. When searching for a specific article or journal, be sure to enter the name of the journal on your browser to see if it has been added to the Internet or if the Web address has changed since this printing.

Academy of Management Review
Ohio Northern University
PO Box 209, 300 S. Union St.
Ada, OH 45810.
http://www.aom.pace.edu/amr/
Scholarly journal for the organizational sciences publishes academically rigorous, conceptual papers that advance the science and practice of management.

Administration and Society
Virginia Polytechnic Institute and State University
Center for Public Administration and Public Affairs
Blacksburg, VA 24061
http://www.sagepub.com/
This journal strives to advance the understanding of public and human service organizations, their administrative processes, and their effects on society.

Administrative Science Quarterly
Cornell University
Johnson Graduate School of Management
425 Caldwell Hall
Ithaca, NY 14853-2602
http://www.gsm.cornell.edu/ASQ/asq.html

Top-rated journal for research in administrative and organization theory.

American Journal of Public Health
1015 15th St., NW,
Washington, DC 20005
http://www.apha.org/journal/AJPH2.htm
A monthly publication of articles in both general and specialized areas of the science, art, and practice of public health.

American Political Science Review
Michigan State University
303 South Kedzie Hall
East Lansing, MI 48824-1032
http://www.ssc.msu.edu/~apsr/
Leading journal in political science, with occasional articles on public policy making and public organizations.

American Politics Quarterly
http://www.sageltd.co.uk/journals/details/j0091.html
Articles examine and explore topics in every area of government, from local and state to regional and national.

American Review of Public Administration
University of Missouri–Kansas City
Cookingham Institute of Public Affairs
Bloch School of Business and Public Administration
Kansas City, MO 64110
http://www.sageltd.co.uk/journals/details/j0212.html
One of the leading journals in its field, dedicated to the study of public affairs and public administration; features articles that address rapidly emerging issues in the field.

Annals of the American Academy of Political and Social Science
http://www.asc.upenn.edu/aapss/annals.html
Published bimonthly, the *Annals* is a collection of single-theme issues exploring topics of current concern.

Australian Journal of Public Administration
University of Queensland
Royal Institute of Public Administration
Department of Government
St. Lucia, Queensland 4067 Australia
For those interested in Australian public administration and comparative analysis.

Brookings Review
1775 Massachusetts Ave., NW
Washington, DC 20036
http://www.brook.edu/press/review/rev_des.htm
Quarterly publication summarizes articles from recent books and studies published by the Brookings Institution on matters of public policy.

California Management Review
University of California, Berkeley
Haas School of Business
350 Barrows Hall
Berkeley, CA 94720
http://www.haas.berkeley.edu/News/cmr/index.html
This high-quality journal publishes articles that are both research-based and address issues of current concern to managers.

Canadian Public Administration
150 Eglington Ave. E., Suite 305
Toronto, Ontario Canada M4P IE8
http://www.cmpa.ca/sl10.html
For those interested in Canadian public administration and comparative analysis.

Colloqui: Cornell Journal of Planning and Urban Issues
Cornell University
106 West Sibley Hall
Ithaca, N.Y. 14853
http://www.crp.cornell.edu/organizations/colloqui/
Founded in 1985 as a forum for practitioners, faculty, and students in planning and related fields, *Colloqui* strives to present planning issues from a wide range of social, political, economic, geographic, and historical perspectives.

The Electronic Hallway Journal
http://www.hallway.org/journal/
A case journal for public policy and administration.

Evaluation Review
http://www.sagepub.com/
Offers the latest applied evaluation methods used in a wide range of

disciplines and provides up-to-date articles on the latest quantitative and qualitative methodological developments, as well as commentaries on related applied-research issues.

The Executive
Ohio Northern University
Academy of Management Executive
PO Box 39, 300 South Union
Ada, OH 45810-0039
Newsletter version of the American Management Association journal.

Foreign Affairs
58 E. 68th St.
New York, NY 10021
http://www.sagepub.com/
Dedicated to promoting improved understanding of international affairs.

Foreign Policy
Carnegie Endowment for International Peace
1179 Massachusetts Ave.
Washington DC 20036
http://www.foreignpolicy.com/index.html
Launched in 1970 to encourage fresh and more vigorous debate on the vital issues confronting U.S. foreign policy.

GAO Journal
U.S. General Accounting Office
Office of Public Affairs
Room 6901
Washington, DC 20548
http://www.gao.gov/
Published by the U.S. General Accounting Office; focuses on accountability, integrity, and reliability involving fiscal issues in government.

Governance
Blackwell Publishers
238 Main St.
Cambridge, MA 02142
http://www.blackwellpublishers.co.uk/asp/journal.asp?ref=0952-1895
An international journal providing a forum for the theoretical and practical discussion of executive politics, public policy, administration, and the organization of the state.

Governing
Congressional Quarterly, Inc.
2300 N. St., NW, Suite 760
Washington, DC 20037
http://www.governing.com
Popular journal with emphasis on the political and administrative management of state and local governments.

Government Executive
National Journal, Inc.
1730 M St., NW, 11th Floor
Washington, DC 20036
http://www.govexec.com
Government's business magazine, focusing on management issues and agencies at the federal level.

Government Productivity News
PO Box 17433
Austin, TX 78755-0435

Government Technology
A monthly journal detailing technological solutions to problems of state and local governments.

Government Union Review
http://www.psrf.org/gur.html
Journal that traces labor management relations at the federal, state, and local levels.

Harvard Business Review
PO Box 52622
Boulder, CO 80321-2622
http://www.hbsp.harvard.edu/products/hbr/index.html
Major journal that publishes a variety of administrative articles by top experts in the field.

Human Relations
http://www.wkap.nl/journalhome.htm/0018-7267
An international interdisciplinary forum for the publication of high-quality original papers across a wide range of the social sciences.

Human Resource Management
Themes related to personnel administration with no distinction between the public and private sectors.

Industrial and Labor Relations Review
http://www.ilr.cornell.edu/depts/ILRrev/
A journal devoted to public and private sectors in industrial relations.

International Journal of Public Administration
Pennsylvania State University
Institute of State and Regional Affairs
Harrisburg, PA 17057
Public administration journal with a comparative and international emphasis.

Journal of Accounting and Public Policy
http://www.elsevier.com/inca/publications/store/5/0/5/7/2/1/505721.pub.html
Discusses the interaction of accounting and public policy in both the private and public sectors.

Journal of Collective Negotiations in the Public Sector
http://www.baywood.com/site/new2/viewbook.cfm?id=100131&c=10148287
Presents clear discussions of the problems involved in negotiating contracts, resolving impasses, strikes and grievances, and administering contracts in the various areas of public employment.

Journal of Criminal Justice
http://www.elsevier.com/inca/publications/store/3/6/6
Focuses on issues of importance to crime research and the criminal justice system.

Journal of Criminal Law and Criminology
http://www.press.uillinois.edu/journals/jclc/html
Top-ranked journal publishes articles on policy and administration of law enforcement.

Journal of Organizational Behavior
http://www.interscience.wiley.com/jpages/0894-3796/
Aims to report and review the growing research in the industrial/organizational psychology and organizational behavior fields around the world.

Journal of Organizational Behavior Management
http://www.haworthpressinc.com
Publishes research and review articles, case studies, discussions, and book reviews on the topics that are critical to today's organizational development practitioners.

Journal of Police Science and Administration
Published by the International Association of Chiefs of Police.

Journal of Policy Analysis and Management
University of California
Association for Public Policy Analysis and Management
Berkeley, CA 94720
http://www.qsilver.queensu.ca/appam/services/jpam
Outlet for graduate and undergraduate public policy programs, research institutions, and individuals in the public policy and management fields.

Journal of Political Economy
http://www.journals.uchicago.edu/JPE/hom.html
PE has been presenting significant research and scholarship in economic theory and practice since its inception in 1892. Publishing analytical, interpretive, and empirical studies, the journal presents work in traditional areas as well as in such interdisciplinary fields as the history of economic thought and social economics.

Journal of Politics
http://www.jstor.ac.uk/journals/00223816.html
Important regional political science journal.

Journal of Public Administration Research and Theory
Rutgers University
J-PART Department 4010
New Brunswick, NJ 08903
http://www.jstor.ac.uk/journals/00223816.html
International interdisciplinary quarterly devoted to building the body of knowledge of public administration.

Journal of Public Affairs Education
http://www.naspaa.org/jpae-ad.htm
This journal is dedicated to advancing teaching and learning in public affairs, including the fields of policy analysis, public administration, public management, and public policy.

Journal of Public Policy
http://www.cup.cam.ac.uk/journals/jnlscat/pup/pup.html
A British journal covering a wide range of policy issues.

Journal of State Government
The Council of State Governments
PO Box 11910
Lexington, KY 40578

Journal of the American Planning Association
http://planning.org/pubs/japarof.html
Covers land-use planning in the public sector.

Journal of Urban Affairs
College of Public Service
St. Louis University
McGannon Hall, Ste. 232
3750 Lindell Blvd.
St. Louis, MO 63108-3342
http://www.udel.edu/uaa/journal.html
The official journal of the Urban
  Affairs Association, the only inter-
  national professional organization
  for urban scholars and practitioners.

*Journal of Urban Analysis and
Management*
State University of New York
Harriman College for Urban and
  Policy Studies
Stony Brook, NY 11790

Management Review
Published by the American Management Association, includes surveys
  of books for executives, critical
  reviews of recent works, and a listing of recent publications received
  from publishers.

*Management: The Magazine for
Government Managers*
Published by the U.S. Office of Personnel Management and focuses on
  public personnel administration.

Monthly Digest of Tax Articles
A publication that addresses recent tax
  issues.

National Civic Review
National Civic League Press
1445 Market St., Ste. 300
Denver, CO 80202-1728
http://www.josseybass.com/JBJournals/
ncr.html

Publishes brief articles on a wide variety of urban public policy issues.

National Journal
A weekly publication designed as a
  monitor of all federal actions, but
  especially in the executive agencies.

National Tax Journal
http://www.ntanet.org/national_tax_
journal.htm
A periodical on issues of government
  finance and taxation.

*New Directions in Public Administration
Research*
Florida Atlantic University
School of Public Administration
220 E. Second Ave.
Fort Lauderdale, FL 33301

Nonprofit Management and Leadership
Focuses on managing and leading
  nongovernment not-for-profit
  organizations.

*Organizational Behavior and Human
Decision Processes*
http://www.academicpress.com/obhdp
Features articles that describe original
  empirical research and theoretical
  developments in all areas of human
  decision processes.

Organization Studies
University of Cambridge
The Judge Institute of Management
  Studies
Fitwilliam House, 32 Trumpington St.
Cambridge, CB2 IQY United
  Kingdom

Personnel Manager's Legal Reporter
A monthly newsletter about legislation and court rulings affecting personnel managers in the public and private sectors.

Philippine Journal of Public Administration
For those interested in Southeast Asian administration and comparative analysis.

Policy Sciences
http://www.wkap.nl/journalhome.htm/ 0032-2687
With an interdisciplinary and international focus, this journal encourages different perspectives and especially welcomes conceptual and empirical innovation.

Policy Studies Journal
http://www.siu.edu/departments/cola/ polysci/psj/welcome.html
Addresses a wide range of public policy issues at all levels of government.

Policy Studies Review
Arizona State University
Policy Studies Organization
School of Justice Studies
Tempe, AZ 85287

Public Administration
Royal Institute of Public Administration
PO Box 87
Oxford, OX2 ODT England
For those interested in British administration and comparative analysis; also lists recent British government publications.

Public Administration Quarterly
Journal with a broad orientation on public administration; also contains job listings.

Public Administration Review
ASPA
1120 G St., NW, Ste. 700
Washington, DC 20005-2885
http://www.aspanet.org/par/sumsma. htm
The most significant American journal concerned with public administration.

Public Administration Times
http://www.aspanet.org/patimes/ ocframes.htm
Newsletter of the American Society for Public Administration; contains job announcements.

Public Budgeting and Financial Management
Pennsylvania State University
Institute of State and Regional Affairs
Middleton, PA 17057

Public Finance Quarterly
http://www.sagepub.com/Shopping/ Journal.asp?id=4667
University of New Orleans
College of Business Administration
New Orleans, LA 70148
Professional forum devoted to U.S. policy-oriented economic research and theory.

Public Management
ICMA
777 N. Capitol St., NE
Washington, DC 20002-4201.
http://www.bookstore.icma.org

Devoted to the profession of local government management with concise, timely articles on specific topics, editorial commentary, and selected departments.

The Public Manager
The Bureaucrat, Inc.
12007 Titian Way
Potomac, MD 20854
http://www.feiaa.org/Public%20Manager.htm
Short articles with a federal emphasis.

Public Personnel Management
IPMA
1617 Duke St.
Alexandria, VA 22314
http://www.ipma-hr.org/pubs/ppm/ppmlist.html
Features groundbreaking articles on labor relations, assessment issues, comparative personnel policies, government reform, and more.

Public Productivity and Management Review
Jossey-Bass Publishers
350 Sansome St.
San Francisco, CA 94104
http://www.sagepub.co.uk/journal/usdetails/j0190.html
Focuses on the need for greater understanding of issues in public productivity and public management.

Public Productivity Review
National Center for Public Productivity
John Jay College
City University of New York
445 W. 59th St.
New York, NY 10019

Publius
Temple University
1616 Walnut St.
Philadelphia, PA 19103
http://www.lafayette.edu/publius
Devoted to intergovernmental relations and federalism.

Review of Public Personnel Administration
Devoted to all aspects of the field, particularly at the state and local levels of government.

Society
Applies social science research to contemporary social and public policy problems.

Solutions
Published by the Council of State Governments. Focuses on specific policy questions and options, such as lobbying reform. Formerly called *State Trends and Forecasts*.

Spectrum: The Journal of State Government
http://secure.csa.org/cgi-bin/StatesnewsCSGStores.storefront/
Features leading edge public policy information from think tanks, government agencies, and other research agencies.

State and Local Government Review
University of Georgia
Carl Vinson Institute of Government
Athens, GA 30602-4582

State Government News
http://secure.csa.org/cgi-bin/StatesnewsCSGStores.storefront/

Provides nonpartisan information on state government trends, political protocol, and leaders in state government making a difference.

Urban Affairs Quarterly
http://www.sagepub.com/Shopping/Journal.asp?id=4693
A leading scholarly journal on urban issues and themes.

Washington Monthly
http://www.washingtonmonthly.com/
Lively and entertaining liberal journalistic publication with provocative articles on politics and public bureaucracy, as well as on policy issues. Book review section.

Glossary

accountability a political principle according to which agencies or organizations, such as those in government, are subject to some form of external control, causing them to give a general accounting of, and for, their actions; an essential concept in democratic public administration (see p. 50).

achievement-oriented criteria standards for making personnel judgments based on an individual's demonstrated, job-related competence (see p. 294).

adjudication a quasi-judicial power delegated to agencies by Congress, under which agencies apply existing laws or rules to particular situations in case-by-case decision making; related term: *adjudicatory proceeding* (see p. 444).

Administrative Careers with America (ACWA) revised testing procedure for entrance examinations into the federal civil service, established in 1990 by President Bush (see p. 30).

administrative discretion the ability of individual administrators in a bureaucracy to make significant choices affecting management and operation of programs for which they are responsible; particularly evident in systems with separation of powers; related terms: *discretionary authority, discretionary power* (see p. 39).

administrative efficiency a normative model of administrative activity, characterized by concentration of power (especially in the hands of chief executives), centralization of governmental policy making, exercise of power by experts and professional bureaucrats, separation of politics and administration, and emphasis on technical or scientific rationality (arrived at by detached expert analysis); the principal alternative to the "pluralist democracy" model (see p. 47).

administrative law an important body of American law pertaining to the legal authority of public administrative entities to perform their duties, and to the limits necessary to control those agencies; administrative law has been created both by judicial decisions (especially in the national government courts) and by statute (principally in the form of Administrative Procedure Acts, enacted by both national and state governments) (see p. 433).

administrative law judge member of the executive branch who performs quasi-judicial functions (see p. 446).

Administrative Procedure Act of 1946 a basic law upon which all federal administrative procedures are based (see p. 441).

advisory opinion one means used by some U.S. regulatory entities to secure voluntary compliance with regulatory requirements; involves issuance of a memorandum indicating how the entity (for example, the FTC) would decide an issue if it were presented formally (see p. 446).

affirmative action   in the context of public personnel administration, a policy or program designed to bring into public service greater numbers of citizens who were largely excluded from public employment in previous years; also, the use of goals and timetables for hiring and promoting women, blacks, and other minorities as part of an equal employment opportunity program (see p. 44).

American Society for Public Administration (ASPA) Code of Ethics   effort by the nation's leading professional association of public administrators to draw up and enforce a set of standards for official conduct (see p. 210).

ascriptive criteria   standards for making personnel judgments that are based on attributes or characteristics other than skills or knowledge (see p. 294).

authority   power defined according to a legal and institutional framework and vested in a formal structure (a nation, organization, profession, or the like); power exercised through recognized, legitimate channels (see p. 7).

backdoor financing   the practice of eliminating discretionary decision-making control from the appropriations stage of the budgetary process (see p. 363).

bargaining or political model   of communication assumes the presence in an organization of considerable sustained conflict, strong tendencies toward secrecy, and motives of expediency on the part of most individuals (see p. 176).

before-versus-after studies   evaluation and comparison of results before and after program implementation to determine what results, if any, were achieved (see p. 408).

benchmarking   a quality and productivity improvement methodology which examines those organizations that are best at performing a certain process or set of processes (for example, employee relations) and then transplanting the methods into one's own organization (see p. 419).

bilateral bargaining   collective bargaining negotiations in which only management and labor are represented (see p. 306).

Bipartisan Commission on Entitlement and Tax Reform   projected in 1994 that major changes were necessary to prevent entitlement spending from consuming the entire federal budget by the year 2012 (see p. 363).

"blame and claim" strategy   situation where politicians "blame" bureaucrats and bureaucrats "claim" not to have the authority to act (see p. 422).

block grants   a form of grant-in-aid in which the purposes to be served by the funding are defined very broadly by the grantor, leaving considerable discretion and flexibility in the hands of the recipient (see p. 128).

bonded indebtedness   revenue-raising tool for governments to issue notes or promises to pay a certain amount (principal) at a certain time (maturity date) at a particular rate of interest (see p. 345).

bounded rationality   the notion that there are prescribed boundaries, controls, or upper and lower limits on the decision-making abilities of individuals within organizations (see p. 224).

brainstorming   free-form and creative technique for collecting and discussing ideas from all participants without criticism or judgment (see p. 267).

broadbanding   the consolidation of existing job classifications into fewer and broader categories, reducing complexity and specialization in job classifications (see p. 298).

Brownlow Report recommendations for reform of the federal government from a 1937 committee appointed by President Franklin Roosevelt, chaired by Louis Brownlow, and including respected scholars and practitioners in the emerging discipline of public administration (see p. 291).

Budget Enforcement Act the informal title of the Omnibus Budget Reconciliation Act, signed into law on November 5, 1990; an extension of the Gramm–Rudman–Hollings Act requiring that all new spending be offset by either new taxes or reductions in expenditures; provided for a special five-year process for deficit reduction, made permanent changes in the congressional budget process, changed the treatment of Social Security revenues in the U.S. federal budget, and established limits on federal discretionary spending (see p. 358).

budget obligations orders placed, contracts awarded, services rendered, or other commitments made by government agencies during a given fiscal period that require expenditure of public funds during the same or some future period (see p. 360).

budget outlays agency expenditures during a given fiscal period, fulfilling **budget obligations** incurred during the same or a previous period (see p. 360).

bureaucracy (1) a formal organizational arrangement characterized by division of labor, job specialization with no functional overlap, exercise of authority through a vertical hierarchy (chain of command), and a system of internal rules, regulations, and record keeping; (2) in common usage, the administrative branch of government (national, state, or local) in the United States; also, individual administrative agencies of those governments (see p. 4).

bureaucratic accountability principles of political accountability applied in an effort to control bureaucratic power (see p. 94).

bureaucratic imperialism the tendency of agencies to try to expand their program responsibilities (see p. 78).

bureaucratic neutrality a central feature of bureaucracy whereby it carries out directives of other institutions of government (such as the chief executive or the legislature) in a politically neutral way, without acting as a political force in its own right; a traditional notion concerning bureaucratic behavior in Western governments; also called *political neutrality* (see p. 38).

bureaucratic resistance self-serving feature of administrative agencies that emphasizes gradualism, slowness, and political caution when dealing with newly selected political leadership in the executive branch (see p. 246).

capitalist system an economic system where the means of production are owned by private citizens (see p. 41).

casework refers to services performed by legislators and their staff on behalf of constituents (see p. 96).

categorical grant a form of grant-in-aid with purposes narrowly defined by the grantor, leaving the recipient relatively little choice as to how the grant funding is to be used, substantively or procedurally (see p. 119).

central clearance a key role played by the Office of Management and Budget (OMB) regarding review of agency proposals for legislation to be submitted to Congress, with OMB approval required for the proposals to move forward. A similar role or pattern exists in many state governments and some local governments, in the relationship among chief executives, administrative agencies, and legislatures. Central clearance also is practiced with regard to submission of budget proposals from executive-branch agencies to legislatures, during the budget-making process (see p. 241).

centralization an organizational pattern focusing on concentrating power at the top on an organization (see p. 181).

checks and balances a governing principle, following from separation of powers, which creates overlapping and interlocking functions among the executive, legislative, and judicial branches of government. These include: the president's power to veto an act of Congress (and Congress's power to override a presidential veto by a two-thirds majority); the Senate's power to confirm or reject presidential appointments to executive and judicial positions, and the power of the courts to determine the constitutionality of the actions of other branches (see p. 39).

chronic fiscal stress a condition confronting increasing numbers of governments and public agencies, resulting from a combination of economic inflation, declining productivity, slower economic growth, and taxpayer resistance to a larger tax burden (see p. 480).

1964 Civil Rights Act landmark legislation prohibiting discrimination by the private sector in both employment and housing (see p. 324).

Civil Service (Pendleton) Act a law formally known as the Civil Service Act of 1883 (sponsored by Ohio Senator George Pendleton), establishing job-related competence as the primary basis for filling national government jobs; created the U.S. Civil Service Commission to oversee the new "merit" system (see p. 290).

Civil Service Reform Act of 1978 comprehensive law designed to reinforce merit principles, protect whistle-blowers, delegate personnel authority to agencies, reward employees for measurable performance, and make it easier to discharge incompetent workers; created the **Federal Labor Relations Authority (FLRA), Office of Personnel Management (OPM), Senior Executive Service (SES),** and the Merit Systems Protection Board (MSPB) (see p. 309).

Clayton Act 1914 law that prohibits price discrimination to eliminate competition or create a monopoly (see p. 435).

clientelism a phenomenon whereby patterns of regularized relationships develop and are maintained in the political process between individual government agencies and particular economic groupings; e.g., departments of agriculture, labor, and commerce, working with farm groups, labor groups, and business organizations, respectively (see p. 21).

closed systems organizations that, in systems theory, have very few internal variables and relationships among those variables, and little or no vulnerability to forces in the external environment (see p. 165).

Code of Federal Regulations source of all laws that authorize regulatory agency actions (see p. 445).

collective bargaining a formalized process of negotiation between "management" and "labor"; involves specified steps, in a specified sequence, aimed at reaching an agreement (usually stipulated in contractual form) on terms and conditions of employment, covering an agreed-on period of time; a cycle that is repeated on expiration of each labor–management contract or other agreement (see p. 305).

Commission on Economy and Efficiency established in 1909 by President William Howard Taft (1909–1913); recommended that a national budgetary process be instituted under direction of the president (see p. 352).

communication vital formal and informal processes of interacting within and between individuals and units within an organization, and between organizations (see p. 171).

community control legal requirements that groups affected by political decisions must be represented on decision-making boards and commissions (see p. 59).

comparable worth extended the "equal pay for equal work" principle to develop criteria for compensation based on the intellectual and physical demands of the job, not market determination of its worth (see p. 324).

Congressional Budget and Impoundment Control Act of 1974 changed the congressional budget process and revised timetables for consideration of spending bills; created the Congressional Budget Office (see p. 364).

Congressional Budget Office (CBO) created in 1974, this is the budget and financial planning division of the U.S. Congress. See **Congressional Budget and Impoundment Control Act of 1974** (see p. 340).

consensual or consensus-building model of communication assumes that by cooperation instead of power struggles and political trade-offs, administrators may seek to reach agreement with potential adversaries as a means of furthering mutual aims (see p. 176).

consent order one means used by some U.S. regulatory entities to secure voluntary compliance with regulatory requirements; involves a formal agreement between the entity and an industry or industries in which the industry agree to cease a practice if the regulatory entity drops punitive actions aimed at the practice (see p. 446).

constituency any group or organization interested in the work and actions of a given official, agency, or organization, and a potential source of support for it; also, the interests (and sometimes geographic area) served by an elected or appointed public official (see p. 89).

contracting out a practice under which private-sector contractors provide designated goods or services to governments, or to individual agencies, for an agreed-upon fee; an example both of a "twilight zone" between public and private sectors, and of public-sector responses to growing fiscal stress; services contracted for include trash collection and fire protection; see also **privatization** (see p. 388).

controlled experimentation involves comparisons of two groups of similar people, one served by the program and another (control group) not served, or served differently; the most expensive and least practiced form of evaluation (see p. 409).

co-optation a process in organizational relations whereby one group or organization acquires the ability to influence activities of another, usually for a considerable period of time (see p. 60).

coordination the process of bringing together divided labor; efforts to achieve coordination often involve emphasis on common or compatible objectives, harmonious working relationships, and the like; linked to issues involving communication, centralization-decentralization, federalism, and leadership (see p. 171).

cost-benefit analysis technique designed to measure relative gains and losses resulting from alternative policy or program options; emphasizes identification of the most desirable **cost-benefit ratio,** in quantitative or other terms (see p. 200).

cost-benefit ratios   the proportional relationship between expenditure of a given quantity of resources and the benefits derived therefrom; a guideline for choosing among alternatives, of greatest relevance to the rational model of decision making (see p. 200).

Council of Economic Advisors (CEA)   the president's chief advisory and research source for economic advice. Consists of three economists (one appointed as chair) and assists the White House in preparing various economic reports (see p. 346).

crisis of legitimacy   a political condition in which elected officials fail to receive a vote of confidence and are perceived to lack the legal authority and right to make binding decisions for the majority of the population (see p. 503).

critical path method (CPM)   a management approach to **program implementation** (related to PERT) in which a manager attempts to assess the resource needs of different paths of action, and to identify the path with the smallest margin of extra resources needed to complete all assigned program activities (the "critical path") (see p. 401).

Cuban missile crisis   dangerous confrontation between the Soviet Union (Russia) and the United States during the Kennedy administration (1962) over the shipment and deployment of Russian nuclear missiles in Cuba (see p. 255).

customer service standards   explicit standards of service quality published by federal agencies and part of the reinventing government initiative (see p. 421).

cutback management or "downsizing"   current fiscal pressures on public organizations have spawned the need for "downsizing" in many places, forcing leaders to use a variety of new tactics. At the same time, they must strive to maintain organization morale and performance levels, while holding to a minimum the negative effects of organizational decline (see p. 270).

cybernetics   emphasizes organizational feedback that triggers appropriate adaptive responses throughout an organization; a thermostat operates on the same principle (see p. 166).

debureaucratize   strategy to decentralize and deregulate the public sector by reductions in force, promoting greater flexibility in personnel decisions, and increasing result-oriented incentives to reduce "overhead" costs (see p. 488).

decentralization   an organizational pattern focused on distributing power broadly within an organization (see p. 181).

decision analysis   the use of formal mathematical and statistical tools and techniques, especially computers and sophisticated computer models and simulations, to improve decision making (see p. 220).

decision making   a process in which choices are made to change (or leave unchanged) an existing condition and to select a course of action most appropriate to achieving a desired objective (however formalized or informal the objective may be), while minimizing risk and uncertainty to the extent deemed possible; the process may be characterized by widely varying degrees of self-conscious "rationality" or by willingness of the decision maker to decide incrementally, without insisting on assessment of all possible alternatives, or by some combination of approaches (see p. 198).

deficit   the amount by which governmental outlays exceed governmental receipts in a fiscal year (see p. 340).

dependent regulatory agencies (DRAs)   regulatory units or subdivisions of executive agencies (see p. 442).

deregulation   strategy to reduce or remove regulations in a particular sector (see p. 468).

direct spending   a category of outlays from budget authority provided in law other than appropriations acts, entitlements, and budget authority for food stamps; sometimes called mandatory spending (see p. 340).

discretionary spending   a category of budget authority that comprises budgetary resources (except those provided to fund direct-spending programs) in appropriations acts (see p. 340).

distributive policies   policy actions such as subsidies or tax deductions that deliver widespread benefits to individuals or groups who often do not bear the costs (see p. 387).

diversity   reflects the goal of many affirmative action programs to diversify the workforce to reflect the population demographics (makeup) at the affected jurisdiction (see p. 284).

earmarking   revenues are "earmarked" for designated purposes (such as elementary, secondary, and higher education, road construction and maintenance, or operating game preserves), leaving the bureaucracy without discretion to change them (see p. 373).

egalitarianism   a philosophical concept stressing individual equality in political, social, economic, and other relations; in the context of public personnel administration, the conceptual basis for "government by the common person" (see p. 290).

empowerment   an approach to citizen participation or management that stresses extended customer satisfaction, examines relationships among existing management processes, seeks to improve internal agency communications, and responds to valid customer demands; in exchange for the authority to make decisions at the point of customer contact, all "empowered" employees must be thoroughly trained, and the results must be carefully monitored (see pp. 61, 486).

entitlements   programs of government financial assistance (mainly to individuals) created under legislation that defines eligibility standards but places no limit on total budget authority; the level of outlays is determined solely by the number of eligible persons who apply for authorized benefits, under existing law (see p. 340).

entrepreneurial government   emphasizes productivity management, measurable performance, privatization, and change (see p. 7).

1972 Equal Employment Opportunity Act   amended Title VII, the Civil Rights Act of 1964, designed to strengthen the authority of the Equal Employment Opportunity Commission (EEOC) to enforce antidiscrimination laws in state and local governments as well as in private organizations with fifteen or more employees (see p. 324).

Equity Pay Act of 1963   prohibited gender-based (or other) discrimination in pay for individuals engaged in the same type of work (see p. 324).

exception principle   an assumption in traditional administrative thinking that chief executives do not have to be involved in administrative activities unless some problem or disruption of routine activity occurs — that is, when there is an exception to routine operations (see p. 253).

executive budgets   budgets prepared by chief executives and and their central budget offices for submission to the legislature for analysis, consideration, review, change, and enactment (see pp. 242, 351).

Executive Order (EO) 10925 (1961) issued by President Kennedy, this EO required for the first time that "affirmative action" guidelines be used to prohibit discrimination in employment by federal agencies and contractors (see p. 324).

Executive Order (EO) 10988 issued by President Kennedy in 1962, this order extended the right to organize and bargain collectively to all national government employees (see p. 308).

Executive Schedule compensation schedule for Federal Senior Executive Service (see p. 295).

externalities the economic consequences or impacts of federal grants-in-aid at the regional and local level (see p. 118).

external (legal-institutional) checks codes of conduct, laws, rules, and statutes that serve as safeguards to insure that individual actions are ethical (see p. 213).

federalism a constitutional division of governmental power between a central or national government and regional governmental units (such as states), with each having some independent authority over its citizens (see p. 107).

Federal Labor Relations Authority (FLRA) replaced the Federal Labor Relations Council and increased the strength of this bipartisan, three-member panel to supervise the creation of bargaining units, union elections, and deal with labor–management relations in federal agencies (see p. 309).

Federal Labor Relations Council created by Executive Order 11491 in 1969 by President Nixon to slightly expand federal workers' rights to join unions and bargain collectively (see p. 309).

Federal Mediation and Conciliation Service mediates negotiation disputes between public employees and federal managers (see p. 309).

Federal Register a listing of all proposed and active federal regulations (see p. 444).

Federal Reserve System an independent board that serves as the central bank of the United States. The "Fed" administers banking, credit, and monetary policies and controls the supply of money available to member banks (see p. 346).

Federal Service Impasses Panel resolves impasses when either party in collective bargaining negotiations feels that no further progress can be made toward settlement of disputed issues (see p. 309).

Federal Trade Commission (FTC) independent regulatory commission charged with enforcing antitrust acts, including the Sherman and Clayton Acts, to protect consumers against unfair trade practices (see p. 390).

First Hoover Commission (1947–1949) was chaired by former president Herbert Hoover and tried to reduce the number of federal agencies created during World War II; recommended an expansion of executive budgetary powers (see p. 353).

fiscal federalism the complex of financial transactions, transfers of funds, and accompanying rules and regulations that increasingly characterizes national–state, national–local, and state–local relations (see p. 114).

fiscal mismatch differences in the capacity of various governments to raise revenues, in relation to those governments' respective abilities to pay for public services which they are responsible for delivering (see p. 115).

fiscal policy refers to government actions aimed at development and stabilization of the private economy, including taxation and tax policy, expenditures, and management of the national debt. Monetary and credit controls are also related to fiscal policy (see p. 341).

formal communication   official written documentation within an organization including electronic mail, memoranda, minutes of meetings, and records. Forms the framework for organizational intent and activity (see p. 172).

formal theory of organization   stresses formal, structural arrangements within organizations, and "correct" or "scientific" methods to be followed in order to achieve the highest degree of organizational efficiency; examples include Weber's theory of bureaucracy and Taylor's "scientific management" approach (see p. 149).

formula grant   a type of national government grant-in-aid available to states and local governments for purposes that are ongoing and common to many government jurisdictions; distributed according to a set formula that treats all applicants uniformly, at least in principle; has the effect of reducing grantors' administrative discretion. Examples are aid to the blind and aid to the elderly (see p. 119).

freedom of information (FOI) law   legislation passed by Congress and some state legislatures establishing procedures through which private citizens may gain access to a wide variety of records and files from government agencies; a principal instrument for breaking down bureaucratic secrecy in American public administration (see p. 51).

free-market competition   basis of U.S. and other free-enterprise economic systems where the means of production and distribution of goods and services are owned by private corporations or individuals, and the government role in the economy is minimal (see p. 432).

full-time equivalent (FTE) employees   the actual number of full-time government personnel plus the number of full-time people who would have been needed to work the hours put in by part-time employees (see p. 286).

functional overlap   a phenomenon of contemporary American bureaucracy whereby functions performed by one bureaucratic entity may also be performed by another; conflicts with Weber's notions of division of labor and specialization (see p. 150).

fundamentalism   the practice of certain religious groups that adhere to strict beliefs and literal interpretation of a set of basic principles (see p. 479).

"gain-sharing"   analogous to "profit-sharing" in the private sector, allows public agencies to share a portion of the savings accrued from implementing productivity improvements (see p. 423).

game theory   a modern theory viewing organizational behavior in terms of competition among members for resources; based on distinctly mathematical assumptions and employing mathematical methods (see p. 166).

garbage can theory of organizational choice   a theory of organizational decision making applicable to organizations in which goals are unclear, technologies are imperfectly understood, histories are difficult to interpret, and participants wander in and out; such "organized anarchies" operate under conditions of pervasive ambiguity, with so much uncertainty in the decision-making process that traditional theories about coping with uncertainty do not apply (see p. 227).

General Accounting Office (GAO)   the investigative arm of Congress that helps Congress oversee federal programs and operations to assure accountability to the American people through a variety of activities including financial audits, program reviews, investigations, legal support, and policy/program analyses (see p. 412).

General Schedule (GS)   pay scale for federal employees, based on grades and steps (see p. 295).

global interdependence   the growing web of interrelationships—in social, economic, cultural, political, technological, institutional, and policy respects— among nations and peoples around the world; particularly significant as it relates to our abilities to communicate globally, and to the speed with which challenges found in one part of the world become a part of the governing environment in other locales (see p. 489).

goal articulation   a process of defining and clearly expressing goals generally held by those in an organization or group; usually regarded as a function of organization or group leaders; a key step in developing support for official goals (see p. 264).

goal congruence   agreement on fundamental goals; refers to the extent of agreement among leaders and followers in the organization on central objectives; in practice, its absence in many instances creates internal tensions and difficulties in goal definition (see p. 210).

gobbledygook   misleading jargon or meaningless technical terms often used to purposely obscure communications within organizations (see p. 175).

Government Performance and Results Act (GPRA)   commonly called the Results Act, requires federal managers to plan and measure performance in new ways; an invaluable collection of resources, tools, models, and guidance is available through the act's Web site to assist in the Results Act implementation (see p. 415).

government regulation   government activity designed to monitor and guide private economic competition; specific actions (characterized as economic regulation) have included placing limits on producers' prices and practices, and promoting commerce through grants or subsidies; other actions emerging more recently (termed social regulation) have included regulating conditions under which goods and services are produced and attempting to minimize product hazards and risks to consumers (see p. 432).

Gramm–Rudman–Hollings Act   the informal title for the Balanced Budget and Emergency Deficit Control Act of 1985, which mandated steadily decreasing national government annual budget deficits through fiscal year 1991 (see p. 340).

grants-in-aid   money payments furnished to a lower level of government to be used for specified purposes and subject to conditions spelled out in law or administrative regulation (see p. 116).

gridlock   derived from term referring to traffic that is so congested that cars cannot move; government is so divided that no consistent policy direction can be established (see p. 92).

gross national product (GNP)   the sum of goods and services produced by the economy, including personal consumption, private investments, and government spending (see p. 345).

groupthink   a mode of thinking that people engage in when they are deeply involved in a cohesive in-group, when members striving for unanimity override their motivation to realistically appraise alternative courses of action; facilitated by insulation of the decision group from others in the organization and by the group's leader promoting one preferred solution or course of action (see p. 222).

gubernatorial   a term which refers to anything concerning the office of state governor — for example, gubernatorial authority or gubernatorial influence (see p. 122).

Hawthorne or "halo" effect   tendency of those being observed to change their behavior to meet the expectations of researchers; named after a factory in Hawthorne, Illinois, where studies took place in the late 1920s and early 1930s (see p. 155).

hierarchy   a characteristic of formal bureaucratic organizations; a clear vertical "chain of command" in which each unit is subordinate to the one above it and superior to the one below it; one of the most common features of governmental and other bureaucratic organizations (see p. 148).

hierarchy of needs   a psychological concept formulated by Abraham Maslow holding that workers have different kinds of needs that must be satisfied in sequence — basic survival needs, job security, social needs, ego needs, and personal fulfillment in the job (see p. 161).

homeostasis   a concept within open-systems theory referring to a process of spontaneous self-stabilization in the relationships among various parts and activities of a complex organization, thereby keeping it functioning in the face of disturbances in the organization's environment (see p. 165).

House Ways and Means Committee   the primary committee in Congress concerned taxation and fiscal policy (see p. 348).

human relations   theories of organization stressing workers' noneconomic needs and motivations on the job, seeking to identify these needs and how to satisfy them, and focusing on working conditions and social interactions among workers (see p. 154).

human resources development (HRD)   the training and staff development of public employees designed to improve job performance (see p. 284).

impasse procedures   in the context of labor–management relations and collective bargaining, procedures that can be called into play when collective negotiations do not lead to agreement at the bargaining table; these include mediation, fact finding, arbitration, and referendum (in some combination, or following one another should one procedure fail to resolve the impasse) (see p. 312).

impoundment   in the context of the budgetary process, the practice by a chief executive of withholding final spending approval of funds appropriated by the legislature, in a bill already signed into law; may take the form of deferrals or rescissions; presidential authority to impound limited by Congress since 1974 (see p. 364).

incrementalism   a model of decision making that stresses making decisions through limited successive comparisons, in contrast to the rational model; also focuses on simplifying choices rather than aspiring to complete problem analyses, on the status quo rather than abstract goals as a key point of reference, on "satisficing" rather than "maximizing," and on remedying ills rather than seeking positive goals (see p. 202).

independent regulatory boards and commissions   delegated authority by Congress to enforce both executive and judicial authority in the application of government regulations (see p. 432).

individualism   a philosophical belief in the worth and dignity of the individual, particularly as part of a political order; holds that government and politics should regard the well-being and aspirations of individuals as more important than those of the government (see p. 42).

informal communication   all forms of communication, other than official written documentation, among members of an organization. Supplements official communications within an organization (see p. 172).

information superhighway   nickname for the World Wide Web (see p. 469).

information technology (IT)   refers to the use of computers, linked-area network (LAN) systems, the World Wide Web, and the Internet to improve the delivery of government services and enhance the capacity of individuals and organizations to gather information (see p. 10).

information theory   a modern theory of organization that views organizations as requiring constant input of information in order to continue functioning systematically and productively; assumes that a lack of information will lead to chaos or randomness in organizational operations (see p. 166).

innovation   the introduction of something new into an organization (see p. 268).

institutional   top-level leadership which is concerned primarily with achieving the long-term goals of the organization (see p. 259).

instruments, or tools, of leadership   various mechanisms such as legislative support, policy initiatives, and emergency decision-making powers available to chief executives to help direct bureaucratic behavior (see p. 238).

interest groups   private organizations representing a portion (usually small) of the general adult population; they exist in order to pursue particular public policy objectives and seek to influence government activity so as to achieve their objectives (see p. 78).

intergovernmental relations (IGR)   all the activities and interactions occurring between or among governmental units of all types and levels within the American federal system (see p. 107).

internal (personal) checks   personal values of, and actions taken by, individuals who are concerned with behaving in an ethical and moral manner (see p. 213).

Internal Revenue Service (IRS)   responsible for administration of federal tax policy and collection of revenue from individuals and corporations (see p. 390).

Iran-Contra affair   scandal in the Reagan–Bush administrations (1986–1987) over alleged involvement of high-level officials in the sale of weapons to Iran and the diversion of proceeds to arm the U.S.-backed "Contra" rebels in Nicaragua (see p. 248).

iron triangle   see *subsystem* (see p. 89).

issue networks   in the context of American politics (especially at the national level), open and fluid groupings of various political actors (in and out of government) attempting to influence policy; "shared-knowledge" groups having to do with some aspect or problem of public policy; lacking in the degree of permanence, commonality of interests, and internal cohesion characteristic of subsystems (see p. 92).

item veto (or line-item veto)   a constitutional power available to more than forty of America's governors, under which they may disapprove some provisions of a bill while approving the others (see p. 243).

job action   any action taken by employees (usually unionized) as a protest against an aspect of their work or working conditions; includes, but is not limited to, strikes or work slowdowns (see p. 314).

judicial review   the constitutional power of the courts to review the actions of executive agencies, legislatures, or decisions of lower courts to determine whether judges, legislators, or administrators acted appropriately (see p. 98).

jurisdiction   in bureaucratic politics, the area of programmatic responsibility assigned to an agency by the legislature or chief executive; also, a term used to describe the territory within the boundaries of a government entity, such as "a local jurisdiction" (see p. 78).

Justice Department   cabinet-level executive agency responsible for the enforcement of federal law (see p. 390).

knowledge explosion   a social phenomenon of the past forty years, particularly in Western industrial nations, creating new technologies and vast new areas of research and education; examples include biogenetic engineering, space exploration, mass communications, nuclear technology, and energy research (see pp. 67, 478).

labor–management relations   the formal setting in which negotiatons over pay, working conditions, and benefits take place (see p. 305).

lateral or cross-functional communication   patterns of oral and written communication within organizational networks that are interdisciplinary and typically cut across vertical layers of hierarchy (see p. 173).

leader as catalyst and innovator   a formalized conception of the "spark plug" role in a group setting. As part of the catalyst role, a leader is also expected to introduce innovations into an organization (see p. 267).

leader as coordinator   (and integrator) involves bringing some order to the multitude of functions within a complex organization (see p. 266).

leader as crisis manager   involves coping with both immediate and longer-term difficulties, more serious than routine managerial challenges (see p. 269).

leader as director   refers to the challenge of bringing some unity of purpose to the organization's members (see p. 263).

leader as gladiator   a leadership role in which the leader seeks to promote the work of an organization, often in an effort to secure additional resources, as well as defending the organization in the external environment (see p. 269).

leader as motivator   a key task centering on devices such as tangible benefits, positive social interaction, work interest, encouragement by job supervisors, and leadership that is self-confident, persuasive, fair, and supportive (see p. 265).

learning organizations   a concept of organizations emphasizing the importance of encouraging new patterns of thinking and interaction within organizations to foster continuous learning and personal development (see p. 169).

legislative intent   the goals, purposes, and objectives of a legislative body, given concrete form in its enactments (though actual intent may change over time); bureaucracies are assumed to follow legislative intent in implementing laws (see p. 38).

legislative oversight   the process by which a legislative body supervises or oversees the work of the bureaucracy in order to ensure its conformity with legislative intent (see p. 38).

legitimacy   the acceptance of an institution or individual such as a government, family member, or state governor as having the legal and publicly recognized right to make and enforce binding decisions (see p. 206).

liberal democracy   a fundamental form of political arrangement founded on the concepts of popular sovereignty and limited government (see p. 41).

limited government   refers to devices built in to the Constitution that effectively limit the power of government over individual citizens (see p. 41).

line functions   substantive activities of an organization, related to programs or policies for which the organization is formally responsible, and usually having direct impact on outside clienteles; the work of an organization directed toward fulfilling its formal mission(s) (see p. 180).

line-item budgeting   the earliest approach to modern executive budget making, emphasizing control of expenditures through careful accounting for all money spent in public programs; facilitated central control of purchasing and hiring, along with completeness and honesty in fiscal accounting (see p. 352).

line-item veto   a constitutional power available to more than forty of America's governors — and, on a limited basis, to the president — with which they may disapprove a specific expenditure item within an appropriations bill instead of having to accept or reject the entire bill (see p. 95).

locality pay   adjustments to federal pay scales that make allowances for higher- or lower-cost areas where employees live (see p. 303).

Malcolm Baldrige National Quality Awards   created by Public Law 100–107, and signed into law on August 20, 1987; the award program led to the creation of a new public–private partnership. Principal support for the program comes from the Foundation for the Malcolm Baldrige National Quality Awards (see p. 418).

management by objectives (MBO)   a management technique designed to facilitate goal and priority setting, development of plans, resource allocation, monitoring progress toward goals, evaluating results, and generating and implementing improvements in performance (see p. 401).

managerial   leadership that emphasizes midlevel supervisory skills and coordination between *technical* and senior-level *institutional* leaders (see p. 259).

mandatory spending   a category of outlays from budget authority provided in laws other than appropriations acts, entitlements, and budget authority for food stamps; see also **direct spending** (see p. 340).

Medicaid   federal health care program operated by the states to assist the poor (see p. 121).

merit pay   an approach to compensation in personnel management founded on the concept of equal pay for equal contribution (rather than for equal activity); related to, and dependent on, properly designed and implemented performance appraisal systems; applied to managers and supervisors in grades GS-13 through GS-15 in the national executive branch, under provisions of the **Civil Service Reform Act of 1978** (see p. 295).

merit system   a system of selection (and, ideally, evaluation of) administrative officials on the basis of job-related competence, as measured by examinations and professional competence (see p. 150).

mixed scanning   a model of decision making that combines the rational-comprehensive model's emphasis on fundamental choices and long-term consequences with the incrementalists' emphasis on changing only what needs to be changed in the immediate situation; emphasizes short-term decisions (see p. 204).

modern organization theory a body of theory that emphasizes empirical examination of organizational behavior, interdisciplinary research employing varied approaches, and attempts to arrive at generalizations applicable to many different kinds of organizations (see p. 163).

money supply the amount of money available to individuals and institutions in society (see p. 346).

monopolistic practices a situation in which a certain company or group of companies controls the production and distribution system of that market to exclude all other competitors (see p. 432).

multilateral bargaining public-sector collective bargaining negotiations that include the broadest number of affected public employee groups (see p. 306).

multiple referral a legislative tactic that has strengthened the power of Congress over political subsystems (see p. 91).

National Labor Relations Board (NLRB) an independent federal agency created in 1935 to enforce the National Labor Relations Act; conducts secret-ballot elections to determine whether employees want union representation, and investigates and remedies unfair labor practices by employers and unions (see p. 390).

National Partnership for Reinventing Government (NPRG) (formerly known as the National Performance Review) see **"reinventing goverment"** (see p. 36).

nepotism a form of favoritism based on hiring family members or relatives (see p. 289).

nonprofit or "third-sector" organizations nongovernmental tax-exempt institutions, such as churches, hospitals, private colleges and universities, the United Way, and the Boy Scouts and Girl Scouts, which provide quasi-governmental services to many local communities using volunteers (see p. 22).

Occupational Safety and Health Administration (OSHA) the mission of OSHA is to save lives, prevent injuries, and protect the health of America's workers. To accomplish this, federal and state governments must work in partnership with the more than 100 million working people and their six and a half million employers who are covered by the Occupational Safety and Health Act of 1970 (see p. 390).

Office of Management and Budget (OMB) an important entity in the Executive Office of the President that assists the president in assembling executive-branch budget requests, coordinating programs, developing executive talent, and supervising program management processes in national government agencies (see p. 15).

Office of Personnel Management (OPM) a key administrative unit in the national government operating under presidential direction, responsible for managing the national government personnel system, consistent with presidential personnel policy (see p. 294).

Omnibus Budget Reconciliation Act of 1993 extended the provisions of earlier legislation through 1998 and established stricter limits on discretionary spending (see p. 371).

open-systems theory a theory of organization that views organizations not as simple, "closed" bureaucratic structures, separate from their surroundings, but as highly complex entities, facing considerable uncertainty in their operations, and constantly interacting with their environment; assumes that organizational components will seek an "equilibrium" among the forces pressing on them and their own responses to those forces (see also **homeostasis**) (see p. 165).

operational goal   a specific and measurable goal for organizational attainment (see p. 392).

operations research (OR)   a set of specific decision-making and analytical tools used in systems theory, modeling, and quantitative research to determine how best to utilize resources (see p. 397).

organizational change   a theory of organization that focuses on those characteristics of an organization that promote or hinder change; assumes that demands for change originate in the external environment and that the organization should be in the best position to respond to them (see p. 166).

organizational development   a theory of organization that concentrates on increasing the ability of an organization to solve internal problems of organizational behavior as one of its routine functions; primarily concerned with identification and analysis of such problems (see p. 28).

organizational humanism   a set of organization theories stressing that work holds intrinsic interest for the worker, that workers seek satisfaction in their work, that they want to work rather than avoid it, and that they can be motivated through systems of positive incentives (such as participation in decision making and public recognition for work well done) (see p. 159).

organizational structure   the types of organizational unit designed to achieve a particular policy goal (see p. 85).

organized anarchies   organizations in which goals are unclear, technologies are imperfectly understood, histories are difficult to interpret, and participants wander in and out; decision making in such organizations is characterized by pervasive ambiguity, with so much uncertainty in the decision-making process that traditional theories about coping with uncertainty do not apply (see p. 227).

"overhead bureaucracy"   increased costs of administering government programs imposed by mandates to include those affected by policy-making decisions; program efficiency tends to decrease as participation increases (see p. 485).

"overhead democracy"   majority control through political representatives who supervise administrative officers responsible and loyal to their superiors for carrying out the directions of the elected representatives (see p. 484).

parliamentary form of government   a form of government practiced in most democratic nations, including France, Germany, the United Kingdom, and Japan in which the chief executive and top-level ministers are themselves members of the legislature (see p. 38).

participatory democracy   a political and philosophical belief in direct involvement by effected citizens in the processes of governmental decision making; believed by some to be essential to the existence of democratic government; related term: *citizen participation* (see p. 43).

partisanship   political party pressures on elected members of Congress, state legislature, or local boards and commissions (see p. 92).

patronage   selection of public officials on the basis of political loyalty rather than merit, objective examination, or professional competence (see p. 149).

"pay-as-you-go" (PAYGO) procedure requiring that spending increases be offset by decreases in annual appropriations so as not to increase the deficit (see p. 371).

Pendleton Act a law formally known as the Civil Service Act of 1883 (sponsored by Ohio Senator George Pendleton), establishing job-related competence as the primary basis for filling national government jobs; created the U.S. Civil Service Commission to oversee the new "merit" system; see also **Civil Service Act** (see p. 290).

performance appraisal a formal process used to document and evaluate an employee's job performance, typically used to reinforce management's assessment of the quality of an individual's work, punish workers who are "below standard," and reward others with bonuses, higher salaries, and promotions (see p. 320).

performance budgeting an approach to modern executive budget making that gained currency in the 1930s, emphasizing not only resources acquired by an agency but also what it did with them; geared to promoting effective management of government programs in a time of growing programmatic complexity (see p. 352).

pervasive ambiguity a situation of long-term uncertainty that pervades the decision-making environment of an organization (see p. 228).

picket-fence federalism a term describing a key dimension of American federalism — intergovernmental administrative relationships among bureaucratic specialists and their clientele groups, in the same substantive areas; suggests that allied bureaucrats at different levels of government exercise considerable power over intergovernmental programs. See also **vertical functional autocracies** (see p. 123).

planning and analysis the process of deliberately defining and choosing operational goals of an organization, analyzing alternative choices for resource distribution, and choosing methods to achieve those goals over a specified time period; an increasingly important tool for public management (see p. 392).

pluralism a social and political concept stressing the appropriateness of group organization, and diversity of groups and their activities, as a means of protecting broad group interests in society; assumes that groups are good and that bargaining and competition among them will benefit the public interest (see p. 42).

pluralist democracy a normative model of administrative activity, characterized by dispersion of power and suspicion of any concentration of power; exercise of power by politicians, interest groups, and citizens; political bargaining and accommodation; and an emphasis on individuals' and political actors' own determination of interests as the basis for policy making; the principal alternative to the **administrative efficiency** model (see p. 47).

policy analysis the systematic investigation of alternative policy options and the assembly and integration of evidence for and against each; emphasizes explaining the causes of policy problems and how public policies are put into effect (see p. 394).

policy development a general political and governmental process of formulating relatively concrete goals and directions for government activity and proposing an overall framework of programs related to them; usually but not always regarded as a chief executive's task (see p. 237).

policy implementation a general political and governmental process of carrying out programs in order to fulfill specified policy objectives; a responsibility chiefly of administrative agencies, under chief-executive and/or legislative guidance; also, the activities directed toward putting a policy into effect (see p. 237).

political corruption   all forms of bribery, favoritism, kickbacks, and legal as well as illegal rewards; commonly associated with reward systems where partisan patronage is in use; more generally, patterns of behavior in government associated with providing access, tangible benefits, etc. to some more than others, on an "insider" basis (see p. 215).

politically neutral competence   the idea that appointments to civil service positions should be made on the basis of demonstrated job competence, and not based on age, ethnicity, gender, politics, or race (see p. 284).

political persuasion or "jawboning"   the power of the chief executive to convince legislators, administrators, and the general public that his or her policies should be adopted; jawboning is quite literally the primary tactic, i.e., talking, used by presidents, governors, or mayors to achieve this goal (see p. 236).

political rationality   a concept advanced by Aaron Wildavsky suggesting that behavior of decision makers may be entirely rational when judged by criteria of political costs, benefits, and consequences, even if irrational according to economic criteria; emphasizes that political criteria for "rationality" have validity (see p. 225).

popular sovereignty   government by the ultimate consent of the governed, which implies some degree of popular participation in voting and other political actions, although this does not necessarily mean mass or universal political involvement (see p. 41).

POSDCORB   acronym standing for the professional watchwords of administration: **P**lanning, **O**rganizing, **S**taffing, **D**irecting, **CO**ordinating, **R**eporting, **B**udgeting (see p. 26).

position classification   a formal task of American public personnel administration intended to classify together jobs in different agencies that have essentially the same types of functions and responsibilities, based on written descriptions of duties and responsibilities (see p. 297).

postindustrialism   a social and economic phenomenon emerging in many previously industrialized nations; characterized by a relative decline in the importance of production, labor, and durable goods, and an increase in the importance of knowledge, new technologies, the provision of services, and leisure time (see p. 482).

power vacuum   where power to govern is splintered, there will inevitably be attempts by some to exercise that power which is not clearly defined and is, therefore, "up for grabs" (see p. 39).

preemptions   the assumption of state or local program authority by the federal government (see p. 112).

privatization   a practice in which governments either join with, or yield responsibility outright to, private-sector enterprises, for provision of services previously managed and financed by public entities; a pattern especially evident in local government service provision, though with growing appeal at other levels of government (see p. 25).

procedural due process   legal term that refers to the legal rules that govern a specific case (see p. 462).

procedural fairness assures fairness in the adjudication process (see p. 462).

productivity the measurable relationship between the results produced and the resources required for production; a quantitative measure of the efficiency of the organization (see p. 413).

productivity bargaining labor–management negotiations that link productivity improvements to employee wage increases, as an alternative to reductions-in-force (see p. 313).

Professional Air Traffic Controllers Organization (PATCO) now defunct union that once represented the nation's air traffic controllers in labor negotiations (see p. 314).

program evaluation the systematic examination of government actions, policies, or programs to determine their success or failure; used to gain knowledge of program impacts, establish accountability, and influence continuation of termination of government activities (see p. 406).

program evaluation and review technique (PERT) a management technique of **program implementation** in which the sequence of steps for carrying out a project or program is mapped out in advance; involves choosing necessary activities and estimating time and other resources required (see p. 400).

program implementation a general political and governmental process of carrying out programs in order to fulfill specified policy objectives; a responsibility chiefly of administrative agencies, under chief executive and/or legislative guidance; also, the activities directed toward putting a policy into effect (see p. 398).

project grant a form of grant-in-aid available to states and localities, by application, for an individual project; more numerous than formula grants, but with less overall funding by the federal government (see p. 119).

Proposition 209 ballot initiative in California that repealed all affirmative action and preferential hiring programs for state jobs and admissions to state colleges and universities (see p. 327).

protective regulation advantages certain groups or individuals by granting special access or licenses, used with professionals (see p. 441).

public administration (1) all processes, organizations, and individuals acting in official positions associated with carrying out laws and other rules adopted or issued by legislatures, executives, and courts (many activities are also concerned with formulation of these rules); (2) a field of academic study and professional training leading to public-service careers at all levels of government (see p. 8).

public cynicism and distrust negative public opinion about politics and government reflected in opinion polls and low voter turnouts (see p. 502).

public-interest groups (PIGs) organized lobbying groups which represent collective interests, i.e., nonbusiness or labor, in influencing public policy. Examples are Common Cause and Greenpeace (see p. 60).

public management a field of practice and study central to public administration that emphasizes internal operations of public agencies and focuses on managerial concerns related to control and direction, such as planning, organizational maintenance, information systems, budgeting, personnel management, performance evaluation, and productivity improvement (see p. 9).

public personnel administration (PPA)   the policies, processes, and procedures designed to recruit, train, and promote the men and women who manage government agencies (see p. 284).

public policy   (1) the organizing framework of purposes and rationales for government programs that deal with specified societal problems; (2) the complex of programs enacted and implemented by government (see p. 384).

rational   decision making is derived from economic theories of how to make the "best" decisions; involves efforts to move toward consciously held goals in a way the requires the smallest input of scarce resources; assumes the ability to separate ends from means, rank all alternatives, gather all possible data, and objectively weigh alternatives; stressing rationality in the process of reaching decisions (see p. 199).

reconciliation process   an important step in congressional budgeting, when Congress makes adjustments in existing law to achieve conformity with annual spending targets adopted in each year's concurrent resolution; these adjustments can take the form of spending reductions, revenue increases, or both (see p. 369).

redistributive policies   deliberate efforts by governments to shift the allocation of valued goods in society from one group to another; highly controversial and often accompanied by bitter political conflicts (see p. 387).

reductions-in-force (RIFs)   systematic reductions or "downsizing" in the number of personnel positions allocated to a government agency or agencies; usually the result of higher-level personnel management policy decisions related to other policy objectives (including budget cuts and executive reorganizations) (see p. 248).

reflexive   an organizational or individual goal related primarily to survival and maintenance; "inward-oriented" as opposed to a goal focusing on external impacts (see p. 206).

regulatory body   refers to all types of dependent and independent regulatory boards, commissions, law enforcement agencies, and executive departments with regulatory authority (see p. 433).

regulatory federalism   an approach to intergovernmental relations under which federal agencies use regulations as opposed to grants to influence state and local governments (see p. 134).

regulatory policies   establish restrictions on the behavior of those subject to the regulations, aim to protect certain groups, range broadly in scope, and are often enforced against businesses (see p. 387).

reinventing government   the Clinton administration initiative based on the best-selling 1992 book *Reinventing Government: How the Entrepreneurial Spirit Is Transforming the Public Sector*, by David Osborne and Ted Gaebler. The book documents successful public-sector efforts to apply market-based, quality, and customer service principles to government. See also **National Partnership for Reinventing Government** (see p. 36).

relational leadership   leaders must not only be competent at traditional skills such as goal setting, conflict management, and motivation, but must be able to acquire information from group members and adapt their leadership styles to fit the needs of followers (see p. 263).

reorganization   authority delegated by Congress to the executive branch to add or subtract staff positions, or to restructure organizational arrangements, to achieve policy goals as well as increased economy, efficiency, and effectiveness of bureaucratic agencies (see p. 250).

representation   once referred to a general principle of legislative selection based on the number of inhabitants or amount of territory in a legislative district. But *adequate, fair, and equal* representation has become a major objective of many who feel they were denied it in the past and are now seeking greater influence, particularly in administrative decision making (see p. 41).

representative democracy   representatives are nominated and elected from individual districts. They compose a legislature that makes binding decisions for its society (see p. 43).

representativeness   groups that have been relatively powerless should be represented in government positions in proportion to their numbers in the population (see p. 41).

reregulation   decision by Congress or an administrative agency to reregulate (see p. 469).

results-oriented   government programs that focus on performance in exchange for granting greater discretionary decision-making power to managers (see p. 422).

reverse discrimination   unfavorable actions against white males to achieve affirmative action goals to hire and promote more women and minorities (see p. 326).

reverse pyramid   a conception of organization structure, especially in service organizations, whereby managerial duties focus on providing necessary support to frontline employees (particularly those whose work centers around information and information technology) who deal directly with individuals seeking the organization's services (see p. 10).

revolution of rising expectations   a social phenomenon of the period since World War II, affecting many nations, in which people who have been relatively poor have sought to increase their level of prosperity both as individuals and as groups; related in part to faith in technological and social advances (see p. 481).

rule making   a quasi-legislative power delegated to agencies by Congress; a rule issued under this authority represents an agency statement of general applicability and future effect that concerns the rights of private parties and has the force and effect of law (see p. 444).

rule of three   a procedure usually followed by the U.S. Office of Personnel Management in narrowing the list of people most qualified for a particular job opening in a national government agency; three names are sent to the agency, which then makes the final selection based on test scores and other considerations (see p. 301).

scientific management   a formal theory of organization developed by Frederick Winslow Taylor in the early 1900s; concerned with achieving efficiency in production, rational work procedures, maximum productivity, and profit; focused on management's responsibilities and on "scientifically" developed work procedures based on "time and motion" studies (see p. 151).

Second Hoover Commission   1955 blue-ribbon commission appointed by President Eisenhower and chaired by former president Hoover to study higher-level positions in the civil service (see p. 291).

Securities and Exchange Commission (SEC)   responsible for regulation of stocks, securities, and investments (see p. 436).

self-regulatory policies protective regulations that either advantage certain professions or classes, or remove from the government the power to regulate (see p. 388).

Senate Finance Committee the principal Senate committee concerned with revenue generation, taxation, and the operations of the **Internal Revenue Service (IRS)** (see p. 348).

Senior Executive Service (SES) established in the national **Civil Service Reform Act of 1978;** designed to foster professional growth, mobility, and versatility among career officials (and some "political" appointees); incorporated into national government personnel management an emphasis on performance appraisal and merit-pay concepts, as part of both the SES and broader merit-system reform (see **Civil Service Reform Act of 1978**) (see p. 291).

sequestration the withholding of budgetary resources provided by discretionary or direct spending legislation, following various procedures under the **Gramm–Rudman–Hollings Act** of 1985 and the **Budget Enforcement Act** of 1990; the withholding of budget authority, according to an established formula, up to the dollar amount that must be cut in order to meet the deficit-reduction target (see p. 369).

shared vision a foundation of core values within which leaders, managers, and employees interact and upon which everything else in the organization is based (see p. 267).

Sherman Antitrust Act first major antitrust legislation, passed in 1890, which made it illegal to fix prices or to monopolize an industry (see p. 435).

single state agency requirement a requirement contained in federal grants designating only one agency to administer national grants, and to establish direct relationships with its counterparts in the national government bureaucracy (see p. 123).

situational approach a method of analyzing leadership in a group or organization that emphasizes factors in the particular leadership situation, such as leader–follower interactions, group values, and the work being done (see p. 260).

social-demographic changes shifts in the population and economies of various regions that impact the delivery of public services (see p. 66).

social regulatory initiatives government actions in the late 1960s and early 1970s to regulate new social areas involving individual health, environmental protection, and public safety; resulted in the creation of several regulatory bodies (see p. 439).

span of control the number of people an individual supervises within a subunit of the organization. Each supervisor should have only a limited number of subordinates to oversee; this expands the chain of command to produce the needed ratio of supervisors to subordinates at each level, in the interest of overall coordination (see p. 184).

specialized language technical vocabulary used by bureaucratic agencies, one effect of which is to restrict access and outside influence (see p. 80).

staff functions originally defined to include all of an organization's support and advisory activities that facilitated the carrying out of "line" responsibilities and functions; more recently, redefined by some to focus on planning, research, and advisory activities (thus excluding budgeting, personnel, purchasing, and other functions once grouped under the "staff" heading) (see p. 180).

stakeholders   bureaucrats, elected officials, groups of citizens, and organized and unorganized interests affected by the decisions of federal, state, and local governments; those having a stake in the outcome of public policies; see also **interest groups, issue networks, subsystem** (see p. 9).

statistical process control (SPC)   the use of statistics to control critical processes within organizations; frequently used with TQM and **Theory Z** Japanese management techniques (see p. 169).

strategic planning   a process used by an organization to formulate a mission statement, consider environmental opportunities, threats, strengths, and weaknesses, identify areas for strategic action, conduct **cost-benefit analysis** to evaluate and select actions, draw up implementation plans, and incorporate **operational goals** into annual budgets (see p. 393).

substantive   an organizational goal focusing on the accomplishment of tangible programmatic objectives (see p. 206).

subsystem   in the context of American politics (especially at the national level), any political alliance uniting some members of an administrative agency, a legislative committee or subcommittee, and an interest group according to shared values and preferences in the same substantive area of policy making; sometimes called an **iron triangle** (see p. 89).

summitry   in national government budget making, the practice of initiating negotiations among leaders of Congress and the White House, involving top Democrats meeting with top Republicans (usually away from public view), in efforts to confront more effectively the seemingly intractable budget (and budget deficit) challenges of the past two decades (see p. 377).

sunk costs   in the context of organizational resources committed to a given decision, any cost involved in the decision that is irrecoverable; resources of the organization are lessened by that amount if it later reverses its decision (see p. 223).

sunset law   provision in laws that government agencies and programs have a specific termination date (see p. 51).

sunshine law   an act passed by Congress and by some states and localities requiring that various legislative proceedings (especially those of committees and subcommittees) and various administrative proceedings be held in public rather than behind closed doors; one devise for increasing openness and accountability (see p. 51).

symbolic actions   proposals for policy changes that serve some limited political purpose, but do not threaten the current situation (see p. 386).

symbolic goals   organizational objectives reflecting broad, popular political purposes, frequently unattainable (see p. 207).

systems analysis   an analytical technique designed to permit comprehensive investigation of the impacts within a given system of changing one or more elements of that system; in the context of analyzing policies, emphasizes overall objectives, surrounding environments, available resources, and system components (see p. 169).

systems theory   a theory of social organizations holding that organizations — like biological organisms — may behave according to inputs from their environment, outputs resulting from organizational activity, and feedback leading to further inputs; also, that change in any one part of a group or organizational system affects all other parts (see p. 164).

task forces   temporary cross-functional teams responsible for achieving a particular goal, often drawn from several departments within a larger agency; typically disbanded after the goal is accomplished (see p. 252).

taxation   a primary means by which governments raise revenues for public services; taxes can be collected from individuals and corporations on income (earned and unearned), profits, property value, sales, and services (see p. 344).

tax expenditure financing   revenue losses from provisions in the federal, state, or local tax codes that allow a special exclusion, exemption, or deduction from gross income or that provide a special tax credit, preferential rate of tax, or a deferral of tax liability (see p. 345).

technical   leadership that focuses on achieving a particular task within a subunit of an organization (see p. 258).

technological change   rapidly emerging patterns of change (related in part to the knowledge explosion) in communication, medical, and transportation technologies, among others, with significant implications both for the societal challenges confronting government and for the means and resources increasingly available to government for conducting public affairs (see pp. 167, 479).

Theory X   model of behavior within organizations that assumes that workers need to be motivated by extrinsic (external) rewards or sanctions (punishments) (see p. 160).

Theory Y   model of organizational behavior that stresses self-motivation, participation, and intrinsic (internal) job rewards (see p. 160).

Theory Z   Japanese management system that stresses deliberative, "bottom-up" collective accountability and decision making, long-term planning, and closer relationships among managers and workers (see p. 168).

time-trend projection   the comparison of preprogram data with actual postprogram data (see p. 408).

total quality management (TQM)   a management approach that encourages organizationwide commitment, teamwork, and better quality of results by providing incentives to increase the success of the whole enterprise. Elements of TQM include commitment to meeting customer-driven quality standards; employee participation or empowerment to make decisions at the point closest to the customer; actions based on data, facts, outcome measures, results, and statistical analysis; commitment to process and continuous quality improvements; and organizational changes and teamwork to encourage implementation of the above elements (see p. 168).

traits approach   a traditional method (now used less widely by scholars) of analyzing leadership in a group or organization; assumes that certain personality characteristics such as intelligence, ambition, tact, and diplomacy distinguish leaders from others in the group (see p. 260).

transitive   goal an organizational goal that, if achieved, would have an impact on an organization's external environment; a goal concerned more with external than with internal consequences of organizational actions (see p. 206).

tunnel vision   results from a fear of mistakes, missed deadlines, and focus on a narrow work environment, which limits the ability to see the organization's activities as a whole (see p. 266).

unfunded mandates   federal (or state) laws or regulations that impose requirements on other governments, often involving expenditures by affected governments, without providing funds for implementation (see p. 107).

vertical functional autocracies associations of federal, state, and local professional administrators who manage intergovernmental programs; also referred to as **picket-fence federalism** (see p. 123).

veto power the constitutional power of the elected chief executive to overrule an appropriation, law or decision by the legislature. At the national government level, requires a two-thirds majority of both houses of Congress to override (see p. 243).

whistle-blowers those who make any disclosure of legal violations, mismanagement, gross waste of funds, abuse of authority, or dangers to public health or safety, whether the disclosure is made within or outside the formal chain of command (see p. 216).

zone of acceptance refers to the extent to which a follower is willing to be led and to obey the leader's commands or directives; concept originally proposed by Chester Barnard, who wrote about leadership in 1930s (see p. 156).

References

Chapter 1: *Approaching the Study of Public Administration*

1. Remarks of President Bill Clinton, February 17, 1993 (emphasis added).
2. Charles T. Goodsell, *The Case for Bureaucracy: A Public Administration Polemic*, 3rd ed. (Chatham, N. J.: Chatham House, 1994), especially Chapter 2.
3. Goodsell, pp. xi–xii (emphasis added). Possible consequences of this intense criticism of bureaucracy and bureaucrats are discussed in Bernard Rosen, "Effective Continuity of U.S. Government Operations in Jeopardy," *Public Administration Review*, 43 (September/October 1983), 383–92, especially pp. 383–86; H. Brinton Milward and Hal G. Rainey, "Don't Blame the Bureaucracy!" *Journal of Public Policy*, 3 (May 1983), 149–68; and Bruce Adams, "The Frustrations of Government Service," *Public Administration Review*, 44 (January/February 1984), 5–13.
4. For an expansion of this theme, see Goodsell, *The Case for Bureaucracy;* and Richard J. Stillman II, *The American Bureaucracy: The Core of Modern Government*, 2nd ed. (Chicago: Nelson-Hall, 1996).
5. Dwight Waldo, "Introduction: Trends and Issues in Education for Public Administration," in Guthrie S. Birkhead and James D. Carroll, eds., *Education for Public Service 1979* (Syracuse: Maxwell School of Citizenship and Public Affairs, Syracuse University, 1979), pp. 13–26, at pp. 25–26.
6. See, for example, B. Guy Peters, *The Politics of Bureaucracy: A Comparative Perspective*, 3rd ed. (New York: Longman, 1989); and Kenneth J. Meier, *Politics and the Bureaucracy: Policy Making in the Fourth Branch of Government*, 3rd ed. (Monterey, Calif.: Brooks/Cole, 1993).
7. See, for example, John Naisbitt and Patricia Aburdene, *Megatrends 2000: Ten New Directions for the 1990s* (New York: William Morrow, 1990).
8. See William G. Ouchi, *The M-Form Society* (Reading, Mass.: Addison-Wesley, 1984). For discussion of the changing expectations of managers and leaders, see Warren H. Schmidt and Jerome P. Finnigan, *The Race Without a Finish Line* (San Francisco: Jossey-Bass, 1992), Chapters 5–11.
9. See Harold Seidman and Robert Gilmour, *Politics, Position, and Power: From the Positive to the Regulatory State*, 4th ed. (New York: Oxford University Press, 1986).
10. See Albert Gore, *Common Sense Government: Works Better and Costs Less* (New York: Random House, 1995), pp. 40–52.

11. The TVA is perhaps the most extensively studied agency in the history of our nation. See, among others, David Lilienthal's spirited book *TVA: Democracy on the March* (New York: Harper and Brothers, 1944); Philip Selznick's unflattering *TVA and the Grass Roots: A Study in the Sociology of Formal Organization* (Berkeley and Los Angeles: University of California Press, 1949); Roscoe C. Martin, ed., *TVA: The First Twenty Years* (University, Ala. and Knoxville, Tenn.: University of Alabama Press and University of Tennessee Press, 1956); Erwin C. Hargrove and Paul K. Conkin, eds., *TVA: Fifty Years of Grass-roots Bureaucracy* (Urbana, Ill.: University of Illinois Press, 1983); Steven M. Neuse, "TVA at Age Fifty — Reflections and Retrospect," *Public Administration Review*, 43 (November/December 1983), 491–99; and Michael R. Fitzgerald and Steven M. Neuse, eds., "TVA: The Second Fifty Years — A Symposium," *Public Administration Quarterly*, 8 (Summer 1984), 138–259.

12. Perhaps the best sources detailing the nature of the Iran-Contra scandal are *President's Special Review Board: The Tower Commission Report* (New York: Bantam Books and Times Books, 1987), and Lawrence Walsh, *Final Report of the Independent Counsel for Iran-Contra Matters* (Washington, D.C.: U.S. Court of Appeals for the D.C. Circuit, 1993).

13. James Q. Wilson, "The Rise of the Bureaucratic State," *The Public Interest*, 41 (Fall 1975), 77–103, at p. 88. See also Stephen Skowronek, *Building a New American State: The Expansion of National Administrative Capacities, 1877–1920* (New York: Cambridge University Press, 1982); and Louis Galambos, ed., *The New American State: Bureaucracies and Policies since World War II* (Baltimore: The Johns Hopkins University Press, 1987).

14. James L. Perry and Kenneth L. Kraemer, eds., *Public Management: Public and Private Perspectives* (Palo Alto, Calif.: Mayfield, 1983); Barry Bozeman, "Dimensions of 'Publicness': An Approach to Public Organization Theory," in Barry Bozeman and Jeffrey Straussman, eds., *New Directions in Public Administration* (Pacific Grove, Calif.: Brooks/Cole, 1984), pp. 46–62; Michael Lipsky and Steven Rathgeb Smith, "Nonprofit Organizations, Government, and the Welfare State," in Frederick S. Lane, ed., *Current Issues in Public Administration*, 5th ed.(New York: St. Martin's, 1994), pp. 414–436; and Hal G. Rainey, *Understanding and Managing Public Organizations* (San Francisco: Jossey-Bass, 1996).

15. This discussion draws especially on Joseph L. Bower, "Effective Public Management: It Isn't the Same as Effective Business Management," *Harvard Business Review*, 55 (March/April 1977), 131–40. See also Gordon Chase and Betsy Reveal, *How to Manage in the Public Sector* (Reading, Mass.: Addison-Wesley, 1983).

16. For a useful discussion of distinctly *public* management, see Barry Bozeman and Jeffrey D. Straussman, *Public Management Strategies: Guidelines for Managerial Effectiveness* (San Francisco: Jossey-Bass, 1990). Another perspective on public versus private management can be found in Barry Bozeman, *All Organizations Are Public* (San Francisco: Jossey-Bass, 1987).

17. This section relies especially on Alan A. Altshuler, "The Study of American Public Administration," in Alan A. Altshuler and Norman C. Thomas, eds., *The Politics of the Federal Bureaucracy*, 2nd ed. (New York: Harper & Row, 1977). See also, among others, Nicholas Henry, *Public Administration and Public Affairs*, 7th ed. (Englewood Cliffs, N.J.: Prentice-Hall, 1999); Frederick C. Mosher, ed., *American Public Administration: Past, Present, Future* (University, Ala.: University of Alabama Press, 1975); Dwight Waldo, *The Study of Public Administration* (New York: Random House, 1955);

and Waldo, *The Enterprise of Public Administration* (Novato, Calif.: Chandler & Sharp, 1980).

18. Quoted by Altshuler, "The Study of American Public Administration," p. 2.
19. Altshuler, "The Study of American Public Administration," p. 3; Henry, *Public Administration and Public Affairs*, pp. 24–25. See also Luther Gulick and Lyndall Urwick, eds., *Papers on the Science of Administration* (New York: Institute of Public Administration, 1937).
20. Rowland Egger, "The Period of Crisis: 1933 to 1945," in Frederick C. Mosher, ed., *American Public Administration: Past, Present, Future* (University, Ala.: University of Alabama Press, 1975), pp. 49–96, at p. 55.
21. Ibid., pp. 91–92.
22. Altshuler, "The Study of American Public Administration," p. 3.
23. See James W. Fesler, "Public Administration and the Social Sciences: 1946 to 1960," in Frederick C. Mosher, ed., *American Public Administration: Past, Present, Future* (University, Ala.: University of Alabama Press, 1975), pp. 97–141.
24. Altshuler, "The Study of American Public Administration," p. 5.
25. Herbert A. Simon, "The Proverbs of Administration," *Public Administration Review*, 6 (1946), 53–67.
26. Altshuler, "The Study of American Public Administration," pp. 10–11.
27. Ibid., p. 13.
28. Henry, *Public Administration and Public Affairs*, pp. 44–46.
29. The academic field of public administration is treated also by Joseph A. Uveges Jr., ed., *Public Administration: History and Theory in Contemporary Perspective* (New York: Marcel Dekker, 1982); Keith M. Henderson, *The Study of Public Administration* (Lanham, Md.: University Press of America, 1984); Brack Brown and Richard J. Stillman II, *A Search for Public Administration* (College Station, Tex.: Texas A & M University Press, 1986); Naomi Lynn and Aaron Wildavsky, eds., *Public Administration: The State of the Discipline* (New York: McGraw-Hill, 1990); Robert B. Denhardt and Barry R. Hammond, *Public Administration in Action: Readings, Profiles, and Cases* (Pacific Grove, Calif.: Brooks/Cole, 1992); and William C. Johnson, *Public Administration: Policy, Politics and Practice*, 2nd ed. (Madison, Wisc.: Brown and Benchmark, 1996); David H. Rosenbloom, *Public Administration: Understanding Management, Politics and Law in the Public Sector*, 4th ed. (New York: McGraw-Hill, 1998); Jay M. Shafritz and E. W. Russell, *Introducing Public Administration*, 2nd ed. (New York: Addison-Wesley Longman, 2000); Richard J. Stillman II, *Public Administration: Concepts and Cases*, 7th ed. (Boston: Houghton Mifflin, 2000).

Chapter 2: Public Administration, Democracy, and the Political System

1. David Osborne and Ted Gaebler, *Reinventing Government: How the Entrepreneurial Spirit is Transforming the Public Sector* (Reading, Mass.: Addison-Wesley, 1992); David Osborne and Peter Plastrik, *Banishing Bureaucracy: Five Stages for Reinventing Government* (Reading, Mass.: Addison-Wesley, 1997).
2. Donald F. Kettl and John J. DiIulio, eds., *Inside the Reinvention Machine* (Washington, D.C." The Brookings Institution, 1995).
3. Our discussion of this subject is based on the excellent treatment by Richard S. Page in "The Ideological-Philosophical Setting of American Public Administration," in Dwight Waldo, ed., *Public Administration in a Time of Turbulence* (Scranton, Pa.:

Chandler, 1971), pp. 59–73. See also Douglas Yates, *Bureaucratic Democracy: The Search for Democracy and Efficiency in American Government* (Cambridge, Mass.: Harvard University Press, 1982; paperback edition, 1987), pp. 10–13. There are other ways, however, to view the public interest; see, for example, Glendon Schubert, *The Public Interest* (Glencoe, Ill.: The Free Press, 1960; reprinted, 1982).

4. Herbert Kaufman, "Administrative Decentralization and Political Power," *Public Administration Review*, 29 (January/February 1969), 3–15, at p. 5 (emphasis added).

5. Though given renewed emphasis in recent decades, the idea of direct participation dates back to the founding of the Republic. Douglas Yates cites historian Andrew Hacker, a scholarly expert on the political thought of James Madison. Hacker suggests that Madison recognized the need for government to "regulate the activities of groups in society" but that Madison also "wanted groups to have a positive role in making governmental policy." See Yates, *Bureaucratic Democracy*, pp. 10–11.

6. This discussion draws on a commentary written by public administration scholar Dwight Waldo and cited by Page in "The Ideological-Philosophical Setting," p. 62. Waldo's *The Administrative State: A Study of the Political Theory of American Public Administration*, 2nd ed. (New York: Holmes and Meier, 1984) is a valuable examination of the evolution of American thinking regarding public administration.

7. Page, "The Ideological-Philosophical Setting," p. 63.

8. This balanced view of power held by the framers finds an analogy in the writings a century later of Woodrow Wilson, one of the foremost administrative reformers. In his famous essay, "The Study of Administration" (1887), Wilson advanced the "politics–administration dichotomy" and the notion of bureaucratic neutrality. What is not as well remembered is that Wilson also argued that administrators should exercise "large powers and unhampered discretion." The principal emphasis of Wilson's essay may be reinterpreted by giving more weight to his prescription for what Jameson Doig has called "administrative energy and administrative discretion." See Doig, "'If I See a Murderous Fellow Sharpening a Knife Cleverly': The Wilsonian Dichotomy and the Public Authority Tradition," *Public Administration Review*, 43 (July/August 1983), 292–304, especially pp. 292–94. The quote cited is from p. 294.

9. See Martin Landau, "Redundancy, Rationality, and the Problem of Duplication and Overlap," *Public Administration Review*, 29 (July/August 1969), 346–58.

10. Yates, *Bureaucratic Democracy*, pp. 31–33.

11. In *Bureaucratic Democracy*, Douglas Yates offers a thoughtful and carefully crafted approach to how these values can, in fact, be reconciled. See also John Rohr, *To Run a Constitution: The Legitimacy of the Administrative State* (Lawrence, Kans.: University Press of Kansas, 1986); Laurence J. O'Toole Jr., "Doctrines and Developments: Separation of Powers, the Politics–Administration Dichotomy, and the Rise of the Administrative State," *Public Administration Review*, 47 (January/February 1987), 17–25; John P. Burke, "Reconciling Public Administration and Democracy: The Role of the Responsible Administrator," *Public Administration Review*, 49 (March/April 1989), 180–85; and John A. Rohr, "The Constitutional Case for Public Administration," in Gary L. Wamsley et al., *Refounding Public Administration* (Newbury Park, Calif.: Sage, 1990).

12. Emmette S. Redford, *Democracy in the Administrative State* (New York: Oxford University Press, 1969), pp. 19–22.

13. Useful and insightful discussions of accountability — and of the related concern for bureaucratic responsibility discussed in Chapter 3 of this book — can be found in

John P. Burke, *Bureaucratic Responsibility* (Baltimore: The Johns Hopkins University Press, 1986); Barbara S. Romzek and Melvin J. Dubnick, "Accountability in the Public Sector: Lessons from the Challenger Tragedy," *Public Administration Review*, 47 (May/June 1987), 227–38; Douglas Yates, *Bureaucratic Democracy: The Search for Democracy and Efficiency in American Government* (Cambridge, Mass.: Harvard University Press, 1982; paperback edition, 1987), especially Chapter 6; Bernard Rosen, *Holding Government Bureaucracies Accountable*, 2nd ed. (Westport, Conn.: Greenwood Press, 1989); Ronald C. Moe and Thomas H. Stanton, "Government-Sponsored Enterprises as Federal Instrumentalities: Reconciling Private Management with Public Accountability," *Public Administration Review*, 49 (July/August 1989), 321–29; and Barbara S. Romzek and Melvin J. Dubnick, "Issues of Accountability in Flexible Personnel Systems," in Patricia W. Ingraham, Barbara Romzek, and associates, eds., *New Paradigms for Government: Issues for the Changing Public Service* (San Francisco: Jossey-Bass, 1994).

14. Theodore J. Lowi, *The End of Liberalism: The Second Republic of the United States*, 2nd ed. (New York: Norton, 1979).

15. William B. Eimicke, *Public Administration in a Democratic Context: Theory and Practice* (Beverly Hills, Calif.: Sage, 1974), p. 17. On a related theme, see Gregory Streib, "Professional Skill and Support for Democratic Principles: The Case of Local Government Department Heads in Northern Illinois," *Administration & Society*, 24 (May 1992), 22–40.

16. In this regard, see Joel D. Aberbach and Bert A. Rockman, "Mandates or Mandarins? Control and Discretion in the Modern Administrative State," *Public Administration Review*, 48 (March/April 1988), 606–12.

17. Harold C. Relyea, "Introduction," in Harold C. Relyea, ed., "Symposium on the Freedom of Information Act," *Public Administration Review*, 39 (July/August 1979), 310–32, at p. 310.

18. *The Freedom of Information Act*, Hearings before the Subcommittee on Information, Justice, and Agriculture, Committee on Government Operations, U.S. House of Representatives, 98th Congress, 2nd session (Washington, D.C.: U.S. Government Printing Office, 1985), pp. 33–34 and 693–94.

19. The FOIA Act was amended to make it easier for businesses to block the release of trade secrets in 1986. See *Congressional Quarterly Weekly Report*, 44 (September 27, 1986), 2325. See also Lotte E. Feinberg and Harold C. Relyea, eds., "Symposium: Toward a Government Information Policy — FOIA at 20," *Public Administration Review*, 46 (November/December 1986), 603–39; Karen J. Maschke and John S. Klemanski, "State-Level Bureaucratic Response to Requests for Information: Public Access and State Freedom of Information Laws," paper presented at the annual meetings of the American Political Science Association, Washington, D.C., September 1988; U. Lynn Jones, "See No Evil, Hear No Evil, Speak No Evil: The Information Control Policy of the Reagan Administration," *Policy Studies Journal*, 17 (Winter 1988–1989), 243–60; and William H. Abrashkin and Ernest Winsor, *Freedom of Information in Massachusetts* (Westport, Conn.: Auburn House, 1989).

20. The following discussion relies on Tess Chichioco, "Making It Hard to Get Records; Government Agencies Are Using Computers to Hinder Disclosure under the Freedom of Information Act," *Editor & Publisher*, 123 (March 31, 1990), 16; Jane E. Kirtley, "Electronic Roadblocks to Freedom of Information: A Press Perspective," *Bulletin of the American Society for Information Science*, 17 (August/September 1991),

10–11; Debra Gersh, "Government Information Protected: Supreme Court Reverses Lower Court Rulings; Says Complete Disclosure of Reports on Haitian Refugees Is Not Necessary under FOIA," *Editor & Publisher*, 124 (December 21, 1991), 24; Kate Doyle, "Hiding Space: NASA's Tips for Avoiding Scrutiny," *Columbia Journalism Review*, 31 (July/August 1992), 18–19; Terry Anderson, "My Paper Prison," *The New York Times Magazine*, April 4, 1993, p. 34; Margo Nash, "The Anderson File," *The Nation*, 256 (April 19, 1993), 509; Mark Fitzgerald, "President Clinton and FOI Laws," *Editor & Publisher*, 126 (May 8, 1993), 16–17; Mark Fitzgerald, "Losing Access to Public Records," *Editor & Publisher*, 126 (May 15, 1993), 9; Debra Gersh, "New FOIA Directives Issued," *Editor & Publisher*, 126 (October 9, 1993), 18–19; Debra Gersh Hernandez, "The FOIA and the White House," *Editor & Publisher*, 126 (November 20, 1993), 22–23; Michael K. Frisby, "Clinton Lawyer Secured U.S. Subpoena to Prevent Release of Whitewater Files," *The Wall Street Journal*, January 6, 1994, p. A14; and "Reno Seeks to Speed Up Release of Some Documents," *The Wall Street Journal*, February 4, 1994, p. A12. See also Edward Greer, "There Goes FOIA," *The Progressive*, 54 (September 1990), 16–17; Teresa Simmons, "Banking On Secrecy: With Our Banks About to Go the Way of Our S&Ls, It's Time We Made the Freedom of Information Act Cover Financial Institutions, Too," *Washington Monthly*, 22 (December 1990), 31–37; "Weight of the Evidence," *Editor & Publisher*, 125 (April 11, 1992), 6; Debra Gersh, "Secrecy as Usual," *Editor & Publisher*, 125 (April 11, 1992), 12–15; and "FOIA Act Weakened by California Supreme Court," *Editor & Publisher*, 126 (July 3, 1993), 26.

21. See, among others, Gary H. Anthes, "Federal Groups Urge Openness," *Computerworld*, 24 (July 30, 1990), 89; Seth Shulman, "Freedom of Information in the Computer Era," *Technology Review*, 93 (July 1990), 14–15; and M. L. Stein, "Computers and the FOIA," *Editor & Publisher*, 123 (June 9, 1990), 16–17.

22. See Mark Fitzgerald, "Privatizing Government Secrecy: As Governments Contract Out More Responsibility to Private Business, Public Access to This Information Is Being Squeezed," *Editor & Publisher*, 126 (April 24, 1993), 36–37.

23. See Bill Kizorek, "Information Access: Is There a Balance?" *Security Management*, 35 (December 1991), 98–99; and Evan I. Schwartz, "Americans Fear Data Raiders Are Snatching Their Privacy," *Business Week*, December 21, 1992, 860.

24. See Gordon P. Whitaker, "Coproduction: Citizen Participation in Service Delivery," *Public Administration Review*, 40 (May/June 1980), 240–46. See also Jeffrey L. Brudney and Robert E. England, "Toward a Definition of the Coproduction Concept," *Public Administration Review*, 43 (January/February 1983), 59–65; and Charles Levine, "Citizenship and Service Delivery: The Promise of Coproduction," in H. George Frederickson and Ralph Clark Chandler, eds., "Citizenship and Public Administration: Proceedings of the National Conference on Citizenship and Public Service," *Public Administration Review*, 44 (March 1984), 178–87.

25. The quest for community control has its roots in the social upheavals of the mid- and late 1960s and early 1970s. See, among others, Alan Altshuler, *Community Control: The Black Demand for Participation in Large American Cities* (New York: Pegasus, 1970); and Joseph Zimmerman, *The Federated City: Community Control in Large Cities* (New York: St. Martin's, 1972).

26. For a broad-ranging assessment of organized citizen activity, see Harry C. Boyte, *The Backyard Revolution: Understanding the New Citizen Movement* (Philadelphia: Temple University Press, 1980). The redlining and uranium mining cases are discussed at

length in Boyte's work. See also, Neil S. Mayer, *Neighborhood Organizations and Community Development: Making Revitalization Work* (Washington, D.C.: The Urban Institute Press, 1984); Harry C. Boyte, Heather Booth, and Steve Max, eds., *Citizen Action and the New Populism* (Philadelphia: Temple University Press, 1986); Sarah F. Liebschutz, "Neighborhood Revitalization in the United States: The Decentralization Dynamic," *Public Administration Quarterly*, 14 (Spring 1990), 86–107; and Frances Moore Lappe and Paul Martin Du Bois, *The Quickening of America: Rebuilding Our Nation, Remaking Our Lives* (San Francisco: Jossey-Bass, 1994); and Lucy Brewer, *Public Works Administration: Current Public Policy Perspectives* (Thousand Oaks, Calif.: Sage Publications: 1997).

27. Rosenbaum, "The Paradoxes of Public Participation," p. 373 (emphasis added).

28. Roscoe C. Martin, *Grass Roots* (University, Ala.: University of Alabama Press, 1957).

29. The description comes from a speech by U.S. Senator Daniel Patrick Moynihan (D-New York), delivered at Syracuse University, May 8, 1969; cited in Harold Seidman and Robert Gilmour, *Politics, Position, and Power: From the Positive to the Regulatory States*, 4th ed. (New York: Oxford University Press, 1986), pp. 207–08.

30. See Mary Grisez Kweit and Robert W. Kweit, *Implementing Citizen Participation in a Bureaucratic Society: A Contingency Approach* (New York: Praeger, 1982).

31. For other perspectives on various aspects of citizen participation, see Steven M. Neuse, "From Grass Roots to Citizen Participation: Where We've Been and Where We Are Now," *Public Administration Quarterly*, 7 (Fall 1983), 294–309; Robert M. O'Brien, Michael Clarke, and Sheldon Kamieniecki, "Open and Closed Systems of Decision Making: The Case of Toxic Waste Management," *Public Administration Review*, 44 (July/August 1984), 334–40; Curtis Ventriss, "Emerging Perspectives on Citizen Participation," *Public Administration Review*, 45 (May/June 1985), 433–40; Ned Crosby, Janet M. Kelly, and Paul Schaefer, "Citizens Panels: A New Approach to Citizen Participation," *Public Administration Review*, 46 (March/April 1986), 170–78.

32. This discussion relies in part on Eimicke, *Public Administration in a Democratic Context*, pp. 33–44.

33. Redford, *Democracy in the Administrative State*, p. 44.

34. Ibid., p. 69 (emphasis added).

35. Thompson, "Bureaucracy in a Democratic Society," p. 207 (emphasis added).

36. See, among others, Brian J. Cook, "The Representative Function of Bureaucracy: Public Administration in Constitutive Perspective," *Administration & Society*, 23 (February 1992), 403–29, and Fred W. Riggs, "Bureaucracy and the Constitution," *Public Administration Review*, 54 (January/February 1994), 65–72.

37. Joel D. Aberbach and Bert A. Rockman, "From Nixon's Problem to Reagan's Achievement: The Federal Executive Reexamined," in Larry Berman, *Looking Back on the Reagan Presidency* (Baltimore and London: The Johns Hopkins University Press, 1990), pp. 175–94, at p. 192.

38. One recent study examined what effects of representativeness could be observed in government policy and administration. See Kenneth J. Meier and Joseph Stewart Jr., "The Impact of Representative Bureaucracies: Educational Systems and Public Policies," *American Review of Public Administration*, 22 (September 1992), 157–71.

39. After each decennial (ten-year) census, the U.S. Bureau of the Census makes available many volumes of data that illuminate the changes in American society. This section relies on summary treatments of census data found in Theodore H. White's *The Making of the President 1960* (New York: Atheneum, 1961), Chapter 8, "Retrospect on

Yesterday's Future," and *The Making of the President 1972* (New York: Atheneum, 1973), Chapter 6, "The Web of Numbers"; President's Commission for a National Agenda for the Eighties, *A National Agenda for the Eighties* (New York: New American Library, 1981), Chapter 2, "The Demographic Background: Toward a Portrait of America in the Eighties"; various reports published in the mid- and late 1980s by the U.S. Bureau of the Census, Department of Commerce; and summary data published in the 1990 U.S. Census of Population.

40. See, for examples, Barry Bozeman and Dianne Rahm, "The Explosion of Technology," in James L. Perry, ed., *Handbook of Public Administration* (San Francisco: Jossey-Bass, 1989), pp. 54–67; Richard R. Davis, *The Web of Politics: The Internet's Impact on the American Political System* (New York: Oxford University Press, 1999); G. David Garson, *Information Technology and Computer Applications in Public Administration: Issues and Trends* (Hershey, Pa.: Idea Group Publishing, 1999); Kevin A. Hill and John E. Hughes, *Cyberpolitics: Citizen Activism in the Age of the Internet* (Lanham, Md.: Rowland and Littlefield, 1998); Wayne Rash Jr., *Politics on the Nets: Wiring the Political System* (New York: W.H. Freeman, 1997).

41. See Alvin Toffler, *Power Shift: Knowledge, Wealth, and Violence at the Edge of the Twenty-First Century* (New York: Bantam, 1990).

Chapter 3: Bureaucratic Politics and Bureaucratic Power

1. See Allan W. Lerner and John Wanat, "Fuzziness and Bureaucracy," *Public Administration Review*, 43 (November/December 1983), 500–09. This "fuzziness" and its consequences (among other factors) prompt administrators to nurture favorable ties with legislatures as institutions and with individual legislators.

2. Norton E. Long, "Power and Administration," *Public Administration Review*, 9 (Autumn 1949), 257–64, at p. 258.

3. Ibid., pp. 258–59.

4. Ibid., p. 259.

5. Lerner and Wanat, "Fuzziness and Bureaucracy," p. 502.

6. Matthew Holden, "Imperialism in Bureaucracy," *American Political Science Review*, 60 (December 1966), 943–51, at p. 951. (emphasis added).

7. Francis E. Rourke, *Bureaucracy, Politics, and Public Policy*, 3rd ed. (Boston: Little, Brown, 1984).

8. See Anthony Downs, *Inside Bureaucracy* (1967. Reprint Prospect Heights, Ill.: Waveland Press, 1994), Chapter 10, especially pp. 118–27; and Martin Landau, "Redundancy, Rationality, and the Problem of Duplication and Overlap," *Public Administration Review*, 29 (July/August 1969), 346–58.

9. Rourke, *Bureaucracy, Politics, and Public Policy*, p. 94.

10. Albert Gore, *Common Sense Government: Works Better and Costs Less* (New York: Random House, 1995).

11. For an introduction to the theoretical roles and political activities of interest groups in American politics, see Jeffrey M. Berry, *The Interest Group Society*, 3rd ed. (New York: Longman, 1997); Allan J. Cigler and Burdett A. Loomis, *Interest Group Politics*, 5th ed. (Washington, D.C.: CQ Press, 1998); V. O. Key Jr., *Politics, Parties, and Pressure Groups*, 5th ed. (New York: Crowell, 1964), especially Chapters 2–6; Lester W. Milbrath, *The Washington Lobbyists* (Chicago: Rand McNally, 1963). Interactions between agencies and interest groups are examined (with other topics) by Glenn

Abney in "Lobbying by the Insiders: Parallels of State Agencies and Interest Groups," *Public Administration Review*, 48 (September/October 1988), 911–17; by Jeanne Nienaber Clarke and Daniel McCool in *Staking Out the Terrain: Power Differentials among Natural Resource Management Agencies* (Albany, N.Y.: State University of New York Press, 1985); by Martha Derthick in *Agency Under Stress: The Social Security Administration in American Government* (Washington, D. C.: The Brookings Institution, 1990); Todd Kunioka and Lawrence S. Rothenberg, "The Politics of Bureaucratic Competition: The Case of Natural Resource Policy," *Journal of Policy Analysis and Management*, 12 (Fall 1993), 700–25.

12. The literature on subsystem politics includes Emmette S. Redford, *Democracy in the Administrative State* (New York: Oxford University Press, 1969), especially Chapter 4; Ernest S. Griffith and Francis R. Valeo, *Congress: Its Contemporary Role*, 5th ed. (New York: New York University Press, 1975); and A. Lee Fritschler and James M. Hoefler, *Smoking and Politics: Policy Making and the Federal Bureaucracy*, 5th ed. (Upper Saddle River, N.J.: Prentice-Hall, 1995).

13. This discussion relies on Roger H. Davidson and Walter J. Oleszek, *Congress and Its Members*, 3rd ed. (Washington, D.C.: CQ Press, 1990), pp. 212–14, and "Members' Health Concerns Now Center on Turf Wars," *Congressional Quarterly Weekly Report*, 51 (October 9, 1993), 2734–35.

14. Our thanks to an anonymous reviewer for suggesting discussion of these phenomena in this context.

15. See Hugh Heclo, "Issue Networks and the Executive Establishment," in Anthony King, ed., *The New American Political System* (Washington, D.C.: American Enterprise Institute for Public Policy Research, 1978), at pp. 103.

16. Ibid., p. 104.

17. *Bloomington-Normal Pantagraph*, July 2, 1980, p. A-4 (emphasis added).

18. See, among others, Joseph P. Harris, *Congressional Control of Administration* (Washington, D.C.: The Brookings Institution, 1964), and Allen Schick, "Politics through Law: Congressional Limitations on Executive Discretion," in Anthony King, ed., *Both Ends of the Avenue: The Presidency, the Executive Branch, and Congress in the 1980s* (Washington, D.C.: American Enterprise Institute for Public Policy Research, 1983), pp. 154–84, especially pp. 170–79.

19. Lawrence C. Dodd and Richard L. Schott, *Congress and the Administrative State* (New York: Wiley, 1979), p. 183. This book (especially Chapters 5 and 6) is one of the best studies of change within Congress and its relationship to changes in legislative oversight. In this regard, see also Morris P. Fiorina, *Congress: Keystone of the Washington Establishment*, 2nd ed. (New Haven: Yale University Press, 1989), especially Chapters 5 and 7. The development of the constituent-service emphasis is examined in John R. Johannes, *To Serve the People: Congress and Constituency Service* (Lincoln, Neb.: University of Nebraska Press, 1984); More generally, see Douglas Arnold, *Congress and the Bureaucracy* (New Haven, Conn.: Yale University Press, 1980); David Mayhew, *Congress: The Electoral Connection* (New Haven, Conn.: Yale University Press, 1974); Randall B. Ripley and Grace A. Franklin, *Congress, the Bureaucracy, and Public Policy*, 5th ed. (Monterey, Calif.: Brooks/Cole, 1991); John R. Wright, *Interest Groups and Congress: Lobbying Contributions and Influence* (Boston: Allyn and Bacon, 1996); Jeffrey M. Berry, *The Interest Group Society*, 3rd ed. (New York: Longman, 1997); and William P. Browne, *Groups, Interests, and Public Policy* (Washington, D.C.: Georgetown University Press, 1998).

20. *Congressional Quarterly Weekly Report*, 42 (July 21, 1984), 1, 797.

21. See Joel D. Aberbach, *Keeping a Watchful Eye: The Politics of Congressional Oversight* (Washington, D.C.: The Brookings Institution, 1990).

22. Fiorina, *Congress: Keystone of the Washington Establishment*, p. 80. See also James Q. Wilson, "The Rise of the Bureaucratic State," *The Public Interest*, 41 (Fall 1975), 77–103, at p. 103. For a study of legislative influence on the activities of public administrators in two state governments, see Richard C. Elling, "State Legislative Influence in the Administrative Process: Consequences and Constraints," *Public Administration Quarterly*, 7 (Winter 1984), 457–81.

23. See, for example, Linda Harriman and Jeffrey D. Straussman, "Do Judges Determine Budget Decisions? Federal Court Decisions in Prison Reform and State Spending for Corrections," *Public Administration Review*, 43 (March/April 1983), 343–51; Donald L. Horowitz, "The Courts as Guardians of the Public Interest," *Public Administration Review*, 37 (March/April 1977), 148–54; David H. Rosenbloom, "Public Administration and the Judiciary: The "New Partnership," *Public Administration Review*, 47 (January/February 1987), 75–83; and Jeffrey D. Straussman, "Courts and Public Purse Strings: Have Portraits of Budgeting Missed Something?" *Public Administration Review*, 46 (July/August 1986), 345–51.

24. Horowitz, "The Courts as Guardians of the Public Interest," p. 150.

25. For insightful discussion of the relationships between government officials and the press, see, among others, Stephen Hess, *The Government–Press Connection* (Washington, D.C.: The Brookings Institution, 1984); and Charles Press and Kenneth VerBurg, *American Politicians and Journalists* (Glenview, Ill.: Scott, Foresman, 1988). A selection from Press and VerBurg's book appears as "Bureaucrats and Journalists," in Frederick S. Lane, ed., *Current Issues in Public Administration*, 4th ed. (New York: St. Martin's, 1990), pp. 225–34.

26. See Jameson Doig, "'If I See a Murderous Fellow Sharpening a Knife Cleverly': The Wilsonian Dichotomy and the Public Authority Tradition," *Public Administration Review*, 43 (July/August 1983), 292–304, especially pp. 292–94.

27. See, among others, Richard C. Elling, "Bureaucratic Accountability: Problems and Paradoxes; Panaceas and (Occasionally) Palliatives," *Public Administration Review*, 43 (January/February 1983), 82–89; John P. Burke, *Bureaucratic Responsibility* (Baltimore: The Johns Hopkins University Press, 1986); William M. Pearson and Van A. Wigginton, "Effectiveness of Administrative Controls: Some Perceptions of State Legislators," *Public Administration Review*, 46 (July/August 1986), 328–31; Mary Grisez Kweit and Robert W. Kweit, "The Reagan Administration and Governmental Accountability," paper delivered at the annual meeting of the American Political Science Association, Chicago, September 1987; Cheryl M. Miller and Deil S. Wright, "Administrative Accountability in State Government: Perceptions of Executive and Legislative Influence over State Administrative Agencies," paper delivered at the annual meeting of the American Political Science Association, Washington, D.C., September 1988; Bernard Rosen, *Holding Government Bureaucracies Accountable*, 2nd ed. (Westport, Conn.: Greenwood Press, 1989); and Dan B. Wood and Richard W. Waterman, *Bureaucratic Dynamics* (Boulder, Colo.: Westview Press, 1994); David N. Ammons, "Overcoming the Inadequacies of Performance Measurement in Local Government: The Case of Libraries and Leisure Services," *Public Administration Review*, 55 (January/February, 1995) 37–47; and William T. Gormley Jr., "Account-

ability Battles in State Administration," in Frederick S. Lane, *Current Issues in Public Administration* (Boston: Bedford/St. Martin's, 1999) pp. 123–40.

Chapter 4: Federalism and Intergovernmental Relations

1. Albert Gore, *Common Sense Government: Works Better and Costs Less* (New York: Random House, 1995), p. 18.
2. William Anderson, *Intergovernmental Relations in Review* (Minneapolis: University of Minnesota Press, 1960), p. 3, cited by Deil S. Wright, *Understanding Intergovernmental Relations*, 3rd ed. (Monterey, Calif.: Brooks/Cole, 1988), p. 14.
3. Wright, *Understanding Intergovernmental Relations*, p. 15.
4. Richard H. Leach, *American Federalism* (New York: Norton, 1970), p. 59–63. See also chapters 3 and 11.
5. Russell L. Hanson, "The Intergovernmental Setting of State Politics," in Virginia Gray, Herbert Jacob, and Kenneth N. Vines, eds., *Politics in the American States: A Comparative Analysis*, 4th ed. (Boston: Little Brown, 1983), p. 28 (emphasis added).
6. The passage quoted appears on page 25 of the decision. This decision overturned a precedent established nearly a decade earlier in *National League of Cities v. Usery*, 426 U.S. 833 (1976).
7. See Cynthia Cates Colella, "State Sovereignty and the NLC Doctrine: Was It Worth All the Effort?" paper presented at the national conference of the American Society for Public Administration, 1985; Martha Derthick, "American Federalism: Madison's Middle Ground in the 1980s," *Public Administration Review*, 47 (January/February 1987), 66–74, especially pp. 70–71; David M. O'Brien, "Federalism as a Metaphor in the Constitutional Politics of Public Administration," *Public Administration Review*, 49 (September/October 1989), 411–19; Eugene W. Hickok Jr., "Federalism's Future Before the U.S. Supreme Court," *Annals of the American Academy of Political and Social Science*, 509 (May 1990), 73–82; Charles Wise and Rosemary O'Leary, "Is Federalism Dead Or Alive in the Supreme Court?" *Public Administration Review*, 52 (November/December 1992), 559–72.
8. For a more general examination of the preemption issue, see Joseph F. Zimmerman, *Federal Preemption: The Silent Revolution* (Ames, Iowa: Iowa State University Press, 1991).
9. Russell L. Hanson, "The Intergovernmental Setting of State Politics," in Virginia Gray, Herbert Jacob, and Kenneth N. Vines, eds., *Politics in the American States: A Comparative Analysis*, 4th ed. (Boston: Little, Brown, 1983), p. 35.
10. For a comprehensive overview of national government aid to cities prior to the 1960s, see Roscoe C. Martin, *The Cities and the Federal System* (New York: Atherton, 1965).
11. Michael D. Reagan and John G. Sanzone, *The New Federalism*, 2nd ed. (New York: Oxford University Press, 1981), p. 33.
12. See, in this connection, Donald F. Kettl, *Government by Proxy: (Mis?) Managing Federal Programs* (Washington, D.C.: Congressional Quarterly Press, 1988).
13. Reagan and Sanzone, *The New Federalism*, pp. 37–43. See also Parris N. Glendening and Mavis Mann Reeves, *Pragmatic Federalism: An Intergovernmental View of American Government*, 2nd ed. (Pacific Palisades, Calif.: Palisades Publishers, 1984), pp. 253–56, and Carol E. Cohen, "State Fiscal Capacity and Effort: An Update," *Intergovernmental Perspective*, 15 (Spring 1989), 15–20.

14. The following description relies on Reagan and Sanzone, *The New Federalism*, Chapter 3. See also George E. Hale and Marian Lief Palley, *The Politics of Federal Grants* (Washington, D.C.: Congressional Quarterly Press, 1981), pp. 18–21.

15. This discussion relies on Arnold M. Howitt, *Managing Federalism: Studies in Intergovernmental Relations* (Washington, D.C.: Congressional Quarterly Press, 1984), pp. 27–28.

16. Ibid., p. 28.

17. Reagan and Sanzone, *The New Federalism*, pp. 125–26.

18. For further information on developments in grant funding (covering both federal and state aid), see, among others, Richard P. Nathan and Fred C. Doolittle, "Federal Grants: Giving and Taking Away," *Political Science Quarterly*, 100 (Spring 1985), 53–74; and Kevin Eddins, "Two Studies Note Federal, State Aid to Cities Declined over Decade [1983–1993]," *Nation's Cities Weekly*, 16 (September 20, 1993), 10.

19. See Daniel J. Elazar, *American Federalism: A View from the States*, 3rd ed. (New York: Harper & Row, 1984), pp. 85–91.

20. Ironically, it was under Eisenhower — a Republican president — that a systematic effort was made to define broad national goals in the late 1950s. See President's Commission on National Goals, *Goals for Americans* (Englewood Cliffs, N.J.: Prentice-Hall, 1960).

21. See James L. Sundquist, with the collaboration of David W. Davis, *Making Federalism Work: A Study of Program Coordination at the Community Level* (Washington, D.C.: The Brookings Institution, 1969), pp. 3–6. For a more recent examination of the Johnson years, see David M. Welborn and Jesse Burkhead, *Intergovernmental Relations in the American Administrative State: The Johnson Presidency* (Austin: University of Texas Press, 1989).

22. Harold Seidman and Robert Gilmour, *Politics, Position, and Power: From the Positive to the Regulatory State*, 4th ed. (New York: Oxford University Press, 1986), p. 197.

23. U.S. Advisory Commission on Intergovernmental Relations, *Urban America and the Federal System* (Washington, D.C.: U.S. Advisory Commission on Intergovernmental Relations, October 1969), p. 5.

24. Terry Sanford, *Storm over the States* (New York: McGraw-Hill, 1967), p. 80.

25. David B. Walker, "Federal Aid Administrators and the Federal System," *Intergovernmental Perspective*, 3 (Fall 1977), 10–17, at p. 17 (emphasis added).

26. See Hale and Palley, *The Politics of Federal Grants*. See also Lawrence D. Brown, James W. Fossett, and Kenneth T. Palmer, *The Changing Politics of Federal Grants* (Washington, D.C.: The Brookings Institution, 1984).

27. One illustration of this involved a decision in North Kansas City, Missouri, to build a senior citizens' center with GRS funds, while nearby Kansas City incorporated the dollars into its annual budget. When GRS stopped, North Kansas City needed only to find funding for maintenance and upkeep of the center; Kansas City, on the other hand, had to eliminate $24 million from its operating budget — and took most of it out of street lighting, an essential service that most central cities must provide to their citizens. Our thanks to an anonymous reviewer for providing this example.

28. This portion of the block grants discussion rests on the treatment of Reagan and Sanzone, *The New Federalism*, Chapter 5, and Wright, *Understanding Intergovernmental Relations*, Chapter 6. See also Reagan and Sanzone, *The New Federalism*, pp. 131–46, and Hale and Palley, *The Politics of Federal Grants*, pp. 107–11. For treatment of the CDBG program, see, among others, Ruth Ross, ed., "The Community Development

Block Grant Program," *Publius: The Journal of Federalism*, 13 (Summer 1983), 1–95, and Eric B. Herzik and John P. Pelissero, "Decentralization, Redistribution, and Community Development: A Reassessment of the Small Cities CDBG Program," *Public Administration Review*, 46 (January/February 1986), 31–36.

29. Wright, *Understanding Intergovernmental Relations*, pp. 212–13.

30. U.S. Advisory Commission on Intergovernmental Relations, *Block Grants: A Comparative Analysis* (Washington, D. C.: ACIR, 1979), p. 39.

31. This discussion of the Reagan block grants relies principally on U.S. Advisory Commission on Intergovernmental Relations, *A Catalog of Federal Grant-in-Aid Programs to State and Local Governments: Grants Funded, FY 1984*, Report M-139 (Washington, D.C.: U.S. Government Printing Office, December 1984). See also Wright, *Understanding Intergovernmental Relations*, pp. 213–16.

32. *A Catalog of Federal Grant-in-Aid Programs to State and Local Governments*, p. 2.

33. Among other sources on GRS, see Richard P. Nathan, Allen D. Manvel, Susannah E. Calkins, and associates, *Monitoring Revenue Sharing* (Washington, D.C.: The Brookings Institution, 1975); Richard P. Nathan, Charles F. Adams Jr., and associates, *Revenue Sharing: The Second Round* (Washington, D.C.: The Brookings Institution, 1977); and David A. Caputo and Richard L. Cole, "City Officials and General Revenue Sharing," *Publius: The Journal of Federalism*, 13 (Winter 1983), 41–54.

34. For further information on the more recent block grants, see, among others, Timothy J. Conlan, "The Politics of Federal Block Grants: From Nixon to Reagan," *Political Science Quarterly*, 99 (Summer 1984), 247–70; Conlan, "Federalism and Competing Values in the Reagan Administration," *Publius: The Journal of Federalism*, 16 (Winter 1986), 29–47; and Conlan, *New Federalism: Intergovernmental Reform from Nixon to Reagan* (Washington, D.C.: The Brookings Institution, 1988); George E. Peterson et al., *The Reagan Block Grants: What Have We Learned?* (Washington, D.C.: Urban Institute Press, 1986); and Wright, *Understanding Intergovernmental Relations*, pp. 213–16.

35. David Swain, "Block Grants Make Little or No Difference: A Local Perspective," *Public Administration Quarterly*, 7 (Spring 1983), 4–21, at pp. 15–17 (emphasis added). See also Robert W. Burchell, James H. Carr, Richard Florida, and James Nemeth, *The New Reality of Municipal Finance: The Rise and Fall of the Intergovernmental City* (New Brunswick, N.J.: Rutgers University, Center for Urban Policy Research, 1984); and Anthony G. Cahill and Joseph A. James, "Responding to Municipal Fiscal Distress: An Emerging Issue for State Governments in the 1990s," *Public Administration Review*, 52 (January/February 1992), 88–94.

36. U.S. Office of Management and Budget, *Special Analyses: Budget of the United States Government, Fiscal Year 1990* (Washington, D.C.: U.S. Government Printing Office, 1989), p. H-26.

37. One indication of the growing stature of state governments is the increasing interest devoted to them by scholarly observers. See, among others, Malcolm L. Goggin, *Policy Design and the Politics of Implementation: The Case of Child Health Care in the American States* (Knoxville, Tenn.: The University of Tennessee Press, 1987); John Herbers, "The New Federalism: Unplanned, Innovative, and Here to Stay," *Governing*, 1 (October 1987), 28–37; Jeffrey Stonecash, "Fiscal Centralization in the American States: Findings from Another Perspective," *Public Budgeting and Finance*, 8 (Winter 1988), 81–89; David R. Berman and Lawrence L. Martin, "State–Local Relations: An Examination of Local Discretion," *Public Administration Review*, 48 (March/April

1988), 637–41; Dennis Dresang and James Gosling, *Politics, Policy, and Management in the American States* (White Plains, N.Y.: Longman, 1989); Carl E. Van Horn, ed., *The State of the States*, 3rd ed. (Washington, D.C.: CQ Press, 1996); Deborah D. Roberts, "Carving Out Their Niche: State Advisory Commissions on Intergovernmental Relations," *Public Administration Review*, 49 (November/December 1989), 576–80; Sarah F. Liebschutz, *Bargaining Under Federalism: Contemporary New York* (Albany, N.Y.: State University of New York Press, 1991); and David C. Nice, *Policy Innovation in State Government* (Ames, Iowa: Iowa State University Press, 1994).

38. See, for example, David Osborne, *Laboratories of Democracy* (Boston: Harvard Business School Press, 1988).

39. See, among others, Catherine H. Lovell et al., *Federal and State Mandating on Local Government — Issues and Impacts*, Report to the National Science Foundation, June 1979; Max Neiman and Catherine Lovell, "Federal and State Mandating: A First Look at the Mandate Terrain," *Administration and Society*, 14 (November 1982), 343–72; Donald F. Kettl, *The Regulation of American Federalism* (Baton Rouge: Louisiana State University Press, 1983; paperback text edition, Baltimore: John Hopkins University Press, 1987); and Jane Massey and Jeffrey D. Straussman, "Another Look at the Mandate Issue: Are Conditions-of-Aid Really So Burdensome?" *Public Administration Review*, 45 (March/April 1985), 292–300.

40. Kettl, *The Regulation of American Federalism*, pp. 3–4.

41. Ibid., pp. 4–5.

42. Ibid., p. 4. See also William T. Gormley, Jr., "Food Fights: Regulatory Enforcement in a Federal System," *Public Administration Review*, 52 (May/June 1992), 271–80.

43. C. Gregory Buntz and Beryl A. Radin, "Managing Intergovernmental Conflict: The Case of Human Services," *Public Administration Review*, 43 (September/October 1983), 403–10, at p. 406.

44. Kettl, *The Regulation of American Federalism*, pp. 5–6. For details of implementation problems with the ADA, see Jay W. Spechler, *Reasonable Accommodation: Profitable Compliance with the Americans with Disabilities Act* (Delray Beach, Florida: St. Lucie Press, 1996).

45. See, among others, John Kincaid, "From Cooperative to Coercive Federalism," *Annals of the American Academy of Political and Social Science*, 509 (May 1990), 139–52; Frank Shafroth, "Senate Starts Action on Mandates; They're Listening and Taking Notes, Too," *Nation's Cities Weekly*, 16 (November 8, 1993), 1–2; Shannon Fountain, "Administration Steps Up Mandate Relief Efforts Following October Executive Order," *Nation's Cities Weekly*, 17 (January 24, 1994), 2; Frank Shafroth, "Governors Join NLC [National League of Cities] Effort to Curb Mandates," *Nation's Cities Weekly*, 17 (February 7, 1994), 14; Jeff Fletcher, "Mayors Blast Unfunded Mandates," *Nation's Cities Weekly*, 17 (February 7, 1994), 1–2; "California May Sue U.S.," *The New York Times*, 143 (February 11, 1994), p. A8; and William Davis, "Borut [NLC Executive Director] Urges ACIR to Study Effects of Mandates," *Nation's Cities Weekly*, 17 (February 21, 1994), 1.

46. For an account of one state–local conflict over mandates, see Tommy Darensbourg, "Louisiana Municipalities Secure Victory Against State-Mandated Costs," *Nation's Cities Weekly*, 14 (October 28, 1991), 4.

47. See, for example, Seidman and Gilmour, *Politics, Position, and Power*, Chapter 10.

48. See, for example, Catherine H. Lovell, "Some Thoughts on Hyperintergovernmentalization," in Richard H. Leach, ed., *Intergovernmental Relations in the 1980s* (New

York: Marcel Dekker, 1983), pp. 87–97. The realities of managing in the context of contemporary IGR are carefully examined in Howitt, *Managing Federalism: Studies in Intergovernmental Relations;* Peter J. May and Walter Williams, *Disaster Policy Implementation: Managing Programs Under Shared Governance* (New York: Plenum, 1986); and Kettl, *Government by Proxy.* A study valuable for its emphasis on positive aspects of federalism is Paul E. Peterson, Barry G. Rabe, and Kenneth K. Wong, *When Federalism Works* (Washington, D.C.: The Brookings Institution, 1986).

Other sources that examine diverse aspects of contemporary IGR as well as focusing on the future course of IGR include David C. Nice, *Federalism: The Politics of Intergovernmental Relations* (New York: St. Martin's, 1987); James L. Walker, "Federalism, the Commerce Clause, and Federal Control over Local Activities: Turning Wheat into Chaff?" paper presented at the annual meeting of the American Political Science Association, Chicago, September 1987; Thomas J. Anton, *American Federalism and Public Policy: How the System Works* (Philadelphia: Temple University Press, 1989); Janice C. Griffith, ed., *Federalism: The Shifting Balance* (Chicago: American Bar Association [Urban, State, and Local Government Law Section], 1989); Deil S. Wright, "Federalism, Intergovernmental Relations, and Intergovernmental Management: Historical Reflections and Conceptual Comparisons," *Public Administration Review*, 50 (March/April 1990), 168–78; and, also by Wright, "Policy Shifts in the Politics and Administration of Intergovernmental Relations, 1930s–1990s," *Annals of the American Academy of Political and Social Science*, 509 (May 1990), 60–72; Daphne A. Kenyon and John Kincaid, *Competition Among States* and *Local Governments: Efficiency and Equity in American Federalism* (Washington, D.C.: Urban Institute Press, 1991); Alice M. Rivlin, "A New Vision of American Federalism," *Public Administration Review*, 52 (July/August 1992), 315–20; Neal Peirce, "Federalism Reform in the 1990s: The First Bold Proposal," *Spectrum: The Journal of State Government*, 65 (Fall 1992), 44–45; and David B. Walker, *The Rebirth of Federalism* (Chatham, N.J.: Chatham House, 1995).

Chapter 5: Organizational Theory

1. H. H. Gerth and C. Wright Mills, *From Max Weber: Essays in Sociology* (New York: Oxford University Press, 1946), pp. 196–203.
2. Julien Freund, *The Sociology of Max Weber* (New York: Vintage Books, 1969), pp. 142–48.
3. Frederick W. Taylor, *The Principles of Scientific Management* (New York: Norton, 1967); first published in 1911.
4. For a humorous, first-person account of life with two other time-and-motion experts, see Frank B. Gilbreth and Ernestine Gilbreth Carey, *Cheaper by the Dozen*, rev. ed. (New York: Crowell, 1963).
5. Hindy Lauer Schachter, *Frederick Taylor and the Public Administration Community: A Reevaluation* (Albany, N.Y.: State University of New York Press, 1989). See also Robert Kanigel, *One Best Way: Frederick Winslow Taylor and the Enigma of Efficiency* (New York: Viking Press, 1997).
6. See Luther Gulick and Lyndall Urwick, eds., *Papers on the Science of Administration* (New York: Institute of Public Administration, 1937).
7. Ibid., pp. 1–46. A contemporary analysis of the foundations of these and other principles can be found in Robert E. Goodin and Peter Wilenski, "Beyond Efficiency: The

Logical Underpinnings of Administrative Principles," *Public Administration Review*, 44 (November/December 1984), 512–17.

8. The best source on the Hawthorne experiments is F.J. Roethlisberger and William J. Dickson, *Management and the Worker* (Cambridge, Mass.: Harvard University Press, 1939). See also Elton Mayo, *The Human Problems of an Industrial Civilization* (Boston: Harvard Business School, 1933), for a statement of Mayo's general approach to his research.

9. Roethlisberger and Dickson, *Management and the Worker*, p. 522.

10. See the summary of findings in Amitai Etzioni, *Modern Organizations* (Englewood Cliffs, N.J.: Prentice-Hall, 1964), at pp. 34–35.

11. See Chester Barnard, *The Functions of the Executive* (Cambridge, Mass.: Harvard University Press, 1938), especially pp. 92–94. See also William G. Scott, "Barnard on the Nature of Elitist Responsibility," *Public Administration Review*, 42 (May/June 1982), 197–201, and William G. Scott and Terence R. Mitchell, "The Universal Barnard: His Meta-Concepts of Leadership in the Administrative State," *Public Administration Quarterly*, 13 (Fall 1989), 295–320.

12. Warren G. Bennis, "Organizational Developments and the Fate of Bureaucracy," in Fred A. Kramer, ed., *Perspectives on Public Bureaucracy*, 3rd ed. (Cambridge, Mass.: Winthrop, 1981), pp. 5–25, at pp. 11–12. See also James G. March and Herbert A. Simon, *Organizations* (New York: Wiley, 1958), pp. 83–88.

13. The following is taken from Ralph White and Ronald Lippitt, "Leader Behavior and Member Reaction in Three 'Social Climates,'" in Dorwin Cartwright and Alvin Zander, eds., *Group Dynamics, Research and Theory*, 3rd ed. (New York: Harper & Row, 1968), pp. 527–53. Other studies of leadership include Fred E. Fiedler, *A Theory of Leadership Effectiveness* (New York: McGraw-Hill, 1967); Fred E. Fiedler and Martin Chemers, *Leadership and Effective Management* (Glenview, Ill.: Scott, Foresman, 1974); Philip Selznick, *Leadership in Administration: A Sociological Interpretation* (Berkeley, Calif.: University of California Press, 1984); and Robert H. Guest, Paul Hersey, and Kenneth H. Blanchard, *Organizational Change Through Effective Leadership*, 2nd ed. (Englewood Cliffs, N.J.: Prentice-Hall, 1986). See also Chapter 7.

14. See, for example, Etzioni, *Modern Organizations*, p. 44.

15. Robert Blauner, *Alienation and Freedom: The Factory Worker and His Industry* (Chicago: University of Chicago Press, 1964).

16. Douglas McGregor, *The Professional Manager* (New York: McGraw-Hill, 1967), and *The Human Side of Enterprise: Twenty-fifth Anniversary Printing* (New York: McGraw-Hill, 1985).

17. Chris Argyris, *Personality and Organization* (New York: Harper & Row, 1957), and *Integrating the Individual and the Organization* (New Brunswick, N.J.: Transaction Publishers, 1990).

18. Frederick Herzberg, Bernard Mausner, and Barbara Synderman, *The Motivation to Work* (New York: Wiley, 1959); and Herzberg, *Work and the Nature of Man* (Cleveland: World, 1966); and Rensis Likert, *New Patterns of Management* (New York: McGraw-Hill, 1961).

19. See Abraham H. Maslow, *Motivation and Personality*, 2nd ed. (New York: Harper & Row, 1970), pp. 35–58.

20. Robert Dubin, "Industrial Worker Worlds: A Study of the 'Central Life Interests' of Industrial Workers," *Social Problems*, 4 (May 1956), 136–40. See also Dubin's "Per-

sons and Organization," in Robert Dubin, ed., *Human Relations in Administration, with Readings*, 4th ed. (Englewood Cliffs, N.J.: Prentice-Hall, 1974).

21. H. Roy Kaplan and Curt Tausky, "Humanism in Organizations: A Critical Appraisal," *Public Administration Review*, 37 (March/April 1977), 171–80.

22. John M. Pfiffner and Frank P. Sherwood, *Administrative Organization* (Englewood Cliffs, N.J.: Prentice-Hall, 1960).

23. Jay M. Shafritz and Philip H. Whitbeck, eds., *Classics of Organization Theory* (Oak Park, Ill.: Moore Publishing, 1978), Introduction to Part III, "The Systems Perspective," p. 119.

24. A basic source applying systems theory to the political process is David Easton, *A Framework for Political Analysis* (Chicago: University of Chicago Press, 1979).

25. This discussion draws on James D. Thompson, *Organizations in Action* (New York: McGraw-Hill, 1967), pp. 3–24.

26. Ibid.

27. Ibid., pp. 6–7.

28. Two other excellent sources in this area are Walter Buckley, *Sociology and Modern Systems Theory* (Englewood Cliffs, N.J.: Prentice-Hall, 1967); and Daniel Katz and Robert L. Kahn, *The Social Psychology of Organizations*, 2nd ed. (New York: Wiley, 1978). See also Robert M. O'Brien, Michael Clarke, and Sheldon Kamieniecki, "Open and Closed Systems of Decision Making: The Case of Toxic Waste Management," *Public Administration Review*, 44 (July/August 1984), 334–40.

29. See Stafford Beer, *Cybernetics and Management* (New York: Wiley, 1959); Karl Deutsch, *The Nerves of Government* (New York: The Free Press, 1963); and Katz and Kahn, *The Social Psychology of Organizations*.

30. See, among others, Jerald Hage and Michael Aiken, *Social Change in Complex Organizations* (New York: Random House, 1970).

31. See Larry Kirkhart and Neely Gardner, eds., "Symposium on Organization Development," *Public Administration Review*, 34 (March/April 1974), 97–140; Paul R. Lawrence and Jay W. Lorsch, *Developing Organizations: Diagnosis and Action* (Reading, Mass.: Addison-Wesley, 1969); and Gerald Zaltman, Robert Duncan, and Jonny Holbeck, *Innovations and Organizations* (New York: Wiley, 1973).

32. See, in this connection, Harold J. Leavitt, Louis R. Pondy, and David M. Boje, *Readings in Managerial Psychology*, 4th ed. (Chicago: University of Chicago Press, 1988).

33. William G. Ouchi, *Theory Z — How American Business Can Meet the Japanese Challenge* (New York: Avon Books, 1982).

34. See, for example, Ronald Contino and Robert M. Lorusso, "The Theory Z Turnaround of a Public Agency," *Public Administration Review*, 42 (January/February 1982), 66–72; Michael E. Milakovich, "Total Quality Management in the Public Sector," *National Productivity Review*, 10 (Spring 1991), 195–215.

35. See, for example, Stephen Bryant and Joseph Kearns, "Workers' Brains as Well as Their Bodies: Quality Circles in a Federal Facility," *Public Administration Review*, 42 (March/April 1982), 144–50; James Bowman, "Quality Circles: Promises, Problems and Prospects in Florida," *Public Personnel Management*, 18 (1989), 375–403.

36. Bryant and Kearns, "Workers' Brains as Well as Their Bodies," p. 144.

37. Peter M. Senge, *The Fifth Discipline: The Art and Practice of the Learning Organization* (New York: Doubleday, 1990); Peter M. Senge, Charlotte Roberts, Richard Ross, Bryan Smith, and Art Kleiner, *The Fifth Discipline Fieldbook* (New York: Currency Doubleday, 1994); Sarita Chawla and John Renesch, eds., *Learning Organizations:*

Developing Cultures for Tomorrow's Workplace (Portland, Ore.: Productivity Press, 1994); Robert L. Dilworth, "Institutionalizing Learning Organizations in the Public Sector," *Public Productivity and Management Review*, 19 (June 1996), 407–421.

38. Communication in the small group is treated in John F. Cragan and David W. Wright, *Communication in Small Group Discussion: An Integrative Approach*, 3rd ed. (St. Paul, Minn.: West, 1991). Sources on communication theory include David K. Berlo, *The Process of Communication* (New York: Holt, Rinehart and Winston, 1960); and Daniel Katz and Robert L. Kahn, *The Social Psychology of Organizations*, 2nd ed. (New York: Wiley, 1978). Sources on communication in organizations include Gerald M. Goldhaber, *Organizational Communication*, 5th ed. (Dubuque, Iowa: Wm C. Brown, 1990); and H. Wayland Cummings, Larry W. Long, and Michael L. Lewis, *Managing Communication in Organizations: An Introduction*, 2nd ed. (Dubuque, Iowa: Gorsuch Scarisbrick, 1987).

39. See, among his other works, Marshall McLuhan, *Understanding Media: The Extensions of Man* (New York: McGraw-Hill, 1964).

40. An amusing treatment of gobbledygook can be found in James H. Boren, *When in Doubt, Mumble: A Bureaucrat's Handbook* (New York: Van Nostrand Reinhold, 1972), Chapter 2. See also Robert W. King, "Communicate Good Like a Bureaucrat Should," *The Bureaucrat*, 13 (Spring 1984), 20.

41. For further treatment of communication in administrative contexts, see Herbert A. Simon, *Administrative Behavior*, 3rd ed. (New York: The Free Press, 1976), Chapter 8; Hindy Lauer Schachter, *Public Agency Communication: Theory and Practice* (Chicago: Nelson-Hall, 1983); and James L. Garnett, *Communicating for Results in Government: A Strategic Approach for Public Managers* (San Francisco: Jossey-Bass, 1992).

42. See, for example, Harold Seidman and Robert Gilmour, *Politics, Position, and Power: From the Positive to the Regulatory State*, 4th ed. (New York: Oxford University Press, 1986), Chapter 10, especially p. 223; and J. D. Williams, *Public Administration: The People's Business* (Boston: Little, Brown, 1980), p. 226.

43. Seidman and Gilmour, *Politics, Position, and Power*, p. 223.

44. Williams, *Public Administration: The People's Business*, Chapter 10, develops these themes more fully.

45. See James L. Sundquist with the collaboration of David W. Davis, *Making Federalism Work: A Study of Program Coordination at the Community Level* (Washington, D.C.: The Brookings Institution, 1969), p. 17. The original categorization was suggested by Charles Lindblom. See also Herbert Kaufman, "Organization Theory and Political Theory," *American Political Science Review*, 58 (March 1964), 5–14, at p. 7.

46. Sundquist, *Making Federalism Work*, p. 18.

47. For other perspectives on this topic, see Allen Schick, "The Coordination Option," in Peter Szanton, ed., *Federal Reorganization: What Have We Learned?* (Chatham, N.J.: Chatham House, 1981), pp. 85–113.

48. Leonard D. White, *Introduction to the Study of Public Administration*, 3rd ed. (New York: Macmillan, 1948), p. 30.

49. Allen W. Imershein, Larry Polivka, Sharon Gordon-Girvin, Richard Chackeriam, and Patricia Martin, "Service Networks in Florida: An Analysis of Administrative Decentralization and Its Effects on Service Delivery," *Public Administration Review*, 46 (March/April 1986), 161–69.

50. Paul Appleby, *Big Democracy* (New York: Alfred A. Knopf, 1945), p. 104.

51. See Frederick C. Thayer, *An End to Hierarchy and Competition: Administration in the Post-Affluent World*, 2nd ed. (New York: Franklin Watts/New Viewpoints, 1980).
52. Warren G. Bennis and Philip E. Slater, *The Temporary Society* (New York: Harper & Row, 1968), p. 56.
53. Ibid.
54. Michael E. Milakovich, *Improving Service Quality: Achieving High Performance in the Public and Private Sectors* (Delray Beach, Fla.: St. Lucie Press, 1995).
55. Thompson, *Organizations in Action*, pp. 8–9; March and Simon, *Organizations*; Richard M. Cyert and James G. March, *A Behavioral Theory of the Firm* (Englewood Cliffs, N.J.: Prentice-Hall, 1963); and Herbert A. Simon, *Administrative Behavior: A Study of Decision–Making Processes in Administrative Organizations*, 4th ed. (New York: The Free Press, 1997).
56. See, among others, Brian R. Fry, *Mastering Public Administration: From Max Weber to Dwight Waldo* (Chatham, N.J.: Chatham House, 1989).

Chapter 6: Decision Making in Administration

1. Herbert A. Simon, "Administrative Decision Making," *Public Administration Review*, 25 (March 1965), 31–37, at pp. 35–36.
2. An extensive literature has grown up in the area of decision making, including David Braybrooke and Charles E. Lindblom, *A Strategy of Decision* (London: Collier-Macmillan, 1963); William J. Gore, *Administrative Decision Making: A Heuristic Model* (New York: Wiley, 1964); William J. Gore and J. W. Dyson, *The Making of Decisions* (New York: The Free Press, 1964); Charles E. Lindblom, "The Science of 'Muddling Through,'" *Public Administration Review*, 19 (Spring 1959), 79–88; Allan W. Lerner, *The Politics of Decision Making: Strategy, Cooperation and Conflict* (Beverly Hills, Calif.: Sage, 1976); Stephen Worchel, Wendy Wood, and Jeffry A. Simpson, eds., *Group Process and Productivity* (Newbury Park, Calif.: Sage, 1991); Herbert A. Simon, Robin L. Marris, and Massimo Egidi, *Economics, Bounded Rationality, and the Cognitive Revolution* (Brookfield, Vt.: E. Elgar Publishing, 1992); Young B. Choi, *Paradigms and Conventions: Uncertainty, Decision Making, and Entrepreneurship* (Ann Arbor: University of Michigan Press, 1993); and Herbert A. Simon, *Administrative Behavior*, 4th ed. (New York: The Free Press, 1997).
3. Anthony Downs, *An Economic Theory of Democracy* (New York: Harper & Row, 1957), p. 4.
4. Ibid., p. 5.
5. Ibid., pp. 4–5 (emphasis added).
6. Lindblom, "The Science of 'Muddling Through,'" p. 81.
7. This discussion relies on Lindblom, "The Science of 'Muddling Through'"; Anthony Downs, *Inside Bureaucracy* (Boston: Little, Brown, 1967; reprint edition published by Waveland Press, Prospect Heights, Ill., 1994); and Aaron Wildavsky, *The Politics of the Budgetary Process*, 4th ed. (Boston: Little, Brown, 1984). See also Robert A. Heineman, William T. Bluhm, Steven A. Peterson, and Edward N. Kearny, *The World of the Policy Analyst: Rationality, Values and Politics*, 2nd ed. (Chatham, New Jersey: Chatham House, 1997), esp. Chapter 2.
8. The reference is to "The Science of 'Muddling Through.'" See also Lindblom's; *The Intelligence of Democracy* (New York: The Free Press, 1965), *The Policy-Making Process* (Englewood Cliffs, N.J.: Prentice-Hall, 1968), *Politics and Markets* (New York: Basic

Books, 1977), and "Still Muddling, Not Yet Through," *Public Administration Review*, 39 (November/December 1979), 517–26.

9. Simon, "Administrative Decision Making," p. 33.

10. Yehezkel Dror, "Muddling Through — 'Science' or Inertia," in "Governmental Decision Making" (a symposium), *Public Administration Review*, 24 (September 1964), 153–57.

11. Amitai Etzioni, "Mixed Scanning: A 'Third' Approach to Decision Making," *Public Administration Review*, 27 (December 1967), 385–92.

12. Ibid., pp. 389–90 (emphasis added).

13. Ibid. (emphasis added).

14. For a thoughtful statement in defense of incrementalism in the planning process, see Sam Pearsall, "Multi-Agency Planning for Natural Areas in Tennessee," *Public Administration Review*, 44 (January/February 1984), 43–48. Etzioni has called for a reassessment of classical/economic rationality itself in a penetrating work, *The Moral Dimension: Toward a New Economics* (New York: The Free Press, 1990). See also Mary Zey, ed., *Decision Making: Alternatives to Rational Choice Models* (Newbury Park, Calif.: Sage, 1992).

15. Lawrence B. Mohr, "The Concept of Organizational Goal," *American Political Science Review*, 67 (June 1973), 470–81, at p. 475.

16. Ibid., pp. 475–76.

17. Lawrence B. Mohr, "The Concept of Organizational Goal," *American Political Science Review*, 67 (June 1973), 470–81, at p. 474.

18. See Arnold Meltsner, *Policy Analysts in the Bureaucracy* (Berkeley: University of California Press, 1976).

19. See Downs, *Inside Bureaucracy*, Chapter 8.

20. Ibid., p. 88.

21. Meltsner, *Policy Analysts in the Bureaucracy*.

22. F. J. Roethlisberger and William J. Dickson, *Management and the Worker* (Cambridge, Mass.: Harvard University Press, 1939); John M. Pfiffner and Frank P. Sherwood, *Administrative Organization* (Englewood Cliffs, N.J.: Prentice-Hall, 1960).

23. See, for example, Alexander George, "The Case for Multiple Advocacy in Making Foreign Policy," *American Political Science Review*, 66 (December 1972), 751–95.

24. Stephen K. Bailey, "Ethics and the Public Service," in Roscoe C. Martin, ed., *Public Administration and Democracy* (Syracuse, N.Y.: Syracuse University Press, 1965), p. 293.

25. "Big Losers in Decision Include Nofziger, Deaver," *Congressional Quarterly Weekly Report*, 46 (July 2, 1988), 1795.

26. Associated Press wire-service story, appearing in the *Bloomington* (Ill.) *Pantagraph*, January 8, 1989, p. A-8.

27. *Washington Post* wire-service story, appearing in the *Bloomington* (Ill.) *Pantagraph*, July 6, 1989, p. A-6.

28. *Memphis Commercial-Appeal*, July 28, 1989, p. A-2. For a broad treatment of the HUD scandals, see Irving Welfeld, *HUD Scandals: Howling Headlines and Silent Fiascoes* (New Brunswick, N.J.: Transaction Publishers, 1992).

29. See Carl J. Friedrich, "Public Policy and the Nature of Administrative Responsibility," *Public Policy*, 1 (1940), 3–24; and Herman Finer, "Administrative Responsibility and Democratic Government," *Public Administration Review*, 1 (Summer 1941), 335–50.

30. Finer, "Administrative Responsibility and Democratic Government," p. 335 (emphasis added).

31. Ibid., p. 337.

32. DeWitt C. Armstrong III and George A. Graham, "Ethical Preparation for the Public Service," *The Bureaucrat*, 4 (April 1975), 6–23, at p. 6 (emphasis added).

33. Cited by Joseph A. Califano Jr., "Richard Nixon: The Resignation Option," *The Bureaucrat*, 2 (Summer 1973), 222–31, at p. 225.

34. Ibid., p. 226 (emphasis added).

35. For further discussion of ethics in public administration, see Joel L. Fleishman, Lance Liebman, and Mark H. Moore, eds., *Public Duties: The Moral Obligations of Government Officials* (Cambridge, Mass.: Harvard University Press, 1981); Ralph Clark Chandler, "The Problem of Moral Reasoning in American Public Administration: The Case for a Code of Ethics," *Public Administration Review*, 43 (January/February 1983), 32–39; Louis C. Gawthrop, *Public Sector Management, Systems, and Ethics* (Bloomington: Indiana University Press, 1984); York Willbern, "Types and Levels of Public Morality," *Public Administration Review*, 44 (March/April 1984), 102–08; Dennis F. Thompson, "The Possibility of Administrative Ethics," *Public Administration Review*, 45 (September/October 1985), 555–61; John A. Rohr, *Ethics for Bureaucrats: An Essay on Law and Values*, 2nd ed., revised and expanded (New York: Marcel Dekker, 1989); Terry L. Cooper, *The Responsible Administrator: An Approach to Ethics for the Administrative Role*, 3rd ed. (San Francisco: Jossey-Bass, 1990); Mark Moore and Malcolm Sparrow, *Ethics in Government: The Moral Challenge of Public Leadership* (Englewood Cliffs, N.J.: Prentice-Hall, 1990); Sheldon S. Steinberg and David T. Austern, *Government, Ethics, and Managers: A Guide to Solving Ethical Dilemmas in the Public Sector* (Westport, Conn.: Praeger, 1990); William M. Timmins, *A Casebook of Public Ethics and Issues* (Monterey, Calif.: Brooks/Cole, 1990); Harold F. Gortner, *Ethics for Public Managers* (Westport, Conn.: Praeger, 1991); W. J. Michael Cody and Richardson R. Lynn, *Honest Government: An Ethics Guide for Public Service* (Westport, Conn.: Praeger, 1992); Jonathan P. West, Evan Berman, and Anita Cava, "Ethics in the Municipal Workplace," in *Municipal Yearbook 1994* (Washington, D.C.: International City/County Management Association, 1994), pp. 3–16; Evan M. Berman and Jonathan P. West, "Values Management in Local Government: A Survey of Progress and Future Directions," *Review of Public Personnel Administration*, 14 (Winter 1994), 6–23; and James S. Bowman, ed., *Ethical Frontiers in Public Management: Seeking New Strategies for Resolving Ethical Dilemmas* (San Francisco: Jossey-Bass, 1994).

36. Sources on administrative corruption include *Fraud in Government Programs: How Extensive Is It? Can It Be Controlled? A Report to the Congress of the United States by the Comptroller General*, General Accounting Office Report No. AFMD-82-3 (Washington, D.C.: U.S. Government Printing Office, November 6, 1981); Simcha B. Werner, "New Directions in the Study of Administrative Corruption," *Public Administration Review*, 43 (March/April 1983), 146–54; and James S. Larson, "Fraud in Government Programs: A Secondary Analysis," *Public Administration Quarterly*, 7 (Fall 1983), 274–93.

37. This discussion relies primarily on Jonathan P. West, Evan Berman, and Anita Cava, "Ethics in the Municipal Workplace," in *The Municipal Yearbook 1993* (Washington, D.C.: International City/County Management Association, 1993), pp. 3–16; Evan M. Berman and Jonathan P. West, "Values Management in Local Government: A Survey of Progress and Future Directions," *Review of Public Personnel Administration*, 14

(Winter 1994), 6–23; Sheldon S. Steinberg and David T. Austern, *Government, Ethics and Managers: A Guide to Solving Ethical Dilemmas in the Public Sector* (Westport, Conn,: Praeger, 1990); Harold F. Gortner, *Ethics for Public Managers* (Westport, Conn.: Praeger, 1991); and W.J. Michael Cody and Richardson R. Lynn, *Honest Government: An Ethics Guide for Public Service* (Westport, Conn.: Praeger, 1992).

38. Simon, "Administrative Decision Making," p. 31.

39. See, for example, James N. Danzinger, William H. Dutton, Rob Kling, and Kenneth L. Kraemer, *Computers and Politics: High Technology in American Local Governments* (New York: Columbia University Press, 1982); Kenneth L. Kraemer and James N. Danzinger, "Computers and Control in the Work Environment," *Public Administration Review*, 44 (January/February 1984), 32–42; and Stuart S. Nagel, *Decision-Aiding Software: Skills, Obstacles, and Applications* (New York: St. Martin's, 1991).

40. Simon, "Administrative Decision Making," p. 33.

41. An outstanding analysis of the problem of obtaining reliability in organizational communications can be found in Martin Landau's "Redundancy, Rationality, and the Problem of Duplication and Overlap," *Public Administration Review*, 29 (July/August 1969), 346–58. The argument that multiple channels of communication can increase the accuracy of messages going to the same receiver has been made by Downs, *Inside Bureaucracy*, Chapter 10. Arthur Schlesinger and Richard Neustadt have described persuasively how various American presidents have made use of multiple channels. See Schlesinger's "Roosevelt as Chief Administrator," in Francis E. Rourke, ed., *Bureaucratic Power in National Politics*, 3rd ed. (Boston: Little, Brown, 1978), pp. 257–69, especially pp. 259–63; and Neustadt's *Presidential Power and the Modern Presidents* (New York: The Free Press, 1991), Chapter 7.

42. Irving L. Janis, *Groupthink*, 2nd ed. (Boston: Houghton Mifflin, 1982), p. 9.

43. Ibid., p. 257. Public managers at all levels, in grappling with similar problems of "in-group" advice, frequently solicit the opinions of outside advisors. Although this course of action is often useful, it has its own pitfalls. See Howell S. Baum, "The Advisor as Invited Intruder," *Public Administration Review*, 42 (November/December 1982), 546–52.

44. See Downs, *Inside Bureaucracy*, Chapter 14.

45. James D. Thompson, *Organizations in Action* (New York: McGraw-Hill, 1967), p. 9. See also John Forester, "Bounded Rationality and the Politics of Muddling Through," *Public Administration Review*, 44 (January/February 1984), 23–31.

46. Aaron Wildavsky, *The Politics of the Budgetary Process*, 2nd ed. (Boston: Little, Brown, 1974), outlined concisely the nature of political rationality, pp. 189–94.

47. Ibid. (emphasis added).

48. Wildavsky (ibid., p. 190) made a similar point with regard to advocates of budgetary reform in the national government.

49. Landau, "Redundancy, Rationality, and the Problem of Duplication and Overlap," especially pp. 350–53.

50. Ibid., pp. 349–50. For an appraisal of the potential benefits of redundancy in public organizations, see Jonathan B. Bendor, *Parallel Systems: Redundancy in Government* (Berkeley: University of California Press, 1985).

51. See Michael D. Cohen, James G. March, and Johan P. Olsen, "People, Problems, Solutions, and the Ambiguity of Relevance," in James G. March and Johan P. Olsen,

eds., *Ambiguity and Choice in Organizations* (Bergen, Norway: Universitetsforlaget, 1976), pp. 24–37. The passage cited appears in the preface to the volume, at p. 8.

Chapter 7: Chief Executives and the Challenges of Administrative Leadership

1. See, among others, Louis Fisher, *The Politics of Shared Power: Congress and the Executive*, 2nd ed. (Washington, D.C.: Congressional Quarterly Press, 1987); Edward Paul Fuchs, *Presidents, Management, and Regulation* (Englewood Cliffs, N.J.: Prentice-Hall, 1988); Dennis D. Riley, *Controlling the Federal Bureaucracy* (Philadelphia: Temple University Press, 1987); Donald F. Kettl, *Government by Proxy: (Mis?)Managing Federal Programs* (Washington, D.C.: Congressional Quarterly Press, 1988); and John J. Dilulio, Gerald Garvey, and Donald F. Kettl, *Improving Government Performance: An Owner's Manual* (Washington D.C.: The Brookings Institution, 1993).

2. For an enlightening study of the Long years, see T. Harry Williams, *Huey Long* (New York: Knopf, 1969). Three useful, and contrasting, studies of Chicago's Mayor Daley are Mike Royko, *Boss: Richard J. Daley of Chicago* (New York: Dutton, 1971); Len O'Connor, *Clout: Mayor Daley and His City* (Chicago: Henry Regnery, 1975); and Milton Rakove, *Don't Make No Waves . . . Don't Back No Losers: An Insider's Analysis of the Daley Machine* (Bloomington: Indiana University Press, 1975). Political developments in Chicago after Daley's death in 1976 are examined in Samuel K. Gove and Louis H. Masotti, eds., *After Daley: Chicago Politics in Transition* (Urbana: University of Illinois Press, 1982).

3. See Thad L. Beyle and J. Oliver Williams, eds., *The American Governor in Behavioral Perspective* (New York: Harper & Row, 1972); Larry Sabato, *Goodbye to Good-Time Charlie: The American Governorship Transformed*, 2nd ed. (Washington, D.C.: Congressional Quarterly Press, 1983); Thad L. Beyle, "Governors," in Virginia Gray, Herbert Jacob, and Robert B. Albritton, eds., *Politics in the American States: A Comparative Analysis*, 5th ed. (Glenview, Ill.: Scott, Foresman, 1990), pp. 201–51; Thad L. Beyle, ed., *Governors and Hard Times* (Washington, D.C.: Congressional Quarterly Press, 1992); and Thad L. Beyle, State Government: *CQ's Guide to Current Issues and Activities 1993–1994* (Washington, D.C: Congressional Quarterly Press, 1993).

4. See Richard E. Neustadt, *Presidential Power and the Modern Presidents* (New York: The Free Press, 1991).

5. Douglas Fox, *The Politics of City and State Bureaucracy* (Pacific Palisades, Calif.: Goodyear Publishing, 1974), p. 25.

6. See, among others, Peggy Heilig and Roger J. Mundt, *Your Voice at City Hall: Politics, Procedures, and Policies of District Representation* (Albany: State University of New York Press, 1984); Glenn Abney and Thomas Lauth, *The Politics of State and City Administration* (Albany: State University of New York Press, 1986); Robert W. Kweit and Mary Grisez Kweit, *People and Politics in Urban America* (Pacific Grove, Calif.: Brooks/Cole, 1990); and Kim Hill and Kenneth Mladenka, *Democratic Governance in American States and Cities* (Pacific Grove, Calif.: Brooks/Cole, 1992).

7. Studies of presidential leadership, in particular, that deal with the interrelationships among these arenas include Frank Kessler, *The Dilemmas of Presidential Leadership: Of Caretakers and Kings* (Englewood Cliffs, N.J.: Prentice-Hall, 1982), and Bert A. Rock-

man, *The Leadership Question: The Presidency and the American System* (New York: Praeger, 1984).

8. See, for example, Glenn Abney and Thomas P. Lauth, "The Governor as Chief Administrator," *Public Administration Review*, 43 (January/February 1983), 40–49.

9. For details on government response to disasters, see Saundra K. Schneider, "Government Response to Disaster: The Conflict Between Bureaucratic Procedures and Emergent Norms," *Public Administration Review*, 53 (March/April 1992), 135–45.

10. See Fisher, *The Politics of Shared Power*, especially Chapter 6; Donald Axelrod, *Budgeting for Modern Government*, 2nd ed. (New York: St. Martin's, 1995); John Cranford, *Budgeting for America*, 2nd ed. (Washington, D.C.: Congressional Quarterly Press, 1989); Howard E. Shuman, *Politics and the Budget: The Struggle between the President and the Congress*, 3rd ed. (Englewood Cliffs, N.J.: Prentice-Hall, 1992); Aaron Wildavsky, *The New Politics of the Budgetary Process*, 2nd ed. (New York: HarperCollins, 1992); and Chapter 10.

11. See the discussion of this office in Fuchs, *Presidents, Management, and Regulation*, Chapter 4.

12. Carl W. Stenberg, "States under the Spotlight: An Intergovernmental View," *Public Administration Review*, 45 (March/April 1985), 319–26, at p. 321.

13. See, among others, Duane Lockard, ed., "A Mini-Symposium: The Strong Governorship: Status and Problems," *Public Administration Review*, 36 (January/February 1976), 90–98, at p. 96; Coleman Ransone, *The American Governorship* (Westport, Conn.: Greenwood Press, 1982); Beyle, "Governors," in Gray, Jacob, and Albritton, eds., *Politics in the American States: a Comparative Analysis*; and Beyle, *Governors and Hard Times*.

14. Terry Sanford, *Storm over the States* (New York: McGraw-Hill, 1967), p. 30.

15. Some question has been raised as to whether the item veto effectively enables a governor to restrain the growth of state budgetary expenditures. See David C. Nice, "The Item Veto and Expenditure Restraint," *Journal of Politics*, 50 (May 1988), 487–99. See also Fisher, *The Politics of Shared Power*, pp. 209–14; and "A Bush Line-Item Veto?," *Congressional Quarterly Weekly Report*, 47 (October 28, 1989), 2848.

16. There is an extensive literature on the decision-making powers of city managers. See David N. Ammons and Charldean Newell, *City Executives: Leadership Roles, Work Characteristics, and Time Management* (Albany: State University of New York Press, 1989); H. George Frederickson, *Ideal and Practice* (Washington, D.C.: International City and County Management Press, 1989); and Richard J. Stillman II, *Preface to Public Administration: A Search for Themes and Direction* (New York: St. Martin's, 1991).

17. Harold Seidman and Robert Gilmour, *Politics, Position, and Power: From the Positive to the Regulatory State*, 4th ed. (New York: Oxford University Press, 1986), p. 104.

18. Seidman and Gilmour, *Politics, Position, and Power*, p. 86 (emphasis added). See also p. 228.

19. See Hugh Heclo, *A Government of Strangers: Executive Politics in Washington* (Washington, D.C.: The Brookings Institution, 1977).

20. This generalization held true for the period 1960–1972; see Heclo, pp. 103–4.

21. Ibid.

22. Heclo, *A Government of Strangers*, pp. 144 and 148 (emphasis added).

23. See Cronin, *The State of the Presidency*, Chapter 7.

24. This treatment of the Reagan management strategy is taken from Richard P. Nathan, *The Administrative Presidency* (New York: Wiley, 1983), Chapters 6 and 7.

25. Ibid., p. 69 (emphasis added).

26. See President's Special Review Board, *The Tower Commission Report* (New York: Bantam Books and Times Books, 1987).

27. Other policy "ailments" that have been the subject of reorganizational "cures" are noted in Seidman and Gilmour, *Politics, Position, and Power*, p. 4.

28. Herbert Kaufman, "Reflections on Administrative Reorganization," in Joseph A. Pechman, ed., *Setting National Priorities: The 1978 Budget* (Washington, D.C.: The Brookings Institution, 1977), pp. 391–418, at p. 392. This discussion relies extensively on Kaufman's treatment.

29. Ibid., pp. 392–94.

30. Ibid., p. 402. For further discussion of executive reorganization, see Peter Szanton, ed., *Federal Reorganization: What Have We Learned?* (Chatham, N.J.: Chatham House, 1981), especially Lester M. Salamon, "The Question of Goals"; I. M. Destler, "Reorganization: When and How?"; and, also by Destler, "Implementing Reorganization" (pp. 58–84, 114–30, and 155–70, respectively); and Walter F. Baber, "Reform for Principle and Profit," *The Bureaucrat*, 13 (Summer 1984), 33–37.

31. John C. Donovan, *The Policy Makers* (New York: Pegasus, 1970), p. 48; Margaret Jane Wyszomirski, "The De-Institutionalization of Presidential Staff Agencies," *Public Administration Review*, 42 (September/October 1982), 448–58; and John Hart, *The Presidential Branch* (Elmsford, N.Y.: Pergamon, 1987).

32. Arthur Schlesinger Jr., *The Coming of the New Deal* (Boston: Houghton Mifflin, 1958), especially pp. 521–29 and 533–37.

33. See Anthony Downs, *Inside Bureaucracy* (Boston: Little, Brown, 1967; reprint edition published by Waveland Press, Prospect Heights, Ill., 1994), pp. 116–18.

34. See Herbert Kaufman, with the collaboration of Michael Couzens, *Administrative Feedback: Monitoring Subordinates' Behavior* (Washington, D.C.: The Brookings Institution, 1973).

35. Downs, *Inside Bureaucracy*, pp. 118–26.

36. Graham Allison, *Essence of Decision: Explaining the Cuban Missile Crisis* (Boston: Little, Brown, 1971), pp. 122–23.

37. For an interesting account of Rockefeller's tenure as governor of New York, see Robert H. Connery and Gerald Benjamin, *Rockefeller of New York: Executive Power in the Statehouse* (Ithaca, N.Y.: Cornell University Press, 1979).

38. Ralph M. Stogdill, *Handbook of Leadership: A Survey of Theory and Research* (New York: The Free Press, 1974), pp. 167–69.

39. See Fred E. Fiedler, *Leader Attitudes and Group Effectiveness* (Urbana: University of Illinois Press, 1958; reprinted, Westport, Conn: Greenwood Press, 1981); also by Fiedler, *A Theory of Leadership Effectiveness* (New York: McGraw-Hill, 1967); Fred E. Fiedler and Martin Chemers, *Leadership and Effective Management* (Glenview, Ill.: Scott, Foresman, 1974); Stogdill, *Handbook of Leadership*; Robert C. Tucker, *Politics as Leadership* (Columbia and London: University of Missouri Press, 1981); Philip Selznick, *Leadership in Administration: A Sociological Interpretation* (Berkeley: University of California Press, 1984); Robert H. Guest, Paul Hersey, and Kenneth H. Blanchard, *Organizational Change through Effective Leadership*, 2nd ed. (Englewood Cliffs, N.J.: Prentice-Hall, 1986); James M. Kouzes and Barry Z. Posner, *The Leadership Challenge: How to Get Extraordinary Things Done in Organizations* (San Francisco:

Jossey-Bass, 1987); Peter B. Smith and Mark F. Peterson, *Leadership, Organizations, and Culture* (Newbury Park, Calif.: Sage, 1988); William G. Scott and Terence R. Mitchell, "The Universal Barnard: His Meta-Concepts of Leadership in the Administrative State," *Public Administration Quarterly*, 13 (Fall 1989), 295–320; Warren Bennis, *Why Leaders Can't Lead: The Unconscious Conspiracy Continues* (San Francisco: Jossey-Bass, 1989); Rourke, Francis E., "Responsiveness and Neutral Competence in American Bureaucracy," *Public Administration Review*, 52 (November/December 1992), 539–46; Peter Block, *Stewardship: Choosing Service over Self-Interest* (San Francisco: Berrett-Koehler, 1993.

40. Fiedler, in *A Theory of Leadership Effectiveness,* discusses varieties of work situations as they relate to leadership. See especially his Chapter 7.

41. James D. Thompson, *Organizations in Action* (New York: McGraw-Hill, 1967), p. 10. This discussion relies on Thompson's treatment of the Parsons formulation; see also Talcott Parsons, *Structure and Process in Modern Societies* (New York: The Free Press, 1960).

42. Thompson, Ibid.

43. Ibid. (emphasis added).

44. Mary Parker Follett, "The Giving of Orders," in Jay M. Shafritz and Albert C. Hyde, eds., *Classics of Public Administration*, 3rd ed. (Pacific Grove, Calif.: Brooks/Cole, 1992), pp. 66–74; reprinted from Henry C. Metcalf, ed., *Scientific Foundations of Business Administration* (Baltimore: Williams & Wilkins, 1926).

45. Ibid., p. 67.

46. Fred E. Fiedler, "Style or Circumstance: The Leadership Enigma," *Psychology Today,* 2 (March 1969), 39–43.

47. Wilfred H. Drath, "Changing Our Minds about Leadership," *Issues & Observations,* Greensboro, N.C.: Center for Creative Leadership, Vol. 16 (No. 1), 1996, p. 1-4.

48. See, for example, Harry Levinson, "Criteria for Choosing Chief Executives," *Harvard Business Review*, 58 (July/August 1980), 113.

49. See Anthony Downs, *Inside Bureaucracy* (Boston: Little, Brown, 1967; reprint edition published by Waveland Press, Prospect Heights, Ill., 1994), p. 88.

50. See, for example, Stogdill, *Handbook of Leadership*, and the discussion of authoritarian leadership style in the Iowa experiment, in Ralph White and Ronald Lippitt, "Leader Behavior and Member Reaction in Three 'Social Climates,'" in Dorwin Cartwright and Alvin Zander, eds., *Group Dynamics: Research and Theory*, 3rd ed. (New York: Harper & Row, 1968), pp. 527–53.

51. Fiedler, *A Theory of Leadership Effectiveness*, p. 147. See the preceding discussion of situational factors.

52. For a case study of the importance of bureaucratic routines, see Graham Allison, *Essence of Decision: Explaining the Cuban Missile Crisis* (Boston: Little, Brown, 1971). Consideration is given to problems of innovation in, among others, Warren G. Bennis, ed., *American Bureaucracy* (New Brunswick, N.J.: Transaction Books, 1970), pp. 111–87, especially pp. 135–64; and Guest et al., *Organizational Change through Effective Leadership*. It should be noted that leadership can just as easily resist innovation desired by members as the other way around. Under the circumstance of leaders resisting innovation sought by followers, the task of "leader as director" will be considerably frustrated as leadership and followership goals grow further apart.

53. See, among others, Peter F. Drucker, *Management: Tasks, Responsibilities, Practices* (New York: Harper & Row, 1974), Chapter 38.

54. See Stogdill, *Handbook of Leadership*, pp. 365–70.

55. For more on leadership effectiveness, see Paul Hersey and John E. Stinson, eds., *Perspectives in Effectiveness* (Athens, Ohio: Center for Leadership Studies, Ohio University, and Ohio University Press, 1980); and Harry Levinson, *Executive* (Cambridge, Mass.: Harvard University Press, 1981).

56. Victor A. Thompson, "How Scientific Management Thwarts Innovation," in Bennis, ed., *American Bureaucracy*, pp. 121–33, especially pp. 123–24. See also James D. Thompson, *Bureaucracy and Innovation* (University, Ala.: University of Alabama Press, 1969).

Chapter 8: Public Personnel Administration and Human Resource Development

1. Herbert Kaufman, "Administrative Decentralization and Political Power," *Public Administration Review*, 29 (January/February 1969), 3–15. See also Chapter 2 of this book.

2. N. Joseph Cayer, *Public Personnel Administration in the United States*, 2nd ed. (New York: St. Martin's, 1986), p. 1.

3. N. Joseph Cayer, *Managing Human Resources: An Introduction to Public Personnel Administration* (New York: St. Martin's, 1980), pp. 6–11.

4. Seymour Martin Lipset and William Schneider, *The Confidence Gap: Business, Labor, and Government in the Public Mind*, rev. ed. (Baltimore, Md.: The Johns Hopkins University Press, 1987), p. 81.

5. See Frederick C. Mosher, "The Changing Responsibilities and Tactics of the Federal Government," *Public Administration Review*, 40 (November/December 1980), 541–48, at p. 543.

6. U.S. Bureau of the Census, *Public Employment in 1995* (Washington, D.C.: U.S. Government Printing Office, 1996).

7. Frederick C. Mosher, *Democracy and the Public Service*, 2nd ed. (New York: Oxford University Press, 1982), Chapters 3 and 4; Nicholas Henry, *Public Administration and Public Affairs*, 7th ed. (Englewood Cliffs, N.J.: Prentice-Hall, 1998).

8. Frederick C. Mosher, "Professions in Public Service," *Public Administration Review*, 38 (March/April 1978), 144–50, at pp. 145–46.

9. Cayer, *Managing Human Resources*, p. 35.

10. It is also true, however, that managers must find ways to deal with the pressures generated by these conflicting personnel approaches. One way to address this problem is suggested in Debra W. Stewart, "Managing Competing Claims: An Ethical Framework for Human Resource Decision Making," *Public Administration Review*, 44 (January/February 1984), 14–22.

11. See Anne Freedman, *Patronage: An American Tradition* (Chicago: Nelson-Hall, 1993).

12. See William Winter, Chair, National Commission on the State and Local Public Service, *Hard Truths/Tough Choices: An Agenda for State and Local Reform* (Albany: Nelson Rockefeller Institute of Government, State University of New York–Albany, 1993), pp. 28–29.

13. Carolyn Ban and Patricia W. Ingraham, "Retaining Quality Federal Employees: Life After PACE," *Public Administration Review*, 48 (May/June 1988), 708–18, at p. 713.

14. Ban and Ingraham point out that the "pendulum swing" from central (OPM) to decentralized (agency) examination processes is typical of historical cycles of reform

in national government personnel management. See their concluding remarks, ibid., p. 716.

15. The quote is taken from David Broder's column about Campbell, published not long after he became Civil Service Commission head. The column appeared under the headline "New Look in Civil Service," in the *Bloomington* (Ill.) *Pantagraph*, May 25, 1977, p. A-4.

16. *Report and Recommendations of the National Commission on the Public Service to the Committee on Post Office and Civil Service, U.S. House of Representatives* (Washington, D.C.: U.S. Government Printing Office, 1989), p. 38.

17. *Report and Recommendations of the National Commission on the Public Service*, p. 35.

18. "Bush Signs Order Allowing Pay Hikes," an Associated Press wire service story appearing in the *Memphis* (Tenn.) *Commercial-Appeal*, December 27, 1989, p. A-2.

19. "Federal Panel Will Urge Higher Pay for Lawmen," a *New York Times* news service story appearing in the *Memphis* (Tenn.) *Commercial-Appeal*, December 25, 1989, p. A-2.

20. This discussion is drawn from Cayer, *Managing Human Resources* (New York: St. Martin's, 1980), pp. 176–77; Lee C. Shaw and R. Theodore Clark Jr., "The Practical Differences Between Public and Private Sector Collective Bargaining," *UCLA Law Review*, 19 (1972), 867–86; and Harry H. Wellington and Ralph K. Winter Jr., "The Limits of Collective Bargaining in Public Employment," in Wellington and Winter, eds., *The Unions and the Cities* (Washington, D.C.: Brookings, 1971), pp. 12–32.

21. Cayer, *Managing Human Resources*, p. 182. See also Richard C. Kearney, *Labor Relations in the Public Sector*, 2nd ed. (New York: Marcel Dekker, 1992), p. 39.

22. Our thanks to an anonymous reviewer for this information.

23. This discussion is taken from Kearney, *Labor Relations in the Public Sector*, pp. 57–63.

24. For a discussion of developments in the 1980s, see Douglas M. McCabe, "The Federal-Sector Mediation and Labor-Management Relations Process: The Federal-Sector Management Experience," *Public Personnel Management*, 19 (Spring 1990), 103–22.

25. Cayer, *Managing Human Resources*, p. 172.

26. *Congressional Quarterly Weekly Report*, 36 (October 14, 1978), 2950. See also David Rosenbloom, "The Federal Labor Relations Authority," pp. 370–88, in David Rosenbloom and Patricia Ingraham, eds., "Symposium: The Federal Civil Service Reform Act of 1978," *Policy Studies Journal*, 17 (Winter 1988–1989), 311–447.

27. See Vice President Al Gore, *Creating a Government That Works Better and Costs Less*, pp. 134–37.

28. Alan Edward Bent and T. Zane Reeves, *Collective Bargaining in the Public Sector* (Menlo Park, Calif.: Benjamin/Cummings Publishing, 1978), p. 21.

29. Cayer, *Managing Human Resources*, p. 174.

30. Kearney, *Labor Relations in the Public Sector*, p. 67.

31. As reported in *Governing*, 7 (January 1994), 15.

32. Marvin J. Levine and Eugene C. Hagburg, *Public Sector Labor Relations* (St. Paul, Minn.: West Publishing, 1979), p. 65 (emphasis added).

33. The following discussion relies on Levine and Hagburg, *Public Sector Labor Relations*, pp. 78–85 and 93–95; Cayer, *Managing Human Resources*, pp. 178–89; Bent and Reeves, *Collective Bargaining in the Public Sector*, Chapter 2; and Kearney, *Labor Relations in the Public Sector*, Chapter 3. See also Donald Klingner, "Public Sector Collective Bargaining: Is the Glass Half Full, Half Empty, or Broken?" *Review of Public*

Personnel Administration, 13 (Summer 1993), 19–28; and Donald Klingner and John Nalbandian, *Public Personnel Management,* 3rd ed. (Englewood Cliffs, N.J.: Prentice-Hall, 1993).

34. Levine and Hagburg, *Public Sector Labor Relations,* p. 79.

35. Cayer, *Managing Human Resources,* p. 189. These comments draw on Cayer, pp. 189–91.

36. For a critique of the view that merit and collective bargaining necessarily are in conflict, see David Lewin and Raymond D. Horton, "The Impact of Collective Bargaining on the Merit System in Government," *The Arbitration Journal,* 30 (September 1975), 199–211. An answer to that critique can be found in Joel M. Douglas, "State Civil Service and Collective Bargaining: Systems in Conflict," *Public Administration Review,* 52 (March/April 1992), 162–71.

37. See Richard C. Kearney's introduction to Kearney, ed., "Public Sector Labor Relations: A Symposium," *Review of Public Personnel Administration,* 13 (Summer 1993), p. 5.

38. For one example, see Jim Armshaw, David G. Carnevale, and Bruce Waltuck, "Cooperating for Quality: Union–Management Partnership in the U.S. Department of Labor," in Kearney, ed., "Public Sector Labor Relations: A Symposium," pp. 94–107.

39. The following overview of the CSRA is adapted from James S. Bowman, "Introduction," in James S. Bowman, ed., "Symposium on Civil Service Reform," *Review of Public Personnel Administration,* 2 (Summer 1982), 1–3, at p. 1; and Lawrence S. Buck, "Executive Evaluation: Assessing the Probability for Success in the Job," in Nicholas P. Lovrich, Jr., ed., "Performance Appraisal Reforms in the Public Sector: The Promise and Pitfalls of Employee Evaluation: A Symposium," *Review of Public Personnel Administration,* 3 (Summer 1983), 63–72, at p. 63. See also, among others, Charlotte Hurley, "Civil Service Reform: An Annotated Bibliography," *Review of Public Personnel Administration,* 2 (Summer 1982), 59–90; Patricia W. Ingraham and Carolyn Ban, eds., *Legislating Bureaucratic Change: The Civil Service Reform Act of 1978* (Albany: State University of New York Press, 1984); *The Senior Executive Service,* Hearings before the Subcommittee on Civil Service, Committee on Post Office and Civil Service, U.S. House of Representatives, 98th Congress, 2nd Session (Washington, D.C.: U.S. Government Printing Office, 1984); and Rosenbloom and Ingraham, eds.,"Symposium: The Federal Civil Service Reform Act of 1978." For discussion of contemporary pressures within the Senior Executive Service, see Gerald Barkdoll and Nina Mocniak, "Strategically Managing the SES Crisis of 1994," *The Public Manager: The New Bureaucrat,* 22 (Spring 1993), 27–30.

40. Testimony of Alan K. Campbell, *The Senior Executive Service,* p. 314.

41. Whether protections for whistle-blowers have, in fact, operated as projected is open to question. See, among others, James S. Bowman, "Whistle Blowing: Literature and Resource Materials," *Public Administration Review,* 43 (May/June 1983), 271–76; "Whistleblowers," *Congressional Quarterly Weekly Report,* 47 (August 12, 1989), 2103; Philip H. Jos, Mark E. Tompkins, and Steven W. Hays, "In Praise of Difficult People: A Portrait of the Committed Whistleblower," *Public Administration Review,* 49 (November/December 1989), 552–61; and Jack Anderson and Dale Van Atta, "Whistle-Blower Hot Lines Lack Trust," *Washington Post,* July 23, 1990, p. D-8.

42. Testimony of Rep. Patricia Schroeder, *The Senior Executive Service,* p. 373. See also *Political Appointees in Federal Agencies,* testimony before the Congress of the United States by Bernard L. Ungar, Director of Federal Human Resource Management

Issues, GAO, October 26, 1989; General Accounting Office Report GAO/T-GGD-90–4 (Washington, D.C.: U.S. Government Printing Office, 1989).

43. Panel discussion on civil service reform, held at a conference honoring Alan K. Campbell, Syracuse, New York, June 19, 1993.

44. In this connection, see, among others, James P. Pfiffner, "Political Public Administration," *Public Administration Review*, 45 (March/April 1985), 352–56.

45. Bernard Rosen, "Effective Continuity of U.S. Government Operations in Jeopardy," *Public Administration Review*, 43 (September/October 1983), 383–92, especially pp. 383–86.

46. U.S. Office of Personnel Management, "Affirmative Employment Statistics" (Washington, D.C.: U.S. Government Printing Office, 1990); cited in Christopher Cornwell and J. Edward Kellough, "Women and Minorities in Federal Government Agencies: Examining New Evidence from Panel Data," *Public Administration Review*, 54 (May/June 1994), 265–70, at p. 265.

47. Cornwell and Kellough, "Women and Minorities in Federal Government Agencies," p. 265.

48. See Gregory B. Lewis, "Men and Women toward the Top: Backgrounds, Careers, and Potential of Federal Middle Managers," paper presented at the annual meetings of the American Society for Public Administration, April 1990, Los Angeles, California; cited in Meredith Ann Newman, "Gender and Lowi's Thesis: Implications for Career Advancement," *Public Administration Review*, 54 (May/June 1994), 277–84, at p. 277. Data for 1974 and 1984 were taken from *Distribution of Male and Female Employees in Four Federal Classification Systems, A Report to the Congress of the United States by the Comptroller General*, General Accounting Office Report GAO/GGD-85–20 (Washington, D.C.: U.S. Government Printing Office, November 27, 1984), Table 1.

49. U.S. Merit Systems Protection Board, *A Question of Equity: Women and the Glass Ceiling in the Federal Government* (Washington, D.C.: U.S. Government Printing Office, October 1992); as cited in Gore, *Creating a Government That Works Better and Costs Less*, p. 213.

50. See, among others, Gregory B. Lewis, "Progress toward Racial and Sexual Equality in the Federal Civil Service?" *Public Administration Review*, 48 (May/June 1988), 700–07; John Nalbandian, "The U.S. Supreme Court's 'Consensus' on Affirmative Action," *Public Administration Review*, 49 (January/February 1989), 38–45; William G. Lewis, "Toward Representative Bureaucracy: Blacks in City Police Organizations, 1975–1985," *Public Administration Review*, 49 (May/June 1989), 257–68; Mary E. Guy, ed., *Women and Men of the States: Public Administrators at the State Level* (Armonk, N.Y.: M. E. Sharpe, 1992); Stephen B. Knouse, Paul Rosenfeld, and Amy Culbertson, eds., *Hispanics in the Workplace* (Newbury Park, Calif.: Sage, 1992); and Albert Mills and Peta Tancred, eds., *Gendering Organizational Analysis* (Newbury Park, Calif.: Sage, 1992). For treatment of another dimension of public-sector diversity, see Pan Suk Kim and Gregory B. Lewis, "Asian Americans in the Public Service: Success, Diversity, and Discrimination," *Public Administration Review*, 54 (May/June 1994), 285–90.

51. "Reverse Discrimination Claim Rejected," a *Los Angeles Times* wire service story, appearing in the *Bloomington* (Ill.) *Pantagraph*, January 8, 1985, p. A-1. The case was *Bushey v. New York State Civil Service Commission*, 84–336.

52. See David H. Rosenbloom, "The Declining Salience of Affirmative Action in Federal Personnel Management," *Review of Public Personnel Administration*, 4 (Summer 1984), 31–40. Rosenbloom argues, however, that progress toward a socially representative public workforce can still be maintained even if his prediction proves correct.

53. See also Anne Freedman, "Doing Battle with the Patronage Army: Politics, Courts, and Personnel Administration in Chicago," *Public Administration Review*, 48 (September/October 1988), 847–59, and, also by Freedman, *Patronage: An American Tradition*.

54. See Anne Freedman, "Commentary on Patronage," *Public Administration Review*, 54 (May/June 1994), 313.

55. See Philip L. Martin, "The Hatch Act in Court: Some Recent Developments," *Public Administration Review*, 33 (September/October 1973), 443–47, at p. 443.

56. This discussion relies on Gore, *Creating a Government That Works Better and Costs Less*.

57. See Paul Volcker, Chair, *Leadership for America: Rebuilding the Public Service: The Report of the National Commission on the Public Service and the Task Force Reports to the National Commission on the Public Service* (Lexington, Mass: Lexington Books, 1990).

58. See, in this regard, Paul Volcker, *Public Service: The Quiet Crisis* (Washington, D.C.: American Enterprise Institute, 1988).

Chapter 9: Government Budgeting

1. Aaron Wildavsky, *The New Politics of the Budgetary Process*, 2nd ed. (New York: HarperCollins, 1992), p. 272.

2. See, among others, Jeffrey D. Straussman, "A Typology of Budgetary Environments: Notes on the Prospects for Reform," *Administration and Society*, 11 (August 1979), 216–26.

3. Wildavsky, *The New Politics of the Budgetary Process*, p. xxiv (emphasis added). Wildavsky examines the rise of budgetary dissensus in Chapters 4–6.

4. Jesse Burkhead, *Government Budgeting* (New York: Wiley, 1956), pp. 59–60 (emphasis added). See also Howard E. Shuman, *Politics and the Budget: The Struggle between the President and the Congress*, 3rd ed. (Englewood Cliffs, N.J.: Prentice-Hall, 1992), Chapter 5.

5. Burkhead, Government Budgeting, p. 63.

6. See *Budget of the United States Government, Fiscal Year 1997* (Washington, D.C.: U.S. Government Printing Office, 1996); and *Budget of the United States Government, Fiscal Year 1997: Historical Tables* (Washington, D.C.: U.S. Government Printing Office, 1995). An intriguing examination of the nation's difficulties with continuing deficits can be found in Robert Heilbroner and Peter Bernstein, *The Debt and the Deficit: False Alarms/Real Possibilities* (New York: W. W. Norton, 1989). See also David P. Calleo, *The Bankrupting of America: How the Federal Budget Is Impoverishing the Nation* (New York: William Morrow and Company, 1992).

7. For an insightful study of the Federal Reserve Board, see Donald F. Kettl, *Leadership at the Fed* (New Haven, Conn.: Yale University Press, 1986).

8. Robert D. Lee Jr., and Ronald W. Johnson, *Public Budgeting Systems*, 4th ed. (Rockville, Md.: Aspen Publishing, 1989), p. 337 (emphasis added).

9. See Robert J. Samuelson, "An Economic Minefield," *National Journal*, 12 (November 22, 1980), 1969–72, at p. 1969.

10. Lee and Johnson, *Public Budgeting Systems*, p. 33.

11. Charles L. Schultze, *The Politics and Economics of Public Spending* (Washington, D.C.: Brookings, 1968), p. 8. Schultze notes (pp. 7–8) that when Alexander Hamilton was George Washington's treasury secretary, he established a central executive budget that gave broad discretion to the executive and "contained the potential for development of a centrally planned budget and a deliberate allocation of resources among competing agencies." Jefferson, however, ended that practice, opposing Hamilton's preferences for a strong central government and a strong executive within it. See also Naomi Caiden, "Paradox, Ambiguity, and Enigma: The Strange Case of the Executive Budget and the United States Constitution," *Public Administration Review*, 47 (January/February 1987), 84–92.

12. Lee and Johnson, *Public Budgeting Systems*, p. 7. This description of early local government reform efforts relies on their treatment found on pp. 7–9.

13. Ibid., p. 7. State governments have continued to be active in budgetary reforms of various kinds and with varying degrees of effectiveness. See, for example, Stanley B. Botner, "The Use of Budgeting/Management Tools by State Governments," *Public Administration Review*, 45 (September/October 1985), 616–20; and Robert B. Albritton and Ellen M. Dran, "Balanced Budgets and State Surpluses: The Politics of Budgeting in Illinois," *Public Administration Review*, 47 (March/April 1987), 143–52. Another perspective on state budgeting can be found in Joel A. Thompson and Arthur A. Felts, "Politicians and Professionals: The Influence of State Agency Heads in Budgetary Success," *Western Political Quarterly*, 45 (March 1992), 153–68.

14. Lee and Johnson, *Public Budgeting Systems*, p. 72.

15. Allen Schick, *Budget Innovation in the States* (Washington, D.C.: Brookings, 1971), p. 7 (emphasis added).

16. Allen Schick, "A Death in the Bureaucracy: The Demise of Federal PPB," *Public Administration Review*, 33 (March/April 1973), 146.

17. This discussion of ZBB relies on the following sources: Peter A. Pyhrr, "The Zero-Base Approach to Government Budgeting," *Public Administration Review*, 37 (January/February 1977), 1–8; Frank D. Draper and Bernard T. Pitsvada, "ZBB — Looking Back after Ten Years," *Public Administration Review*, 41 (January/February 1981), 76–83.

18. William Greider, "The Education of David Stockman," *The Atlantic Monthly*, 248 (December 1981), 27–54, at pp. 30 and 36. Based on interviews with Stockman, this article clearly lays out key assumptions made by the Reagan administration and by Stockman, in particular, during the pivotal first year of the Reagan presidency.

19. Stockman's view of the true nature of supply-side economics is discussed in Greider, "The Education of David Stockman," pp. 46–47. See also Shuman, *Politics and the Budget*, Chapter 8.

20. Regarding proposed budget cuts in intergovernmental aid, see, among others, "Cities, States Say Cuts in Aid Will Create an Unfair Burden," *Congressional Quarterly Weekly Report*, 43 (February 16, 1985), 291–94; and Chapter 4 of this book.

21. Executive Office of the President, *Budget of the United States, Fiscal Year 1995* (Washington, D.C.: Government Printing Office, 1994), p. 235.

22. See the *New York Times*, February 8, 1994, pp. A1, A12, and A13 for an overview of the Clinton FY 95 budget proposals. See also *Congressional Quarterly Weekly Report*, 52 (February 14 and February 21, 1994), for an extended discussion of the Clinton

budget, and *Budget of the United States Government, Fiscal Year 1995* (Washington, D.C.: U.S. Government Printing Office, 1994).

23. See, among others, J. Richard Aronson and John L. Hilley, *Financing State and Local Governments*, 4th ed. (Washington, D.C.: Brookings, 1986), and Glenn Abney and Thomas P. Lauth, *The Politics of State and City Administration* (Albany: State University of New York Press, 1986).

24. This discussion relies extensively on Lee and Johnson, *Public Budgeting Systems*, Chapter 9.

25. Lance T. LeLoup, *Budgetary Politics*, 4th ed. (Brunswick, Ohio: King's Court, 1988), p. 302.

26. Lee and Johnson, *Public Budgeting Systems*, pp. 187–88. In addition to the formal responsibilities discharged during the authorization and appropriations stages, there are opportunities for Congress to attempt to assert greater general control over executive agencies. Examples include adding "limitation amendments" to appropriations bills and enacting temporary authorizations. See Allen Schick, "Politics through Law: Congressional Limitations on Executive Discretion," in Anthony King, ed., *Both Ends of the Avenue: The Presidency, the Executive Branch, and Congress in the 1980s* (Washington, D.C.: American Enterprise Institute for Public Policy Research, 1983), pp. 154–84, at pp. 170–75.

27. Wildavsky, *The New Politics of the Budgetary Process*, Chapter 7.

28. Bipartisan Commission on Entitlement and Tax Reform, "Interium Report to the President" (Washington, D.C.: The Commission, 1994), p. 6.

29. See, among others, LeLoup, *Budgetary Politics*, Chapters 5 and 6.

30. Betts and Miller, "More about the Impact of the Congressional Budget and Impoundment Control Act," p. 114.

31. See, among others, Allen Schick, *Congress and Money: Budgeting, Spending, and Taxing* (Washington, D.C.: The Urban Institute, 1980); Donald Axelrod, *Budgeting for Modern Government* (New York: St. Martin's, 1995), Chapter 8; and Shuman, *Politics and the Budget*, Chapter 7.

32. These heightened tensions in Congress are a reflection, to some degree, of the changes in the overall context of budgetary decision making in recent years. See Schick, "Incremental Budgeting in a Decremental Age," *Policy Sciences*, 16 (September 1983), 1–25.

33. See Walter J. Oleszek, *Congressional Procedures and the Policy Process*, 3rd ed. (Washington, D.C.: Congressional Quarterly Press, 1988), pp. 67–68.

34. Axelrod, *Budgeting for Modern Government*, p. 201. This overview of the Gramm–Rudman–Hollings process draws substantially on Axelrod's discussion.

35. Craig Rimmerman, "Deficit Politics, Gramm–Rudman–Hollings, and the Deadlock of Democracy," paper presented at the annual meetings of the American Political Science Association, Washington, D.C., September 1988, p. 14.

36. Axelrod, *Budgeting for Modern Government*, pp. 201–202.

37. Quoted in Rimmerman, "Deficit Politics, Gramm–Rudman–Hollings, and the Deadlock of Democracy," p. 13.

38. For a detailed summary of revised deficit targets, discretionary spending limits, and timetables of sequestration through FY 1995, see Edward Davis and Robert Keith, *Budget Enforcement Act of 1990: A Brief Summary, CRS Report for Congress* (Washing-

ton, D.C.: Congressional Research Service, Library of Congress, November 1990), pp. 1–11; see also Axelrod, *Budgeting for Modern Government*, p. 203–209.

39. Wildavsky, *The New Politics of the Budgetary Process*, pp. 530 and 532.
40. See Vice President Albert Gore, *Creating a Government That Works Better and Costs Less: The Report of the National Performance Review* (New York: Times Books, Random House, 1993), pp. 13–14.
41. See, among others, Jerry McCaffery, ed., "Special Issue: The Impact of Resource Scarcity on Urban Public Finance," *Public Administration Review*, 41 (January 1981); Robert W. Burchell and David Listokin, eds., *Cities under Stress: The Fiscal Crises of Urban America* (New Brunswick, N.J.: Rutgers University, Center for Urban Policy Research, 1982); Elaine B. Sharp and David Elkins, "The Impact of Fiscal Limitation: A Tale of Seven Cities," *Public Administration Review*, 47 (September/October 1987), 385–92; Helen F. Ladd and John Yinger, *America's Ailing Cities: Fiscal Health and the Design of Urban Policy* (Baltimore and London: The Johns Hopkins University Press, 1989); and Thomas Swartz and Frank Bonello, *Urban Finance under Siege* (Armonk, N.Y.: M. E. Sharpe, 1993).
42. Former House Budget Committee Chairman James Jones (D-Okla.) once observed: "It's not the [congressional] budget process that's irritating people. It's that dividing scarcer resources is not as easy as dividing growing resources." See Oleszek, *Congressional Procedures and the Policy Process*, p. 68.
43. Schick, "The Road from ZBB," p. 180.
44. Donald Kettl, "Myths, Trends, and Traditions in the Budgetary Process," paper presented at annual meetings of the American Political Science Association, Washington, D.C., September 1988, p. 4.
45. This observation was made in Hedrick Smith, *The Power Game* (New York: Random House, 1988), pp. 658–59; cited in Rimmerman, "Deficit Politics, Gramm–Rudman–Hollings, and the Deadlock of Democracy," p. 12.
46. Wildavsky, *The New Politics of the Budgetary Process*, p. xx.
47. Schick, "Incremental Budgeting in a Decremental Age," p. 24 (emphasis added).

Chapter 10: Public Policy and Management

1. See Murray Edelman, *The Symbolic Uses of Politics*, with a new Afterword (Urbana: University of Illinois Press, 1985).
2. Theodore Lowi, "American Business, Public Policy Case-Studies, and Political Theory," in *World Politics*, 16 (July 1964), 677–715; Randall B. Ripley and Grace A. Franklin, *Congress, The Bureaucracy, and Public Policy*, 5th ed. (Pacific Grove, Calif: Brooks/Cole, 1991).
3. This discussion is taken from James E. Anderson, *Public Policy Making*, 3rd ed. (New York: Holt, Rinehart and Winston, 1984), pp. 113–16.
4. David Osborne and Ted Gaebler, *Reinventing Government: How the Entrepreneurial Spirit Is Transforming the Public Sector* (Lexington, Mass: Addison-Wesley, 1992), p. 31, Appendix A, and Chapter 10, pp. 290–98.
5. See, among many others, E. S. Savas, *Privatizing the Public Sector* (Chatham, N.J.: Chatham House, 1982); James Ferris and Elizabeth Graddy, "Contracting Out: For What? With Whom?" *Public Administration Review*, 46 (July/August 1986), 332–44; Ted Kolderie, "The Two Differing Concepts of Privatization," *Public Administration*

Review, 46 (July/August 1986), 285–91; Harold J. Sullivan, "Privatization of Public Services: A Growing Threat to Constitutional Rights," *Public Administration Review*, 47 (November/December 1987), 461–67; Ronald C. Moe, "Exploring the Limits of Privatization," *Public Administration Review*, 47 (November/December 1987), 453–60; Lyle C. Fitch, "The Rocky Road to Privatization," *American Journal of Economics and Sociology*, 47 (January 1988), 1–14; David R. Morgan and Robert E. England, "The Two Faces of Privatization," *Public Administration Review*, 48 (November/December 1988), 979–87; Ronald C. Moe and Thomas H. Stanton, "Government-Sponsored Enterprises as Federal Instrumentalities: Reconciling Private Management with Public Accountability," *Public Administration Review*, 49 (July/August 1989), 321–29; John A.Rehfuss, *Contracting Out in Government: A Guide to Working with Outside Contractors to Supply Public Services* (San Francisco: Jossey-Bass, 1989); John G. Heilman and Gerald W. Johnson, *The Politics and Economics of Privatization: The Case of Wastewater Treatment* (Tuscaloosa: The University of Alabama Press, 1992); and H. Brinton Milward, "Implications of Contracting Out: New Roles for the Hollow State," in Patricia W. Ingraham, Barbara Romzek, and Associates, eds., *New Paradigms for Government: Issues for the Changing Public Service* (San Francisco: Jossey-Bass, 1994).

6. Donald F. Kettl, *Sharing Power: Public Governance and Private Markets* (Washington, D.C.: The Brookings Institution, 1993).

7. See, for example, Lynton K. Caldwell, *Science and the National Environmental Policy Act: Redirecting Policy through Procedural Reform* (Tuscaloosa: The University of Alabama Press, 1982); Charles O. Jones, *An Introduction to the Study of Public Policy*, 3rd ed. (Monterey, Calif.: Brooks/Cole, 1984), Chapter 2, especially pp. 34–35; Amitai Etzioni, *Public Policy in a New Key* (New Brunswick, N.J.: Transaction Publishers, 1992); Gerald Garvey, *Facing the Bureaucracy: Living and Dying in a Public Agency* (San Francisco: Jossey-Bass, 1993); Marc K. Landy, Marc J. Roberts, and Stephen R. Thomas, *The Environmental Protection Agency: From Nixon to Clinton*, expanded edition (New York: Oxford University Press, 1994); and A. Lee Fritschler, and James M. Hoefler, *Smoking and Politics: Policy Making and the Federal Bureaucracy*, 5th ed. (Upper Saddle River, N.J.: Prentice-Hall, 1996).

8. Fritschler, *Smoking and Politics*, p. 49.

9. Anderson, *Public Policy Making*, pp. 97–100.

10. See, among others, Lewis G. Bender and James A. Stever, eds., *Administering the New Federalism* (Boulder, Colo.: Westview, 1986); Robert Jay Dilger, *National Intergovernmental Programs* (Englewood Cliffs, N.J.: Prentice-Hall, 1989); Paul E. Peterson, Barry G. Rabe, and Kenneth K. Wong, *When Federalism Works* (Washington, D.C.: The Brookings Institution, 1986); and David Walker, *The Rebirth of Federalism* (Chatham, N.J: Chatham House, 1995).

11. Quoted in Peter H. Rossi and Sonia R. Wright, "Evaluation Research: An Assessment of Theory, Practice, and Politics," *Evaluation Quarterly*, 1 (February 1977), 5–52, at p. 23.

12. Bertram M. Gross, "Planning: Developing Purposefulness," in Frederick S. Lane, ed., *Managing State and Local Government: Cases and Readings* (New York: St. Martin's, 1980), pp. 243–50, at p. 243.

13. See Paul C. Nutt and Robert W. Backoff, *Strategic Management of Public and Third Sector Organizations: A Handbook for Leaders* (San Francisco: Jossey-Bass, 1992); Mark

Moore, *Creating Public Value: Strategic Planning in Government* (Cambridge, Mass: Harvard University Press, 1995); Jack Koteen, *Strategy Management in Public and Non-Profit Organizations: Managing Public Concerns in an Era of Limits* (Westport, Conn.: Praeger Publishers, 1997); and Paul Joyce, *Strategic Management for the Public Services* (Buckingham, Eng.: Open University Press, 1999).

14. Gerald L. Barkdoll, "Concentering: A Useful Preplanning Activity," *Public Administration Review*, 43 (November/December 1983), 556–60, at p. 556.

15. For more information related to planning, see, among others, Leonard I. Ruchelman, *A Workbook in Program Design for Public Managers* (Albany: State University of New York Press, 1985); and Barton Wechsler and Robert W. Backoff, "Policy Making and Administration in State Agencies: Strategic Management Approaches," *Public Administration Review*, 46 (July/August 1986), 321–27.

16. Jacob B. Ukeles, "Policy Analysis: Myth or Reality?" in Norman Beckman, ed., "Symposium on Policy Analysis in Government: Alternatives to 'Muddling Through,'" *Public Administration Review*, 37 (May/June 1977), 223–28, at p. 223. See also Yvonna Lincoln and Egon Guba, "Research, Evaluation, and Policy Analysis: Heuristics for Disciplined Inquiry," *Policy Studies Review*, 5 (February 1986), 546–65; and E. S. Quade, *Analysis for Public Decisions*, 3rd ed. (New York: Elsevier, 1989).

17. See, among others, M. E. Hawkesworth, *Theoretical Issues in Policy Analysis* (Albany: State University of New York Press, 1988); Robert A. Heineman, William T. Bluhm, Steven A. Peterson, and Edward N. Kearny, *The World of the Policy Analyst* (Chatham, N.J.: Chatham House, 1990); Barry Bozeman and Jeffrey D. Straussman, *Public Management Strategies: Guidelines for Managerial Effectiveness* (San Francisco: Jossey-Bass, 1990); and Barry Bozeman, ed., *Public Management: The State of the Art* (San Francisco: Jossey-Bass, 1993).

18. Ukeles, "Policy Analysis: Myth or Reality?" pp. 26–27.

19. This discussion relies on Harry P. Hatry, Louis Blair, Donald Fisk, and Wayne Kimmell, "An Illustrative Checklist for Assessing Program Analyses," in Harry P. Hatry et al., *Program Analysis for State and Local Governments*, 2nd ed. (Washington, D.C.: The Urban Institute, 1987).

20. This discussion relies on Barry Bozeman, *Public Management and Policy Analysis* (New York: St. Martin's, 1979), pp. 267–76.

21. Ibid., pp. 269–70.

22. Bozeman, *Public Management and Policy Analysis*, pp. 308–09.

23. Ibid., p. 270.

24. Adapted from Jones, *An Introduction to the Study of Public Policy*, p. 166.

25. Jeffrey L. Pressman and Aaron Wildavsky, *Implementation*, 3rd ed. (Berkeley: University of California Press, 1984) p. xx (emphasis added).

26. See Randall B. Ripley and Grace A. Franklin, *Bureaucracy and Policy Implementation* (Homewood, Ill.: Dorsey, 1982); Walter Williams et al., *Studying Implementation: Methodological and Administrative Issues* (Chatham, N.J.: Chatham House, 1982); Robert T. Golembiewski and Alan Kiepper, "Lessons from a Fast-Paced Public Project: Perspectives on Doing Better the Next Time Around," *Public Administration Review*, 43 (November/December 1983), 547-56; Laurence J. O'Toole Jr. and Robert S. Montjoy, "Interorganizational Policy Implementation: A Theoretical Perspective," *Public Administration Review*, 44 (November/December 1984), 491-503; M.A. Levin and B. Ferman, *The Political Hand: Policy Implementation and Youth Employment Programs* (New York: Pergamon, 1985); Peter J. May and Walter Williams, *Disaster*

Policy Implementation: Managing Programs under Shared Governance (New York: Plenum, 1986); Malcolm L. Goggin, *Policy Design and the Politics of Implementation: The Case of Child Health Care in the American States* (Knoxville: The University of Tennessee Press, 1987); Richard Nathan, *Turning Promises into Performance: The Management Challenge of Implementing Workfare* (New York: Columbia University Press, 1993); and Robert C. Myrtle and Kathleen H. Wilber, "Designing Service Delivery Systems: Lessons from the Development of Community-Based Systems of Care for the Elderly," *Public Administration Review*, 54 (May/June 1994), 245–52.

27. Fritschler, and James M. Hoefler, *Smoking and Politics*, pp. 48–49.

28. Jones, *An Introduction to the Study of Public Policy*, p. 34.

29. Malcolm M. Feeley and Austin D. Sarat, *The Policy Dilemma: Federal Crime Policy and the Law Enforcement Assistance Administration* (Minneapolis: University of Minnesota Press, 1981). See also Thomas E. Cronin, Tania Z. Cronin, and Michael E. Milakovich, *U.S. v. Crime in the Streets* (Bloomington: Indiana University Press, 1981).

30. Pressman and Wildavsky, *Implementation*, pp. 99–100.

31. This discussion relies on Nicholas Henry, *Public Administration and Public Affairs*, 6th ed. Englewood Cliffs, N.J.: Prentice-Hall, 1994, pp. 161–62.

32. Peter F. Drucker, *The Practice of Management* (New York: Harper & Row, 1954).

33. Bruce H. DeWoolfson Jr., "Public Sector MBO and PPB: Cross Fertilization in Management Systems," *Public Administration Review*, 35 (July/August 1975), 387–94; Michael L. Moore and K. Dow Scott, "Installing Management by Objectives in a Public Agency: A Comparison of Black and White Managers, Supervisors, and Professionals," *Public Administration Review*, 43 (March/April 1983), 121–26; and James E. Swiss, "Establishing a Management System: The Interaction of Power Shifts and Personality under Federal MBO," *Public Administration Review*, 43 (May/June 1983), 238–45.

34. Peter F. Drucker, "What Results Should You Expect? A Users' Guide to MBO," in Jong S. Jun, ed., "Symposium on Management by Objectives in the Public Sector," *Public Administration Review*, 36 (January/February 1976), 12–19, at p. 18.

35. See Swiss, "Establishing a Management System: The Interaction of Power Shifts and Personality under Federal MBO," p. 239.

36. Drucker, "What Results Should You Expect? A Users' Guide to MBO," p. 13.

37. Frank P. Sherwood and William J. Page Jr., "MBO and Public Management," in Jong S. Jun, ed., "Symposium on Management by Objectives in the Public Sector," *Public Administration Review*, 36 (January/February 1976), 5–12, at p. 9.

38. See, among others, Stephen K. Bailey and Edith K. Mosher, *ESEA: The Office of Education Administers a Law* (Syracuse, N.Y.: Syracuse University Press, 1968); Jerome T. Murphy, "Title I of ESEA: The Politics of Implementing Federal Education Reform," *Harvard Educational Review*, 41 (February 1971), 35–63; and Milbrey W. McLaughlin, *Evaluation and Reform: The Elementary and Secondary Education Act of 1965/Title I* (Cambridge, Mass.: Ballinger, 1975).

39. Bailey and Mosher, *ESEA*, p. 3.

40. Murphy, "Title I of ESEA," pp. 35-36 (emphasis added).

41. Ibid., p. 43.

42. Joseph S. Wholey, "The Role of Evaluation and the Evaluator in Improving Public Programs," *Public Administration Review*, 36 (November/December 1976), 679–83, at p. 680.

43. Ibid., p. 681.

44. Donald T. Campbell, "Reforms as Experiments," *American Psychologist*, 24 (April 1969), 409–29, at p. 419 (emphasis added).

45. See Thomas R. Dye, *Understanding Public Policy*, 7th ed. (Englewood Cliffs, N.J.: Prentice-Hall, 1992), pp. 354–55; and Charles Jones, *An Introduction to the Study of Public Policy*, Chapter 9. See also Joseph S. Wholey, *Evaluation and Effective Public Management* (Boston: Little, Brown, 1983); Steven Cohen, *The Effective Public Manager: Achieving Success in Government* (San Francisco: Jossey-Bass, 1988); and Peter H. Rossi and Howard E. Freeman, *Evaluation: A Systematic Approach*, 4th ed. (Newbury Park, Calif.: Sage, 1989).

46. Jones, *An Introduction to the Study of Public Policy*, p. 199.

47. This discussion of evaluation designs is taken from Harry P. Hatry, Richard E. Winnie, and Donald M. Fisk, *Practical Program Evaluation for State and Local Governments*, 2nd ed. (Washington, D.C.: The Urban Institute, 1981), Chapter 3.

48. See, for example, Donald T. Campbell and Julian C. Stanley, *Experimental and Quasi-Experimental Designs for Research*, 2nd ed. (Chicago: Rand McNally, 1966), especially pp. 23 and 25; and Kenneth J. Meier and Jeffrey L. Brudney, *Applied Statistics for Public Adminstration*, 4th ed. (Fort Worth, Tex: Harcourt Brace, Jovanovich, 1997), pp.143–54.

49. Murphy, "Title I of ESEA," pp. 41–43.

50. James Q. Wilson, "On Pettigrew and Armor," *The Public Interest*, 31 (Spring 1973), 132–34.

51. Murphy, "Title I of ESEA," p. 43 (emphasis added).

52. Jones, *An Introduction to the Study of Public Policy*, pp. 218–24. See also E. J. Meeham, *The Quality of Federal Public Housing: Programmed Failure in Public Housing* (Columbia: University of Missouri Press, 1979); Beverly A. Cigler and Michael L. Vasu, "Housing and Public Policy in America," *Public Administration Review*, 42 (January/February 1982), 90–96; and Robert W. Kweit and Mary Grisez Kweit, *People and Politics in Urban America* (Pacific Grove, Calif.: Brooks/Cole, 1990), Chapter 14, pp. 324–31.

53. Larry Polivka and Laurey T. Stryker, "Program Evaluation and the Policy Process in State Government: An Effective Linkage," *Public Administration Review*, 43 (May/June 1983), 255–59, at p. 258 (emphasis added).

54. Campbell, "Reforms as Experiments," pp. 409–10 (emphasis added).

55. Ibid., p. 410 (emphasis added).

56. Martin A. Strosberg and Joseph S. Wholey, "Evaluability Assessment: From Theory to Practice in the Department of Health and Human Services," *Public Administration Review*, 43 (January/February 1983), 66–71, at p. 66 (emphasis added). See also Ruchelman, *A Workbook in Program Design for Public Managers*.

57. Other useful sources on program and policy evaluation include "Mini-Symposium on Program Evaluation — The Human Factor," *Public Administration Review*, 44 (November/December 1984), 525–38; Theodore H. Poister, "Linking Program Planning, Evaluation, and Management: Will It Ever Happen?" *Public Administration Review*, 46 (March/April 1986), 179–83; and Dennis Palumbo, ed., *The Politics of Program Evaluation* (Newbury Park, Calif.: Sage, 1987).

58. Edward K Hamilton, "Productivity: The New York City Approach," in Chester A. Newland, ed., "Symposium on Productivity in Government," *Public Administration Review*, 32 (November/December 1972), 739–850, at pp. 784–95. See also John Matzer Jr., ed., *Productivity Improvement Techniques: Creative Approaches for Local Gov-*

ernment (Washington, D.C.: International City Management Association, 1986); Robert O. Brinkerhoff and Dennis E. Dressler, *Productivity Measurement: A Guide for Managers and Evaluators* (Newbury Park, Calif.: Sage, 1989); and Deborah Cutchin, "Municipal Executive Productivity: Lessons from New Jersey," *Public Productivity and Management Review*, 13 (Spring, 1990), 245–70. For discussion of productivity from other perspectives, see Stephen Worchel, Wendy Wood, and Jeffry A. Simpson, eds., *Group Process and Productivity* (Newbury Park, Calif.: Sage, 1991); and Mary Ellen Guy, "Workplace Productivity and Gender Issues," *Public Administration Review*, 53 (May/June 1993), 279–82.

59. Jeff Leeds, "Federal Benefits to Be Available at ATM Terminals," a *Los Angeles Times* news service story appearing in the *Miami Herald*, June 1, 1994, p. 3.

60. Donald F. Kettl, "Beyond the Rhetoric of Reinvention: Driving Themes of the Clinton Administration's Management Reforms," *Governance*, 7 (July 1994), 307–14.

61. Robert S. Kravchuk and Ronald W. Schack, "Designing Effective Performance-Measurement under the Government Performance and Results Act of 1993," *Public Administration Review*, 56, (July/August, 1996), 348–59.

62. See, among others, Michael Weir, "Efficiency Measurement in Government," *The Bureaucrat*, 13 (Summer 1984), 38–42; Thomas J. Cook, ed., "Symposium: Performance Measurement in Public Agencies," *Policy Studies Review*, 6 (August 1986), 61–170; George Downs and Patrick Larkey, *The Search for Government Efficiency: From Hubris to Helplessness* (New York: Random House, 1986); and James E. Swiss, *Public Management Systems* (Englewood Cliffs, N.J.: Prentice-Hall, 1991).

63. David Carr and Ian Littman, *Excellence in Government: Total Quality Management in the 1990s* (Arlington, Va.: Coopers and Lybrand, 1990); Michael E. Milakovich, "Enhancing the Quality and Productivity of State and Local Government," *National Civic Review*, 79 (May/June 1990), 266–77; Milakovich, "Total Quality Management for Public Sector Productivity Improvement," *Public Productivity and Management Review*, 14 (Fall 1990), 19–32; Milakovich, "Total Quality Management in the Public Sector," *National Productivity Review*, 10 (Spring 1991), 195–215; Ronald J. Stupak, "Driving Forces for Quality Improvement in the 1990s," *The Public Manager: The New Bureaucrat*, 22 (Spring 1993), 32; Milakovich, "Leadership for Public Service Quality Management," *The Public Manager*, 22 (Fall 1993), 49–52; and James Bowman, "At Last, an Alternative to Performance Appraisal: Total Quality Management," *Public Administration Review*, 54 (March/April, 1994), 129–36.

64. James E. Swiss, "Adapting Total Quality Management (TQM) to Government," *Public Administration Review*, 52 (July/ August 1992), 356–62. For other critical reviews of TQM, see Steven Cohen and Ronald Brand, *Total Quality Management in Government: A Practical Guide for the Real World* (San Francisco: Jossey-Bass, 1993); Albert C. Hyde, "Barriers in Implementing Quality Management," *The Public Manager: The New Bureaucrat*, 22 (Spring 1993), 33; and Laura A. Wilson and Robert F. Durant, "Evaluating TQM: The Case for a Theory-Driven Approach," *Public Administration Review*, 54 (March/April 1994), 137–47.

65. William V. Rago, "Adapting Total Quality Management (TQM) to Government: Another Point of View," *Public Administration Review*, 54 (January/February 1994), 61–65; and Joseph Sensenbrenner, "Quality Comes to City Hall," *Harvard Business Review*, 69 (March/April 1991), 64–75.

66. Robert S. Kravchuk and Robert Leighton, "Implementing Total Quality Management in the States," *Public Productivity and Management Review*, 17 (Fall 1993), 71–82;

and Evan Berman, Michael E. Milakovich, and Jonathan P. West, "Implementing TQM in the States," *Spectrum: The Journal of State Government*, 67 (Spring 1994), 6–13.

67. Jonathan P. West, Evan Berman, and Michael E. Milakovich, "Total Quality Management in Local Government," *Municipal Yearbook* 1994 (Washington, D.C.: International City/County Management Association, 1994), pp. 14–26.

68. Stanley A. Brown, *Total Quality Service: How Organizations Use It to Create a Competitive Advantage* (Englewood Cliffs, N.J.: Prentice-Hall, 1992); Ronald Gilbert, *The TQS Factor and You* (Boca Raton, Fla.: Business Performance Publications, 1992); and Michael E. Milakovich, *Improving Service Quality* (Delray Beach, Fla.: St. Lucie Press, 1995).

69. Paul Volcker, Chair, *Leadership for America: Rebuilding the Public Service: The Report of the National Commission on the Public Service and the Task Force Reports to the National Commission on the Public Service* (Lexington, Mass: Lexington Books, 1990); William Winter, Chair, National Commission on the State and Local Public Service, *Hard Truths/Tough Choices: An Agenda for State and Local Reform* (Albany: Nelson Rockefeller Institute of Government, State University of New York-Albany, 1993); Vice President Albert Gore Jr., *From Red Tape to Results: Creating a Government That Works Better and Costs Less — Report of the National Performance Review* (New York: Times Books, Random House, 1993). Numerous other studies and reports have also focused on many of the same questions addressed by these commissions. See, for example, Patricia W. Ingraham and Donald F. Kettl, eds., *Issues for the American Public Service* (Chatham, N.J.: Chatham House, 1992); Donald F. Kettl, John J. Dilulio, Jr., and Gerald Garvey, *Improving Government Performance: An Owner's Manual* (Washington, D.C.: The Brookings Institution, 1993); Frank J. Thompson, ed., *Revitalizing the State and Local Public Service: Strengthening Performance, Accountability and Citizen Confidence* (San Francisco: Jossey-Bass, 1993); and John J. Dilulio, Jr., ed., *Deregulating the Public Service: Can Government Be Improved?* (Washington, D.C.: The Brookings Institution, 1994).

70. "Social Security Tops in Customer Service," Dalbar Financial Services, Inc., Boston, Mass., press release, May 3, 1995.

71. For an elaboration of this debate, see James H. Svara, "Reforming or Dismantling Government?" *Public Administration Review*, Vol. 56 (July/August 1996), 400–406.

72. Gore, *National Performance Review*, p. 17. Like TQM, the Report of the NPR — as well as the whole concept of reinventing government — has been subjected to some sharp criticism. See, among others, Charles Goodsell, "Re-Invent Government, or Re-Discover It?" *Public Administration Review*, 53 (January/February 1993), 85–87; John J. Dilulio Jr., "Reinventing the Dinosaur?" *Brookings Review*, 11 (Fall 1993), 5; David Segal, "What's Wrong with the Gore Report," *Washington Monthly*, 25 (November 1993), 18–23; Ronald C. Moe, "The 'Reinventing Government' Exercise: Misinterpreting the Problem, Misjudging the Consequences," *Public Administration Review*, 54 (March/April 1994), 111–22; James R. Thompson and V. Dale Jones, "Reinventing Government: The Role of Theory in Reform Implementation," paper presented at the annual meetings of the Midwest Political Science Association, Chicago, April 1994; Rob Gurwitt, "Entrepreneurial Government: The Morning After," *Governing*, 7 (May 1994), 34–40; Donald F. Kettl, "Reinventing Government? Appraising the National Performance Review" (Washington, D.C.: The Brookings Institution Center for Public Management), CTM Report, August 1994, 94–102;

and Donald F. Kettl and John J. DiIulio, Jr., eds., *Inside the Reinvention Machine* (Washington, D.C.: The Brookings Institution, 1995).

Chapter 11: Government Regulation and Administrative Law

1. Paul W. MacAvoy, *The Regulated Industries and the Economy* (New York: Norton, 1979), pp. 17–24. See also Louis M. Kohlmeier Jr., *The Regulators: Watchdog Agencies and the Public Interest* (New York: Harper & Row, 1969), pp. 307–09; Eugene Bardach and Robert Kagan, eds., *Social Regulation* (San Francisco: Institute for Contemporary Studies, 1982); David P. McCaffrey, *OSHA and the Politics of Health Regulation* (New York: Plenum, 1982); Robert E. Litan and William D. Nordhaus, *Reforming Federal Regulation* (New Haven, Conn.: Yale University Press, 1983), pp. 43–44; Richard A. Harris and Sidney M. Milkis, *The Politics of Regulatory Change: A Tale of Two Agencies* (New York: Oxford University Press, 1989), focusing on the Federal Trade Commission and the Environmental Protection Agency; and A. Lee Fritschler and James M. Hoefler, *Smoking and Politics: Policy Making and the Federal Bureaucracy,* 5th ed. (Upper Saddle River, N.J.: Prentice-Hall, 1996).
2. Robert S. Lorch, *Democratic Process and Administrative Law,* rev. ed. (Detroit, Mich.: Wayne State University Press, 1980), p. 59 (emphasis added).
3. This terminology is consistent with the usage suggested in Kenneth J. Meier, "The Impact of Regulatory Organization Structure: IRCs or DRAs?" *Southern Review of Public Administration,* 3 (March 1980), 427–43. We are indebted to an anonymous reviewer for suggesting this clarification.
4. Fritschler and Hoefler, *Smoking and Politics,* pp. 54–55.
5. For further examination of state-level regulation, see, among others, Patty D. Renfrow and David J. Houston, "A Comparative Analysis of Rulemaking Provisions in State Administrative Procedure Acts," *Policy Studies Review,* 6 (May 1987), 657–65. Jeffrey E. Cohen, *The Politics of Telecommunications Regulation: The States and the Divestiture of AT&T* (Armonk, N.Y.: M. E. Sharpe, 1992); and Evan J. Ringquist, *Environmental Protection at the State Level: Politics and Progress in Controlling Pollution* (Armonk, N.Y.: M. E. Sharpe, 1993).
6. Morton Grodzins, *The American System: A New View of Government in the United States* (Chicago: Rand McNally, 1966), pp. 75–80.
7. William Lilley III and James C. Miller III, "The New 'Social Regulation,'" *The Public Interest,* 47 (Spring 1977), 49–61, at pp. 52–53 (emphasis added).
8. James L. Regens, Thomas M. Dietz, and Robert W. Rycroft, "Risk Assessment in the Policy-Making Process: Environmental Health and Safety Protection," *Public Administration Review,* 43 (March/April 1983), 137–45, at p. 138.
9. Ibid. (emphasis added).
10. Thomas Moss and Barry Lubin, "Risk Analysis: A Legislative Perspective," in Chester R. Richmond, Phillip J. Walsh, and Emily D. Copenhaver, eds., *Health Risk Analysis* (Philadelphia: Franklin Institute Press, 1981), p. 30; cited by Regens, Dietz, and Rycroft, "Risk Assessment in the Policy-Making Process," p. 138.
11. Regens, Dietz, and Rycroft, "Risk Assessment in the Policy-Making Process," p. 138. See also George C. Eads and Michael Fix, *Relief or Reform? Reagan's Regulatory Dilemma* (Washington, D.C.: Urban Institute Press, 1984), Chapter 5, "Social Regulation: Competing Diagnoses and Remedies"; and Leonard A. Cole, *Element of Risk: The Politics of Radon* (Washington, D.C.: AAAS Press, 1993).

12. Herbert Kaufman, *Red Tape* (Washington, D.C.: The Brookings Institution, 1977), Chapter 2.

13. Albert Gore, Jr., *Common Sense Government Works Better and Costs Less* (New York: Random House, 1995), p. 40.

14. Fritschler and Hoefler, *Smoking and Politics*, p. 108.

15. This discussion is based on Meier, "The Impact of Regulatory Organization Structure," especially pp. 440–42.

16. This description of the rule-making process is taken from *Federal Register: What It Is and How to Use It* (Washington, D.C.: Office of the Federal Register, National Archives and Records Service, General Services Administration, 1980).

17. Fritschler and Hoefler, *Smoking and Politics*, pp. 138–39.

18. Ibid., p. 66.

19. See, for example, Seymour Scher, "Regulatory Agency Control through Appointment: The Case of the Eisenhower Administration and the NLRB," *Journal of Politics*, 23 (November 1961), 667–88; cited by James E. Anderson, *Public Policy Making*. 3rd ed (New York: Holt, Rinehart and Winston, 1984), p. 160.

20. Erwin G. Krasnow, Lawrence D. Longley, and Herbert A. Terry, *The Politics of Broadcast Regulation*, 3rd ed. (New York: St. Martin's, 1982), Chapter 2.

21. Ibid., Chapter 3. For an interesting case study of regulatory politics involving the FCC, see James L. Baughman, *Television's Guardians: The FCC and the Politics of Programming, 1958–1967* (Knoxville: The University of Tennessee Press, 1985).

22. *Federal Register: What It Is and How to Use It*, p. 2.

23. See *Government Executive*, 22 (January 1990), 10.

24. The quote is taken from the second edition (1978) of *The Politics of Broadcast Regulation*, p. 28.

25. William L. Cary, *Politics and the Regulatory Agencies* (New York: McGraw-Hill, 1967), p. 4.

26. Mark V. Nadel, *The Politics of Consumer Protection* (Indianapolis, Ind.: Bobbs-Merrill, 1971), p. 29; quoted by Fritschler and Hoefler, *Smoking and Politics*, p. 12. See also William F. West, "The Growth of Internal Conflict in Administrative Regulation," *Public Administration Review*, 48 (July/August 1988), 773–82.

27. *U.S. News & World Report*, March 28, 1977, p. 49.

28. Interview with Representative (later Senator) Steven D. Symms (R-Idaho), in *U.S. News & World Report*, June 13, 1977, 51–52.

29. Interview with Dr. David T. Carr, in *U.S. News & World Report*, June 13, 1977, pp. 51–52.

30. Donald Dalrymple, assistant counsel to the House Interstate and Foreign Commerce Subcommittee on Health and the Environment, quoted in *Congressional Quarterly Weekly Report*, 35 (July 2, 1977), p. 1348.

31. "OSHA Toxic Regulations Expanded," Associated Press wire service story, appearing in the *Bloomington* (Ill.) *Pantagraph*, August 20, 1987, p. D-1.

32. "EPA Warns about Groundwater Pollution," Associated Press wire service story, appearing in the *Bloomington* (Ill.) *Pantagraph*, December 15, 1988, p. D-2.

33. "Rewards for Insider Trapping Tips," Associated Press wire service story, appearing in the *Bloomington* (Ill.) *Pantagraph*, June 29, 1989, p. D-1.

34. "Buckling Up for Work," an editorial appearing in the *Washington Post*, July 16, 1990, p. A-10.

35. "ICC Bans Smoking on Buses," Associated Press wire service story, appearing in the *Bloomington* (Ill.) *Pantagraph*, December 19, 1990, p. D-1.

36. "New Meat Label Rules Anger Industry," Associated Press wire service story, appearing in the *Bloomington* (Ill.) *Pantagraph*, November 5, 1993, pp. D-1 and D-2.

37. Steven A. Holmes, "In 4 Years, Disabilities Act Hasn't Improved Jobs Rate." *New York Times*, October 23, 1994.

38. Peter Jacobsen, "Historical Overview of Tobacco Legislation and Regulation," *Journal of Social Issues*, 53 (1997), 75.

39. A. Lee Fritschler, *Smoking and Politics: Policy Making and the Federal Bureaucracy* (Upper Saddle River, N.J.: Prentice Hall, 1989).

40. See Jacobsen, "Historical Overview of Tobacco Legislation and Regulation," pp. 79–84.

41. David Kessler, "The Food and Drug Administration's Regulation of Tobacco Products," *The New England Journal of Medicine*, 335 (13), 1996, 988.

42. "The Tobacco Settlement" *Policy.com* March 16, 1998 <http://www.policy.com/issuewk/98/0316/031698a.html>.

43. "Statement of John R. Garrison, CEO, American Lung Association on Global Tobacco Bailout," *Corporate Watch On-line* <http:/www.corpwatch.org/feature/tobacco/lung.html>.

44. Action on Smoking and Health, *Appendices to the Report of the Koop-Kessler Advisory Committee on Tobacco Policy and Public Health*, 1998 <http://www.ash.org/appendix.html>.

45. Lorch, *Democratic Process and Administrative Law*, p. 32.

46. Ibid. (emphasis added).

47. Phillip J. Cooper, *Public Law and Public Administration*, 2nd ed. (Englewood Cliffs, N.J.: Prentice-Hall, 1988), p. 6 (emphasis added); see also, Leif Carter and Christine Harrington, *Administrative Law and Politics* (New York: HarperCollins, 1991); Peter L. Strauss, ed., Todd Rakoff, W. A. Gellhorn, *Gellhorn and Byse's Administrative Law: Cases and Comments* (Westbury, N.Y.: Foundation Press, 1995); and Kenneth F. Warren, *Administrative Law in the Political System*, 3rd ed. Upper Saddle River, N.J.: Prentice-Hall, 1997), pp. 24–25.

48. Lorch, *Democratic Process and Administrative Law*, p. 61.

49. Kenneth F. Warren, *Administrative Law and the Political System*, pp. 24–25.

50. The discussions of rule making and adjudication rely primarily on Lorch, *Democratic Process and Administrative Law*, Chapters 5 and 6; and Cooper, *Public Law and Public Administration*, Chapters 5 and 6 (respectively); see also Warren, *Administrative Law in the Political System*, Chapters 5 and 6.

51. See Lorch, *Democratic Process and Administrative Law*, pp. 102–05.

52. The following discussion relies on Cooper, *Public Law and Public Administration*, pp. 119–23.

53. Lorch, *Democratic Process and Administrative Law*, p. 115.

54. Cooper, *Public Law and Public Administration*, p. 114.

55. Ibid., pp. 233–39.

56. We are especially indebted to Marla Calhoon for her assistance in gathering case-related materials for this section, and to Professor Thomas Eimermann for his valuable suggestions along the way.

57. Warren, *Administrative Law in the Political System*, p. 271.

58. This account relies on Warren, ibid., pp. 230–231.

59. Warren, *Administrative Law in the Political System*, p. 233.

60. See Lorch, *Democratic Process and Administrative Law*, especially Chapter 1. For a comprehensive treatment of both regulatory policy and administrative law, see David H. Rosenbloom and Richard D. Schwartz, eds., *Handbook of Regulation and Administrative Law* (New York: Marcel Dekker, 1994).

61. See, among others, U.S. Supreme Court Associate Justice Stephen Breyer, *Regulation and Its Reform* (Cambridge, Mass.: Harvard University Press, 1982); and Litan and Nordhaus, *Reforming Federal Regulation*.

62. See Litan and Nordhaus, *Reforming Federal Regulation*, Chapter 5, especially pp. 100–13. For an overview of presidential efforts to increase control of regulatory bodies, see Howard Ball, *Controlling Regulatory Sprawl: Presidential Strategies from Nixon to Reagan* (Westport, Conn.: Greenwood Press, 1984). See also Marc K. Landy, Marc J. Roberts, and Stephen R. Thomas, *The Environmental Protection Agency: From Nixon to Clinton*, expanded edition (New York: Oxford University Press, 1994).

63. For a case study of reform in a specific context, see James R. Temples, "The Nuclear Regulatory Commission and the Politics of Regulatory Reform: Since Three Mile Island," *Public Administration Review*, 42 (July/August 1982), 355–62. See also Lynton K. Caldwell, *Science and the National Environmental Policy Act: Redirecting Policy through Procedural Reform* (Tuscaloosa: The University of Alabama Press, 1982), and DeWitt John, *Civic Environmentalism: Alternatives to Regulation in States and Communities* (Washington, D.C.: Congressional Quarterly Press, 1993).

64. Regarding airline deregulation and its impacts, see, among others, Steven Morrison and Clifford Winston, *The Economic Effects of Airline Deregulation* (Washington, D.C.: The Brookings Institution, 1986); and Anthony Brown, *The Politics of Airline Deregulation* (Knoxville: The University of Tennessee Press, 1987). For an incisive analysis of airline deregulation, trucking, and telecommunications industry, see Martha Derthick and Paul J. Quirk, *The Politics of Deregulation* (Washington, D.C.: The Brookings Institution, 1985). An interesting examination of the early rise of trucking regulation is found in William R. Childs, *Trucking and the Public Interest: The Emergence of Federal Regulation, 1914–1940* (Knoxville: The University of Tennessee Press, 1985).

65. This discussion relies on Litan and Nordhaus, *Reforming Federal Regulation*, pp. 127–31; Kenneth J. Meier, *Regulation: Politics, Bureaucracy, and Economics* (New York: St. Martin's, 1985), p. 3; and data drawn from *Budget of the United States Government, 1982 — Appendix* (Washington, D.C.: U.S. Government Printing Office, 1981); *Budget of the United States Government, 1986 — Appendix* (Washington, D.C.: U.S. Government Printing Office, 1985); *Budget of the United States Government, 1991 — Appendix* (Washington, D.C.: U.S. Government Printing Office, 1990); and *Budget of the United States Government, 1995 — Appendix* (Washington, D.C.: U.S. Government Printing Office, 1994).

66. Michael R. Gordon, "Will Reagan 'Turn Business Loose' if Business Wants to Stay Regulated?" *National Journal*, 13 (January 3, 1981), 10–13, at p. 10.

Chapter 12: Conclusion: Public Administration in a Time of Rapid Social Change

1. James D. Carroll, "Putting Government's House in Order," *Maxwell News and Notes*, 13 (Fall 1978), 2 (published by the Maxwell School of Citizenship and Public Affairs; Syracuse University; Syracuse, N.Y.).

2. Frederick C. Mosher, "The Public Service in the Temporary Society," *Public Administration Review*, 31 (January/February 1971), 47–62, at p. 49.

3. These paradoxes were first noted by public administration scholar Dwight Waldo in 1972, and if anything are more noticeable now than then. Dwight Waldo, "Developments in Public Administration," *Annals of the American Academy of Political and Social Science*, 404 (November 1972), 217–45, at p. 219.

4. Mosher, "The Public Service in the Temporary Society," p. 51. The phrase overhead democracy was used originally by Emmette Redford in *Democracy in the Administrative State* (New York: Oxford University Press, 1969), p. 70.

5. David P. Snyder, "The Intolerant Society: An Assessment of Our Evolving Institutional Environment," *The Bureaucrat*, 3 (October 1974), 247–69, at p. 256.

6. See Alice Rivlin, *Reviving the American Dream: The Economy, the States, and the Federal Government* (Washington, D.C.: The Brookings Institution, 1992).

7. Russ Linden, "Business Process Reengineering: Newest Fad, or Revolution in Government?" *Public Management*, 75 (November 1993), 9–12. See also Michael Hammer and James Champy, *Reengineering the Corporation* (New York: Harper Business, 1993), and Jay Chatzkel and Paul R. Popick, "Reengineering Experiments in Three Federal Organizations," *The Total Quality Review*, 4 (March/April 1994), 57–67.

8. See, for example, Charles Handy, *The Age of Unreason* (Cambridge, Mass.: Harvard Business School Press, 1989); and Sarah F. Liebschutz, "Neighborhood Revitalization in the United States: The Decentralization Dynamic," *Public Administration Quarterly*, 14 (Spring 1990), 86–107.

9. See, for example, Richard C. Elling, "The Line in Winter: An Academic Assessment of the First Report of the National Commission on the State and Local Public Service"; Raymond W. Cox III, "The Winter Commission Report: The Practitioner's Perspective"; and Delmer D. Dunn, "Public Affairs, Administrative Faculty, and the Winter Commission Report," *Public Administration Review*, 54 (March/April 1994), 107–08, 108–09, and 109–10, respectively.

10. See, among others, James S. Bowman, "Teaching Ethics in Public Administration," in Richard Heimovics and AnnMarie Rizzo, eds., *Innovations in Teaching Public Affairs and Administration* (monograph published jointly by Florida International University, Miami, and the University of Missouri–Kansas City, 1981), pp. 79–90; and Dalton S. Lee, "The Challenge of Teaching Public Administration Ethics," *The Political Science Teacher*, 2 (Fall 1989), 1–3.

11. See David H. Rosenbloom, "Public Administrative Theory and the Separation of Powers," *Public Administration Review*, 43 (May/June 1983), 219–27.

12. See Michael W. Dolan, "Administrative Law and Public Administration," *Public Administration Review*, 44 (January/February 1984), 86–89, at p. 86; and Chapter 12 of this book.

13. Waldo, "Developments in Public Administration," p. 243 (emphasis added).

14. Mosher, "The Public Service in the Temporary Society," p. 60 (emphasis added).

15. See, for example, Leo Herbert, Larry N. Killough, and Alan Walter Steiss, *Governmental Accounting and Control* (Monterey, Calif.: Brooks/Cole, 1984).

16. See Michael J. Wriston, "In Defense of Bureaucracy," *Public Administration Review*, 40 (March/April 1980), 179–83, especially p. 180; and Charles T. Goodsell, *The Case for Bureaucracy: A Public Administration Polemic*, 3rd ed. (Chatham, N.J.: Chatham House, 1994).

17. Wriston, "In Defense of Bureaucracy," p. 180.

18. See Robert E. Litan and William D. Nordhaus, *Reforming Federal Regulation* (New Haven, Conn.: Yale University Press, 1983), p. 132.

19. See, among others, Alan Stone, *Regulation and Its Alternatives* (Washington, D.C.: Congressional Quarterly Press, 1982); Susan J. Tolchin and Martin Tolchin, *Dismantling America: The Rush to Deregulate* (Boston: Houghton Mifflin, 1983); and Larry N. Gerston, Cynthia Fraleigh, and Robert Schwab, *The Deregulated Society* (Pacific Grove, Calif.: Brooks/Cole, 1988).

20. In this connection, see, among others, Patricia A. Wilson, "Power, Politics, and Other Reasons Why Senior Executives Leave the Federal Government," *Public Administration Review*, 54 (January/February 1994), 12–19.

21. See James P. Pfiffner, "The Challenge of Federal Management in the 1980s," *Public Administration Quarterly*, 7 (Summer 1983), 162–82, at pp. 172–74; Thomas W. Kell, "Negative Views Undermine Public Enterprise," *The Public Manager: The New Bureaucrat*, 22 (Spring 1993), 51–54. A somewhat different viewpoint about presidential efforts to undermine the bureaucracy may be found in Neil Skene, "Assault on Bureaucracy Never Materialized," *Congressional Quarterly Weekly Report*, 50 (November 7, 1992), 3608. See also Report of the National Commission on the Public Service (the Volcker Commission), *Leadership for America: Rebuilding the Public Service* (Lexington, Mass.: Lexington Books, 1989).

22. The National Performance Review has attracted some pointed criticism. See, among others, Jon Meacham, "What Al Gore Might Learn the Hard Way," *Washington Monthly*, 25 (September 1993), 16–20; and David Segal, "What's Wrong with the Gore Report," *Washington Monthly*, 25 (November 1993), 18–23.

23. A. Lee Fritschler, *Smoking and Politics: Policy Making and the Federal Bureaucracy*, 5th ed. (Englewood Cliffs, N.J.: PrenticeHall, 1996), p. 148,(emphasis added).

24. E. Samuel Overman, "Public Management: What's New and Different?" *Public Administration Review*, 44 (May/June 1984), 275–78, at p. 278. For a useful overview of public management, see G. David Garson and E. Samuel Overman, *Public Management Research in the United States* (New York: Praeger, 1983).

25. See Charles Goodsell's review of Osborne and Gaebler's work, entitled "Re-Invent Government, or Re-Discover It?" *Public Administration Review*, 53 (January/February 1993), 85–87.

26. Ronald C. Moe, "The 'Reinventing Government' Exercise: Misinterpreting the Problem, Misjudging the Consequences," *Public Administration Review*, 54 (March/April 1994), 111–22; DeLeon, Linda and Robert B. Denhardt, "The Political Theory of Reinvention," *Public Administration Review*, 60 (March/April 2000): pp. 89–98.

27. See, for example, Francis Rourke, "The 1993 John Gaus Lecture: Whose Bureaucracy Is This, Anyway? Congress, the President and Public Administration," *PS: Political Science & Politics*, 26 (December 1993), 687–91.

28. Hindy Lauer Schachter, *Reinventing Government or Reinventing Ourselves: The Role of Citizen Owners in Making a Better Government* (Ithaca, N.Y.: State University of New York Press, 1996).

29. John J. DiIulio, Jr., "Reinventing the Dinosaur?" *Brookings Review*, 11 (Fall 1993), 5.

30. Segal, "What's Wrong with the Gore Report."

31. "Environmentalists Warned to Ease Attacks on EPA," an Associated Press story appearing in the *Bloomington* (Ill.) *Pantagraph*, December 9, 1984, p. A7 (emphasis added).

32. Rosenbloom, "Public Administrative Theory and the Separation of Powers," p. 225 (emphasis added).

33. See, among others, James O. Freedman, *Crisis and Legitimacy* (New York: Cambridge University Press, 1978); cited by Rosenbloom, "Public Administrative Theory and the Separation of Powers," p. 225.

34. Mark A. Abramson and Sandra Baxter, "The Senior Executive Service: A Preliminary Assessment from One Department," paper presented at a 1981 symposium on civil service reform, and reprinted in *The Senior Executive Service*, pp. 483–513; the premises referred to appear at p. 512.

35. "GOP Finds Fed Not All Bad," *Bloomington* (Ill.) *Pantagraph*, March 26, 1981, p. A10.

36. Attitudes toward government and bureaucracy are discussed in Kaufman, "Fear of Bureaucracy: A Raging Pandemic"; Richard L. McDowell, "Sources and Consequences of Citizen Attitudes toward Government," in H. George Frederickson and Ralph Clark Chandler, eds., "Citizenship and Public Administration: Proceedings of the National Conference on Citizenship and Public Service," *Public Administration Review*, 44 (March 1984), 152–56; and Seymour Martin Lipset and William Schneider, *The Confidence Gap: Business, Labor, and Government in the Public Mind*, rev. ed. (Baltimore, Md.: The Johns Hopkins University Press, 1987).

37. Adapted from the written comments of an anonymous reviewer, to whom we owe a considerable debt for these very salient and perceptive observations.

38. Alan D. Monroe, *Public Opinion in America* (New York: Harper & Row, 1975), p. 292.

39. Waldo, "Developments in Public Administration," p. 244. See also Waldo, *The Enterprise of Public Administration* (Novato, Calif.: Chandler & Sharp, 1980), and *The Administrative State*, 2nd ed. (New York: Holmes and Meier, 1984).

40. David Broder, "Ethics in Government?" *Washington Post* syndicated column appearing in the *Bloomington* (Ill.) *Pantagraph*, April 12, 1981, p. A8 (emphasis added).

Index